T0189828

Communications
in Computer and Information Science 1045

Commenced Publication in 2007
Founding and Former Series Editors:
Phoebe Chen, Alfredo Cuzzocrea, Xiaoyong Du, Orhun Kara, Ting Liu,
Krishna M. Sivalingam, Dominik Ślęzak, Takashi Washio, and Xiaokang Yang

Editorial Board Members

Simone Diniz Junqueira Barbosa
  Pontifical Catholic University of Rio de Janeiro (PUC-Rio),
  Rio de Janeiro, Brazil
Joaquim Filipe
  Polytechnic Institute of Setúbal, Setúbal, Portugal
Ashish Ghosh
  Indian Statistical Institute, Kolkata, India
Igor Kotenko
  St. Petersburg Institute for Informatics and Automation of the Russian
  Academy of Sciences, St. Petersburg, Russia
Junsong Yuan
  University at Buffalo, The State University of New York, Buffalo, NY, USA
Lizhu Zhou
  Tsinghua University, Beijing, China

More information about this series at http://www.springer.com/series/7899

Mayank Singh · P. K. Gupta ·
Vipin Tyagi · Jan Flusser ·
Tuncer Ören · Rekha Kashyap (Eds.)

Advances in Computing and Data Sciences

Third International Conference, ICACDS 2019
Ghaziabad, India, April 12–13, 2019
Revised Selected Papers, Part I

 Springer

Editors
Mayank Singh
University of KwaZulu-Natal
Durban, South Africa

Vipin Tyagi
Department of Computer Science
and Engineering
Jaypee University of Engineering
and Technology
Guna, Madhya Pradesh, India

Tuncer Ören
School of Electrical Engineering
and Computer Science
University of Ottawa
Ottawa, ON, Canada

P. K. Gupta
Computer Science and Engineering
Jaypee Institute of Information
Technology
Waknaghat, Himachal Pradesh, India

Jan Flusser
ÚTIA AV ČR
Institute of Information Theory
and Automation
Prague 8, Praha, Czech Republic

Rekha Kashyap
CSE Department
Inderprastha Engineering College
Ghaziabad, Uttar Pradesh, India

ISSN 1865-0929   ISSN 1865-0937   (electronic)
Communications in Computer and Information Science
ISBN 978-981-13-9938-1   ISBN 978-981-13-9939-8   (eBook)
https://doi.org/10.1007/978-981-13-9939-8

This Springer imprint is published by the registered company Springer Nature Singapore Pte Ltd.
The registered company address is: 152 Beach Road, #21-01/04 Gateway East, Singapore 189721, Singapore

Preface

Computing techniques like big data, cloud computing, machine learning, the Internet of Things etc. are playing the key role in processing of data and retrieval of advanced information. Several state-of-art techniques and computing paradigms have been proposed based on these techniques. This volume contains papers presented at the Third International Conference on Advances in Computing and Data Sciences (ICACDS 2019) held during April 12–13, 2019, at Inderprastha Engineering College, Ghaziabad, UP, India. The conference was organized specifically to help researchers, academics, scientists, and industry come together and to derive benefits from the advances of next-generation computing technologies in the areas of advanced computing and data sciences.

The Program Committee of ICACDS 2019 is extremely grateful to the authors who showed an overwhelming response to the call for papers submitting over 621 papers in two tracks in advanced computing and data sciences. All submitted papers went through a peer review process and finally 112 papers were accepted for publication in Springer's CCIS series. We are very thankful to our reviewers for their efforts in finalizing the high-quality papers.

The conference featured many distinguished personalities including Prof. K. K. Agarwal, Chairman-NAAC, Prof. J. S. P. Rai, Vice Chancellor Jaypee University of Engineering and Technology, Raghogarh, Guna; Prof. Rajkumar Buyya, University of Melbourne, Australia; Prof. Viranjay M. Srivastava, University of KwaZulu-Natal, Durban, South Africa; Prof. Baisakhi Chakraborty, National Institute of Technology, Durgapur; Prof. Parteek Bhatia, Thapar Institute of Engineering and Technology, Patiala, India; Prof. S. K. Mishra, Majmaah University, Saudi Arabia; Prof. Arun Sharma, Indira Gandhi Delhi Technical University for Women, India; Prof. Prathmesh Churi, NMIMS University, Mumbai; Dr. Anup Girdhar, CEO and Founder, Sedulity Solutions & Technology, India, among many others. We are very grateful for the participation of all speakers in making this conference a memorable event.

The Organizing Committee of ICACDS 2019 is indebted to Prof. B. C. Sharma, Director Inderprastha Engineering College, for the confidence that he invested in us in organizing this international conference, and all the faculty and staff of the CSE Department, IPEC, Ghaziabad for their support in organizing the conference and for making it a grand success.

We would also like to thank Dr. Divya Jain, JUET Guna; Dr. Neelesh Jain, JUET Guna; Dr. Prateek Pandey, JUET Guna; Dr Nilesh Patel, JUET Guna; Dr. Ratnesh Litoriya, JUET Guna; Mr. Kunj Bihari Meena, JUET Guna; Dr. Deepshikha Tiwary, Thapar University Patiala; Dr. Ghanshyam Raghuwanshi, Manipal University, Jaipur; Dr. Vibhash Yadav, REC Banda; Dr. Sandhya Tarar, GBU Noida; Mr. Nishant Gupta, MGM CoET, Noida; Mr. Rohit Kapoor, SK Info Techies; Mr. Akshay Chaudhary and

Ms. Akansha Singh from GISR Foundation; Mr. Deepak Singh, Mr. Atul Kumar, and Ms. Shivani Gupta from Consilio Intelligence Research Lab for their support. Our sincere thanks to Consilio Intelligence Research Lab, GISR Foundation, Print Canvas, IP Moment, Aptron, VGeekers and Tricky Plants for sponsoring the event.

June 2019   Mayank Singh
                                                                   P. K. Gupta
                                                                   Vipin Tyagi
                                                                   Jan Flusser
                                                                   Tuncer Ören
                                                                   Rekha Kashyap

Organization

Steering Committee

Chief Patron

Vinay Kumar Pathak   APJAKTU, Lucknow, India
(Vice-chancellor)
S. S. Jain (Chairman)   Inderprastha Engineering College, Ghaziabad, India

Patron

B. C. Sharma (Director)   Inderprastha Engineering College, Ghaziabad, India

Steering Committee

Alexandre Carlos Brandão   UNIFEI, Brazil
  Ramos
Mohit Singh   Georgia Institute of Technology, USA
H. M. Pandey   Edge Hill University, UK
M. N. Hooda   BVICAM, Delhi, India
S. K. Singh   IIT BHU, Varanasi, India
Jyotsna Kumar Mandal   University of Kalyani, West Bengal, India

Honorary Chairs

Viranjay M. Srivastava   University of KwaZulu-Natal, Durban, South Africa
V. K. Singh   Inderprastha Engineering College, Ghaziabad, India

General Chairs

Mayank Singh   University of KwaZulu Natal, Durban, South Africa
Rekha Kashyap   Inderprastha Engineering College, Ghaziabad, India

Advisory Board Chairs

Tuncer Ören   University of Ottawa, Canada
Jan Flusser   Institute of Information Theory and Automation,
         Czech Republic

Technical Program Committee Chairs

P. K. Gupta   Jaypee University of Information Technology, Solan,
         India
Vipin Tyagi   Jaypee University of Engineering & Technology,
         Guna, India

Program Chairs

Ulrick Klauck   Aalen University, Germany
Shailendra Mishra   Majmaah University, Saudi Arabia

Conveners

Gaurav Agrawal   Inderprastha Engineering College, India
Sandhya Tarar   Gautam Buddha University, India

Co-conveners

Prathamesh Churi   NMIMS University, India
Shikha Badhani   DU, India

Conference Chairs

Ravi Tomar   University of Petroleum and Energy Studies, India
Jagendra Singh   Inderprastha Engineering College, India

Conference Co-chairs

Lavanya Sharma   Amity University, India
Vibhash Yadav   Rajkiya Engineering College Banda, India
Rakesh Saini   DIT University, India
Abhishek Dixit   Tallinn University of Technology, Estonia
Vipin Deval   Tallinn University of Technology, Estonia

Organizing Chairs

Pooja Tripathi   Inderprastha Engineering College, India
Mandeep Katre   Inderprastha Engineering College, India

Organizing Secretariat

Chahat Sharma   Inderprastha Engineering College, India
Krista Chaudhary   Krishna Engineering College, Ghaziabad, India
Umang Kant   Krishna Engineering College, Ghaziabad, India

Creative Head

Deepak Singh   Consilio Intelligence Research Lab, India

Marketing Head

Akshay Chaudhary   GISR Foundation, India

Organizing Committee

Registration

Tripti Sharma	Inderprastha Engineering College, India
Amrita Bhatnagar	Inderprastha Engineering College, India
Kirti Jain	Inderprastha Engineering College, India
Harshita	Inderprastha Engineering College, India

Publication

Jagendra Singh	Inderprastha Engineering College, India

Cultural

Diksha Dani	Inderprastha Engineering College, India
Anjali Singhal	Inderprastha Engineering College, India
Nidhi Agrawal	Inderprastha Engineering College, India
Prachi	Inderprastha Engineering College, India

Transportation

Mandeep Katre	Inderprastha Engineering College, India
Pushendra Singh	Inderprastha Engineering College, India
Shailendra Singh	Inderprastha Engineering College, India
Alok Katiyar	Inderprastha Engineering College, India
Sandeep Agrawal	Inderprastha Engineering College, India

Hospitality

Neeta Verma	Inderprastha Engineering College, India
Gaurav Srivastava	Inderprastha Engineering College, India
Vanshika Gupta	Inderprastha Engineering College, India
Udit Bansal	Inderprastha Engineering College, India

Stage Management

Sweeta Bansal	Inderprastha Engineering College, India
Chahat Sharma	Inderprastha Engineering College, India
Anchal Jain	Inderprastha Engineering College, India

Technical Session

Pranshu Saxena	Inderprastha Engineering College, India
Anjali Singhal	Inderprastha Engineering College, India
Diksha Dani	Inderprastha Engineering College, India
Alka Singhal	Inderprastha Engineering College, India
Jagendra Singh	Inderprastha Engineering College, India
Sneh Prabha	Inderprastha Engineering College, India
Pooja Singhal	Inderprastha Engineering College, India

Shweta Chaku	Inderprastha Engineering College, India
Naman Sharma	Inderprastha Engineering College, India
Preeti	Inderprastha Engineering College, India
Kumud Alok	Inderprastha Engineering College, India

Finance

Gaurav Agrawal	Inderprastha Engineering College, India
Mandeep Katre	Inderprastha Engineering College, India
Amit Sharma	Inderprastha Engineering College, India
Vipin Kumar Singhal	Inderprastha Engineering College, India

Food

Archana Agrawal	Inderprastha Engineering College, India
Harendra Singh	Inderprastha Engineering College, India
Swapna Singh	Inderprastha Engineering College, India
Shraddha Srivastava	Inderprastha Engineering College, India
Shiva Soni	Inderprastha Engineering College, India

Advertising

Monika Bansal	Inderprastha Engineering College, India
Shelly Gupta	Inderprastha Engineering College, India
Kamna Singh	Inderprastha Engineering College, India

Press and Media

Monika Bansal	Inderprastha Engineering College, India
Chahat Sharma	Inderprastha Engineering College, India
Bharti	Inderprastha Engineering College, India

Editorial

Pranshu Saxena	Inderprastha Engineering College, India

Sponsored by

Consilio Intelligence Research Lab

Co-sponsored by

GISR Foundation
IP Moment
Print Canvas
VGeekers
Tricky Plants

Contents – Part I

Contents – Part II

Data Sciences

Comparative Analysis of Cognitive Neurodynamics on AMIGOS Dataset Versus Prepared Dataset

Rubleen Kaur[✉], Rupali Gill, and Jaiteg Singh

Chitkara University Institute of Engineering and Technology,
Chitkara University, Chandigarh, Punjab, India
oberoi23rubleen@gmail.com,
{rupali.gill,jaiteg.singh}@chitkara.edu.in

Abstract. Cognitive Neurodynamics is the scientific field that is concerned with the study of biological processes of brain and aspects that underlie cognition. The specific focus of cognition is on neural connections that are involved in the mental process. So the resultant of cognitive states which consists of thoughts, perception, memory, experiences predicted the state of emotional behaviour in human. There are two parts of brain which are responsible for cognition and emotional states in human i.e. Amygdala and frontal cortex of brain. In this paper, a correlation analysis is being done on the basis of common feature set choosen between self- prepared dataset and public access dataset. The public domain dataset named AMIGOS is choosen for research analysis, as it is prepared on (14 + 2) electrodes. In both datasets same number of electrodes are used. Experimental results confirm that accuracy of both datasets are compatible with each other. AMIGOS dataset shows 80.12% accuracy and prepared dataset shows 74.62% accuracy using SVM classifier.

Keywords: Cognition · Emotion · Neurodynamics ·
Electroencephalography (EEG) · AMIGOS · Arousal · Valence ·
Neuromarketing · Neuroscience · STBD (Spatio-Temporal Brain Data) ·
SVM (Supervised Vector Machine)

1 Introduction

Cognitive Neuroscience tries to correlate preference measure with neural measure. Neural measure could actually be used to detect behaviour evidences for predicting marketing actions. In this present study, the authors used EEG to predict preference measures and neural measure in response to commercial advertisements. As such, these EEG measures provide real world outcomes. Neuromarketing, applying neuroscience methods and techniques because brain data is less noisy as compared to other data obtained through conventional methods. Neuroscience provides comprehensive introduction to understand how consumer make decision in purchasing products. Consumer Neuroscience and Neuromarketing both are dealing with consumer behaviour. Neuroscience term is related to academic literature and Neuromarketing term is somehow related to industry [4]. To study consumer behaviour in day to day life, neuroscientific

M. Singh et al. (Eds.): ICACDS 2019, CCIS 1045, pp. 3–12, 2019.
https://doi.org/10.1007/978-981-13-9939-8_1

tools are required to study. In neuroscientific tools such as EEG, fMRI, used to generate neural outcomes of brain with respect to any marketing stimuli. To deeply study these measures, it is important to know the main tasks of brain such as cognition and emotion.

Emotion and cognition are two excellent code of behavior for understanding the nature of neurodynamics, a specific focus on neural connections of brain that are involved in the mental process. From neuroscience perspective, there is a dynamic interaction between emotional processing areas and cognitive centers of brain [5]. The focus analysis of this research work is to address the correlation between neural, mental and behavioral states.

This paper is organized as follow. In Sect. 2, literature work is introduced. Then in Sect. 3 problem statement is described. In Sect. 4, Comparison is done between different methodologies. After that in Sect. 5, datasets are introduced. Further, in Sect. 6, SVM classifier is introduced. In Sect. 7, results are discussed. Section 8, presented conclusion and future work.

2 Background

In paper [6], traditional market research method are not capable to capture the customers' emotional responses. So consumer neuroscience uses neuroscientific tools to capture quantitative measure of marketing stimuli such as pricing decision, brand images, brand preference.

Consumer neuroscience is also known as Neuromarketing but there is a distinction between two terms. Consumer Neuroscience refers to academic literature and Neuromarketing refers to the industrial term. Many consumer neuroscience papers provide the explanation of neuroscientific tools in their studies but there is no appropriate information about full range of neuroscientific tools and which tool is appropriate for Neuromarketing research [9].

These Neuroscientific tools are used to detect emotional behaviour of human. There are two most commonly used theories of emotion: Plutchik and James Russell. In this research work, Russell theory of emotion is chosen for categorizing emotions. Russell suggested a 2-D circular space to represent emotions, containing arousal and valence as dimensions. Valence measures positive or negative affectivity. Arousal measures the calmness to excitement of the information. Arousal represented by vertical axis whereas valence represented by horizontal axis and the center between vertical and horizontal axis represents neutral valence and medium level of arousal. This model is known as Circumplex model of emotion [13]. This model is commonly used to represent external stimuli in affective states.

In brain, neurons are fundamental processing element which are interconnected and can exchange information with each other. Inspired by structure of brain neurons Spiking neural network has been developed [19].

To meaningfully interpret the cognitive mechanism of brain, an appropriate methodology is required to analyse the complex multivariate STBD. EEG is a kind of STBD (spatio- temporal brain data) and has been used to analyse preferences and decision- making stated by [23]. So emotional experience arises from organic changes that occur in the body due to some arousal activity [26].

In Paper [31], there is a circuit in the center of the brain that is responsible for the substrates of the emotion. During 20 years of research throughout the 1960 and 1970, afferent input from heart affects perception and behaviour. In summary evidence clearly demonstrates that afferent signals from heart influencing the cortical activity of brain.

3 Problem Definition

Buying behaviour is a decision process and act of people are involved in purchasing goods. There are three queries generated in order to analyse consumer buying behaviour:

1. What influences consumer purchases
2. What are the changing factors in society
3. Why they make the decision they do

So to analyse these changing factors revolving around the consumer in order to analyse the decision making process. As none of the research work used low cost device. So in this AMIGOS research work, cost effective device is used to detect human emotions in real time applications in medical, merchandising, neuromarketing etc. There is a need to create strong methodological foundation for strengthening the relationship between neurodynamics and consumer neuroscience. The goal of this paper is to tap consumer emotions to understand the marketing practices.

4 Comparison of Methodologies

This segment gives an overview of neuroscience tools and techniques available for Neuromarketing researchers [10]. There are various companies which designed EEG device for research purpose. Out of which two are low-cost consumer grade EEG devices: the Emotiv EPOC+ and the Neurosky Mind Wave. The accuracy rate of Emotiv Epoc is 75% and Neurosky device is 50% [13]. The headset used in this work is made by EMOTIV EPOC+ company having 14(+2) channels and designed for human brain research to access the brain data. If the comparative analysis being done for both methods, then there is not much difference between these two methods. The Prepared dataset is based on proposed technique as discussed in previous paper [1]. The method of extracting data is based on same technique i.e. EEG but the use of stimuli in both cases is different. In AMIGOS, movie trailer stimuli is used and in prepared dataset, advertisement video stimuli is being used.

4.1 Steps to Compare AMIGOS Versus Prepared Dataset

1. Convert both datasets into meaningful form.
2. Analyse both datasets by making inference rules.
3. Extract the features from both datasets.

4. Categorize features into minimum, maximum and average range.
5. Classify responses into various classes depending on Russell's model.

In Table 1, there is a classification of emotion states depending on Russell's model. The emotion states are bored, excited, angry and so on are taken to differentiate them into arousal-valence scale.

Table 1. Categorisation of emotion scale.

States	Category
Bored	LAHV
Excited	HAHV
Angry	HALV
Frustrated	HALV
Sad	LALV
Fatigue	LALV
Alert	HALV
Depress	LALV
Sleepy	LAHV
Happy	HAHV

5 Dataset

5.1 AMIGOS Dataset

AMIGOS means AMIGOS dataset is used for multimodal research of affect and personality traits based on individual mood and groups. The dataset is collected using EMOTIV EPOC+ headset of 14 electrodes. The proposed work is carried over a dataset of 40 participants on 16 different videos. The dataset includes participant id, experiment id, arousal, valence, dominance, liking readings of respective videos. With respect to these readings participants are categorized into different classes of emotions as in Table 2.

5.2 Prepared Dataset

The dataset is prepared by using EMOTIV EPOC+ headset of 16 electrodes. The number of participants used in this dataset is 30 as discussed in previous paper [1]. There is an environment setup for every participant such as 60 s of rest is inserted after watching every advertisement video. So the mind should be relaxed for the next advertisement. A proper sitting environment is provided with a 30 cm distance from laptop screen.

Table 2. AMIGOS dataset description.

Database content	
Number of participants	40
Number of videos	16
Videos duration	1 min affective highlight
Rating scales	I. Bored
	II. Excited
	III. Angry
	IV. Frustrate
	V. Sad
	VI. Fatigue
	VII. Alert
	VIII. Depress
	IX. Sleepy
	X. Happy
Recorded signals	Psychological signals

5.3 Correlation Analysis Between Two Datasets

The rating scale used for the both datasets is same. But the number of participants and videos are different. The goal of the experiment is to extract features of various emotional responses from human subjects while they were tested on visual human stimuli. The extracted features of AMIGOS experiment is the Spectral Power of each electrode in the form of alpha, beta, gamma, delta waves which is same for prepared datset. Emotiv control panel is used to detect these brainwaves and classify the frequency level of brainwaves in the form various emotional states as stated by Russell's model in Fig. 1 (Table 3).

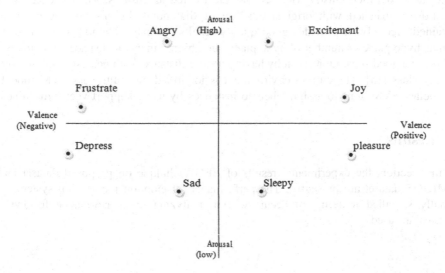

Fig. 1. Valence-arousal model of emotion [2].

Table 3. Prepared dataset description.

Database content	
Number of participants	30
Number of videos	20
Videos duration	1 min affective highlight
Rating scales	I. Bored
	II. Excited
	III. Angry
	IV. Frustrate
	V. Sad
	VI. Fatigue
	VII. Alert
	VIII. Depress
	IX. Sleepy
	X. Happy
Recorded signals	Psychological signals
Software used	Emotive Xavier Control Panel

6   Radial Kernel Support Vector Classifier (Multi Model Regression)

In this paper to classify the emotional behaviour of participants, SVM classifier is used. In SVM model, all participants recordings of with respective video is taken as vectors and then classify them into various classes using hyperplane. In this paper, SVM classification is combined with SVM regression which is SVM based multimodal prediction technique. The classification of features into 10 classes of emotion is studied successfully through SVM code. During classification, it is observed that which point is lying near to which cluster. Here classes are treated as clusters. Then it check that emotion is matched with original emotion of that point. In this way accuracy is obtained precisely. It provides good quality results for many learning tasks. It constructs hyperplane or number of hyperplanes in a high dimensional space. Hyperplane, achieved a good separation result by having a large distance from nearest training point of any class [15]. The current environment is identified by multi-class SVM model. Multiclass SVM aims to assign labels to instances by using support vector machines.

7   Results

In this section, the experimental results of EEG technique on proposed dataset and AMIGOS dataset are presented. The performance of emotion recognition systems is usually specified in terms of accuracy. For analyzing the performance following metrics are used:

$$Accuracy(Acc.) = Number\ of\ Correct\ Predictions/Total\ Number\ of\ Cases \quad (6.1)$$

$$Error\ Rate(ER) = False\ rate/Total\ Number\ of\ Cases \quad (6.2)$$

$$Precision = True\ positives/True\ Positives + False\ Positives \quad (6.3)$$

$$Recall = True\ Positives/True\ Positives + False\ Negatives \quad (6.4)$$

$$F1\ Score = 2 * Precision * Recall/Precision + Recall \quad (6.5)$$

The outcome shows that the interest level of all the users are not same. It varies from person to person mental state [17]. Experimental results shows the difference in terms of accuracy between original state and predicted state using SVM. Below in Table 4 following features are selected to classify the data into emotion scale.

Table 4. Feature selection

Features	Min	Average	Max
Interest	0.140091	0.631061	0.977023
Engagement	0.447019	0.644323	0.8515637
Excitement	0.12	0.38242	1
Focus	0.213	0.57992	1

The experimental result presents the difference between the accuracy level of both datasets. Both metrics are calculated by using confusion matrix. Then Recall and precision is calculated in order to track error rate (Table 5).

Table 5. Confusion matrix of prepared dataset

Class	True Bored	True Excited	True Angry	True Frustrated	True Sad	True Fatigue	True Alert	True Depress	True Sleepy	True Happy
P.Bored	56	17	0	0	3	0	0	6	6	0
P.Excited	13	70	0	0	0	0	0	0	0	6
P.Angry	1	5	40	10	1	0	0	1	0	0
P.Frustrated	0	0	0	73	9	1	0	3	1	3
P.Sad	0	0	0	0	74	7	0	0	10	0
P.Fatigue	0	0	0	0	10	30	0	0	13	0
P.Alert	0	9	0	0	0	0	12	0	0	0
P.Depress	4	0	0	0	2	0	0	15	1	0
P.Sleepy	0	0	0	0	2	1	0	0	50	4
P.Happy	0	1	0	1	0	0	2	0	4	25

This prepared model is tested for emotions by using SVM algorithm. These ten emotions lie in different-different quadrants according to arousal-valence model. By using this model the predicted accuracy is 74.62%. This model is tested for emotions by using SVM algorithm. These ten emotions lie in different- different quadrants according to arousal-valence model. By using AMIGOS model the predicted accuracy is 80.12% (Table 6).

Table 6. Confusion matrix of AMIGOS dataset

Class	True Bored	True Excited	True Angry	True Frustrated	True Sad	True Fatigue	True Alert	True Depress	True Sleepy	True Happy
P.Bored	63	15	0	0	0	0	0	0	0	0
P.Excited	0	69	0	0	0	0	0	0	0	9
P.Angry	0	0	49	5	0	0	0	0	0	0
P. Frustrated	0	0	0	78	0	9	0	0	0	0
P.Sad	0	0	0	0	69	0	0	0	20	0
P.Fatigue	0	0	0	0	0	59	0	0	9	0
P.Alert	0	5	0	0	0	0	49	0	0	0
P.Depress	0	0	0	0	2	0	0	48	2	0
P.Sleepy	0	0	0	0	0	0	0	0	55	2
P.Happy	0	10	0	0	0	0	0	0	0	55

Below in Table 7 accuracy metrics are used to determine the precision rate between observed dataset with respect to existing dataset.

Table 7. Accuracy measures

S. no	Dataset	Accuracy	Recall	Precision	F1 score
1.	Prepared	74.4	0.325	0.6363	0.4301
2.	AMIGOS	80.12	0.299	0.835	0.44032

8   Conclusion and Future Scope

The AMIGOS and prepared datasets are verified by using SVM model which predicts the accuracy of class attributes. There is not much difference in the accuracy scale of both datasets. This model is tested for ten emotions by using SVM algorithm. These ten emotions lie in different-different quadrants according to arousal-valence model. As per the accuracy obtained by this model is higher than other researchers, who are also using SVM but on different datasets [15].

Many researchers tries to attempt their research in the field of emotions. This is a new field, research work in this field is very less. Because no one actually predicts the human inner reside feeling but there is an attempt to understand human nature by using emotions.

In future work, there is an attempt to use large number of participants in dataset, to obtain more precise results.

References

1. Kaur, R., Gill, R., Singh, J.: Cognitive emotion measures of brain. In: Proceedings of 13th INDIACom; INDIACom-2019; 6th International Conference on "Computing for Sustainable Global Development", 13–15 March 2019, pp. 59–63 (2019)
2. Russell, J.A.: A circumplex model of affect. J. Pers. Soc. Psychol. **39**, 1161–1178 (1980)
3. Consoli, D.: A new concept of marketing: the emotional marketing. BRAND Broad Res. Account. Negot. Distrib. **1**, 52–59 (2010)
4. Harris, J.M., Ciorciari, J., Gountas, J.: Consumer neuroscience for marketing researchers. J. Consum. Behav. **17**, 239–252 (2018)
5. Atmanspacher, H., Rotter, S.: Interpreting neurodynamics: concepts and facts. Cogn. Neurodyn. **2**, 297–318 (2008)
6. Daugherty, T., Hoffman, E., Kennedy, K., Nolan, M.: Measuring consumer neural activation to differentiate cognitive processing of advertising: revisiting Krugman. Eur. J. Market. **52**, 182–198 (2018)
7. Lee, N., Brandes, L., Chamberlain, L., Senior, C.: This is your brain on neuromarketing: reflections on a decade of research. IEEE J. Market. Manage. **33**, 878–892 (2017)
8. Hanson, C., Caglar, L.R., Hanson, S.J.: Attentional bias in human category learning: the case of deep learning. Front. Psychol. **9**, 374–384 (2006)
9. Tortella-Feliu, M., Morillas-Romero, A., Balle, M., Llabrés, J., Bornas, X., Putman, P.: Spontaneous EEG activity and spontaneous emotion regulation. Int. J. Psychophysiol. **94**, 365–372 (2014)
10. Deco, G., Rolls, E.T.: Neurodynamics of biased competition and cooperation for attention: a model with spiking neurons. J. Neurophysiol. **94**, 295–313 (2005)
11. Yadava, M., Kumar, P., Saini, R., Roy, P.P., Dogra, D.P.: Analysis of EEG signals and its application to neuromarketing. Multimed. Tools Appl. **76**, 19087–19111 (2017)
12. Maskeliunas, R., Damasevicius, R., Martisius, I., Vasiljevas, M.: Consumer-grade EEG devices: are they usable for control tasks? PeerJ **76**, 1746–1749 (2016)
13. Gao, Y., Lee, H.J., Mehmood, R.M.: Deep learning of EEG signals for emotion recognition. In: 2015 IEEE International Conference, pp. 1–5. IEEE (2015)
14. Ruiz-Padial, E., Ibáñez-Molina, A.J.: Fractal dimension of EEG signals and heart dynamics in discrete emotional states. Biol. Psychol. **137**, 42–48 (2018)
15. Cao, J., Mao, X., Luo, Q.: Neurodynamic system theory and applications. Abstr. Appl. Anal. **2013**, 639 (2013)
16. Plutchik, R.: The circumplex as a general model of the structure of emotions and personality. Am. Psychol. Assoc. **52**, 1301–1310 (1997)
17. Gloor, P., Guberman, A.H.: The temporal lobe & limbic system. Can. Med. Assoc. J. **157**, 1597–1603 (1997)
18. Subramanian, R., Wache, J., Abadi, M.K., Vieriu, R.L., Winkler, S., Sebe, N.: ASCERTAIN: emotion and personality recognition using commercial sensors. IEEE Trans. Affect. Comput. **2**, 147–160 (2018)
19. Vecchiato, G., et al.: How to measure cerebral correlates of emotions in marketing relevant tasks. Cogn. Comput. **6**, 856–871 (2014)

20. Kasabov, N.K.: NeuCube: a spiking neural network architecture for mapping, learning and understanding of spatio-temporal brain data. Neural Netw. **52**, 62–76 (2014)
21. Cushing, C.A., Adams, R.B., Ward, N., Albohn, D.N., Steiner, T.G., Kveraga, K.: Neurodynamics and connectivity during facial fear perception: the role of threat exposure and signal congruity. Sci. Rep. **8**, 2776–2796 (2018)
22. Boksem, M.A.S., Smidts, A.: Brain responses to movie trailers predict individual preferences for movies and their population-wide commercial success. J. Market. Res. **52**, 482–492 (2015)
23. Chinmayi, R., Nair, G.J., Soundarya, M., Poojitha, D.S., Venugopal, G., Vijayan, J.: Extracting the features of emotion from EEG signals and classify using affective computing. In: International Conference on Wireless Communications, Signal Processing and Networking (WiSPNET), pp. 2032–2036. IEEE (2017)
24. Wang, H., Coble, C., Bello, P.: Cognitive-affective interactions in human decision-making: a neurocomputational approach. In: Proceedings of the Twenty-Eighth Annual Conference of the Cognitive Science Society, vol. 28, pp. 2341–2346 (2006)
25. McCraty, R.: Heart-brain neurodynamics: the making of emotions, pp. 76–110. HeartMath Research Center, Institute of HeartMath, Boulder Creek, 03-015 (2003)
26. Andreassi, J.L.: Psychophysiology, Human Behavior & Physiological Response, 5th edn. Lawrence Erlbaum, London (2007)
27. Astolfi, L., et al.: The track of brain activity during the observation of TV commercials with the high-resolution EEG technology. Comput. Intell. Neurosci. **2009**, 7 (2009). Article ID 652078
28. Banich, M.T., Compton, R.: Cognitive Neuroscience. Cengage Learning, Wadsworth (2010)
29. Bartra, O., McGuire, J.T., Kable, J.W.: The valuation system: a coordinate-based meta-analysis of BOLD fMRI experiments examining neural correlates of subjective value. NeuroImage **76**, 412–427 (2013)
30. Baumgartner, T., Knoch, D., Hotz, P., Eisenegger, C., Fehr, E.: Dorsolateral and ventromedial prefrontal cortex orchestrate normative choice. Nature Neurosci. **14**, 1468–1474 (2011)
31. Baumgartner, T., Schiller, B., Rieskamp, J., Gianotti, L.R.R., Knoch, D.: Diminishing parochialism in intergroup conflict by disrupting the right temporo-parietal junction. Soc. Cogn. Affect. Neurosci. **9**, 653–660 (2014)
32. Bechara, A., Damasio, H., Damasio, A.R., Lee, G.P.: Different contributions of the human amygdala and ventromedial prefrontal cortex to decision-making. J. Neurosci. **19**, 5473–5481 (1999)
33. Bechara, A., Tranel, D., Damasio, H.: Characterization of the decision-making deficit of patients with ventromedial prefrontal cortex lesions. Brain **123**, 2189–2202 (2000)
34. Duvinage, M., Castermans, T., Petieau, M., Hoellinger, T., Cheron, G., Dutoit, T.: Performance of the Emotiv Epoc headset for P300-based applications. Biomed. Eng. Online **12**, 56 (2013)
35. Svozil, D., Kvasnicka, V., Pospichal, J.: Introduction to multi-layer feed-forward neural networks. Chemometr. Intell. Lab. Syst. **39**, 43–62 (1997)
36. Lekshmi, S.S., Selvam, V., Rajasekaran, M.P.: EEG signal classification using principal component analysis and wavelet transform with neural network. In: 2014 International Conference on Communications and Signal Processing (ICCSP), pp. 687–690. IEEE (2014)
37. Kotler, P.: Consumer Neuroscience. MIT Press, Cambridge (2017)
38. Bhardwaj, A., et al.: Classification of human emotions from EEG signals using SVM and LDA classifiers. In: 2nd International Conference on Signal Processing and Integrated Networks (SPIN). IEEE (2015)

Business Forecasting in the Light of Statistical Approaches and Machine Learning Classifiers

Prasun Chakrabarti[1,2]([⊠]), Biswajit Satpathy[1], Siddhant Bane[3],
Tulika Chakrabarti[4]([⊠]), Narendra S. Chaudhuri[5], and Pierluigi Siano[6]

[1] Department of Business Administration, Sambalpur University,
Sambalpur 768019, Odisha, India
[2] ITM Universe, Vadodara 391510, Gujarat, India
drprasun.cse@gmail.com
[3] Department of Computer Science and Engineering, ITM Universe,
Vadodara 391510, Gujarat, India
[4] Department of Chemistry, Sir Padampat Singhania University,
Udaipur 313601, India
tulika.chakrabarti20@gmail.com
[5] Department of Computer Science and Engineering,
Indian Institute of Technology, Indore 453552, Madhya Pradesh, India
[6] Department of Industrial Engineering, University of Salerno,
Via Giovanni Paolo II, 132, 84084 Fisciano SA, Italy

Abstract. The paper focuses a non-conventional approach using Poisson and Binomial distributions for optimum strategic business forecasting. An analysis has been carried out based on profit-loss statistics of consecutive ten years. Relevance of Poisson distribution in business forecasting is shown. Relevance of Binomial distribution in business forecasting is also shown. Curve fitting has been applied to reveal further some discovered facts related to gain analysis. Linear Regression, Exponential, Parabolic, Power function, Logarithmic, polynomial of degree 2 and 4 curves are shown as cases. Novel facts related to business forecasting in the light of machine learning classifiers have been pointed out leading to new directions in the field of research in business analytics.

Keywords: Curve fit · Business forecasting · Machine learning classifiers

1 Introduction

Strategic development or review [1] deals with an analysis of the factors external to a business that affects strategy. Marketing Myopia [2] also indicates the essence of investigation of sales and profit in case of strategic uncertainty. In certain cases due to some external stochastic events [3], statistical analysis has to be carried out based upon prediction and forecasting. Point estimation [4] and Artificial Neural Network [5] also facilitate towards accurate modeling in business forecasting. Based on best curve fitting [6], mathematical expressions can be obtained which will suffice towards framing an optimum business strategy. Finding the facts leading to some directions in business thought based on statistical established theories [7] is a research challenge.

© Springer Nature Singapore Pte Ltd. 2019
M. Singh et al. (Eds.): ICACDS 2019, CCIS 1045, pp. 13–21, 2019.
https://doi.org/10.1007/978-981-13-9939-8_2

Rare work has been done in business forecasting in the light of machine learning classifiers whereby this research definitely leads to a new direction in the process of business forecasting.

2   Relevance of Poisson and Binomial Distributions in Business Forecasting

Business forecasting [8] and relevant simulation based modeling [9] plays a pivotal role towards optimum strategic management. Sensing profit or loss at specific timing instants is a part of the exercise. In a specific time period, the number of occurrences of any stochastic event, either profit or loss, has to be counted and therein lies the significance of Poisson distribution [10]. Suppose n is the frequency of business analysis within a specific period of observation, y be a counting process representing the event loss within time period t and m be the mean of Poisson distribution. If the strategic decision is framed then risk margin has to be noted as a threshold [11]. Considering at most k number of incidence of event loss in a year, the mathematical representation is

$$P(y <= k) = e^{-m}(1 + m + m^2/2! + m^3/3! + \ldots\ldots\ldots + m^k/k!). \qquad (1)$$

The frequency of incidence of event loss that occurs in disjoint time intervals is independent. The event $\{X = s\}$ indicates the number of successes e.g. business profit and $\{Y = n-s\}$ as the number of failures e.g. business loss. The probabilistic representation is given by $p^s(1-p)^{n-s}$. Now the incidence of the event profit can be governed by $\binom{n}{s}$ ways. Herein lays the essence of validity of Binomial distribution.

Table 1. Analysis of profit-loss as per ten consecutive years (n = 10 and m = 3.6)

Timing instants of observation representing y_i, i = 1 to 10	Probability of Success p(s)	Risk margin k	Poisson Distribution P (y <= k)
1	0.7	4	0.7806
2	0.6	5	0.8946
3	0.8	3	0.6025
4	0.9	2	0.3799
5	0.5	6	0.9554
6	0.7	4	0.7806
7	0.6	5	0.8946
8	0.5	6	0.9554
9	0.6	5	0.8946
10	0.9	2	0.3799

3   Business Forecasting Based on Curve Fitting

Prediction in business in effective way suffices the increase in probability of gain in future [12]. As per the concept pointed out in Sect. 2 and the Table 1, the curve fitting e.g. p(s) against P(y >= k) has been performed and related inference is drawn.

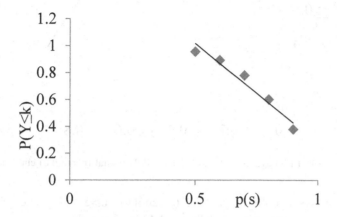

Fig. 1. Plot of p(s) against P(Y <= k) using Linear regression based curve fitting

Figure 1 points out the curve fitting based on the linear regression. Prediction is governed by the equation $y = -1.4692x + 1.7509$.

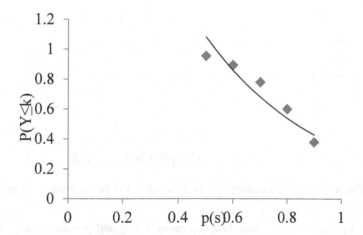

Fig. 2. Plot of p(s) against P(Y <= k) using Exponential curve fitting

Figure 2 points out the exponential curve fitting and prediction is governed by the equation $y = 3.4443e^{-2.313x}$.

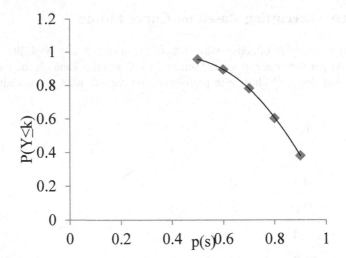

Fig. 3. Plot of p(s) against P(Y <= k) using Polynomial (parabolic) curve fitting

Figure 3 points out the polynomial (parabolic) curve fitting and prediction is governed by the equation $y = -2.7833x^2 + 2.4559x + 0.4234$.

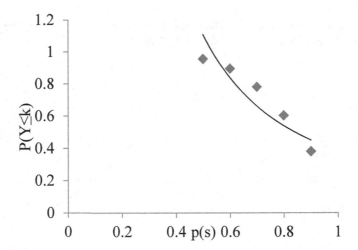

Fig. 4. Plot of p(s) against P(Y <= k) using Power function curve fitting

Figure 4 points out the power function curve fitting and prediction is governed by the equation $y = 0.3828x^{-1.535}$

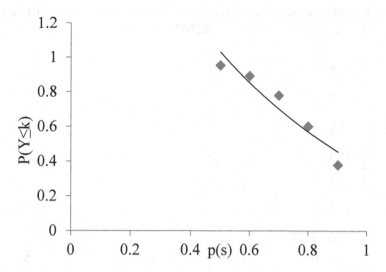

Fig. 5. Plot of p(s) against P(Y <= k) using Logarithmic curve fitting

Figure 5 points out the logarithmic curve fitting and prediction is governed by the equation: $y = -0.983ln(x) + 0.3521$. Based on the aforementioned graphical analysis, it is evident that the prediction of Poisson distribution on the basis of futuristic probability of success yield optimum accuracy estimate in the case of polynomial (parabolic) curve fitting.

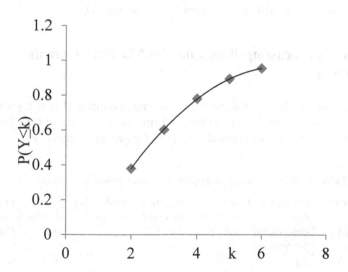

Fig. 6. Plot of k against P(Y <= k) using polynomial (degree 2) curve fitting

Figure 6 points out the polynomial (degree 2) curve fitting and prediction is governed by the equation $y = -0.0278x^2 + 0.3667x - 0.243$.

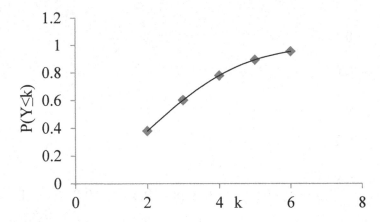

Fig. 7. Plot of k against P(Y <= k) using polynomial (degree 4) curve fitting

Figure 7 indicates the polynomial (degree 4) curve fitting and prediction is governed by the equation $y = 0.0013x^4 - 0.0211x^3 + 0.0974x^2 + 0.0532x + 0.0321$. On the basis of the supervised machine learning and figures from Table 1, a forecasting can be done based on the risk margin (k) and the Poisson distribution P(y <= k). The graphical analysis based on Figs. 6. and 7. clearly indicates best curve fitting in case of polynomials of degree 2 and 4 respectively. This will facilitate to predict the futuristic loss and accordingly the risk management has to be framed.

4 Business Forecasting Based on the Machine Learning Classifiers

The business gain analysis using machine learning classifiers [13] is a great research challenge. The sole objective is to extract information from dataset (see Table 2) and transform into meaningful categorical data [14] for proper forecasting.

Table 2. Business analysis dataset for classification using *Weka 3.8.1*

Timing instants of observation representing y_i, i = 1 to 10	Frequency of data observation per year (n)	Instances of event gain (X)	Instances of event loss (Y)	Probability of Success p(s)	Risk margin (k)	Poisson Distribution P(y <= k)
1	10	7	3	0.7	4	0.7806
2	10	6	4	0.6	5	0.8946
3	10	8	2	0.8	3	0.6025

(continued)

Table 2. (*continued*)

Timing instants of observation representing y_i, i = 1 to 10	Frequency of data observation per year (n)	Instances of event gain (X)	Instances of event loss (Y)	Probability of Success p(s)	Risk margin (k)	Poisson Distribution P(y <= k)
4	10	9	1	0.9	2	0.3799
5	10	5	5	0.5	6	0.9554
6	10	7	3	0.7	4	0.7806
7	10	6	4	0.6	5	0.8946
8	10	5	5	0.5	6	0.9554
9	10	6	4	0.6	5	0.8946
10	10	9	1	0.9	2	0.3799

We have used popular, open-source data mining tool Weka (version *8.3.1*) [15] for the analysis purpose. On the basis of supervised filter applied on instances, the experimental results have been obtained (see Table 3).

Table 3. Quantitative parameters of various machine learning classifiers using cross-validation 10-fold in Weka 8.3.1

Classifiers	Kappa statistic	True positive rate	False positive rate	Precision	Recall	ROC area	Accuracy (%)
BayesNet (class balancer)	1.000	1.000	0.000	1.000	1.000	1.000	100
Complement BayesNet (class balancer)	0.625	0.813	0.188	0.864	0.813	0.813	81.3
HMM and Naïve Bayes (class balancer)	0.000	0.500	0.500	0.250	0.500	0.500	50
Logistic, SGD, KStar and LWL (function classifier under class balancer)	1.000	1.000	0.000	1.000	1.000	1.000	100
Multilayer Perceptron (function classifier under class balancer)	0.875	0.938	0.063	0.944	0.938	1.000	93
Simple Logistic (function classifier under class balancer)	0.000	0.500	0.500	0.250	0.500	1.000	50
SMO (function classifier under class balancer)	0.625	0.813	0.188	0.864	0.813	0.813	81.3
Voted Perceptron (function classifier)	0.000	0.500	0.500	0.250	0.500	0.469	50
BFTree (tree classifier under class balancer)	−0.250	0.375	0.625	0.214	0.375	0.750	37.5

(*continued*)

Table 3. (*continued*)

Classifiers	Kappa statistic	True positive rate	False positive rate	Precision	Recall	ROC area	Accuracy (%)
Random Forest and Random Tree (tree classifier under class balancer)	1.000	1.000	0.000	1.000	1.000	1.000	100
REPTree (tree classifier under class balancer)	0.000	0.500	0.500	0.250	0.500	1.000	50
BayesNet and Naïve Bayes (resample)	1.000	1.000	0.000	1.000	1.000	1.000	100
Complement BayesNet (resample)	0.750	1.000	0.250	0.800	1.000	0.875	87.5
HMM (resample)	0.000	0.500	0.500	0.250	0.500	0.500	50
Logistic, SGD, Multilayer perceptron (function classifier under resample)	1.000	1.000	0.000	1.000	1.000	1.000	100
Simple logistic (function classifier under resample)	−0.250	0.375	0.625	0.214	0.375	0.750	37.5
SMO (function classifier under resample)	0.750	0.875	0.125	0.900	0.875	0.875	87.5
Voted Perceptron (function classifier under resample)	0.000	0.500	0.500	0.250	0.500	0.000	50
IBK, KStar, LWL (lazy classifier under resample)	1.000	1.000	0.000	1.000	1.000	1.000	100
BFTree (tree classifier under resample)	−0.25	0.375	0.625	0.214	0.375	0.750	37.5
J48, Random Forest, Random Tree (tree classifier under resample)	1.000	1.000	0.000	1.000	1.000	1.000	100
RepTree	−0.125	0.438	0.563	0.233	0.438	0.875	43.8

5 Conclusions

In the view of the simulation using Weka 3.8.1 tool based on dataset as mentioned in Table 2, we state the following inferences:

  i. Using class balancer, BayesNet provides best accuracy and optimum business forecasting.
 ii. Using function classifier under class balancer category, Logistic, SGD, KStar and LWL provide best accuracy.

iii. Using tree classifier under class balancer category, Random Forest and Random Tree provide best accuracy.

iv. Using resample, BayesNet and Naïve Bayes provide best accuracy.

v. Using function classifier under resample category, Logistic, SGD, Multilayer perceptron provides best accuracy.

vi. Using lazy classifier under resample category, IBK, KStar, LWL provide best accuracy.

vii. Using tree classifier under resample category, J48, Random Forest and Random Tree provide best accuracy.

The paper points out certain research inferences based on Poscurve fitting in business forecasting. Machine learning based classifiers facilitate towards business forecasting using Weka *3.8.1* as the simulator. Using class balancer and resample category, investigations have been carried out towards yielding best accuracy by the classifiers.

References

1. Aaker, D.A.: Strategic Market Management. Wiley, New Jersey (2005)
2. Levitt, T.: Marketing Myopia. Harvard Business Review, pp. 45–56, July–August (1960)
3. Olofsson, P.: Probability, Statistics, and Stochastic Processes. Wiley, New Jersey (2005)
4. Giri, P.K., Banerjee, J.: Introduction to Statistics. Academic Publishers, Cambridge (1999)
5. Mitchell, T.M.: Machine Learning. Tata McGraw Hill Companies, Inc., New York (1997)
6. Cobb, C.W., Paul, D.H.: A theory of production. Am. Econ. Rev. Suppl. **18**, 139–165 (1925)
7. Samuelson, A.P.: Economics, 10th edn. McGraw-Hill Book Company, New York (1976)
8. Hanke, J.E., Wichern, D.W.: Business Forecasting. Pearson Education Inc., London (2009)
9. Gordon, G.: System Simulation. Pearson Education, Inc., London (1978)
10. Casella, G., Berger, R.L.: Statistical Inference. Duxbury Advanced Series Thomson Learning, Pacific Grove (2002)
11. Tony, M.: Principles of Strategic Management. Taylor & Francis, London (2007)
12. Udo, S., Len, T., Michael, G.: Business Forecasting. Wiley, New York (2016)
13. Shwartz, S.S., David, S.B.: Understanding Machine Learning: From Theory to Algorithms. Cambridge University Press, Cambridge (2014)
14. Agresti, A.: Categorical Data Analysis. Wiley, New York (1990)
15. Richard, R.: Data Mining: A Tutorial-Based Primer. CRC Press, New York (2016)

Real Time Prediction of American Sign Language Using Convolutional Neural Networks

Shobhit Sinha⑩, Siddhartha Singh⑩, Sumanu Rawat⑩, and Aman Chopra⁽✉⁾⑩

Manipal Institute of Technology, Manipal 576104, Karnataka, India
shobhit.sinha19@gmail.com, singh.siddhartha23@gmail.com,
sumanurawat12@gmail.com, amanchopra64@gmail.com

Abstract. The American Sign Language (ASL) was developed in the early 19th century in the American School for Deaf, United States of America. It is a natural language inspired by the French sign language and is used by around half a million people around the world with a majority in North America. The Deaf Culture views deafness as a difference in human experience rather than a disability, and ASL plays an important role in this experience. In this project, we have used Convolutional Neural Networks to create a robust model that understands 29 ASL characters (26 alphabets and 3 special characters). We further host our model locally over a real-time video interface which provides the predictions in real-time and displays the corresponding English characters on the screen like subtitles. We look at the application as a one-way translator from ASL to English for the alphabet. We conceptualize this whole procedure in our paper and explore some useful applications that can be implemented.

Keywords: American Sign Language · Convolution Neural Network · Image processing · Video processing

1 Introduction

The National Institute on Deafness and Other Communication Disorders is an organization that conducts biomedical research processes of hearing, balance, smell, taste, voice, speech, and language. Their statistics dictate that within the USA, 3 in every 1000 people are born with a certain degree of impaired hearing capacity in one or both ears. Around 30 million people above the age of 12 years have hearing loss in both ears. A number of solutions have been developed to ease communication without being able to hear clearly.

The American Sign Language provides a wide array of symbols, actions, and movements which enables communication without sound. It has a vast scope, hence for the purpose of conceptualization, we have concentrated our research on the ASL Alphabet dataset only. In this paper, we develop a Convolutional Neural Network model using the Keras library. After making sure that the CNN

© Springer Nature Singapore Pte Ltd. 2019
M. Singh et al. (Eds.): ICACDS 2019, CCIS 1045, pp. 22–31, 2019.
https://doi.org/10.1007/978-981-13-9939-8_3

model is trained with a high accuracy metric, we host our model to enable real-time prediction. We provide a video input through the webcam. Each frame is then decolorized and augmented for efficient processing. Using optimal multi-processing for hosting the model on multiple CPU cores simultaneously, we are able to make a real-time prediction on live video stream input with negligible latency. This method can play a great role in developing state of the art real time sign language detection software for people who have difficulty in speaking and hearing. This could bridge the communication gap which persists between impaired people.

A brief about the objective of this paper has been mentioned in Sect. 2. A discussion about previous works and research done in this field has been mentioned under Sect. 3. Section 4 talks about the methodology which has been used to extract the most influential features. Section 5 explains the real-time prediction of the video and finally, the paper ends with Sect. 6 and Sect. 7 presenting the results and conclusion respectively.

2 Objective

In this paper, we have proposed a Machine Learning Software Application that is capable of acting as a one-way translator for sign languages. Our application makes real-time predictions on the 26 ASL alphabet and 3 special characters enabling anyone to understand ASL if they know the English alphabet. Due to computational limitations, we have performed our experiments on a small section of ASL. This concept can be extended to the complete ASL and even more sign languages if appropriate datasets are available. Our objective is to provide such real-time translators for sign languages and weaken the communication barrier caused due to the variety and complexity of sign languages.

3 Related Work

A number of studies have been performed in the fields of gesture recognition, sign language translation, and image recognition and varied approaches have been taken to solve similar problems. In this section, we will take a look at a few of such researches. Classification of large image datasets using Convolutional neural networks is proposed in [8]. The authors have documented their submission to the image net challenge where they use 1.3 million images to train a Convolutional Neural Network and the resulting model consists of 60 million parameters. This research was a milestone in works related to the use of CNN for image recognition.

In work [14], an approach for Indian sign language recognition has been proposed. The authors have processed the input image and each entry is compared with a large database of existing images to give out the most likely output. This comparison has been sped up with the use of multiprocessing and GPU computing. The authors go on to write about how they converted their output into an audio format to facilitate communication further.

The following paper [10] delves into the field of Human-Computer Interaction on the basis of hand gesture recognition. The authors of the paper have used Kinect sensors to record the depth and color information of the subject to come to more robust and accurate conclusions about hand shape and structure. A successful experiment is recorded in the paper wherein the application is used to play a game of Rock Paper Scissors. Apart from the above-mentioned works, there has been a lot of time, effort and resources put into the research directing to understanding gestures of the human body, with the goal of making meaningful conclusions without having to type your instructions into a computer. The paper [13] used Hidden Markov Models to develop a single view camera system that recognizes hand gestures. The authors in [4] proposed a 2 level approach to solve the real-time hand gesture recognition. They used two levels of approach using Haar-like features and AdaBoost. The system presented in the paper [7] uses skin detection and hand contour comparison algorithm to detect and track a bare hand in a cluttered background via bag of features and SVM (Support Vector Machines). The paper [9] presents a software which aims to present a real time of hand gesture on basis of detection of some shape based features like orientation, Centre of mass centroid, fingers status, thumb in positions of raised or folded fingers of hand. In work [11] authors have extracted features such as Eigen vectors and Eigen values for recognition and have used principal component analysis for gesture recognition. In work [12] the authors have performed segmentation on skin pixels and have also used depth information in parallel to get better results. They have used SVM for the final classification. The paper [5] discusses sign language recognition using linguistic sub units. They have used Markov models to encode the temporal changes between sub-units and sequential pattern boosting to apply discriminative feature selection. [2] segments the hand and then uses Hilbert space-filling curve to extract a feature vector invariant to translation, scaling, and stretching. Paper [1] showcases a method for automatic recognition of finger-spelling in Indian sign language using the back-propagation algorithm through artificial neural networks.

4 Methodology

The methodology of the system has been shown in Fig. 1.

4.1 Data Set Description

The ASL dataset [3] which is downloaded from Kaggle consists of all 26 alphabets of English language and 3 special characters namely delete, nothing and space. The dataset is divided into different directories for different alphabets and special characters. Each directory contains approx 3000 images out of which 80% is used for training and 20% is used for validation. The image size of the dataset is 200×200 pixels and the image resolution is 72 pixels/in. The size of the entire dataset is 1.11 GB.

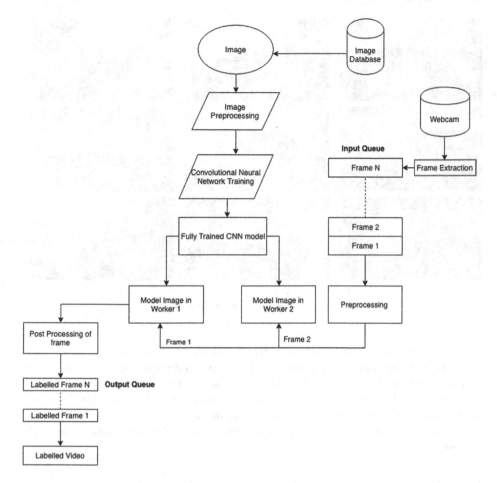

Fig. 1. Block diagram of methodology

4.2   Data Pre Processing

To build a good image classifier model we need a huge dataset. Having a small dataset, approx. 3000 per class in our case (87,000 images in total), can lead to poor accuracy of the model. Data augmentation is done to artificially increase the dataset. The ImageDataGenerator API of keras is used to generate real-time augmented data. Performing actions like changing the height and the width, rotating the image, zooming in and out, horizontal and vertical flip, changing sheer intensity and changing the brightness level will create artificial data for the model to improve the accuracy. Certain data preprocessed images have been shown in Fig. 2. As a preprocessing step, we are reducing the dimensions of the image and scaling the image pixels to [0, 1] to make it trainable on the resources available to us.

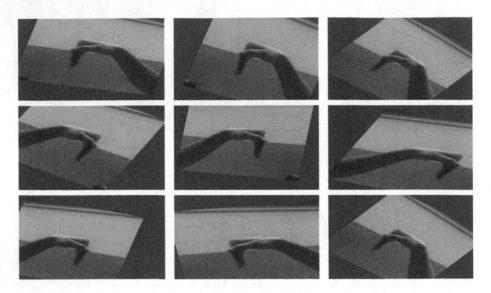

Fig. 2. Data pre processing steps

The ASL dataset, available at Kaggle, comes as a separate directory for every class. After extracting the class name from the paths a numpy array of labels are created which is the binarized for the CNN model. The LabelBinarizer enables us to convert the human readable string of class labels into one hot encoded labels to improve the prediction done by the model.

The data is randomly partitioned into two sections 80% for training and 20% for testing.

4.3   Model

The aim was to develop a model capable of predicting ASL alphabets and special characters with very high accuracy. Since the input of this model is an image, we decided to use the CNN architecture for this model. The model contains multiple convolutional layers, pooling layers, ReLU layers, and a fully connected layer.

Random shuffling was done while reading the data into memory to make sure that the training and testing images are not the same every time. The image dimensions are reduced and the pixels are scaled to [0, 1]. Before training the dataset is randomly divided into two sections – 80% for training and 20% for validation. The model consists of Conv2D layers having filters 32, 64 and 128. We purposely increased the filter size of Conv2D layers because the deeper we go in the network, the smaller the spatial dimensions of our volume, and the more filters we learn. The architectural design of the CNN model is showing in Fig. 3. In this layer the padding used is "same" because we want the output layer should be of the same length as the input layer. The kernel size of these layers is (3,3).

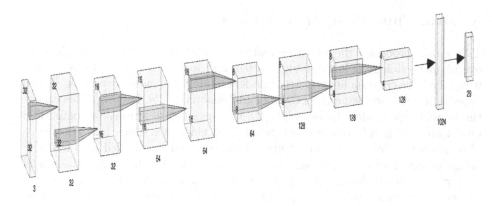

Fig. 3. CNN architecture

Activation Layer: ReLU or Rectified Linear Unit is used as the activation function in this model. The ReLU is nothing but $R(x) = Max(0, x)$ i.e when x is less than 0 the value is 0 and for $x > 0$ the value is x where x is the input to the neuron. Some of the advantages of ReLU are Sparse activation, better gradient propagation, Efficient computation and Scale-invariant. We use ReLU activation layer only for the hidden layers, and for the output layer we are using SoftMax function because it gives the probability for classifying the image in different classes.

Pooling Layer: The basic job of pooling layer is to provide downsampling operations. This plane is responsible for reducing the dimensionality of the feature maps thus decreasing the number of subsequent parameters to learn. Using the MaxPooling2D API we added the pooling layer in our model to reduce the dimensionality of the image by reducing the number of pixels. In our model, we are using a pool size of 3×3 for the initial layer and then 2×2 for subsequent layers. The pool size in Max-Pooling is decreased towards the end layers of the model to make sure that the spatial dimensions are not reduced too quickly.

Dropout: Dropout layer is important in a model to avoid overfitting. After each layer, we're dropping some percentage of neurons to make sure that not one neuron is fully responsible for any feature. The dropout forces the layer to learn the same feature with a different set of neurons and thus avoiding the overfitting. In our model, the dropout is 25% in the intermediate layers and 50% in the fully connected layer.

Fully Connected Layer: The fully connected layer serves as a linear combinatorial function for the nonlinear activation maps produced in the last convolutional layer of the CNN. It is an easy way to learn to combine the different activations that would lead to a correct classification of the given image. Of course, due to a large number of parameters that are usually present in these fully connected layers, it is often very computationally expensive.

5   Real Time Prediction of Video

This paper processes the video in real time. The following diagram gives an overall methodology of how the video is being processed. The model was trained using the Keras python library. After model training, the model was saved. Video processing was done using OpenCV [6] and Tensorflow [15]. For tensorflow to use the saved Keras model, the model had to be converted to tensorflow compatible model and the graph was thus extracted. The video is nothing but a sequence of a number of frames in time. Video processing can be divided into multiple image processing tasks. ASL sign in each frame was classified using the model that we developed. We made use of inbuilt webcam as the source of video for the classifier. Since the frame rate of the video was pretty high and a GPU environment wasn't available, we had to improvise and use multiprocessing and a queue mechanism to make the process as fast and smooth as possible. OpenCV was used to extract frames from the video source. Each frame required some pre-processing to be done which acted as a blocking operation for the next frame extraction operation. To solve this a queue was implemented to hold the next set of frames until the time preprocessing was being performed on the preceding frames. Since the system used had dual cores, a set of worker threads were spawned. Image of the model was loaded in both the set of workers so that they can act as individual classifiers and increase the speed of computation.

6   Results

The CNN model trained on 87,000 ASL images gave an accuracy of **96.03%**. Figure 4 depicts the Loss and accuracy vs Epoch number of the model. It can be seen that with the increasing number of epochs the accuracy increased

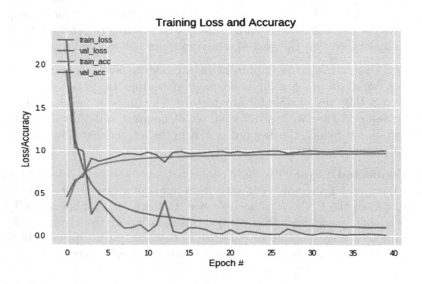

Fig. 4. Loss/Accuracy vs Epoch graph

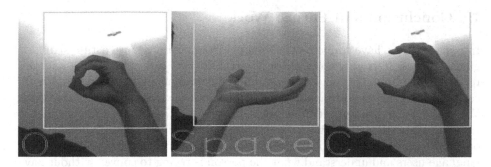

Fig. 5. Results for letter O, space and C

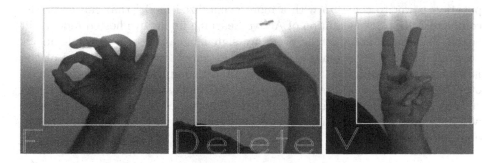

Fig. 6. Results for letter F, delete and V

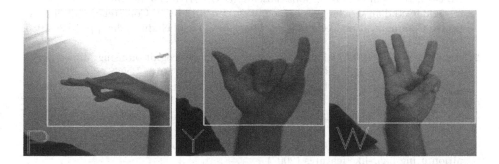

Fig. 7. Results for letter P, Y and W

substantially and the loss values decreased. The model was successfully used by a real time system, which could detect sign language with minimal latency. Example predictions of the system have been shown in Figs. 5, 6 and 7.

7   Conclusion and Future Work

In our paper, we have trained a CNN model from nothing but existing sign language images. It is easy to generate a database for projects like this and the reward is manifold. Our experiments were focused on a small part of the American Sign Language, for which we were able to produce strikingly accurate results. We produce the live output of symbols shown to a webcam, with a negligible time lag, almost as if viewing a video with subtitles. We strongly believe that our approach can prove to be useful in helping people to communicate with sign language users and understand what the person is trying to convey without having to be proficient in American Sign Language. CNN turned out to be perfect for this application.

As a part of future work, we suggest using better hardware and more computation power to come up with a more generalized model that can cover the complete ASL. Implementation of Active Learning in our live hosted model will enable the contribution of the everyday sign language users. It would inculcate our model with a sense of dialects and varied shapes and forms of the human hand. The authors of this paper plan to implement this approach on other sign languages and eventually host this application on public platforms such as Android and the web, free of cost. We sincerely hope that our research will help people with difficulty in speaking and listening and will improve the quality of their life.

References

1. Adithya, V., Vinod, P.R., Gopalakrishnan, U.: Artificial neural network based method for Indian sign language recognition. In: 2013 IEEE Conference on Information & Communication Technologies, Thuckalay, Tamil Nadu, India, pp. 1080–1085 (2013)
2. Ragab, A., Ahmed, M., Chau, S.-C.: Sign language recognition using hilbert curve features. In: Kamel, M., Campilho, A. (eds.) ICIAR 2013. LNCS, vol. 7950, pp. 143–151. Springer, Heidelberg (2013). https://doi.org/10.1007/978-3-642-39094-4_17
3. ASL Alphabet. Image dataset for alphabets in the American sign language. https://www.kaggle.com/grassknoted/asl-alphabet
4. Emil, M., Chen, P.Q., Georganas, N.D.: Real-time vision-based hand gesture recognition using haar-like features (2007)
5. Cooper, H., Ong, E.-J., Pugeault, N., Bowden, R.: Sign language recognition using sub-units. J. Mach. Learn. Res. 13(1), 2205–2231 (2012)
6. Bradski, G.: The OpenCV library. DR DOBBS J. Softw. Tools 120, 122 (2000)
7. Dardas, N.H., Georganas, N.D.: Real-time hand gesture detection and recognition using bag-of-features and support vector machine techniques. IEEE Trans. Instrum. Measurment (2011)
8. Krizhevsky, A., Sutskever, I., Hinton, G.E.: ImageNet classification with deep convolutional neural networks. In: Pereira, F., Burges, C.J.C., Bottou, L., Weinberger, K.Q. (eds.) Advances in Neural Information Processing Systems, vol. 25, pp. 1097–1105 (2012)

9. Nikam, A.S., Ambekar, A.G.: Sign language recognition using image based hand gesture recognition techniques. In: 2016 Online International Conference on Green Engineering and Technologies (IC-GET), Coimbatore, pp. 1–5 (2016)

10. Ren, Z., Meng, J., Yuan, J., Zhang, Z.: Robust hand gesture recognition with the kinect sensor. In: Proceedings of the 19th ACM International Conference on Multimedia (MM 2011), pp. 759–760. ACM, New York (2011)

11. Sawant, S.N., Kumbhar, M.S.: Real time sign language recognition using PCA. In: 2014 IEEE International Conference on Advanced Communications, Control and Computing Technologies, Ramanathapuram, pp. 1412–1415 (2014)

12. Raheja, J.L., Mishra, A., Chaudhary, A.: Pattern Recognit. Image Anal. **26**, 434 (2016). https://doi.org/10.1134/S1054661816020164

13. Starner, T.E.: Visual recognition of American sign language using hidden Markov models. Master's thesis, Massachusetts Institute of Technology, Cambridge (1995)

14. Madhuri, Y., Anitha, G., Anburajan, M.: Vision-based sign language translation device. In: 2013 International Conference on Information Communication and Embedded Systems, ICICES 2013, pp. 565–568 (2013). https://doi.org/10.1109/ICICES.2013.6508395

15. Abadi, M., et al.: TensorFlow: large-scale machine learning on heterogeneous systems (2015). http://www.tensorflow.org

Hybridization of Fuzzy Min-Max Neural Networks with kNN for Enhanced Pattern Classification

Anil Kumar[(✉)] and P. S. V. S. Sai Prasad

School of Computer and Information Sciences,
University of Hyderabad, Hyderabad, Telangana, India
`anilhcu@uohyd.ac.in, saics@uohyd.ernet.in`

Abstract. Fuzzy Min-Max Neural Networks (FMNN) is a single epoch learning Pattern Classification algorithm with several advantages for online learning. The information loss due to Contraction step of FMNN leads to several improvements in literature such as MLF, FMCN etc. These approaches do not use Contraction step and provide additional structures in FMNN for decision making in overlapped regions overcoming the problem of Contraction with the cost of an increase in training complexity of FMNN. This work proposes a hybridization of FMNN with kNN algorithm for achieving the ability to handle decision making in overlapped regions without altering the structure of FMNN. Comparative studies with existing approaches over benchmark decision systems have proved the utility of the proposed kNN-FMNN approach.

Keywords: Fuzzy Min-Max Neural Network · FMNN · Fuzzy sets · Neural networks · Classification · kNN · Hybrid system · MLF

1 Introduction

In 1965, Zadeh [16] introduced the new concept called Fuzzy sets, to manipulate the imprecise data into the fuzzy pattern. The Fuzzy logic aims at creating approximate human reasoning that is helpful on cognitive decision making. Several Hybrid systems were developed with Fuzzy sets combining other soft computing models such as artificial neural networks, expert systems and genetic algorithm etc. [6,12,14,18,19].

A hybrid system like the combination of the artificial neural network with fuzzy logic has proved their effectiveness in being helpful for real-world problems [6]. In 1992, Simpson [15] proposed Fuzzy Min-Max Neural Network (FMNN) classifier based on fuzzy hyperboxes. The union of fuzzy hyperboxes represents individual decision classes. A hyperbox is defined as a region in n-dimensional pattern space characterized by minimum points, maximum points and fuzzy membership function. FMNN learning algorithm computes the min-max points of hyperboxes to acquire knowledge. These placing and adjustment

© Springer Nature Singapore Pte Ltd. 2019
M. Singh et al. (Eds.): ICACDS 2019, CCIS 1045, pp. 32–44, 2019.
https://doi.org/10.1007/978-981-13-9939-8_4

of hyperboxes create a granular structure of pattern in pattern space which is useful for pattern classification. This method also constitutes with several salient learning features like online learning, non-linear separability and non-parametric classification, thus, making FMNN more flexible.

FMNN has been applied successfully in different applications such as fault detection, lung cancer, medical data analysis, classification of music and text classification etc. [1,4,9–13,20].

However, FMNN is facing problems due to contraint of the size of hyperboxes and contraction process which may lead to gradation error in classification [8,17]. Several developments have been proposed for FMNN in order to overcome its limitation and for enhanced classification.

In 2000, Gabrys et al. [7] proposed a generalization and extension based on FMNN known as General Fuzzy Min-Max Neural Network (GFMNN) that incorporates a significant modification on conventional FMNN with the new fuzzy membership function and hyperbox expansion criteria. But they used the same contraction process as FMNN that tempered the acquired knowledge in the boundary region causing gradation error in classification.

Many researchers have achieved an innovative way to exclude the contraction process to retains overlapping information for better pattern classification. In 2004, Bargiela et al. [2] proposed a new classifier known as Inclusion/Exclusion Fuzzy Hyperbox classifier (EFC) using an inclusion hyperboxes that includes input patterns belonging to the same class, and exclusion hyperboxes (erroneous hyperboxes) that includes input patterns in a confusion region of a different class. However, this method resulted in the reduction in classification accuracy owing to the removal of exclusion hyperboxes.

In 2007, Nandedkar et al. [8] introduced a novel concept called Fuzzy Min-Max Neural Network classifier with Compensatory Neuron Architecture (FMCN). This method can protect the min-max points of confusion overlap region to enhance the learning algorithm as this information is highly significant for pattern classification. Although this method did not allow the overlapped hyperboxes to be expanded for next time which tends to increase in cardinality of hyperboxes, thus increasing the time and space complexity.

In 2007, Zhang et al. [17] proposed a new approach called as Data Core Based Fuzzy Neural Network (DCFMN) to overcome the limitation in FMCN with the help of geometrical centre and data core of hyperbox which can additionally benefit to handle noisy data. Hence, this method results in high classification accuracy than other prominent approaches like GFMNN, FMCN, EFC and also classical FMNN. In 2014, Devtalab et al. [3] proposed a new method called Multi-Level Fuzzy Min-Max Neural Network (MLF) classifier employing a multi-level tree structure to classify the pattern. Each level of model operates the smaller hyperboxes to handle the confusion region problem. It resulted in the enhancement of classification accuracy in the boundary region compared with existing approach GFMNN, EFC, FMCN, DCFMN and FMNN.

The above-mentioned improvement to FMNN has been obtained at an increased cost of training as additional is added to the simple three-layer architecture of FMNN. This motivated us to explore for the methodology for achieving the better classification accuracies without resorting to modification of the structure of FMNN. The proposed work introduces hybridization of k Nearest Neighbour algorithm in FMNN as kNN-FMNN classifier for dealing with overlapping regions without change of Neural Network structure of FMNN. We perform the experiments on benchmark dataset mentioned in [3] to establish the importance of kNN-FMNN. Comparative experiments are conducted against the existing approaches GFMNN, EFC, FMCN, DCFMN and MLF respectively for establishing the relevance of the proposed approach.

The remaining part in this paper is organized as follows: Sect. 2 briefly introduces the basics of FMNN for Classification. Section 3 gives the proposed kNN-FMNN algorithm. Section 4 provides the experiments and analysis of results. Paper ends with the conclusion.

2   Fuzzy Min-Max Neural Network

In 1992, Simpson [15] proposed the single-pass dynamic network structure with salient learning features as online learning, non-linear separability and non-parametric classification, to deal with pattern classification using fuzzy systems known as the fuzzy min-max neural network (FMNN). It is a supervised learning neural network that uses n-dimensional hyperbox fuzzy sets to represent pattern spaces [15]. FMNN learning process creates and adjusts hyperboxes in n-dimensions space for all decision classes in the pattern space.

(a)

(b)

Fig. 1. (a) Hyperbox, (b) Overlapped region by two hyperboxes

Each hyperbox is determined by min points, max points with corresponding fuzzy membership function, defined as:

$$B_j = \{X, V_j, W_j, f(X, V_j, W_j)\} \quad \forall X \in I^n \tag{1}$$

where X is the input pattern, V_j and W_j are the minimum and maximum points of B_j hyperbox. I^n is the n-dimensional unit pattern space.

The fuzzy membership function (b_j) defined in Eq. (2):

$$b_j(X_h) = \frac{1}{2n} \sum_{i=1}^{n} [max(0, 1 - max(0, \gamma.min(1, x_{hi} - w_{ji})))$$
$$+ max(0, 1 - max(0, \gamma.min(1, v_{ji} - x_{hi})))] \tag{2}$$

where $X_h = (x_{h1}, x_{h2}, ..., x_{hn})$ is input pattern in n dimensional space and, $V_j = (v_{j1}, v_{j2}, ..., v_{jn})$ and $W_j = (w_{j1}, w_{j2}, ..., w_{jn})$ are the corresponding min points and max points for hyperbox B_j. γ is the sensitive parameter that regulates how fast the membership decreases as the distance between A_h and B_j increases.

FMNN training is a single epoch algorithm. For each training pattern, the learning involves three stages: (1) Expansion (2) Overlap Test (3) Contraction Process of Hyperboxes. During the training phase, when an input pattern enters into the network, the network tries to accommodate into one of existing same class hyperbox that gives full membership value. Otherwise, the network attempts to find the closest same label hyperbox which have the highest membership degree. The input pattern attempts to expand the particular hyperbox, bounded by expansion criteria given in Eq. (3). The range of user-defined parameter theta in Eq. (3) is $(0 < \theta < 1)$ and controls the volume of hyperbox.

$$\sum_{i=1}^{n} (max(w_{ji}, x_{hi}) - min(v_{ji}, x_{hi})) \leq n\theta \tag{3}$$

When the condition in Eq. (3) is satisfied, the Hyperbox expands to incorporate the input pattern by adjusting the min and max points by using the Eqs. (4) and (5).

$$v_{ji}^{new} = min(v_{ji}^{old}, x_{hi}) \quad \forall i = 1, 2, 3, \ldots, n. \tag{4}$$

$$w_{ji}^{new} = max(w_{ji}^{old}, x_{hi}) \quad \forall i = 1, 2, 3, \ldots, n. \tag{5}$$

If the condition Eq. (3) is not satisfied, a point hyperbox is created with minimum and maximum value same as the input pattern.

After the expansion process, the overlap test [15] examines the overlap for the expanded hyperbox with all hyperboxes of other decision classes. Two hyperboxes don't overlap as long as there is at least one dimension at which they are not overlapping. If there is an overlap in all dimensions, then the test determine the dimension at which the smallest overlap occurs. If overlap test results in identifying the dimension having the smallest overlap, the contraction steps [15] adjust the hyperboxes along that dimension resulting in non-overlapping hyperboxes.

For example in Fig. 1b, both hyperboxes have overlapped in all dimensions. Overlap test determines that the least overlap exist horizontal dimension. The contraction step adjusts the hyperboxes along this dimension and resulting adjusting hyperboxes are given with a bold outline.

In testing an FMNN for a given test pattern x, the fuzzy membership of x into all the hyperboxes is computed. The test pattern x is classified to the decision class corresponding to the hyperbox achieving highest fuzzy membership.

3 Proposed kNN-FMNN Algorithm

Classical FMNN algorithm [15], described in Sect. 2, results in non-overlapping among the hyperbox of different classes. This results in information loss existing in the overlapping (boundary) region and results in the possibility of objects of one class being absolute members of hyperboxes of other class. The defuzzification of the overlapping region affects the generalizability of the FMNN. The existing approaches [2,3,7,8,17] dealing with the representation of overlapping region by avoiding overlapping and contraction process, are resulting in increasing the complexity of FMNN structure. The proposed kNN-FMNN approach aims at retaining the simple structure of FMNN while having the ability to deal with decision making in overlapping regions.

In kNN-FMNN approach, the kNN classification algorithm is used for decision making when a testing pattern falls into an overlapping region.

kNN classification algorithm doesn't have any training phase. For every input test pattern, the distance is evaluated between the test pattern with all the training patterns. The nearest k training patterns are selected as the nearest neighbours. Based on the classes of those k nearest neighbours, voting is conducted, and the test pattern is characterized to majority class of nearest neighbours. But in the presence of large training data, kNN requires significant testing time.

FMNN gives a natural way to group the nearest objects into the granular structure of hyperbox. So, using this we can restrict the space in which k nearest neighbour computation needs to be performed. This aspect we are employing in dealing with respect to overlapping region of FMNN testing algorithm.

The rest of section described the training and testing phases of kNN-FMNN algorithms given in Algorithms 1 and 2 respectively.

3.1 Training of kNN-FMNN Algorithm

Let DT represents the set of the training pattern, and FM represents the FMNN model be constructed. Initially, FM is empty, and as training proceeds, hyperboxes are added to the FM model extending the representation of hyperbox H in FMNN, given in Sect. 2. The index list of objects belonging to H is maintained in our approach. For each input pattern x belonging to DT, only the expansion step is performed to preserve the overlapping region. In traditional FMNN based on expansion criteria, given in Eq. (3) , hyperbox can expand non-uniformly in a different dimension as cumulative widths of all dimensions needs to be less than $n\theta$. This can result in a narrow strip of hyperboxes along few dimension and found to be unsuitable for decision making with respect to kNN. To overcome this, we have adopted the modified expansion criteria given by Gabriel et al. [7] in their work on General Fuzzy Min-Max Neural Network for Clustering and Classification (GFMNN). For a hyperbox H with V and W as min and max points, and x as the input pattern, the modified expansion criteria is given in Eq. (6).

$$\forall_{i=1\ldots n}(\max(w_{ji}, x_{hi}) - \min(v_{ji}, x_{hi}) \leq \theta \tag{6}$$

This modified expansion criteria bounds every width of hyperbox on each dimension by θ and helps in generation of more uniform hyperboxes found suitable for kNN based decision making.

Algorithm 1. Training of kNN-FMNN

Input : DT:Training Samples, γ, θ
Output: Learning Model FM
1 Let FM: FMNN model (Initial empty);
2 **for** *every x in DT* **do**
3   **if** *FM.Belong(x) == True* **then**
4   H = FM.HMemb(x);
5   FM.Save(H,x);
6   **else**
7   H = FM.HMemb(x);
8   **if** *H exist* **then**
9   **if** $Exp_H(x) == True$ **then**
10   FM.Expand(H,x);
11   FM.Save(H,x);
12   **else**
13   FM.Create(x);
14   FM.Save(H,x);
15   **end**
16   **else**
17   FM.Create(x);
18   FM.Save(H,x);
19   **end**
20   **end**
21 **end**
22 Return FM

For every training pattern x, the method $Belongs(x)$ finds fuzzy membership value of x with all hyperboxes pertaining to class of x using Eq. (2) and determine whether there exists a hyperbox giving full membership of one to x.

$$Belong(x) = \{\exists h \in HBS \mid Memb_h(x) == 1 \ \& \ class(x) == class(h)\} \quad (7)$$

where HBS represents a set of hyperboxes.

If $Belongs(x)$ is true, x is added to the hyperbox giving the full membership without resulting in any modificaiton of hyperbox. Otherwise using $HMemb(x)$ the hyperbox H giving the highest membership is obtained. In case of the existence of such H, if expansion criteria are satisfied the hyperbox H is expanded using Eqs. (4) and (5) and object x stored as a member of resulting hyperbox. In case of expansion criteria not being met, or no hyperbox of a corresponding class existing, a point hyperbox is created using $Create(x)$, and x is added to the point hyperbox created.

3.2 Testing of kNN-FMNN Algorithm

Let DS be a set of testing sample. For every testing pattern x in DS, we compute the fuzzy membership value with all hyperboxes in FM. Because the overlapping among hyperboxes is allowed in the training phase, it is possible to obtain absolute membership of 1 to multiple hyperboxes. The $absMemb(x)$ returns all the hyperboxes giving full membership. If this set is empty, then the testing pattern is not belonging to any of hyperboxes and decision is taken like traditional FMNN testing by assigning the decision class corresponding to nearest hyperbox. In case $absMemb(x)$ return a non-empty collection of hyperboxes then the purity of collection is examined. The resulting collection is pure if only if all hyperboxes correspond to a single decision class and in which case, without ambiguity that class is assigned to the testing pattern. In case of impurity objects belonging to all this hyperboxes collected in $LocalSet$ function and kNN is performed locally for determining the decision class of x. The descriptions of functions used is given below:

$absMemb(x) = \{h \in HBS \mid Memb_h(x) == 1\}$: Collection of hyperboxes which have full membership for the object x.

$pure(absMemb(x)) = \{\forall h_1, h_2 \in absMemb(x) \mid class(h_1) == class(h_2)\}$: Collection of all hyperboxes that containing x correspond to same decision class.

$Members(h)$: Collecting the objects belonging to hyperbox h.

$LocalSet(absMemb(x)) = \bigcup_{h \in absMemb(x)} (Members(h))$.

$knnlocal(LocalSet(absMemb(x)), x)$: applying kNN methods on selected objects.

Algorithm 2. Testing of kNN-FMNN Algorithm

Input : DS: Testing Samples, Learning Model FM, k

1 **for** *every x in DS* **do**
2 | Compute fuzzy membership of x with all hyperboxes of FM model;
3 | **if** $|absMemb(x)| > 1$ **then**
4 | | **if** *pure(absMemb(x)) == True* **then**
5 | | | Classify x as $absMemb(x).class$;
6 | | **else**
7 | | | HO $= LocalSet(absMemb(x))$;
8 | | | Classify x using $knnlocal(HO, x).class$
9 | | **end**
10 | **else**
11 | | Classify x to highest membership hyperbox class
12 | **end**
13 **end**

---

4 Experiments

4.1 Performance Comparison with MLF [3] Approach

For evaluating the performance of kNN-FMNN, we have adopted the experimentation model given in [3] for MLF algorithm. In [3], MLF algorithm's performance was compared with popular variants of FMNN such as FMNN [15], GFMNN [7], EFC [2], FMCN [8] and DCFMN [17] in the aspects of average mis-classification, average number of hyperboxes produced and computational time given in milliseconds. The experiments were conducted on a synthesized and standard datasets. Furthermore, The stratified 3-fold cross-validation technique was performed on the original dataset to comprehend the model's ability. The original dataset was partitioned into three subsets. In each iteration, one group was retained for the testing part and, the remaining two groups were used for training the model. This validation continues for three times (in each fold).

Table 1. Benchmark datasets

Dataset	Attributes	Objects	Decision classes
Iris	3	150	3
Breast Cancer	30	569	2
Glass	9	214	6
Ionosphere	32	351	2
Thyroid	21	7200	3
Wine	13	178	3
Parkinson	22	195	2
Ozone layer	72	1848	2
Spambase	57	4597	2

In this paper, we have conducted experiments on kNN-FMNN following the same procedure given in [3]. The system configuration used for our experiments is CPU: Intel i5 7500, Clock Speed: 3.40 GHz × 4, RAM: 8 GB DDR4, OS: Ubuntu 16.04 LTS 64 bit and Software: Rstudio Version 1.1.456. The configuration for experimentation in [3] for MLF and associated algorithms is CPU:core 2 dual, Clock Speed: 1.3 MHz and Ram: 4 GB.

The experiments are conducted on nine benchmarks numeric dataset, collected from the UCI machine learning repository [5] which were used in MLF [3] experimentation. The description of numeric datasets used is shown in Table 1. The synthesized datasets used in [3] were not experimented because of unavailability of datasets. Here, we employed different expansion criterion (theta = 0.2 and 0.3) on kNN-FMNN with γ as 0.4 and 'k' in kNN is set to 3.

All experiment results of the kNN-FMNN with other FMNN methods are listed in Table 2. The results given for MLF and associated algorithms are reproduced from [3] for comparison. The best result under each category for each dataset is shown in boldface.

Table 2. Comparative experiment results

Dataset	Method	Classification (%)			No. of Hyperbox	Time (ms)
		Min	Max	Average		
Iris	GFMNN	81.33	96.67	86.33	37.5	175
	EFC	88.67	96.67	91.31	42.0	54
	FMCN	90.00	97.33	92.76	63.6	44
	DCFMN	92.11	97.33	94.66	37.7	50
	MLF	**95.33**	97.33	**96.33**	56.3	60
	kNN-FMNN ($\theta = 0.2$)	94.0	96.0	94.66	22.3	20
	kNN-FMNN ($\theta = 0.3$)	94.0	**98.0**	96.0	**13**	15
Breast Cancer	GFMNN	55.51	95.74	78.35	154	1586
	EFC	58.44	94.27	79.34	183	629
	FMCN	68.58	95.30	83.16	244	472
	DCFMN	84.15	95.74	90.54	190	416
	MLF	93.69	96.48	95.59	227	1451
	kNN-FMNN ($\theta = 0.2$)	**94.66**	**96.82**	**96.13**	164	700
	kNN-FMNN ($\theta = 0.3$)	94.70	96.85	95.6	**79.6**	347
Glass	GFMNN	43.48	66.67	49.79	56	583
	EFC	35.27	66.63	42.53	89	115
	FMCN	29.47	66.63	41.26	394	96
	DCFMN	29.47	66.67	39.97	77	114
	MLF	56.04	68.12	60.32	227	225
	kNN-FMNN ($\theta = 0.2$)	**60.56**	**76.05**	**65.91**	49	41
	kNN-FMNN ($\theta = 0.3$)	56.33	69.01	63.54	**35.6**	33
Ionosphere	GFMNN	42.74	89.46	68.93	**120**	2163
	EFC	33.33	87.46	62.12	150	424
	FMCN	46.15	89.46	78.43	271	329
	DCFMN	79.54	**93.45**	87.77	132	448
	MLF	83.76	**93.45**	89.30	184	909
	kNN-FMNN($\theta = 0.2$)	**88.03**	91.45	**90.02**	146.6	399
	kNN-FMNN($\theta = 0.3$)	87.17	90.59	88.88	121.3	308
Thyroid	GFMNN	30.59	85.39	61.37	57	345
	EFC	74.89	90.87	85.30	**66**	116
	FMCN	74.89	90.87	85.78	116	94
	DCFMN	74.89	93.17	89.76	**66**	103
	MLF	75.34	94.52	90.88	72	152
	kNN-FMNN ($\theta = 0.2$)	**94.72**	**95.29**	**94.86**	327	16542
	kNN-FMNN ($\theta = 0.3$)	94.12	94.37	94.26	255	13811
Wine	GFMNN	85.00	96.67	92.91	129	817
	EFC	92.22	96.67	94.47	133	234
	FMCN	92.22	97.33	94.47	183	160
	DCFMN	92.22	97.33	94.53	124	127
	MLF	92.22	97.33	94.61	133	274
	kNN-FMNN ($\theta = 0.2$)	**93.33**	100	96.08	91	95
	kNN-FMNN ($\theta = 0.3$)	**93.33**	100	**96.64**	**55.6**	63
Parkinson	GFMNN	76.41	82.97	80.83	98	786
	EFC	40.77	78.97	74.66	111	256
	FMCN	40.77	82.56	75.54	207	216
	DCFMN	67.70	83.08	78.97	99	265
	MLF	77.95	84.10	83.49	111	302
	kNN-FMNN ($\theta = 0.2$)	**87.69**	**96.92**	**92.30**	81.6	163
	kNN-FMNN ($\theta = 0.3$)	86.15	**96.92**	91.79	**53.3**	109

Table 2. (*continued*)

Dataset	Method	Classification (%)			No. of Hyperbox	Time (ms)
		Min	Max	Average		
Ozone layer	GFMNN	41.66	92.16	79.84	929	61481
	EFC	77.13	92.95	87.38	1031	27221
	FMCN	90.05	92.87	91.89	2759	30850
	DCFMN	73.79	92.60	87.51	988	24694
	MLF	89.92	92.78	91.12	1314	49699
	kNN-FMNN ($\theta = 0.2$)	96.80	96.42	**97.41**	1034.6	28436
	kNN-FMNN ($\theta = 0.3$)	**96.94**	**96.75**	96.32	**531**	14208
SpamBase	GFMNN	39.90	83.39	54.15	293	86696
	EFC	43.21	81.04	56.78	700	12988
	FMCN	67.67	86.91	75.42	4982	6310
	DCFMN	71.95	86.91	80.70	693	98644
	MLF	82.89	89.39	88.41	7614	76929
	kNN-FMNN ($\theta = 0.2$)	**89.29**	88.31	88.68	550	12686
	kNN-FMNN ($\theta = 0.3$)	87.40	**90.14**	**89.21**	**254.3**	4974

4.2   Analysis of Results

The computational complexity of FMNN training algorithm is proportional to the cardinality of hyperboxes created. In addition to the cardinality of hyperboxes, the cost of complex structures such as a compensatory neuron, exclusion hyperboxes and hierarchical layers in algorithms like FMCN, DCFMN and MLF increases the complexity. The computational time reported in Table 2 validates the same as kNN-FMNN achieved training much lesser time compared to MLF and other approaches. The computational efficiently of kNN-FMNN is due to adapting FMNN with only the expansion step and also achieving much lesser cardinality of hyperboxes compared to other approaches.

From Fig. 3, it is observed that the average number of hyperbox creation is less than other FMNN methods except for thyroid dataset because of sparsity in the dataset. As the number of hyperboxes created thyroid dataset is more, the computation training time is higher only for this dataset.

Figure 2 depicts the experimental result of classification accuracy. It is observed that in all the datasets, kNN-FMNN with theta (0.2 or 0.3) achieved similar or better classification accuracy compared to MLF and other approaches.

kNN-FMNN has achieved significantly better classification accuracies in Parkinson, Ozone layer, Glass and Thyroid datasets. For example for Parkinson dataset, by using the kNN-FMNN algorithm with user-defined parameter ($\theta = 0.2$), obtained 92.3% of average classification accuracy with 81 average number of hyperboxes creation respectively, whereas MLF gave 83.49% accuracy along with 111 hyperboxes.

We have experimented kNN-FMNN with several theta (θ) values, and all the results were not reported due to space contraint. It is observed that for less theta values such as 0.02, the cardinality of hyperboxes is huge and for high theta values such as 0.9, the cardinality of hyperboxes is less in the cost of

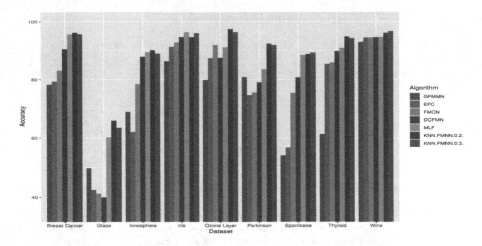

Fig. 2. Comparison of average classification accuracy

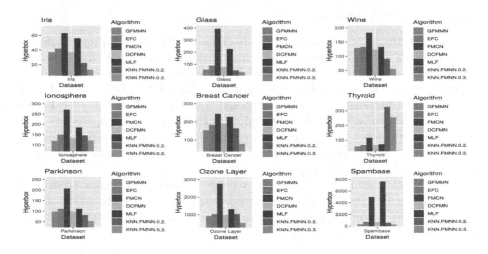

Fig. 3. Comparison of average hyperbox size

misclassification. The best result (minimization of the cardinality of hyperboxes, maximation of classification accuracy) are obtained for theta values between 0.2 to 0.3, and the same is recommended.

5   Conclusion

Several improvements were proposed for the Fuzzy Min-Max Neural Network to overcome limitations arise due to contraction step. These extensions have resulted in adding additional complexity to FMNN thus increasing the training time. This work proposed kNN-FMNN as hybridization of FMNN with kNN for overcoming the contraction step in FMNN. The proposed approach resulted in building the classification model with a fewer number of hyperboxes and achieving good classification accuracy by utilizing kNN locally for disambiguating classification decision in the overlapping region. The experimental results have established that kNN-FMNN achieved better classification accuracy than existing approaches such as MLF, FMCN, DCFMN, EFC, GFMNN in less computation time. In future, attempts will be done for proposing parallel and distributing kNN-FMNN for achieving scalability in large-scale decision systems.

References

1. Ahmed, A.A., Mohammed, M.F.: SAIRF: a similarity approach for attack intention recognition using fuzzy min-max neural network. J. Comput. Sci. **25**, 467–473 (2018)
2. Bargiela, A., Pedrycz, W., Tanaka, M.: An inclusion/exclusion fuzzy hyperbox classifier. KES J. **8**, 91–98 (2004)
3. Davtalab, R., Dezfoulian, M.H., Mansoorizadeh, M.: Multi-level fuzzy min-max neural network classifier. IEEE Trans. Neural Netw. Learn. Syst. **25**, 470–482 (2014)
4. Deshmukh, S., Shinde, S.: Diagnosis of lung cancer using pruned fuzzy min-max neural network. In: 2016 International Conference on Automatic Control and Dynamic Optimization Techniques (ICACDOT), pp. 398–402, September 2016
5. Dheeru, D., Karra Taniskidou, E.: UCI machine learning repository (2017). http://archive.ics.uci.edu/ml
6. Fullér, R.: Introduction to Neuro-Fuzzy Systems. Advances in Soft Computing, vol. 2. Physica-Verlag, Heidelberg (2000)
7. Gabrys, B., Bargiela, A.: General fuzzy min-max neural network for clustering and classification. IEEE Trans. Neural Netw. **11**(3), 769–783 (2000)
8. Nandedkar, A.V., Biswas, P.K.: A fuzzy min-max neural network classifier with compensatory neuron architecture. In: Proceedings of the 17th International Conference on Pattern Recognition, ICPR 2004, vol. 4, pp. 553–556, August 2004
9. Quteishat, A., Lim, C.P.: Application of the fuzzy min-max neural networks to medical diagnosis. In: Lovrek, I., Howlett, R.J., Jain, L.C. (eds.) KES 2008. LNCS (LNAI), vol. 5179, pp. 548–555. Springer, Heidelberg (2008). https://doi.org/10.1007/978-3-540-85567-5_68
10. Quteishat, A., Lim, C.P.: A modified fuzzy min-max neural network with rule extraction and its application to fault detection and classification. Appl. Soft Comput. **8**(2), 985–995 (2008)
11. Sadeghian, P., Wilson, C., Goeddel, S., Olmsted, A.: Classification of music by composer using fuzzy min-max neural networks. In: 2017 12th International Conference for Internet Technology and Secured Transactions (ICITST), pp. 189–192, December 2017
12. Sayaydeh, O.N., Mohammed, M.F., Lim, C.P.: A survey of fuzzy min max neural networks for pattern classification: variants and applications. IEEE Trans. Fuzzy Syst. **27**, 1 (2018)
13. Seera, M., Wong, M.D., Nandi, A.K.: Classification of ball bearing faults using a hybrid intelligent model. Appl. Soft Comput. **57**, 427–435 (2017)

14. Shuang, F., Chen, C.L.P.: Fuzzy restricted boltzmann machine and deep belief network: a comparison on image reconstruction. In: 2017 IEEE International Conference on Systems, Man, and Cybernetics (SMC), pp. 1828–1833, October 2017
15. Simpson, P.K.: Fuzzy min-max neural networks. I. Classification. IEEE Trans. Neural Netw. **3**(5), 776–786 (1992)
16. Zadeh, L.: Fuzzy sets. Inf. Control **8**(3), 338–353 (1965)
17. Zhang, H., Liu, J., Ma, D., Wang, Z.: Data-core-based fuzzy min-max neural network for pattern classification. IEEE Trans. Neural Netw. **22**(12), 2339–2352 (2011)
18. Zhou, S., Chen, Q., Wang, X.: Fuzzy deep belief networks for semi-supervised sentiment classification. Neurocomputing **131**, 312–322 (2014)
19. Zimmermann, H.: Fuzzy Sets and Expert Systems. Springer, Dordrecht (2001). https://doi.org/10.1007/978-94-010-0646-0_10
20. Zobeidi, S., Naderan, M., Alavi, S.E.: Effective text classification using multi-level fuzzy neural network. In: 2017 5th Iranian Joint Congress on Fuzzy and Intelligent Systems (CFIS), pp. 91–96, March 2017

Individualized Patient-Centered Type 2 Diabetes Recommender System

Nishat Afreen$^{(\boxtimes)}$, Shrey Singh, and Sanjay Kumar

Department of Computer Science and Engineering, NIT Jamshedpur,
Jamshedpur 831014, India
mail.nishatafreen@gmail.com, shrey.singh1991@gmail.com,
sanjay.cse@nitjsr.ac.in

Abstract. Diabetes mellitus is unfolding as a global health challenge in today's society. The rapid advancement in the information and communication technology coupled with the burgeoning demand for data connectivity have carved the path for increased opportunities for diabetes self-management. This paper explores the use of a mobile application as a tool for providing patient-tailored diet to help improve clinical outcomes. To achieve this objective, it utilizes the abilities of two machine learning models - artificial neural network and XGBoost. Based on the diabetic profile of a patient, XGBoost regressor is used to predict the total calorie consumption and the artificial neural network is used to predict the percentage of carbohydrates, proteins, and fats in the daily diet. The values of RMSE proves the efficacy of both the machine learning models. These predicted values are then used to prepare a user adaptive diet chart by giving the user the freedom to consider his preferences within the range of predicted values. This work aims not only to educate the Type 2 Diabetes patients on their disease but also ensure a healthy lifestyle and keep diabetes in check avoiding any bothersome surprises.

Keywords: Type 2 Diabetes · Recommender system · Diet ·
Lifestyle modification · Machine learning

1 Introduction

Diabetes Mellitus is a group of metabolic disorders affecting more than 500 million people worldwide. Diabetes demands ongoing medical care and patient self-management to prevent diabetes progression and long-term complications [1]. Self-management refers to the tasks carried out by an individual to facilitate diabetes self-care [2]. Traditional education about a disease predominantly involves generic information whereas the primary focus should be the self-management of the disease. The need for diabetes self-management pertains to all types of diabetes like type 1, type 2, and gestational diabetes, however, this paper focuses on only Type 2 Diabetes (T2D). The main causes of T2D are genetics, lifestyle, and physical activity [3]. Lifestyle modifications can play a vital role in controlling T2D by monitoring body intake as well as body activities. This paper focuses

© Springer Nature Singapore Pte Ltd. 2019
M. Singh et al. (Eds.): ICACDS 2019, CCIS 1045, pp. 45–54, 2019.
https://doi.org/10.1007/978-981-13-9939-8_5

on regulating the body intake to keep diabetes in check. This study follows a user-centered approach to provide a user adaptive diet plan to reduce their total dependence on drugs only.

Around 90% of the people diagnosed with diabetes mellitus have T2D. Diet and eating behavior play a vital role in the onset and progression of T2D. In the early stages, the changes in eating habits can defer the need for medications. In later stages, proper diet can manage the disease well and keep diabetes in a controlled state. Following a diet chart can help a patient self-manage their disease. Our paper propounds a recommender system that recommends patient-tailored diet based on the diabetic profile of an individual.

Preparing a personalized diet chart for an individual patient is in itself a challenging task. The first challenge is that diet chart should be tailor fit to the diabetic and the related medical profile of a patient. Applying a case-based approach to address this challenge is a very difficult task as it requires exploring all the possible cases and conditions for the recommendation. Therefore, with the help of machine learning, we let our system learn to customize the individualized diet. The personalized dietary recommendations include the total calorie consumption as well as the percentage of carbohydrates, proteins, and fats in the diet. The second challenge is that the recommended diet chart provided to the individual patients must be economically and geographically favorable. To overcome this difficulty, we provide the patient the freedom to select the food items within the range of dietary suggestions given by the recommender system.

Our diabetic diet recommender system takes into consideration both the healthfulness of the diet as well as the user's food choice. Both the factors carry equal prominence in influencing the diet recommendation model. A healthy diet, with appropriate nutrition value, neglecting the likes and dislikes of a user may not be welcomed by the user. The user's food choice is influenced by many factors like personal preferences, economic condition, food item availability, culture, and religion etc. Our diabetic diet recommender system cannot rely only on the user likings as it needs to combine the factors of healthfulness as well as user preferences to provide tailored meal suggestions.

2   Related Work

Automated analysis and interpretation of patient's data would be beneficial in providing personalized feedbacks and alerts. The decision support tools play a vital role in processing the complex data and providing assistance in medication, lifestyle modification or insulin dosage. Preuveneers et al. [4] propounded a location-aware prototype system for managing the disease of type 1 insulin-dependent diabetes patients. Their application relies on GSM cellular data and hidden Markov model to monitor the user location and to infer the user activity for the purpose of assisting the patients to take decisions on daily drug dosage. The commercial applications like RapidCalc Diabetes Manager for iPhone [5] proffer insulin dosage suggestion opposed to lifestyle modification on the basis of data entered by the user pertaining to food intake, physical activities, and blood glucose level. The applications Insulin Calculator [6] and Insulin Dose Calculator [7] records the consumption of carbohydrates and monitors the blood glucose to adjust the insulin dosage. The mobile applications providing drug assistance always carry a potential risk of the aftermath of inaccurate drug suggestion. This calls for the necessity of guidance of government rules and regulations.

Wang et al. explored an artificial neural network (ANN) and multivariate logistic regression (MLR) model to classify the patients at high risk of T2D on the basis of demographic, lifestyle and anthropometric data [8]. Rahman et al. [9] presented a hybrid rough set reasoning model to predict the type of diabetes and identify the trends to manage type 1 as well as type 2 diabetes. In Hussein et al.'s approach [10], a chronic disease diagnosis recommender system is proposed using multiple decision tree classification algorithms to predict chronic diseases risks like diabetes. Medina-Moreira et al. [11] introduced a collaborative filtering technique based recommender system for diabetes self-management. In another approach by Bankhele et al. [12], an Android application is built to provide diet and exercise recommendations to diabetic patients through user-based collaborative filtering using Pearson Correlation to measure the similarity between the user and a similar user in the database. The most recent work is that of Norouzi et al. [13] who designed a knowledge based and constrained based reasoning food recommender system through the use of roulette wheel algorithm.

3   Proposed Work

The recommender system proposed in this paper, as depicted in Fig. 1, help the type 2 diabetes patients to prepare their respective diet chart according to their diabetic profile. This system incorporates a 3 tier system comprising of the user, application, and the server where the application acts as an intermediate component in the communication between the user and the server. The user submits his/her diabetic profile as input to the application, which in turn sends the data to the server for processing by the machine learning algorithms. The machine learning algorithm calculates the calorie intake per day as well as the percentage of carbohydrates, proteins, and fats personalized to every individual. The calculated values are fed back to the application. Within this range of values, the end user is free to prepare the personalized diet chart according to his/her preferences. This controlled diet can help to regulate the type 2 diabetes in patients.

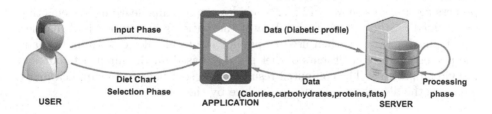

Fig. 1. Architecture of recommender system

3.1   Input Phase

The input phase is comprised of two types of input: the personal user profile and the diabetic profile. The personal profile pertains to the information needed during the registration phase (Age, Sex, Body Mass Index (BMI), Blood pressure etc.). The diabetic profile includes three crucial diabetes test – Random Blood Sugar (RBS), Fasting Blood Sugar (FBS) and Oral Glucose Tolerance Test (OGTT). Since diabetes can develop long-term complications like the risk of developing cardiovascular disease, liver damage, kidney damage etc., therefore, the diabetic profile of our application includes the other facets and need for Co-Morbidity Assessment of patient in addition to blood glucose test. The data collected from the user in the application comprises of the attributes as specified in the Table 1 These attributes are selected by taking into account both the medical practitioner's expertise as well as data availability limitations.

Table 1. User parameters

User parameters		
User profile	Diabetic profile	Co-morbidity assessment
Age(in years)	Random blood sugar (RBS)	Renal Function Test
Sex	Fasting blood sugar (FBS)	Creatinine Serum
Body Mass Index (BMI) [kg/m^2]	Oral Glucose Tolerance Test (OGTT)	Creatinine Urine
Systolic Blood pressure [mm Hg]		Liver Function Test
Diastolic Blood pressure [mm Hg]		Alanine Transaminase (SGPT)
Year of Diagnosis		Aspartate Aminotransferase (SGOT)
PLA Score		
		Lipid Profile Test
		Total Cholesterol
		Low Density Lipoprotein (LDL)
		High Density Lipoprotein (HDL)
		Triglycerides

3.2   Processing Phase

The inputs provided by the user in our application is processed on the server. The processing stage, as shown in Fig. 2, includes the machine learning systems that are trained on the pre-processed data of the patients in a supervised manner. The trained network is then used to predict the total calorie consumption and the percentage of constituents of diet per day based on the input attributes of individual patients. The computed result is then sent back to the application to facilitate the diet chart selection procedure by the user.

Machine Learning System. The machine learning (ML) system acts as a readily available dietitian who avails the diabetic profile of the users and predicts its diet metrics. The ML system is a supervised system trained on thousands of diabetic patient's data. The predicted output of the ML system consists of 4 values computed by two different ML algorithms - Artificial Neural Network and XGBoost [14]. XGBoost utilizes the patient's data to predict the total calorie consumption of a user per day and artificial neural network evaluates the percentage of carbohydrates, proteins, and fats per day.

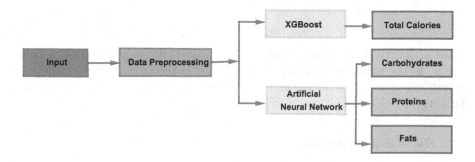

Fig. 2. Flowchart of processing phase

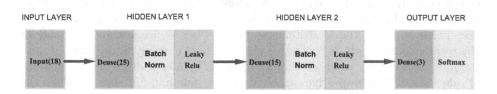

Fig. 3. Architecture of model 2 (artificial neural network)

A multilayer perceptron (MLP) ANN with a configuration of $18 \times 25 \times 15 \times 3$ is used as shown in the Fig. 3. The layers use batch normalization to diminish the internal covariate shift [15]. Both the hidden layers use Leaky Rectified Linear Unit (Leaky ReLU) as the non-linear activation function which allows a small, non-zero gradient when the neurons are not active [16].

$$z_1' = w_1 * I + b_1 \qquad where \ w_1 \in R^{M_{L_1} \times M_{L_2}} \tag{1}$$

$$z_1 = \begin{cases} \alpha * z_1' \ if \ z_1' < 0 \\ z_1' \qquad if \ z_1' \geq 0 \end{cases} \tag{2}$$

For layer $L_3(HiddenLayer2)$,

$$z_2' = w_2 * z_1 + b_2 \qquad where \ w_2 \in R^{M_{L_2} \times M_{L_3}} \tag{3}$$

$$z_1 = \begin{cases} \alpha * z_2' \ if \ z_2' < 0 \\ z_2' \qquad if \ z_2' \geq 0 \end{cases} \tag{4}$$

For layer $L_4(OutputLayer)$,

$$z_3' = w_3 * z_3 + b_1 \qquad where \; w_3 \in R^{M_{L_3} \times M_{L_4}} \tag{5}$$

$$z_{3_j} = \frac{e^{z_{3_j}'}}{\sum\limits_{k=1}^{K} e^{z_{3_k}'}} \qquad for \; j = 1,2....K \quad where \; K = M_{L_4} \tag{6}$$

$$\hat{y} = [z_{3_1}, z_{3_2}, ...z_{3_K}] \tag{7}$$

where M_{L_i} is the number of neurons in layer i, w_i is the weight matrix, b_i is the bias, z_i' is the weighted sum of the neurons, z_i is the output of the non-linear activations, α is the negative slope coefficient of Relu activation function, $\hat{y}$ is the output of ANN.

3.3   Diet Chart Selection

Merely providing generic information of diet to keep diabetes in control would not be sufficient. Significant effort needs to be done to improve the eating habits and altering the daily diet. The output of the processing phase i.e. the total calories consumed per day and the percentage of carbohydrates, fats and proteins in it. The total calories consumed per day is distributed into 4 meals a day. The user needs to select the food items as per his/her choice within the range of the total calories (with its respective percentage of carbohydrate, proteins, and fats) allocated to per meal per day. Every food item contains a certain amount of calories and their respective carbohydrate, protein and fat content. When the user selects a food item, the remaining amount of the allocated calories, proteins and fats is decreased. This type of diet chart selection procedure makes it easier to recommend the user-specific diet to regulate diabetes.

The food items available for diet selection procedure are either whole (E.g. egg, apple, banana etc.) or can be taken in fractional amount i.e per gram (E.g. flour, rice, lentils, vegetables etc.). Some foods are consumed directly and some are combined in an appropriate amount to prepare a recipe to be consumed. Rather than suggesting a recipe recommendation application, we are providing a platform to the user to select the raw food items consumable within the range of its nutritional value (total allocated calories and respective carbohydrates, proteins, and fat content). A dish is made up of a combination of many raw food items. The nutrition values of the individual raw food items sum up to the total nutritional value of a dish. The diet chart selection problem is solved by a combination of integer 0/1 and fractional knapsack problem [17,18]. The profit our knapsack problems pertains to the priority of the food item selection by the user.

4 Experiment

4.1 Dataset Preprocessing and Set up

Data preparation was one of the most vital parts of the research, partly because data is the key element to obtain an accurate regression target and partly because such patient-tailored data containing diabetic profiles as well as related comorbidity profiles was not available. The dataset of 10087 Type 2 diabetic patients consisting of 18 attributes as depicted in input phase was collected from Rajendra Institute of Medical Sciences (RIMS Ranchi). With the help of a panel of dietitians, the corresponding output values (the total calorie consumption, the content of carbohydrates, proteins, and fats per day) of all the training examples are carefully populated in the dataset. The data is normalized to make the data comparable across the features. This training dataset is then used to train the machine learning systems (ANN and XGBoost [14]) in a supervised manner. XGBoost has a built-in routine to handle the missing data. The erroneous data are taken care of by the validations of the application in the input phase.

4.2 Methodology

The overall process of developing machine learning algorithms comprises of two phases- the model selection phase where an appropriate architecture can be selected that can generalize the data well and the training phase where the selected model can be trained on the dataset and cross-validated.

Model Selection Phase. Previous research has demonstrated that multilayer feedforward perceptron can perform well on supervised learning tasks like classification and regression. In order to have the best possible results, we performed many rounds of MLP network architecture selection and refit the models on the training dataset. The network architecture selection comprised of selecting the number of hidden layers and the number of neurons in each of the layers. The driving force for refitting the model was to obtain a model that can generalize the data well. After a random run of experiments, two hidden layers were constructed and the optimal number of nodes in the hidden layers was fixated at 25 and 18. 3 outputs were selected for MLP to represent the fraction of the carbohydrates, proteins, and fat in the diet per day. Softmax was used as non-linear activation at the output layer as all the 3 outputs add up to 1.

XGBoost seemed to outperform both linear regression as well as artificial neural network in terms of computation speed and accuracy to predict by the total calorie consumption by a patient per day.

Training Phase. The dataset is split into the training set (80%) and test set (20%) respectively. Therefore, the machine learning models (MLP and XGBoost) were trained on a dataset of 8069 patients and validated on 2018 patient data. We performed random selection on various hyperparameters of machine learning models to obtain low bias and low variance models. The values of the tuned hyperparameters are presented in the Table 2. The MLP was trained for 25 epochs and the weights were learned by minimizing the Mean Squared Error Loss function with Adaptive Moment Estimation (ADAM) [19] as an optimizer. A range of learning rate from 0.01 to 0.0001 was explored for the optimizer. To prevent overfitting, a dropout of 0.20 was introduced in both the hidden layers. XGBoost Regressor converged with a Mean Absolute Error. On experimenting with other combinations of hyperparameters, it was observed that either the results were worse or the gain in performance was negligible.

Table 2. Hyperparameters of machine learning models.

Hyperparameter	
ANN	18:25:15:3 network; activation_function = LeakyRelu; output_layer = softmax; Adam optimizer; learning_rate = 0.0001; batch_size = 128; shuffle = true; dropout = 0.2; no_of_epochs = 125
XGBoost	n_estimators = 1000; learning_rate = 0.07; max_depth = 3; min_child_ weight = 1.5; gamma = 0; subsample = 0.8; colsample_bytree = 0.8

5   Results and Analysis

5.1   Comparison and Performance Analysis

In order to provide patient-tailored meal suggestions, the problem was divided into two subproblems - prediction of the total calorie consumption (Model1) and prediction of the percentage of carbohydrates, proteins, and fats (Model2) in the daily diet. The regression objective of predicting the total calorie consumption of patients can be evaluated by various machine learning models like linear regression, ANN, tree-based models, etc. Therefore, the same experiment with a dataset of 10087 patients was applied to linear regression, ANN and XGBoost to seek the best performer. Linear regression tends to underfit and it is no surprise as the relationship between the features and the regressor is linear in linear regression. As illustrated in Fig. 4, ANN overfits and fails to achieve our objective of a low bias and low variance model. XGBoost is the most robust algorithm as it checks the possibility of both underfitting and overfitting.

In order to obtain an apple to apple comparison, the performance of our experiment is evaluated with three performance metrics - RMSE, EVar and R^2. The comparison of the performance of these three machine learning methods on the three stated evaluation metrics is presented in Table 3. Results depict that XGBoost wins over the other by a wide margin. The second problem of predicting the percentage of carbohydrates, proteins, and fats in the daily diet can be considered as a multivariate regression problem with an additional constraint of 3 outcomes summing up to 1. We found the architecture of the neural network shown in Fig. 3 the most appropriate to solve our problem. It can be observed that both Model1 (XGBoost) and Model2 (ANN) perform considerably well.

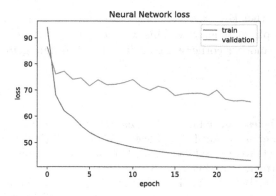

Fig. 4. Overfitting of ANN

Table 3. Comparison of machine learning algorithms for Model1

Model	Root mean square error (RMSE)	Explained variance score (EVar)	R^2 score
Linear regression	345.56186	0.86525	0.85254
ANN	86.64294	0.96621	0.95216
XGboost	46.20606	0.98198	0.97988

5.2 Results

The RMSE of Model1 (XGBoost) for predicting the total calorie consumption was computed to be 46.20606 and Model2 (ANN), for predicting the percentage of carbohydrates, proteins, and fats, converged at RMSE 0.98213.

6 Conclusion and Future Work

The main contribution of this paper is to provide a novel approach to help manage T2D taking into account both the patient's preferences as well as the significance of the healthfulness of diet in providing recommendations to T2D patients. This study provides a holistic approach that inputs the diabetic profile of the patients and feeds it to machine learning models. This work demonstrates that a simple two-model approach can produce nearly optimal results. It explores the capabilities of both artificial neural network and XGBoost in predicting the total calorie consumption as well as the percentage of carbohydrates, proteins, and fats in the daily diet. The results substantiate that the machine learning models not only run fast but also provides superior prediction competence. The evaluation depicts outstanding performance with high accuracy. The participation of the user in the diet chart selection stands outs our approach from related approaches. The other key area that plays a major role in preventing and managing diabetes is physical activity. This work can be extended to the regulation of daily exercise, another cornerstone of diabetes self-management.

References

1. American Diabetes Association, et al.: Diabetes Care **35**, S11 (2012)
2. Powers, M.A., et al.: J. Acad. Nutr. Diet. **115**(8), 1323 (2015)
3. Kavakiotis, I., Tsave, O., Salifoglou, A., Maglaveras, N., Vlahavas, I., Chouvarda, I.: Comput. Struct. Biotechnol. J. **15**, 104 (2017)
4. Preuveneers, D., Berbers, Y.: Proceedings of the 10th International Conference on Human Computer Interaction with Mobile Devices and Services, pp. 177–186. ACM (2008)
5. Gilport, Gilport Enterprises, 8 November 2010. itunes.apple.com/in/app/rapidcalc-diabetes-manager/id400469609?mt=8
6. Google play store play.google.com/store/apps/details?id=com.ltmod.insulincalculator&hl=en_GB
7. Google play store. play.google.com/store/search?q=insulindosecalculator&c=apps&hl=en_GB
8. Wang, C., et al.: Diabetes Res. Clin. Pract. **100**(1), 111 (2013)
9. Ali, R., Hussain, J., Siddiqi, M.H., Hussain, M., Lee, S.: Sensors **15**(7), 15921 (2015)
10. Hussein, A.S., Omer, W., Li, X., Ati, M.: GLOBAL HEALTH, The First International Conference on Global Health Challenges, Venice, Italy (2012)
11. Medina-Moreira, J., Apolinario, O., Luna-Aveiga, H., Lagos-Ortiz, K., Paredes-Valverde, M.A., Valencia-García, R.: A collaborative filtering based recommender system for disease self-management. In: Valencia-García, R., Lagos-Ortiz, K., Alcaraz-Mármol, G., Del Cioppo, J., Vera-Lucio, N., Bucaram-Leverone, M. (eds.) Technologies and Innovation. CITI 2017. CCIS, vol. 749, pp. 60–71. Springer, Cham (2017). https://doi.org/10.1007/978-3-319-67283-0_5
12. Bankhele, S., Mhaske, A., Bhat, S., Shinde, S.: Int. J. Comput. Appl. **167**, 5 (2017)
13. Norouzi, S., et al.: Arch. Iran. Med. (AIM) **21**, 10 (2018)
14. Chen, T., Guestrin, C.: Proceedings of the 22nd ACM SIGKDD International Conference on Knowledge Discovery and Data Mining, pp. 785–794. ACM (2016)
15. Ioe, S., Szegedy, C.: International Conference on Machine Learning, pp. 448–456 (2015)
16. Xu, B., Wang, N., Chen, T., Li, M.: arXiv preprint arXiv:1505.00853 (2015)
17. Balas, E., Zemel, E.: Oper. Res. **28**(5), 1130 (1980)
18. Ishii, H., Ibaraki, T., Mine, H.: Math. Program. **13**(1), 255 (1977)
19. Kingma, D.P., Ba, J.: arXiv preprint arXiv:1412.6980 (2014)

CAD Data Computing for Component Type Realization and Assembly Sequence Generation

Umeshchandra Mane[1(✉)], Venkatesh Jonnalagedda[2],
and Balaji Dabade[3]

[1] Mechanical Engineering Department, Shri Guru Gobind Singhji Institute
of Engineering and Technology, Nanded 431606, Maharashtra, India
umeshmane1986@gmail.com
[2] Nanded 431606, Maharashtra, India
meghavenkatesh@gmail.com
[3] Production Engineering Department, Shri Guru Gobind Singhji Intitute
of Engineering and Technology, Nanded 431606, Maharashtra, India
bmdabade@gmail.com

Abstract. Computer Aided Design (CAD) packages are widely used to create mathematical modelling of product's geometry at the time of design and development phase. This CAD model involves very complicated definition of geometrical entities and interpretation of the same for assembly planning is an open research area. Most of the currently used assembly planning approaches hugely depends on human expert's intervention. Current practices mostly use, only component name definition out of CAD data to identify component type which is likely to fail if the industry is using different language or number system to define component names. This paper presents a novel CAD data computation system for component type realization and assembly sequence generation. The developed system works automatically and independent of component names so that manual errors can be avoided. Assembly sequence generation helps in reducing complexity to be analyzed by human expert.

Keywords: Computer Aided Design · Data computing ·
Component type realization · Assembly sequence generation

1 Introduction

Computer Aided Design (CAD) is a technology, seamlessly integrated in the fields like analysis, simulation, manufacturing, etc. Usability of CAD data is being explored very rapidly making it an unavoidable instance in product development. Assembly planning and production planning are such area where researchers are contributing to enhance the automated usage of CAD data. In such packages, assembly definition of a product

V. Jonnalagedda—Quintessence Engineering Consultant LLP (Former Head of Mechanical Engineering Department Shri Guru Gobind Singhji Institute of Engineering and Technology).

© Springer Nature Singapore Pte Ltd. 2019
M. Singh et al. (Eds.): ICACDS 2019, CCIS 1045, pp. 55–63, 2019.
https://doi.org/10.1007/978-981-13-9939-8_6

consists of geometry and topological representation of each component and relationships of interrelating components. Specialized graphical interface is provided by CAD software, but manual analysis is a tedious task as it involves invisible components due to overlapping surfaces. CAD model provides enough information for graphic display of the assembly, but it is inadequate for assembly planning" [1].

2 Literature Review

Currently available methods hugely depend on human expert interaction for assembly sequence generation. Bourjault et al. [2] developed an algorithm to generate feasible sequences in which precedence relationship information is given by human expert. Homem et al. [3] proposed And/Or graph to represent all subassembly states, such And/Or graph becomes very complicated if the product is having a greater number of parts. Directed graphs [4–7] are used to represent partial assembly sequences in compact way. Experts are needed to analyze product definition and geometrical blocking relationships. A lot of research is going on for automatically using CAD data in assembly planning phase. Reddy and Ghosh [1] proposed an approach for generation of assembly sequences based on geometric and mobility constraints. Vigano and Gomez [8] proposed automatic approach to obtain initial feasible assembly sequences using spatial interaction and some empirical formulae. Sotiris et al. [9] used AR technology to identify the precedencies by conducting intersection test for each component. Li-Ming and Xun [10] proposed a system through which precedencies are identified based on information relating to interference and stability of components. In this approach, component types are identified based on the name of the components and some assembly sequences are automatically assigned. George et al. [11] developed a system which generates precedence diagram by using CAD data. This method also depends on component name definition to delete/hide fastener components. Riadh et al. [12] used feature simplification to generate assembly sequence. Li et al. [13] developed a system naming "AutoAssem" for assembly planning which provides assembly sequence planning functions. Yu et al. [14] proposed an approach to generate sequential exploded view with the help of extended interference matrices. Belhadj et al. [15] proposed an approach to generate subassembly from CAD model. Kheder et al. developed an approach to optimize DSP with the integration of artificial intelligence techniques in a CAD environment [16] model sub-assemblies.

All above studies infer that component type realization can be beneficial in assembly sequence generation. Component type realization can also help in Assembly Sequence Planning, Assembly Path Planning, Assembly Line Balancing, Assembly Line Design, plant layout, location of component storage and retrieval systems, location of material handling equipment and some other production planning decisions etc. Component categorization based on names of the components has been used for assembly planning. This kind of categorization system is likely to fail if the industry is using different language or number system to identify a component [17]. Also, dependence on component's name make system to rely on user input and existing component name library for correctness of the output.

This paper presents a system for component type realization and assembly sequence generation without any expert's intervention by computing CAD data. Developed system automatically analyzes any sort of complex product with minimal interaction of user with CAD environment.

3 Proposed Approach

The CAD data of a product includes mathematical equations of every components' geometry and information about every components' relative location with other components. Those mathematical equations are used to represent vertices, edges and surfaces for multiple components. Interpretation of relationships between each mathematical equation is computationally challenging. The system extracts physical properties like mass, volume, area, number of relationships, center of gravity, location of component, etc. Analyzing any product with the help of human expert takes a lot of time and is likely to have errors due to visibility limits. A system is developed which successfully extracts information from CAD data and automatically realizes type of the components involved in the product definition. This system also extracts the location of each component of the assembly which is further used for assembly sequence generation. This section elaborates every step involved in the system.

3.1 Extract the Physical Properties of Each Component

CAD data of a product includes dimensions, geometry, relationships and material specification of each component. System extracts Mass, Volume, Area, Coordinates for Center of Gravity (C. G. coordinates) of each component which is saved in spreadsheet application. Relationships of each component with other components are also extracted by using mating condition and it is saved in relationship matrix/graph. Table 1 shows the extracted product features.

3.2 Read the Occupation Dimensions of Each Component in Global Coordinate System

Every component in a product is located at a specific position in global coordinate system. Minimum and maximum coordinate dimensions are measured by using bounding box for each component in global X, Y and Z coordinate system as shown in Fig. 1. Table 2 shows the occupation dimensions for knuckle joint. This information is used to realize components sharing same space e.g. a bolt or pin fastening two different components will be sharing same space with respective fastened components.

3.3 Identify the Relationship and Envelopment of Each Component with Respect to Other Components

Occupation information collected in previous step is in the form of coordinate dimensions. This step establishes the relativity of each component with other components in the form of envelopment. Envelopment of one component with respect to other component is identified based on overlapping of orthographic views. If one component's all orthographic views are inside the other component's respective orthographic views then such component is considered as completely enveloped component in to other component [17]. If a specific component is having all orthographic views partially overlapping with other component's respective orthographic views, then such components are considered as partially enveloped components. The information regarding envelopment is categorized in three different types which are partial envelopment, major envelopment (C.G. of one component lies in other enveloping component) and complete envelopment. In envelopment matrix, complete envelopment is indicated with 'C', major envelopment is indicated with 'M' and partial envelopment is indicated with 'P' as shown in Fig. 2.

Table 1. Product features for knuckle joint

Type of mating condition in between different parts of the assembly			Parts of assembly	Mass of each part	Volume of each part	Area of each part	C.G. coordinate		
Part name	Part name	Mating type					X	Y	Z
Fork	Pin	Contact	Fork	3.63	462540	70305	0	−40	0
Fork	Collar	Contact	Pin	0.93	118595	18692	0	0	2
Fork	Eye	Contact	Taper pin	0.01	1178.1	981.75	0	0	−65
Pin	Taper pin	Contact	Collar	0.10	12173	5263.3	0	0	−65
Pin	Collar	Contact	Eye	3.25	413043	40664	0	8	0
Pin	Eye	Contact							
Taper pin	Collar	Contact							
Collar	Eye	Contact							

Table 2. Occupation dimensions for knuckle joint

Parts of assembly	Bounding box origin coordinate			Bounding box length in coordinate direction		
	X	Y	Z	X	Y	Z
Fork	40	−100	−60	80	140	120
Pin	−25	−25	−80	50	50	150
Taper pin	−2	−30	−68	5	60	5
Collar	−25	−25	−70	50	50	10
Eye	−40	−40	−40	80	100	80

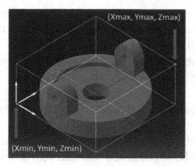

Fig. 1. Bounding box specifications for one component.

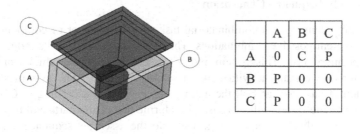

	A	B	C
A	0	C	P
B	P	0	0
C	P	0	0

Fig. 2. Sample Product and its envelopment matrix.

3.4 Component Type Realization

CAD data includes complete geometry definition of the product but lacks the realization of type of component. Realization of component type based on CAD definition has not yet studied intensively and some of the approaches are dependent on name of component in CAD file defined by the user. In this approach, CAD data computation is used to realize components in three different types that is Main components, Connectors and Secondary Connectors. Conditions to identify the same is explained below.

Conditions for Connector Component Realization. Connector component are used for connecting assembly components e.g. screw, bolt, key, etc. Those are identified by using following rules.

Condition 1. Component should have contact with at least two other heavier components than self-weight.
Condition 2. Component should have envelopment with at least two other components satisfying above condition.

Conditions for Secondary Connector Component Realization. Secondary connectors are those which are used to lock the Connector components identified in above step e.g. washers, nuts, O-rings etc. Those are identified by using following rules.

Condition 1. Component should have contact with a connector component.
Condition 2. Component should have less weight than the connector component satisfying above condition.
Condition 3. Component should have envelopment with connector component satisfying above two conditions.

Conditions for Main Component Realization. All the remaining components after identification of connectors and secondary connectors are considered as main components. Main components are generally fastened with the help of connectors (i.e. fasteners) or else they can be self-fastened with the help of integral design features (i.e. threads, press locks, gravity constraints etc.).

3.5   Assembly Sequence Generation

The Assembly planning is a combinatorial task. For 'n' number of components there can be n! different possible combinations. This complexity needs to be reduced to ease assembly planners' task. This system finds an assembly sequence which can play as a guideline for downstream activities like assembly planning. The system starts with identification of base part and all the main parts are ranked according to CG distance from base part. The system follows basic thumb rule that nearer parts will be assembled first. System uses the flowchart in Fig. 3 to find the assembly sequence among main parts and flowchart in Fig. 4 is used to establish assembly sequence among connector parts. Algorithm uses following conditions to find base part.

Condition 1. Base part should not be a connector or secondary connector.

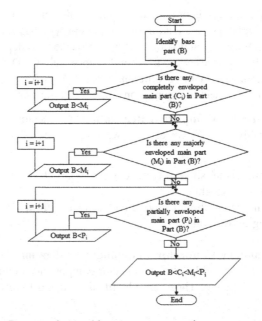

Fig. 3. Process of assembly sequence generation among main parts.

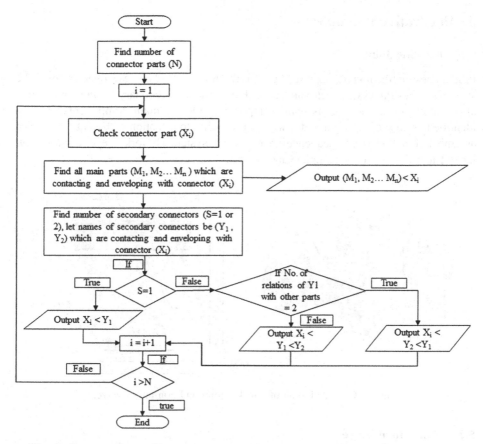

Fig. 4. Process of assembly sequence generation among parts connected to connectors.

Condition 2. Base part should have relationship with at least two other components.

Condition 3. Base part should have highest self-weight.

4 Implementation

The system is implemented in CATIA V5-R19 software package and Visual Basic Application Programming Interface (VB-API) is used for carrying out data extraction from ".CATProduct" file. System automatically extracts physical properties and occupation information and exports to spreadsheet application i.e. MS Excel in this case. A special program developed in MS VBA uses the data from spreadsheet and gives the output of component type realization and assembly sequence generation.

5   Illustrative Examples

5.1   Knuckle Joint

Product design file of knuckle joint (Fig. 5) is randomly tested on developed system. The system realizes Pin as Connector and Taper Pin, Collar as Secondary Connectors system also realizes Fork and Eye as main components. Out of main components, Fork is identified as base component and it will be preceding to selection of Eye at the time of assembly. Final assembly sequence generated by system is "fork < eye < Pin < Collar < Taper Pin" which is complete and correct.

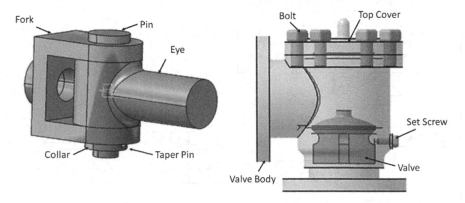

Fig. 5. CAD definition of knuckle joint and non-return valve.

5.2   Non-return Valve

Non-Return Valve consisting of 10 different components is tested on developed system. This system successfully identifies 6 bolts, 1 locating screw as connectors. System also identifies Valve body, Valve and Top Cover as main components in the product. System starts with identifying valve body as base component keeping it as first component in assembly sequence. This main component is sharing relationship with other two main components that is valve and top cover. As valve cover is completely included in body, preference is given to the same and is kept succeeding Valve Body in assembly sequence. Final assembly sequence generated is "Valve Body < Valve < Locating Screw < Top Cover < Bolt 1 < Bolt 2 < Bolt 3 < Bolt 4 < Bolt 5 < Bolt 6" which is also correct.

6   Conclusions

The paper presented an approach to automatically realize the type of components and to generate the precedence relationships by using CAD data. The developed system extracts physical properties and occupational information of each part and saves in MS Excel application. Component type realization and occupational information is used for assembly sequence generation process. Most of the currently available approaches depend on component name, pattern matching, Case-Based reasoning to categorize the type of components [10–12], whereas system presented in this paper proposes novel CAD data computation approach to realize component types. Main intention of the proposed system is to generate assembly sequence early in the design phase so that it can guide downstream activities like assembly line design, plant layout and design phase itself. In future, assembly constraints like required tools, fixtures or handling equipment can be captures in the developed system and advanced optimization algorithms can play a big role in optimizing downstream activities e.g. assembly line design.

References

1. Reddy, G., Ghosh, K.: A simplified and efficient representation for evaluation and selection of assembly sequences. Comput. Ind. **50**, 251–264 (2003)
2. Bourjault, A.: Contribution a une approche methodologique de l' assemblage automatid: elaboration automatique des sequences operatoires. Ph.D. thesis, Department of Mechanical Engineering, University of Franche-Comte, France (1984)
3. Homem, D.L.S., Sanderson, A.C.: A correct and complete algorithm for the generation of mechanical assembly sequences. In: Proceedings IEEE International Conference on Robotics and Automation, pp. 56–61 (1989)
4. Prenting, T., Battaglin, R.: The precedence diagram: a tool for analysis in assembly line balancing. J. Ind. Eng. **15**(4), 208–213 (1964)
5. Qin, Y.F., Xu, Z.G.: Assembly process planning using a multi-objective optimization method. In: International Conference on Mechatronics and Automation, pp. 593–598 (2007)
6. Sinanoglu, C., Boklu, H.R.: An assembly sequence planning system for mechanical parts using neural network. Assem. Autom. **25**, 38–52 (2005)
7. Chen, G., Zhou, J., Cai, W., Lai, X., Lin, Z., Menassa, R.: A framework for an automotive body assembly process design system. Comput. Aided Des. **38**(5), 531–539 (2006)
8. Vigano, R., Gomez, G.: Automatic assembly sequence exploration without precedence definition. Int. J. Interact. Des. Manuf. **7**, 79–89 (2013)
9. Sotiris, M., George, P., Loukas, R., George, C.: Assembly support using AR technology based on automatic sequence generation. CIRP Ann.-Manuf. Technol. **62**, 9–12 (2013)
10. Li-Ming, O., Xun, X.: Relationship matrix based automatic assembly sequence generation from a CAD model. Comput.-Aided Des. **45**, 1053–1067 (2013)
11. George, P., Christos, T., Nikolaos, P., Dimitris, M., George, C.: Assembly precedence diagram generation through assembly tiers determination. Int. J. Comput. Integr. Manuf. **29** (10), 1045–1057 (2016)
12. Riyadh, B., Imen, B., Moez, T., Nizar, A.: Assembly sequences plan generation using features simplification. Adv. Eng. Softw. **119**, 1–11 (2018)
13. Li, D.X., Wang, C., Bi, Z., Yu, J.: AutoAssem: an automated assembly planning system for complex products. IEEE Trans. Ind. Inf. **8**(3), 669–678 (2012)
14. Yu, J., Li, D.X., Bi, Z., Wang, C.: Extended interference matrices for exploded view of assembly planning. IEEE Trans. Ind. Inf. **11**, 279–286 (2014)
15. Belhadj, I., Trigui, M., Benamara, A.: Subassembly generation algorithm from a CAD model. Int. J. Adv. Manuf. Technol. **87**, 2829–2840 (2016)
16. Kheder, M., Trigui, M., Aifaoui, N.: Optimization of disassembly sequence planning for preventive maintenance. Int. J. Adv. Manuf. Technol. **90**, 1337–1339 (2017)
17. Umeshchandra, M., Venkatesh, J., Balaji, D.: Rule based system to generate Hierarchical Directed Graph for mechanical assemblies. Manuf. Lett. **19**, 29–34 (2019)

Methods to Distinguish Photorealistic Computer Generated Images from Photographic Images: A Review

Kunj Bihari Meena and Vipin Tyagi[(✉)]

Jaypee University of Engineering and Technology, Raghogarh, Guna, MP, India
dr.vipin.tyagi@gmail.com

Abstract. Uses of digital images have increased multifold in last few years in various important fields such as virtual reality, gaming, social media, magazine, news papers, medical, legal issues, law, academics etc. At the same time, image editing and rendering tools have also evolved significantly. With the help of computers and such advanced image rendering tools it is possible to create photorealistic computer graphics images effortlessly. It is very difficult to discriminate such photorealistic computer graphics images from actual photographic images taken from digital cameras by human visual system. If computer generated images are used with malicious intentions it creates negative impact on the society. Therefore, several methods have been proposed in last few years to distinguish computer generated images from photographic images. This paper presents a comprehensive review of the existing methods. A classification of all existing methods is also provided based on the use of feature extraction techniques and classifier used. Accordingly, all the existing methods are grouped into four categories: statistical feature based, acquisition process based, visual feature based, and hybrid feature based methods. This paper also reviews publically available related image datasets and suggests the future directions.

Keywords: Image forgery detection · Computer graphics ·
Photorealistic computer generated images · Photographic images ·
Support Vector Machine · SVM · RGB color model · Classification accuracy ·
Feature extraction

1 Introduction

The involvement of digital images is ubiquitous in today's age of digital media. The digital images are the prominent carrier of digital information. Images are used in several fields such as virtual reality, film industry, advertisement and marketing, magazine, news agencies, medical field, laws, defense, surveillance system and security, legal issues, insurance, social media etc. The authenticity of a digital image play vital role in these applications. Due to rapid growth of multimedia tools, and 2D and 3D rendering software it becomes easy job to create computer graphics with high photorealism. Hence, in most of the situations Computer Generated (CG) images cannot be differentiated from the actual photographic (PG) images which are captured using digital camera by human eyes. Figure 1 shows three examples of CG images (first row) and three examples of PG

© Springer Nature Singapore Pte Ltd. 2019
M. Singh et al. (Eds.): ICACDS 2019, CCIS 1045, pp. 64–82, 2019.
https://doi.org/10.1007/978-981-13-9939-8_7

images (second row). It is obvious that CG images may be maliciously used in the aforementioned fields to mislead the people. For an instance, a political leader may create computer generated fake image of any leader of opposition party to defame him. The number of fake images produced before forensic departments relating to legal issues has increased multifold in last few years [1–3]. Recently, using artificial intelligence and virtual reality, a synthesizing Obama project was developed to simulate facial expressions of Obama [4]. Several researchers have focused their attention to develop methods to differentiate between CG and PG images in last few years. Birajdar and Mankar [5] have reviewed few methods to differentiate CG images from PG images. Tokuda et al. [6] have studied several methods and introduced four hybrid methods FUS1, FUS2, FUS3, and FUS4 by combining two or more features extraction techniques and classifiers by implementing 17 existing methods. In 2016, Holmes et al. [7] have conducted two experiments based on human visual system by hiring 250 persons from Amazon's Mechanical Turk online work force to classify images as CG or PG image. On the basis of experiments, authors have suggested that classification accuracy can be improved if trained experts judge images instead of untrained people. Ng et al. [8] surveyed various methods proposed during 2004-2011 to differentiate CG images from PG images. In this study, the authors have classified existing methods into five categories: image formation based, natural image statistics based, steganalysis based, visual cues based, and combined features based methods.

Fig. 1. Examples of computer generated images (first row) and photographic images (second row) [9]

These aforementioned review articles are not complete review articles, e.g. [5] includes only small section related to this field. Similarly, [8] reviews classification methods till 2011 only. In this study we have found total of 52 research articles that proposed the methods to differentiate CG images from PG images. Year-wise statistics of these 52 research papers is illustrated in Fig. 2. From Fig. 2, it can be observed that 8 methods have been proposed in year 2011, whereas no related research paper is available in year 2015.

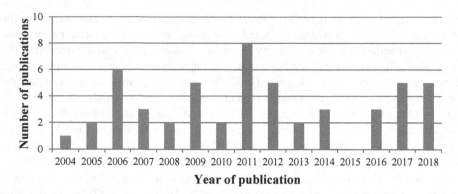

Fig. 2. Number of publications that addressed methods to differentiate between CG and PG images over last 15 years

The common workflow of the methods to differentiate between CG and PG images is presented in Fig. 3. Brief description of each of the steps mentioned in workflow is presented as follows:

Pre-processing: Input image is pre-processed (optionally) in the methods in order to reduce computational cost or to improve the classification accuracy. Common pre-processing operations includes: conversion from RGB color space model to HSV or YCbCr color space model or grayscale image. The methods proposed in [10–13] have extracted features in HSV color space, whereas, YCbCr color space model is used in the methods proposed in [14–16].

Feature Extraction: Feature extraction techniques plays vital role in any method to discriminate CG images from PG images. Selection of robust feature extraction technique can reduce the time complexity at the same time it can also improve the classification accuracy significantly [17]. Hence, much effort was given to explore various types of feature extraction mechanisms in the literature. Common feature extraction techniques to represent input image are Discrete Wavelet Transform (DWT) [18], cotourlet [19], curvelet [19], fractal geometry [20], traces of demosaicing [21], 2D histogram features [22], ResNet-50 model [23], and VGG19 network [24] etc.

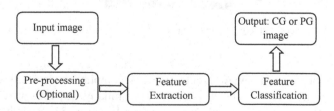

Fig. 3. Common workflow of methods to distinguish CG images from PG images

Feature Classification: The selection of suitable feature classification technique directly affects the classification accuracy as each classifier has different nature in terms of learning algorithm. Hence, various feature classification techniques have also investigated in the literature. Commonly used classifiers includes Support Vector Machine (SVM) [18, 19, 25, 26], Convolution Neural Network (CNN) [23, 27, 28], Deep learning [23], Fishers's Linear Discriminant (FLD) [29, 30], genetic algorithm [15], AdaBoosting learning algorithm [31] etc.

This paper presents two separate classifications for the methods to differentiate between CG and PG images available in literature; first classification is based on feature extraction techniques, whereas second classification is based on feature classifier used. In first classification, the methods have been categorized as: statistical feature based, acquisition process based, visual feature based, hybrid feature based, and miscellaneous feature based methods. The statistical distribution of all 52 methods according to this classification is presented in Fig. 4. From Fig. 4, it can be observed that most of the proposed methods are based on statistical feature extraction techniques. In the second classification, the basis of categorization is feature classifier used to classify input image as CG or PG. Based on this classification all 52 methods have been categorized into four groups as: SVM based, neural network based, Fishers's linear discriminant based, and miscellaneous classifier based methods. Statistical distribution of all 52 methods according to this classification is presented in Fig. 5. It can be concluded that SVM classifier is widely preferred classifier and neural network based classifiers are the second most preferred choice. Besides SVM based, neural network based, and FLD based classifiers, other classifiers like genetic algorithm, AdaBoosting learning algorithm, threshold based classifiers are also employed in [15], [31], and [21] respectively.

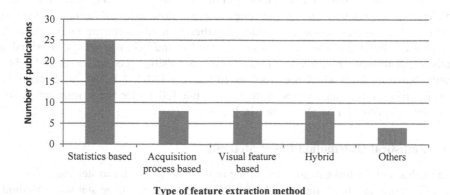

Fig. 4. Feature extraction techniques based distribution of the methods to differentiate between CG and PG images

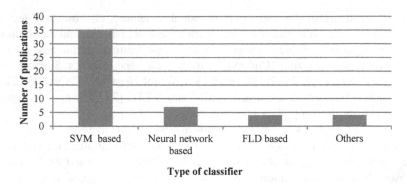

Fig. 5. Classifier based distribution of the methods to distinguish CG images from PG images

The rest of the paper is arranged as follows: in Sect. 2 detailed classification of the methods to differentiate between CG and PG images is presented. Section 3 describes publically available image datasets of comprise photographic images and photorealistic computer graphics. At last, Sect. 4 summarizes the work and also suggests possible future directions.

2 Methods to Differentiate Between CG and PG Images

As described in Sect. 1, the methods to differentiate between CG and PG images have two crucial steps: feature extraction and feature classification. Effectiveness of any method depends on the selection of appropriate feature extraction technique and also the selection of suitable classification technique. After assessing several research articles, we have found that in literature, authors have explored different types of feature extraction techniques and feature classifiers. Based on feature extraction techniques used, the methods to differentiate between CG and PG images have classified as statistical distribution based, visual feature based, acquisition process based, and hybrid feature based methods which are described in Sects. 2.1, 2.2, 2.3, and 2.4. Section 2.5 presents other miscellaneous methods that do not fall under these four categories. Complete classification is also shown in Fig. 6.

2.1 Statistical Distribution Based Methods

The methods under this category follow the basic concept similar to steganalysis that is the CG images can be distinguished from PG images based image statistics. Methods based on statistical distribution are further classified as frequency transform based methods and texture based methods.

2.1.1   Frequency Transform Based Methods

The statistical distribution based methods that are related to the frequency transform based feature extraction techniques fall under this category. First time, Farid et al. [18] introduced image statistical model using first four order statistics of wavelet coefficients in different subbands. In this method, total 216 features were calculated and then SVM classifier was employed to classify image as CG or PG. Based on the experiments conducted on the images dataset of 40, 000 PG and 6,000 CG images, the authors have confirmed that the classification accuracy is 71%. Wang et al. [30] proposed a method using statistics of wavelet coefficient histograms and FLD classifier; and achieved 91% classification accuracy with relatively low feature vector length of 144. Chen et al. [32] investigated a method using SVM classifier and statistical moments of wavelet coefficient in HSV color space. This method attains 94% classification accuracy on the image dataset of 1000 CG and 1000 PG images.

Cui et al. [33] developed an algorithm based on similar features as [32] in Discrete Fourier Transform domain. The authors have suggested that this method secured 94% accuracy on Columbia image dataset. Chen et al. [15] proposed a method based on wavelet based statistical features in YCbCr color space. In this method genetic algorithm is used as a classifier to classify feature vectors of size 100 on Columbia image dataset to secure 82.3% classification accuracy. Chen et al. [26] introduced a method based on alpha-stable distribution model and wavelet based statistic to distinguish CG images from PG images. This method also exploits SVM classifier and achieves 97.6% accuracy on the image dataset mentioned in [32]. Sutthiwan et al. [34] introduced a method based transition probability matrix in Discrete Cosine Transform (DCT) domain. In this method, the authors have extracted feature in Y and Cb components as high correlation found in the features of these two components.

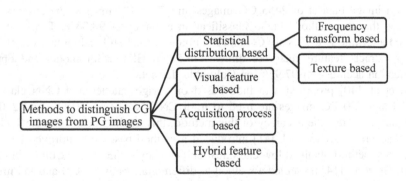

Fig. 6. Classification of the methods to differentiate between CG and PG images based on feature extraction mechanism

Sutthiwan [22] introduced a method based on statistical moments of 1-D and 2-D characteristic functions and then 780 features are extracted and supplied to SVM classifier. Further, boosting feature selection is employed to reduce the feature dimensionality up to 390. However this method has low classification accuracy (88%) on Columbia image dataset. Lu et al. [35] developed an algorithm based on multiresolution decomposition and higher order local autocorrelation. Bo et al. [36] introduced a method by employing Benford's law and SVM classifier. This method has low computation cost as it uses feature vector of length 54. Classification accuracy of this method is 91.6% on dataset of 2400 CG and 2400 PG images. Guo et al. [12] proposed a method by utilizing multiwavelet and SVM classifier in HSV color space. Contourlet and SVM based method to differentiate CG images from PG images was proposed by Ozparlak et al. [19]. However, this method has low classification accuracy of 82.68% on image dataset of 5000 CG and 5000 PG images.

Fan et al. [37] devised a method based on contourlet transform and SVM classifier in HSV color space model. Wang et al. [11] introduced a method using Quaternion Wavelet Transform (QWT) and SVM classifier. Based on experiments performed on a dataset of 7500 CG images and 7500 PG images, the authors have suggested that their method performs better than [18] and [19]. Birajdar et al. [38] introduced a mechanism to classify CG and PG images based on DWT binary statistical image features. In this method, input RGB image is first converted into grayscale, then 256 features are extracted, finally SVM is used to classify images as CG or PG. Further, fuzzy entropy based feature selection technique is applied to select appropriate features. Recently, Wang et al. [39] proposed a method based on quaternion skewness and kurtosis. The authors claim that their method shows 19% better classification accuracy as compared to method introduced in [18].

2.1.2   Texture Based Methods

The statistical based methods that extract image statistical features using local patch or texture are listed in this section. Li et al. [16] discovered a technique based on Local Binary Patterns (LBP). Total 59 features are extracted per image in YCbCr color model and then these features are supplied to SVM classifier. By conducting set of experiments on image dataset of 2455 CG images and 2455 PG images, the authors have suggested that the method obtains classification accuracy as 98.33%. Tan et al. [13] designed a technique to classify CG and PG images based on local ternary count. This method extracts feature vector of dimension 54 in HSV color model and obtains classification accuracy of 97.95% on Columbia dataset.

Yu et al. [40] proposed a method based on image patches and CNN classifier. 750 CG and 750 PG images are used to train CNN, whereas 250 CG and 250 PG images are used test the accuracy of this method, this method achieves 98.5% classification accuracy. Deng et al. [41] introduced a method based on improved LBP and SVM. This method obtained low classification accuracy of 83.3% on Columbia image dataset. He et al. [14] presented a method to differentiate between CG and PG images by extracting image features using Schmid filter bank algorithm in YCbCr color model. This method applied CNN and recurrent neural network classifiers.

2.1.3   Other Statistical Methods

This section presents statistical based methods that do not fall under above two categories. Rocha et al. [42] introduced a method based progressive randomization technique and SVM classifier. In this method, the feature dimension was only 96, hence it required less time to process an image (6.1 s per image of size 512×512 pixels). Li et al. [43] proposed a method using second-order difference statistics and LDA

Table 1. Comparative study of existing methods to distinguish CG image from PG images that are based on statistical distribution

Method	Features extracted	Classifier used	Feature length	Accuracy	Dataset
Farid et al. [18]	First and higher-order wavelet statistics and error predictors	SVM	216	71%	40000 PG and 6000 CG images
Wang et al. [30]	Wavelet coefficient histograms	FLD	144	91%	1000 CG and 1000 PG images
Rocha et al. [42]	Progressive randomization technique	SVM	96	97.2%	40 000 PG and 6000 CG image
Chen et al. [32]	Statistical moments, wavelet coefficient	SVM	234	94%	1000 CG and 1000 PG images
Cui et al. [33]	DFT	SVM	78	94%	Columbia dataset
Chen et al. [15]	Wavelet	Genetic Algo.	100	82.3%	Columbia dataset
Chen et al. [26]	Wavelet decomposition coefficients	SVM	135	97.6%	1000 CG and 1000 PG images
Sutthiwan et al. [34]	DCT	SVM	150	94.2%	Columbia dataset
Li et al. [16]	Second order statistic	LDA	144	95.5%	Columbia dataset
Sutthiwan et al. [22]	2D histogram feature	SVM	780	88%	Columbia dataset
Wu et al. [29]	Histogram	FLD	112	95.3%	1000 CG and 1000 PG images
Lu et al. [35]	2D-DWT	SVM	225	98%	Columbia dataset
Bo et al. [36]	DCT	SVM	54	91.6%	2400 CG and 2400 PG images
Guo et al. [12]	Multiwavelet	SVM	192	92.79%	Columbia dataset
Ozparlak et al. [19]	Contourlet	SVM	768	82.68%	5000 CG and 5000 PG images
Fan et al. [37]	Contourlet	SVM	384	93.51%	Columbia dataset

(continued)

Table 1. (*continued*)

Method	Features extracted	Classifier used	Feature length	Accuracy	Dataset
Li et al. [16]	LBP	SVM	59	98.33%	2455 CG and 2455 PG images
Wang et al. [11]	Quaternion wavelet	SVM	576	94.87%	7500 CG and 7500 PG images
Tan et al. [13]	Local ternary count	SVM	54	97.95%	Columbia dataset
Rahmouni et al. [44]	11-bin histogram	CNN	256	93.20%	1800 CG and 1800 PG images
Yu et al. [40]	CNN	CNN	–	98.50%	1000 CG and 1000 PG images
Birajdar et al. [38]	DWT	SVM	256	87.72%	Columbia dataset
Deng et al. [41]	LBP	SVM	128	83.3%	Columbia dataset
He et al. [14]	ResNet-50 model	CNN-RNN	800	93.87%	6800 CG and 6800 PG images
Wang et al. [39]	Quaternion central moments in color quaternion	SVM	864	98.89%	7500 CG and 7500 PG images

classifier in HSV color model. Wu et al. [29] proposed a method based on statistics of histogram of image and FLD classifier. Rahmouni et al. [44] suggested a method based on 11-bin histogram statistics and Convolutional Neural Network (CNN) with a custom pooling layer. The experiments have carried out on dataset of 1800 CG and 1800 PG images by extracting feature of size 256. This method secured 93.20% classification accuracy on this dataset. Table 1 presents a comparative study of existing methods to distinguish CG image from PG images that are based on statistical distribution.

2.2   Visual Features Based or Geometry Based Methods

This section reviews the methods that are based on visual features or geometry of an image such as color, texture, edge properties, and surface smoothness etc. Basic idea of the methods under this category is that the computer generated images have simpler textures, less color variation, and simpler scenes as compared to photographic images.

First time, Athitsos et al. [45] developed a method to distinguish computer graphics from real images based on visual content and geometry of an image. Multiple decision tree algorithm is trained by feeding 1025 CG and 643 PG images. Ng et al. [25]

developed a model to differentiate between CG and PG images based on natural image statistics extracted from local patch of an input image. Ng et al. also developed an online project [10] to classify CG images and PG images by implementing three different techniques based on geometry, wavelet, and cartoon features. Chen et al. [31] introduced a technique based on farthest neighbor histogram feature introduced in [45]. This technique employed AdaBoosting learning algorithm as a classifier and the method is evaluated on large dataset of 36,000 CG and 35,000 PG images.

Wu et al. [46] developed a method based on visual features derived from color, edge, saturation and texture features. SVM classifier is used to classify images as CG or PG. Pan et al. [47] introduced a method based on fractal dimension by capturing the difference in color perception between CG images and PG images. Nguyen et al. [48] introduced a method to distinguish computer generated human faces from natural faces taken from camera. This method uses face asymmetry information as a feature, then SVM is used as a classifier. Zhang et al. [49] introduced a technique by combining two

Table 2. Comparative study of existing methods to distinguish CG image from PG images that are based on visual features

Method	Features extracted	Classifier used	Feature length	Accuracy	Dataset
Ng et al. [25]	Fractal geometry	SVM	108	82.00%	Internet
Athitsos et al. [45]	Visual content	Multiple decision trees	9	86%	1025 CG and 643 PG images
Ng et al. [10]	Patch-based image statistic	SVM	24	83%	Columbia dataset
Chen et al. [31]	Farthest neighbor histogram feature	AdaBoosting algorithm	9	86%	36,000 CG and 35,000 PG images
Wu et al. [46]	Color, ratio of saturated pixels	SVM	–	91.50%	1044 CG and 1114 PG images
Pan et al. [47]	Fractal geometry	SVM	20	91.20%	1500 CG and 1500 PG images
Nguyen et al. [48]	Face asymmetry information	SVM		89%	200 CG and 200 PG images
Zhang et al. [49]	Local edge patches and key sampling points in accordance with Voronoi cells	SVM	256	95.7%	Columbia dataset

visual features local edge patches and key sampling points in accordance with Voronoi cells. Table 2 presents a comparative study of existing methods to distinguish CG image from PG images that are based on visual features.

2.3   Acquisition Process Based Methods

The generation process of CG image and PG images are totally different. Figure 7 shows acquisition process of a digital image that is captured using any digital camera. The common steps include camera lens, Color Filter Array (CFA), camera sensor, CFA interpolation, post-processing (white balancing, gamma correction, color enhancement, low-pass filtering). Each of these steps introduce a unique signature in digital image which are not present in CG images as CG images follow different process of generation (Fig. 8). Therefore many researchers have developed methods to differentiate CG images from PG images based on these acquisition process based differences.

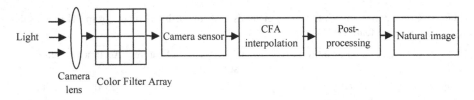

Fig. 7. Image acquisition process of photographic image [50]

Fig. 8. Image acquisition process of computer generated image [50]

Ng et al. [20] proposed a method based on gamma correction and SVM classifier. This method achieves classification accuracy 83.5% on Columbia dataset. Dehnie et al. [51] developed method based on pattern noise. Dirik et al. [52] discovered a technique using traces of demosaicking and chromatic aberration. Khanna et al. [53] introduced a mechanism based on residual pattern noise that exist in images obtained from digital cameras and scanners. Gallagher et al [21] suggested a method based on traces of demosaicing and threshold based classification. Peng and Zhou [50] introduced a method using properties of the CFA interpolation and photo response non-uniformity noise. The method obtained high classification accuracy using SVM classifier up to 99.43%. This method also shows good results under JPEG compression and additive noise. Peng et al. [54] proposed a method based on multifractal theory and the characteristics of PRNU. Yao et al. [55] introduced a method based on sensor pattern noise and CNN classifier. The authors claimed that this method achieves 100% accuracy on image dataset of 1800 CG and 1800 PG images. Table 3 presents a comparative study of existing methods to distinguish CG images from PG images that are based on acquisition process based features.

Table 3. Comparative study of existing methods to distinguish CG image from PG images that are based on acquisition process based features

Method	Features extracted	Classifier used	Feature length	Accuracy	Dataset
Ng et al. [20]	Gamma correction	SVM	192	83.5%	Columbia dataset
Dehnie et al. [51]	Sensor pattern noise	-	1	72.0%	300 CG and 300 PG images
Dirik et al. [52]	Traces of demosaicking and chromatic aberration	SVM	76	99.9%	1800 CG and 1800 PG images
Khanna et al. [53]	Residual pattern noise	SVM	–	91.5%	1000 CG and 1000 PG images
Gallagher et al. [21]	Traces of demosaicing	Threshold based classifier	1	98.4%	Columbia dataset
Peng and Zhou [50]	CFA interpolation	SVM	9	99.43%	1200 CG and 1200 PG images, Columbia Dataset
Peng et al. [54]	PRNU Noise	SVM	8	98.99%	3000 CG and 3000 PG images, Columbia dataset
Yao et al. [55]	Sensor pattern noise	Deep Learning	128	100%	1800 CG and 1800 PG images

2.4 Hybrid Features Based Methods

Sankar et al. [56] introduced a hybrid method based on local patch statistics features and texture interpolation. Peng et al. [57] developed a technique by combining statistical features, PRNU characteristics, and fractal dimension. This method uses SVM classifier and achieves 97.30% accuracy on dataset of 2400 CG and 2400 PG images. Tokuda et al. [6] described a hybrid method by combining various features. Chen et al. [58] introduce a hybrid method by combining sensor pattern noise based statistics and histogram features to distinguish CG images from PG images. Wang et al. [59] proposed a method based on statistical features and texture similarity. SVM classifier is employed in this method to classify CG and PG images. This method works well under basic post-processing operation like additive noise, JPEG compression etc. Zhang et al. [60] proposed a method by merging features of visual descriptor and wavelet based statistics. Conotter and Cordin [61] described a hybrid method based on wavelet based features and sophisticated pattern noise statistics. Peng et al. [62] introduced a method based on 9 dimensions of histogram features and 9 dimensions of multi-fractal spectrum features This method gets 98.69% classification accuracy on dataset of 7500 CG and 7500 PG images using SVM classifier. Table 4 presents a comparative study of existing methods to distinguish CG images from PG images that are based on hybrid features.

Table 4. Comparative study of existing methods to distinguish CG image from PG images that are based on hybrid features

Method	Features extracted	Classifier used	Feature length	Accuracy	Dataset
Sankar et al. [56]	Texture interpolation, and patch statistics based features	Two class	557	90%	Columbia dataset
Peng et al. [57]	Hybrid	SVM	75	97.30%	2400 CG and 2400 PG images
Tokuda et al. [6]	FUS4	SVM	13	97%	4850 CG and 4850 PG images
Peng et al. [62]	Regression model fitness features	SVM	24	98.69%	7500 CG and 7500 PG images
Conotter et al. [61]	Denoising filter	SVM	228	70.1%	8000CG and 8000 PG images
Chen et al. [58]	Pattern noise statistics and histogram features	LSSVM	68	88.25%	Columbia dataset
Wang et al. [59]	Statistical feature	SVM	70	98%	Columbia dataset
Zhang et al. [60]	Visual features and wavelet statistics	SVM	222	87.6%	Columbia dataset

2.5   Miscellaneous Features Based Methods

Pan et al. [63] introduced a method based on hidden Markov tree. This method secures average accuracy up to 84.6% on Columbia dataset. Rezende et al. [23] introduced a method using ResNet-50 model and CNN. This method was evaluated on the large dataset of 4850 CG and 4850 PG images, method gained classification accuracy up to 97%, however, feature length is very high as 2048. Recently, He proposed [27] a technique to differentiate between CG and PG images using VGG-19 and ResNet network. This method achieves 95% accuracy on the dataset mention in [23] using CNN classifier. Meanwhile, Nguyen [24] also employed VGG- 19 network to extract the features from an image. Then CNN classifier is used to classify image as CG and PG image. This method obtains 100% classification accuracy on image dataset of 1800 CG and 1800 PG images. Table 5 presents comparative study of existing methods to distinguish CG images from PG images that are based on miscellaneous features.

Table 5. Comparative study of existing methods to distinguish CG image from PG images that are based on miscellaneous features

Method	Features extracted	Classifier used	Feature length	Accuracy	Dataset
Pan et al. [63]	Hidden Markov tree	SVM	135	84.60%	Columbia
Rezende et al. [23]	ResNet-50 model	CNN	2048	97%	4850 CG and 4850 PG images
He [27]	ResNet-50 model and VGG19 network Fold	CNN	–	96%	4850 CG and 4850 PG images
Nguyen et al. [24]	VGG-19 network	CNN	–	100%	1800CG and 1800 PG images

3 Image Datasets Available

Table 6 shows several publicly available datasets that are commonly used by authors to evaluate the performance of their proposed methods.

Table 6. Description of various available datasets related to classification of computer generated images and photographic images

Dataset	Total images	Resolution	Description
Columbia Image Database [9]	800 CG and 800 PG images	700 × 500 pixels to 3000 × 2000 pixels	800 CG images are taken from the Internet and 800 PG images from Google image search and personal collections
Tokuda dataset [6]	4850 CG and 4850 PG images	4608 × 3456 pixels	Collected from different websites and Art-CG gallery database [64]
Rahmouni dataset [44]	1800 CG and 1800 PG images	1920 × 1080 pixels to 4900 × 3200 pixels	CG images are taken from Level-Design Reference Database [65] and PG images are collected from RAISE dataset [66]

4 Conclusion and Future Directions

This paper presented a comprehensive review of the methods to distinguish computer generated images from actual photographic images. The existing methods have been classified based on two different criteria: first classification is based on techniques used to extract the features from the input image. Accordingly, the methods have been categorized as: statistical feature based, acquisition process based, visual feature based, and hybrid feature based methods. Whereas second classification is based on classifier used, according to this classification the methods in literature are categorized as SVM based, neural network based, and Fisher's linear based methods. It has been observed that most of the methods are based on statistical feature extraction technique and SVM classier. In this survey following issues related to classification of computer graphics and photographic images are observed: (1) low classification accuracy especially under various common post-processing operations, (2) higher computation complexity due to higher feature dimension, (3) lack of generalization of method for various image datasets, (4) lack of availability of image dataset. These limitations can be improved by using feature extraction technique that can represent an image effectively using low feature dimension, and by applying better feature classifier. In this study, we have observed that the methods based on convolution neural network classifier perform best among all other methods. In future these methods can be enhanced to distinguish computer generated videos from actual video captured using digital cameras.

References

1. Tyagi, V.: Understanding Digital Image Processing. CRC Press (2018)
2. Meena, K.B., Tyagi, V.: Image forgery detection: survey and future directions. In: Shukla, R. K., Agrawal, J., Sharma, S., Singh Tomer, G. (eds.) Data, Engineering and Applications, pp. 163–194. Springer, Singapore (2019). https://doi.org/10.1007/978-981-13-6351-1_14
3. Ansari, M.D., Ghrera, S.P., Tyagi, V.: Pixel-based image forgery detection: a review. IETE J. Educ. **55**, 40–46 (2014). https://doi.org/10.1080/09747338.2014.921415
4. Seitz, S.S.S.M., Kemelmacher-Shlizerman, I.: Synthesizing obama: learning lip sync from audio. ACM Trans. Graph. **36**, 95 (2017)
5. Birajdar, G.K., Mankar, V.H.: Digital image forgery detection using passive techniques: a survey. Digit. Investig. **10**, 226–245 (2013). https://doi.org/10.1016/j.diin.2013.04.007
6. Tokuda, E., Pedrini, H., Rocha, A.: Computer generated images vs. digital photographs : a synergetic feature and classifier combination approach. J. Vis. Commun. Image Represent. **24**, 1276–1292 (2013). https://doi.org/10.1016/j.jvcir.2013.08.009
7. Holmes, O., Banks, M.S., Farid, H.: Assessing and improving the identification of computer generated portraits. ACM Trans. Appl. Percept. **13**, 1–12 (2016). https://doi.org/10.1145/2871714
8. Ng, T.T., Chang, S.F.: Discrimination of computer synthesized or recaptured images from real images. In: Sencar, H., Memon, N. (eds.) Digital Image Forensics, pp. 275–309. Springer, New York (2013). https://doi.org/10.1007/978-1-4614-0757-7_10
9. Ng, T., Chang, S., Hsu, J., Pepeljugoski, M.: Columbia Photographic Images and Photorealistic Computer Graphics Dataset (2005)
10. Ng, T., Chang, S.: An online system for classifying computer graphics images from natural photographs. In: Proceedings of SPIE 6072, Security, Steganography, and Watermarking of Multimedia Contents VIII, 607211, pp. 397–405 (2006). https://doi.org/10.1117/12.650162
11. Wang, J., Li, T., Shi, Y., Lian, S., Ye, J.: Forensics feature analysis in quaternion wavelet domain for distinguishing photographic images and computer graphics. Multimed. Tools Appl. **76**, 23721–23737 (2016). https://doi.org/10.1007/s11042-016-4153-0
12. Guo, K., Wang, R.: A new method for detecting computer-generated images based on multiwavelets. J. Inf. Comput. Sci. **8**, 1449–1456 (2011)

13. Tan, D.Q., Shen, X.J., Qin, J., Chen, H.P.: Detecting computer generated images based on local ternary count. Pattern Recognit. Image Anal. **26**, 720–725 (2016). https://doi.org/10.1134/S1054661816040167
14. He, P., Jiang, X., Sun, T., Member, S., Li, H.: Computer graphics identification combining convolutional and recurrent neural network. IEEE Signal Process. Lett. **25**, 1369–1373 (2018). https://doi.org/10.1109/LSP.2018.2855566
15. Chen, W., Shi, Y.Q., Xuan, G., Su, W.: Computer graphics identification using genetic algorithm. In: IEEE International Conference on Pattern Recognition, pp. 1–4 (2009). https://doi.org/10.1109/ICPR.2008.4761552
16. Li, Z., Ye, J., Shi, Y.Q.: Distinguishing computer graphics from photographic images using local binary patterns. In: Shi, Y.Q., Kim, H.-J., Pérez-González, F. (eds.) IWDW 2012. LNCS, vol. 7809, pp. 228–241. Springer, Heidelberg (2013). https://doi.org/10.1007/978-3-642-40099-5_19
17. Talib, A., Mahmuddin, M., Husni, H., George, L.E.: Influencing factors on classification of photographic and computer generated images. J. Comput. **4**, 74–79 (2012)
18. Lyu, S., Farid, H.: How realistic is photorealistic? IEEE Trans. Signal Process. **53**, 845–850 (2005)
19. Ozparlak, L., Avcıbas, I.: Differentiating between images using wavelet-based transforms: a comparative study. IEEE Trans. Inf. Forensics Secur. **6**, 1418–1431 (2011)
20. Ng, T., Chang, S., Hsu, J., Xie, L.: Physics-motivated features for distinguishing photographic images and computer graphics. In: Proceedings of ACM Multimedia, pp. 239–248 (2005)
21. Gallagher, A.C., Chen, T.: Image authentication by detecting traces of demosaicing. In: 2008 IEEE Computer Society Conference on Computer Vision and Pattern Recognition Workshops, CVPR Workshop (2008). https://doi.org/10.1109/CVPRW.2008.4562984
22. Sutthiwan, P., Ye, J., Shi, Y.Q.: An enhanced statistical approach to identifying photorealistic images. In: Ho, A.T.S., Shi, Yun Q., Kim, H.J., Barni, M. (eds.) IWDW 2009. LNCS, vol. 5703, pp. 323–335. Springer, Heidelberg (2009). https://doi.org/10.1007/978-3-642-03688-0_28
23. De Rezende, E.R.S., Ruppert, G.C.S., Archer, C.T.I.R.: Exposing computer generated images by using deep convolutional neural networks. In: 30th SIBGRAPI Conference on Graphics, Patterns and Images, pp. 71–78, Niteroi, Brazil (2017)
24. Nguyen, H.H., Nozick, V.: Modular convolutional neural network for discriminating between computer-generated images and photographic images. In: 13th International Conference on Availability, Reliability and Security, Hamburg, Germany (2018)
25. Ng, T., Chang, S.: Classifying photographic and photorealistic computer graphic images using natural image statistics, New York, NY 10027 (2004)
26. Chen, D., Li, J., Wang, S., Li, S.: Identifying computer generated and digital camera images using fractional lower order moments. In: 4th IEEE Conference on Industrial Electronics and Applications, pp. 230–235 (2009). https://doi.org/10.1109/ICIEA.2009.5138202
27. He, M.: Distinguish computer generated and digital images: a CNN solution. Concurr. Comput. Pract. Exp. **4788**, 1–10 (2018). https://doi.org/10.1002/cpe.4788
28. Yu, I.J., Kim, D.G., Park, J.S., Hou, J.U., Choi, S., Lee, H.K.: Identifying photorealistic computer graphics using convolutional neural networks. In: Proceedings - International Conference on Image Processing, ICIP, pp. 4093–4097 (2018). https://doi.org/10.1109/ICIP.2017.8297052
29. Wu, R., Li, X., Bin, Y.: Identifying computer generated graphics via histogram features. In: 2011 18th IEEE International Conference on Image Processing, pp. 1973–1976 (2011)
30. Wang, Y., Moulin, P.: On discrimination between photorealistic and photographic images. In: IEEE International Conference on Acoustics, Speech and Signal Processing (2006)

31. Chen, Y., Li, Z., Li, M., Ma, W.Y.: Automatic classification of photographs and graphics. In: 2006 IEEE International Conference on Multimedia Expo, ICME 2006 - Proceedings 2006, pp. 973–976 (2006). https://doi.org/10.1109/ICME.2006.262695

32. Chen, W., Shi, Y.Q.: Identifying computer graphics using HSV color model and statistical moments of characteristic functions. In: IEEE International Conference on Multimedia, pp. 1123–1126, Beijing, China (2007). https://doi.org/10.1109/ICME.2007.4284852

33. Cui, X., Tong, X., Xuan, G.: Discrimination between photo images and computer graphics based on statistical moments in the frequency domain of histogram. In: Chinese Information Hiding Workshop, Nanjing, China, pp. 276–279 (2007)

34. Sutthiwan, P., Cai, X., Shi, Y.Q., Zhang, H.: Computer graphics classification based on Markov process model and boosting feature selection technique. In: Proceedings - International Conference on Image Process, ICIP, pp. 2913–2916 (2009). https://doi.org/10.1109/ICIP.2009.5413344

35. Lu, W., Sun, W., Chung, F.L., Lu, H.: Revealing digital fakery using multiresolution decomposition and higher order statistics. Eng. Appl. Artif. Intell. **24**, 666–672 (2011). https://doi.org/10.1016/j.engappai.2011.01.002

36. Bo, X., Junwen, W., Guangjie, L., Yuewei, D.: Photorealistic computer graphics forensics based on leading digit law. J. Electron. **28**, 1933–1936 (2011). https://doi.org/10.1007/s11767-011-0474-3

37. Fan, S., Wang, R., Zhang, Y., Guo, K.: Classifying computer generated graphics and natural images based on image contour information. J. Inf. Comput. Sci. **10**, 2877–2895 (2012)

38. Birajdar, G.K., Mankar, V.H.: Computer graphic and photographic image classification using local image descriptors. Def. Sci. J. **67**, 654–663 (2017)

39. Wang, J., Li, T., Luo, X., Shi, Y., Liu, R., Jha, S.K.: Identifying computer generated images based on quaternion central moments in color quaternion. IEEE Trans. Circuits Syst. Video Technol. **PP**, 1 (2018). https://doi.org/10.1109/TCSVT.2018.2867786

40. Yu, I.-J., Kim, D.-G., Park, J.-S., Hou, J.-U., Choi, S.: Identifying photorealistic computer graphics using convolutional neural networks. In: IEEE International Conference on Image Processing, pp. 4093–4097 (2017)

41. Deng, L.I.N., Liu, C., Sun, Y.: Photorealistic computer graphics identifying algorithm based on improvement local binary pattern. In: International Conference on Artificial Intelligence and Engineering Applications, pp. 834–838 (2017)

42. Rocha, A., Goldenstein, S.: Is it fake or real? In: Brazilian Symposium Computer Graphics Image Processing (2006)

43. Li, W., Zhang, T., Zheng, E., Ping, X.: Identifying photorealistic computer graphics using second-order difference statistics. In: International Conference on Fuzzy Systems and Knowledge Discovery, pp. 2316–2319 (2010)

44. Rahmouni, N., et al.: Distinguishing computer graphics from natural images using convolution neural networks. In: 2017 IEEE Workshop on Information Forensics and Security (WIFS), pp. 228–241 (2017)

45. Athitsos, V., Swain, M.J., Frankel, C.: Distinguishing photographs and graphics on the World Wide Web. In: IEEE Workshop on Content-Based Access Image Video Libraries (1997)

46. Wu, J., Kamath, M.V., Poehlman, S.: Detecting differences between photographs and computer generated images. In: 24th IASTED International Conference on Signal Processing, Pattern Recognition, and Applications, pp. 268–273 (2006)

47. Pan, F., Chen, J., Huang, J.: Discriminating between photorealistic computer graphics and natural images using fractal geometry. Sci. China Ser. F Inf. Sci. **52**, 329–337 (2009). https://doi.org/10.1007/s11432-009-0053-5

48. Dang-Nguyen, D.-T., Boato, G., De Natale, F.G.B.: Discrimination between computer generated and natural human faces based on asymmetry information. In: 20th European Signal Processing Conference, pp. 1234–1238, Bucharest, Romania (2012)
49. Zhang, R., Wang, R.-D., Ng, T.-T.: Distinguishing photographic images and photorealistic computer graphics using visual vocabulary on local image edges. In: Shi, Y.Q., Kim, H.-J., Perez-Gonzalez, F. (eds.) IWDW 2011. LNCS, vol. 7128, pp. 292–305. Springer, Heidelberg (2012). https://doi.org/10.1007/978-3-642-32205-1_24
50. Peng, F., Zhou, D.: Discriminating natural images and computer generated graphics based on the impact of CFA interpolation on the correlation of PRNU. Digit. Investig. **11**, 1–9 (2014). https://doi.org/10.1016/j.diin.2014.04.002
51. Dehnie, S., Taha, S., Memon, N.: Digital image forensics for identifying computer generated and digital camera images. In: IEEE International Conference on Image Processing, pp. 2313–2316 (2006)
52. Dirik, A.E., Bayram, S., Memon, N.D.: New features to identify computer generated images. In: International Conference on Image Processing, pp. 2–6 (2007). https://doi.org/10.1109/ICIP.2007.4380047
53. Khanna, N., Chiu, G.T., Allebach, J.P., Delp, E.J.: Forensic techniques for classifying scanner, computer generated and digital camera images. In: IEEE International Conference on Acoustics, Speech and Signal Processing, pp. 1653– 1656 (2008)
54. Peng, F., Shi, J., Long, M.: Identifying photographic images and photorealistic computer graphics using multifractal spectrum features of PRNU. In: IEEE International Conference on Multimedia and Expo, pp. 1–6 (2014)
55. Yao, Y., Hu, W.: Distinguishing computer-generated graphics from natural images based on sensor pattern noise and deep learning. Adv. Sens. Pattern Noise Used Multimed. Forensics Count. Forensic **18**, 1–11 (2018). https://doi.org/10.3390/s18041296
56. Sankar, G., Zhao, V., Yang, Y.H.: Feature based classification of computer graphics and real images. In: IEEE International Conference on Acoustics Speech Signal Processing - Proceedings, ICASSP, pp. 1513–1516 (2009). https://doi.org/10.1109/ICASSP.2009.4959883
57. Peng, F., Liu, J., Long, M.: Identification of natural images and computer generated graphics based on hybrid features. Int. J. Digit. Crime Forensics. **4**, 1–16 (2012). https://doi.org/10.4018/jdcf.2012010101
58. Chen, Z.: A novel photographic and computer graphic composites detection method. In: National Conference on Information Technology and Computer Science, pp. 935–938 (2012)
59. Wang, X., Liu, Y., Xu, B., Li, L., Xue, J.: A statistical feature based approach to distinguish PRCG from photographs. Comput. Vis. Image Underst. **128**, 84–93 (2014). https://doi.org/10.1016/j.cviu.2014.07.007
60. Zhang, R., Wang, R.: Distinguishing photorealistic computer graphics from natural images by imaging features and visual features. In: International Conference on Electronics, Communications and Control, pp. 226–229 (2011)
61. Conotter, V., Cordin, L.: Detecting photographic and computer generated composites. In: SPIE Symposium on Electronic Imaging (2011)
62. Peng, F., Zhou, D., Long, M., Sun, X.: Discrimination of natural images and computer generated graphics based on multi-fractal and regression analysis. Int. J. Electron. Commun. **71**, 72–81 (2016)
63. Pan, F., Huang, J.: Discriminating computer graphics images and natural images using hidden Markov Tree Model. In: Kim, H.-J., Shi, Y.Q., Barni, M. (eds.) IWDW 2010. LNCS, vol. 6526, pp. 23–28. Springer, Heidelberg (2011). https://doi.org/10.1007/978-3-642-18405-5_3

64. Art-CG gallery database. http://cggallery.itsartmag.com
65. Piaskiewicz, M.: Level-design reference database. http://level-design.org/referencedb/
66. Dang-Nguyen, D., Pasquini, C., Conotter, V.: Raise: a raw images dataset for digital image forensics. In: 6th ACM Multimedia Systems Conference, pp. 219–224 (2015)

A Novel Approach for Automatic Diagnosis of Skin Carcinoma from Dermoscopic Images Using Parallel Deep Residual Networks

Rahul Sarkar$^{(\boxtimes)}$, Chandra Churh Chatterjee, and Animesh Hazra

Department of Computer Science and Engineering,
Jalpaiguri Government Engineering College, Jalpaiguri 735102, West Bengal, India
{rs2018,ccc2025,animesh.hazra}@cse.jgec.ac.in

Abstract. Basal cell carcinoma and squamous cell carcinoma are known to be the two most widespread variety of skin cancer. In this study, we introduce a novel state of the art deep neural network for skin carcinoma detection. The proposed network requires training two identical subnetworks to perform extensive feature extraction for accurate classification. These subnetworks are designed following the deep residual learning paradigm to boost up the loss optimization. The units in each convolution layer use the separable convolution algorithm in order to conserve parameter space, which in turn allows us to design the costly classification network architecture described in this study. Our model achieved an AUROC score of 0.997, 1.000 and 0.998 for basal cell carcinoma, squamous cell carcinoma, and benign skin lesion classification respectively. Here, we explain the working of the aforementioned network and discuss in details the state of the art performance achieved by it.

Keywords: CLAHE · Grad-CAM · Residual learning · RMSprop · Separable convolution

1 Introduction

Skin cancer is considered to be the most widespread cancer variant with 2,000 mortalities arising from basal cell carcinoma (BCC) and squamous cell carcinoma (SCC) alone, in the U.S. [1]. Basal cell carcinoma is the most common variant of skin cancer followed by squamous cell carcinoma. In 2017, an estimate of 95,360 new cases of skin carcinoma was diagnosed along with an estimated death toll of 13,590, in the U.S. [2]. However, a timely diagnosis can prove to be crucial for the successful treatment of skin carcinoma. In this study, we introduce a state of the art network for basal and squamous cell carcinoma diagnosis from dermoscopic images of skin lesion obtained from the ISIC dataset [3].

The proposed model is a combination of a pair of parallel identical networks which operate on the images with kernel dimensions that are the transpose of each other. The parallel network structure aids error minimization along with varying

© Springer Nature Singapore Pte Ltd. 2019
M. Singh et al. (Eds.): ICACDS 2019, CCIS 1045, pp. 83–94, 2019.
https://doi.org/10.1007/978-981-13-9939-8_8

feature extraction in either branch at the same level. The availability of more features aids the accurate detection of the disease from the images. Also, residual learning [4] is used in order to optimize the error in the network while simultaneously boosting the classification accuracy. Separable convolution [5] has also been incorporated in order to optimize the parameter space required by the model and at the same time reducing the time complexity of the network compared to a traditional convolution algorithm. The novelty of our model lies in its unique parallel residual network structure and the choice of the convolution algorithm used.

The images mentioned above have also been preprocessed by applying a denoising algorithm followed by a contrast limited enhancement algorithm in order to optimize the classification performance. Special channel selection for the images has also been done to optimize the performance of the model as described in the sections below. The validity of performance of the model was verified by monitoring the class activation maps of the convolution layers of the model alongside its training curves. A stable model was thus obtained, capable of reproducing the optimal results on the dataset in question. An outstanding accuracy of 97.86% along with an AUROC score of 0.997, 1.000 and 0.998 for BCC, SCC and benign skin lesion respectively was obtained. The proposed network along with the dataset used can be found at https://github.com/RahulSkr/skinCarcinomaDetection.

The rest of the paper dives into the details of the working and evaluation of the model and is arranged in the following manner: Sect. 2 discusses the works related to skin carcinoma diagnosis from dermoscopic images using the existing statistical models and compares the performance of our model with them; Sect. 3 explains in details the dataset preparation and model development phases; Sect. 4 discusses the results obtained by the model. Finally, Sect. 5 concludes the study and discusses its future scope.

2   Related Works

A study on several existing works towards the diagnosis of the skin carcinoma was performed and the superiority of our proposed methodology was established with respect to these works. All these works are summarized in a nutshell below.

Skin carcinoma has been studied for a long time and the very first works on the diagnosis of the skin carcinoma are in the year 2004 which include the detection of basal cell carcinoma using electrical impedance and neural networks by Dua et al. [6]. It involves two methods, one where PCA algorithm is applied in MATLAB for performing the preprocessing task and the second method, where the impedance of the tissues, size, and location of the skin lesion are calculated. Both methods are followed by an artificial neural network (ANN) for training and stimulating the data containing impedance values. Discrimination of skin carcinoma lesions based upon their textual attributes using wavelets and classification between healthy and affected skin tissues using support vector machines were described by Chaudhry et al. [7] in the year 2007.

Table 1. Summary of some of the existing statistical models used to diagnose skin carcinoma

Author	Year	Employed methodology	Accuracy
Chaudhry et al. [7]	2007	Wavelets over SVM classifier	89%
Masood et al. [14]	2015	Self Supervised Learning Model	89%
Singh et al. [9]	2016	K-means clustering and MC-SVM classifier	94.4%
Suganya [10]	2016	Feature extraction and SVM classifier	96.8%
Kharazmi et al. [11]	2016	Vascular features analysis using Random forest	96.5%[a]
Zhang et al. [13]	2017	Transfer learning on InceptionV3	86.54%
Esteva et al. [12]	2017	Transfer learning on InceptionV3 CNN	72.1%
Our methodology	-	**Parallel deep residual learning**	**97.86%**

[a]In terms of AUC score of classifying BCC images from benign

Multiclass classification of several skin cancer types was explained by Shimizu et al. [8]. Here four class (melanoma, basal cell carcinoma, nevi, and seborrhoeic keratosis) classification was performed using two models: a layered model with task decomposition strategy and flat models treated as baselines. Border detection was performed followed by feature extraction along with interpolation for the multiclass classification. A K-means clustering algorithm was used for preprocessing followed by classification using MC-SVM (multi-class support vector machine), which is described by Singh et al. [9], in the year 2016. In the same year, a model using SVM classifier for classification of skin lesions was proposed by Suganya [10]. The SVM classifier was used for binary classifications between two sets of skin lesions, which were then combined to perform the multiclass classification. Kharazmi et al. [11] described the detection and segmentation of vascular structures of skin lesions followed by BCC classification, where 12 vascular features were extracted which were then fed to a random forest classifier.

Esteva et al. [12] explained a transfer learning model based on the Inception V3 architecture in the year 2017. The model was trained for 21 different classes and tested against 21 certified dermatologists where the CNN achieved an accuracy of $72.1 \pm 0.9\%$. Another transfer learning algorithm based on Inception V3 network was developed by Zhang et al. [13].

An overview of the aforementioned methodologies which acquired high performance scores is summarized in Table 1.

3 Proposed Methodology

Deep learning paradigms are quite powerful when working with image data. However, for complex data, deep and complex models are necessary. If trained using gradient-based learning techniques, these models become prone to the dangers of *accuracy degradation* and increasing loss (caused by the problem of *vanishing gradient*) with an increase in depth of the model. In order to design an ideal model against the dataset in question we follow certain deep learning paradigms to overcome such problems. Additionally, the image data used in our study has been extensively processed to optimize the performance of the model.

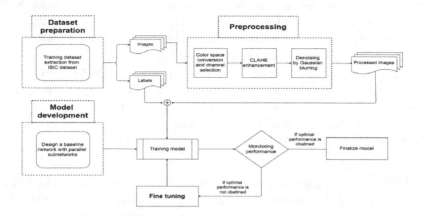

Fig. 1. Overview of the proposed methodology

Figure 1 provides a brief overview of the proposed methodology and Fig. 2 shows a *3D* representation of the proposed network. In the sections below we discuss the training data and the proposed model in details.

3.1   Dataset Preparation

Data pertaining to skin carcinoma was extracted from the ISIC dataset with appropriate labels. The ISIC dataset is considered as a benchmark with respect to skin cancer image data collection. Out of 23,906 images of lesions, 2169 are diagnosed as being melanoma positive, 19,373 are diagnosed as benign, 615 skin carcinoma positive images (586 BCC positive and 29 SCC positive images) and the rest belonging to several other classes. For our study, we use a total of 700 images: 300 benign skin lesion images, 300 BCC positive images and an augmented set of 100 SCC positive images (in order to suffice for the lack of images in this class).

3.2   Preprocessing

Images are resized to dimensions (224×224), maintaining their inherent aspect ratio. This is done by resizing the images to either a height or width of 224 (whichever dimension being larger in the original image) and scaling the other dimension while maintaining the aspect ratio. This resized image is then overlaid on a null matrix of resolution (224×224). The matrix thus obtained is used to derive image matrices in CIELAB and grayscale color space. These derived matrices are merged to obtain a 4 channel image matrix consisting of channels of CIELAB color space and grayscale color space.

Denoising of Images. Images are denoised using the Gaussian blurring algorithm. The Gaussian filter works based on the Gaussian function defined below:

$$G(x, y) = \frac{1}{2\pi\sigma^2} \times \exp\left(-\frac{x^2 + y^2}{2\sigma^2}\right). \tag{1}$$

Clearly, from Eq. 1 the function is separable in two dimensions and is hence relatively faster than other blurring algorithms. All channels in the 4 channel image matrix (mentioned above) undergo this blurring phase and the resultant matrix is then enhanced as explained in the section below.

Enhancement of Images. We prefer not to enhance the grayscale channel. The rest of the channels in the matrix are enhanced following CLAHE enhancement algorithm. Now, to enhance an image means to modify its L^*-channel or *lightness*-channel of the image. Thus, we apply the CLAHE algorithm over the L^*-channel alone.

In the CLAHE algorithm, image is divided into smaller regions and contrast limited enhancement is performed on each of these regions, which prevents noise-enhancement. These smaller regions are then combined using bilinear interpolation to eliminate region boundaries. It should also be mentioned that we perform denoising prior to enhancement, which eliminates the possibility of noise enhancement in the images.

3.3 Model Development

Convolution neural networks are known to be well compatible with image data. However, with an increase in depth of these networks the accuracy can be seen to decrease, this can be referred to as *accuracy degradation*. This is caused due to the loss in the momentum moving forward. Again, during backward propagation, the loss is found to saturate at a much higher value compared to a network with fewer layers and training on the same dataset. This phenomenon is known as *vanishing gradient* problem. In addition, the proposed network is seen to exceed hardware capacity when trained using traditional convolution operation. Hence, we use depthwise separable convolution instead of a traditional convolution operation, in order to optimize parameter complexity. The model development has been discussed in details in the sections below.

Convolution Layer. As already mentioned, we use separable convolution for our model. In case of traditional convolution algorithm, we can define the parameter complexity and the computation cost respectively as:

$$\rho = k \times k \times f_{in} \times f_{out} \tag{2}$$

$$\kappa = \rho \times d_{in} \times d_{in} \tag{3}$$

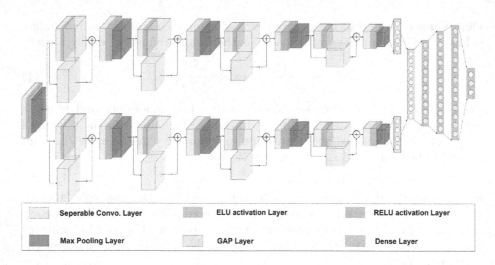

Fig. 2. A 3D representation of the proposed network

Here, k represents the dimension of the kernel in each direction, f_{in} and f_{out} are the number of feature maps fed as input and obtained as output from a convolution layer and finally d_{in} is the dimension of the input feature map in each direction. The first convolution layer of our model accepts an image of resolution (224×224), we find the parameter complexity and computational cost to be $\rho = \mathbf{512}$ and $\kappa = \mathbf{2.57e7}$ using traditional convolution algorithm. Whereas, using depthwise separable convolution we can rewrite Eqs. 2 and 3 respectively as follows:

$$\rho_{ds} = k \times k \times f_{in} + f_{in} \times f_{out} \tag{4}$$

$$\kappa_{ds} = \rho_{ds} \times d_{in} \times d_{in} \tag{5}$$

From Eqs. 4 and 5 we can find the parameter and computational cost while using depthwise separable convolution to be $\rho_{ds} = \mathbf{96}$ and $\kappa_{ds} = \mathbf{4.82e6}$ respectively. Clearly, using depthwise separable convolution proves to be cost effective. In addition to this, the number of kernels in separable convolution operation for a given dimension and with the same number of input and output feature maps is obviously greater (as the convolution operation is divided into spatial convolution followed by a point-wise convolution operation), so the computation time is lower as compared to traditional convolution.

Residual Structure of the Network. From the model architecture illustrated in Fig. 2, the residual structure of the network can be determined. The identical structure of the branches is clear from the figure. Each branch consists of 4 *residual modules*. Each of these modules has an identity mapping to aid the propagation of the loss throughout the network.

The error obtained at a lower level gets degraded while moving upwards throughout the network. This happens because every layer propagates the gradient of the loss to the previous layer and as a result, the loss thus propagated becomes vanishingly small. To alleviate this problem Kaiming He et al. proposed the introduction of an identity mapping in the network. Figure 3 shows the fundamental residual block used in our model. Evidently, this results in a lower cross-entropy loss and a higher accuracy of **0.0767** and 97.86% respectively as opposed to a loss and accuracy of **0.3011** and 92.86% in case of a plain network (with no identity connections).

Finally, we use global average pooling to obtain a 1D vector from each branch and merge these into a single vector which is then fed to a fully connected or FC layer.

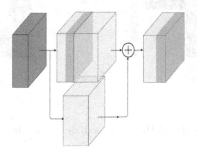

Fig. 3. Residual module as seen in our network

4   Result and Discussion

In order to optimize the model, we monitor its loss, accuracy and AUROC score along with the class activation maps of the convolution layers of the network. The model was fine tuned by modifying the number of residual modules (or blocks) in each branch and by tweaking the number of feature maps fed in and obtained out of these modules. In this section, we discuss in details about the training setup for the model along with results to support the said setup.

4.1   Experimental Setup

The proposed network is built using the Keras framework. Optimization is performed using RMSprop optimizer, which is known to adjust the learning rate automatically. However, we do provide a means to reduce the learning rate, should the model stagnate. Early stopping technique is used to obtain the best weights for the model before it overfits the dataset. In addition, we use Variance scaling to initialize random weights to the units of the model from a *normal* distribution centered around zero (as we do not know the ideal weights of the units, we can consider half of them to be positive and the other half to be negative). The model was trained on 560 images and validated using the remaining 140 images (no images overlap with each other from the training and validation set).

4.2   Confusion Matrix and Related Performance Metrics

The confusion matrices illustrated in Fig. 4a and b show the performance of the proposed and plain model on the validation set respectively. Performance metrics derived from the confusion matrix which evaluate the classification ability of the model for each class is shown in Table 2.

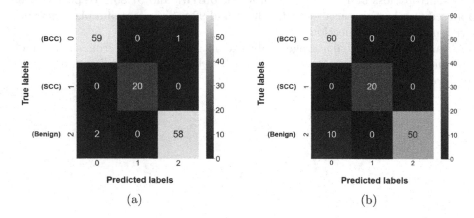

Predicted labels   Predicted labels
(a)   (b)

Fig. 4. (a) Confusion matrix of the proposed network; (b) Confusion matrix of the plain network

In Table 2 below we compare the performance of the proposed network with its plain counterpart. Also, the overall accuracies of the proposed network and its plain counterpart are **97.86%** and **92.86%** respectively.

Table 2. Comparison of the performance of the proposed model with its plain counterpart

Performance metrics	Proposed network (kernel size = (4×4))			Plain network (kernel size = (4×4))		
	BCC	SCC	Benign	BCC	SCC	Benign
Accuracy	**0.979**	**1.000**	**0.979**	0.929	1.000	0.929
Specificity	**0.975**	**1.000**	**0.986**	0.875	1.000	1.000
Sensitivity	**0.983**	**1.000**	**0.966**	1.000	1.000	0.833
Precision	**0.967**	**1.000**	**0.983**	0.857	1.000	1.000
F_1 score	**0.975**	**1.000**	**0.975**	0.923	1.000	0.909

Both networks have a parallel subnetwork structure, in which kernels in one branch have dimensions (1×4) and kernels in the adjacent branch have dimensions (4×1).

4.3 Performance Curves

Figure 5 illustrates the various performance curves for the proposed model. A comparison of the training accuracy and loss curves of the various kernel sizes used for each branch is shown in Fig. 5a and b respectively. Additionally, the ROC curves (along with the respective AUC scores) for the proposed network is shown in Fig. 5c, along with an enhanced view of the top-left portion of the curves (see Fig. 5d).

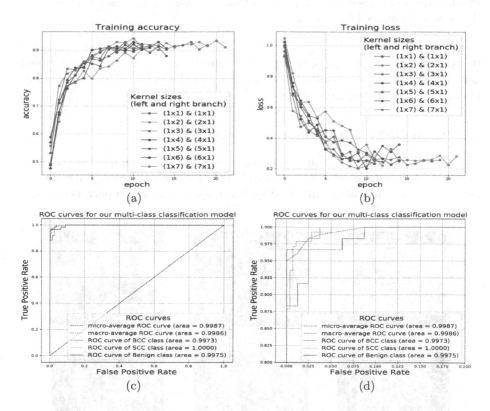

Fig. 5. (a) shows the comparison of the training accuracy curves for various kernel sizes; (b) shows the comparison of the training loss curves for various kernel sizes; (c) shows the ROC curves for the proposed model; (d) shows an enhanced view of the top left portion of the ROC curves shown in Fig. 5c

Figure 6a and b show the comparison of the accuracy and loss curves of the plain and proposed network. From the figures it is clear that the plain network

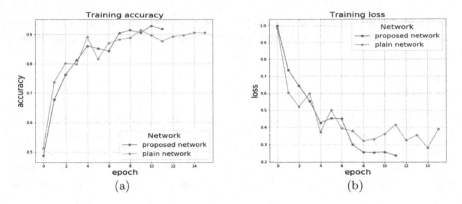

Fig. 6. (a) and (b) show the comparison of the training accuracy and loss curves of the plain and proposed model respectively

stops training with a high saturated loss value as compared to the proposed network, which in turn results in low accuracy of the model. This problem has already been addressed in Sect. 3.3.

4.4 Grad-CAM Visualization

To validate the classification ability of the model we monitor the gradient weighted class activation maps (grad-CAMs) of the convolution layers in the network. Class activation maps visualize the regions of importance under

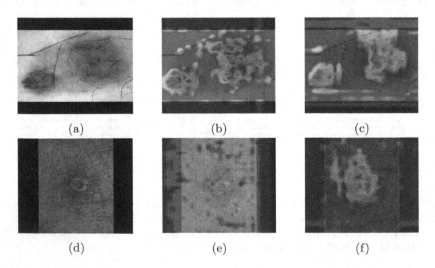

Fig. 7. (a) and (d) show the processed images; (b) and (e) show the grad-CAMs for last conv. layer of branch in which kernel sizes are (1×4); (c) and (f) show the grad-CAMs for last conv. layer of branch in which kernel sizes are (4×1)

consideration by a layer. Grad-CAMs provide a method to visualize these regions while preserving their spatial information, which is lost in the fully connected layers.

The grad-CAMs of the last convolution layers for each branch is shown in Fig. 7. From the above figure, it is clear that both branches accurately identify the lesions in the images, which leads to accurate classification.

5 Conclusion and Future Scope

In this study, we propose a novel, state of the art algorithm for accurate diagnosis of skin carcinoma, from dermoscopic images of skin lesion. We also show how our algorithm outperforms the existing statistical models for the same classification task. Our proposed model addresses the issue of accuracy degradation while dealing with the problem of vanishing gradient. Additionally, the proposed network being designed using depthwise separable convolution, is both parameter cost and time efficient. Saving the parameter space allows for an increase in depth of the model which (in our case) has resulted in a better performance than the existing models.

As a future scope of this study, we intend to extend the model's classification ability by including more classes of skin cancer available in the ISIC dataset. This will ensure a complete automation in the process of diagnosis of skin cancer from dermoscopic images by our model, thereby making it a state of the art algorithm for skin cancer diagnosis.

References

1. Cancer.Net: Skin cancer (non-melanoma): statistics. https://www.cancer.net/cancer-types/skin-cancer-non-melanoma/statistics. Accessed 2019
2. American Cancer Society: Cancer facts and figures 2017. https://www.cancer.org/content/dam/cancer-org/research/cancer-facts-and-statistics/annual-cancer-facts-and-figures/2017/cancer-facts-and-figures-2017.pdf. Accessed 2019
3. ISIC Archive: Melanoma project. https://www.isic-archive.com. Accessed 2019
4. Chollet, F.: Xception: deep learning with depthwise separable convolutions, pp. 1800–1807, July 2017
5. He, K., Zhang, X., Ren, S., Sun, J.: Deep residual learning for image recognition. In: 2016 IEEE Conference on Computer Vision and Pattern Recognition (CVPR), pp. 770–778, June 2016
6. Dua, R., Beetner, D.G., Stoecker, W.V., Wunsch, D.C.: Detection of basal cell carcinoma using electrical impedance and neural networks. IEEE Trans. Biomed. Eng. **51**(1), 66–71 (2004)
7. Chaudhry, M.A., Ashraf, R., Jafri, M.N., Akbar, M.: Computer aided diagnosis of skin carcinomas based on textural characteristics, pp. 125–128, December 2007
8. Shimizu, K., Iyatomi, H., Celebi, M.E., Norton, K., Tanaka, M.: Four-class classification of skin lesions with task decomposition strategy. IEEE Trans. Biomed. Eng. **62**(1), 274–283 (2015)
9. Singh, S.K., Jalal, A.S.: A robust approach for automatic skin cancer disease classification, pp. 1–4, August 2016

10. Suganya, R.: An automated computer aided diagnosis of skin lesions detection and classification for dermoscopy images, pp. 1–5, April 2016
11. Kharazmi, P., AlJasser, M.I., Lui, H., Wang, Z.J., Lee, T.K.: Automated detection and segmentation of vascular structures of skin lesions seen in dermoscopy, with an application to basal cell carcinoma classification. IEEE J. Biomed. Health Inform. **21**(6), 1675–1684 (2017)
12. Esteva, A., et al.: Dermatologist-level classification of skin cancer with deep neural networks. Nature **542**, 115–118 (2017)
13. Zhang, X., Wang, S., Liu, J., Tao, C.: Computer-aided diagnosis of four common cutaneous diseases using deep learning algorithm, pp. 1304–1306, November 2017
14. Masood, A., Al-Jumaily, A., Anam, K.: Self-supervised learning model for skin cancer diagnosis, pp. 1012–1015, April 2015

Identification of Various Neurological Disorders Using EEG Signals

Aarti Sharma[1(✉)], J. K. Rai[2], and R. P. Tewari[3]

[1] Department of ECE, Inderprastha Engineering College,
Site-IV, Ghaziabad, India
aartibhavya@gmail.com
[2] Department of ECE, ASET, Amity University, Noida, India
[3] Department of Applied Mechanics, MNNIT, Allahabad, India

Abstract. Activity of human body is controlled by human brain. Identification of different neurological disorders from EEG signals is still a challenging task. In this paper EEG dataset of forty eight subjects (twelve - epileptic, twelve - normal, twelve - schizophrenic and twelve – alzheimer) have been investigated and it is evident from the findings that remarkable difference exists for extracted features. Six statistical features have been extracted from the dataset of afore-mentioned neurological disorders. Extensive variation in extracted features exists for different neurological disorders. Principal features are selected by calculating Euclidean Distance between different feature vectors. Mean, median and mode are proven to be the best features. The findings are statistically validated using one way analysis of variance (ANOVA).

Keywords: Electroencephalography (EEG) · Features · Epilepsy · Alzheimer · Schizophrenia

1 Introduction

Neurological disorders take huge cost on individual and health care systems. After cardiovascular disease neurological disorders are the main cause of death. Since 1990 deaths from neurological disorders have increased by 37% [1]. Dataset from different modalities like brain scans, electroencephalography (EEG) can be used for detection of the neurological disorders. In this paper EEG dataset of alzheimer's, epilepsy and schizophrenia subjects have been analyzed in context of disorder detection.

Epilepsy is the most common disorder that affect 0.6-0.8% of world population. Most adverse consequence of epilepsy is that it can happen anywhere anytime [2]. Numerous algorithms have been designed for detection and prediction of epileptic seizure [3]. Due to ease of recording and good temporal resolution EEG signal is the preferred choice for the researchers.

Other neurological disorder that is taken into consideration is Alzheimer Disease (AD). Alzheimer is a progressive neurological disorder that occurs due to degeneration of neurons in the cerebral cortex area [4]. AD progress through three stages i.e. Mild Cognitive Impairment (MCI), moderate and severe. Many algorithms have been reported in literature with the help of which AD can be detected at an early stage using

© Springer Nature Singapore Pte Ltd. 2019
M. Singh et al. (Eds.): ICACDS 2019, CCIS 1045, pp. 95–103, 2019.
https://doi.org/10.1007/978-981-13-9939-8_9

EEG signals [5]. MCI and AD cause EEG signals to slow down. Detection of AD at early stage will be helpful to the family members so that preventive measures like timely intake of medicines can be taken to delay the symptoms of the disease. Increment in power in low frequency bands (delta and theta) and decrement in high frequency bands (alpha and beta) is used as a signature for detection of AD from EEG signals [6]. Power spectral density and coherence has also been used to detect irregularities in EEG signals of AD subjects [7].

Third most common brain disorder is schizophrenia that has been taken into consideration. Schizophrenia is a kind of depression which causes consistent anxiety among the patients [8–10]. This kind of disorder can be detected by regular interviews with the patient and family members. It has been reported in the literature that schizophrenia disorder can also be detected using EEG signals [11].

No work has been reported in literature in which dataset from all the disorders have been studied collectively. In this paper EEG data for all neurological disorders and dataset of the normal subjects have been analyzed.

This paper presents preprocessing and segmentation of EEG data followed by the extraction of statistical features. Epoch of one minute from each data has been considered. Number of channels used for recording of EEG data is different for each disorder, so features have been extracted from each channel. The main objective of this paper is to identify the feature set with the help of which neurological disorders can be detected. This paper is structured as follows: in Sect. 2 EEG data set for epilepsy, AD, schizophrenia and normal subjects is presented. Section 3 explains the methodology. Features used are explained in Sect. 4. Finally results and conclusions are presented in Sect. 5 and Sect. 6 respectively.

2 EEG Dataset

In this study four different data sets are explored. The first dataset contains EEG recording of AD subjects. Second dataset contains EEG recording of epileptic subjects. Third and fourth groups of data consist of EEG recording from schizophrenic and normal subjects.

2.1 EEG Data of AD Subjects

EEG data of AD subjects that has been investigated in this study is already analyzed in [12]. The data has been recorded by placing 16 electrodes on scalp. Sampling frequency of data is 1024 Hz and recording duration is one minute. Analysis has been done for the dataset of one minute duration. For one minute duration number of samples will be 60 * 1024.

2.2 EEG Data of Epileptic Subjects

Dataset used for epileptic subjects is available at [13]. Sampling rate is 256 Hz. Detailed description about the dataset is available in [14].

2.3   EEG Data of Schizophrenic and Normal Subjects

Dataset for schizophrenic and normal subjects is made available by [15]. Recording duration for the dataset is one minute with sampling rate of 128 Hz.

3   Methodology

Abundance of features are available in literature [8, 16] for seizure prediction, alzheimer and schizophrenia detection. None of the work has been reported in which all the neurological disorders have been evaluated jointly. In this work features from all the disorders have been evaluated simultaneously. Figure 1 describes block diagram for identification of neurological disorders which consists of feature extraction and statistical validation phase.

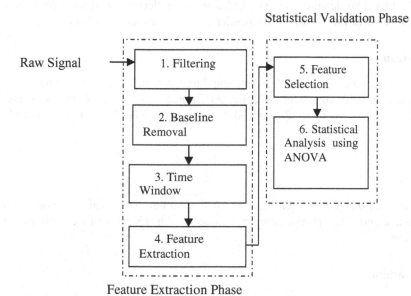

Fig. 1.   Block diagram of proposed methodology

Feature extraction stage consists of four steps while statistical validation stage consists of two steps. All the steps for detection of neurological disorders have been described below:

Step 1: Raw EEG signals for various neurological disorders are filtered out by using FIR filters.

Step 2: Signals from all EEG channels are shifted from the baseline due to muscle and eye blink artifacts. Muscle and eye blink artifacts have been removed by subtracting average of signals from all EEG channel from individual EEG channel.

Step 3: EEG Signals for various neurological disorders are segmented into smaller signals by using non-overlapping window. One minute duration has been considered for the analysis.

Step 4: From the signals of different neurological disorders, statistical features have been extracted from different window segment. All the extracted features have been explained in Sect. 4.

Step 5: Prominent features from the extracted features have been selected using Euclidean Distance (ED) between different feature vectors.

Step 6: The findings are statistically validated using one way ANOVA.

4 Feature Computation

Considering that numbers of channels used for acquisition of brain signals are different for each dataset so, features are extracted from each electrode and then averaged out. Extracted features for neurological disorder detection are enlisted below:

4.1 Mean

Depending on window length of one minute duration and sampling rate, total numbers of samples for EEG signals of epileptic, AD, normal and schizophrenic subjects are 60 * 256, 60 * 1024, 60 * 128 and 60 * 128 respectively. Mean can be calculated using (1)

$$\mu = \frac{\sum x}{N} \tag{1}$$

where, μ is the mean, x is EEG signal and N is total number of samples. For epileptic, AD, normal and schizophrenic subject's value of N is 15360, 61440, 7680 and 7680 respectively.

4.2 Variance

Variance measures degree of adjacency between different data points. Variance is calculated using (2).

$$\sigma^2 = \frac{(x - \mu)^2}{N} \tag{2}$$

where, σ is the variance, μ is mean and N is the total number samples.

4.3 Mode

Mode is defined as the value which occurs most frequently in the given dataset.

4.4   Median

Median is defined as the middle value in the given dataset. For finding median of the given time series data values are arranged in the ascending order and then the middle value is sorted out.

4.5   Mobility

Mobility is defined as the square root of variance of first derivative of the signal $x(t)$ divided by variance of signal $x(t)$. It is calculated using (3).

$$Mobility = \sqrt{\frac{\text{var}\left(\frac{dx}{dt}\right)}{\text{var}(x)}} \tag{3}$$

4.6   Complexity

Complexity indicates the similarity of shape of signal to pure sine wave. Complexity is calculated using (4).

$$Complexity = \frac{mobility\left(\frac{dx}{dt}\right)}{mobility(x)} \tag{4}$$

5   Results

Detection of neurological disorders from EEG signals described in Sect. 3 has been carried out using MATLAB. EEG signals before and after removal of various artifacts for epileptic subjects are shown in Fig. 2 and Fig. 3 respectively.

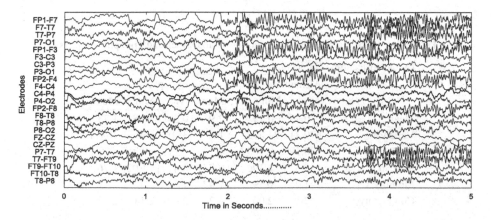

Fig. 2. EEG signals of epileptic subjects before pre-processing

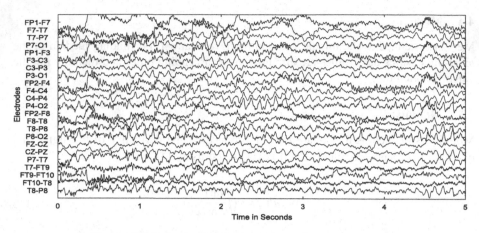

Fig. 3. EEG signals of epileptic subjects after pre-processing

Analysis has been done for forty eight subjects (twelve for each neurological disorder). The average, minimum and maximum results of extracted features is illustrated in Table IA and Table 1B respectively.

Table 1A. Extracted features from dataset of normal and schizophrenic subjects

Extracted features	Subjects					
	Normal			Schizophrenic		
	Avg.	Min	Max	Avg.	Min	Max
Mean	4.7	−2.9	10.9	2.4	−3.9	4.1
Variance	153054	76196.74	253986	98554.5	60025.2	174439
Mode	4.8	−21.16	19.45	2.8	−20.75	14.2
Median	3.8	0.1	19.39	−0.5	−11.7	16.33
Mobility	0.5	0.42	0.55	0.4	0.35	0.5
Complexity	2.2	1.89	2.57	2.4	2.14	2.87

Table 1B. Extracted features from dataset of alzheimer and epileptic subjects

Extracted features	Subjects					
	Alzheimer			Epilepsy		
	Avg.	Min	Max	Avg.	Min	Max
Mean	0.73	−0.29	2.9	0.38	−0.8	1.73
Variance	679.41	24.892	1959	3816	569	10311
Mode	0.59	0.4097	1.763	−383	−759	−78.1
Median	0.33	$1.39e^{-17}$	0.845	0.41	−1.02	1.76
Mobility	1.25	0.59	1.47	1.47	1.42	1.54
Complexity	2.5	2.06	4.2	2.09	2.14	2.87

Maximum value of extracted features is observed from normal subjects. Extracted feature magnitude is in decreasing order for normal, schizophrenic, alzheimer and epilepsy. Data is plotted for different neurological disorders by considering mean as a feature in Fig. 4. It is evident from Fig. 4 that maximum value of mean is observed from normal subjects.

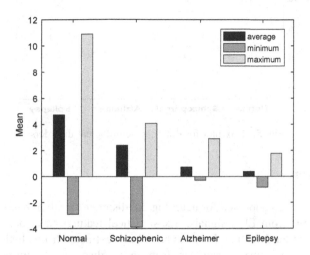

Fig. 4. Mean from EEG signals of different subjects

Since there are six classes of feature vector, so inter class distance between different classes is measured. Suppose feature vectors from two classes are $(a_1, a_2, \ldots\ldots\ldots\ldots a_N)$ and $(b_1, b_2, \ldots\ldots\ldots\ldots b_N)$ respectively. ED between these classes is measured using (5).

$$ED = \sqrt{(a_1 - b_1)^2 + (a_2 - b_2)^2 + \ldots\ldots\ldots(a_N - b_N)^2} \qquad (5)$$

Greater the value of ED, more inter class distance exists between different classes and more prominent is the feature for neurological disorder detection. Mean, Median and Mode are proven to be the best features in context of disorder detection.

Above mentioned findings are statistically validated using one way ANOVA. ANOVA1 tests null hypothesis that the samples from different neurological disorders have the same feature against the alternative hypothesis that extracted features are not same. Obtained p value is $5.95e^{-06}$. So, the null hypothesis that no difference exists between different neurological disorders is rejected. Figure 5 shows box plot for samples from different neurological disorders. It can be observed from Fig. 5 that remarkable difference exists between different groups of data.

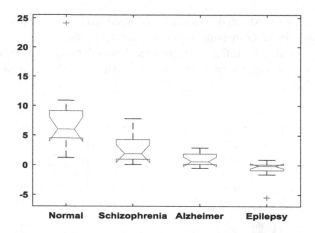

Fig. 5. Box plot for different neurological disorders

6   Conclusion

This work presents an approach for neurological disorder detection based on extracting statistical features from EEG signals. Six statistical features have been extracted for neurological disorder detection. Features have been extracted from all channels for one second duration and twelve samples from each disorder. Features showing the remarkable difference between different classes have been selected using ED. Mean, Median and Mode are found to be the best features. Selected features show noteworthy variation so it offers a good prospect in neurological disorder detection.

Developing algorithm that can help in detection of different neurological disorders will be a great help to society. With an aim of developing convenient devices for real life use our future research directions would be: (1) Development of more practical computerized algorithm that can differentiate between different neurological disorders. (2) Testing the abovementioned approach on larger database. (3) Integration of the features with other features like electrocardiogram (ECG) and electro myogram (EMG) signals of the same subjects to eliminate different artifacts.

References

1. Siuly, S., Zhang, Y.: Medical big data: neurological disease diagnosis through medical data analysis. J. Data. Sci. Eng. **1**(2), 54–64 (2016)
2. Fisher, R.S., et al.: Operational classification of seizure types by the international league against epilepsy: position paper of ILAE Commission for classification and terminology. Epilepsia **58**(4), 522–530 (2017)
3. Freestone, D.R., Karoly, P.J., Cook, V.: A forward looking review of seizure prediction. Curr. Opin. Neurol. **30**, 1–5 (2017)
4. Alzhemier Association, Alzheimer Disease Facts and Figures, Alzheimer Dementia, vol. 13 (2017)

5. Jumeily, D.A., Iram, S.F., Vialatte, B., Fergus, P., Hussain, P.: A novel method for early diagnosis of Alzheimer disease based on EEG signals. Sci. World J. **2015**, 1–11 (2015). Article ID 931387
6. Jutgla, E.G., et al.: Diagnosis of Alzheimer's disease from EEG by means of synchrony measures in optimized frequency bands. In: IEEE Conference on Engineering in Medicine and Biology Society, San Diego, CA, USA, pp. 4266–4270 (2012)
7. Dauwels, J., Vialatte, F.B., Cichocki, A.: On the early diagnosis of Alzheimer's disease from EEG signals: a mini-review. In: Wang, R., Gu, F. (eds.) Advances in Cognitive Neurodynamics (II), pp. 709–716. Springer, Dordrecht (2011). https://doi.org/10.1007/978-90-481-9695-1_106
8. Boostani, R., Sadatnezhad, K., Sabeti, M.: An efficient classifier to diagnose of schizophrenia based on the EEG signals. Expert Syst. Appl. **36**(3), 6492–6499 (2009)
9. Howes, O.D., Murray, R.M.: Schizophrenia an integrated socio developmental-cognitive model. Lancet **383**(9929), 1677–1687 (2014)
10. Patel, K.R., Cherian, J., Gohil, K., Atkinson, D.: Schizophrenia: overview and treatment options. J. Managed Care Hosp. Formulary Manage. **39**(9), 638–645 (2014)
11. Timashev, S.F., Panishev, O.Y., Polyakov, Y.S., Kaplan, A.Y.: Analysis of cross correlation in electroencephalogram signals as an approach to proactive diagnosis of schizophrenia. Phys. A **391**(4), 1179–1194 (2012)
12. Kulkarni, N.N., Bairagi, B.K.: Extracting salient features for EEG based diagnosis of Alzheimer's disease using SVM classifier. IETE J. Res. **63**(1), 1–11 (2017)
13. Goldberger, A.L., et al.: PhysioBank, PhysioToolkit and PhysioNet: components of a new research resource for complex physiological signals. Circulation **101**(23), e215–e220 (2000)
14. Sharma, A., Rai, J.K., Tewari, R.P.: Prior forecasting of epileptic seizure and localization of epileptogenic region. J. Biomed. Eng. Appl. Basis Commun. **29**(2), 1–16 (2017)
15. http://brain.bio.msu.ru/eeg_schizophrenia.htm
16. Wang, S., Wong, S.: A novel reinforcement learning framework for online adaptive seizure prediction. In: IEEE Conference on Bioinformatics and Biomedicine, Hong Kong, China, pp. 494–504 (2010)

Neural Networks Based Cancer Classification Model Using CT-PET Fused Images

S. Srimathi[1(✉)], G. Yamuna[1], and R. Nanmaran[2]

[1] Department of Electronics and Communication Engineering,
Annamalai University, Annamalai Nagar,
Chidambaram 608002, Tamilnadu, India
srimathinanmaran@gmail.com, yamuna.sky@gmail.com
[2] Department of Electronics and Instrumentation Engineering,
Annamalai University, Annamalai Nagar,
Chidambaram 608002, Tamilnadu, India

Abstract. Classification of cancer determines appropriate treatment and help determines the prognosis which can reduce mortality rate and healthcare treatment cost. In this work neural network based efficient classification model is proposed. The various steps, Pre processing, Image fusion, Feature extraction, Image segmentation, classification and performance evaluation has been followed in this work. Linear Contrast enhancement technique is used for image enhancement. Two images from two different sources namely CT and PET scan are fused to make use the advantage of both imaging techniques. PET scans allow healthcare Professionals to examine the functions of the body, including oxygen use and glucose metabolism. CT scans allow healthcare Professionals to evaluate detailed images of internal organs. When these medical images are merged, they often lead to a faultless diagnosis. For this, discrete wavelet transform based image fusion algorithm is developed. Marker controlled watershed Algorithm is used to segment the area which is affected by cancer. The various color features, shape features and texture based features are extracted from the segmented image data set which will be given as input to neural network. Back Propagation algorithm is used to train the neural network. The classifier determines the Cancer images as two different cases either benign or malignant. The performance of the neural classifier is determined using the performance parameters like Accuracy, Sensitivity and Specificity. The proposed neural network classifier when fused image is given as input, it provides Accuracy of 90%, sensitivity of 92% and Specificity of 88%.

Keywords: Tumor · Classification · Image fusion · Watershed algorithm · Neural networks

1 Introduction

Early detection of cancer plays an important role in healthcare industry. Nowadays the mortality rate of cancer is increased due to detection of cancer in severe stage. Before the infectious disease could strike, we can kill the grinding poverty. Thus it leads less threaten to life. A tenuous and composite disease, it was hard to detect and treat.

© Springer Nature Singapore Pte Ltd. 2019
M. Singh et al. (Eds.): ICACDS 2019, CCIS 1045, pp. 104–116, 2019.
https://doi.org/10.1007/978-981-13-9939-8_10

Sporting cases rises with expansion of microscopy and scientific knowledge [1]. Many researches have explained that the developing stage of the disease is highly related with the survival likelihood of patients. So there is a need of constructive and easy method for detecting cancer is Pivotal [2]. It is important that if we treat and detect the cancer in early stage the possibility of survival rate will increase. In Global context, this interprets into nearly 3 lakhs lives that could be rescued every year as a result of prior detection. As such, emerging techniques that can help to detect and treat cancer at prior stages can have a great influence on survival and standard life of cancer patients. In order to achieve this novel fusion based cancer classification model is proposed in this paper. The combination of PET and CT scanned image is a powerful technique to diagnose cancer at early stage. These fused images are considered for further segmentation and classification procedures which can provide more detailed features and some additional features when compared to CT or PET scanned images are considered individually.

2 Methodology

As shown in Fig. 1, the proposed work is carried out in five stages namely Preprocessing, Image Fusion, Image Segmentation, Feature Extraction and Classification. Dental CT and PET scan images of cancer are digitized and given as the input. The input image is preprocessed to remove the noise. Next, the enhanced image is fused together using Discrete Wavelet Transform to gain the advantages of both imaging techniques. Segmentation of affected area is obtained by applying watershed algorithm to fused image. By applying GLCM extraction procedure various features are extracted and these features are stored in neural network. These features can be compared with new features while testing the ability of neural network and thus a neural network can be used to identify whether the input fused image is benign or malignant in nature.

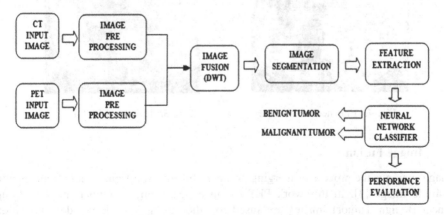

Fig. 1. Architecture of proposed cancer classification model

2.1   Image Preprocessing

The first stage is the Image Preprocessing. The input image which is obtained is preprocessed so that the resultant image is free from the noise. In this paper, Linear Contrast enhancement pre processing method is used which linearly expands the original digital values. Resizing of input image is also done to make it compatible for image fusion input. The CT image (Liver cancer) and PET Image (Liver cancer) are taken as input images as shown in Figs. 2 and 3. The enhanced images are shown in Figs. 4 and 5.

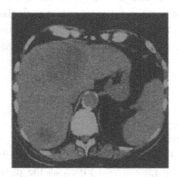

Fig. 2. Input CT image (Liver cancer-Benign)

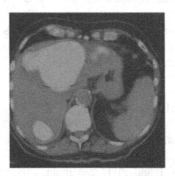

Fig. 3. Input PET image (Liver cancer-Benign)

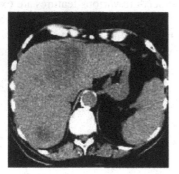

Fig. 4. Enhanced CT image

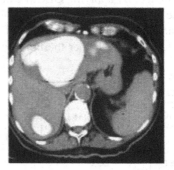

Fig. 5. Enhanced PET image

2.2   Image Fusion

Image fusion is the process of merging pertinent information from various sources into a single image [3]. In this work PET (Lung cancer-Benign Tumor) and CT (Lung cancer-Benign Tumor) images are fused together using Two Level decomposition DWT and the fused images will be used for further classification procedures.

2.2.1   Discrete Wavelet Transform Based Image Fusion

A Discrete wavelet transform (DWT) is a frequency domain transform where the wavelets are discretely sampled. Temporal resolution of wavelet transform is the key advantage, when compared to Fourier Transform. It represents both frequency and location details [4].

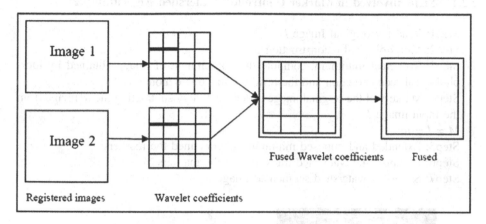

Fig. 6. Block Diagram of DWT based image fusion

The entire process of image fusion is mathematically given by Eq. (1) below:

$$I(x,y) = DWT^{-1}(\varphi(DWT(I_1(x,y)), DWT(I_2(x,y)))). \tag{1}$$

Where DWT is a Discrete wavelet transform, $I_1(x, y)$ and $I_2(x, y)$ are input images and φ is fusion rule. DWT^{-1} is the inverse discrete wavelet transform (IDWT). The core concept of image fusion using DWT is explained in Fig. 6. The fused image of CT and PET input image is shown in Fig. 7.

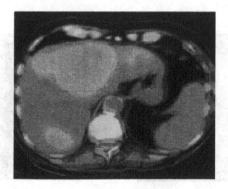

Fig. 7. Fused CT-PET image

2.3   Image Segmentation Using Marker Controlled Watershed Algorithm

The watershed transform is a morphological gradient based segmentation technique [5]. Concept of markers is used to control over segmentation in images. Various steps involved in marker controlled watershed algorithm are explained below.

2.3.1   Steps Involved in Marker Controlled Watershed Algorithm [12]

Step1: Read the original Image I

Step2: Morphological reconstruction of I

Step3: To detect minimum, compute the compliment of image obtained by morphological reconstruction and the resulted image is denoted as Ic

Step4: Markers of the original image is determined by subtracting the Ic image from the input image I.

$M = I - Ic$

Step5: Extended and imposed minimum, we obtained the markers

Step6: Compute the watershed transform of the markers

Step7: Show the watershed segmented image

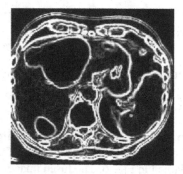

Fig. 8. Gradient magnitude of fused image

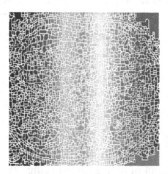

Fig. 9. Watershed transform of gradient magnitude

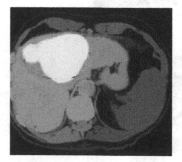

Fig. 10. Opening by reconstruction

Fig. 11. Segmented cancer area

From Figs. 8, 9, 10 and 11 are the sequential steps of watershed Algorithm based segmentation of images [6]. Gradient magnitude and wavelet transform of gradient images are shown in Fig. 8 and Fig. 9 respectively. Further opening by reconstruction and segmented images are shown in Fig. 10 and Fig. 11 respectively.

2.4   Feature Extraction

Feature extraction inculpates lessening the amount of data required to describe a large set of features [7]. Shape based features namely Area, Perimeter and Pixel based features namely Maximum Intensity, Minimum Intensity, Mean Intensity and statistical features like Contrast, Energy, Correlation, Homogeneity, and Entropy are extracted and fed into Artificial neural network (ANN) classifier as an input to classify cancer as either Benign or Malignant. Shape based features and Pixel based features are extracted using Matlab region properties function while the statistical features are extracted using gray-level co-occurrence matrix (GLCM) [8]. A data set contains 25 sample image of Liver cancer Benign tumor category from which 225 extracted features and 25 sample image of Liver cancer Malignant tumor category from which 225 features is created and given as input to ANN classifier during training and testing stage. Given an image I, of size $N \times N$, the co-occurrence, matrix P can be defined in Eq. (2). The offset $(\Delta x, \Delta y)$ is the distance between the pixel of interest and its neighbors.

$$P(i,j) = \sum_{X=1}^{N} \sum_{Y=1}^{N} = 1 \qquad \begin{array}{l} \text{If } I(x, y) = I(X + \Delta X, Y + \Delta Y) = I \\ 0 \text{ otherwise} \end{array} \qquad (2)$$

2.4.1   Shape Based Features

(i) Perimeter

Distance around the boundary of the tumor region returned as a scalar. Perimeter is calculated by measuring the distance between pixels around the border of the tumor region.

2.4.2   Pixel Based Features

(ii) Maximum Intensity
It is the value of pixel with the greatest intensity in the cancer affected region.

(iii) Minimum Intensity
It is the value of pixel with the lowest intensity in the cancer affected region.

(iv) Mean Intensity
It is the Mean of all the intensity values in the cancer affected region.

2.4.3 Statistical Features (Texture Based Features) [7]

(v) **Contrast**

Contrast is the measurement of pixel intensities in the cancer affected region and its neighbors above image. It is mathematically defined in Eq. (3).

$$C = \sum_{n=0}^{N-1} n^2 \sum_{i=0}^{N-1} \sum_{j=0}^{N-1} P(i,j). \tag{3}$$

Where n = |i − j|.

(vi) **Energy**

The amount of pixels that are repeated in the cancer affected region is called as Energy. It is mathematically defined in Eq. (4).

$$\mu = \frac{1}{MN} \sum_{i=1}^{N} \sum_{j=1}^{N} P(i,j). \tag{4}$$

(vii) **Correlation**

Correlation is the measurement of dependency of two or more variables. It is mathematically defined in Eq. (5).

$$\eta = \sum_{i=0}^{N-1} \sum_{j=0}^{N-1} P(i,j) \frac{(i - \mu x)(j - \mu y)}{\sigma x \sigma y}. \tag{5}$$

Where $\mu x, \mu y$ are the Mean values of x and y
$\sigma x, \sigma y$ are the Standard deviation of x and y

(viii) **Homogeneity**

Homogeneity is the measurement of local resemblance in an image. It is mathematically defined in Eq. (6).

$$H = \sum_{i=0}^{N-1} \sum_{j=0}^{N-1} \frac{P(i,j)}{1 + (i - j)^2}. \tag{6}$$

(ix) **Entropy**

It is the measure of degree of randomness in the image. It is mathematically defined in Eq. (7).

$$E = \sum_{i=0}^{N-1} \sum_{j=0}^{N-1} P(i,j) \log P(i,j). \tag{7}$$

Various features extracted from segmented image (Fig. 11) are tabulated in first row of Table 1. Second row of table is the extracted features of segmented lung cancer-Malignant tumor image.

Table 1. Extracted features from segmented image

Extracted features	Benign tumor	Malignant tumor
Perimeter (cm)	40	120
Maximum intensity	252	254
Minimum intensity	2	1
Mean intensity	124	122
Contrast	0.241	0.715
Energy	0.176	0.587
Correlation	0.275	0.753
Homogeneity	1.264	2.062
Entropy	4.672	7.432

2.5   Classification Using Artificial Neural Networks

Automated classifiers can be useful for healthcare professionals in differentiate benign and malignant patterns of cancer [11]. Thus, in this paper, an artificial neural network ANN which can be served as an automated classifier is investigated. In this paper back propagation algorithm is used for training ANN [9]. The nine extracted features from segmented image (Table 1) are given as input to ANN. The error of ANN is mathematically given as in Eq. (8).

$$e = t - y \tag{8}$$

Where e is error, t is the target output and y is the actual output.

3   Performance Evaluations

The next step after implementing ANN classification is to find the effectiveness of the model. In this work Performance measures such as Accuracy, Sensitivity, Specificity, False Positive Rate (FPR), Precision, and Negative Predictive Value are evaluated to verify the performance of ANN Classifier [13]. For the proposed work 50 images were chosen randomly.

3.1 True Positive (TP) and True Negative (TN)

If the classifier predicts a cancer image as cancer image, it is the case of True Positive (TP). Similarly, when a classifier identifies a Non cancer image as a non-cancerous image, it is the case of True Negative (TN).

3.2 False Positive (FP) and False Negative (FN)

When the classifier predicts a Non cancerous image as cancer image, it is case of False Positive (FP). Similarly, when a classifier identifies a cancer image as a non-cancerous image, it is the case of False Negative (FN).

3.3 Accuracy

Accuracy is the measure of correct prediction of the classifier in overall data sets. It is mathematically written in Eq. (9) as

$$ACCURACY = \frac{(TN + TP)}{(TN + FP + FN + TP)} \tag{9}$$

3.4 Sensitivity

Sensitivity is the measures of actual positive image category that are correctly identified as such positive image category. It is mathematically written in Eq. (10).

$$SENSITIVITY = \frac{TP}{(TP + FN)} \tag{10}$$

3.5 False Positive Rate (FPR)

$$FPR = \frac{FP}{(FP + TN)} \tag{11}$$

The false positive rate is calculated as the ratio between the numbers of negative image category is wrongly categorized as positive (false positives) and the total number of actual negative image category regardless of classification. It is mathematically written in Eq. (11).

3.6 Specificity

Specificity is the measures of actual negative image category that are correctly identified as such negative image category. It is mathematically written in Eq. (12)

$$\text{SPECIFICITY} = \frac{\text{TN}}{(\text{TN} + \text{FP})} \tag{12}$$

3.7 Precision

Precision also called as positive predictive value [10] is the fraction of relevant images with the recovered images. It is mathematically written in Eq. (13) as

$$\text{PRECISION} = \frac{\text{TP}}{(\text{FP} + \text{TP})} \tag{13}$$

3.8 Negative Predictive Value (NPV)

Percentage of normal structures detected that does not really represent abnormalities. It is mathematically written in Eq. (14) as

$$\text{NPV} = \frac{\text{TN}}{(\text{TN} + \text{FN})} \tag{14}$$

The confusion matrix and Evaluated results are tabulated in Tables 2 and 3 as below

Table 2. Confusion matrix

		Predicted	
		Negative	Positive
Actual	Negative	TN (22)	FN (2)
	Positive	FP (3)	TP (23)

Table 3. Evaluated results

Parameters	Values (%)
Accuracy	90
Sensitivity	92
False positive rate	12
Specificity	88
Precision	88.46
Negative predictive value	91.67

3.9   ROC (Receiver Operating Characteristics) Plot

Area under curve (AUC) provides an overall measure of performance across all possible classification thresholds. From the ROC plot (Fig. 12) of we can see that AUC is closer to 1 for both benign and malignant cases hence performance of ANN is excellent.

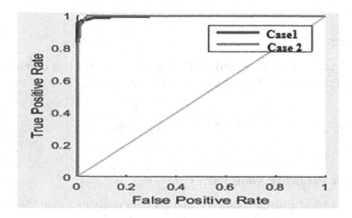

Fig. 12. ROC plot of True Positive rate versus False Positive rate in which blue color line belongs to *Case1 (Benign)* and yellow color line belongs to *Case2 (Malignant)* (Color figure online)

3.10   Performance Comparison

The performance measures such as Accuracy sensitivity FPR and Specificity are compared with existing neural network classifier [9] when non fused images are given as input to neural network. From Table 4 we can see the proposed neural network based classifier performs better when fused image is given as input.

Table 4. Comparison of classifier performance with Existing method

Parameters	Without fusion image input [9]	Fused image input (Proposed)
Accuracy	87.5	90
Sensitivity	87.5	92
False positive rate	12.5	12
Specificity	87.5	88

4 Conclusion

CT and PET medical images are taken as two input images. Linear Contrast enhancement technique is developed for image enhancement. Then discrete wavelet transform based image fusion algorithm is developed to fuse two input images. Then Marker controlled watershed Algorithm is developed to segment the area which is affected by cancer. Five texture based features were extracted using GLCM method and three pixel based features, one shape based features are also considered to improve the Performance of classification. All these nine features were extracted from the segmented image and given as input to Artificial neural network (ANN) to identify the cancer, either benign (not spreads to neighbour cells) or Malignant (Spreads to neighbour cells). The performance of the neural classifier is determined using the performance parameters like Accuracy, Sensitivity and Specificity. The proposed neural network classifier when fused image is given as input, it provides (Table 4) Accuracy of 90%, sensitivity of 92%, Specificity of 88%, False Positive Rate of 12%, Precision of 88% and Negative Predictive Value of 91.67% and When compare to existing neural network classifier the proposed neural network classifier performs better when fused image is given as input. The main drawback of this proposed work is Processing of data is very slow when images are fused together. The two images that we are interested in fusion need to be of same size which is not possible all the time so we need to resize the images to make it compatible for image fusion.

References

1. Rastogi, T., Hildesheim, A., Sinha, R.: Opportunities for cancer epidemiology in developing countries. IEEE Trans. **53**, 1011–1024 (2017)
2. Sunny Auyang, Y.: Magneto-thermal modeling of biological tissues: a step toward breast cancer detection. IEEE ncer **4**, 909–917 (2004)
3. Chao, Z., Zhang, K., Li, Y.J.: An image fusion algorithm using wavelet transform. Chin. J. Electron. **32**, 750–753 (2013)
4. Chen, M., Di, H.: Study on optimal wavelet decomposition level for multi-focus image fusion. J. Optoelectron. Adv. Mater. **31**, 64–67 (2004)
5. Lu, N., Ke, X.Z.: A segmentation method based on gray-scale morphological filter and watershed algorithm for touching objects image. In: Fourth International Conference on Fuzzy Systems and Knowledge Discovery (2007)
6. Wei-bin, C., Xin, Z.: A new watershed algorithm for cellular image segmentation based on mathematical morphology. In: IEEE International Conference on Machine Vision and Human-Machine Interface (2010)
7. Haralick, R.E., Shanmugam, K., Dinstein, I.: Textural features for image classification. IEEE Trans. Syst. Man Cybern. **SMC-3**(6), 610 (1973)
8. Thamaraichelvi, B., Yamuna, G.: Gray level co-occurrence matrix features based classification of tumor in medical images. J. Eng. Appl. Sci. **11**, 11403–11414 (2016)
9. Layek, K., Das, S., Samanta, S.: DWT based sonoelastography prostate cancer image classification using back propagation neural network. IEEE Trans. **1**, 66–71 (2016)

10. Salahuddin, T., et al.: Breast cancer image classification using pattern based hyper conceptual sampling method. Inform. Med. Unlocked **13**, 176–185 (2018)
11. Sendhil Kumar, K., Venkatalakshmi, K., Karthikeyan, K.: Lung cancer detection using image segmentation by means of various evolutionary algorithms. Comput. Math. Methods Med. **1**, 1–16 (2019)
12. Agrawal, D., Kulshreshtha, V., Sharma, P.: Brain tumor detection using K-means clustering and threshold segmentation. Int. J. Adv. Res. Sci. Eng. Technol. **5**(3), 5333–5340 (2018)
13. Chehade, W.E.H., Kader, R.A., El-Zaart, A.: Segmentation of MRI images for brain cancer detection. J. Eng. Appl. Sci. **10**(11), 835–844 (2018)

A Deep Learning Approach to Speech Recognition of Digits

Gagan Gopinath, Joel Kiran Kumar$^{(\boxtimes)}$,
Nirmit Shetty, and S. S. Shylaja

Department of Computer Science and Engineering,
PES University, Bengaluru, Karnataka, India
gagan.28.1.97@gmail.com, joelkiran45@gmail.com,
nirmit123@gmail.com, shylaja.sharath@pes.edu

Abstract. One of the technologies gaining an increasing popularity in recent years has been speech recognition. This technology has a widespread user base ranging from organizations to individuals for the various benefits it provides. Today, there are a great deal of virtual voice assistants in the market- Siri, Cortana and Alexa, to name a few. However, they all require an active internet connection and aren't supported on all devices. We have built a digit recognition system that works offline on desktop and mobile devices. This speech-to-text system can recognize a sequence of digits spoken between 0 and 9 and distinguish variations such as "double two" and "triple six". Our approach involves recording a digit sequence audio as input and pre-processing it by extracting the peak amplitudes, followed by Mel Frequency Cepstral Coefficients (MFCC) feature extraction and finally feeding the feature vector to an artificial neural network that outputs the most probable class. We then exported the model to a minimized configuration that is simple to use on mobile platform. We obtained an accuracy of 87% for the validation set and 86% for the test set.

Keywords: Android development · Artificial neural networks ·
Feature extraction · Speech recognition

1 Introduction

Speech recognition features a considerable history with numerous innovations. As of late, this sphere has gained from advances in big data and deep learning. The advances are proved not solely by the spurt of scholarly papers printed but more significantly by the global industry adoption of a range of deep learning strategies in coming up with and deploying speech recognition systems. Speech recognition technology and also the voice user interfaces (VUIs) we use to interact with have become so reliable that they currently make errors only 5.5% of the time, which is about the same error rate as a human.

The goal of automatic speech recognition (ASR) is the conversion of human speech into spoken words. When an individual speaks a word, they cause their voice to form a time-varying pattern of sounds which are nothing but waves of pressure that propagate through air. A sensor such as a microphone captures the sound and turns it into a sequence of numbers depicting the change in pressure over time. This time pressure signal gets

© Springer Nature Singapore Pte Ltd. 2019
M. Singh et al. (Eds.): ICACDS 2019, CCIS 1045, pp. 117–126, 2019.
https://doi.org/10.1007/978-981-13-9939-8_11

converted to a time frequency energy signal by the automatic speech recognition system. The system has been trained using a set of labeled speech sounds and labels the sounds it comes across. To form a textual representation of what was said, these acoustic labels are combined with models of word sequences and pronunciations. It can be a difficult task as human speech signals are extremely variable because of varying speaker attributes, speaking styles and uncertain environmental noises [1].

It is fairly acknowledged that hidden Markov models (HMMs) have been extremely productive in dealing with sequences of variable length and also modeling the temporal behavior of speech signals through a sequence of states, every one of which is related with a particular probability distribution of observations. [2] talks about a speech recognition system for isolated digits of English language using the HMM toolkit which has an accuracy of 95%. Similarly [3] achieves the same using Mel-Frequency Cepstral Coefficients (MFCC) and dynamic time warping algorithms and has an accuracy of 90.5%. MFCC is among the most widely used feature extractor in automatic speech recognition. [4] talks about an alternate knowledge base approach using MATLAB – DSP tool kit to identify isolated spoken digits with an 89% success rate.

Reference [5] is an offline speech recognition system built for desktop applications by CMU research known as CMU Sphinx. It includes a collection of libraries and tools for speech recognition development that can be associated with speech supported applications. However, the accuracy is very low when it comes to recognition of digits. Reference [6] is a research blog that explains about building a basic speech recognition network that identifies ten different words. The tutorial builds a model that tries to classify an audio clip of one second length as either "yes", "no", "stop", "go", "up", "down", "left", "right", "on", or "off". Our application stands out from existing models as it can recognize not just isolated digits but also a sequence of digits spoken along with variations such as "double four" and "triple two". Currently there are a great deal of virtual voice assistants in the market -Siri, Cortana and Alexa, to name a few. However, they all require an active internet connection and aren't supported on all devices. Our digit recognition system is real-time and works on desktop and mobile devices without connecting to the internet.

We describe our approach and methodology in Sect. 2. In Sect. 3 we summarize and interpret the results. Finally, in Sect. 4 we conclude and list future enhancements.

2   Methodology

For the implementation we used Keras, which is a Python based open-source neural network library [7]. Keras can be run on top of TensorFlow (an open-source machine learning framework [8]). We used Android Studio IDE [9] for building our Android application.

2.1   Dataset Collection

There are no readily available datasets online for digit recordings. Google's audio dataset [10] is available, but not for Indian accents. Hence, we had to manually collect each recording. We collected audio samples of one second duration from a wide range of people with different accents. The total number of samples collected were approximately 3000 which included 10 samples for each class from each speaker. The samples were recorded using a single channel at 16 kHz sampling rate, chunk size of 1024 bytes and in .wav format.

2.2 Pre-processing Step

To account for the various background noises that might be present when our application is being used, we mixed 6 types of noise to our recordings using Audacity [11] (an open-source digital audio editor) to simulate the actual environment of usage. Whenever either a single digit or a sequence of digits is recited, there is a peak amplitude for each digit. We extract only the peaks by splitting whenever there is a dip in amplitude as illustrated in Fig. 1, after which we get a sequence of peaks for the recited digits that we then pass through a filter to remove any leading/trailing silence or background noise.

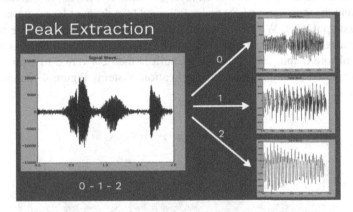

Fig. 1. A signal represented using Amplitude (y-axis) vs Time (x-axis) graph, split based on the peak amplitudes.

2.3 Training

The speech audio input of 1 s length is recorded using a microphone. Once the dataset is collected, we have 12 classes namely 0–9, double and triple. Noise and silence in the data are removed or stripped and only the peak amplitudes remain. We then feed the audio to MFCC for feature extraction and specify the count of features required, in our case we have chosen 60 features (represented in Fig. 2) as the performance was found to be better with this number. MFCC by default does signal processing, which involves applying discrete Fourier transform to the signal, followed by applying Mel scale to the signal, followed by applying logarithmic function to the signal, followed by extracting cepstral coefficients, and finally applying inverse Fourier transform to the signal.

```
[-230.96957642,  171.77231254,  -39.42159665,   71.52483118,
   -8.41686161,   -6.61962217,    3.89361165,  -15.2129247 ,
   -8.17144073,  -13.38055722,   -9.4173859 ,   -5.72768474,
    0.60169693,  -13.24752414,   11.31222591,    8.78414484,
  -10.99531276,    8.4223977 ,   -1.76496519,   -2.94715317,
   -0.33170247,    2.69732572,   -5.44098831,  -11.07903626,
   -1.79232414,   -1.17207721,    0.52590674,   -3.02910207,
   -4.57664463,    0.24864186,   -0.57710713,   -5.98112304,
   -2.42103682,   -1.43986763,  -11.13688052,   -4.49616301,
   -5.44376548,   -7.01693491,   -0.99630079,   -4.03065697,
    2.08991078,   -3.87672439,    2.22605132,    3.44188906,
   -3.56503124,    2.80481485,    4.49262954,    1.53353626,
    1.76958097,    4.90373744,    1.88380735,    8.5771721 ,
    8.11576295,    4.54152861,    6.98318929,    0.80406685,
    0.26468113,    0.53300813,    1.34037993,    1.80229661]
```

Fig. 2. An MFCC feature vector with 60 features.

The cepstral coefficients are the features, which are then fed to the deep neural network for training. Our neural network comprises of an input layer containing 60 nodes, 3 hidden layers and an output layer containing 12 nodes. Figure 3 is a rough illustration of the same. The first hidden layer contains 100 nodes, the second contains 100 nodes and the third contains 80 nodes followed by a dropout layer, output of which is fed to the output layer. We have used Adam optimizer with a learning rate of 0.00001 along with categorical cross entropy [12] as our loss function. The input gets mapped to the most probable output class. The model built is then converted to a protobuf (.pb) file and integrated with the Android application system. Figure 4 summarises the training phase.

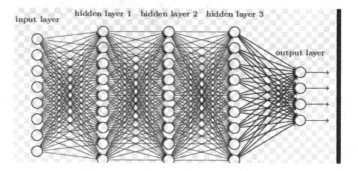

Fig. 3. A sample representation of our deep neural network. Source: http://neuralnetworksanddeeplearning.com/chap6.html

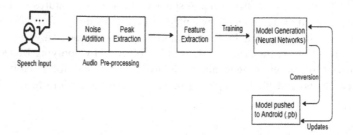

Fig. 4. Overview of training phase.

2.4   Testing

The application can then be launched on Android. Recording of the digits happens on the app via the device's microphone and the corresponding digits will be displayed. If a continuous sequence of digits is spoken, the audio file is split into individual digit audio files and the same procedure as mentioned above in the training phase applies for individual digit prediction. Figure 5 outlines the testing phase.

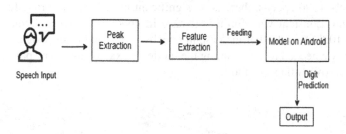

Fig. 5. Overview of testing phase.

2.5   On Android

Firstly, we had to replicate the pre-processing steps done on desktop during training of the model, on Android. The libraries in Python used to perform audio pre-processing and feature extraction were not readily available in Java. The process involved accessing chunks of data from the .wav file, removing background noise below the mentioned threshold and splitting the audio file based on leading/trailing silence. Each of these audio files now had to be predicted by feeding it to the model. The next step was to convert the model saved on desktop in .h5 format (a grid format suitable for storing multi-dimensional arrays of numbers) to. pb format, which is compact and easy to work with on mobile platform [13].

The steps followed to convert the .h5 file included freezing the model (weights that were variables during the training phase had to be converted to constants) [14], matching intermediate node names with output nodes and model optimization. The model is then exported to .pb format and should be stored in the Assets folder of the Android project to make it accessible. The TensorFlow Java API has exposed all the required methods through the TensorFlowInferenceInterface class. The core of TensorFlow is written in C++, whereas Android is written in Java and there is no communication medium between the two. Hence, the interface establishes a linking between them.

3   Results and Discussions

3.1   Graphical Results

The dataset was divided into 80% for the training phase and 20% for the testing phase. The 80% was again split 80–20 for training and validations sets respectively. As depicted in Fig. 6, initially, there is a steep increase in the accuracy for both validation and training sets as the number of epochs/iterations increase, but as soon as it reaches approximately 1000 epochs, there is no significant increase in accuracy for validation and it remains constant with further increase in epochs. However, training accuracy approaches 100% with further increase in epochs, which indicates a sign of overfitting [15]. Hence, we needed to stop training the model at exactly the elbow point, so that we didn't end up overfitting our model.

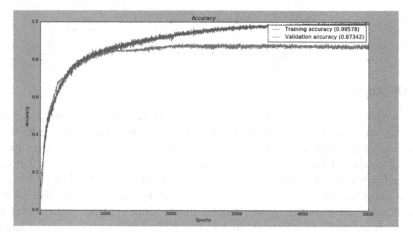

Fig. 6.   Accuracy (y-axis) vs Epochs (x-axis).

Figure 7 depicts the loss function value as the number of epochs increase. A loss function (or cost function) maps an event onto a real number that represents some associated "cost" with the event. The loss function used for training the model is categorical_crossentropy. Lower the loss function value, the better is the predicted output. From the above graph, we can see that as the number of epochs increase initially, there is a steep decrease in the loss function value for both validation and training sets and after a certain point the loss function value almost remains constant for validation, while for training it approaches 0. This is a clear indication of overfitting. Hence, we stopped training the model at this elbow point.

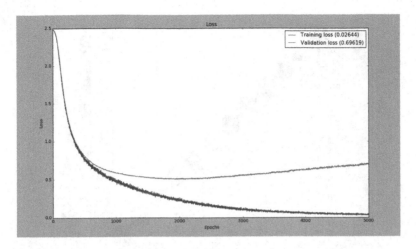

Fig. 7. Loss (y-axis) vs Epochs (x-axis).

3.2 Confusion Matrix

A confusion matrix is a table typically used to describe the performance of a classifier on a test data set for which the true values are known. In the relative color scale shown to the right of Fig. 8, darker the color, more the correct predictions made by the model. Each column depicts a set of samples that were predicted to belong to the corresponding label. Here, the first column represents all the clips that were predicted to be double, the second all those that were predicted to be eight and so on. Similarly, each row depicts clips by their actual labels (Fig. 9).

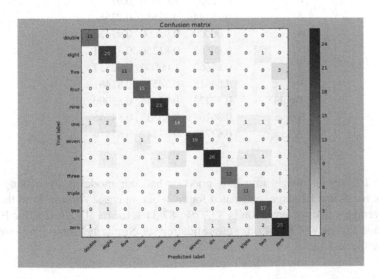

Fig. 8. Validation set confusion matrix. True labels depicted on x-axis and predicted labels on y-axis (Color figure online)

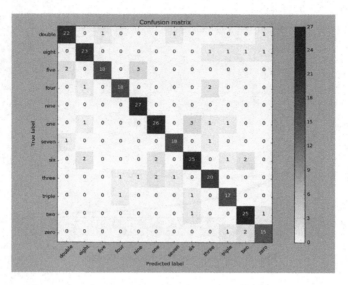

Fig. 9. Test set confusion matrix. True labels depicted on x-axis and predicted labels on y-axis.

Table 1. Validation set summary

Classification	Precision	Recall	F1 score
0	0.86667	0.92857	0.89655
1	0.83333	0.86957	0.85106
2	1.00000	0.78571	0.88000
3	0.93750	0.88235	0.90909
4	0.95833	1.00000	0.97872
5	0.73684	0.73684	0.73684
6	1.00000	0.95000	0.97436
7	0.86667	0.81250	0.83871
8	0.86667	1.00000	0.92857
9	0.84615	0.78571	0.81481
Double	0.77273	0.94444	0.85000
Triple	0.86207	0.83333	0.84746
Average	0.87720	0.87342	0.87316

Table 1 gives an insight into how good or bad our model is by making use of precision, recall and F1 score, calculated for each output class. As seen from the above figure, average value for precision is 87.77%, 87.34% for recall, 87.32% for F1 score and average accuracy of 87.34% for the validation set. Similarly, Table 2 represents the scores for the test set.

Table 2. Test set summary.

Classification	Precision	Recall	F1-score
0	0.8800	0.8800	0.8800
1	0.85185	0.85185	0.85185
2	0.94737	0.78261	0.85714
3	0.90000	0.85714	0.87805
4	0.87097	1.00000	0.93103
5	0.86667	0.81250	0.83871
6	0.90000	0.90000	0.90000
7	0.83333	0.78125	0.80645
8	0.80000	0.80000	0.80000
9	0.80952	0.89474	0.85000
Double	0.83333	0.92593	0.87719
Triple	0.83333	0.83333	0.83333
Average	0.85975	0.85811	0.85733

4   Conclusion and Future Work

We have built an offline digit recognition system, which is a speech-to-text system that does real time prediction using deep neural networks. It can recognize a sequence of digits spoken between 0–9 for different accents and also handle variations such as "double four" and "triple one". We achieved a test accuracy of 86%. The same model can be exported to Android and used by mobile applications. Some of the use cases for the application could be hands-free dialling, lift operation or Aadhaar number verification. The target audience could be people with physical disabilities, the visually impaired or senior citizens.

Further enhancements that we plan to work on include collecting more training samples from a wider diversity of speakers to further improve the accuracy, reduce the latency for output prediction, classifying non-digit words as "unknown", reduce the effect of background noise, handle variations such as hundred, thousand, twenty-five, thirty-nine, etc. and finally, support different regional Indian languages.

References

1. Forsberg, M.: Why is Speech Recognition Difficult? (2003)
2. Pawar, G.S., Morade, S.S.: Isolated English language digit recognition using Hidden Markov Model toolkit. Int. J. Adv. Res. Comput. Sci. Softw. Eng. 4(6) (2014)
3. Periyavaram, V.: Knowledge Base approach for spoken digit recognition. http://www.csc. villanova.edu/~nlp/pres2/periyavaram.ppt
4. Somaiya, K.J.: Isolated digit recognition using MFCC AND DTW (2012)
5. Carnegie Mellon University. CMUSphinx Open Source Speech Recognition, 8 November 2017. https://cmusphinx.github.io/wiki/tutorial/

6. TensorFlow.org. Simple Audio Recognition, 13 January 2018. https://www.tensorflow.org/tutorials/sequences/audio_recognition
7. https://keras.io/
8. https://www.tensorflow.org/
9. https://developer.android.com/studio
10. Speech commands dataset version 2 (2018). https://storage.cloud.google.com/download.tensorflow.org/data/speech_commands_v0.02.tar.gz
11. https://www.audacityteam.org/
12. Gomez, R.: Understanding Categorical Cross-Entropy Loss, 23 May 2018. https://gombru.github.io/2018/05/23/cross_entropy_loss/
13. Niroshan, A.: Step By Step Guide To Run Your Trained Neural Network Model On Android, 29 August 2017. https://medium.com/@nirosh
14. Agarwal, P.: Deploying a Keras Model on Android, 25 October 2017. https://medium.com/@thepulkitagarwal
15. EliteDataScience: Overfitting in Machine Learning: What It Is and How to Prevent It, 7 September 2017. https://elitedatascience.com/overfitting-in-machine-learning

An Architecture for Analysis of Mobile Botnet Detection Using Machine Learning

Ashok Patade[✉] and Narendra Shekokar

DJSCE, University of Mumbai, Mumbai, India
{ashok.patade,narendra.shekokar}@djsce.ac.in

Abstract. The smart-phone has become a critical cybernetic victim especially of cellular botnets. The current exploration examines mobile botnet attacks for Android smart-phone launched from a Windows based PC and detects those attacks using an ensemble machine learning classification algorithm. This investigation is to breach the gap to develop malware framework in perspective of headers' field examination of PE format with Machine Learning algorithm used. The Homogeneous architecture model proposed in this investigation chooses the most representative subset of the features toward accurate classification of botnet traffic. The ensemble classification technique used in this architecture consists of four machine learning algorithms namely; Random Forest, Gradient Boosting Algorithm, Extreme learning machine and eXtreme Gradient Boosting. After exhaustive literature survey, it is concluded that the architecture proposed in this investigation is unique homogeneous combination of four algorithm mention above. The efficiency of the proposed architecture is evaluated on existing data-set CLaMP (Classification of Malware with PE headers). It has been evaluated on a ClaMP data-set to achieve better botnet detection accuracy relative to its peer techniques.

Keywords: Mobile botnet attack detection · Malware analysis · Cyber-security · Ensemble learning

1 Introduction

In the domain of cyber security a botnet is defined as a interconnected web of compromised or susceptible PCs or electronic gadgets which are controlled or can be accessed remotely by the botmaster using a Command and Control (C&C) channel. This C&C channel can be operated by means of bluetooth, WiFi or SMS. The compromised framework is named as a bot which has vulnerabilities and makes ready for the intrusion of the botmaster. The C&C channel can be utilized for correspondence between the botmaster and the individual bots in the botnet. In the event that the gullible client is utilizing the cell phone, a significant number of the time one keep messages in the message box which is as of now read. An aggressor uses such as of now read messages to perform assaults

© Springer Nature Singapore Pte Ltd. 2019
M. Singh et al. (Eds.): ICACDS 2019, CCIS 1045, pp. 127–139, 2019.
https://doi.org/10.1007/978-981-13-9939-8_12

on such cell phones. Utilizing this system an aggressor can take classified data like financial balance, individual contact and utilize this data for the malevolent exercises.

The current investigation proposes a homogeneous architecture for mobile botnet detection on android phones using an ensemble machine learning model. The aim is to choose the most representative subset of the features or attributes from the network traffic generated by a compromised bot and utilize it toward accurate classification or estimation of mobile botnet traffic. The efficacy of the technique is underlined by conducting broad experiments on existing dataset viz. CLaMP (Classification of Malware with PE headers). The ensemble classification model used in the proposed architecture uses non parametric probabilistic frameworks that have gained significance in the field of predictive analytics. Their mathematical models are described in Sect. 4.

We are explaining basic of the mobile botnet and feature selection in machine learning in this Section. In Sect. 2 the literature survey is presented in which findings of the mobile botnet attacks and use of machine learning algorithm in the mobile botnet detection using feature selection are presented. In Sect. 3 the proposed system for detecting mobile botnet attack launched from Windows PC to target Android phones is described. The mathematical model for the detection mechanism of this architecture using machine learning classification is presented in this Section. Section 4 presents the results of the architecture measured on the CLaMP (Classification of Malware with PE headers) datasets against existing techniques. The conclusion of this investigation is presented in Sect. 5.

1.1 Basic of Botnet and Mode of Communication and Propagation for Mobile Botnet

The term Botnet is a combination of robot and network. The botnet is available in various architectures like centralized, peer to peer, hybrid etc. Botnets can be outlined utilizing Personal PCs and in addition cell phones. A versatile botnet, much the same as a PC botnet, is a sort of malware that runs naturally once introduced on a gadget without portable antivirus programming. As the botnet develops, each tainted cell phone gets added to a system of bots overseen by a botmaster cybercriminal.

1.2 Background of Machine Learning

Only two levels of headings should be numbered. Lower level headings remain unnumbered; they are formatted as run-in headings.

Arthur Samuel (1959) characterizes Machine learning as, "Field that enables PCs to learn without being expressly programmed" [12, 13].

- **Supervised learning:** It encourages the PC to accomplish something, at that point let it utilize it's recently discovered information to do learning [7, 10, 14].

- **Unsupervised learning:** Unsupervised learning let the PC figure out how to accomplish something, and utilize this to decide structure in information [11,17,18].
- **Semi-Supervised Machine Learning**
  Issues where you have a lot of information (X) and just a portion of the information is marked (Y) are called Semi-Supervised Machine learning issues [15,16,19].

Machine learning algorithm used for classification of malware mobile botnet with feature selection are briefly explained below:

Random Forest. Random forest is a troupe technique which is built by a few choice trees to vote on the order (or relapse) assignment and created by (Breiman 2001). (Horning 2010) In Random forest, part traits are picked arbitrarily, so the connection between's trees is diminished bringing about enhanced forecast precision. In Random forest calculation, the quantity of trees and the highlights to build trees are picked by the client. Be that as it may while preparing Random forest in Weka, there is no need to pick the quantity of highlights, Weka satisfies this activity by thinking of some as capacity foundation (Ali, Khan, Ahmad and Maqsood 2012).

Gradient Boosting Algorithm. Slope boosting [6] is a champion among the most serious strategies for building perceptive models. Boosting left whether a frail learner can be changed to end up better. Leeway of the angle boosting structure is that another boosting estimation should be deduced for each adversity work. Choice trees are used as the feeble learner in slope boosting.

Extreme Learning Machine. The core of Extreme learning machine [5], known as ELM, is that the learning parameters of nodes, including input weights and inclination, are discretionarily doled out and require not be tuned while the yield weights can be sensibly controlled by the fundamental summed up in reverse engendering. The main parameter should have been characterized is the quantity of nodes. Contrasted and other customary learning calculations for SLFNs, ELM gives to a great degree quicker learning rate, better speculation execution and with slightest human intercession.

EXtreme Gradient Boosting. XGBoost [3], is an updated passed on tendency boosting library expected to be significantly successful, versatile and flexible. It realizes machine learning computations under the Gradient Boosting framework. XGBoost gives a parallel tree boosting (generally called GBDT, GBM) that handle various data science issues in a snappy and correct way.

1.3   Feature Selection Methods

Aside from models with implicit component determination, most methodologies for decreasing the quantity of indicators can be set into two primary classifications. Utilizing the wording of [9]:

- *Wrapper* strategies assess various models utilizing methods that include and additionally expel indicators to locate the ideal mix that boosts show execution.
- *Filter* techniques assess the importance of the indicators beyond the prescient frameworks and therefore display just the indicators consisting of a certain category of measure [25].

1.4   PE Header and Export Table

In this subsection, a delineation of the Windows smaller executable (PE) header of combined executables and the Export table is given.

PE is the neighborhood Win32 record sort out. Each win32 executable (beside VxDs and 16-bit DLLs) utilizes PE record orchestrate. 32bit DLLs, COM archives, OCX controls, Control Panel Applets (.CPL records) and .NET executables are all PE sort out. Undoubtedly, even NT's piece mode drivers use PE archive compose. It is basic to consider Windows PE archive for two reasons: Adding code to executables (e.g. keygen imbuement or including handiness) and physically emptying executables. With respect to the last said, most shareware nowadays comes "stuffed" in order to give an extra layer of security.

In a stuffed executable, the import tables are typically pulverized and data is consistently mixed. The packer inserts code to empty the archive in memory upon execution, and a short time later bounces to the principal area reason for the record (where the primary program truly starts executing). In case we make sense of how to dump this memory region after the packer completed emptying the executable, in any case we need to settle the regions and import tables before our application will run.

PE Header

Any parallel executable record (paying little respect to operating systems prominently present in electronic gadgets such as Unix or Windows) needs to join a header to depict its arrangement: e.g., the base area of its code region, data portion, and the once-over of limits that know how to be carried from the executable, et cetera. Right once the record is performed by the working structure, the OS essentially scrutinizes this header info, and after that piles the twofold data from the archive to occupy the substance of the code/data bits of the area space aimed at the relating system. Exactly when the archive is logically associated (i.e., the structure calls it depend on upon are not statically associated in the executable), the OS needs to count on its import table to make sense of wherever to find the areas of these structure purposes.

Most twofold executable records on Windows seeks after the going with organization: **DOS Header** (64 bytes), **PE Header, sections** (code and data).

DOS Header starts with charm number 4D 5A 50 00, and the former 4 bytes is the region of PE header in the twofold executable record. Distinctive arenas are not all captivating. The PE header holds in a general sense more information and all the all the extra stimulating. In Fig. 1, you find the organization of PE Header.

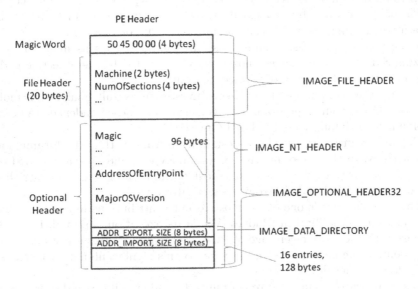

Fig. 1. Structure of PE header

Export Table

The primary area of IMAGE_DATA_DIRECTORY of the voluntary header field has facts of the fare table. By Fig. 1, it is derived that the 4 bytes arranged at PE 0x78 (i.e., balance 120 bytes) is the relative area (concerning DLL base area) of the fare table, and the accompanying byte (at balance 0x7C) is the proportion of the fare table.

1.5 Homogeneous Ensemble Model

Homogeneous ensemble models use multiple models of the same type for classifying or regressing the result. The intuition behind such a technique is to simultaneously use multiple weak predictors to build a strong predictor. Ensemble methods are of two types: Homogeneous and heterogeneous. Usually ensemble models use bagging "bootstrap resampling" method for Ensemble learning. A final meta model is build from initially models by polling, averaging etc. Every individual model uses various preparing sets, by using bootstrap, it utilizes numerous variants of preparing set. Such a group meta calculation of machine learning is made for enhancing the exactness of machine learning calculation for both relapse and grouping.

2 Related Work

In this section we are focusing on the work which is closer to the current research exertion.

[21] and Storm, separates itself from different types of malware (infections, Trojan ponies, worms) by its capacity to set up a control channel that enables its tainted customers to work as an organized group, or botnet.

Some security scientists planned assault methodologies as mention in [4], utilizing SMS benefit messages known as "Quiet SMS" to the objective gadget to execute the DOS (Denial of Service) assault.

Open source community is active to investigate assault analysis on mobile platform. Open source programming ventures for correspondence framework development including OpenBTS and OpenBSC [1,27].

[23] and Conficker is regarded as a significant framework for performing malicious activity. In the age of internet based honeypots, the malware named conficker has been regarded as one of the most harmful and malicious cyber threat that has affected PC and electronic gadgets worldwide.

The iKee [22] bot is one of the most recent contributions in cell phone malware, focusing on jailbroken iPhones. While its execution is straightforward in contrast with the most recent age of PC-based malware, its suggestions exhibit the potential augmentation of crimeware to this significant new wilderness of handheld customer devices.

Lastly, Researchers in [24], present multi day vulnerabilities and shortcomings they found in the Short Message Service (SMS) convention, which permit the inserting of high limit clandestine channels.

2.1 Literature Review of Highlight Choice and Machine Learning

The accompanying area discusses commitment of [8,20,26] in determination of various system activity highlights utilized in versatile botnet discovery and how unique machine learning calculations used to accomplish the best arrangement precision.

[26], investigate the viability of various blend of highlights to accomplish the best order exactness. They benchmark stream based factual highlights effectively utilized in the current examinations and break down their relative viability. They utilized three element choice techniques, for example, eigenvalue or spectral techniques such as Correlation Attribute Identification (CFS), Principal Component Analysis (PCA), and Minimum repetition most extreme importance (mRMR), to kill less discriminative highlights from other applicant highlights. In spite of the fact that their last list of capabilities demonstrated a high recognition rate of with 99% on a preparation dataset which incorporates modest number of botnets, they accomplished 75% identification precision on a testing dataset which contains considerably more unique kinds of botnet.

[8], examine in their investigation, the impact of the choice of various system activity stream exporters. To achieve this, they assess five distinctive activity stream exporters; Maji et al., Tranalyzer and Netmate utilizing five unique classifiers C4.5, SVM, ANN, Bayesian systems, and Naive Bayes. They direct a progression of analyses on open botnet datasets. As indicated by their test results, the best arrangement exactness is accomplished by utilizing Tranalyzer with C4.5 classifier.

In [20], featured imperative highlights utilized in versatile botnet Detection, subsequent to applying highlight choice on the extricated include set, three surely understood machine learning calculations to be specific; SVM, Random Forest and Logistic Regression are assessed to accomplish best botnet discovery exactness.

They utilize three component determination strategies to pick the most agent subset of the highlights toward precise grouping of botnet activity.

In our understanding, but for (Markel and Bilzor 2014), no further malware framework work has been ended in perspective of headers' field examination. In view of our writing audit we have investigate our discoveries in the accompanying area.

2.2 Review and Analysis

Mobile Botnets have been castoff for a variety of malicious doings and they have ripe and have become exceptionally cultured over the years. Understanding and disassembling these nets needs vigorous investigation and collaboration between private and government areas. There are very few attempts to detect and evaluate mobile botnet attacks using Machine Learning. PE file format on Windows OS is first time evaluated in current research work with Machine Learning algorithm: Random forest, Stochastic Gradient boosting, Extreme learning machine and XGBoost. A representative set of features to identify mobile botnets is built from varying network traffic features. An ensemble machine learning model is used in the proposed architectures to detect mobile botnet for android smartphone.

2.3 Problem Statement

Public WiFi networks are increasing in the current age of digitization for smart phones users. However, such networks offer benefits as well as challenges from the perspective of cyber security. They offer an anonymous channel for launching cyber attacks over the internet. Hence, it is necessary for securing smart phones which are getting attacked by public WiFi networks by building an efficient detection framework that can aid the system administrators of such public WiFi networks. The homogeneous architecture proposed in this inquiry aims to offer such a framework. The current inquiry focuses on mobile botnet attacks launched from Windows PC on remote Android phones. The scope of the investigation is defined with these restrictions as such category of attacks are increasing in scale and frequency.

3   Proposed Architecture for Analysis of Mobile Botnet Detection Using Machine Learning for Android

Thus, in the preceding sections the background information of predictive analytics/machine learning, mobile botnets, PE file format, feature selection and ensemble models was provided. The homogeneous architecture is built from the assimilation of these concepts. It selects or leads to the identification of the most representative subset of the features or variables (dependent variables) toward accurate classification (ground truth labeling) of mobile botnet traffic on android phones. The extensive experiments are performed on existing dataset viz. CLaMP (Classification of Malware with PE headers). The ensemble model used in the proposed architecture consists of four well-known machine learning algorithms namely; Random Forest, Gradient Boosting Algorithm, Extreme learning machine and eXtreme Gradient Boosting. The homogeneous architecture uses this for the first time to achieve best mobile botnet detection accuracy.

3.1   Ensemble Model for Classification

A Ensemble model is worked with the end goal of machine learning. The segments of this gathering are arrived at the midpoint of for getting the meta model.

3.2   Detection Mechanism - Mobile Botnets

In the first stage, numerous features as API calls, strings, also code behaviours are takeout statically as well as dynamically to arrest the appearances of the file examples for dissimilar mode of statement and spread for Mobile Botnet. In the second stage, smart methods of ML classification are used to mechanically classify the file examples interested in dissimilar classes/objects built on the examination of feature representations. Note that these Machine Learning malware indicators for botnet mostly vary on the feature demonstration and the employed machine learning techniques.

In these patterns, the uncovering is typically a pipeline course as revealed in below figure. Figure 2 displays the general procedure of malware detection using Machine Learning practises using PE file format.

- **Windows PE file Network Capture.** This step use Python scripts to collect the PE file samples from the network. This sample used to create the dataset.
- **Embedded Feature Extraction.** A python script as mentioned in the [2] which extract all the values from all three key PE headers. DOS_Header, FILE_HEADER AND OPTIONAL_HEADER. If any error occurs then the values will be allocated as zero for that header. Many PE files don't have DOS_Header then all the header will be assigned '0'.
- **ML Classification Model Construction.** It evaluated the performance of four non-parametric supervised learning algorithm namely Random Forest, Gradient Boosting Algorithm, Extreme learning machine and eXtreme Gradient Boosting using "Caret" package.

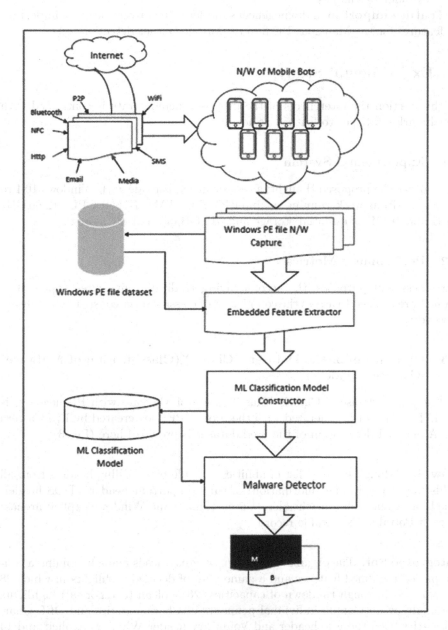

Fig. 2. Process of Malware detection using ML classification & feature selection algorithm

- **ML Classification Model.** Final model is a homogeneous model of the above four techniques.
- **Feature importance.** homogeneous model will analyze the most important features for the Malicious PE files for Mobile Botnet detection.

4   Experimental Study

In this Section the aftereffects of the proposed demonstrate is contrasted with benchmark strategies to feature its adequacy.

4.1   Experimental System

To approve the proposed thought, a test situation is made with Windows 10 Pro Operating framework running on Intel(R) Core(TM) i7-5660 CPU @2.60 GHz CPU and 16 GB of essential storage and 512 GB of auxiliary storage.

4.2   Performance Metrics

For assessment purposes, the accompanying traditional measures appeared in Table 1 are utilized to assess the completing of classification-constructed malware discovery.

4.3   Description of the Dataset - ClaMP (Classification of Malware with PE Headers)

In the study, Dataset - ClaMP (Classification of Malware with PE headers) is used. The dataset is generated with the tool - "PEFile" created by Ero Carrera [2]. A detailed description of the used dataset is provided here (Fig. 3):

Raw Set. Rough features list of abilities is made by expelling headers from all fields (segments/header information) of three important headers (DOS header, File Header and Voluntary header, plus customary and Windows-explicit arenas) in each Portable Executable record.

Integrated Set. The organized rundown of capacities is made by joining a couple picked unrefined features and a game plan of decided highlights in which 28 are same as in rough rundown of capacities, 26 boolean (categorical) highlights are made by developing individual pennants of Characteristics and DLL Characteristics from the File header and Voluntary header Windows explicit and 14 remain deduced highlights.

Table 1. Measures of classification-based malware detection performance

Measures	Specification
True Positive (TP)	Quantity of file examples accurately categorized as malicious
True Negative (TN)	Quantity of file examples accurately categorized as benign
False Positive (FP)	Quantity of file examples incorrectly categorized as malicious
False Negative (FN)	Quantity of file examples incorrectly categorized as benign
TP Rate (TPR)	$TP/(TP+FN)$
FP Rate (FPR)	$FP/(FP+TN)$
Accuracy (ACY)	$(TP+TN)/(TP+TN+FP+FN)$

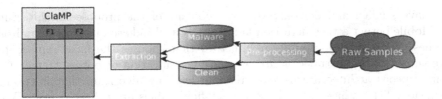

Fig. 3. CLaMP (Classification of Malware with PE headers)

4.4 Comparison with Previous Works

The proposed homogeneous architecture is evaluated against the below baselines techniques:

David et al. (2016) have discussed the sorted out examination of numerous arenas of PE header and communicated that seeing these highlights boost the malware distinguishing proof frequency.

Bai et al. (2014) devise API and DLL requests close by numerous unrefined estimations of PE headers. Examination through (Bai et al. 2014) effort won't state flawless virtues or blames of the anticipated exertion yet aimed at evaluated results (Tables 2 and 3).

Table 2. Comparison of proposed homogeneous architecture with baselines on CLAMP (Raw dataset)

Technique	Sensitivity	Specificity	Precision
David et al. (2016)	0.86	**0.98**	0.95
Bai et al. (2014)	0.89	0.96	**0.96**
Markel and Bilzor (2014)	**0.936**	0.95	0.93
Proposed technique	**0.936**	0.92	0.91

Table 3. Comparison of proposed homogeneous architecture with baselines on CLAMP (Integrated dataset)

Technique	Sensitivity	Specificity	Precision
David et al. (2016)	0.95	**0.986**	0.91
Bai et al. (2014)	0.86	0.90	0.82
Markel and Bilzor (2014)	0.93	0.94	0.90
Proposed technique	**0.968**	0.96	**0.93**

5 Conclusion

We have studied and demonstrated the efficacy of the proposed architecture for Mobile botnet attack detection launched from Windows platform to android phones. We have proposed an architecture that chooses the most representative subset of the features toward accurate classification of botnet traffic. The homogeneous architecture uses a ensemble learning algorithm that is trained on header field values only. These header field values are collected from Windows PE file. Accuracy as well as several performance metrics have been used to evaluate the performance of proposed technique with respect to several state of the art baselines. Analysis of the results show that the proposed framework of the current inquiry outperforms the other frameworks on several measures or otherwise achieves comparable performance.

References

1. Burgess, D.A., Samra, H.S., et al.: The OpenBTS project (2008). http://openbts. sourceforge.net, http://openBTS.org
2. Carrera, E.: x5: Reverse engineering automation with Python
3. Chen, T., He, T., et al.: XGBoost: extreme gradient boosting
4. Croft, N.J., Olivier, M.S.: A silent SMS denial of service (DoS) attack (2007)
5. Ding, S., Zhao, H., Zhang, Y., Xu, X., Nie, R.: Extreme learning machine: algorithm, theory and applications. Artif. Intell. Rev. **44**(1), 103–115 (2015)
6. Friedman, J.H.: Greedy function approximation: a gradient boosting machine. Ann. Stat. **29**, 1189–1232 (2001)
7. Gentyala, V.: Geolocation events based auto theme changer for browsers. Int. J. Adv. Res. Comput. Sci. **4**(3) (2013)
8. Haddadi, F., Zincir-Heywood, A.N.: Benchmarking the effect of flow exporters and protocol filters on botnet traffic classification. IEEE Syst. J. **10**(4), 1390–1401 (2016)
9. John, G.H., Kohavi, R., Pfleger, K.: Irrelevant features and the subset selection problem. In: Machine Learning Proceedings 1994, pp. 121–129. Elsevier, Amsterdam (1994)
10. Nerurkar, P.: Review of data storage by fusion drive in MAC. Int. J. Adv. Res. Comput. Sci. **4**(3), 256–259 (2013)
11. Nerurkar, P., Bhirud, S.: Modeling influence on a social network using interaction characteristics. Int. J. Comput. Math. Sci. **6**(8), 152–160 (2017)

12. Nerurkar, P., Chandane, M., Bhirud, S.: Community detection using node attributes: a non-negative matrix factorization approach. In: Verma, N.K., Ghosh, A.K. (eds.) Computational Intelligence: Theories, Applications and Future Directions - Volume I. AISC, vol. 798, pp. 275–285. Springer, Singapore (2019). https://doi.org/10.1007/978-981-13-1132-1_22

13. Nerurkar, P., Chandane, M., Bhirud, S.: A comparative analysis of community detection algorithms on social networks. In: Verma, N.K., Ghosh, A.K. (eds.) Computational Intelligence: Theories, Applications and Future Directions - Volume I. AISC, vol. 798, pp. 287–298. Springer, Singapore (2019). https://doi.org/10.1007/978-981-13-1132-1_23

14. Nerurkar, P., Pavate, A.: Study of AngularJS: a client side Javascript framework for single page applications. Int. J. Contemp. Res. Comput. Sci. Technol. 1(4), 92–96 (2015)

15. Nerurkar, P., Pavate, A., Shah, M., Jacob, S.: Analysis of probabilistic models for influence ranking in social networks. In: Iyer, B., Nalbalwar, S.L., Pathak, N.P. (eds.) Computing, Communication and Signal Processing. AISC, vol. 810, pp. 215–223. Springer, Singapore (2019). https://doi.org/10.1007/978-981-13-1513-8_23

16. Nerurkar, P., Pavate, A., Shah, M., Jacob, S.: Performance of internal cluster validations measures for evolutionary clustering. In: Iyer, B., Nalbalwar, S.L., Pathak, N.P. (eds.) Computing, Communication and Signal Processing. AISC, vol. 810, pp. 305–312. Springer, Singapore (2019). https://doi.org/10.1007/978-981-13-1513-8_32

17. Nerurkar, P., Shirke, A., Chandane, M., Bhirud, S.: Empirical analysis of data clustering algorithms. Procedia Comput. Sci. **125**, 770–779 (2018)

18. Nerurkar, P., Shirke, A., Chandane, M., Bhirud, S.: A novel heuristic for evolutionary clustering. Procedia Comput. Sci. **125**, 780–789 (2018)

19. Pavate, A., Nerurkar, P., Ansari, N., Bansode, R.: Early prediction of five major complications ascends in diabetes mellitus using fuzzy logic. In: Nayak, J., Abraham, A., Krishna, B.M., Chandra Sekhar, G.T., Das, A.K. (eds.) Soft Computing in Data Analytics. AISC, vol. 758, pp. 759–768. Springer, Singapore (2019). https://doi.org/10.1007/978-981-13-0514-6_72

20. Pektaş, A., Acarman, T.: Effective feature selection for Botnet detection based on network flow analysis (2017)

21. Porras, P., Saidi, H., Yegneswaran, V.: A multi-perspective analysis of the storm (Peacomm) worm. Technical report (2007)

22. Porras, P., Saïdi, H., Yegneswaran, V.: An analysis of the iKee.B iPhone Botnet. In: Schmidt, A.U., Russello, G., Lioy, A., Prasad, N.R., Lian, S. (eds.) MobiSec 2010. LNICST, vol. 47, pp. 141–152. Springer, Heidelberg (2010). https://doi.org/10.1007/978-3-642-17502-2_12

23. Porras, P.A., Saidi, H., Yegneswaran, V.: A foray into Conficker's logic and rendezvous points (2009)

24. Rafique, M.Z., Khan, M.K., Alghatbar, K., Farooq, M.: Embedding high capacity covert channels in Short Message Service (SMS). In: Park, J.J., Lopez, J., Yeo, S.-S., Shon, T., Taniar, D. (eds.) STA 2011. CCIS, vol. 186, pp. 1–10. Springer, Heidelberg (2011). https://doi.org/10.1007/978-3-642-22339-6_1

25. Saeys, Y., Inza, I., Larrañaga, P.: A review of feature selection techniques in bioinformatics. Bioinformatics **23**(19), 2507–2517 (2007)

26. Samani, E.B.B., Jazi, H.H., Stakhanova, N., Ghorbani, A.A.: Towards effective feature selection in machine learning-based botnet detection approaches. In: 2014 IEEE Conference on Communications and Network Security, pp. 247–255 (2014)

27. Welte, H.: Report of OpenBSC GSM field test August 2009, HAR2009, Vierhouten, The Netherlands (2009)

Thyroid Prediction Using Machine Learning Techniques

Sagar Raisinghani[1]([✉]), Rahul Shamdasani[1], Mahima Motwani[1],
Amit Bahreja[1], and Priya Raghavan Nair Lalitha[2]

[1] Department of Computer Engineering, University of Mumbai,
Vivekanand Education Society's Institute of Technology, Mumbai, India
{2015sagar.raisinghani,2015rahul.shamdasani,
2015mahima.motwani,2015amit.bahreja}@ves.ac.in
[2] Computer Engineering Department,
Vivekanand Education Society's Institute of Technology, Mumbai, India
priya.rl@ves.ac.in

Abstract. Thyroid is a critical medical condition which can be caused either due to increased levels of TSH (Thyroid Stimulating Organ) or due to some infection in thyroid organs itself. The machine learning algorithms have been employed to model the prediction and diagnosis of thyroid patients. A variety of these algorithms including Decision trees, Random forest, Support vector machine, Artificial Neural Network and Logistic regression have been widely used in development of predictive models of thyroid disease. The paper presents a review of recent ML algorithms applied in the prediction and diagnosis of thyroid detection. The proposed system is used for thyroid disease prediction of patients, based on various symptoms and reports of thyroid. With comparative study, different ML techniques are used by the proposed system to achieve better accuracy in disease prediction. Among these, Decision tree algorithm is found to be better with the accuracy of 99.46%.

Keywords: Machine learning · Predictive models · Thyroid prediction · Thyroid diagnosis · Thyroid classification

1 Introduction

According to the survey [9], it states that on an average one out of 38000 people in the world are suffering from congenital hypothyroidism. In developing countries like India, there are almost 42 million people suffering from thyroid disease. It seems to be more common among Indians, especially this ratio in Mumbai is stated as one out of 2640. Now a days more than 25,000 hospitals across the globe collects data on patients in various formats. In the traditional method, the clinical and medical studies are carried out using classical analysis and statistical tests.

Thyroid disease is widely spread in today's world and it often causes severe damage to life and body. It affects functioning of thyroid gland which in turn results into excess secretion of thyroid hormones. Its symptoms include low energy, weight gain, fatigue, inability to tolerate cold, dry skin, slow heart rate, there may be a swelling

M. Singh et al. (Eds.): ICACDS 2019, CCIS 1045, pp. 140–150, 2019.
https://doi.org/10.1007/978-981-13-9939-8_13

in a part of neck. In this disease body goes into auto safe mode in which hormones are generated which pulverize the thyroid organs. It affects the body in an irreversible manner so it is very important to avoid this disease. The avoidance of this disease requires preliminary knowledge of the occurrence of this disease as it is very difficult to cure this disease once it reaches its final stages.

2 Literature Survey

The research paper by Rao and Razia [1] showcased almost all the ML techniques with their basic structure. Out of all the algorithms, ANN showed best result. The major limitation of this method was it didn't explored the Genetic Algorithm for better optimized result.

Prerana et al. [2] proposed the technique of data mining using neural networks that can be used for early prediction of thyroid. The network was trained using back propagation and gradient method working simultaneously. But the variation in layers of various network parameters were not considered during training.

Umadevi et al. [3] worked on the trial of 21 parameters to train the model using classification algorithm. The model was trained using KNN, ANN and fuzzy ANN algorithm and the accuracy was compared. It was evident that Fuzzy ANN performed better than other two classification algorithms. But it is observed that due to few samples for dis-functions of thyroid, the classification between over and under functioning thyroid was difficult.

Ammulu and Venugopal [4] have proposed data mining technique to predict hypothyroidism in the patient. In the research paper, data mining technique is applied on the hypothyroid dataset to determine the positive and the negative cases from the entire dataset. But, the algorithm works only for under functioning thyroid and thus nothing can be said about hyperthyroidism.

Ahmed et al. [5] provides Support vector machine (multi, binary) algorithm for thyroid prediction. The precision value along with confusion matrix was used for evaluation of results. Medical data cleaning was used for filling all the blank spaces. When thyroid disease goes through structural changes it becomes difficult to detect it based on variations of thyroid hormones.

Mahajan et al. [6] have provided a way to detect hypo and hyperthyroid from thermal images using Bayesian classifier. It provided 81.18% accuracy in classification. The major drawback of this algorithm was if the image were not cleared or not processed properly, the results shown differed with a high range than the actual output.

Saiti et al. [7] have proposed thyroid prediction using PNN and support vector machine. Feature selection was done using genetic algorithms. The fitness evaluation contained two terms: (1) accuracy and (2) the number of features selected. When the algorithms were tested without the GA, the accuracy of both the methods was around 85%, but with the help of the GA accuracy obtained was nearly 100%.

The proposed system will even help the new practitioners to improve their analysis skills and predict the disease even without prior knowledge about it. The primary task is to provide thyroid diagnosis at early stages and also attain higher accuracy.

3 Methodology

The patient data provided can be either in structured or unstructured format. The unstructured data is required to be transformed into structured data in order to analyze the data.

3.1 Structured Data

Different approaches are discussed as follows for the better use of structured patient data in health prediction system:

Machine Learning Algorithms. Artificial neural network being an application of machine learning is a very powerful algorithm. It can work on structured data and it is always able to derive pattern from a dataset of any size.

A large number of attributes are considered in the dataset and considering the attributes and the vividness of the data we have shortlisted five algorithms for implementation out of which the best will be selected.

Decision Tree. It is one of the most important classification and prediction method in supervised learning. A decision tree classifier has a tree type structure which provides stability and high accuracy. Decision tree is also referred to as CART (Classification And Regression Trees). Decision tree applies simple if else rules to construct the trees. Decision tree algorithm commonly uses gini index, information gain, chi-square, and reduction in variance to make a strategic split.

Multilayer Feed Forward Neural Network. In neural networks the nodes are initialized these nodes are connected with each other. The line connecting them have a predefined weight, for many years there was no optimized technique to decide these weights, but now these weights are considered to be affecting the prediction results so they need to be optimized for which an iterative method is used which optimizes the results.

Support Vector Machine (SVM). It is a very useful algorithm sometimes in case of large data it gives very good efficiency it is used for classification purpose, it classifies the data into various sets and trains the model using this set and then it successfully predicts the data using this trained model. First it plots the attributes in the graph and separates it broadly using a boundary and the nodes which lie on this boundary are named as the support vectors.

Logistic Regression. Logistic regression conducts regression analysis when the dependent variable has dichotomous results (binary). Logistic regression is a very strong technique for doing predictive analysis. It defines the data very efficiently and explains the relation between one dependent binary variable and one or more nominal independent variable. One of the important consideration done while selecting the logistic regression model is the model fit. Selection of variables is another important because more the number of scrap variable lesser will be efficiency of the algorithm.

Random Forest. Random Forest is a supervised learning algorithm. The general idea behind the bagging method is that a combination of learning models increases the overall result. One big advantage of random forest is, that it can be used for both classification and regression problems, which form the majority of current machine learning systems. Random Forest has almost the same hyper parameters as a decision tree or a bagging classifier.

4 Proposed Model

While training the model, various machine learning algorithms are evaluated and the best is selected. This in turn will help in increasing the efficiency of the system. The attributes which are selected are taken from the health expertise.

4.1 System Architecture

The Fig. 1 below shows the conceptual design of the system that is being proposed. Components of the proposed system are described as following:

Data Pre-processing. The data obtained must be preprocessed into an understandable format. In order to preprocess the data, check out the missing values if any in the dataset. If there are some missing values then they must be replaced with mean, medium or mode of the feature. Then, the categorical data is required to be transformed into numerical data. To apply machine learning algorithm on the dataset, Dataset is split in training and testing set.

Training Set. The training data is then trained using a machine learning algorithm. In decision tree algorithm, all the attributes are tested for the split using cost function, gini index in our case. A root node is obtained after the first split. A higher gini index indicates greater inequality, and thus the split occurs at the attribute which has the least gini index value.

In Support Vector Machine algorithm, the numeric input variables in the thyroid dataset (the columns) form an n-dimensional space. The right hyper-plane is identified that divides the two classes, either class 0 or class 1.

In Random Forest algorithm, a decision tree is an intuitive model and the building block of this algorithm. But, the decision tree algorithm is prone to overfitting as the maximum depth is not limited. Random forest is a model constructed with many decision trees. The model randomly samples the training data points when building trees and considers random subsets of features when splitting nodes.

In logistic regression algorithm, the value of dependent variable is predicted using independent variables. It is assumed that there is a relation between dependent variable and predicted variable. To train the data, coefficients are found that best describes the predictor variables for the linear relation.

Data Pruning. In decision tree algorithm, pruning is done to improve the performance and stability of the tree. The complexity if tree is reduced by removing the less important branches of the tree. Pruning increases the accuracy of the algorithm and also reduce overfitting.

In Support Vector Machine algorithm, reduce the complexity of the function and increase the speed of SVM. Iterative process is used to prune SVM.

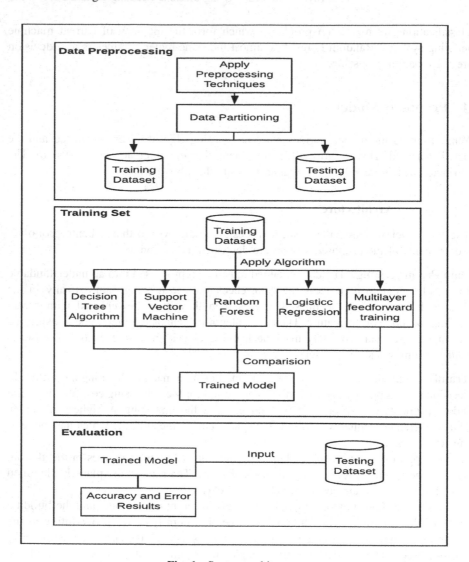

Fig. 1. System architecture

4.2 Process Diagram of Evaluation Method

Referring to the Fig. 2, initially, the data is collected from various sources. The collected data is then normalized. Then the dataset is split to training and testing dataset. For E.g. In decision tree method, prediction of class label for a record starts from the root of the tree. The values of the root attribute are compared with record's attribute. On the basis of comparison, the branch is followed to the corresponding value and jump to the next node. The comparison of the record's attribute with other internal nodes of the tree is continued until a leaf node occurs with predicted class value. The accuracy of each split is calculated using a function. The attribute with least cost is chosen for split. Using same strategy, the groups formed can be subdivided which makes this algorithm recursive in nature. As it has an excessive desire of lowering the cost, it is also called as the greedy algorithm. The root node is always the one which has the least gini score and thus the best classifier. Gini score gives the probability of choosing an item from the set and the probability of that item being misclassified.

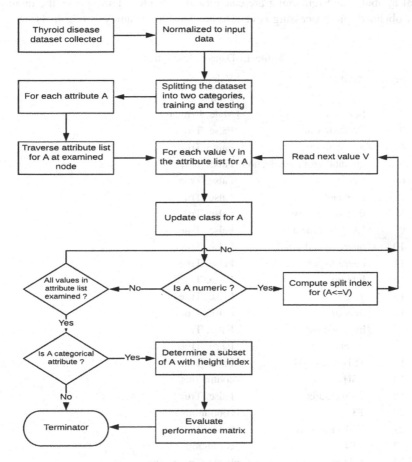

Fig. 2. Process diagram

Gini index is calculated by using:

$$Gini = 1 - \sum_j p_j^2$$

The value of gini index lies between 0 and 1. If the gini score is 0 then this indicates a perfect equality and if the gini score is 1, then this indicates a perfect inequality. The attribute with least gini index is chosen for the split.

4.3   Experimental Setup

Data Description. The dataset is obtained from several sources like thyroid disease dataset from UCI machine learning repository and other such repositories which consists of 10,450 records in total. There are total 29 features, out of which six features are real attributes and remaining are categorical attributes. To improve the quality of dataset obtained, pre-processing is carried out for further analysis (Table 1).

Table 1. Dataset description

Sr. no.	Attribute	Value type
1	Age	continuous
2	Sex	Male, Female
3	On thyroxine	False, True
4	query on thyroxine	False, True
5	on antithyroid medication	False, True
6	sick	False, True
7	pregnant	False, True
8	thyroid surgery	False, True
9	L131 treatment	False, True
10	query hypothyroid	False, True
11	query hyperthyroid	False, True
12	lithium	False, True
13	goitre	False, True
14	tumour	False, True
15	hypopituitary	False, True
16	psych	False, True
17	TSH measured	False, True
18	TSH	continuous
19	T3 measured	False, True
20	T3	continuous
21	TT4 measured	False, True
22	TT4	continuous
23	T4U measured	False, True
24	T4U	continuous
25	FTI measured	False, True
26	FTI	continuous
27	TBG measured	False, True
28	TBG	continuous
29	referral source	WEST, STMW, SVHC, SVI, SVHD, other

Implementation. The dataset collected from the source is classified using decision tree algorithm, random forest algorithm, support vector machine algorithm, logistic regression and multilayer feedforward algorithm. The accuracy for each algorithm is evaluated using performance matrix and the algorithm with highest accuracy is selected for future classifications.

5   Result and Analysis

The data obtained from the source was split in the ratio of 80:20. The training dataset consisted of 8360 training instances and the testing dataset consisted of 2090 testing instances. After training the model with all the 5 algorithms discussed above, the algorithms were tested using the testing dataset. The performance of the model was then evaluated via F1-score, Recall, Precision and Accuracy.

Figure 3 (bar graph to the left) below shows the comparison of the 5 algorithms discussed above on the basis of accuracy. Accuracy measures how well the system is performing under the testing data set. It is the ratio of accurately predicted samples to the total number of sample taken into consideration for the testing process.

$$Ac = CP + CN/N$$

Where,

Ac = accuracy
CP = correctly predicted positive samples
CN = correctly predicted negative samples
N = total Number of samples in the testing dataset

From the above comparison it is observed that Decision tree has the highest accuracy of 99.46%. Random forest algorithm has the accuracy very close to that of decision tree. The next algorithm logistic regression holds the accuracy of 97.5%. Support vector machine algorithm has the accuracy of 96.25% and multilayer feed-forward obtains the last raking with the percentage equal to 95.17%.

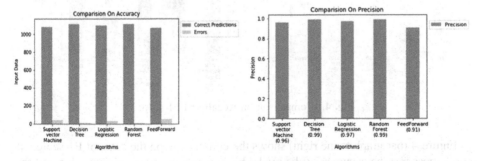

Fig. 3. Comparison on Accuracy and Precision

Figure 3 (bar graph to the right) shows the comparison on the basis of precision. Precision is calculated by considering the ratio of total number of positive samples to the total number of samples which the system reported to be positive

$$Pr = P/NP$$

Where,

Pr = Precision
P = Positive samples
NP = total number of samples reported positive

Decision tree and the random forest algorithm got precision of 0.99 whereas logistic regression has precision of 0.97, support vector machine has precision of 0.96 and multilayer feedforward has least precision of 0.91.

Figure 4 (bar graph to the left) below shows the comparison on the basis of recall. Recall gives the measure of the system's positively predicted value to the total number of positive samples taken into consideration for testing process

$$Recall = P/NP$$

Where,

P = truly predicted positive samples
NP = Total positive samples in the testing set

As it is observed from the Fig. 3, decision tree and random forest algorithm have a recall of 0.99, logistic regression has a recall of 0.97, support vector machine has a recall of 0.96, and multilayer feedforward has a recall of 0.95.

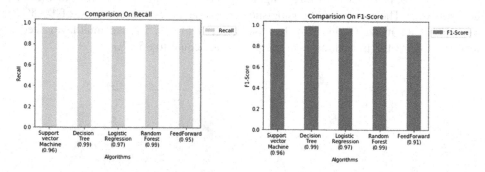

Fig. 4. Comparison on Recall and F1-score

Figure 4 (bar graph to the right) shows the comparison on the basis of F1-score. F1 scores measures the accuracy of the model by considering the Precision value and the recall values simultaneously.

$$F1 \text{ score} = 2 * (Re * Pr)/(Re + Pr)$$

Where,

Re = Recall of the model
Pr = Precision of the model

It can be observed that decision tree and random forest have the highest F1-score of 0.99 whereas multilayer feedforward has the least F1-score of 0.91 (Table 2).

Table 2. Comparisons of various algorithms and parameters

	Accuracy	Precision	Recall	F1 score
SVM	96.25%	0.96	0.96	0.96
Decision Tree	99.46%	0.99	0.99	0.99
Logistic Regression	97.50%	0.97	0.97	0.97
Random Forest	99.30%	0.99	0.99	0.99
Feed Forward	95.17%	0.91	0.95	0.91

6   Conclusion

Thyroid is one of the most important gland of the body which controls metabolism and heart rate of our body. 'T3' and 'T4' are the hormones secreted by this gland which have a major role in controlling the metabolism and temperature of human body. In addition, 27 more parameters are considered in the proposed system using various machine learning algorithms in order to attain better accuracy in disease prediction. Also, after performing a comparative study to find the most accurate and precise algorithm for prediction, it can be concluded that decision tree algorithm gives the most accurate and precise results with the accuracy of 99.46% and precision of 0.99.

7   Future Scope

The proposed system may extended to the Internet of Things (IoT) concepts, which helps in real monitoring of thyroid patients and can predict diseases using ML techniques. Such interfaces provide greater help to patients as well as doctors and it will bring a revolutionary change in medical field as it can predict diseases with minimal errors and maximum efficiency. It makes system feasible for almost every type of user, including elderly and disabled persons.

References

1. Rao, N., Razia, S.: Machine learning techniques for thyroid disease diagnosis. Indian J. Sci. Technol. **9**(28) (2016). https://doi.org/10.17485/ijst/2016/v9i28/93705
2. Prerana, P.S., Taneja, K.: Predictive data mining for diagnosis of thyroid disease using neural network. Int. J. Res. Manag. Sci. Technol. **3**(2), 75–80 (2015). E-ISSN: 2321-3264
3. Umadevi, S., JeenMarseline, K.S.: Applying classification algorithms to predict thyroid disease. Int. J. Eng. Sci. Comput. **7**(10), 15118–15120 (2017)
4. Ammulu, K., Venugopal, T.: Thyroid data prediction using data classification algorithm. Int. J. Innov. Res. Sci. Technol. **4**(2), 208–212 (2017)
5. Ahmed, J., Abdul Rehman Soomrani, M.: TDTD: Thyroid Disease Type Diagnostics. In: 2016, International Conference on Intelligent Systems Engineering (ICISE) (2016). https://doi.org/10.1109/INTELSE.2016.7475160
6. Mahajan, P., Madhe, S.: Hypo and hyperthyroid disorder detection from thermal images using Bayesian classifier. In: 2014 International Conference on Advances in Communication and Computing Technologies (2014). https://doi.org/10.1109/EIC.2015.7230721
7. Saiti, F., Naini, A.A., Tehran, I., Shoorehdeli, M.A., Teshnehlab, M.: Thyroid disease diagnosis based on genetic algorithms using PNN and VM. In: 2009 3rd International Conference on Bioinformatics and Biomedical Engineering (2009). https://doi.org/10.1109/ICBBE.2009.5163689
8. Decision Trees in Machine Learning. https://towardsdatascience.com/decision-trees-in-machine-learning-641b9c4e8052
9. Thyroid disorders in India: An epidemiological perspective. https://www.ncbi.nlm.nih.gov/pmc/articles/PMC3169866/#ref1
10. 7 Types of Artificial Neural Networks for Natural Language Processing. https://medium.com/@datamonsters/artificial-neural-networks-for-natural-language-processing-part-1-64ca9ebfa3b2
11. Thyroid Disease Data Set. http://archive.ics.uci.edu/ml/datasets/thyroid+disease

An Iterative Scheme for a Class of Fractional Order Perturbed Differential Equations

Rupsha Roy[1] and Kotapally Harish Kumar[2(✉)]

[1] School of Basic Sciences, Indian Institute of Technology Indore, Indore 453552, India
phd12124103@iiti.ac.in

[2] Research and Development, Datafoundry Pvt. Ltd., Divyasree Technopolis, Bangalore 560037, India
harish.k@datafoundry.ai

Abstract. This paper presents an existence and uniqueness theorem for a class of fractional order perturbed differential equations using modified quasilinearization method. A convergence analysis is accomplished not only using the monotone properties of the functions involved but also with a relaxation on these properties. The applicability of the proposed scheme is illustrated using examples assuring the uniqueness that the literature fails to achieve and the numerical simulation is done using the pseudo spectral method.

Keywords: Caputo's fractional derivative ·
Modified quasilinearization · Monotone iterations ·
Pseudo spectral method

1 Introduction

Recently, functional differential equations involving fractional order derivatives gained considerable attention of many researchers. The importance of the investigations of such differential equations lies in the fact that they include several dynamic systems as special cases. In this paper, an existence and uniqueness theorem for the initial value problem

$$^cD^q(x(t) - f(t, x(t))) = g(t, x(t)), \qquad x(0) = x_0 \qquad (1)$$

where $f, g \in C([0, T] \times \mathbb{R}, \mathbb{R})$ and $^cD^q$ is the Caputo's fractional derivative of order q with $0 < q \leq 1$ is discussed via modified quasilinearization method. Various versions of fixed point theorem in Banach space, Banach Algebra and partially ordered space are frequently used in the literature to study the existence of the solution of (1). Though the results in [1–4] ensure the existence of solution, they fail to provide uniqueness and any iterative scheme to approximate the solution [2–4]. Extensive research is done for variations of (1) in the literature [5–18].

© Springer Nature Singapore Pte Ltd. 2019
M. Singh et al. (Eds.): ICACDS 2019, CCIS 1045, pp. 151–163, 2019.
https://doi.org/10.1007/978-981-13-9939-8_14

Using the fixed point theorem in partially ordered Banach space [1], recently an interesting successive monotone iterative method is studied for (1). Though this iterative procedure guarantee the existence of the solutions, it fails to ensure the uniqueness. This paper provides an interesting comparison theorem for a class of integral equations. Making use of this comparison theorem and the monotone properties of the functions f and g, the monotonicity of the proposed modified quasilinearization iterative scheme is obtained. To expand the applicability of the proposed scheme, a semilocal convergence theorem is also proved by relaxing the monotone properties of the functions involved. More specifically, a set of sufficient conditions is provided to choose the initial guess which will guarantee not only the convergence of the proposed scheme but also the uniqueness of the solution in the neighborhood of the initial guess. Interesting nontrivial examples are also provided to show the utility of the proposed study. It is important to notice that the literature fails to provide the uniqueness and any iterative procedure for the examples considered. To summarize, the major contributions of this paper are as follow:

1. A new comparison theorem for integral equations.
2. Existence and uniqueness of (1) via a monotone convergence theorem using modified quasilinearization.
3. Existence and uniqueness of (1) via semilocal convergence theorem using modified quasilinearization.

The organization of the paper is as follows. Section 2 provides the relevant results for the main theorem. In Sect. 3, convergence theorems for modified quasilinearization are given. Two examples are solved in Sect. 4 using multi domain pseudo spectral method discussed in [19] which also support the theory proposed.

2   Preliminaries

In this section, some basic definitions and results are presented that are used to prove the main results.

Lemma 1. *Let $f, g \in C([0, T] \times \mathbb{R}, \mathbb{R})$. Then $x(t) \in C[0, T]$ is the solution of*

$$^{c}D^{q}(x(t) - f(t, x(t))) = g(t, x(t)), \qquad x(0) = x_0 \tag{2}$$

iff it is the solution of the integral equation

$$x(t) = x_0 - f(0, x_0) + f(t, x) + \frac{1}{\Gamma q} \int_0^t (t - s)^{q-1} g(s, x(s)) \mathrm{d}s. \tag{3}$$

Definition 21. *A function $v \in C([0, T], \mathbb{R})$ is called a lower solution of (3) if for all $t \in [0, T]$,*

$$v(t) \leq x_0 - f(0, x_0) + f(t, v) + \frac{1}{\Gamma q} \int_0^t (t - s)^{q-1} g(s, v(s)) \mathrm{d}s. \tag{4}$$

It is said to be an upper solution if the inequality is reversed.

Lemma 2. *Let F and G be two continuous functions defined on $[0,T]$. Then the integral equation*

$$x(t) = F(t) + \frac{1}{\Gamma q} \int_0^t (t-s)^{q-1} G(s) x(s) ds \qquad (5)$$

has a unique solution.

Proof. Let $M_1 = \sup_{s \in [0,T]} |G(s)|$. Define a function $\mathscr{F} : C[0,T] \to C[0,T]$ by

$$\mathscr{F}x(t) = F(t) + \frac{1}{\Gamma q} \int_0^t (t-s)^{q-1} G(s) x(s) ds.$$

Then one can easily show that for all $t \in [0,T]$,

$$|\mathscr{F}^n x(t) - \mathscr{F}^n y(t)| \leq \frac{(M_1 T^q)^n}{\Gamma(nq+1)} \|x - y\|$$

$$\|\mathscr{F}^n x - \mathscr{F}^n y\| \leq \frac{(M_1 T^q)^n}{\Gamma(nq+1)} \|x - y\|.$$

Consequently, $\mathscr{F}^n$ is a contraction map for some $n \in \mathbb{N}$ and by contraction principle, $\mathscr{F}$ has a unique fixed point. Hence the result.

Lemma 3. *Let $x \in C([0,T], \mathbb{R})$ and $h \in C([0,T], \mathbb{R}_0^+)$. If x satisfies the inequality*

$$x(t) \leq \frac{1}{\Gamma q} \int_0^t (t-s)^{q-1} h(s) x(s) ds \quad for \ all \ \ t \in [0,T], \qquad (6)$$

then $x(t) \leq 0$ for all $t \in [0,T]$.

Proof. Consider the Banach space $C[0,T]$ with the norm $\|x\|_\rho = \sup_{t \in [0,T]} \dfrac{|x(t)|}{E_q(\rho t^q)}$ where $\rho > 0$ [20]. Define an operator $V : C[0,T] \to C[0,T]$ by

$$Vx(t) = \frac{1}{\Gamma q} \int_0^t (t-s)^{q-1} h(s) x(s) ds.$$

Note that $Vx(t) \leq 0$ for all $x \in C[0,T]$ if $x(t) \leq 0$ where $t \in [0,T]$. Now

$$\|V\| = \sup_{\|x\|_\rho \leq 1} \sup_{t \in [0,T]} \frac{|\int_0^t (t-s)^{q-1} h(s) x(s) ds|}{\Gamma q E_q(\rho t^q)}$$

$$\leq \sup_{\|x\|_\rho \leq 1} \sup_{t \in [0,T]} \frac{M}{\Gamma q E_q(\rho t^q)} \int_0^t (t-s)^{q-1} \frac{|x(s)|}{E_q(\rho s^q)} E_q(\rho s^q) ds$$

$$\|V\| \leq \sup_{t \in [0,T]} \frac{M}{\Gamma q E_q(\rho t^q)} \int_0^t (t-s)^{q-1} E_q(\rho s^q) ds \leq \frac{M}{\rho}$$

where $M = \sup_{t \in [0,T]} |h(t)|$. Choose ρ sufficiently large such that $\frac{M}{\rho} < 1$. Then $(I - V)^{-1} = \sum_{n=0}^{\infty} V^n$. Now if $y(t) \leq 0$ for all $t \in [0,T]$, then $(I - V)^{-1} y(t) = \sum_{n=0}^{\infty} V^n y(t) \leq 0$. (6) can be written as $(I - V)x(t) \leq 0$. Applying $(I - V)^{-1}$ on both sides of the inequality, one can get $x(t) \leq 0$ for all $t \in [0,T]$.

3   Convergence Analysis

This section presents the convergence analysis of modified quasilinearization method in two ways. In the first approach, the convergence of modified quasi-linearization to the solution of (1) is obtained based on monotone properties of f and g. These properties of f and g are relaxed in the second approach to acquire the existence and uniqueness result for (1). For $\alpha_0, \beta_0 \in C[0,T]$, the sector $[\alpha_0, \beta_0]$ is defined by $\{x : \alpha_0(t) \leq x(t) \leq \beta_0(t), \, \forall \, t \in [0,T]\}$. Define $\lambda = x_0 - f(0, x_0)$, $m_1 = \min_{t \in [0,T]} \{\alpha_0, \beta_0\}$ and $m_2 = \max_{t \in [0,T]} \{\alpha_0, \beta_0\}$. Throughout this paper, g_2 denotes the derivative of g with respect to the second variable. The following theorem affirms the convergence of the modified quasilinearization when g has the decomposition $g = u + v$ and $f, u, v, u_2, v_2 \in C([0,T] \times [m_1, m_2])$.

Theorem 1. *Let $\alpha_0, \beta_0 \in C^1([0,T], \mathbb{R})$ be the ordered lower and upper solutions of (3) satisfying $u_2(t, \alpha_0) + v_2(t, \beta_0) \geq 0$ on $[0,T]$. Further suppose that*

(i) *in the sector $[\alpha_0, \beta_0]$, for each fixed t, f and u_2 are nondecreasing and v_2 is nonincreasing in the second variable;*

(ii) *$|f(t_1, x_1) - f(t_2, x_2)| \leq L_1|t_1 - t_2| + L_2|x_1 - x_2|$, $L_1 \geq 0$, $0 \leq L_2 < 1$ for all $(t_i, x_i) \in [0,T] \times [m_1, m_2]$, $i = 1, 2$.*

Then there exist monotone sequences

$$\alpha_{n+1}(t) = \frac{1}{\Gamma q} \int_0^t (t-s)^{q-1}(g(s, \alpha_n) + (u_2(s, \alpha_0) + v_2(s, \beta_0))(\alpha_{n+1} - \alpha_n))ds$$
$$+ f(t, \alpha_n) + \lambda, \tag{7}$$

$$\beta_{n+1}(t) = \frac{1}{\Gamma q} \int_0^t (t-s)^{q-1}(g(s, \beta_n) + (u_2(s, \alpha_0) + v_2(s, \beta_0))(\beta_{n+1} - \beta_n))ds$$
$$+ f(t, \beta_n) + \lambda \tag{8}$$

that converge uniformly and monotonically to the unique solution of (3) in $[\alpha_0, \beta_0]$.

Proof. From Lemma 2, it is clear that (7) and (8) are well defined and has a unique solution for each $n \in \mathbb{N}$. Now using mathematical induction and Lemma 3 the following inequality is obtained for all $n \in \mathbb{N}$.

$$\alpha_0 \leq \alpha_1 \leq \cdots \leq \alpha_n \leq \beta_n \leq \cdots \leq \beta_1 \leq \beta_0 \tag{9}$$

on $[0,T]$. Firstly for $n = 1$, one has to show $\alpha_0 \leq \alpha_1 \leq \beta_1 \leq \beta_0$ on $[0,T]$. Let $p(t) = \alpha_0 - \alpha_1$. Then

$$p(t) \leq f(t, \alpha_0) + \frac{1}{\Gamma q} \int_0^t (t-s)^{q-1}g(s, \alpha_0)ds - f(t, \alpha_0)$$
$$- \frac{1}{\Gamma q} \int_0^t (t-s)^{q-1}(g(s, \alpha_0) + (u_2(s, \alpha_0) + v_2(s, \beta_0))(\alpha_1 - \alpha_0))ds$$

$$p(t) \leq \frac{1}{\Gamma q} \int_0^t (t-s)^{q-1}(u_2(s, \alpha_0) + v_2(s, \beta_0))p(s)ds.$$

By Lemma 3, $p(t) \leq 0$. Thus $\alpha_0 \leq \alpha_1$ on $[0, T]$. Similarly $\beta_1 \leq \beta_0$ on $[0, T]$. Let $p(t) = \alpha_1 - \beta_1$. Then

$$p(t) = f(t, \alpha_0) - f(t, \beta_0) + \frac{1}{\Gamma q} \int_0^t (t - s)^{q-1} (g(s, \alpha_0) - g(s, \beta_0)) ds$$

$$+ \frac{1}{\Gamma q} \int_0^t (t - s)^{q-1} (u_2(s, \alpha_0) + v_2(s, \beta_0))(\alpha_1 - \alpha_0 - \beta_1 + \beta_0) ds$$

$$\leq \frac{1}{\Gamma q} \int_0^t (t - s)^{q-1} (u_2(s, \alpha_0) + v_2(s, \beta_0))(\alpha_0 - \beta_0) ds$$

$$+ \frac{1}{\Gamma q} \int_0^t (t - s)^{q-1} (u_2(s, \alpha_0) + v_2(s, \beta_0))(\alpha_1 - \alpha_0 - \beta_1 + \beta_0) ds$$

$$p(t) \leq \frac{1}{\Gamma q} \int_0^t (t - s)^{q-1} (u_2(s, \alpha_0) + v_2(s, \beta_0)) p(s) ds.$$

By Lemma 3, $p(t) \leq 0$. Thus $\alpha_1 \leq \beta_1$ on $[0, T]$. Assume that (9) is true for $n = k$. That is,

$$\alpha_0 \leq \cdots \leq \alpha_{k-1} \leq \alpha_k \leq \beta_k \leq \beta_{k-1} \leq \cdots \leq \beta_0 \qquad (10)$$

on $[0, T]$. To prove (9), it is enough to show that

$$\alpha_k \leq \alpha_{k+1} \leq \beta_{k+1} \leq \beta_k \qquad (11)$$

on $[0, T]$. Let $p(t) = \alpha_k - \alpha_{k+1}$. Then

$$p(t) = f(t, \alpha_{k-1}) - f(t, \alpha_k) + \frac{1}{\Gamma q} \int_0^t (t - s)^{q-1} (g(s, \alpha_{k-1}) - g(s, \alpha_k)) ds$$

$$+ \frac{1}{\Gamma q} \int_0^t (t - s)^{q-1} (u_2(s, \alpha_0) + v_2(s, \beta_0))(\alpha_k - \alpha_{k-1} - \alpha_{k+1} + \alpha_k) ds$$

$$\leq \frac{1}{\Gamma q} \int_0^t (t - s)^{q-1} (u_2(s, \alpha_0) + v_2(s, \beta_0))(\alpha_{k-1} - \alpha_k) ds$$

$$+ \frac{1}{\Gamma q} \int_0^t (t - s)^{q-1} (u_2(s, \alpha_0) + v_2(s, \beta_0))(\alpha_k - \alpha_{k-1} - \alpha_{k+1} + \alpha_k) ds$$

$$p(t) \leq \frac{1}{\Gamma q} \int_0^t (t - s)^{q-1} (u_2(s, \alpha_0) + v_2(s, \beta_0)) p(s) ds.$$

By Lemma 3, $p(t) \leq 0$. Thus $\alpha_k \leq \alpha_{k+1}$ on $[0,T]$. In a similar way it can be proved that $\beta_{k+1} \leq \beta_k$ on $[0,T]$. Let $p(t) = \alpha_{k+1} - \beta_{k+1}$. Then

$$
p(t) = f(t,\alpha_k) - f(t,\beta_k) + \frac{1}{\Gamma q} \int_0^t (t-s)^{q-1}(g(s,\alpha_k) - g(s,\beta_k))ds
$$

$$
+ \frac{1}{\Gamma q} \int_0^t (t-s)^{q-1}(u_2(s,\alpha_0) + v_2(s,\beta_0))(\alpha_{k+1} - \alpha_k - \beta_{k+1} + \beta_k)ds
$$

$$
\leq \frac{1}{\Gamma q} \int_0^t (t-s)^{q-1}(u_2(s,\alpha_0) + v_2(s,\beta_0))(\alpha_k - \beta_k)ds
$$

$$
+ \frac{1}{\Gamma q} \int_0^t (t-s)^{q-1}(u_2(s,\alpha_0) + v_2(s,\beta_0))(\alpha_{k+1} - \alpha_k - \beta_{k+1} + \beta_k)ds
$$

$$
p(t) \leq \frac{1}{\Gamma q} \int_0^t (t-s)^{q-1}(u_2(s,\alpha_0) + v_2(s,\beta_0))p(s)ds.
$$

By Lemma 3, $p(t) \leq 0$. Hence $\alpha_{k+1} \leq \beta_{k+1}$ on $[0,T]$. Consequently, (11) is proved. To complete the proof, it is enough to show that $\{\alpha_{n+1}\}$ and $\{\beta_{n+1}\}$ are equicontinuous. Define $M_1 = \sup\limits_{\substack{\nu \in [\alpha_0,\beta_0] \\ t \in [0,T]}} \{|g(t,\nu) + 2\beta_0(u_2(t,\alpha_0) + v_2(t,\beta_0))|\}$, $A = \left[\left(L_1 T^{1-q} + \frac{2M_1}{\Gamma(q+1)}\right)\left(\frac{1}{1-L_2}\right) + LL_2 T^{1-q}\right]$ and $L = \sup\limits_{t \in [0,T]} |\alpha_0'(t)|$. For any $t_1 < t_2$ in $t \in [0,T]$ and $n \in \mathbb{N}$,

$$
|\alpha_{n+1}(t_1) - \alpha_{n+1}(t_2)| \leq L_1|t_1 - t_2| + L_2|\alpha_n(t_1) - \alpha_n(t_2)|
$$

$$
+ \frac{M_1}{\Gamma q}\left(\int_0^{t_1} |(t_1-s)^{q-1} - (t_2-s)^{q-1}|ds + \int_{t_1}^{t_2} |(t_2-s)^{q-1}|ds\right)
$$

$$
= L_1|t_1 - t_2| + L_2|\alpha_n(t_1) - \alpha_n(t_2)| + \frac{M_1}{\Gamma(q+1)}(2(t_2-t_1)^q + t_1^q - t_2^q)
$$

$$
|\alpha_{n+1}(t_1) - \alpha_{n+1}(t_2)| \leq L_1|t_1 - t_2| + L_2|\alpha_n(t_1) - \alpha_n(t_2)| + \frac{2M_1(t_2-t_1)^q}{\Gamma(q+1)}. \tag{12}
$$

Now using induction on $n \in \mathbb{N}$, the following inequality is proved.

$$
|\alpha_n(t_1) - \alpha_n(t_2)| \leq A(t_2 - t_1)^q \quad \forall\, n \in \mathbb{N},\ t_1 < t_2 \tag{13}
$$

on $[0,T]$. For the choice of $n = 0$, (12) becomes

$$
|\alpha_1(t_1) - \alpha_1(t_2)| \leq L_1|t_1 - t_2| + L_2|\alpha_0(t_1) - \alpha_0(t_2)| + \frac{2M_1(t_2-t_1)^q}{\Gamma(q+1)}
$$

$$
\leq L_1|t_1 - t_2| + L_2 L|t_1 - t_2| + \frac{2M_1(t_2-t_1)^q}{\Gamma(q+1)}
$$

$$
\leq \left((L_1 + LL_2)T^{1-q} + \frac{2M_1}{\Gamma(q+1)}\right)(t_2 - t_1)^q
$$

$$
|\alpha_1(t_1) - \alpha_1(t_2)| \leq A(t_2 - t_1)^q.
$$

Assume that (13) holds true for $n = 2, 3, \ldots, k$. Now one can easily see that

$$|\alpha_{k+1}(t_1) - \alpha_{k+1}(t_2)| \leq \left(L_1 T^{1-q} + \frac{2M_1}{\Gamma(q+1)}\right)(1 + L_2 + \cdots + L_2^k)(t_2 - t_1)^q$$
$$+ L L_2^{k+1} T^{1-q}(t_2 - t_1)^q$$
$$\leq \left[\left(L_1 T^{1-q} + \frac{2M_1}{\Gamma(q+1)}\right)\left(\frac{1}{1-L_2}\right) + L L_2 T^{1-q}\right](t_2 - t_1)^q \quad (14)$$
$$|\alpha_{k+1}(t_1) - \alpha_{k+1}(t_2)| \leq A(t_2 - t_1)^q.$$

Thus $\{\alpha_n\}$ is equicontinuous. Similarly $\{\beta_n\}$ is also equicontinuous. Now it is clear that the sequences $\{\alpha_n\}$ and $\{\beta_n\}$ are uniformly bounded and equicontinuous on $[0, T]$. Hence by Ascoli-Arzela's Theorem, there exist subsequences $\{\alpha_{n_k}\}$ and $\{\beta_{n_k}\}$ that converge uniformly on $[0, T]$. In view of (9), it follows that sequences $\{\alpha_n\}$ and $\{\beta_n\}$ converge uniformly and monotonically to ρ_1 and ρ_2 respectively. Clearly ρ_1 and ρ_2 are the solutions of (2) and $\rho_1 \leq \rho_2$. Let $p(t) = \rho_2 - \rho_1$. Then

$$p(t) = f(t, \rho_2) - f(t, \rho_1) + \frac{1}{\Gamma q}\int_0^t (t - s)^{q-1}(g(s, \rho_2) - g(s, \rho_1))ds$$

$$= f(t, \rho_2) - f(t, \rho_1) + \frac{1}{\Gamma q}\int_0^t (t - s)^{q-1}g_2(s, \delta)p(s)ds \quad [\rho_1 \leq \delta \leq \rho_2]$$

$$\leq L_2 p(t) + \frac{M}{\Gamma q}\int_0^t (t - s)^{q-1}p(s)ds$$

$$p(t) \leq \frac{M}{(1 - L_2)\Gamma q}\int_0^t (t - s)^{q-1}p(s)ds$$

where $M = \sup\limits_{t\in[0,T]} |u_2(t, \beta_0) + v_2(t, \alpha_0)|$. By Lemma 3, $p(t) \leq 0$. Thus $\rho_1 = \rho_2$. Hence the theorem.

The following semi local theorem ensures the convergence of the modified quasilinearization to the unique solution of (1) when f and g fail to satisfy the monotone properties. More specifically, the following theorem provides a set of sufficient conditions on the initial guess which gives the guarantee of the convergence of the modified quasilinearization to the unique solution of (1) in the neighborhood of the initial guess. For $\alpha_0 \in C[0, T]$, $B(\alpha_0, r)$ denotes the closed ball with center α_0 and radius r.

Theorem 2. Let $\alpha_0 \in C([0, T], \mathbb{R})$ and $B(\alpha_0, r) \subseteq C[0, T]$ and $f, g, g_2 \in C([0, T] \times [-r - \|\alpha_0\|, r + \|\alpha_0\|], \mathbb{R})$. Further assume that

1. there exist M_1, M_2 and M_3 such that $\|\alpha_0 - x_0\| \leq M_1$, $\|g\| \leq M_2$ and $\|g_2\| \leq M_3$, $\forall\, t \in [0, T]$;

2. $|f(t_1, s_1) - f(t_2, s_2)| \le L_1|t_1 - t_2| + L_2|s_1 - s_2|$; $\forall\ (t_i, s_i) \in [0,T] \times [-r - \|\alpha_0\|, r + \|\alpha_0\|]$, $i = 1, 2$, $0 \le L_1$, $0 \le L_2 < 1$;

3. $r \ge \dfrac{M_2 T^q + \Gamma(q+1)(L_1 T + L_2 M_1 + M_1)}{(1 - L_2)\Gamma(q+1) - 2M_3 T^q}$, $3M_3 T^q < (1 - L_2)\Gamma(q+1)$.

Then (3) *has a unique solution in* $B(\alpha_0, r)$. *Moreover, when* $\lambda = x_0 - f(0, x_0)$, *the modified quasilinearization*

$$\alpha_{n+1} = \lambda + f(t, \alpha_n) + \frac{1}{\Gamma q}\int_0^t (t-s)^{q-1}(g(s, \alpha_n) + g_2(s, \alpha_0)(\alpha_{n+1} - \alpha_n))ds \quad (15)$$

is well defined with $\alpha_n \in B(\alpha_0, r)$ *for all* $n \in \mathbb{N}$ *and* $\{\alpha_n\}$ *converges uniformly to the solution* $x(t)$ *of* (3).

Proof. Using Lemma 2, one can conclude that the linear equation (15) has a unique solution for each $n \in \mathbb{N}$. Define $a = \dfrac{L_2\Gamma(q+1) + M_3 T^q}{\Gamma(q+1) - M_3 T^q}$, $\theta_1 = \dfrac{M_2 T^q + \Gamma(q+1)(L_1 T + L_2 M_1 + M_1)}{\Gamma(q+1) - M_3 T^q}$ and $\theta_2 = \dfrac{L_2\Gamma(q+1) + 2M_3 T^q}{\Gamma(q+1) - M_3 T^q}$. Note that

$$\alpha_1(t) - \alpha_0(t) = x_0 - f(0, x_0) + f(t, \alpha_0) + \frac{1}{\Gamma q}\int_0^t (t-s)^{q-1}g(s, \alpha_0)ds$$

$$+ \frac{1}{\Gamma q}\int_0^t (t-s)^{q-1}g_2(s, \alpha_0)(\alpha_1 - \alpha_0)ds - \alpha_0$$

$$|\alpha_1(t) - \alpha_0(t)| \le |f(t, \alpha_0) - f(0, x_0)| + \frac{1}{\Gamma q}\int_0^t (t-s)^{q-1}|g(s, \alpha_0)|ds$$

$$+ \frac{1}{\Gamma q}\int_0^t (t-s)^{q-1}|g_2(s, \alpha_0)||\alpha_1 - \alpha_0|ds + |x_0 - \alpha_0|$$

$$\|\alpha_1 - \alpha_0\| \le L_1 T + (L_2 + 1)\|\alpha_0 - x_0\| + \frac{M_2 T^q}{\Gamma(q+1)} + \frac{M_3 T^q\|\alpha_1 - \alpha_0\|}{\Gamma(q+1)}$$

$$\|\alpha_1 - \alpha_0\| \le \theta_1 < r.$$

Hence $\alpha_1 \in B(\alpha_0, r)$. Assume that for $k = 2, 3, \ldots, n-1$, $\|\alpha_k - \alpha_0\| \leq (1 + a + \cdots + a^{k-1})\theta_1$. Similarly,

$$|\alpha_n(t) - \alpha_0(t)| \leq |f(t, \alpha_{n-1}) - f(0, x_0)| + \frac{1}{\Gamma q} \int_0^t (t-s)^{q-1} |g(s, \alpha_{n-1})| ds$$

$$+ \frac{1}{\Gamma q} \int_0^t (t-s)^{q-1} |g_2(s, \alpha_0)| \|\alpha_n - \alpha_{n-1}\| ds + |x_0 - \alpha_0|$$

$$\|\alpha_n - \alpha_0\| \leq L_1 T + L_2 \|\alpha_{n-1} - x_0\| + \|\alpha_0 - x_0\| + \frac{M_2 T^q}{\Gamma(q+1)}$$

$$+ \frac{M_3 T^q \|\alpha_n - \alpha_{n-1}\|}{\Gamma(q+1)}$$

$$\leq L_1 T + L_2 (\|\alpha_{n-1} - \alpha_0\| + \|\alpha_0 - x_0\|) + M_1 + \frac{M_2 T^q}{\Gamma(q+1)}$$

$$+ \frac{M_3 T^q}{\Gamma(q+1)} (\|\alpha_n - \alpha_0\| + \|\alpha_{n-1} - \alpha_0\|)$$

$$\leq L_1 T + \left(L_2 + \frac{M_3 T^q}{\Gamma(q+1)} \right) (1 + a + \cdots + a^{n-2})\theta_1 + L_2 M_1$$

$$+ M_1 + \frac{M_2 T^q}{\Gamma(q+1)} + \frac{M_3 T^q}{\Gamma(q+1)} \|\alpha_n - \alpha_0\|$$

$$\|\alpha_n - \alpha_0\| \leq \frac{M_2 T^q + \Gamma(q+1)(L_1 T + L_2 M_1 + M_1)}{\Gamma(q+1) - M_3 T^q}$$

$$+ \frac{(L_2 \Gamma(q+1) + M_3 T^q)(1 + a + \cdots + a^{n-2})\theta_1}{\Gamma(q+1) - M_3 T^q}$$

$$= \theta_1 + a(1 + a + \cdots + a^{n-2})\theta_1 = (1 + a + \cdots + a^{n-1})\theta_1$$

$$\|\alpha_n - \alpha_0\| \leq \frac{\theta_1}{1-a}.$$

Hence $\alpha_n \in B(\alpha_0, r)$ for all $n \in \mathbb{N}$. Similarly, using induction on $n \in \mathbb{N}$, one can easily obtain $\|\alpha_n - \alpha_{n-1}\| \leq \theta_2^{n-1} \theta_1$, for all $n \in \mathbb{N}$. Now,

$$\|\alpha_{k+n} - \alpha_k\| \leq \|\alpha_{k+n} - \alpha_{k+n-1}\| + \cdots \|\alpha_{k+2} - \alpha_{k+1}\| + \|\alpha_{k+1} - \alpha_k\|$$

$$\leq \theta_2^{k+n-1} \theta_1 + \cdots + \theta_2^{k+1} \theta_1 + \theta_2^k \theta_1$$

$$= \theta_2^k (1 + \theta_2 + \cdots + \theta_2^{n-1})\theta_1$$

$$\|\alpha_{k+n} - \alpha_k\| \leq \frac{\theta_2^k}{1 - \theta_2} \theta_1.$$

Note that $\|\alpha_{k+m} - \alpha_k\| \to 0$ as $k \to \infty$. Thus $\{\alpha_n\}$ is a Cauchy sequence and hence converges to $x(t)$ (say). From (15) it can be concluded that $x(t)$ is the solution of (2). To show the uniqueness of the solution of (2), suppose x_1 and x_2 be any two solutions of (2). Let $p(t) = x_1 - x_2$. Then

$$p(t) = f(t, x_1) - f(t, x_2) + \frac{1}{\Gamma q} \int_0^t (t-s)^{q-1} (g(s, x_1) - g(s, x_2)) ds$$

$$= f(t, x_1) - f(t, x_2) + \frac{1}{\Gamma q} \int_0^t (t-s)^{q-1} \int_0^1 g_2(s, \theta x_1 + (1-\theta)x_2) p(s) d\theta ds$$

$$|p(t)| \leq \frac{1}{\Gamma q} \int_0^t (t-s)^{q-1} \int_0^1 |g_2(s, \theta x_1 + (1-\theta)x_2) p(s)| d\theta ds + |f(t, x_1) - f(t, x_2)|$$

$$\leq L_2 |p(t)| + \frac{M_3}{\Gamma q} \int_0^t (t-s)^{q-1} |p(s)| ds$$

$$|p(t)| \leq \frac{M_3}{(1-L_2)\Gamma q} \int_0^t (t-s)^{q-1} |p(s)| ds.$$

By Lemma 3, $|p(t)| \leq 0$. Hence $x_1 = x_2 = x(t)$ is the unique solution of (2) in $B(\alpha_0, r)$.

4   Examples

In this section, examples are provided to demonstrate the proposed theory. Based on the proposed iterative procedure, for specific choices of f and g, existence and uniqueness result for (1) is verified and solved numerically. In particular, at each step, the linear integral equation in the iterative procedure is solved numerically using multi-domain pseudo spectral method discussed in [19]. Interesting examples are also provided in which the proposed theorems ensure both existence as well as uniqueness while the literature [2,3] fails to ensure the uniqueness. For all the numerical simulations, the following stopping criterion $\|\alpha_{n+1} - \alpha_n\| \leq 10^{-8}$ is used. Throughout this section, N denotes the number of grid points, h denotes the step size and M denotes number of iterations.

Example 1. Consider the initial value problem

$$^cD^q \left(x(t) - \frac{tx(t)}{6} \right) = \frac{x^2(t) + x(t)}{3} + g(t); \quad x(0) = 0 \tag{16}$$

where $g(t) = -\dfrac{t^2 + t}{3} + \dfrac{t^{1-q}}{\Gamma(2-q)} - \dfrac{t^{2-q}}{3\Gamma(3-q)}$. For the choice of $T = 1$, $\alpha_0 = 0$, $\beta_0 = 2t$, $u(t, x) = g(t, x)$, $v(t, x) = 0$, $L_1 = \dfrac{2}{3}$ and $L_2 = \dfrac{1}{3}$, all the hypotheses of Theorem 1 are satisfied. Hence (16) has a unique solution in the sector $[0, 2t]$. Table 1 gives the number of iterations and error for the proposed scheme. It is interesting to note that though the results in [1–3] ensure the existence, they fail to confirm uniqueness. Moreover, [2,3] fail to propose any iterative procedure to approximate the solution numerically.

Table 1. Numerical results for (16) when $N = 5$ and $h = 1$.

q	0.9	0.7	0.5	0.3
M	15	17	21	35
Error	6.2727×10^{-4}	9.4479×10^{-4}	7.8542×10^{-4}	5.6033×10^{-4}

Example 2. Consider the initial value problem

$$^{c}D^{q}\left(x(t) - \frac{x^{3}(t)}{300} \right) = \frac{\cos x(t)}{500} + g(t); \quad x(0) = 0 \tag{17}$$

where $g(t) = -\dfrac{\cos t^{2}}{500} + \dfrac{\Gamma(3)t^{2-q}}{\Gamma(3-q)} - \dfrac{\Gamma(7)t^{6-q}}{300\Gamma(7-q)}$. For the choice of $T = 1$, $\alpha_0 = 0$, $L_1 = 0$, $L_2 = 0.0324$, $M_1 = 0$, $M_2 = 1.502$, $M_3 = 0.002$, $r = 1.8$ and $q = 0.3$, all the hypotheses of the Theorem 2 are satisfied. Hence the initial value problem (17) has a unique solution in $B(0, 1.8)$. Table 2 gives the number of iterations and error for the proposed scheme. Note that the theorem discussed in [1] fails to guarantee the existence of the solution of (17) as $g(t, x)$ does not satisfy the monotone property. Moreover, though the results in [2, 3] guarantee the existence of the solution, they fail to confirm the uniqueness and to propose an iterative procedure to approximate the solution numerically.

Table 2. Numerical results for (17) when $N = 8$ and $h = 1$.

q	0.9	0.7	0.5	0.3
M	8	6	7	7
Error	6.7468×10^{-4}	6.9898×10^{-4}	3.6104×10^{-4}	1.2777×10^{-4}

5   Conclusion

This paper presents two convergence results for modified quasilinearization to prove the existence and uniqueness for fractional order perturbed differential equations. Though there are many works in the literature confirming the existence of solutions, this study cater to the uniqueness as well as employment of an iterative procedure to approximate the solution that are rarely seen.

Acknowledgement. The authors wish to express their utmost gratitude to Prof. V. Antony Vijesh, IIT Indore for his valuable suggestions and guidance.

References

1. Somjaiwang, D., Ngiamsunthorn, P.S.: Existence and approximation of solutions to fractional order hybrid differential equations. Adv. Differ. Equ. **2016**, 278–288 (2016). https://doi.org/10.1186/s13662-016-0999-8
2. Herzallah, M.A.E., Baleanu, D.: On fractional order hybrid differential equations. Abstr. Appl. Anal. **2014**, 7 (2014). https://doi.org/10.1155/2014/389386. Article ID 389386
3. Agarwal, R.P., Zhou, Y., He, Y.: Existence of fractional neutral functional differential equations. Comput. Math. Appl. **59**, 1095–1100 (2010). https://doi.org/10.1016/j.camwa.2009.05.010
4. Zhou, Y., Jiao, F.: Existence of extremal solutions for discontinuous fractional functional differential equations. Int. J. Dyn. Syst. Differ. Equ. **2**, 237–252 (2009). https://doi.org/10.1504/IJDSDE.2009.031104
5. Khan, H., Tunc, C., Chen, W., Khan, A.: Existence theorems and Hyers-Ulam stability for a class of hybrid fractional differential equations with p-Laplacian operator. J. Appl. Anal. Comput. **8**, 1211–1226 (2018). https://doi.org/10.11948/2018.1211
6. Dhage, B.: Quadratic perturbations of periodic boundary value problems of second order ordinary differential equations. Differ. Equ. Appl. **2**(4), 465–486 (2010). https://doi.org/10.7153/dea-02-28
7. Dhage, B.: Basic results in the theory of hybrid differential equations with mixed perturbations of second type. Funct. Differ. Equ. **19**(1–2), 87–106 (2012). https://doi.org/10.1186/s13662-017-1407-8
8. Dhage, B.: Differential inequalities for hybrid fractional differential equations. J. Math. Inequal. **7**(3), 453–459 (2013). https://doi.org/10.7153/jmi-07-40
9. Dhage, B., Jadhav, N.S.: Basic results in the theory of hybrid differential equations with linear perturbations of second type. Tamkang J. Math. **44**(2), 171–186 (2013). https://doi.org/10.5556/j.tkjm.44.2013.1086
10. Dhage, B., Lakshmikantham, V.: Basic results on hybrid differential equations. Nonlinear Anal. Hybrid Syst. **4**, 414–424 (2010). https://doi.org/10.1016/j.nahs.2009.10.005
11. Noroozi, H., Ansari, A., Dahaghin, M.S.: Existence results for the distributed order fractional hybrid differential equations. Abstr. Appl. Anal. **2012**, 16 (2012). https://doi.org/10.1155/2012/163648. Article ID 163648
12. Lu, H., Sun, S., Yang, D., Teng, H.: Theory of fractional hybrid differential equations with linear perturbations of second type. Bound. Value Probl. **2013**, 23–38 (2013). https://doi.org/10.1186/1687-2770-2013-23
13. Hilal, K., Kajouni, A.: Boundary value problems for hybrid differential equations with fractional order. Adv. Differ. Equ. **2015**, 183–202 (2015). https://doi.org/10.1186/s13662-015-0530-76
14. Yan, R.A., Sun, S.R., Wang, D.W.: The existence of solutions for boundary value problems of two types fractional perturbation differential equations. J. Appl. Math. Comput. **48**, 187–203 (2015). https://doi.org/10.1007/s12190-014-0798-x
15. Abbas, A., Benchohra, M., N'Guerekata, G.M.: Topics in fractional differential equations. Developments in Mathematics, vol. 27. Springer, New York (2012). https://doi.org/10.1007/978-1-4614-4036-9
16. Sitho, S., Ntouyas, S.K., Tariboon, J.: Existence results for hybrid fractional integro-differential equations. Bound. Value Probl. **2015**, 113–125 (2015). https://doi.org/10.1186/s13661-015-0376-7

17. Sun, S., Zhao, Y., Han, Z., Li, Y.: The existence of solutions for boundary value problem of fractional hybrid differential equations. Commun. Nonlinear Sci. Numer. Simulat. **17**, 4961–4967 (2012). https://doi.org/10.1016/j.cnsns.2012.06.001

18. Zhao, Y., Sun, S., Han, Z., Li, Q.: Theory of fractional hybrid differential equations. Comput. Math. Appl. **62**, 1312–1324 (2011). https://doi.org/10.1016/j.camwa.2011.03.041

19. Maleki, M., Kajani, M.T.: Numerical approximations for Volterra's population growth model with fractional order via a multi-domain pseudospectral method. Appl. Math. Model. **39**, 4300–4308 (2015). https://doi.org/10.1016/j.apm.2014.12.045

20. Chandhini, G., Prashanthi, K.S., Vijesh, V.A.: A radial basis function method for fractional darboux problems. Eng. Anal. Bound. Elem. **86**, 1–18 (2017). https://doi.org/10.1016/j.enganabound.2017.10.001

A Novel Algorithm to Compute Stable Groups in Signed Social Networks

Lakshmi Satya Vani Narayanam[1](✉) and Satish V. Motammanavar[2](✉)

[1] PES University, Bangalore, India
vani.nls@gmail.com
[2] R.V. College of Engineering, Bangalore, India
drsatishmath@gmail.com

Abstract. This paper presents two new problems in the context of signed social networks and then conducts a systematic analysis of the same. These problems essentially deal with finding groups of specific cardinality that satisfy certain *stability* requirements. In particular, we define two notions of stability in signed social networks, namely *internal stability* and *external stability*. We call a group internally stable if the difference between positive edges and negative edges within the group is maximum. A group for which the difference between positive incoming edges and negative incoming edges from outside the group, is maximum, is externally stable. Based on these notions of internal and external stability, we define two important problems: The *comprehensively stable group problem* and the *internally stable group problem*. Given an integer k, the comprehensively stable group problem deals with finding a group of k nodes that satisfies both internal stability and external stability. This problem is applicable in the context of finding trustworthy well-functioning committees to take decisions in signed networks. Given an integer k, the internally stable group problem deals with finding a group of k nodes that satisfies internal stability. In this paper, we first study the computational aspects of these two problems. We first prove that both these problems are hard computationally. We then present computationally efficient algorithms for these problems that are approximate in spirit. We then show the efficacy of the proposed algorithms by using real life signed social networks.

Keywords: Signed social networks · Directed graphs · Stable groups · Team formation · Committee selection · Approximation algorithm

1 Introduction

Online social networks offer several opportunities to discover interesting behavioral patterns as well as useful knowledge patterns [12,13]. There has been significant interest from users in terms of participating in such online social networks wherein participation refers to registration or engagement with other users. All users on such social networking platforms form connections amongst each other

© Springer Nature Singapore Pte Ltd. 2019
M. Singh et al. (Eds.): ICACDS 2019, CCIS 1045, pp. 164–176, 2019.
https://doi.org/10.1007/978-981-13-9939-8_15

using tweets, votes, posts etc. Through these connections, users develop rich relationships with one another. However, as pointed out in [13], most of the existing algorithms/approaches that make use of network analysis generally assume these connections to be simply *unsigned* pairwise links. Such assumptions fail to capture the richness of the relationships among the users. These assumptions can lead to analysis that is inaccurate or even flawed in some cases, depending on the role and strength of negative links in the context of the particular social network. For example, in the case of social influence propagation, it has been assumed that each connection will try to positively influence a node about a particular idea/product. However it is not always the case, since on online social networks, users are also negatively influenced by some of their connections where the action done by a "foe" prompts the person to do the opposite action (such as voting for a competitor candidate) [14]. Yet another scenario that accommodates negative links is the *disapproval* voting systems which allow a user to cast negative votes [4]. Therefore, it is important for network analysis algorithms to account for the presence of sign on edges in the network.

We refer to a social network as signed if there exists both positive and negative links [12,13] in the literature. In such networks, the *sign* of each edge refers to either positive or negative. Depending on the underlying context, positive sign of an edge indicates friendship or trust or compatibility; and negative sign of an edge indicates agony or distrust or incompatibility.

We are interested in defining and finding a *stable* group in a social network by taking into account the *sign* of the edges. In particular, we propose two types of stability for any group of nodes in the signed social network and we refer them *internal stability* and *external stability*. Internal stability of a group of people (or nodes) requires more positive edges and less negative edges among them. External stability of a group requires more number of positive edges and less number of negative edges directed towards them from the members outside the group.

By building upon the above two notions of stability, we deal with two problems in this paper. In the first problem, ***Comprehensively Stable Group*** (CSG) problem, we define a stable group to be both externally stable and internally stable. Finding such groups are relevant in situations where both types of edges – intra group and incoming edges to the group are important. As an example, to form a committee which needs to come with a decision that affects the entire population, it is important that the committee selected should minimize distrust by having less negative edges among themselves and maximize trust by having more positive edges among themselves. If this is not met, it might lead to a situation where the chosen committee fails to make a decision. Similarly, it is also important that the members in the formed committee are trusted by other non-committee members of the network, for the committee to be trusted and the decision to be widely accepted.

The next problem deals with forming ***Internally Stable Group*** (ISG) which requires more positive edges in the group and less negative edges. Such a scenario is important where a team needs to be formed which can work constructively and efficiently on a project. As an illustration, assume that a manager has to choose a team of K individuals to work on a project and he is aware of the sign of the edges that exist between individuals in the network. The manager now wants to choose a team having more positive edges and less negative edges. If however manager chooses a team which consists of individuals who do not work well with each other (i.e. has a lot number of negative edges amongst each other), then it is highly probable that the team won't be able to function properly and deliver projects in time.

Both the problems support several practical use cases. These problems have not been considered before in the context of signed networks. Given an integer k, the problem of finding stable groups of size k has relevance in the domain of both committee formation and team formation. Both of the problems are challenging. Naïve algorithms for both of the problems require searching over all the subsets of size k of set of vertices (V) in the network. This means searching over $\binom{V}{k}$ potential subsets and then choosing the best set which maximizes the given objective function, depending on the problem.

1.1 Our Contributions

The key contributions can be summarized as follows:

- *Algorithms:* We propose scalable and efficient greedy algorithms to solve both the CSG and ISG problems.
- *Proofs and Analysis:* Showing that both the problems are computationally hard, and further show the approximation guarantees of the greedy algorithms so proposed.
- *Experimental Evaluations:* We test our approach using the data arising from signed social networks and some of them are large in size. We show that our methods are scalable and effective.

Below describes the contents of various sections in this paper. Section 2 provides a brief summary of relevant research work from the literature. Section 3 presents a few notations and formally defines the proposed problems. Section 4 presents the key results derived in this paper. Then Sect. 5 shows the experimental results and Sect. 6 formally concludes this paper by bringing out certain important future research directions.

2   Relevant Work

The relevant work in the literature can be categorized into two categories: signed social network analysis and team formation problems.

Analysis of Signed Social Networks: There has been a lot of papers recently which talk about analysis of signed social networks. Brzozowski et al. studied the positive and negative relationships that exist on Essembly [5]. Kunegis et al. computed the global properties of the foe/friendship Slashdot network [10].

Leskovec et al. [13] dealt with evaluating the theories of signed social networks. Signed social networks have also been used in various existing problem settings such as link-prediction [1,6,13,18], community detection [2,17] and information diffusion [14]. Most of the modern day online social networks do not explicitly model the negative relations between users. Therefore, another line of work exists in trying to infer the negative edges from other auxiliary information available on these platforms. Hassan et al. proposed an approach to construct a signed social network from a text in an online discussion post [8]. Maniu et al. also presents an approach to infer signed social network from interactions on user generated content in Wikipedia [16].

Team Formation Problem: Lappas *et al.* deals with finding a team of people which satisfies the required skill set by minimizing the communication cost among the team [11]. A lot of work has been done after this seminal work. Majumder *et al.* considers capacitated version of the problem of forming teams [15]. Later Aris *et al.* focused on studying online variant of forming teams [3]. However, there is no prior work in the literature that deals with team formation over signed social networks.

3   Notation and Definitions

Let us first define a directed and unweighted graph $G = (V, E)$, where V is a set of n nodes and E is a set of m directed edges among the vertices in V. We define a sign function $s : E \rightarrow \{+1, -1\}$ such that, for each directed edge $(i, j) \in E$, let $s(i, j)$ denote the sign of the edge (i, j) and we interpret this as follows: if $s(i, j) = +1$, then the sign of the edge (i, j) is positive; else if $s(i, j) = -1$, then negative. From now on, we refer to the tuple (G, s) as the *signed graph*. Now, we formally define the two proposed notions: internal stability and external stability.

Definition 1 (Internal Stability). *For any $S \subseteq V$, we define internal stability of S to be the difference between the number of positive edges among the nodes in S and the number of negative edges among the nodes in S. That is, internal stability of S is $|\{(i, j) \ni i \in S, j \in S \; s(i, j) = +1\}| - |\{(i, j) \ni i \in S, j \in S \; s(i, j) = -1\}|$.*

Definition 2 (External Stability). *For any $S \subseteq V$, let $I^+(S)$ to be the set of all nodes in $V \setminus S$ from which there is at least one positive edge to some node in S. Also let $I^-(S)$ to be the set of all nodes in $V \setminus S$ from which there is at least one negative edge to some node in S. We define external stability of S to be the difference between the number of nodes in $I^+(S)$ and the number of nodes in $I^-(S)$.*

Note that the external stability of a set is defined in terms of the nodes outside the set having positive/negative edges to the nodes in the set. This is because we are interested in measuring the trust of the set from the view point of the nodes outside that set. Though there could be other ways of defining the external stability using positive and negative edges, we work with the above definition in this paper. We now formally define both the CSG problem and the ISG problem.

3.1   Comprehensively Stable Group (CSG) Problem

Let $S \subset V$ be a subset of vertices in G. Let $N(S)$ to be the set of all nodes from which either at least a positive or at least a negative edge exists to some node in S. Now define $I^+(S)$ to be the set of nodes having at least one positive link from some node in $V \setminus S$ to S and, on similar lines, define $I^-(S)$ to be the set of nodes having at least one negative link from some node in $V \setminus S$ to S. That is, $I^+(S) = \{j \in N(S) \ : \exists i \in S, \ \ni \ s(j,i) = +1\}$ and $I^-(S) = \{j \in N(S) \ : \exists i \in S, \ \ni \ s(j,i) = -1\}$. Then, the internal stability of the set S is $|\{(i,j) \ \ni \ i \in S, \ j \in S \ s(i,j) = +1\}| - |\{(i,j) \ \ni \ i \in S, \ j \in S \ s(i,j) = -1\}|$ and the external stability of the set S is $|I^+(S)| - |I^-(S)|$.

Definition 3 (Comprehensive Stability). *The comprehensive stability of a set of nodes is defined to be the sum of its internal stability and its external stability. We denote this by $\sigma_C(.)$.*

That is, for the set $S \subseteq V$, its comprehensive stability is $\sigma_C(S) = |\{(i,j) \ \ni \ i \in S, \ j \in S \ s(i,j) = +1\}| - |\{(i,j) \ \ni \ i \in S, \ j \in S \ s(i,j) = -1\}| + |I^+(S)| - |I^-(S)|$. We now formally define the problem of identifying a group of specific size having maximum comprehensive stability.

Definition 4 (Comprehensively Stable Group (CSG) Problem). *Given a directed graph $G = (V, E)$ and an integer $k < |V|$, the problem of comprehensively stable group is to determine a set $S \subset V$ of size k such that $\sigma_C(S)$ is maximized.*

3.2   Internally Stable Group (ISG) Problem

Let $S \subset V$ be a subset of vertices in G. Then, the internal stability of the set S is $|\{(i,j) \ \ni \ i \in S, \ j \in S \ s(i,j) = +1\}| - |\{(i,j) \ \ni \ i \in S, \ j \in S \ s(i,j) = -1\}|$. We denote the internal stability of a set to be $\sigma_I(.)$. We now formally define the problem of identifying a group of specific size having maximum internal stability.

Definition 5 (Internally Stable Group (ISG) Problem). *Given a directed graph $G = (V, E)$ and an integer $k < |V|$, the problem of internally stable group is to determine a set $S \subset V$ of size k such that $\sigma_I(S)$ is maximized.*

4   Our Approach

Here we initially consider the CSG problem and then we consider ISG problem.

4.1   Algorithm for the CSG Problem

We first show that the comprehensively stable group problem is computationally hard by a reduction from the well known set cover problem.

Lemma 1. *The comprehensively stable group problem is NP-hard.*

Proof: Consider an arbitrary instance of the NP-complete set cover problem, defined by a collection of subsets $T_1, T_2, \ldots, T_m$ of a ground set $U = \{1, 2, \ldots, n\}$. We wish to know whether there exist k of these subsets whose union is equal to U. We show that this can be viewed as a special case of the CSG problem.

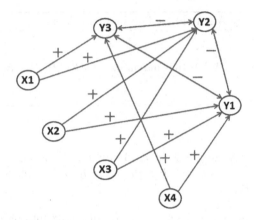

Fig. 1. A stylized example corresponding to the CSG problem

Given any arbitrary instance of the set cover problem, we construct a directed graph (G, s) with positive and negative links as follows. Introduce a node x_i in G corresponding to each element $i \in U$ and also introduce a node y_j in G corresponding to each set T_j. This leads to a total of $n + m$ nodes in G. Now create signed edges in G as follows: introduce a directed edge (x_i, y_j) with positive sign whenever $i \in T_j$; and introduce two directed edges (y_{j1}, y_{j2}) and (y_{j2}, y_{j1}) both with negative signs for every pair T_{j1} and T_{j2}. This leads to a total of $|T_1| + |T_2| + \ldots + |T_m|$ positive edges and a total of $m(m-1)$ negative edges in G. Figure 1 presents a stylized example of constructing G from the following instance of the set cover problem: $U = \{1, 2, 3, 4\}$, $T_1 = \{2, 3, 4\}$, $T_2 = \{1, 2, 3\}$, $T_3 = \{1, 4\}$, and $k = 2$.

The set cover problem is equivalent to deciding if there is a set S of k nodes in G such that $\sigma_C(S) = n - m - k$. If we have a solution to the set cover problem, then we can construct S with all vertices corresponding to the sets in the solution of the set cover problem. In this case, clearly $\sigma_C(S) = [n - (m - k)] - 2k$ because $|I^+(S)| = n$ (as the nodes in S correspond to a solution of the set cover problem), $|I^-(S)| = m - k$ (as the k vertices corresponding to the sets in the solution of set cover problem have negative links to $m - k$ vertices in G) and the term $-2k$

corresponds to internal stability. On the other hand, if we have a set S with k nodes such that $\sigma_C(S) = n - m - k$, then the set cover problem is also solvable as the sets corresponding to the nodes in S form a solution to the set cover problem.   ∎

Since the comprehensively stable group problem is computationally hard, we now present an approximation algorithm as shown in Algorithm 1. There are k iterations in Algorithm 1 and in each iteration of this algorithm we greedily select a node that maximizes the comprehensive stability of the currently constructed set S. In the following lemma, we derive the approximation guarantee of Algorithm 1.

Algorithm 1. Greedy Algorithm - The CSG Problem

1: Set $S \leftarrow \phi$
2: **for** $i = 1$ to k **do**
3:    Choose a node $n_i \in V \setminus S$ that maximizes $\sigma_C(S \cup \{n_i\}) - \sigma_C(S)$
4:    Set $S \leftarrow S \cup \{n_i\}$
5: **end for**

Lemma 2. *The greedy algorithm (i.e. Algorithm 1) approximates the comprehensive stability of any set of size k within a ratio of $(1 - e^{-H_k})$ where H_k is the k-th harmonic number.*

Proof: Let S^* be the optimal set of size k with maximum spread and $\sigma_C(S^*)$ be the value of its spread. Let S_i be the set of all nodes chosen by the end of i-th iteration of Algorithm 1 and X_i be the contribution of the i-th node towards maximizing the spread. That is $X_i = \sigma_C(S_i) - \sigma_C(S_{i-1})$ (note that $S_0 = \phi$). First, consider X_1 and the following holds:

$$X_1 \geq \frac{\sigma_C(S^*)}{k} \tag{1}$$

$$\Rightarrow \quad \sigma_C(S^*) - X_1 \leq \sigma_C(S^*)\left(1 - \frac{1}{k}\right). \tag{2}$$

Next, consider X_2 and the following holds:

$$X_2 \geq \frac{\sigma_C(S^*) - X_1}{k - 1} \tag{3}$$

$$\Rightarrow \quad \sigma_C(S^*) - X_1 - X_2 \leq \sigma_C(S^*)\left(1 - \frac{1}{k}\right)\left(1 - \frac{1}{k-1}\right). \tag{4}$$

Proceeding along similar lines, we get

$$\sigma_C(S^*) - \sum_{i=1}^{i=k} X_i \leq \sigma_C(S^*) \Pi_{i=1}^{i=k}\left(1 - \frac{1}{k-i+1}\right). \tag{5}$$

$$\Rightarrow \frac{\sum_{i=1}^{i=k} X_i}{\sigma_C(S^*)} \geq 1 - \Pi_{i=1}^{i=k}\left(1 - \frac{1}{k-i+1}\right)$$
$$\geq 1 - e^{-\frac{1}{k}} e^{-\frac{1}{k-1}} \ldots e^{-1}$$
$$= 1 - e^{-H_k}.$$

This completes the proof. ∎

4.2   Algorithm for the ISG Problem

Here we first show that the ISG problem is NP-hard. Then we present an approximation algorithm to address this problem.

We show the computational intractability of ISG problem by a reduction from the well known dense k-subgraph problem [7,9]. Towards this end, we first define the density of a graph as follows.

Definition 6 (Density). *The density $d_{G'}$ of a graph $G' = (V', E')$ is its average degree. That is, $d_{G'} = \frac{2|E'|}{|V'|}$. When G' is clear from the context, we simply denote the density to be d.*

Definition 7 (DkS Problem). *The dense k-subgraph (DkS) problem has as input an undirected graph $G' = (V', E')$ (on n vertices) and a parameter k. The output is G^*, a subgraph of G' induced on k vertices, such that G^* is of maximum density and we denote this by $d^*(G', k)$.*

It is known that the dense k-subgraph problem is a NP-hard [7,9].

Lemma 3. *The internally stable group problem is NP-hard.*

Proof: We prove the claim by a reduction from the dense k-subgraph problem. An instance of the dense k-subgraph problem consists of a graph $G' = (V', E')$ and a constant k, and the solution is a maximum density subgraph with k nodes. Let $n = |V'|$. Using this, we now construct an instance of the ISG problem. In other words, we construct a signed graph (G, s) as follows. There are $n+1$ nodes in G where the first n nodes corresponds to the n nodes in G'. For each edge $(i, j) \in E'$, we construct two positive signed edges in G such that $s(i, j) = +1$ and $s(j, i) = +1$. Also we create a negative edge from node n to node $n+1$ in G. That is, we have a total of $n+1$ nodes and $2|E|+1$ signed edges in G. Now, it is easy to see that a set $S \subseteq V$ such that $|S| = k$ is the solution to the dense k-subgraph problem if and only if it is a solution to the ISG problem. The ISG problem is a special case of the dense k-subgraph problem which implies that the ISG problem is NP-hard. ∎

Table 1. Description of three benchmark signed social network data sets

Data set	No. of nodes	No. of edges	Fraction of positive edges	Fraction of negative edges
Slashdot	82144	549202	77.39%	22.61%
Epinions	131828	841372	85.29%	14.71%
Wiki-Vote	7118	107080	78.41%	21.59%

Since the internally stable group problem is computationally hard, we present an approximation algorithm as shown in Algorithm 2. In this algorithm, the choice of the first node into the final solution set is tricky. Since we look for internal stability, any node in the given network qualifies to be the first node in the final solution. Hence we iterate over each node being chosen as the first node in the solution set and then we choose the remaining $k - 1$ nodes in $k - 1$ iterations in a greedy fashion that maximizes the internal stability of the currently constructed solution set. In what follows, we derive the approximation guarantee of Algorithm 2.

Algorithm 2. Greedy Algorithm - The ISG Problem

1: $S^* \leftarrow \phi$
2: **for** $j = 1$ to $|V|$ **do**
3:     Set $S \leftarrow \{j\}$
4:     **for** $i = 2$ to k **do**
5:         Choose a node $n_i \in V \setminus S$ that maximizes $\sigma_I(S \cup \{n_i\}) - \sigma_I(S)$
6:         Set $S \leftarrow S \cup \{n_i\}$
7:     **end for**
8:     **if** $\sigma_I(S^*) < \sigma_I(S)$ **then**
9:         $S^* \leftarrow S$
10:    **end if**
11: **end for**

Lemma 4. *The greedy algorithm (i.e. Algorithm 2) approximates the internal stability of any set of size k within a ratio of $(1 - e^{-H_k})$ where H_k is the k-th harmonic number.*

The proof of this lemma is straightforward using the arguments similar to that in Lemma 2.

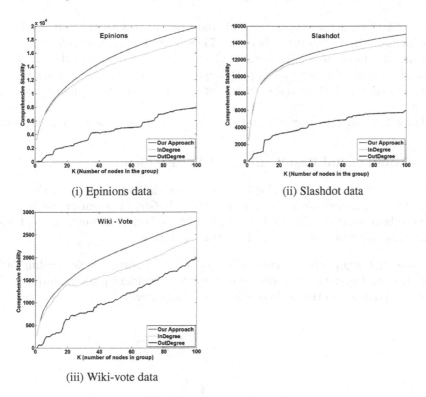

(i) Epinions data   (ii) Slashdot data

(iii) Wiki-vote data

Fig. 2. Performance comparison of the proposed algorithm for the CSG problem against heuristics on three benchmark network data sets: Epinions, Slashdot, and WikiVote

5   Experimental Evaluation

Here we demonstrate the efficacy of the proposed algorithms using three benchmark signed social network data sets. We now describe these data sets briefly.

1. Slashdot Data Set [13]: This social media platform is a news platform with focus on technology-driven topics. This platform allows users to label other users with positive and negative labels. There are 82144 users in this network with 549202 links among them. Of all these links, 77.39% are positive and the remaining negative [13].

2. Epinions Data Set [13]: This social media platform supports who-trust-whom relations among the consumers. All the trust relationships interact and form a *Web of Trust*, which is then combined with the review ratings to determine which reviews should be shown to the user. There are 131828 users in this network and 841372 links among them. Among these links, 85.29% are positive and the remaining negative [13].

3. Wiki-Vote Data Set [12,13]: This data set deals with the voting relationships of users in Wikipedia. There are 7118 users in this network and 107080 links among them. Here links are signed wherein a positive (negative) link indicates (does not indicate) the support/approval of one user to another user for admin status. Of all these links, 78.41% are positive and the remaining negative [12,13].

Table 1 briefly describes the statistics associated with these three data sets.

5.1   Experimental Results for the CSG Problem

In the context of the CSG problem, we evaluate the performance of the greedy algorithm (i.e. Algorithm 1) (and we refer to this *Greedy* hereafter) with that of two standard heuristics for the CSG problem based on well known graph theory techniques. We now outline these heuristics as follows:

- In the first algorithm, we choose the top k nodes sorted in descending order of their in-degree where in-degree is the sum of incident positive and negative edges. We refer to this *InDegree* heuristic hereafter.

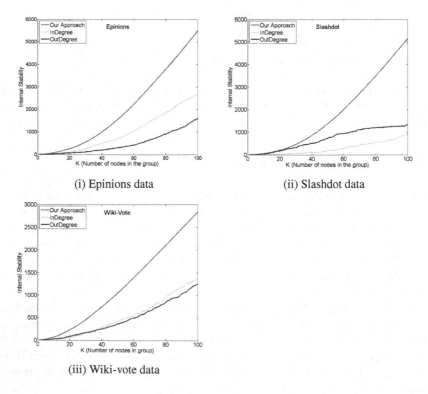

(i) Epinions data   (ii) Slashdot data

(iii) Wiki-vote data

Fig. 3. Performance comparison of the proposed algorithm for the ISG problem against heuristics on three benchmark network data sets: Epinions, Slashdot, and WikiVote

– In the second algorithm, we choose the top k nodes sorted in descending order of their out-degree, where out-degree is the sum of outgoing positive and negative edges. These top k nodes are considered as a group and it's performance is evaluated in terms of comprehensive stability. We refer to this *OutDegree* heuristic hereafter.

We conduct experimentation using the above three data sets. Figure 2 shows that the performance of our proposed algorithm is superior to that of the above heuristics.

5.2 Experimental Results for the ISG Problem

For the ISG problem, we show the performance of the greedy algorithm (i.e. Algorithm 2) (and we refer to this *Greedy* hereafter) with that of two standard heuristics as defined above. We conduct experimentation of these algorithms and heuristics using the above three data sets. From Fig. 3, it is clear that our proposed greedy algorithm outperforms the heuristics.

6 Conclusions

This paper focused on enriching the analysis of signed social networks by considering two new problems. We presented the formal definitions of these two problems and then dealt with the computational aspects of the same. We also validated the efficacy of the proposed algorithms by using three real world signed social network data sets.

The work in this paper can be extended in several ways. One interesting direction for future work could be to see whether we can further improve the approximation guarantee of the algorithms proposed for the CSG and ISG problems. Another interesting direction for future work is to find groups of nodes that not only satisfy the stability requirements, but also the *connectivity* requirements. Note that the stable groups that we determine both in the CSG problem context and the ISG problem context need not be connected.

References

1. Agrawal, P., Garg, V., Narayanam, R.: Link label prediction in signed social networks. In: Proceedings of 23rd International Joint Conference on Artificial Intelligence (IJCAI) (2013)
2. Amelio, A., Pizzuti, C.: Community mining in signed networks: a multiobjective approach. In: ASONAM, pp. 95–99 (2013)
3. Anagnostopoulos, A., Becchetti, L., Castillo, C., Gionis, A., Leonardi, S.: Online team formation in social networks. In: Proceedings of 21st International Conference on World Wide Web, pp. 839–848 (2012)
4. Brams, S.J., Fishburn, P.C.: Approval Voting. Birkhauser, Boston (1983)
5. Brzozowski, M.J., Hogg, T., Szabo, G.: Friends and foes: ideological social networking. In: Proceedings of the ACM SIGCHI Conference on Human Factors in Computing Systems (CHI) (2008)

6. Chiang, K.Y., Natarajan, N., Tewari, A., Dhillon, I.S.: Exploiting longer cycles for link prediction in signed networks. In: Proceedings of ACM CIKM, pp. 1157–1162 (2011)
7. Feige, U., Kortsarz, G., Peleg, D.: The dense k-subgraph problem. Algorithmica **29**, 410–421 (2001)
8. Hassan, A., Abu-Jbara, A., Radev, D.: Detecting subgroups in online discussions by modeling positive and negative relations among participants. In: Proceeding of EMNLP-CoNLL 2012 Proceedings of the 2012 Joint Conference on Empirical Methods in Natural Language Processing and Computational Natural Language Learning, pp. 59–70 (2012)
9. Khuller, S., Saha, B.: On finding dense subgraphs. In: Proceedings of ICALP, pp. 597–608 (2009)
10. Kunegis, J., Lommatzsch, A., Bauckhage, C.: The slashdot zoo: mining a social network with negative edges. In: Proceedings of 18th WWW, pp. 740–750 (2009)
11. Lappas, T., Liu, K., Terzi, E.: Finding a team of experts in social networks. In: Proceedings of International Conference on Knowledge Discovery and Data Mining, pp. 467–476 (2009)
12. Leskovec, J., Huttenlocher, D., Kleinberg, J.M.: Predicting positive and negative links in online social networks. In: Proceedings of World Wide Web (WWW), pp. 641–650 (2010)
13. Leskovec, J., Huttenlocher, D., Kleinberg, J.M.: Signed networks in social media. In: Proceedings of the 28th ACM SIGCHI Conference on Human Factors in Computing Systems (CHI), pp. 1361–1370 (2010)
14. Li, Y., Chen, W., Wang, Y., Zhang, Z.L.: Influence diffusion dynamics and influence maximization in social networks with friend and foe relationships. In: Proceedings of the Web Search and Data Mining (WSDM) (2013)
15. Majumder, A., Datta, S., Naidu, K.V.M.: Capacitated team formation problem on social networks. In: Proceedings of 18th ACM SIGKDD International Conference on Knowledge Discovery and Data Mining, pp. 1005–1013 (2012)
16. Silviu, M., Bogdan, C., Talel, A.: Building a signed network from interactions in Wikipedia. In: DBSocial, pp. 19–24 (2011)
17. Traag, V.A., Bruggeman, J.: Community detection in networks with positive and negative links. Phys. Rev. **80**, 036115 (2009)
18. Yang, S.H., Smola, A.J., Long, B., Zha, H., Chang, Y.: Friend or frenemy? Predicting signed ties in social networks. In: Proceedings of SIGIR, pp. 555–564 (2012)

Deep Convolution Neural Network Based Denoiser for Mammographic Images

Gurprem Singh[✉], Ajay Mittal, and Naveen Aggarwal

UIET, Panjab University, Chandigarh, India
gurpremsingh94@gmail.com, {ajaymittal,navagg}@pu.ac.in

Abstract. Denoising is an important image pre-processing operation required to improve the image quality. In the past, several image denoising solutions have been put forth with varying performances. Recently, deep-learning based approaches have given better results than conventional algorithms. While these methods offer promising results on denoising of natural images, their application to medical imaging is yet to be fully explored. In this study, mammographic images, which are generally corrupted with Gaussian noise, have been effectively denoised using a deep convolution neural network. The model proposed in this work outshines various existing state-of-the-art solutions. Our model achieves a structural similarity index (SSIM) of 0.98 and value of 41.53 dB for peak signal to noise ratio (PSNR).

Keywords: Image processing · Deep-learning · Computer vision · Convolution neural networks · Mammographs · SSIM · PSNR

1 Introduction

Images are unavoidably corrupted with different kinds of noise distributions due to several factors occurring during acquisition, transmission and storage processes. In general, several noise distributions like Gaussian, Poisson, Rayleigh, Rician, Speckle, Salt-and-Pepper degrade the images. In the case of X-ray images, Gaussian and Poisson noise distributions are mostly present. Mammograms which are X-ray images of breasts are susceptible to corruption by Gaussian noise. In X-ray imaging, there exists a trade-off between the patient's exposure to radiation and the quality of the image. The radiation dosage cannot exceed a certain threshold to prevent patients from its harmful effects. However, decreasing radiation dosage leads to the addition of noise to output images [1]. In case of medical domain, accuracy and precision of the scans is of supreme importance for the purpose of diagnosis, determining the stage and level of disease, identification of tumorous or unwanted tissue masses. Noise can add artefacts to these images leading to false diagnosis, thus obstructing the proper treatment of the patient. The noisy image also hampers effective feature extraction from images. Thus, image quality is significant for diagnosis and patient care. The machines, as well as humans, require noise-free images for proper analysis. In

© Springer Nature Singapore Pte Ltd. 2019
M. Singh et al. (Eds.): ICACDS 2019, CCIS 1045, pp. 177–187, 2019.
https://doi.org/10.1007/978-981-13-9939-8_16

order to filter out the noise to enhance image quality, various image processing techniques are used.

Image denoising aims to eliminate or reduce the degradation caused by noise so as to obtain an image with enhanced quality to be used in further applications and analysis. It is a low-level computer vision task, which acts as a base for other high-level tasks like segmentation, classification, etc. Mathematically it can be represented as:

$$\hat{I}(x, y) = I(x, y) + N(x, y) \tag{1}$$

where some noise N(x,y) corrupts the original image I(x, y) producing $\hat{I}$(x, y), the noisy image. The denoising algorithms try to estimate I(x, y) from $\hat{I}$(x, y) while assuming N(x, y) to be following a specific well-defined function. Researchers have proposed several methods in the last few decades for image denoising. There are classical techniques including but not limited to simple linear and non-linear filters. Then there are frequency domain noise filtering algorithms using discrete Fourier transforms, wavelets, etc. Further, there are fuzzy based noise detection and filtering methods, dictionary learning and sparse representation based algorithms. Additionally, Block-Matching and 3D filtering (BM3D) [2], Weighted Nuclear Norm Minimization (WNNM) [3], Non-Local means filtering (NL) [4] are some techniques utilising domain transformations. With recent advances in computation powers, development of deep-learning solutions has exploded. The deep-learning solutions based on multi-layer perceptron, convolution neural networks, convolution auto-encoders have been proposed for natural image denoising. However, medical imaging still needs more exploration by the deep-learning solutions. In 2016, Convolution Denoising auto-encoder (CNN DAE) [5] was proposed for the task. However, the network used was shallow, and the image size used was 64 × 64. The level of detail is vital for disease diagnosis in medical images. In the case of mammograms, one needs a noise-free image for detection of lesions and calcification masses.

In this work, a deep CNN model trained with X-ray images of mammograms is presented. The images are resized from the original size of 1024 × 1024 to 256 × 256, and 512 × 512 to study how resizing of images impacts the denoising performance of deep CNN model. The results of our model are compared with state-of-the-art methods like BM3D, WNNM, CNN DAE.

The paper is organized as follows: Section 2 explains previous related work. Section 3 discusses the methods and materials which includes model architecture details, dataset details, and experimental setup. In Sect. 4, results and discussion are presented. Finally, in Sect. 5 the conclusion is drawn and the scope for further work is presented.

2   Related Work

Image denoising methods have evolved from simple median filtering to domain transforms and non-local filters; from dictionary-learning and sparse-coding based methods to more recent deep-learning based solutions. The following subsections give a brief about traditional and deep-learning based methods:

2.1 Traditional Methods

Before the popularity of deep-learning based solutions, various methods were proposed for image denoising. There existed various local filters and their variations. These are further divided into linear and non-linear filters. Linear filters include mean, harmonic, contra-harmonic filters, etc. Non-linear filters, also called order-statistic filters, include median, min-max, Wiener filters, etc. Then there are non-local filters like NL means which use self-similarity between patches and calculates a denoised output based on the weighted average of these patches.

Furthermore, there are wavelets [6], discrete Fourier and cosine transform, curvelets [7] which work in a transformed representation of an image and filter out the noisy coefficients before inverting image back to the spatial domain. The Bayes-Least-Squares with a Gaussian-Scale-Mixture (BLS-GSM) [8] and BM3D also fall in transform domain filtering methods. BM3D separates the 2D noisy patches of the image into 3D data groups. The 3D data group is composed of 2D transforms like DCT, DFT etc. within a group along with 1D Haar transform across groups. BM3D makes use of self-similarity between different image patches. In WNNM, image non-local self-similarity is exploited for the task of denoising.

Furthermore, there are dictionary-based and sparse-coding based denoising methods like K-SVD [9]. It is an iterative procedure based on the generalization of the k-means clustering algorithm. The intuition behind this is that the patches in estimated image $\hat{I}(x, y)$ can be depicted as a linear combination of fewer patches from the learned dictionary, which may be static or even dynamic. However, most of these methods have been outperformed by more recent deep-learning based solutions. In Subsect. 2.2, we briefly discuss the evolution of CNNs for medical image analysis and then outline the contemporary deep-learning based image denoising methods.

2.2 Deep-Learning Methods

Since the 1990s, various medical image analysis tasks like micro-calcifications detection in mammogram images [10], lung nodules detection in CT scan images [11] have utilized CNNs. With the coming of GPU capabilities, the CNN usage was revived with better performance. The examples include, but not limited to, lesion classification [12,13], landmark, region and organ localization [14,15], object or lesion detection [16], lesion, organ or substructure segmentation [17], image registration [18], content-based image retrieval, image enhancement [19]. However, other medical image enhancement applications like denoising, intensity normalisation have only observed a restrained usage of deep-learning algorithms [20]. In [21], the authors used an ensemble of deep neural networks using restricted Boltzmann machine for dynamic contrast-enhanced magnetic resonance images of the human brain and [5], a simple shallow network of convolution auto-encoders was used to learn weights for denoising on the mini-MIAS dataset of mammogram images (MMM) [22] and a dental radiography dataset

[23]. However, denoisers based on deep-learning for natural images have seen a lot of development in recent past.

Deep convolution neural networks have been in use for natural image restoration tasks for quite some time now. In [24], Multi-Layer Perceptron (MLP) with several hidden layers was used for image denoising. MLP learns to map noisy image patches onto clean ones. Learning weights in MLPs can be used for several kinds of noise ranging from Gaussian, Poisson, Rician, etc. However, MLPs may pose problems of overfitting and vanishing gradient on the increase in depth. Authors in [25] used a simple convolutional neural network for this task. The structure of CNN provide flexibility to deal with image data and it is adaptable to several kinds of noises corrupting the images without any major changes to the method or architecture. Several advances have been made in case of CNNs like learning and training methods, regularizations, activations like the rectified linear unit and so on. These advances provide better accuracy, less training time which can be utilised for various low and high-level computer vision tasks. Zhang et al. [26] utilised CNN with batch normalisation to propose a model which avoids accuracy saturation as faced by shallow networks. The model proposed in this study is adapted and inspired from DnCNN proposed by Kai Zhang et al. which gave an excellent denoising performance as compared to previous methods. However, the training image size was 180 × 180 which is not quite the case with mammograms, and the model was trained and tested for natural images only. Furthermore, On-Demand Learning algorithm with deep convolutional neural networks given by Gao et al. [27] in 2017 for image restoration to avoid the fixation problem faced by denoisers.

However, the major work has been concentrated on natural images, and there exists a substantial difference between medical imaging and natural imaging modalities. So, this work has been devoted to a specific case of X-ray imaging modality to achieve better denoising capabilities for mammograms. Furthermore, it has been observed that in most of the previous works the images used for experiments were resized to a smaller size. Therefore, this work also explores the impact of scaling down the training images on the performance of denoiser on the original image of a higher scale and size.

3   Methods and Materials

This section describes the method used for denoising the images, the dataset used, the implementation details and system configurations.

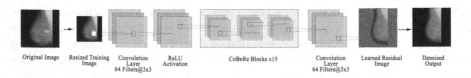

Fig. 1. Model architecture

3.1 Model Architecture

The deep CNN has been used for the denoising of mammogram images in this study. In the proposed CNN model the depth of the network is set to 17 layers as shown in Fig. 1. Convolution layer with 64 filters having (3, 3) size is fed with input images. This is followed by the rectified linear unit (ReLU) activation function layer. After this, there are 15 CoBnRe blocks which consist of 3 parts. Firstly, the convolution layer with 64 filters of size (3, 3). Then the second part applies batch normalisation on the output of the convolution layer. ReLU activation function is further applied to this for non-linearity. In the end, there is a convolution layer which estimates a residual noisy image consisting of one feature map from the output of 15th CoBnRe block. This residual noisy image is subtracted from the noisy input image to get denoised output.

3.2 Training and Testing Data

MIAS-mini(MMM) [22] dataset is used for all the experiments conducted during the study. In the dataset, there are 322 images of mammograms available and all the images are originally of the size 1024×1024. Out of these, 22 images are used as test images in each case and the rest of the data is used to train the model. Two different cases, as outlined in Subsect. 3.3, of image size are considered to study the impact of the resizing training image on the performance of denoiser.

3.3 Experiments

Two cases are considered for the experiments and the training images are prepared by resizing the original images. The two cases are outlined in Table 1. 300 resized images were fed to the model for training and the corruption parameter for Gaussian noise has been set at $\sigma = 25$ and $\mu = 0$. Random Gaussian noise was added to the training image to generate a noisy image. The images were randomly rotated and flipped, in order to augment the training dataset. Keras [28], with tensorflow [29] backend, was used for implementing the model. The model was run on a system with Intel Xeon processor with NVidia M5000 Graphics Processing Unit (GPU). The models were run for fifty epochs with batch size 128 and at a learning rate of 0.001. Adam optimizer was used for learning weights with mean square error as the loss to be optimized. It took approximately 24 h for the model to converge in the case (a) and 70 h in the case (b).

Table 1. The experimental setup

Cases	Training image size	No. of images
Case (a)	256×256	300
Case (b)	512×512	300

4   Results and Discussion

SSIM measures degree of similarity between two images. In this index, one of the images is considered having perfect quality and the other is compared with this image as reference as given by Wang et al. [30]. SSIM is used to compare the results with CNN DAE. The result obtained by the proposed method proved to be significantly better. The average SSIM obtained is 0.98 as compared to 0.81 by CNN DAE as shown in Table 2. This shows that a deeper network outperforms a shallow convolution auto-encoder model. It should also be noted that the tests performed in CNN DAE were performed on 64×64 sized mammogram images, but the results for our model are obtained for 1024×1024 sized images. Our model performs better even for images bigger in size and resolution.

Table 2. Comparison of denoising performance based on SSIM

Method	SSIM (average)
CNN DAE	0.81
NLM	0.89
BM3D	0.92
WNNM	0.93
Proposed	**0.98**

PSNR metric is also employed to gauge the performance of the proposed denoiser with BM3D, WNNM and median filter. The codes for BM3D and WNNM are provided by the respective authors on their website [31,32]. PSNR is generally calculated to measure the quality between the original and reconstructed image. The higher the value of this metric, the superior the quality of the reconstructed output image. In Table 3, the comparison of proposed denoiser with traditional state-of-the-art methods on 22 test images of mammograms is presented. It can be observed that better results were obtained in case (b) of the proposed method where an input training image was resized to 512×512 rather than resizing to 256×256. It proves the robustness of the proposed method and additionally shows that re-sizing the training image can impact the performance of denoiser on test images carrying bigger size and higher resolution. Also, the graph presenting loss in Fig. 2 shows that the initial mean squared error loss is low in case (b) as compared to case (a). However, the impact of re-sizing needs further investigation and more in-depth analysis.

The fact that a deeper network is at a better position to learn the feature maps for noisy and clean image targets contribute to a better performance by the proposed model. Also, in the auto-encoder model, there is down-sampling of the input image by using maxpool layer. The image is then upsampled in the decoder phase to reconstruct the image. This maxpool operation reduces the dimensionality of the input data resulting in loss of information of the original

Table 3. Denoising performance compared with traditional methods based on PSNR

Image	BM3D	WNNM	Median	Case (a)	Case (b)
mdb301	40.36	38.55	31.89	41.46	**41.52**
mdb302	41.33	40.31	31.92	**42.79**	42.78
mdb303	40.73	38.89	31.92	41.89	**42.04**
mdb304	40.68	38.45	31.89	41.87	**41.92**
mdb305	40.09	38.33	31.90	41.11	**41.31**
mdb306	40.77	39.49	31.94	41.90	**42.09**
mdb307	39.26	36.59	31.90	40.23	**40.40**
mdb308	39.83	37.27	31.87	40.81	**41.00**
mdb309	39.81	38.16	31.9	40.81	**40.87**
mdb310	39.88	37.76	31.91	40.94	**41.02**
mdb311	39.97	36.88	31.92	41.13	**41.33**
mdb312	40.17	37.23	31.89	41.41	**41.44**
mdb313	39.56	36.82	31.87	40.32	**40.62**
mdb314	39.56	38.78	31.86	40.44	**40.53**
mdb315	39.67	36.85	31.93	**40.83**	40.82
mdb316	39.71	36.85	31.90	**40.87**	**40.87**
mdb317	42.27	39.61	31.94	**43.89**	43.61
mdb318	42.39	39.51	31.93	43.81	**43.89**
mdb319	39.50	36.91	31.86	40.58	**40.70**
mdb320	39.77	37.2	31.87	40.92	**40.99**
mdb321	40.47	38.26	31.90	**41.78**	41.72
mdb322	40.74	38.04	31.93	42.06	**42.12**
Average	40.23	38.03	31.90	41.45	**41.53**

image, which in turn reduces the resultant SSIM values. In the case of BM3D, the model behaves poorly when dissimilar patterns are observed in the image and the algorithm is unable to exploit the similarity of image patches. Even though mammographic images do not contain very dissimilar patches within the image, the method is still outperformed by the proposed solution. Not only the PSNR comparison but also the visual quality of the denoiser output show that WNNM smoothens the tissues and edges of breasts as shown in Figs. 3 and 4. Also, the denoised image of median filter still carries a grainy appearance. Even in case of BM3D output, the edges of breast appear grainy, whereas in the original image the edges are free from any distortion. Such smoothening and grainy artifacts can be disastrous for patient care as it may leave lesions and calcifications go undetected. However, in the results of the proposed method, the output image is significantly similar to the original image with an SSIM value of 0.9803.

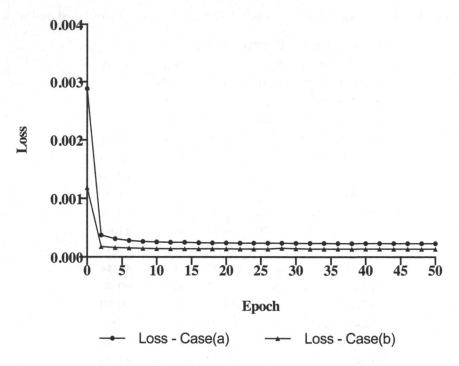

Fig. 2. Training loss with respect to epochs for case (a) and case (b) experiments

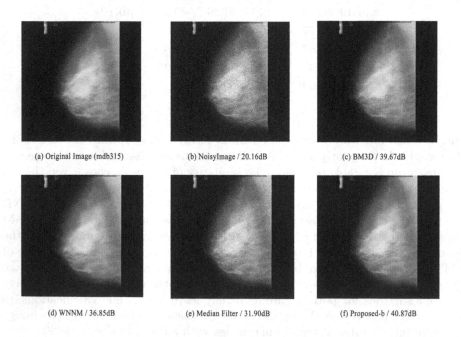

Fig. 3. Denoising result on mdb315 with Gaussian noise $\sigma = 25$

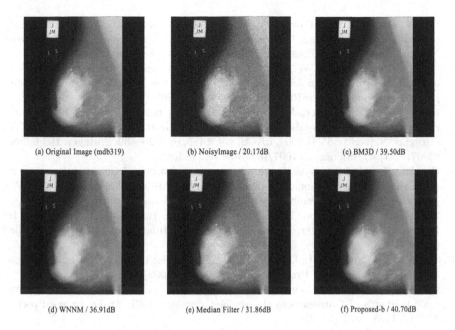

(a) Original Image (mdb319)   (b) NoisyImage / 20.17dB   (c) BM3D / 39.50dB

(d) WNNM / 36.91dB   (e) Median Filter / 31.86dB   (f) Proposed-b / 40.70dB

Fig. 4. Denoising result on mdb319 with Gaussian noise $\sigma = 25$

5   Conclusion

In this work, the application of deep convolution neural network is explored for denoising of mammogram images. The denoising performance of our method outperforms traditional state-of-the-art solutions like BM3D, WNNM and median filtering method based on the PSNR metric. The model also beats CNN DAE, a deep-learning method based on convolution auto-encoders, on SSIM metric by a great margin. It was also shown that performance gains were obtained if images were resized to 512×512 rather than 256×256 for training the model. However, re-sizing the images leads to loss of pixel level details and significant information which is crucial for further analysis and examination especially in case of medical imaging. Therefore, our future work would focus on finding a way to train the model without re-sizing the images. We would like to introduce changes like skip connections, residual learning, and other activation functions, like leaky ReLU, to the model so that the model converges faster and avoids gradient vanishing problem. It would also be of our interest to investigate the utility of transfer learning to achieve remarkable denoising outcome without the need to train model from scratch. Additionally, the model can also be extended to other noise distributions and several other medical imaging modalities.

References

1. Goldman, L.W.: Principles of CT: radiation dose and image quality. J. Nucl. Med. Technol. **35**(4), 213–225 (2007)

2. Dabov, K., Foi, A., Katkovnik, V., Egiazarian, K.: Image denoising with block-matching and 3D filtering. In: Image Processing: Algorithms and Systems, Neural Networks, and Machine Learning, vol. 6064, p. 606414 (2006)
3. Gu, S., Zhang, L., Zuo, W., Feng, X.: Weighted nuclear norm minimization with application to image denoising. In: Proceedings of the IEEE Conference on Computer Vision and Pattern Recognition, pp. 2862–2869 (2014)
4. Kervrann, C., Boulanger, J., Coupé, P.: Bayesian non-local means filter, image redundancy and adaptive dictionaries for noise removal. In: Sgallari, F., Murli, A., Paragios, N. (eds.) SSVM 2007. LNCS, vol. 4485, pp. 520–532. Springer, Heidelberg (2007). https://doi.org/10.1007/978-3-540-72823-8_45
5. Gondara, L.: Medical image denoising using convolutional denoising autoencoders. In: IEEE 16th International Conference on Data Mining Workshops (ICDMW), pp. 241–246. IEEE, December 2016
6. Simoncelli, E.P., Adelson, E.H.: Noise removal via Bayesian wavelet coring. In: Proceedings of IEEE International Conferences on Image Processing, pp. 379–382 (1996)
7. Starck, J.L., Candes, E.J., Donoho, D.L.: The curvelet transform for image denoising. IEEE Trans. Image Process. **11**(6), 670–684 (2002)
8. Portilla, J., Strela, V., Wainwright, M.J., Simoncelli, E.P.: Image denoising using scale mixtures of Gaussians in the wavelet domain. IEEE Trans. Image Process. **12**(11), 1338–1351 (2003)
9. Aharon, M., Elad, M., Bruckstein, A.: K-SVD: an algorithm for designing overcomplete dictionaries for sparse representation. IEEE Trans. Signal Process. **54**(11), 4311 (2006)
10. Zhang, W., Doi, K., Giger, M.L., Wu, Y., Nishikawa, R.M., Schmidt, R.A.: Computerized detection of clustered microcalcifications in digital mammograms using a shift-invariant artificial neural network. Med. Phys. **21**(4), 517–524 (1994)
11. Lo, S.C., Lou, S.L., Lin, J.S., Freedman, M.T., Chien, M.V., Mun, S.K.: Artificial convolution neural network techniques and applications for lung nodule detection. IEEE Trans. Med. Imaging **14**(4), 711–718 (1995)
12. Kawahara, J., Hamarneh, G.: Multi-resolution-tract CNN with hybrid pretrained and skin-lesion trained layers. In: Wang, L., Adeli, E., Wang, Q., Shi, Y., Suk, H.-I. (eds.) MLMI 2016. LNCS, vol. 10019, pp. 164–171. Springer, Cham (2016). https://doi.org/10.1007/978-3-319-47157-0_20
13. Shen, W., Zhou, M., Yang, F., Yang, C., Tian, J.: Multi-scale convolutional neural networks for lung nodule classification. In: Ourselin, S., Alexander, D.C., Westin, C.-F., Cardoso, M.J. (eds.) IPMI 2015. LNCS, vol. 9123, pp. 588–599. Springer, Cham (2015). https://doi.org/10.1007/978-3-319-19992-4_46
14. de Vos, B.D., Wolterink, J.M., de Jong, P.A., Viergever, M.A., Išgum, I.: 2D image classification for 3D anatomy localization: employing deep convolutional neural networks. In: Medical Imaging 2016: Image Processing, vol. 9784, p. 97841Y. International Society for Optics and Photonics, March 2016
15. Yang, D., Zhang, S., Yan, Z., Tan, C., Li, K., Metaxas, D.: Automated anatomical landmark detection ondistal femur surface using convolutional neural network. In: IEEE 12th International Symposium on Biomedical Imaging (ISBI), pp. 17–21. IEEE, April 2015
16. Dou, Q., et al.: Automatic detection of cerebral microbleeds from MR images via 3D convolutional neural networks. IEEE Trans. Med. Imaging **35**(5), 1182–1195 (2016)

17. Brosch, T., Tang, L.Y., Yoo, Y., Li, D.K., Traboulsee, A., Tam, R.: Deep 3D convolutional encoder networks with shortcuts for multiscale feature integration applied to multiple sclerosis lesion segmentation. IEEE Trans. Med. Imaging **35**(5), 1229–1239 (2016)

18. Miao, S., Wang, Z.J., Liao, R.: A CNN regression approach for real-time 2D/3D registration. IEEE Trans. Med. Imaging **35**(5), 1352–1363 (2016)

19. Oktay, O., et al.: Multi-input cardiac image super-resolution using convolutional neural networks. In: Ourselin, S., Joskowicz, L., Sabuncu, M.R., Unal, G., Wells, W. (eds.) MICCAI 2016. LNCS, vol. 9902, pp. 246–254. Springer, Cham (2016). https://doi.org/10.1007/978-3-319-46726-9_29

20. Litjens, G., et al.: A survey on deep learning in medical image analysis. Med. Image Anal. **42**, 60–88 (2017)

21. Benou, A., Veksler, R., Friedman, A., Riklin Raviv, T.: De-noising of contrast-enhanced MRI sequences by an ensemble of expert deep neural networks. In: Carneiro, G., et al. (eds.) LABELS/DLMIA -2016. LNCS, vol. 10008, pp. 95–110. Springer, Cham (2016). https://doi.org/10.1007/978-3-319-46976-8_11

22. Suckling, J., et al.: The mammographic image analysis society digital mammogram database exerpta medica. Int. Congr. Ser. **1069**, 375–378 (1994)

23. Wang, C.W., et al.: A benchmark for comparison of dental radiography analysis algorithms. Med. Image Anal. **31**, 63–76 (2016)

24. Burger, H.C., Schuler, C.J., Harmeling, S.: Image denoising: can plain neural networks compete with BM3D? In: IEEE Conference on Computer Vision and Pattern Recognition (CVPR), pp. 2392–2399. IEEE, June 2012

25. Jain, V., Seung, S.: Natural image denoising with convolutional networks. In: Advances in Neural Information Processing Systems, pp. 769–776 (2009)

26. Zhang, K., Zuo, W., Chen, Y., Meng, D., Zhang, L.: Beyond a Gaussian denoiser: residual learning of deep CNN for image denoising. IEEE Trans. Image Process. **26**(7), 3142–3155 (2017)

27. Gao, R., Grauman, K.: On-demand learning for deep image restoration. In: Proceedings of IEEE Conference on Computer Vision and Pattern Recognition, pp. 1086–1095, October 2017

28. Chollet, F.: Keras Github repository. https://github.com/keras-team/keras

29. Tensorflow. http://www.tensorflow.org

30. Wang, Z., Bovik, A.C., Sheikh, H.R., Simoncelli, E.P.: Image quality assessment: from error visibility to structural similarity. IEEE Trans. Image Process. **13**(4), 600–612 (2004)

31. Image and video denoising by sparse 3D transform-domain collaborative filtering. http://www.cs.tut.fi/~foi/GCF-BM3D/

32. Weighted Nuclear Norm Minimization for Image Denoising, Version 1.0. https://github.com/csjunxu/WNNM_CVPR2014

Detection of Brain Tumor Using Machine Learning Approach

Chadha Megha[⊠] and Jain Sushma

Thapar Institute of Engineering and Technology, Patiala, India
megha.chadha95@gmail.com, sjain@gmail.com

Abstract. Tumor in brain is one of the most dangerous diseases which if not detected at the early stages can even risk the life. Currently, the methods used by neurologists for analysis are not completely error free and states that manual segmentation isn't a good idea. This study presents machine learning based approach for segmentation of brain images and identification of tumor using SVM classification approach which improve the performance, minimize the complexity and works on real time data.

Keywords: Brain tumor · MR images · Segmentation · Detection techniques

1 Introduction

The study of e-health care systems and evolving technology in the recent times let radiologists provide better health care to the patients. Tumor in brain is the uncontrolled mass of tissues on the brain. It is divided into tissues having cancerous cells called benign tumor and tissues with non cancerous cells called malignant tumor. Tumors fall under grade I to grade IV according to World Health Organization [6] where grade I and II are called low grade tumors possessing slow growth. Grade III and IV are high grade tumors which grow rapidly as compared to low grade.

Benign tumor has homogeneity in structure containing active cancer cells. It falls under the category of grade of I or II glioma. However, malignant tumor has non heterogeneous structure containing active cancerous cells falling under the grade category of III or IV. If benign tumors are left untreated, they tend to develop into high grade tumors. Benign tumors can be simply treated with surgery and treatment for malignant tumor is either chemotherapy or radiotherapy or can also be a combination of the two [6].

Segmentation is the process which is adapted to segment the image in order to detect the abnormalities in the brain. As the goal is to detect tumor at the early stages, the MR image of the brain is subjected to undergo through the process of segmentation for further classification. Accordingly, the therapy is suggested by the neurologist [9]. The implementation of the algorithm is done as following:

© Springer Nature Singapore Pte Ltd. 2019
M. Singh et al. (Eds.): ICACDS 2019, CCIS 1045, pp. 188–196, 2019.
https://doi.org/10.1007/978-981-13-9939-8_17

2 Literature Survey

Kaur et al. [1] proposed a research to partition the image into meaningful parts having similar features and properties. All the techniques that are explained are appropriate for medical research in the field of medical image applications. But from the study it is clear that no single method is sufficient for every image type and no all methods are suitable for a particular image type.

Işın A. et al. [2] proposed an approach for layer by layer segmentation and then applying filters on them. Patches of the skull are taken and trained filters and used on them. The classifier used is Deep Neural Network (DNN).

Yuheng et al. [3] concluded with his study of image algorithms that the combination of multiple segmentation methods is very effective, as it makes full use of the advantages of different algorithms on the basis of multi-feature fusion, so as to achieve better segmentation effect.

Kaur et al. [4] presented different image detection and segmentation techniques have been discussed in depth for the segmentation of the image. The application of image engineering can be medical imaging, object recognition etc.

Vaithegi et al. [5] worked on Image binarization is the process of separation of pixel values into two groups, black as background and white as foreground. According to this categorization, thresholding segmentation is done. Thresholding technique was implemented on medical images that remove background by using local mean and standard deviation.

Kumari et al. [8] proposed a research on the basis of classification and feature extraction techniques. SVM was used on 100 brain image, where out of them, mean value was calculated which gave a rough idea if the patient has tumor tissues or not.

Damodharan et al. [10] presented a technique using ANN individually which gives the accuracy of 83% separating the tissues of the brain into WM, GM and CSF.

Arunadevi et al. [11] has proposed a technique of extreme learning machine for classification of brain tumor from 3D MR images. This method obtained an accuracy of 93.2%, the sensitivity of 91.6%, and specificity of 97.8%.

Chaddad et al. [15] proposed a technique for automatic feature extraction for brain tumor detection based on Gaussian mixture model using MR images. The method worked on the principal component analysis and wavelet based features, the performance of the GMM feature extraction is enhanced. Accuracy achieved was 97.05%.

Demirhan et al. [16] presented a new tissue segmentation algorithm using wavelets and neural networks, which claims effective segmentation of brain MR images into the tumor, WM, GM, edema, and CSF.

Roslan et al. [18] presented a methodology where mean was calculated for each image sequence for around 30 MR images. The segmentation was done using thresholding method which produced more accurate and robust images.

Zanaty et al. [20] presented a theory for brain tumor segmentation based on hybrid type of approach, combining FCM, seed region growing, and Jaccard similarity coefficient algorithm to measure segmented GM and WM tissues from MR images. This method obtained an average segmentation of 90% at noise level of 3% and 9%, respectively.

3 Proposed Machine Learning Approach for Segmentation and Classification

See Fig. 1.

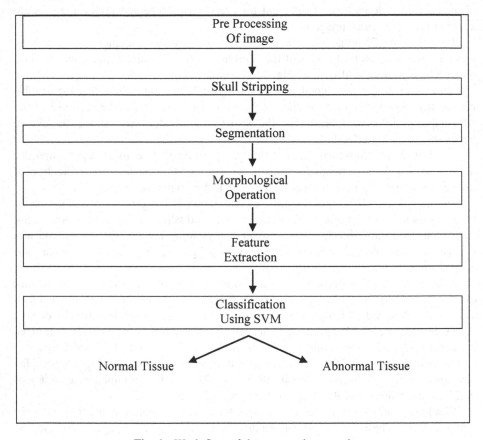

Fig. 1. Work flow of the proposed approach

3.1 Pre Processing

It is the primary step for image analysis. The purpose of pre processing is to remove the extra cranial tissues from the image and enhance the image so that further processing becomes easier for the human. It enhances the features which are important for further processing in the image.

Pre processing of image also improves the signal-noise ratio distorting the noise only leaving the desired parts of the image [2].

3.2   Skull Stripping

It is the process of removal of all the extra tissues in the skull images. It plays a very vital role in image analysis and is of utmost importance for effective examination of the images. The several tissues that can be removed are extra fat, skin, muscles etc. that lies in the brain. There are various skull stripping methods such as morphology-based method, intensity-based methods, deformable-based methods, template-based methods, hybrid methods etc.

An image processed with skull stripping will automatically give better segmentation results and better accuracy in diagnosis of brain tumor [19].

3.3   Segmentation Process

First of all, in the process of segmentation, the MR image is converted into binary image taking in account a threshold value. The selected value for threshold is 128. The pixel values which come to be greater than the threshold value are white, and the pixel values which come out to be smaller than the threshold value are black. Because of these two values, we get the infected area and rest is cropped out.

Now the next job is to eliminate the white pixels. The new cropped image and the original image are taken and divided into two equal parts. The process of morphological erosion gives us the boundaries of the brain images. It is a simple concept for rearranging the obtained pixel values, not having anything to do with the mathematical values. Hence, we take in account only the binary images for this process. We obtain three classes after the erosion process namely white matter, gray matter and cerebral spinal fluid [5]. Following are the types of segmentation:

Edge Based Segmentation: It is the method where edge is considered as the boundary between two regions with properties specific to grey scale. The border of every image is surrounded by a visible closed border and can be calculated by the intensity of the image.

Region Based Segmentation: This method aims at segmenting the similar images into different regions. The segmentation is done with grey values of the image pixels. Further methods are categorised into Region Growing segmentation, Region merging and splitting segmentation depending on the pixels of the image [4].

Threshold Based Segmentation: This method separates the foreground from the background by setting a threshold value. This is how a grey image is converted to binary image which reduces the complexity of the image. The necessary data required for this segmentation is shape and location of object to be detected in the image [4].

Cluster Based Segmentation: This segmentation is specifically used to segment the images with grey level because it is easily applicable on high dimensional image data including colorful images. The pixels in one cluster are similar to each other than other pixels in the cluster. They may belong together in terms of same color or same texture [2].

3.4 Morphological Operations

Operations such as erosion dilation or region filling on the image are applied to binary image to remove the non cerebral tissue from the brain image. The basic concept behind this is to produce a noise free skull stripped image [18]. The process is depicted in Fig. 2 where erosion is done to remove the pixels from the boundaries of the image.

3.5 Feature Extraction Process

In order to collect high level of information such as texture, shape, size, contrast etc., feature extraction is done. By just selecting the prominent features, the accuracy of the diagnosis becomes easy. Gray Level Concurrence Matrix (GLCM) is the most used technique for feature selection in image analysis. First of all the GLCM is calculated and then texture based on GLCM is calculated. It helps in reducing the data and speed ups the algorithm. Not only has the accuracy improved, but the overall performance as well [9]. Some useful features and they methods to calculate them are listed below [7]:

Mean (M): By adding all the pixel values of the image and then dividing it by the total number of pixels, we obtain the mean of an image.

$$M = \left(\frac{1}{a \times b}\right) \sum_{x=0}^{a-1} \sum_{y=0}^{b-1} f(x, y) \tag{1}$$

Standard Deviation (SD): In probability distribution, standard deviation is the second most central point. It is the measure of non-uniformity and the more will be the value, more will be the contrast in the images.

$$SD(\sigma) = \sqrt{\left(\frac{1}{a \times b}\right) \sum_{x=0}^{a-1} \sum_{y=0}^{b-1} (f(x, y) - T)^2} \tag{2}$$

Entropy (E): The degree of randomness in an image is called average information or entropy of an image. A certain image has certain entropy which can describe the texture of the image.

$$E = - \sum_{x=1}^{a-1} \sum_{y=1}^{b-1} f(x, y) \log f(x, y) \tag{3}$$

Skewness (S_k): It is the measure of non symmetric behavior in an image. If an image is considered from the central point, it has to be similar from both left and right sides in order to be symmetric [1].

$$S_k(A) = \left(\frac{1}{a \times b}\right) \frac{\sum (f(x,y) - S)^3}{SD^3} \tag{4}$$

Kurtosis (K$_t$): The probability of random variable is subjected to some shape whether it is flat or peaky which is represented by kurtosis of an image.

$$K_t(X) = \left(\frac{1}{a \times b}\right) \frac{\sum (f(x,y) - M^4|}{SD^4} \tag{5}$$

Energy: Energy is described as the amount of repetition in pixels. It can also be termed as the similar kind of pixels in the image.

$$En = \sqrt{\sum_{x=0}^{a-1} \sum_{y=0}^{n-1} f^2(x,y)} \tag{6}$$

Contrast: It is the measure of the color and brightness of an image with respect to its neighbor over the image [1].

$$C = \sum_{x=0}^{a-1} \sum_{y=0}^{b-1} f^2(x,y) \tag{7}$$

3.6 Support Vector Machine

SVMs are supervised learning models which are used to analyze the data for classification as well as regression. It was invented by Vladimir N. Vapnik which was later modified by Carpis and Vapnik in 1993.

If a training dataset is given, the purpose of SVM is to divide the non-linear transformation into a linear transformation using kernel functions of SVM. In the implementation, the kernel that I've used is Gaussian kernel which has made the classification very easy and convenient. SVM works with hyper planes dividing the dataset into two parameters which maximizes the margin between the non overlapping parameters [13]. The performance in SVM is measured by the accuracy, sensitivity and specificity. We've chosen SVM because it works best even when the data is not linearly separable. It is basically defined by a distinguishing hyperplane. The training dataset gives us the output as a hyperplane which finds a boundary between the two possible outputs (Tables 1 and 2).

Table 1. Statistical analysis of images.

Data	Mean	Standard deviation	Entropy	Skewness	Kurtosis	Energy
Image 1	8.66	43.99	0.65	0.0053	2.89041E–06	10.94
Image 2	11.81	49.11	0.94	0.0065	2.74079E–06	16.37
Image 3	39.4	75.59	3.03	0.01054	1.8506E–06	65.99
Image 4	6.83	39.45	0.45	0.00517	3.3368E–06	8.11
Image 5	11.9	38.81	2.09	0.02002	1.35422E–05	33.17
Image 6	5.33	28.95	1.12	0.01647	2.05493E–05	13.87

Table 2. Confusion matrix defining TP, TN, FP, FN.

Expected outcome	Positive	Negative	Row total
Positive	TP	FP	TP+FP
Negative	TN	FN	TN+FN
Column total	TP+FN	FP+TN	TP+FP+FN+TN

4   Result and Conclusion

The experimental results produced by the proposed technique depict the outcomes as modified image and segmented image followed by skull stripped image (Fig. 3).

The results concluded are based on SVM, BWT [12] and ANN on the basis of criteria of performance such as specificity, sensitivity and accuracy. The detailed analysis shown in the Fig. 2 helps in segmenting the image into WM, GM or CSF. We have also used skull stripping method for the removal of unwanted noise while performing the algorithm. It is observed that tumor detection is more fast and accurate as compared to manual segmentation performed by radiologists. The experimental results

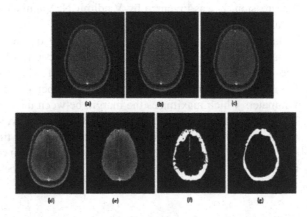

Fig. 2. (a) Original image (b) Background eliminated image (c) Restored image (d) Restored image after contrast modification (e) Skull stripped image (f) Segmentation white image (g) Final image

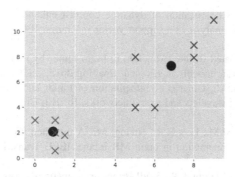

Fig. 3. Output image of SVM classifier

achieved are 83.3% accuracy identifying whether the tissue is normal or abnormal. This technique is suitable for the clinical data of MR images.

In the future, this work can be extended by combining more than one classifier or feature selection method to get better accuracy.

References

1. Kaur, D., Kaur, Y.: Various image segmentation techniques: a review. Int. J. Comput. Sci. Mob. Comput. **3**(5), 809–814 (2014)
2. Işın, A., Direkoğlu, C., Şah, M.: Review of MRI-based brain tumor image segmentation using deep learning methods. Procedia Comput. Sci. **102**, 317–324 (2016)
3. Yuheng, S., Hao, Y.: Image segmentation algorithms overview. arXiv preprint arXiv:1707. 02051 (2017)
4. Kaur, A.: A review paper on image segmentation and its various techniques in image processing. Int. J. Sci. Res. **3**(12), 12–14 (2012)
5. Senthilkumaran, N., Vaithegi, S.: Image segmentation by using thresholding techniques for medical images. Comput. Sci. Eng. **6**(1), 1–13 (2016)
6. American Brain Tumor Association. http://www.abta.org
7. Digital Image Processing PDF. http://www.prenhall.com
8. Kumari, R.: SVM classification an approach on detecting abnormality in brain MRI images. Int. J. Eng. Res. Appl. **3**(4), 1686–1690 (2013)
9. Mahmoudi, M., et al.: Magnetic resonance imaging tracking of stem cells in vivo using iron oxide nanoparticles as a tool for the advancement of clinical regenerative medicine. Chem. Rev. **111**(2), 253–280 (2010)
10. Damodharan, S., Raghavan, D.: Combining tissue segmentation and neural network for brain tumor detection. Int. Arab J. Inf. Technol. (IAJIT) **12**(1), 43–53 (2015)
11. Arunadevi, B., Deepa, S.N.: Texture analysis for 3D classification of brain tumor tissues. Przegląd Elektrotechniczny 342–348 (2013)
12. Alwan, I.M., Jamel, E.M.: Digital image watermarking using Arnold scrambling and Berkeley wavelet transform. Al-Khwarizmi Eng. J. **12**(2), 124–133 (2017)
13. Huo, B., Yin, F.: Research on novel image classification algorithm based on multi-feature extraction and modified SVM classifier. Int. J. Smart Home **9**(9), 103–112 (2015)

14. Torheim, T., et al.: Classification of dynamic contrast enhanced MR images of cervical cancers using texture analysis and support vector machines. IEEE Trans. Med. Imaging **33** (8), 1648–1656 (2014)
15. Chaddad, A.: Automated feature extraction in brain tumor by magnetic resonance imaging using Gaussian mixture models. J. Biomed. Imaging **2015**, 8 (2015)
16. Demirhan, A., Törü, M., Güler, I.: Segmentation of tumor and edema along with healthy tissues of brain using wavelets and neural networks. IEEE J. Biomed. Health Inform. **19**(4), 1451–1458 (2015)
17. Song, T., Jamshidi, M.M., Lee, R.R., Huang, M.: A modified probabilistic neural network for partial volume segmentation in brain MR image. IEEE Trans. Neural Networks **18**(5), 1424–1432 (2007)
18. Roslan, R., Jamil, N., Mahmud, R.: Skull stripping magnetic resonance images brain images: region growing versus mathematical morphology. Int. J. Comput. Inf. Syst. Ind. Manag. Appl. **3**, 150–158 (2011)
19. Benson, C.C., Lajish, V.L.: Morphology based enhancement and skull stripping of MRI brain images. In: International Conference on Intelligent Computing Applications (ICICA), pp. 254–257. IEEE, March 2014
20. Zanaty, E.A.: Determination of gray matter (GM) and white matter (WM) volume in brain magnetic resonance images (MRI). Int. J. Comput. Appl. **45**(3), 16–22 (2012)

Fuzzy Petri Net Representation
of Fuzzy Production Propositions
# of a Rule Based System

Sakshi Gupta[1], Sunita Kumawat[1(✉)], and Gajendra Pratap Singh[2]

[1] Department of Applied Mathematics, Amity School of Applied Sciences,
Amity University Haryana, Gurgaon, India
{sakshi86.10,ksunita86}@gmail.com
[2] Mathematical Sciences and Interdisciplinary Research Lab,
School of Computational and Integrative Sciences, JNU, New Delhi, India
gajendraresearch@gmail.com

Abstract. Petri net is a potential mathematical and graphical modelling tool, used to examine the properties of various complex discrete event and distributed systems. In this paper, a Petri net variant, called Fuzzy Petri net (FPN) has been used to represent Fuzzy Production propositions of a rule based system, where a fuzzy production proposition explains the fuzzy relation among two propositions. For this purpose, another Petri net variant, known as Boolean Petri net (BPN) is considered because of its practical significance. BPNs can be used to represent active and inactive stages of a system like switching circuits; to qualitatively describe gene regulatory interactions etc. The Fuzzy Production propositions of BPN have been represented using Fuzzy Petri net and a precedent-subsequent relation between the two fuzzy propositions of BPNs has been checked using fuzzified propositional algorithm. This relation provides an important property of BPNs based on initial marking of Petri nets and the obtained truth degree of the success node validates the belief strength of this property.

Keywords: Petri net · Fuzzy Petri net · Fuzzy Production proposition ·
Boolean Petri net · Knowledge representation

1 Introduction

Petri nets (PNs) have been and are being successfully applied to model and analyze various Knowledge-based systems (KBSs) like computational distributed systems, discrete-event systems, communication protocols, manufacturing systems, performance evaluation etc. [16]. Different types of biological networks have also been modeled and studied using Petri nets [1, 4, 5, 10, 20]. This is due to their capability to model any graph-based structure [1] and represent the flow of information in any expert system. The concept of Petri nets was first introduced in 1962 by a German Mathematician, Carl Adam Petri in his Doctoral thesis 'Communication with Automata' submitted to the Darmstadt University, West Germany [19]. Thereafter, they are being used as a graphical and mathematical tool for modelling and studying concurrency, conflicts and synchronization in discrete event and distributed systems [16].

© Springer Nature Singapore Pte Ltd. 2019
M. Singh et al. (Eds.): ICACDS 2019, CCIS 1045, pp. 197–210, 2019.
https://doi.org/10.1007/978-981-13-9939-8_18

But classic PNs are not able to properly represent the real-world systems. This is due to continuous growth of the database of real-world knowledge systems, some uncertain and imprecise information may be presented in these systems. Thus, to handle uncertain or vague information, a special subclass of Petri nets, called *Fuzzy Petri nets* (FPNs) has been introduced by Lipp [13] for modelling industrial control systems. Then in 1988, Looney [15] modified PNs using fuzzy reasoning and logic to represent rule-based expert systems. Later, in 1990, a more general FPN model has been proposed by Chen [2] to model knowledge representation and also described a fuzzy reasoning algorithm that automatically performs knowledge reasoning. In [17], authors have augmented the time concept with Fuzzy Petri nets and analyzed how the time factor has impacted the net performance in terms of transition firing and marking of input and the output places. FPNs have been successfully applied in various areas like fault diagnosis systems, biological networks, operational management systems, wireless sensor systems etc. [3, 14, 24, 25].

In this paper, we have taken fuzzy propositions of a rule based system of one subclass of safe Petri nets known as Boolean Petri nets (BPNs) [7–9, 22, 23]. Boolean Petri nets are an emerging and promising class of Petri nets having importance in various application fields like to construct control systems, switching circuits, in genetic regulatory networks and many more [7, 21]. For example, in a genetic regulatory network, gene can be either active or inactive, i.e. gene expression has two states either ON (denoted by '1') or OFF (denoted by '0'). Hence, we can associate a Boolean variable with each gene, denoting the activation or inhibition of that gene [21]. So, BPNs can be used to describe and analyze the interactions between genes. Similarly, in the digital circuits also known as switching circuits, signal has two different states (ON/OFF, 1/0) and these circuits are based on Boolean logic gates [6]. Boolean algebra is a useful mathematical tool for simplifying switching circuits. Hence, performance of these circuits can be easily analyzed using BPNs. In [7], authors have shown "If a Petri net is Boolean, then initial marking for all the places is one". Here, we are checking the converse of this result that *"IF initial marking for all the places is one, THEN it is a Boolean Petri net"* i.e. *"IF initial marking for all the places is one, THEN a Petri net will generate all the binary n-vectors"* using fuzzy rule based modelling. It is achieved by obtaining a sprouting tree which shows a precedent-subsequent relationship between these propositions and the truth degree of goal proposition is also calculated using the truth degree of starting proposition that shows the belief strength of the above property. To do so, the modified version of fuzzy reasoning algorithm proposed in [2] has been used. Then an argument is made by using the obtained sprouted tree and its validity is proved by using the existing methods of proof.

The remaining paper is systematized as follows: Sect. 2 discusses basic concepts of Petri nets, Fuzzy Petri nets and Boolean Petri nets. Section 3 describes the fuzzified propositional algorithm. In Sect. 4, implementation of algorithm is illustrated using the 3 cases. Section 5 discusses the argument formulation and validation. Section 6 gives the conclusions and scope.

2 Petri Nets: Overview

Petri net is defined as a graph, which is directed, weighted, bipartite multigraph having two types of nodes: places and transitions. The *places* represented by circles model the conditions while the *transitions* represented by bars or rectangular boxes model the actions [8, 9, 12]. It is also called condition-event (place-transition) net [11]. The relation between these nodes is represented by connecting them to each other through directed arcs. If there is a directed arc connecting a place (transition) to a transition (place), then the place is known as *input (output)* place of that transition. Some positive integer is assigned to each arc, which signifies the weight of that arc. For the arcs having weight 1, the weight is generally omitted. Some places are assigned with non-negative integers known as *Tokens*. They are represented by using black dots inside a place. The number of tokens inside a place indicate the number of data resources available. *Marking vector* M signifies the state of the Petri net and it tells us the number of tokens present in each place in that state. Mathematically, PNs are defined as [16]:

Definition 1: Petri net is a 5-tuple: $PN = (P, T, F, W, M_0)$; where $P = \{p_1, p_2, \ldots, p_n\}$ and $T = \{t_1, t_2, \ldots, t_m\}$ are respectively the finite non-empty set of places and transitions, with $P \cap T = \emptyset$ and $P \cup T \neq \emptyset$, $F \subseteq (P \times T) \cup (T \times P)$ is a set of arcs, $W : F \rightarrow \{1, 2, 3 \ldots\}$ is a weight function, $M_0 : P \rightarrow \{0, 1, 2, \ldots\}$ is the initial marking vector. It is written as $M_0 = (m_1, m_2, \ldots, m_n)$, where n is the total number of places and each m_i indicates the number of tokens present in each place; $m_i \in \{0, 1, 2, \ldots\}$, where $i = 1, 2, \ldots, n$.

A Petri net is simulated according to transition firing rule. A transition t is *enabled* if all its input places has at least as many tokens as the weight of the arcs connecting those input places to the transition t. When an enabled transition fires, the enable tokens are consumed by the transition and deposited into each of its output places according to the arc weight. The firing of a transition leads to the change in the state of the system and thus modification in the marking. Detailed information of PNs can be found in [18]. Figure 1 illustrates the firing rule of a transition.

Definition 2: If p_i and p_j are respectively the input and output places of any transition $t_l; l = 1, 2, \ldots, m$; then the place p_j is called *immediate reachable* from the place p_i. Let p_k be another place such that p_k is immediate reachable from p_j and p_j is immediate reachable from p_i, then the place p_k is called *reachable* from the place p_i.

For example, in Fig. 1, place p_3 is immediate reachable from the places p_1 and p_2 while p_4 is reachable from the places p_1 and p_2.

Definition 3: The *immediate reachability set* of the place p_i, denoted by $IRS(p_i)$ is the set of places that are immediately reachable from p_i And the *reachability set* of p_i, denoted by $RS(p_i)$ is the set of places that are reachable from p_i. For example, in Fig. 1,

$$IRS(p_1) = \{p_3\}, IRS(p_2) = \{p_3\}, IRS(p_3) = \{p_4\} \text{ and } RS(p_1) = \{p_4\}, RS(p_2)$$
$$= \{p_4\}.$$

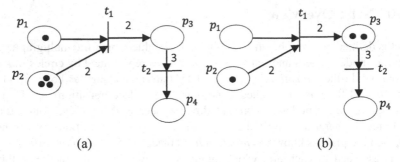

(a)   (b)

Fig. 1. (a) Petri net before firing. Places p_1 and p_2 are the input places and p_3 is an output place of the transition t_1. Place p_3 is the input place and p_4 is an output place of the transition t_2. Here, t_1 is an enabled transition and $M_0 = \{1, 3, 0, 0\}$. (b) Petri net after firing. After firing of transition t_1, one token from p_1 and two tokens from p_2 are consumed and two tokens in p_3 are deposited. New state will be $M_1 = \{0, 1, 2, 0\}$. At this state, no transition is enabled and the Petri net is said to be in dead state, i.e. no transition firing will take place.

Definition 4: The places p_i and p_j are known as *adjacent places* with respect to the transition $t_l; l = 1, 2, \ldots, m$; if both are input places of the transition t_l. For example, in Fig. 1, places p_1 and p_2 are adjacent places with respect to the transition t_1.

However, it is not possible to accurately model many real-world situations using basic Petri nets and also such Petri nets are not able to deal with uncertain or vague data presented in most of the knowledge-based systems. This is because database of expert systems is continuously increasing resulting in growing complexity of these systems. To overcome these shortcomings, an extension of Petri nets knowns as Fuzzy Petri nets (FPNs) is developed for the knowledge representation of complex control processes and fuzzy rule-based expert systems [13, 15].

A Fuzzy Petri net is used to model and study a system having uncertainty. In an FPN, each transition is linked with a certainty factor between 0 and 1 and the token in a place is linked with a truth value between 0 and 1. Also, the number of tokens in a place are constrained to one. According to Chen, Fuzzy Petri net is defined as [2]:

Definition 5: Fuzzy Petri net is an 8-tuple: $FPN = (P, T, Q, I, O, f, \alpha, \beta)$; where P, T and Q are non-empty finite sets of places, transitions and propositions, respectively, $P \cap T \cap Q = \varnothing, |P| = |Q|$, I and O are input and output functions, both from transitions to the set of places, $f : T \rightarrow [0, 1]$ is an association function linking each transition with a certainty factor having real value between 0 and 1, $\alpha : P \rightarrow [0, 1]$ is also an association function indicating the truth degree of each place, $\beta : P \rightarrow Q$ is an association function associating the places to propositions.

In an FPN, a transition t_i is enabled if $\forall p_j \in I(t_i)$, i.e. for all input places p_j of transition t_i, truth degree of each place is greater than or equal to given threshold value λ, i.e. $\alpha(p_j) \geq \lambda$, where $0 \leq \lambda \leq 1$. Then the reasoning process of an FPN is executed by firing the Fuzzy Production propositions and updating the truth value of output place at each step.

A *Fuzzy Production proposition (FPP)* defines a fuzzy relation between two propositions. FPPs are usually expressed using fuzzy 'IF-THEN' proposition in which part of the proposition after 'IF' is the antecedent or precondition and part of the proposition after 'THEN' denotes consequent or postcondition. According to [2, 15], the generalized formula of Fuzzy Production proposition can be stated as follows:

Definition 6: The ith FPP, FP_i is defined as: FP_i : *IF q_j THEN $q_k (\mu_i = a)$*. Here, q_j and q_k are the propositions associated with the places p_j & p_k, i.e. $\beta(p_j) = q_j$ & $\beta(p_k) = q_k$; $\mu_i (0 \leq a \leq 1; 1 \leq i \leq n)$ is the certainty factor associated with the transition t_i and represents the belief strength of the proposition, i.e. $f(t_i) = \mu_i$.

If $\alpha(p_j) = \gamma_j$ *and* $\beta(p_j) = q_j$, i.e. truth degree of proposition q_j associated with the place p_j is γ_j and $\gamma_j \geq \lambda$, then after firing the Fuzzy Production proposition FP_i, the truth degree of the proposition q_k will be $\gamma_k = \gamma_j * \mu_i$. Following is an example of Fuzzy Production proposition:

FP_1: IF your body temperature is above $100\,^{\circ}F$ THEN you have a fever $(\mu_1 = 0.90)$.

Let q_1 "your body temperature is above $100\,^{\circ}F$" and q_2 "you have a fever" be the two propositions of the FP_1. The two propositions q_1 and q_2 will correspond to the two places p_1 and p_2. Let the threshold value be $\lambda = 0.30$ and the truth degree of the proposition q_1 is 0.80, i.e. $\alpha(p_1) = \gamma_1 = 0.80$. The modelling of FP_1 using FPN is shown in Fig. 2.

Fig. 2. FPN of FP_1

In the above FPN model, $P = \{p_1, p_2\}$, $T = \{t_1\}$, $Q = \{q_1, q_2\}$, $I\{t_1\} = p_1$, $O\{t_1\} = \{p_2\}$, $f(t_1) = \mu_1 = 0.90$, $\alpha(p_1) = 0.80$, $\alpha(p_2) = 0$, $\beta(p_1) = q_1$, $\beta(p_2) = q_2$. Since $\gamma_1 \geq \lambda$, so after firing of the FP_1, the truth degree of the proposition q_2 will be $\gamma_2 = \gamma_1 * \mu_1 = 0.72$. It tells us the possibility degree of having a fever is 0.72. The firing of an FPN is shown in Fig. 3.

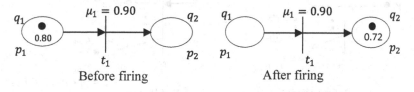

Before firing   After firing

Fig. 3. Firing of a Fuzzy Petri net

The most common Fuzzy Production propositions are [2, 15]:

Type 1: *IF q_j THEN $q_k(\mu_i = a)$* (Fig. 4).

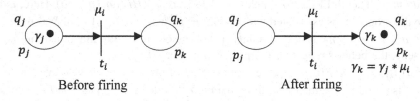

Before firing   After firing

Fig. 4. FPN of Type 1 FPP

Type 2: IF *q_{j1} and q_{j2} and q_{j3} and...and q_{jn} Then $q_k(\mu_i = a)$* (Fig. 5).

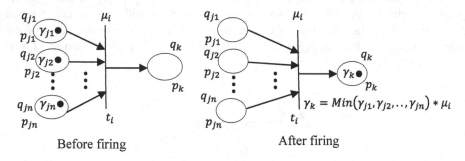

Before firing   After firing

Fig. 5. FPN of Type 2 FPP

Type 3: IF q_j THEN q_{k1} and q_{k2} and ... and $q_{kn}(\mu_i = a)$ (Fig. 6).

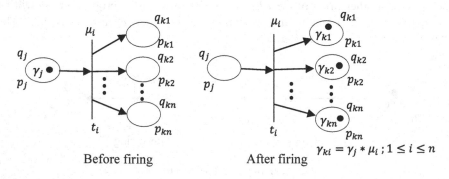

Before firing   After firing

Fig. 6. FPN of Type 3 FPP

Type 4: IF q_{j1} or q_{j2} or ... or q_{jn} THEN $q_k(\mu_i = a)$ (Fig. 7).

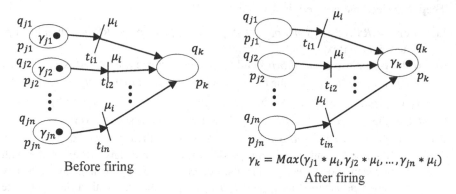

Before firing

$$\gamma_k = Max(\gamma_{j1} * \mu_i, \gamma_{j2} * \mu_i, ..., \gamma_{jn} * \mu_i)$$

After firing

Fig. 7. FPN of Type 4 FPP

In this paper, we have used the special class of 1-safe Petri Nets known as Boolean Petri nets (BPNs). *BPNs* are 1-safe Petri nets which generate all the 2^n binary vectors as marking vectors in its reachability tree [7–9, 22, 23]. For more information on BPNs, see [7, 22].

Here, the Fuzzy Production propositions for the rule based system of BPNs have been taken as input. Three cases have been discussed by taking different certainty factors of the fuzzy production propositions and the truth degree of our goal proposition is calculated using the fuzzified propositional algorithm [2]. The truth degree so obtained shows the belief strength in the precedent-subsequent relation among the starting and final fuzzy propositions of the BPNs.

3 Fuzzified Propositional Algorithm (FPA)

In this section, fuzzified propositional algorithm based on FPNs has been described. The FPA automatically generates the truth degree of the goal proposition by using the truth degree of the initial proposition and also finds whether there exists precedent-subsequent relationship among the initial and goal proposition [2].

FPA generates a tree which gives all the paths from the initial place to the final place. Every vertex of the tree is a 4-tuple represented by $\{p_k, \gamma_k, IRS(p_k), \lambda\}$; where p_k is a place, γ_k is the truth degree of place p_k, $IRS(p_k)$ is the immediate reachability set of the place p_k and λ is the threshold. Let p_s and p_g be the initial and goal place respectively. As explained earlier, the propositions q_s and q_g will be associated with the places p_s and p_g respectively. Let us suppose the truth degree of the starting proposition, q_s entered by the user is γ_s i.e. the truth value of the token in the place p_s is γ_s and the user wants to know what will be γ_g i.e. the truth degree of the proposition q_g. Let $\mu_{xy} = a$ denotes the certainty factor of the condition associated with the propositions q_x and q_y and A_{xy} denote the set of adjacent places of p_x, where $p_y \in IRS(p_x)$. The fuzzified propositional algorithm is briefly explained as follows:

Step 1: Start from the initial proposition q_s and mark the root node of the tree as $\{p_s, \gamma_s, IRS(p_s), \lambda\}$ as $\beta(p_s) = q_s$. This is the non-terminal vertex.

Step 2: Select one non-terminal vertex p_i.

(a) If either $IRS(p_i) = \emptyset$ or $\forall p_k \in IRS(p_i)$, goal place $p_g \notin RS(p_k)$, then label p_i as terminal vertex.

(b) If the goal place $p_g \in IRS(p_i)$ and $\gamma_i \geq \lambda$, then create a new vertex p_g labelled as $\{p_g, \gamma_g, IRS(p_g), \lambda\}$ in the tree with a directed edge marked $\mu_{ig} = a$, from the vertex $\{p_i, \gamma_i, IRS(p_i), \lambda\}$ to the vertex $\{p_g, \gamma_g, IRS(p_g), \lambda\}$, where $\gamma_g = \gamma_i * a$. Here, the vertex $\{p_g, \gamma_g, IRS(p_g), \lambda\}$ will be called a success vertex.

(c) If the goal place $p_g \notin IRS(p_i)$ and $p_g \in RS(p_k)$, then $\forall p_k \in IRS(p_i)$,

   (c.1) If $A_{ik} = \emptyset$ and $\gamma_i \geq \lambda$, and p_k does not occur in any vertex in the path between root vertex p_s and the selected vertex p_i, then generate a new vertex p_k labelled as $\{p_k, \gamma_k, IRS(p_k), \lambda\}$ in the tree with a directed edge marked $\mu_{ik} = a$, from the vertex $\{p_i, \gamma_i, IRS(p_i), \lambda\}$ to the vertex $\{p_k, \gamma_k, IRS(p_k), \lambda\}$, where $\gamma_k = \gamma_i * a$. Here, the vertex $\{p_k, \gamma_k, IRS(p_k), \lambda\}$ will be called a non-terminal vertex.

   (c.2) Else if $A_{ik} = \{p_b, p_c, \ldots, p_z\}$, i.e. p_i has some adjacent places, then the user is requested to insert the truth degree of the propositions $q_b, q_c, \ldots$ and q_z associated with the places $p_b, p_c, \ldots$ and p_z respectively. Let $y_b, y_c, \ldots, y_z$ be the corresponding truth degrees entered by the user.
   Let $h = Min(y_i, y_b, y_c, \ldots, y_z)$.

      (c.2.1) If $h \geq \lambda$, then create a new vertex p_k labelled as $\{p_k, \gamma_k, IRS(p_k), \lambda\}$ in the tree with an edge marked $\mu_{ik} = a$, from the vertex $\{p_i, \gamma_i, IRS(p_i), \lambda\}$ to the vertex $\{p_k, \gamma_k, IRS(p_k), \lambda\}$, where $\gamma_k = h * a$. Here, the vertex $\{p_k, \gamma_k, IRS(p_k), \lambda\}$ will be called a non-terminal vertex.

      (c.2.2) else mark the vertex p_i as a terminal vertex.

Step 3: If no non-terminal vertex remains, then go to Step 4. Else, repeat Step 2.

Step 4: If there is a success node, then there exists a precedent-subsequent relation among the first proposition q_s and goal proposition q_g and the truth degree of the goal proposition q_g will be calculated as:

Let G be a set of success vertices. i.e.

$$G = \{(p_g, r_1, IRS(p_g), \lambda), (p_g, r_2, IRS(p_g), \lambda), \ldots, (p_g, r_m, IRS(p_g), \lambda)\}$$

where $0 \leq r_i \leq 1, 1 \leq i \leq m$.

Then set $T = Max(r_1, r_2, \ldots, r_m)$. The truth degree of the final proposition q_g will be T.

else there does not exist a precedent-subsequent relation among the first and final propositions.

4   Case Study

In this section, we have considered Fuzzy Production propositions corresponding to BPNs and made three different cases. These propositions have been made with the help of [7, 8, 22]. In each case, there is a variation in the certainty factors of each proposition.

The Fuzzy Production propositions for the rule based Boolean Petri nets are:

FP_1: IF $M_n(x) \leq 1 \forall x \in P$ THEN Petri net is 1-bounded $(\mu_1 = a_1)$.

FP_2: IF the number of tokens in a place in PN never exceeds one THEN place is safe $(\mu_2 = a_2)$.

FP_3: IF all the places are safe or Petri net is 1-bounded, THEN Petri net is safe $(\mu_3 = a_3)$.

FP_4: IF a Petri net is safe and it generates all binary n-vectors as marking vectors in its reachability tree THEN Petri net is Boolean Petri net $(\mu_4 = a_4)$.

FP_5: IF a Petri net is Boolean Petri net, THEN $M_0(x) = 1 \forall x \in P, |P| \leq |T|$ and incidence matrix contains negative identity matrix of order n as a submatrix $(\mu_5 = a_5)$.

FP_6: IF a Petri net is safe and $M_0(x) = 1 \forall x \in P$ THEN it can be embedded as an induced subnet of a BPN $(\mu_6 = a_6)$.

FP_7: IF $M_0(x) = 1 \forall x \in P$ THEN Petri net is a Boolean Petri net $(\mu_7 = a_7)$.

Let us denote the above propositions as:

q_1: $M_n(x) \leq 1 \forall x \in P$, q_2: Petri net is 1-bounded
q_3: Number of tokens in a place in PN never exceeds one
q_4: Place is safe, q_5: Petri net is safe
q_6: Petri net generates all binary n-vectors as marking vectors in its reachability tree
q_7: Petri net is Boolean Petri net
q_8: $M_0(x) = 1 \forall x \in P$, q_9: $|P| \leq |T|$
q_{10}: Incidence matrix contains negative identity matrix of order n as a submatrix
q_{11}: Petri net can be embedded as an induced subnet of a BPN

Rewriting the FPPs using the above notations, we have

FP_1: IF q_1 THEN q_2 $(\mu_1 = a_1)$ FP_2: IF q_3 THEN q_4 $(\mu_2 = a_2)$
FP_3: IF q_4 or q_2 THEN q_5 $(\mu_3 = a_3)$ FP_4: IF q_5 and q_6 THEN q_7 $(\mu_4 = a_4)$
FP_5: IF q_7 THEN q_8 and q_9 and q_{10} $(\mu_5 = a_5)$
FP_6: IF q_5 and q_8 THEN q_{11} $(\mu_6 = a_6)$ FP_7: IF q_8 THEN q_7 $(\mu_7 = a_7)$

The user wants to know if there exists any precedent-subsequent relation between the propositions q_1 and q_7. So, our initial and goal propositions are q_1 and q_7 respectively and the corresponding initial and goal places will be p_1 and p_7 as $\beta(p_1) = q_1$ and $\beta(p_7) = q_7$. Assume that the threshold value, $\lambda = 0.30$ and the truth degree of the initial place p_1 given by the user is $\gamma_1 = 0.90$ for all the three cases. The Fuzzy Petri net model of the FPPs of Boolean Petri nets is shown in Fig. 8. The Immediate reachability set, reachability set and set of adjacent places are shown in Table 1 and Table 2 respectively. Let us discuss the three cases:

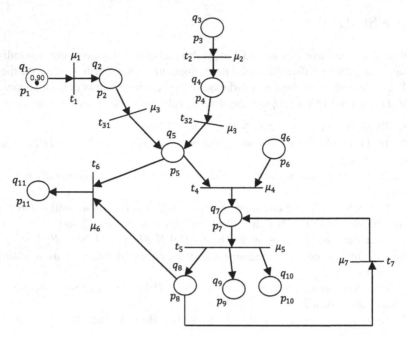

Fig. 8. FPN of FPPs of Boolean Petri net

<table>
<tr><th colspan="3" align="center">Table 1.</th></tr>
<tr><th>Place
p_i</th><th>IRS (p_i)</th><th>RS (p_i)</th></tr>
<tr><td>p_1</td><td>$\{p_2\}$</td><td>$\{p_2,p_5,p_7,p_8,p_9,p_{10},p_{11}\}$</td></tr>
<tr><td>p_2</td><td>$\{p_5\}$</td><td>$\{p_5,p_7,p_8,p_9,p_{10},p_{11}\}$</td></tr>
<tr><td>p_3</td><td>$\{p_4\}$</td><td>$\{p_4,p_5,p_7,p_8,p_9,p_{10},p_{11}\}$</td></tr>
<tr><td>p_4</td><td>$\{p_5\}$</td><td>$\{p_5,p_7,p_8,p_9,p_{10},p_{11}\}$</td></tr>
<tr><td>p_5</td><td>$\{p_7,p_{11}\}$</td><td>$\{p_7,p_8,p_9,p_{10},p_{11}\}$</td></tr>
<tr><td>p_6</td><td>$\{p_7\}$</td><td>$\{p_7,p_8,p_9,p_{10},p_{11}\}$</td></tr>
<tr><td>p_7</td><td>$\{p_8,p_9,p_{10}\}$</td><td>$\{p_7,p_8,p_9,p_{10},p_{11}\}$</td></tr>
<tr><td>p_8</td><td>$\{p_7,p_{11}\}$</td><td>$\{p_7,p_8,p_9,p_{10},p_{11}\}$</td></tr>
<tr><td>p_9</td><td>$\varnothing$</td><td>$\varnothing$</td></tr>
<tr><td>p_{10}</td><td>$\varnothing$</td><td>$\varnothing$</td></tr>
<tr><td>p_{11}</td><td>$\varnothing$</td><td>$\varnothing$</td></tr>
</table>

<table>
<tr><th colspan="3" align="center">Table 2.</th></tr>
<tr><th>Place p_i</th><th>Place p_k</th><th>A_{ik}</th></tr>
<tr><td>p_1</td><td>p_2</td><td>$\varnothing$</td></tr>
<tr><td>p_2</td><td>p_5</td><td>$\varnothing$</td></tr>
<tr><td>p_3</td><td>p_4</td><td>$\varnothing$</td></tr>
<tr><td>p_4</td><td>p_5</td><td>$\varnothing$</td></tr>
<tr><td>p_5</td><td>p_7</td><td>$\{p_6\}$</td></tr>
<tr><td>p_5</td><td>p_{11}</td><td>$\{p_8\}$</td></tr>
<tr><td>p_6</td><td>p_7</td><td>$\{p_5\}$</td></tr>
<tr><td>p_7</td><td>p_8</td><td>$\varnothing$</td></tr>
<tr><td>p_7</td><td>p_9</td><td>$\varnothing$</td></tr>
<tr><td>p_7</td><td>p_{10}</td><td>$\varnothing$</td></tr>
<tr><td>p_8</td><td>p_7</td><td>$\varnothing$</td></tr>
<tr><td>p_8</td><td>p_{11}</td><td>$\{p_5\}$</td></tr>
</table>

Case 1: In this case, the certainty factors taken are:

$$FP_1: \mu_1 = 0.90;\ FP_2: \mu_2 = 0.90;\ FP_3: \mu_3 = 0.95;\ FP_4: \mu_4 = 0.92;\ FP_5: \mu_5 = 0.95;$$
$$FP_6: \mu_6 = 0.90;\ FP_7: \mu_7 = 0.50$$

After implementing the algorithm, the tree obtained is shown in Fig. 9. Since we have got a success node with truth degree $\gamma_7 = 0.71$, showing there exist a precedent-subsequent relation between the first and final propositions. The value of truth degree shows that possibility degree of this relation to be true is 0.71.

Case 2: Here, we have decreased the certainty factor values. The new certainty factors taken are:

$$FP_1: \mu_1 = 0.85; \; FP_2: \mu_2 = 0.80; \; FP_3: \mu_3 = 0.85; \; FP_4: \mu_4 = 0.90; \; FP_5: \mu_5 = 0.80;$$
$$FP_6: \mu_6 = 0.87; \; FP_7: \mu_7 = 0.50$$

After implementing the algorithm, the tree obtained is shown in Fig. 10. Again, we have got a success node but with truth degree $\gamma_7 = 0.58$, which shows there exist a precedent-subsequent relation between the first and final proposition. The lesser value of truth degree shows that as we lower the certainty factors of the FPPs, the possibility degree of this relation to be true also get decreased and in this case, it has become 0.58.

Case 3: In this case, we have further decreased the certainty factor values. The new certainty factors taken are:

$$FP_1: \mu_1 = 0.80; \; FP_2: \mu_2 = 0.75; \; FP_3: \mu_3 = 0.80; \; FP_4: \mu_4 = 0.85; \; FP_5: \mu_5 = 0.75;$$
$$FP_6: \mu_6 = 0.85; \; FP_7: \mu_7 = 0.50$$

After implementing the algorithm, the tree obtained is shown in Fig. 11. Here again, we have got a success node but now with truth degree $\gamma_7 = 0.49$. The occurrence of success node again shows that there exists a precedent-subsequent relation between the first and final proposition. The truth degree value has further decreased, proving that as we keep on lowering the certainty factors of the FPPs, the possibility degree of this relation to be true will also get decreased and in this case, it has become 0.49.

5 Formulation and Validation: An Argument Based on Sprouting Tree

In this section, we will formulate an argument based on the tree obtained in the previous section and then, will check its validity.

In Sect. 4, after applying fuzzified propositional algorithm we have got three trees corresponding to each case, but the path $(p_1 \rightarrow p_2 \rightarrow p_5 \rightarrow p_7)$ to reach the goal place p_7 from the initial place p_1 is same in all the 3 cases. Based on this path, an argument having three premises R_1, R_2, R_3 and conclusion C is obtained which is as follows:

$$R_1: p_1 \rightarrow p_2, R_2: p_2 \rightarrow p_5 \; and \; R_3: p_5 \rightarrow p_7; \quad C: p_1 \rightarrow p_7$$

As defined earlier, the places p_1, p_2, p_5 and p_7 are associated with the propositions q_1, q_2, q_5 and q_7. Using the inference rules and existing methods for validation of an argument, we have proved that our argument $(p_1 \rightarrow p_2, p_2 \rightarrow p_5, p_5 \rightarrow p_7 \therefore p_1 \rightarrow p_7)$ is valid, i.e. whenever all the premises are true, the conclusion is also true. The validation of our argument further strengthens our result obtained in Sect. 4, that "there exist a precedent-subsequent relation between the initial proposition q_1 and final proposition q_7". However, the extent for this to be true will be depending upon the certainty factors of the FPPs.

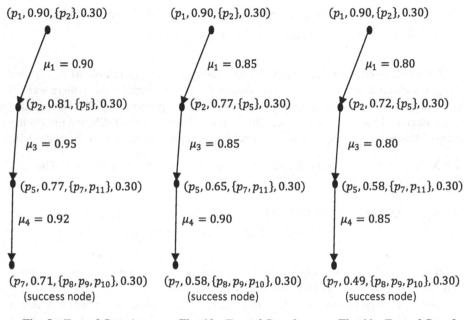

| Fig. 9. Tree of Case 1 | Fig. 10. Tree of Case 2 | Fig. 11. Tree of Case 3 |

6   Conclusions and Scope

In this study, we have shown a precedent-subsequent relation between the initial proposition, "$M_n(x) \leq 1 \, \forall x \in P$" and final proposition, "Petri net is a Boolean Petri net". That is, "IF $M_n(x) \leq 1 \, \forall x \in P$ THEN Petri net is a Boolean Petri net" and this result is also strongly supported by the argument validation proof. Though, the possibility degree of this relation to be true will depend on the certainty factors of the Fuzzy Production propositions given by the user. Since the certainty factors are given by the user and if we know some propositions are true, then the values of certainty factors can be chosen higher, i.e. close to 1. In the first case, the possibility degree of Fuzzy Production proposition "IF $M_n(x) \leq 1 \, \forall x \in P$ THEN Petri net is a Boolean Petri net" to be true is 0.71 which has decreased to 0.58 and to 0.49 in second and third case respectively depending on the certainty factors. In particular, it will also hold if we take initial marking equal to one for all the places i.e. $M_0(x) = 1 \, \forall x \in P$. So, we have proved that IF $M_0(x) = 1 \, \forall x \in P$ THEN Petri net is a Boolean Petri net along with other conditions.

The computational good characterization of Boolean Petri nets and its verification using Fuzzy Petri nets is still an open problem to the researchers. This characterization may save the computational running time and effort of the multi switches circuits used in various applications.

Acknowledgements. The first and second authors are thankful to Department of Applied Sciences, Amity University, Haryana and the third author is thankful to UPOE-II 257 and DST PURSE for providing research facility.

References

1. Chaouiya, C.: Petri net modelling of biological networks. Brief. Bioinform. **8**(4), 210–219 (2007)
2. Chen, S.M., Ke, J.S., Chang, J.F.: Knowledge representation using fuzzy Petri nets. IEEE Trans. Knowl. Data Eng. **2**(3), 311–319 (1990)
3. Hamed, R.I., Ahson, S.I., Parveen, R.: A new approach for modelling gene regulatory networks using fuzzy Petri nets. J. Integr. Bioinform. **7**(1), 113 (2010)
4. Heiner, M., Koch, I., Will, J.: Model validation of biological pathways using Petri nets-demonstrated for apoptosis. Biosystems **75**, 15–28 (2004)
5. Hofestadt, R.: Advantages of Petri-net modeling and simulation for biological networks. Int. J. Biosci. Biochem. Bioinforma. **7**(4), 221–229 (2017)
6. Jain, S., Naik, P.K., Bhooshan, S.V.: Petri nets – an application in digital circuits. In: Proceedings of the ICWET 2010 International Conference & Workshop on Emerging Trends in Technology, p. 1005 (2010). https://doi.org/10.1145/1741906.1742168
7. Kansal, S., Acharya, M., Singh, G.P.: Boolean Petri nets. In: Pawlewski, P. (ed.) Petri nets — Manufacturing and Computer Science, pp. 381–406. In-Tech Global Publisher (2012). ISBN 978-953-51-0700-2, Chapter 17
8. Kansal, S., Singh, G.P., Acharya, M.: On Petri nets generating all the binary n-vectors. Scientiae Mathematicae Japonicae **e-2010**, 113–120 (2010). 71(2), 209–216
9. Kansal, S., Singh, G.P., Acharya, M.: 1-Safe Petri nets generating every binary n-vector exactly once. Scientiae Mathematicae Japonicae, **e-2011**, 127–137 (2011). 74(1) 29–36
10. Koch, I.: Petri nets in systems biology. Softw. Syst. Model. **14**(2), 703–710 (2015)
11. Kumawat, S.: Weighted directed graph: a Petri net-based method of extraction of closed weighted directed euler trail. Int. J. Serv. Econ. Manag. **4**(3), 252–264 (2012)
12. Kumawat, S., Purohit, G.N.: Total span of farm work flow using Petri net with resource sharing. Int. J. Bus. Process Integr. Manag. **8**(3), 160–171 (2017)
13. Lipp, H.-P.: The application of a fuzzy Petri net for controlling complex industrial processes. In: Proceedings of IFAC Conference on Fuzzy Information Control, Marseille, pp. 459–465 (1983)
14. Liu, H.C., You, J.X., Li, Z.W., Tian, G.: Fuzzy Petri nets for knowledge representation and reasoning: a literature review. Eng. Appl. Artif. Intell. **60**, 45–56 (2017)
15. Looney, C.G.: Fuzzy Petri nets for rule-based decision making. IEEE Trans. Syst. Man Cybern. **18**, 178–183 (1988)
16. Murata, T.: Petri nets: properties, analysis and applications. Proc. IEEE **77**(4), 541–580 (1989)
17. Pedrycz, W., Camargo, H.: Fuzzy timed Petri nets. Fuzzy Sets Syst. **140**(2), 301–330 (2003)
18. Peterson, J.L.: Petri Net Theory and the Modeling of Systems. Prentice-Hall, Englewood Cliffs (1981)

19. Petri, C.A.: Communication with automata. Ph.D. dissertation, Technical report. RADC-TR-65-377, Rome Air Development Center, Rome (1966)
20. Reddy, V.N., Mavrovouniotis, M.L., Liebman, M.N.: Petri net representations in metabolic pathways. In: Proceedings of the International Conference on Intelligent Systems for Molecular Biology (1993)
21. Remy, E., Mossé, B., Thieffry, D.: Boolean dynamics of compound regulatory circuits. In: Rogato, A., Zazzu, V., Guarracino, M. (eds.) Dynamics of Mathematical Models in Biology, pp. 43–53. Springer, Cham (2016). https://doi.org/10.1007/978-3-319-45723-9_4
22. Singh, G.P.: Some advances in the theory of Petri nets. Ph.D. thesis, Faculty of Technology, University of Delhi, Delhi, India (2013)
23. Singh, G.P., Kansal, S., Acharya, M.: Embedding an arbitrary 1-safe Petri net in a Boolean Petri net. Int. J. Comput. Appl. **70**(6), 7–9 (2013)
24. Zhou, K.Q., Zain, A.M.: Fuzzy Petri nets and industrial applications: a review. Artif. Intell. Rev. (2016). https://doi.org/10.1007/s10462-015-9451-9
25. Zhou, K.Q., Mo, L.P., Jin, J., Zain, A.M.: An equivalent generating algorithm to model fuzzy Petri net for knowledge-based system. J. Intell. Manuf. **30**(4), 1831–1842 (2019). https://doi.org/10.1007/s10845-017-1355-x

Fraud Detection in Medical Insurance Claim with Privacy Preserving Data Publishing in TLS-N Using Blockchain

Thanusree Mohan[✉] and K. Praveen

TIFAC-CORE in Cyber Security, Amrita School of Engineering, Coimbatore,
Amrita Vishwa Vidyapeetham, Coimbatore, India
thanu2909@gmail.com, k_praveen@cb.amrita.edu

Abstract. Insurance fraud is one of the most serious problem that insurers, consumers and regulators witnessed in the last couple of years affecting availability of insurances. Increase in the cost of the companies, inflated premium is caused by the number of frauds in the medical insurance sector threatening the viability of the insurance companies and also an adverse effect on the profit they incur. Forged documents submitted for claim settlement gets verified due to limited resource availability. Enabling TLS-N in the conversation between the insurance company, policy holder and medical institution curtail life insurance frauds. Data privacy must be given utmost importance while we handle medical insurance scenarios, TLS-N with privacy preserving data publishing schemes facilitates privacy and mitigates content hiding attack. These records stored in blockchain keeps track of the policy details, the medical reports and insurance claims over the period of validity, helps detecting fraud in the insurance claim.

Keywords: Non-repudiation · TLS-N · Privacy preserving data publishing · Hashing · Blockchain · Insurance claim fraud

1 Introduction

In insurance industry, health insurance vertical has been showing an encouraging growth rate. However, this growth rate along with the lack of reliable information and documentation challenges gave in opportunities and incentives to commit fraud [1]. In medical insurance sector, fraud could be committed by anyone from the policy holder, insurance provider, insurance company employee and/or when the employee and the policy holder collude. Identification of a false claim is a challenging proposition since across Indian insurance company the quality of the data is poor along with no robust mechanism of verification like social security number. Common medical insurance frauds are due to the following reasons:

- Bogus claims prepared by physicians
- Wrong representation of the details regarding the medical condition
- Modifying the identity of the provider and recipient
- Billing and incurring wrong charges for services which were not performed
- Fake documentation

© Springer Nature Singapore Pte Ltd. 2019
M. Singh et al. (Eds.): ICACDS 2019, CCIS 1045, pp. 211–220, 2019.
https://doi.org/10.1007/978-981-13-9939-8_19

- Double billing
- Upcoding and Miscoding of procedures

Blockchain is a peer-to-peer decentralized distributed ledger/system which is cryptographically secure. A transaction is the fundamental unit of blockchain [2, 3]. A block is composed of multiple transactions, previous block hash, timestamps, nonce etc. Blockchain could also be referred to as the Internet database that support decentralization. Every node maintains a local copy of the global datasheet. Blockchain works like a public ledger. Applications like financial transactions and IoT uses blockchain technology for an unrivaled security in the Internet. Blockchain technology was referred in the whitepaper by Satoshi Nakomoto, who developed Bitcoin [4]. Ethereum [5] is another most widely used and successful blockchain with built-in Turing-complete programming language which could be used for creating highly flexible smart contracts [6]. Featuring smart contracts makes Ethereum a more effective decentralized platform than bitcoin [7]. Ethereum provides a platform to write user specific decentralized application.

Transport Layer Security (TLS) [10–12] is adopted in most of the present-day HTTP traffic [13] and has transformed the web into a more secure communication platform provides confidentiality, integrity of the content communicated through the web. However, non-repudiation is equally important in the web communication. TLS needs third-party to facilitate this property. Guaranteeing non-repudiation on the internet, we assure that an action performed cannot be denied. TLS-N was developed as an extension to TLS [8, 9] since TLS could not provide non-repudiation. TLS-N was introduced which has the ability to ensure that the conversation between the two entities (generator of the evidence and requester who asks for the evidence) involved in the TLS handshake is genuine by verifying the evidence/proof generation from the TLS-N scheme after the TLS handshake. The TLS communication between the entities share the parameters for enabling TLS-N in the TLS session. The evidence followed by proof are generated and this proof is stored in the blockchain. The verification of the proof is done in TLS-N using Ethereum based smart contract. The paper is structured as follows: Sect. 2 describes about Insurance claim, Third Party Administrator (TPA) and the issues reported in claim frauds. In Sect. 3, TLS-N, its existing architecture and content hiding attack is explained in detail. Section 4 describes privacy preserving in data publishing [14]. Section 5 provides the proposal to issue reported in TLS-N and how we can incorporate it in medical insurance scenario, the use case of updated version of TLS-N in medical insurance claim settlement and an evaluation of this scheme. The paper concludes with Sect. 6.

2 Insurance Claim

Health insurance claims and their settlements have always reported issues in the recent years due to tremendous number of fraud cases reported which affects the insurance company when the insured perform insurance claim fraud and the insured are affected when the insurance company or the TPA reject the insurance claim stating reasons that favor the insurers. The laws relating to insurance claim and settlement had been favoring the insurers than the insured since the start of medical insurance industry [1]. There is always defiance and lack of consistency in the medical insurance industry where the customers are affected in a pernicious way. A general case of processing medical insurance claim is depicted in the Fig. 1. When an insured request for insurance claim, the insured is asked to submit the required proofs and documents to process the reimbursement, this verification is done by the insurer however the process is done either involving a TPA or directly between the insurer and the insured. The details are verified by the insurer and the claim is either approved or rejected. The insured can cater wrong document since there is no proof of authenticity of the document being provided. The documents shared could be forged and the claim would be approved.

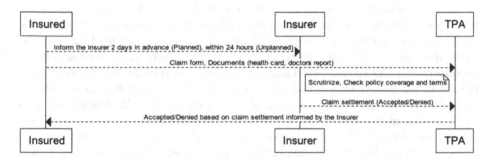

Fig. 1. A general health insurance claim work flow where a TPA is involved

3 TLS-N

TLS-N, with a design similar to content extraction signatures (CES) [15–17] and redactable signatures [18], guarantees generation of a privacy preserving proof of the conversation between the communicating parties involved in the TLS handshake that is used to verify the conversation thereby providing non-repudiation. TLS version 1.3 was extended to TLS-N and it provides privacy preserving and non-interactive proof generation and verification and hence non-repudiation.

Evidence Generation, Proof Generation and Verification
The client and server negotiate the TLS-N parameters during the TLS handshake before the scheme starts. In TLS-N client is referred to as the requester and server as the generator. The records, send and received in TLS communication are mapped based on ordering vector used in TLS-N. Ordering vector would have the sequence of the records from the generator to the requester and vice versa. If record from requester to generator is mapped as r_i identified by a 0, then the record from generator to requester mapped as g_i is identified as 1. Once the handshake is over, the evidence window will begin and the generator will start recording all the conversation that happen between the generator and requester. Using the records which is stored at the evidence buffer in the generator (plaintext records), the salt secret (derived from TLS traffic secret), a hash-chain is computed. Unique salt secrets are generated for the records. If the records are divided into equal sized chunks, then the salt secret input for each of the chunks

would be unique. The Merkle tree is generated using the salt secret, the plain text records, originator information. A small session state is saved by the generator during the TLS-N handshake and it is called TLS-N state. The TLS-N state is updated using the records that are sent and received in TLS communication. The evidence window closes once the requester ask for the evidence through the return evidence message. To compute the evidence, the generator signs the TLS-N state using its own private key. The TLS state contains an ordering vector, timestamp from the beginning of the TLS session and a hash value incorporating all records till the time of evidence window closure. The evidence thus created at the generator is sent to the requester along with records of the conversation that happened before receiving return evidence message. The requester generates a non-repudiable proof from the information received from generator. The requester can generate different kinds of proof. In order to generate proof, the requester uses the evidence provided by the generator and the certificate chain. The requester sends the proof to verifier, who verify the content of the proof. At the verifier end, the verification process is done using an Ethereum based smart contract implementation. The smart contract analyzes the proof, reckons the salt and Merkle tree to recreate the hash chain and verifies the signature. The verifier tries to recreate the evidence from the salt secret, plain-text of record, cipher suite, Oi. Since smart contracts is used in the verification part and smart contracts cannot be modified, the verification process in TLS-N incorporated with Ethereum smart contract makes it tamper proof. The TLS conversation between the requester and generator when TLS-N is enabled and the TLS conversation recreated by the verifier from the information available as proof is shown in Fig. 2.

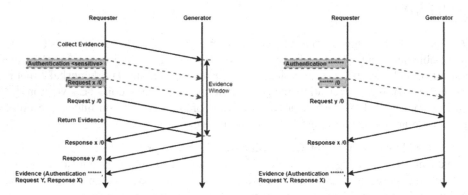

Fig. 2. The packet flow diagram at the requester end and verifier end

Content Hiding Attack

In TLS-N, the requester is allowed to hide content from the records. This feature is exploited when an adversary acts as requester and is allowed to hide important communication content of a variable-length data in order to trick the verifier. During verification the hidden content is not considered and the verifier blindly assumes the content which is hidden is not to be considered for the verification procedure. A scenario where the records are of variable length, the data of sensitive origin and the request data both could be hidden using the content hiding feature in the requester. The resultant proof generated would have variable length hidden content which the verifier would ignore while recreating the Merkle tree, hence a partial Merkle tree would be created from the available parameters. This evidence recreated would have wrong combination of request response pair and thereby gets verified since the final hash of the hash chain and timestamp are all verified at the verifier. As shown in right side image in the Fig. 2, while recreating the conversation, the verifier gets request Y mapped to response for X, which is not the correct conversation that happened however it is verified since the verifier does not check if the hidden content is required or not for the verification process.

4 Privacy Preserving in Data Publishing

There had been tremendous amount of research done on privacy preserving while publishing data that contain sensitive information. Over recent years, data privacy has always been a concern due to data leaks and breaches due to it reported in all sectors over the internet. Anonymity operation [19, 20, 22] approach like generalization and suppression could solve privacy related issues as they preserve the privacy of the data being shared. The purpose of using anonymity algorithms is to prevent exposing the sensitive content. Due to this feature privacy preserving data publishing is showing a drastic implementation in the field of medical institutions where the patient private information and health reports are to be stored with utmost privacy and security. PPDP privacy and anonymity scheme in explained in detail on the paper [23] by Benjamin CM Fung.

5 Proposed Work

Insurance fraud due to false documentation is mainly caused by not having any proper verification mechanism of the documents catered by the policy holder while registering an insurance claim. The authenticity of the documents being catered and non-repudiation on the conversation that happened before the insurance claim process if all recorded in a decentralized oracle then the verification process during the insurance claim could be made easier with more accuracy. Blockchain maintains the authenticity of the data stored however does not provide correctness to the data given to blockchain. Hence, we add proof generated from TLS-N which guarantees content correctness and non-repudiation of the conversation. In order to mitigate content hiding attack, instead of hiding the entire record, the requester is allowed to perform privacy preserving data publishing generalization scheme which would not hide the entire record. Generalization scheme would replace the original value of the record content with semantically consistent but less specific value preserving anonymity.

5.1   Adversary Model

In this paper, the below mentioned use case adversary models are addressed.

- The Requester (insured/policy holder) getting his claim settled by manipulated documents
- The verifier (insurer) manipulating the proof to reject genuine claims

5.2   TLS-N with Blockchain for Medical Insurance Claim Settlement

Medical claims [21] contain sensitive information and it is important to maintain privacy while dealing with medical information. Due to data leak, sensitive information of anyone is readily available a click away. Hence creating fake documents and using it for insurance claim fraud is not a tedious task in present days. Many insurance claim frauds are reported where the policy and claims are taken without the consent or knowledge of the individuals. The medical insurance claim scheme and blockchain incorporation use case is mentioned in the Fig. 3. When an individual register himself for an insurance policy through the website, the TLS-N parameters are shared and enabled during the TLS handshake. During the TLS communication the user caters personal information and updates medical reports/history required for the registration of the individual. The details submitted is verified by the insurance company. Once the policy is issued, the insured request for return evidence message and the insurance company generates the evidence of the records which includes the user details, the medical records and the policy number. Policy number will be unique parameter in the blockchain. The policy holder can now create proof from the evidence maintaining the privacy feature in TLS-N by incorporating generalization scheme of privacy preserving data publishing. The insurance company pushes the evidence and the policy holder pushes the proof to the blockchain. When the policy holder visits the hospital, the hospital verifies the submitted policy ID and details of the insured are genuine by referring the blockchain. This verification result is also added to the blockchain as a record. After verification, the policy holder has medical test done or undergoes treatment, the hospital sends the details to the insured and this evidence and the proof are uploaded in the blockchain which will be further verified by the insurer. Communication between the insured and insurer is shown in Fig. 4 and communication between the insured/patient and the medical institution is shown in Fig. 5.

During the proof submission to the blockchain, the requester could do content hiding attack as mentioned in the Sect. 3, which is mitigated using privacy preserving data publishing generalization mechanism. This could also be misused by applying the scheme on non-sensitive content which is prevented through smart contract verification routine that evaluates the requester have only applied the scheme of generalization to the fields and to the level allowed by the smart contract. The verification process is done in two phases in the proposed architecture. The TLS-N verification can be done when the medical institution needs to verify if the policy details are valid and the check the insured patients' medical records from blockchain. The second verification process done at the insurance company where the medical records and the documents shared by the medical institution are verified using Smart contract and stored in the blockchain.

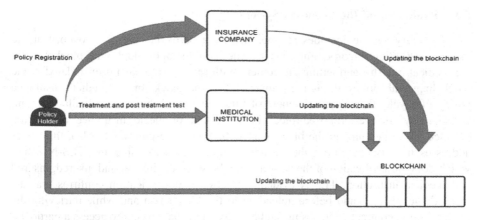

Fig. 3. Medical insurance Blockchain architecture with TLS-N

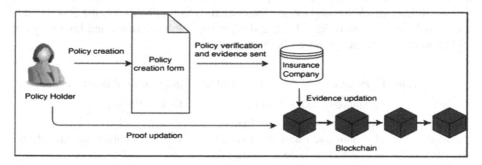

Fig. 4. Communication between the insured and the insurer during policy creation

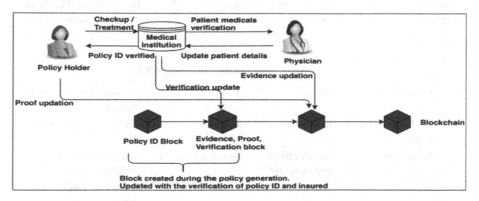

Fig. 5. Communication between the insured and the medical institution during and after the medical checkup and treatment

5.3   Evaluation of the Proposed System

Contemporary system includes storing medical records in central repository at the medical institution. Incorporating this scheme would support deploying blockchain in the medical industry and letting the content with reference to each user updated in the blockchain with policy ID as the primary ID in the block. In the medical insurance policy life-cycle, there is involvement of middlemen and this affects availability and transparency. In the proposed blockchain system, duplicate insurance claims are detected since the entry in the blockchain is based on the policy ID. Also, this paper addresses trust issues within the insurance claim scenario using the TLS-N setup, which does the verification of the conversation between the insurer and insured, insured and medical institution. TLS-N evidence creation and verification confirms that the patient's details are valid before uploading to the blockchain and while retrieving the content, smart contract validates the authenticity of the user trying to access a particular content from the blockchain. Comparison of existing blockchain solution in the medical insurance industry with the proposed scheme is mentioned in the Table 1. Although these blockchains provide confidentiality and authenticity, the level of privacy provided by them differs. Table 2 depicts the fraud scenarios and how they are mitigated in the scheme proposed in this paper.

Table 1. Proposed Scheme with other Blockchain for medical insurance

Feature	Functionality (Blockchain based)	CIA	Privacy
MIStore	Medical Insurance Storage System	✓	×
MedRec	Medical record management system	✓	Permissioned Blockchain
SURETY.AI	AI platform for insurance companies	✓	×
HGD	Architecture for sharing healthcare data	✓	Secure multi-party computing
Proposed Scheme	PPDP in TLS-N using Blockchain for insurance companies	✓	Incorporating TLS-N in communication

Table 2. Fraud scenarios and proposed scheme

No	Fraud scenario	Impact	Solution per proposed scheme
1	Medical identity theft	Manipulate user information	Digital signature in TLS-N
2	Robocalls	Bogus claims on insurance creation and coverage	Entry to blockchain by authorized users
3	Scam	Against Govt and private insurers	Update to blockchain with policy ID
4	Cyber Attacks	Stealing patient details	TLS-N with blockchain
5	Lack of interoperability	Impact the quality and cost to the patient care	Security and trust build in blockchain

6 Conclusion

Insurance claim settlement is becoming a very tedious task over past few years where competitive insurance industry is drastically increasing and one phase where the insurers are trying to lure customers with every possible promise to take policies from their company where the insurance company employees or agents promise the customer of many features which are not part of the claim process and the policy holder gets cheated. On the other hand, the policy holder cheats the insurance provider by submitting false proofs and documents in the insurance claim and gets the claims processed and approved. This happens since there is no proper verification process available to check the authenticity of the proofs being submitted by the policy holder. The solution proposed in the paper solves the TLS-N content hiding attack using generalization of privacy preserving data publishing scheme and incorporating this on a blockchain oracle helps provide immutability to the content related to a policy holder.

References

1. Chudgar, D.: Life Insurance Fraud–Risk Management and Fraud Prevention (2013). papers. ssrn.com
2. Ritzdorf, H., et al.: TLS-N: Non-repudiation over TLS Enabling Ubiquitous Content Signing for Disintermediation. IACR ePrint report 578 (2017)
3. Mazonka, O.: Blockchain: simple explanation. J. Ref. (2016)
4. Nakamoto, S., et al.: Bitcoin: A peer-to-peer electronic cash system (2008). Working Paper
5. Sajana, P., Sindhu, M., Sethumadhavan, M.: On Blockchain Applications: Hyperledger Fabric And Ethereum. Int. J. Pure Appl. Math. **118**(18), 2965–2970 (2018)
6. Buterin, V.: A next-generation smart contract and decentralized application platform. White paper (2014)
7. Fekkes, L., et al.: Comparing Bitcoin and Ethereum (2018)
8. Katz, J., et al.: Handbook of Applied Cryptography. CRC Press, Boca Raton (1996)
9. Delignat-Lavaud, A., et al.: Implementing and proving the TLS 1.3 record layer. In: 2017 IEEE Symposium on Security and Privacy (SP). IEEE (2017)
10. Dierks, T., Allen, C.: RFC 2246: The TLS protocol version 1.0, January 1999. Status: Proposed Standard (1996)
11. Dierks, T., Rescorla, E.: "IETF RFC 4346." The Transport Layer Security (TLS) Protocol Version 1 (2006)
12. Rescorla, E.: The transport layer security (TLS) protocol version 1.3. No. RFC 8446 2018
13. Purohit, M., Kaushik V., Vasudevan, S.K.: Enhanced Link Redirection Interface for Secured Browsing Using Web Browser Extensions. Editorial Preface 4 no. 10 (2013)
14. Sreevidya, B., Rajesh, M., Sasikala, T.: Performance analysis of various anonymization techniques for privacy preservation of sensitive data. In: Hemanth, J., Fernando, X., Lafata, P., Baig, Z. (eds.) ICICI 2018. LNDECT, vol. 26, pp. 687–693. Springer, Cham (2019). https://doi.org/10.1007/978-3-030-03146-6_77
15. Steinfeld, R., Bull, L., Zheng, Y.: Content extraction signatures. In: Kim, K. (ed.) ICISC 2001. LNCS, vol. 2288, pp. 285–304. Springer, Heidelberg (2002). https://doi.org/10.1007/3-540-45861-1_22
16. Bull, L., Squire, D., Zheng, Y.: A hierarchical extraction policy for content extraction signatures. Int. J. Digit. Libr. **4**(3), 208–222 (2004)

17. Wang, C., et al.: A new forward secure content extraction signature scheme. In: 2015 12th International Conference on Fuzzy Systems and Knowledge Discovery (FSKD). IEEE (2015)
18. Chang, E.-C., Lim, C.L., Xu, J.: Short redactable signatures using random trees. In: Fischlin, M. (ed.) CT-RSA 2009. LNCS, vol. 5473, pp. 133–147. Springer, Heidelberg (2009). https://doi.org/10.1007/978-3-642-00862-7_9
19. FeiFei, Z., LiFeng, D., Kun, W., Yang, L.: Study on privacy protection algorithm based on k-anonymity. Phys. Procedia Elsevier **33**, 483–490 (2012)
20. Wang, K., Chen, R., Fung, B.C., Yu, P.S.: Privacy-preserving data publishing: a survey on recent developments. ACM Computing Surveys (2010)
21. Dubovitskaya, A., Xu, Z., Ryu, S., Schumacher, M., Wang, F.: Secure and trustable electronic medical records sharing using blockchain. In: AMIA Annual Symposium Proceedings 2017, p. 650 (2017)
22. Ajun, C.: Slicing: a new approach to privacy preserving data publishing. IJESC Springer (2015)
23. Goryczka, S., Xiong, L., Fung, B.C.M.: m-Privacy for Collaborative Data Publishing. IEEE Trans. Knowl. Data Eng. **26**(10), 2520–2533 (2014)

MR Brain Image Tumor Classification via Kernel SVM with Different Preprocessing Techniques

Asmita Dixit[✉] and Aparajita Nanda[✉]

Department of CS and IT, Jaypee Institute of Information Technology,
Noida-62, India
asmitadixit5778@gmail.com, aparajita.nanda@jiit.ac.in

Abstract. Medical imaging interpretation and analysis requires automatic and exact classification. Several methods have been proposed in the last few years. This paper presents the effect of classification accuracy through different pre-processing techniques in the existing method tested on different Kernel SVM. Occurrence of irregular discontinuities causing bias field effect and intensity variations while capturing MR images requires the pre-processing of images. Three different preprocessing techniques such as Anisotropic diffusion, Homomorphic and Alphatrimmed filters are applied to brain MR images. We first enhance the attributes of the MRI image using these filters individually and then segments the tumor region. The relevant features are extracted from tumor regions and trained in a classifier. For feature extraction Wavelet transform is used, followed by feature reduction by using principle component analysis (PCA). The reduced features are trained with Kernel Support Vector Machine (KSVM) and classifies the tumor in MRI image as malignant and benign. We validate the performance of our approach on a dataset through multiple iterations to calculate the average classification accuracy subject to different preprocessing techniques.

Keywords: MRI · Anisotropic diffusion filter · Segmentation

1 Introduction

Brain tumor is termed as an unnatural cell growth and division of brain tissues which may be cancerous or non-cancerous. These tumor cells are being uncommon, yet very fatal in nature. Hence, early detection leads to a greater probability to cure completely. The two main reasons for brain tumors are radiations and rare genetic condition. Computed tomography (CT), magnetic resonance imaging (MRI) and positron emission tomography (PET) are some of the imaging techniques for brain tumor detection [1]. Doctors evaluate the tumor from the imaging tests and plan the proper medication. It is the size, type and exact location of the tumor cells in brain that is analyzed for treatment progress. Benign tumor is non-cancerous and it will not invade the neighbor cells. Recently, several techniques have been proposed for brain tumor classification. MRI is harmless and able to differentiate neural architecture of brain. MRI imaging technique uses radio wave signal with a very strong magnetic field that intensify the target region

© Springer Nature Singapore Pte Ltd. 2019
M. Singh et al. (Eds.): ICACDS 2019, CCIS 1045, pp. 221–230, 2019.
https://doi.org/10.1007/978-981-13-9939-8_20

to produce its intrinsic structure. At the time of image acquisition, the levels of excitation are tuned to result different MRI sequences. MRI with different modalities yields different level of contrast images which further depicts the structural information. MRI modalities useful in brain tumor classification are T1, T1-Gd, T2, T2-weighted and Fluid Attenuated Inversion Recovery (FLAIR). T1 MRI images differentiate normal tissues; T2 images depict the tumor region through the bright effect of the CSF. T1-Gd easily differentiates boundary of Region of Interest, whereas FLAIR images help to distinguish the edema region by suppressing the water molecule. Figure 1 depicts the MRI sequences.

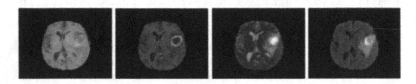

Fig. 1. T1, T1-Gd, T2, FLAIR MRI modalities

Brain tumor malignancy varies from grade I to grade IV. Grade IV tumor are highly malignant whereas tumor if detected at grade I can be easily cured. Brain MRI tumor classification can be achieved by first performing the pre-processing on image with further segmenting the tumor region from MRI, later extracting features for training and lastly testing and performing classification. Pre-processing on MRI brain image is a crucial step for de-noising and enhancing the relevant features present in image. Since, different scanners may be used while taking MR image acquisition of a patient at different times, which may result in large variations of intensity values. Therefore, MR images require pre-processing for certain improvements such as spatial smoothing, motion correction, normalization, distortion correction and bias field correction. Pre-processing plays a significant role as it could be said that the more clarity in imaging details, better will be the segmentation and classification accuracy results. To overcome these issues, different filters for preprocessing like adaptive filter, anisotropic diffusion filter, homomorphic filter, alphatrimmed filter etc. Adaptive filter is used to remove skull and bone tissues, however this situation is found rarely in MRI brain images.

In this paper, we preprocess the MR brain images with anisotropic diffusion filter, homomorphic filter, alphatrimmed filter to obtain an enhanced image with relevant feature quality and examine its effect in classification accuracy. Anisotropic diffusion filter follows the scale-space approach of edge detection to find non-uniformity in image intensity values [2]. Another is homomorphic filter which focuses on frequency domain filtering technique and used for correcting the non-uniform illumination distribution [3]. Another filter used to check the image enhancement is alpha trimmed filter which deals with multiple types of noises [4]. K-means clustering performs segmentation to segment Cerebrospinal fluid (CSF), white matter (WM) and gray matter (GM) portion of brain but lacks segmenting images containing noise [5]. This paper combines Discrete Wavelet Transformation with other thirteen extracted features like Skewness, Contrast, Homogeneity, Correlation, Mean, Energy, Standard deviation, Smoothness, Entropy,

Kurtosis, RMS, Variance and IDM to help find distinct features in tumor classification. Classification accuracy was tested on SVM Linear kernel, SVM Radial Basis Function Kernel and SVM Polynomial kernel for better accuracy results [6, 7].

2 Related Works

Saritha et al., 2013 [8] estimates two class classification of normal and abnormal brain obtaining 100% accuracy in classifying normal brain, 91.3% for stroke, 100% for degenerative disease, 95.7% for classifying brain tumor and infectious disease 91.3%. The concept of spider web plots with entropy values is used for extracting the features and Probabilistic neural network for classification. The only constraint is each time retraining is required with the increase in database. Dataset-75 was classified dividing 15 images in each category collected from Harvard Medical School. Nayak et al., 2016 performs successful segmentation and detection of cancer cells obtaining 99.53% and 100% accuracy with the use of algorithm DWT + PPCA + ADBRF. AdaBoost for classification is simple and robust to noise and outliers also measures missing data. Dataset-66 consists of 7 types of diseases of both normal and abnormal brain: Glioma malignant tumor, meningioma tumor, alzheimer's diseases, pick's, sarcoma and Huntington's disease. Dataset-255 estimates 99.53% accuracy including cerebral toxoplasmosis, herpes encephalitis, chronic subdural hematoma, and multiple sclerosis [9]. Similarly, Isin et al., 2016 describes a study of traditional methods of segmentation as well as the recent trends of deep learning using BRATS Dataset [10]. Their approach focuses on difference between semi automatic and automatic methods. Automatic Segmentation is discriminative and generative as well.

Anitha et al., 2016 [11] implemented a brain MR image tumor classification with 85% accuracy rate for 33 images, 94.28% accuracy for 65 images and 96.6% accuracy with 57 MR images. Adaptive pillar k-means was applied for segmenting tumor region and Self-Organizing Map together with K-nearest Neighbor was applied for two-tier classification.

Menze et al., 2015 suggested a generative brain tumor segmentation model including twenty different segmentation algorithm. These algorithms are applied to a 65 multi-contrast MRI including lower and higher grade glioma images. An accuracy of 74–85% is achieved on BRATS image data-set [12]. Shree et al., 2018 develops a concept which is achieving accuracy rate almost 100% in separating and classifying normal brain tissues and abnormal brain tissues. A combination of gray level co-occurrence matrix (GLCM) for obtaining features and probabilistic neural network (PNN) works as classifier [13]. At the very initial step required pre-processing is performed focusing on improving signal to noise ratio.

Unde et al. 2012 [14] termed new way of edge detection for agile contours on the basis of local adaptive threshold technique through fluctuating energy minimization for contour stoppage at required object borderline. It is able to perform tumor segmentation using thresholding segmentation algorithm. Performance analysis is measured on 512×512 size of image of 16 bit DICOM. Their approach clearly defines the boundaries on images, without any loss of changing curve at object edge and correct segmentation. Sajjad et al., 2018 builds a deep Convolutional Neural Network (CNN) based automatic multi-grade brain MR images tumor classification, obtaining 90.03% accuracy rate for grade I, 89.91% in correctly classifying grade II, 84.11% in judging grade III tumor and 85.50% accuracy achieved for grade IV. The experiment validation is performed on two different datasets; one is the radiopaedia dataset which contains MR brain images 121 in number. Second dataset is a dataset of 3064 brain MR images of modality T1-weighted. The methodology concept applied is initially performing tumor segmentation. Then data augmentation is performed, to increase the amount of data images. Lastly high-level of features are extracted and a convolutional neural network based computer aided system is achieved [15]. Usman et al., 2017 classifies tumor as complete tumor, enhancing tumor and active tumor from BRATS2013 brain MRI dataset. Pre-processing is done to remove the skull region of the brain and to obtain soft brain tissues. Histogram matching is implemented on these skull stripped images. Tumor labels are predicted on the basis of texture based wavelet features extracted. Random forest classifier is for classification. BRATS2013 is broken into high grade and low grade in which 88% complete tumor accuracy, 75% active tumor accuracy and 95% enhancing tumor accuracy rate in high grade. In low grade 81% for complete tumor and 62% accuracy rate for active tumor achieved [16].

3 Proposed Methodology

In proposed methodology, we preprocess the MR brain images with anisotropic diffusion filter, homomorphic filter and alphatrimmed filter to obtain an enhanced image with relevant feature quality and examine its effect in classification accuracy. After that we segment the image with K-means clustering. The paper combines Discrete Wavelet Transformation with other thirteen extracted features. Classification accuracy was tested on SVM Linear kernel, SVM Radial Basis Function Kernel and SVM Polynomial kernel.

The basic methodology for brain tumor classification involves the following steps:

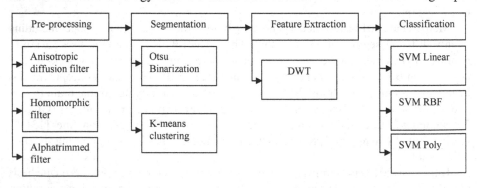

3.1   Pre-Processing

We have done analysis of various pre-processing techniques for tumor classification. Further testing of brain MR images is done by three different filters for analyzing their effect on classification accuracy. There are various brain MR images which require filtering and some do not require. The category of pre-processing varies from the type of distortion effect on the image like is there a requirement of bias field correction, intensity normalization or removal of skull and bone region. Also at time pre-processing is significant for separating brain region and central nervous system.

3.1.1   Anisotropic Diffusion Filter

Anisotropic diffusion filter helps in de-noising the images without erasing significant parts of the image. It is basically used with MR images and in several automated context [2]. With noise level exceeding 3%, it is not possible to maintain the edges for complete removal of noise by Anisotropic diffusion filter [2].

$$\begin{cases} \dfrac{\partial I}{\partial t} = div\lceil c(|\nabla I|)\nabla I\rceil \\ I(t=0) = I_o \end{cases} \tag{1}$$

Where, div(..) denotes the divergence operator, ∇ represents gradient operator, magnitude is | |, for initial image we have I_0 and c() specifies diffusion coefficient. Figure 2 given below depicts the effect of applying Anisotropic Diffusion filter in given sample image of 23 images dataset.

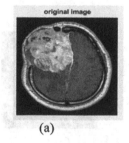 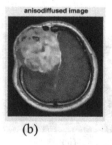

(a)   (b)

Fig. 2. shows (a) original image and (b) effect of Anisotropic Diffusion Filter on sample Brain MRI

3.1.2   Homomorphic Filter

Homomorphic filter contributes in both de-noising and image enhancement. Commonly used for correcting non uniform illumination in images [3]. It simultaneously increases contrast also normalizes the brightness of the image. Homomorphic filters lacks in separation of illumination and reflectance in an image.

$$f(x,y) = i(x,y).r(x,y)$$
$$\ln(f(x,y)) = \ln(i(x,y)) + \ln(r(x,y))$$
$$F(u,v) = I(u,v) + R(u,v)$$
$$N(u,v) = H(u,v).F(u,v) \tag{2}$$
$$n(x,y) = invF(N(u,v))$$
$$nimage(x,y) = \exp(n(x,y))$$

f is the image, i illumination and r is the reflectance.

3.1.3   Alpha-Trimmed Filter

Alpha-trimmed filter is an averaging filter as it calculates average within neighbor window, deleting both highest and lowest gray intensity values. Multiple type noise problems could be easily solved since it combines Gaussian and salt-and pepper filtering method. This filter can be used only where noise density is high. It is not useful in images with low noise density [4].

$$A(x,y) = \frac{1}{NxN - 2P} \sum_{i=P}^{NxN-2P} A_i \tag{3}$$

Where A= image and size square mask ranging from minimum to maximum value is N × N. Parameter P cannot exceed N × N/2, is the size mask is 5 × 5 P could be 3. Figure 3 given below depicts the effect of applying Alpha-Trimmed filter in given sample image of 23 images dataset.

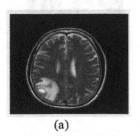
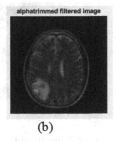

(a)   (b)

Fig. 3. Depicts (a) original image (b) the effect of applying Alpha Trimmed filter in given sample image of 23 images dataset.

3.1.4   Color Based k-Means Segmentation

Color based k-means segmentation technique is considered. Initially Otsu binarization is applied and then k-means clustering. Thirteen features including DWT, Contrast, Correlation, Energy, Homogeneity, Mean, Standard_Deviation, Entropy, RMS, Variance, Smoothness, Kurtosis, Skewness, IDM are extracted.

3.1.5 Classification

Classification accuracy is calculated based on SVM linear classifier, SVMRBF classifier and SVM Polynomial classifier. SVM kernels are memory efficient since it makes decision function via subset of trained values. The different kernels and their mathematical equations are as follows:

Linear SVM

$$f(x) = B(0) + sum(ai^*(x, x_i))$$ (4)

For the representation of new input vector we have x, B(0) and ai are the coefficients evaluated from learning algorithm of trained data.

RBF SVM

$$K(x, x^1) = \exp(\frac{-\|x - x^1\|}{2\sigma^2})$$ (5)

$-\|x\text{-}x^1\|$ calculates the squared Euclidean distance of 2 feature vectors of image K and σ is a free parameter.

Polynomial SVM

$$K(x_i, x_j) = (x_i.x_j + 1)^d$$ (6)

Input space vectors are x_i and x_j i.e., the feature vectors.

4 Experiment

Brain MR images were tested on three different filters for their impact on the image quality. Pre-processing using three different filtering techniques was performed for denoising and enhancing image feature quality. For this Anisotropic Diffusion filter, Homomorphic filter and Alpha Trimmed filter was use. Further, analysis of their effect on classification accuracy was calculated. Experiments were performed in MATLAB2017b. Feature of simple SVM was used and extended to kernel SVM.

4.1 Database

The experiments and accuracy calculation was performed on dataset-66 and other 23 MR images containing benign and malignant tumor effected brains. The datasets have T2-weighted MR images; dataset-66 has images of 256 × 256 resolution, the second dataset has images of different scale variations ranging from minimum 118 × 200 to maximum 235 × 235. The source of dataset was Harvard Medical School website.

Dataset-66 has both normal brain as well as pathological (abnormal) brain MR images. Dataset-66 is categorized in diseases termed as glioma brain tumor, meningioma infected cells, Alzheimer's, Alzheimer's along with visual agnosia, Pick's disease symptoms, sarcoma and Huntington's disease. Figure 4 represents one sample each of the former said brain diseases. Random selection of 16 images in dataset-66 and 7 were selected in remaining 23 MR images. Setting of trained image and validation is represented in Table 1 using 5-fold cross validation.

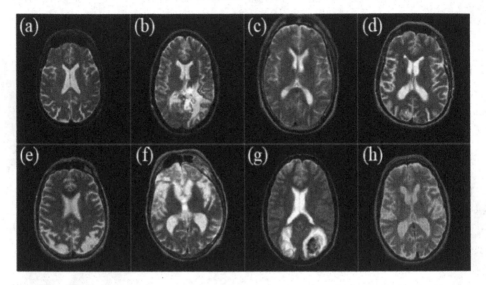

Fig. 4. Sample of brain MRIs: (a) normal brain (b) glioma tumor (c) Meningioma tumor (d) Alzheimer's (e) Alzheimer's along with visual agnosia (f) Pick's disease (g) sarcoma (h) Huntington's disease.

Table 1. Tabular representation of training and validating images (5-fold cross validation)

Total no. images	Trained		Validated	
	Benign	Malignant	Benign	Malignant
66	26	24	10	6
23	11	12	4	3

Classification Accuracy

The paper proposes the effect of pre-processing in the existing DWT+PCA+SVM technique. It depicts the outcome of increased accuracy in the existing technique by adding different pre-processing filters (Table 2).

Table 2. Classification accuracy comparison of 3 different filters in Different Kernel SVM for the same MRI dataset and same number of images:

		SVM Linear	SVM RBF	SVM Poly
With Pre-processing	Anisotropic Diffusion filter	61.53	61.53	58.97
	Homomorphic filter	55	60	58
	Alphatrimmed filter	54	55	57
Without pre-processing		53.84	53.84	53.84

5 Conclusion

This study proposes the effect of classification accuracy through different pre-processing techniques in the existing method tested on different Kernel SVM. This proposed method helps in enhancing the brain MR image in order to distinguish between benign and malignant tumour of the brain. The experiment gives different accuracy results on the basis of three different filters, resulting in noise reduction and increase classification accuracy. Further future work could be focused on multi-level tumor grade classification. Since the binary classification does not provide help in treatment phase. The most important contribution of this paper is to propose a method which helps in exact and detail diagnosis of tumor region.

References

1. Hemanth, D.J., Anitha, J., Naaji, A., Geman, O., Popescu, D.E.: A modified deep convolutional neural network for abnormal brain image classification. IEEE Access **7**, 4275–4283 (2019)
2. Padmashree, S., Nagapadma, R.: Performance measure analysis between anisotropic diffusion filter and bilateral filter for post processing of fractal compressed medical images. Int. J. Comput. Appl. **123**(12), 36–43 (2015)
3. Agrawal, P., Chourasia, V., Kapoor, R., Agrawal, S.: A Comprehensive study of the image enhancement techniques. Int. J. Adv. Found. Res. Comput. (IJAFRC) **1**, 85–89 (2014)
4. Sharma, P., Singh, H.: Improvement of brain tumor feature based segmentation using decision based alpha trimmed global mean filter. Int. J. Comput. Appl. **121**(21), 13–20 (2015)
5. Liu, J., Guo, L.: A new brain MRI image segmentation strategy based on k-means clustering and SVM. In: 2015 7th International Conference on Intelligent Human-Machine Systems and Cybernetics (IHMSC), vol. 2, pp. 270–273. IEEE (2015)
6. Chaplot, S., Patnaik, L.M., Jagannathan, N.R.: Classification of magnetic resonance brain images using wavelets as input to support vector machine and neural network. Biomed. Signal Process. Control **1**(1), 86–92 (2006)
7. El-Dahshan, E.-S.A., Hosny, T., Salem, A.-B.M.: Hybrid intelligent techniques for MRI brain images classification. Digital Signal Process. **20**(2), 433–441 (2010)
8. Saritha, M., Joseph, K.P., Mathew, A.T.: Classification of MRI brain images using combined wavelet entropy based spider web plots and probabilistic neural network. Pattern Recogn. Lett. **34**(16), 2151–2156 (2013)

9. Nayak, D.R., Dash, R., Majhi, B.: Brain MR image classification using two-dimensional discrete wavelet transform and AdaBoost with random forests. Neurocomputing **177**, 188–197 (2016)
10. Işın, A., Direkoğlu, C., Şah, M.: Review of MRI-based brain tumor image segmentation using deep learning methods. Procedia Comput. Sci. **102**, 317–324 (2016)
11. Anitha, V., Murugavalli, S.: Brain tumour classification using two-tier classifier with adaptive segmentation technique. IET Comput. Vision **10**(1), 9–17 (2016)
12. Menze, B.H., et al.: The multimodal brain tumor image segmentation benchmark (BRATS). IEEE Trans. Med. Imaging **34**(10), 1993 (2015)
13. Shree, N.V., Kumar, T.N.R.: Identification and classification of brain tumor MRI images with feature extraction using DWT and probabilistic neural network. Brain Inform. **5**(1), 23–30 (2018)
14. Unde, A.S., Premprakash, V.A. Sankaran, P.: A novel edge detection approach on active contour for tumor segmentation. In: 2012 Students Conference on Engineering and Systems (SCES), pp. 1–6. IEEE, March 2012
15. Sajjad, M., Khan, S., Muhammad, K., Wu, W., Ullah, A., Baik, S.W.: Multi-grade brain tumor classification using deep CNN with extensive data augmentation. J. Comput. Sci. **30**, 174–182 (2019)
16. Usman, K., Rajpoot, K.: Brain tumor classification from multi-modality MRI using wavelets and machine learning. Pattern Anal. Appl. **20**(3), 871–881 (2017)

Attribute-Based Deterministic Access Control Mechanism (AB-DACM) for Securing Communication in Internet of Smart Health Care Things

Ankur Lohachab[✉] and Ajay Jangra[✉]

University Institute of Engineering Technology, Kurukshetra University, Kurukshetra, India
ankurlohachab@gmail.com, er_jangra@yahoo.co.in

Abstract. Internet of Things (IoT) envisages the idea of ubiquitous inter-connectivity, and aims at building smart blocks of next generation technologies by integrating physical world with the Internet. Concepts of IoT are making a huge impact in health sector by facilitating remote medical services including health monitoring, rescue in emergency situations, and so forth. Devices for imaging and diagnosis when embedded with sensors and actuators, build the core of IoT-enabled health care. However, this new paradigm of health care comes along with various security and privacy challenges, such as unauthorized access, that may lead to serious consequences if not handled appropriately. This paper presents an Attribute Based Deterministic Access Control Mechanism (AB-DACM) explicitly designed to ensure secure remote access in medical organisations using Attribute Based Access Control (ABAC) model and Elliptic Curve Cryptography (ECC). Moreover, the proposed authorisation algorithm is validated and verified using Access Control Policy Testing (ACPT) tool.

Keywords: Internet of Things · Smart Health Care · Security ·
Attribute-Based Access Control · Authentication ·
Access Control Policy Testing

1 Introduction

Concept of IoT is re-defining the physical world by means of inter-connecting uniquely identifiable devices [1]. Technologies like Wireless Sensor Networks (WSNs), Artificial Intelligence (AI) based algorithms, different communication interfaces, and Cloud and Fog Computing, collectively form a typical IoT environment. With advancements in Micro-Electro-Mechanical-Systems (MEMS), various applications are being re-designed. Distributed IoT environment offers varying range of applications from generic to specific ones, by providing ancillary smartness to the devices. Now-a-days, major sectors like health care rely on IoT services for better and unprecedented development.

Digital health care ecosystem integrates patients and doctors onto a common platform for intelligent health monitoring by analysing day-to-day human activities. Smart wearable devices facilitate patients with real-time monitoring of their body parameters

© Springer Nature Singapore Pte Ltd. 2019
M. Singh et al. (Eds.): ICACDS 2019, CCIS 1045, pp. 231–243, 2019.
https://doi.org/10.1007/978-981-13-9939-8_21

including glucose, blood pressure, heartbeat, and so forth. Early diagnosis ensures prevention from hazardous illness among the patients. Similarly, smart homes and vehicles provide doctors the facility for operating the toolkits remotely for personalized treatment of the patients. Body Sensor Networks (BSNs) is one of the tremendous technologies which plays a vital role in the mobile health care services [2]. Diverse nature of health sector demands traceability. Although in general terms, traceability can be understood as a process of identifying all the data from its origin till consumption [3]. However, in health sector, it can be defined as the information of the patients from their appointment till treatment, and also afterwards as long as patients are associated with the organization. This abundant amount of data and digitization of medical objects compel us to enforce strong security mechanisms that would not only ensure privacy of their data, but also authorized implementation of the medical devices [4, 5].

There is plethora of challenges in the way of ensuring security of the data collected from the patients and for operating medical devices. Many researchers try to achieve this goal by using steganography techniques for hiding the critical information in an image which can be a viable solution. However, cryptographic techniques are more preferable. The classical encryption algorithms like Advanced Encryption Standard (AES) and River-Shamir-Adleman (RSA) are not suitable for IoT devices as these devices have low power as compared to other battery-powered devices. Hence, there is a need to use cryptographic solutions that are not only light-weight in nature, but also provide better security. Elliptic Curve Cryptography (ECC) provides the same level of security as of AES and RSA with lesser key size which makes it suitable for resource-constrained devices [6].

By considering the requirements of providing stronger authentication and authorization, we develop a framework which will utilize the concept of ECC for producing secure authentication, and Attribute Based Access Control (ABAC) model for ensuring authorization. Moreover, we use Access Control Policy testing (ACPT) tool for validating and verifying the correctness of the proposed algorithm in eXtensible Access Control Markup Language (XACML) format. Rest of the paper is organized as follows. Section 2 presents the related work in the field. Section 3 discusses the proposed framework in detail. Section 4 discusses the results of implementation and analyses various security aspects in detail. Finally, Sect. 5 concludes the paper with future work.

2   Related Work

Traditional model for health care sector followed hospital-centric approach. For instance, when people fell sick, then only they used to visit the hospitals. But in recent years, adoption of IoT based devices in the health care sector provides the facility to the end users that they are able to monitor their health on their own. In some cases, they take prescription without making a physical visit to the hospital. Increase in the use of health care devices is also increasing challenges in terms of privacy and security as attackers are always trying to capture the patient's health record and devices. Nevertheless, researchers are always trying to make efforts for developing better schemes that provide resistance to attacks. This section reviews some of the related access control and authentication schemes as summarized in Table 1.

Moosavi et al. [7] proposed a secure and efficient authentication and authorization mechanism on a prototype IoT-based health care system. The proposed architecture is built using Pandaboard, WiSMotes and SmartRF06, and by using the fundamental concept of certificate based Datagram Transport Layer Security (DTLS) handshake protocol. The authors believe that their architecture is more secure than centralized delegation based architecture, and impact of the Denial of Service (DoS) attacks is reduced up to some extent. They also proved that due to the optimized key management scheme, overhead between sensor nodes and smart gateway reduces up to 26% and communication latency reduces up to 16% between smart gateway and end users. In [8], the authors presented a robust and efficient authentication protocol for health care based applications by using wireless medical sensor networks. They compared their scheme with the authentication protocol proposed by Kumar et al. [9]. Based on their observations, latter is vulnerable to privilege insider and off-line password guessing attacks, and also failed to provide user anonymity. Hence, former is better with higher computational efficiency and stronger security.

Bernabe et al. [10] proposed an access control system TACIoT which provides flexible and trust-aware end-to-end security for IoT devices. The authors claimed that their novel mechanism provides reliable light-weight authorization by considering trust values based on the Quality of Service (QoS), device's social relationships, and reputation. They successfully implemented and evaluated their mechanism on real test-bed designed for non-contained and constrained IoT devices. Pal et al. [11] reduced the number of authentication policies and proposed an access control architecture which

Table 1. Related work – application areas and problems addressed.

Year	Authors	Area	Problems	Solutions
2015 [7]	Moosavi et al.	Smart Health Care	• Resource-constrained sensors cannot perform computational intensive authentication and authorization operations • DoS attacks	• Distributed smart e-health gateways to perform trivial tasks • Distributed nature of architecture
2015 [8]	He et al.		• Security and privacy of sensor collected data	• Anonymous authentication protocol
2016 [10]	Bernabe et al.	IoT applications	• Pervasive communication • Reliability	• End-to-end security • Trust based mechanism
2017 [11]	Pal et al.	Smart Health Care	• Unauthorized access to smart things • ABAC, RBAC and CAPBAC require highly centralized solution and unmanageably large policy base	• Fine-grained access control mechanism • Hybrid mechanism with reduced number of authentication policies
2018 [12]	Cruz-Piris et al.	IoT applications	• Access control for heterogeneous devices • Protection of Internet-based services along with IoT devices	• Modelling Communication procedures as resources • Integrating authorization mechanism with communication protocol

provides fine-grained access control by improving management policies. They described their implementation with hybrid access control by applying attributes, capabilities and roles. This model is formally specified and demonstrated using various use-case scenarios. Cruz-Piris et al. [12] proposed a methodology which is able to protect resources by allowing the modelling of communication actions as resources considering Message Queuing Telemetry Transport (MQTT) as the communication protocol. For access control mechanism, the authors selected Open Authorization (OAuth) 2.0 and User-Managed Access (UMA). They also validated their proposed solution's correctness and evaluated overhead of energy consumption.

3 Proposed Framework

This section discusses the proposed framework in detail along with the preliminary concepts used and system entities involved.

3.1 Preliminaries and System Entities

Elliptic Curve Cryptography. Security of ECC is based on the mathematical equation, specifically trapdoor function, which states that $A \rightarrow B$ can be easily found, but vice versa is not true, i.e., $A \leftarrow B$ cannot be found easily [13]. Among various elliptic curves, WEIERSTRASS curve shown in Fig. 1 is adopted by the National Institute of Standards and Technology (NIST) which uses 384 bits to provide similar security as of 7680 bits of RSA [14]. WEIERSTRASS curve uses the Eq. (3.1) given below –

$$E_p(a, b) : y^2 = x^3 + ax + b \pmod{p}, \tag{3.1}$$

where a and b are constants that are used to define the elliptic curves and $a, b \in Z_p$. Set $Z_p = \{0, 1, 2, 3, 4, \ldots, p-1\}$, where $p > 3$ is a large prime number which satisfies $4a^3 + 27b^2 \bmod p \neq 0$, along with a special point O called as 'point at infinity' or 'zero point'. Various problems are considered in ECC for providing better security, and among these problems, Elliptic Curve Discrete Logarithm Problem (ECDLP) is very popular which says that, if $Q = KP$, where $P, Q \in E_P(a, b)$ and $K \in Z_p$, then computing scalar K is not easy even if we know both P and Q.

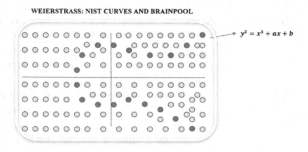

Fig. 1. Weierstrass elliptic curve.

Attribute Based Access Control Model. In ABAC model, subject presents the attributes based on which access can be granted. Two aspects in ABAC are – policy based access control model, and the corresponding architecture model which is able to apply these policies. Attributes are identified by the subjects and objects based on their characteristics. Based on the condition defined by policy rules, permission is granted or denied to the end user [15].

Threat and Functional Assumptions. Formulation of the proposed scheme is based on the below discussed threat and functional assumptions –

1. Interception: An attacker has the capability of eavesdropping the ongoing transmission for collecting the sensitive information [16].
2. Cloud: Devices and smart cards can be used in an independent way with respect to any type of Cloud.
3. Authorization: An attacker may try to use the services without having the appropriate permissions or with stolen access privileges.
4. Privacy: Like privileged insider attack, attackers may try to breach the privacy of the end users for accessing the unauthorized parameters.

System Entities. Proposed scheme involves following entities as discussed below [Fig. 2] –

1. Patients/Data Providers: These are responsible for collecting the data and provide respective data for storing in the Medical Server.
2. Medical Server: It is present in the application support layer which includes Cloud technology. Distributed Cloud Computing technology reduces the workload on a traditional single Cloud center. Now-a-days, some of the common demands of users, such as to use the facilities provided by multiple service providers, need of

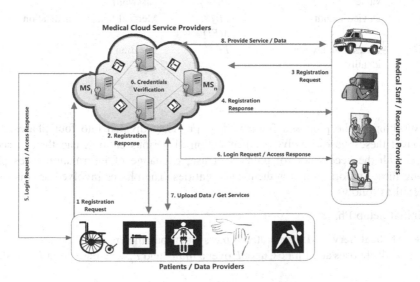

Fig. 2. System model of the proposed scheme.

hybrid Cloud in peak hours of usage, and reduction in time of communication, encourage developers to use next generation Cloud Computing.

3. Medical Staff/Resource Provider: Medical staff is capable of providing the required services and facilities as demanded by the patients.

3.2 Working of the Proposed Scheme

The proposed scheme utilizes some useful notations as summarized in Table 2.

Table 2. Notations used in proposed scheme.

Term	Description	Term	Description
MS	Medical server	BIO_I	Medical staff biometrics
E	Elliptic curve over a finite field F_P	d_info_i	Device information of medical staff
P	Generator of G	OTP	Medical staff device's one-time password
p, n	Large prime numbers	E_X	Medical staff smart card parameters
x, PK	Private and public key of medical server	t_i	Current time stamp
$h_1 ()$	Hash function chosen by medical server	$M1, M1'$	Messages
P_i	Patient	ME	Medical expert
$PID_i,$ $PW_{i\ i}$	Patient's identity and password	$RP, AT,$ IA, PH	Receptionist, attendant, insurance agent, pharmacist
RPW_I	Pseudo random password	$MEXP$	Medical expenditure
r, S	Random number, secret value	$HU_I,$ HPW_I	Medical staff username and password
PD_i	Device identity	$MHY,$ MED	Medical history, medication
$APID_I$	Patients anonymous identity	LOC	Location

Working of the proposed framework is precisely divided into four phases. Execution of these phases involves authentication of various entities, and then in accordance with the access control policies in use, exchange of information takes place among these authorized and authenticated entities. The phases involved are discussed in detail as follows.

1. Initial Setup Phase

- Medical Server MS generates some system parameters as follows –
  - It chooses an Elliptic Curve E over a finite field F_p with base point P of order n.

- It chooses a random private key x and computes public key $PK = xP$.
- It chooses secure and collision-resistant hash functions $h_1()$.
- It keeps x as private and publishes the public parameters $\{E(F_p), P, Ps, h_q\}$.

2. Registration Phase

- **Patient Registration** – In order for patient P_i to get registered at the remote medical server MS, he/she uses the health application portal and sends his/her identity including the wearable device identity (if any) to MS.
  - P_i chooses an identity PID_i, a password PW_i, a random number r, and computes a pseudorandom password RPW_i as –

  $$P_i : RPW_i = h_1(PW_i\|r)$$

  - P_i sends PID_i, RPW_i, r along with device identity PD_i (if any) to MS as –

  $$P_i \rightarrow MS : \{PID_i, RPW_i, r, PD_i\}$$

  - MS checks for the identity collision. If the identity chosen by the patient or device identity already exists, the request is discarded.
  - MS computes the anonymous identity $APID_i$ for the patient as –

  $$MS : APID_i = h_1(PID_i\|r\|x)$$

  and a secret value as –

  $$MS : S_i = h_1(APID_i\|r\|x).$$

  - MS stores $\{APID_i, r, RPW_i, S_i\}$ in its database and also sends the same to the patient.

  $$MS \rightarrow P_i : \{APID_i, r, S_i\}$$

- **Medical Staff Registration** –
  - In order for the Medical Staff to get registered, they choose a username HU_j, password HPW_j.
  - They send the same along with the biometrics information BIO_j and the device information d_info over which OTP can be received to the MS as –

  $$\text{Medical Staff} \rightarrow MS : \{HU_j, HPW_j, BIO_j, d\_info\}$$

- In return, MS issues a smart card to the medical staff with $E_x\{HU_j, HPW_j, BIO_j\}$ stored over it.

3. Mutual Authentication Phase

- Patient Authentication –
  - Whenever a patient wants to store data at the data center or gets the treatment from a medical expert, he/she has to prove his/her legitimacy to the MS. For that the patient sends $\{APD_i', r', S_i'\}$ and the current time stamp t_i to MS.

$$\text{P}_i \rightarrow \text{MS} : \{APD_i', r', S_i'\}$$

  - MS upon receiving the same, computes

$$\text{MS} : S_i = h_1\left(APD_i' || r' || x\right).$$

  If $S_i = S_i'$, implies that the patient's identity is valid.
  - Once the identity of the patient is validated, he/she can upload the data or can get the required services.
- Medical Staff Authentication –
  - In order for hospital staff including Receptionist, Attendant, Medical Expert, Pharmacist, and Insurance Agent to treat the patient under them or to deal with the insurance related aspects, they use the smart card containing the information $\{MS_i, BIO_i\}$ and the OTP received on their devices to access the patient related information from the Cloud data center.

$$\text{M}_1 = \left\{HU_j, HPW_j, BIO_j, OTP\right\} + rxP, \text{M}_1' = rP$$
$$\text{Hospital Staff} \rightarrow \text{MS} : \left(\text{M}_1, \text{M}_1'\right)$$

  - MS checks the information and validates the identity of the respective staff member.

$$\text{MS} : \text{M}_1 - k\text{M}_1' = \left\{HU_j, HPW_j, BIO_j, OTP\right\}$$

  - After validation of the identity, Attribute Based Deterministic Access Control (AB-DAC) maps the information to permissible actions by taking the consensus of the involved entities [Fig. 3].

4. Credential Change Phase

- P_i chooses a new password PW_{inew} computes a new pseudorandom password RPW_{inew} as –

$$\text{P}_i : RPW_{inew} = h_1(PW_{inew} || r)$$

which is sent to MS.

$$\text{P}_i \rightarrow \text{MS} : \{PID_i, RPW_{inew}\}$$

- MS checks for the identity of the patient and stores the new password.

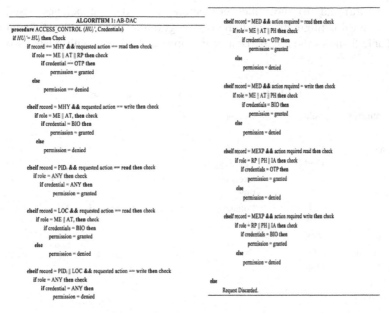

Fig. 3. Pseudo code of attribute based deterministic access control.

4 Results and Discussion

This section presents the implementation of the proposed policy model in XACML format along with security analysis.

4.1 Protocol Results and Comparison

ACPT tool is utilized in order to test and verify the correctness of the policies for device level access control. This tool is used for model specification and composition of policies through the use of rule templates. It also verifies the properties and tests the policies against some specific properties in order to determine security holes. Table 3 shows the initial parameters chosen during the formularization of AB-DAC. Table 4 shows the results for verification and testing AB-DAC model in the proposed scheme.

Table 3. Initial parameter values chosen in AB-DAC.

Parameters	Attribute	Attribute type	Attribute values
Subject	Role	String	ME, RP, AT, IA, PH
	Credentials		OTP, BIO
Resource	Record	String	MHY, ID, LOC, MED, MEXP
Action	MLSDefaultAction	Boolean	Read, Write
Environment	AUTH	Boolean	True, False

Figure 4(a) and (b) show the verification of the defined policies based on the initially defined configuration and proposed algorithm. Based on the different parameters, Table 5 shows the comparison of the proposed scheme with related work.

Table 4. Results based on input parameters.

Input parameters	Value	Output parameters	Value			
			Static		Dynamic	
System name	Fireeye INPUT	No. of Tests/Type	–	–	25	25
Degree of interaction	2	Execution time	32 ms	16 ms	0.249 s	0.936 s
Mode	SCRATCH	Policies mode	Merged	Combined	Merged	Combined
Algorithm	IPOG					
Ignore constraints	NO					
Progress Info, Debug Mode, Verify Coverage	OFF					

Fig. 4. Verification results of AB-DAC algorithm (**a**) Merged policies (**b**) Combined policies.

Table 5. Comparison with other related schemes.

Schemes →	Moosavi et al. [7]	He et al. [8]	Bernabe et al. [10]	Pal et al. [11]	Cruz-Piris et al. [12]	Proposed scheme
Comparison Parameters ↓						
Access control model	–	–	Distributed CapBAC	CapBAC, ABAC, RBAC	User Management Access (UMA)	ABAC
Formal verification	Yes	No	Yes	No	Yes	Yes
Credential-change phase	No	Yes	–	No	–	Yes

4.2 Security Analysis

Our proposed framework satisfies the following security properties –

1. Patient Anonymity – Patient's anonymity is maintained by computing anonymous identity and using the same throughout the communication.
2. Prevention against Masquerade Attacks – Since OTP is sent to the device of medical staff to access patient specific information, an attacker cannot pretend as a legitimate staff member to access the same.
3. One-time Registration – Medical server checks for the identity of the patient or device before registration which ensures that multiple patients or devices cannot register under same identity.
4. Prevention of Forgery Attacks – Use of biometric information of the medical staff before card issuance prevents forgery attacks.
5. Prevention against Stolen Smart Card Attacks – Since medical staff uses OTP received on their devices along with smart cards, if the card gets stolen, an attacker cannot use it without the OTP.

5   Conclusion

Since IoT devices are being used to generate massive scale of attacks in the health care sector, there is a need to develop an architecture that will solace these security problems in a much efficacious way. This paper, presents an Attribute Based Deterministic Access Control Mechanism (AB-DACM) for ensuring security in health care communication scenario. For end-user authorization, Attribute Based Access Control (ABAC) model is utilized, and for authentication, concepts of Elliptic Curve Cryptography (ECC) are used. The authorization algorithm is validated using Access Control Policy Testing (ACPT) tool. For static verification, the execution time is 32 ms for merged policies and 16 ms for combined policies, respectively. On the other hand, for dynamic verification, the execution time is 0.249 s for merged policies, and 0.936 s for combined policies. The results of the implementation show the effectiveness of the proposed model in dynamically changing application requirements and it is best suited for resource-constrained IoT based Smart Health Care environment.

Acknowledgment. The authors would like to acknowledge Dr. Vincent Hu from National Institute of Standards and Technology (NIST) for providing access credentials for ACPT tool.

References

1. Pattabiraman, P., Dhaya, R., Sasidhar, B., Kanthavel, R.: IoV: the future of automobiles. In: Singh, M., Gupta, P.K., Tyagi, V., Sharma, A., Ören, T., Grosky, W. (eds.) ICACDS 2016. CCIS, vol. 721, pp. 158–164. Springer, Singapore (2017). https://doi.org/10.1007/978-981-10-5427-3_17
2. Fortino, G., Ghasemzadeh, H., Gravina, R., Liu, P.X., Poon, C.C., Wang, Z.: Advances in Multi-Sensor Fusion for Body Sensor Networks: Algorithms, Architectures, and Applications: Guest Editorial (2018)
3. Martínez Pérez, M., Dafonte, C., Gómez, Á.: Traceability in patient healthcare through the integration of RFID technology in an ICU in a hospital. Sensors **18**(5), 1627 (2018)
4. Habib, C., Makhoul, A., Darazi, R., Couturier, R.: Health risk assessment and decision-making for patient monitoring and decision-support using wireless body sensor networks. Inf. Fusion **47**, 10–22 (2019)
5. Shen, J., Chang, S., Shen, J., Liu, Q., Sun, X.: A lightweight multi-layer authentication protocol for wireless body area networks. Future Gener. Comput. Syst. **78**, 956–963 (2018)
6. Lohachab, A., Karmabir: Using Quantum Key Distribution and ECC for Secure Inter-Device Authentication and Communication in IoT Infrastructure (2018)
7. Moosavi, S.R., Gia, T.N., Rahmani, A.M., Nigussie, E., Virtanen, S., Isoaho, J., Tenhunen, H.: SEA: a secure and efficient authentication and authorization architecture for IoT-based healthcare using smart gateways. Procedia Comput. Sci. **52**, 452–459 (2015)
8. He, D., Kumar, N., Chen, J., Lee, C.C., Chilamkurti, N., Yeo, S.S.: Robust anonymous authentication protocol for health-care applications using wireless medical sensor networks. Multimedia Syst. **21**(1), 49–60 (2015)
9. Kumar, P., Lee, S., Lee, H.: E-SAP: efficient-strong authentication protocol for healthcare applications using wireless medical sensor networks. Sensors **12**, 1625–1647 (2012)
10. Bernabe, J.B., Ramos, J.L.H., Gomez, A.F.S.: TACIoT: multidimensional trust-aware access control system for the Internet of Things. Soft. Comput. **20**(5), 1763–1779 (2016)
11. Pal, S., Hitchens, M., Varadharajan, V., Rabehaja, T.: On design of a fine-grained access control architecture for securing IoT-enabled smart healthcare systems. In: Proceedings of the 14th EAI International Conference on Mobile and Ubiquitous Systems: Computing, Networking and Services, pp. 432–441. ACM (2017)
12. Cruz-Piris, L., Rivera, D., Marsa-Maestre, I., de la Hoz, E., Velasco, J.R.: Access control mechanism for IoT environments based on modelling communication procedures as resources. Sensors **18**(3), 917 (2018)
13. Gura, N., Patel, A., Wander, A., Eberle, H., Shantz, S.C.: Comparing elliptic curve cryptography and RSA on 8-bit CPUs. In: Joye, M., Quisquater, J.-J. (eds.) CHES 2004. LNCS, vol. 3156, pp. 119–132. Springer, Heidelberg (2004). https://doi.org/10.1007/978-3-540-28632-5_9

14. Lohachab, A.: ECC based inter-device authentication and authorization scheme using MQTT for IoT networks. J. Inf. Secur. Appl. **46**, 1–12 (2019)
15. Ouaddah, A., Mousannif, H., Elkalam, A.A., Ouahman, A.A.: Access control in the Internet of Things: big challenges and new opportunities. Comput. Netw. **112**, 237–262 (2017)
16. Lohachab, A., Karambir, B.: Critical analysis of DDoS—an emerging security threat over IoT networks. J. Commun. Inf. Netw. **3**(3), 57–78 (2018)

An Enhanced Genetic Virtual Machine Load Balancing Algorithm for Data Center

Mala Yadav$^{(\boxtimes)}$ and Jay Shankar Prasad$^{(\boxtimes)}$

School of Computer and Information Science, MVN University Palwal,
Aurangabad 121105, Haryana, India
{12CA9002, jayshankar.prasad}@mvn.edu.in

Abstract. Data centers with cloud computing platform host several resources using numerous virtual machines. Such situations may cause the degradation of performance and violations of service level agreement. These challenges are addressed by providing an efficient load balancing mechanism for data centers, and also the workload must be distributed dynamically between the nodes. In this paper, hybrid meta-heuristic genetic algorithm based load balancing technique using active virtual has been proposed and simulated by Cloud Analyst. Simulation results of this hybrid meta heuristic approach found to be encouraging. Obtained results of the proposed algorithm are compared and analyzed with existing traditional strategy and it outperformed which makes it suitable for the deployment over the data centers.

Keywords: Genetic Algorithm · Load balancing · Cloud computing ·
Cloud Analyst

1 Introduction

Cluster, grid and cloud computing provides enormous computing power through virtualization and resource aggregation. All these technologies, fulfills the user high computing utility requirement. These utility based computing are paid service business model and according to actual utilization, consumers need to pay rather to purchase entire resource. For example, to use the electricity consumers don't need to build a power plant but he/she should purchase the electricity and pay according to the use.

High power computing as a services are available worldwide through Amazon, Google, and Microsoft, and known as Cloud Computing. In cloud computing, the basic computing infrastructure, either to perform high end complex processing or to execute simple programs is knowns as a "cloud," whose basic objective is to offer on demand computing for diverse applications worldwide [1]. Thus, processing and storage "as a service" are the prime concerns.

Cloud computing is defined as "*model for enabling ubiquitous, convenient, on demand network access to a shared pool of configurable computing resources that can be rapidly provisioned and delivered with minimal managerial effort or service provider interaction*" in NIST [2].

Distributed computing deployed over fast internet provides cloud computing to disseminate the task for processing and executing from local workstations to remote

M. Singh et al. (Eds.): ICACDS 2019, CCIS 1045, pp. 244–253, 2019.
https://doi.org/10.1007/978-981-13-9939-8_22

clusters. Through virtualization technology, a single data center (i.e. a high power server) behaves like multiple machines [1]. A new technology cloud computing has significant use and various role in business, but for the practical deployment it needs to handle issues. Load balancing is a critical issue, because all the available task (workload) must be evenly distributed on the entire cloud to ensure that no overloaded and underloaded processor or resources should exist on network. The requirement of efficient load balancing algorithm by Cloud service provider (CSP) in cloud computing platform is still in demand [2]. Thus, several application requests can be distributed over available resources lying with data centers using efficient load balancing approaches. However, to meet the user requirements by efficient resource utilization also enhances the overall performance of the cloud computing environment. Load balancing are centralize or decentralized, static or dynamic depending upon the task handling [3].

In this paper, we proposed and simulated a hybrid genetic algorithm(GA) approach based on priority of best suited available virtual machine(VM) using active virtual machine load balancer. Fusion of active virtual machine load balancer with GA algorithms provide dual optimization and helps in achieving the target of efficient load balancing. CloudAnalyst [23] is based on CloudSim [22] facilitates the simulation and analysis to assess the proposed algorithm. The experimental result shows that modified hybrid algorithm amazingly improves the resource utilization. The rest of paper is organized as follows: Sect. 2 deals about related previous work. Section 3 gives brief overview of simulation tool CloudAnalyst [23]. In Sect. 4, modified hybrid genetic algorithm for load optimization has been proposed and discussed. Section 5 presents the simulation parameters and comparison and analysis of simulation result with state-of-the-art techniques. Section 6 concludes the paper with future directions of the research.

2 Related Work

For load balancing several approaches are found in literature and most of the investigations are categorized in two primary classifications static and dynamic. Static approach require prior knowledge and some prospects about the communication period, executing capability of system, resource requirements for tasks, memory and storage devices capacity. Usually in static approach [3, 4], assignment of task to available resources is done either in deterministic or probabilistic form [3] whereas, dynamic load balancing techniques typically use the current system status in decisions making [4]. The design and critical implementation of such dynamic load balancing algorithm is more complicated and complex than static, however, they provide excellent performance, efficient and accurate solutions also [3, 5].

Both distributed and centralised approaches are used for the design of dynamic strategies with associated pros and cons. In distributed dynamic strategies [6, 7], the load balancing performed by every participating nodes. However, centralized dynamic approach [8, 9] performs load balancing through single node. In semi-distributed approach, the system consists of "n" numbers of partitions called as clusters within the cluster load balancing is according to centralized approach [4]. Grid and cloud computing usually deploys dynamic adaptive approach of load balancing [4].

Minimum Execution Time (MET) parameter to allocate the jobs to available nodes randomly for faster execution and without bothering the current load of the node has been used in [10] and found to be suitable for load balancing. Similarly, AI approach of load balancing suggested by Xu et al. [11] also improved the performance of cloud computing.

Min-Min approach [12, 13], is a static load balancing approach the tasks which has minimum execution time leads the starvation problem whereas, Maximum execution time tasks have to wait for longer time period.

Max-Min Load Balancing Algorithm [14, 15] works almost similar to Min-Min but it first finds the minimum completion time of tasks and then decides the maximum value thus utilizing both the minimum and maximum parameters and able to avoid the starvation.

A dynamic load balancing approach is Equally Spread current execution [16, 17] is considering the task according to priority for allocation in random order. Some times the size of the task can also decide the priority [17]. Here, Larger size or higher priority task, is allocated to the lightly loaded Virtual Machine by providing enough resources and consuming less time leads to optimum throughput [16, 17].

Round Robin algorithm [18] is suitable for static environment it selects the node randomly for allocating a job which is least loaded. First-cum-first-serve (FCFS) approach is applied to assign the resources to the task and organized in circular order in time sharing manner without using priority of the task. In this approach each request gets equal priority but resource utilization is found less efficient [18].

Ant colony optimization (ACO) approach found suitable to avoid the deadlocks in cloud computing [19]. For load balancing, time shared and space shared scheduling approaches are found suitable [19] for less memory consumption and efficient usage [19, 20].

GA based approach assuming equal priority of jobs for load balancing and efficient utilization of resource in cloud environment also guarantees QOS [21].

From the available related work, it is observed that the efficient load balancing algorithm which handles the issues of virtualization is certainly helpful.

3   Cloud Analyst

In real world environment to measure or test the performance is always risky. Simulations helps to overcome from the above situations and reducing the cost end efforts by creating virtual framework. In cloud computing testbeds play significant role [23]. To simulate cloud environment various frameworks are CloudSim [22] and CloudAnalyst [23]. The CloudAnalyst is open source based on CloudSim and can assess social networks tools as per topographical distribution of clients and data centers also [23]. CloudSim provide mere basic facilities like simulation and modelling on cloud [23].

CloudAnalyst accepts input and produces simulation with parameter tuning and using GUI. It can simulate large scale application in terms of processing power and user's workload. Prominent components of the cloud analyst are six virtual demographic regions, user base, data center controller, VM load balancer and internet cloudlet. The user bases are group of users generating traffic however, internet cloudlet are group of users requesting for processing, Data center controller monitors data into VM and load balancer assigns virtual machine for computing.

4 Methodology for Genetic Scheduling Algorithm

Performance optimization objective of Virtual Machines achieved by recognizing the jobs length, capabilities of resources and effectively estimating the underutilized VMs. Consideration of job length parameter help in scheduling the jobs onto the right VMs, help in minimizing the response time and overloaded VM significantly affects the job migrations. Earlier load balancing methods does not use length of task, priority and inherent capabilities of the resources and thus usually found to be overloaded. So the lengthy task and having higher priority results in late response. Round robin task scheduling approach avoids the resource capabilities, task issues and concerns, tasks duration. Thus the long duration and prioritized task consumes higher response times. The proposed method considers the problems of late response, importance of available VMs. Aim is to predict the least utilized VMs and optimum utilization of available resources by balancing the load. Genetic approach in load balancing utilizes the resources efficiently [24, 26] and provide best optimized solution [25]. Genetic operators tuning reduces the response time. Genetic operator enhanced by considering several factors [21]. The data center handles P tasks from Q users. The processing elements of servers deployed within data centers handles these tasks. Thus the processing elements have the complete scenario of utilization.

Let PE be the processing elements then Eq. 1.

$$PE \rightarrow f(FLOPS, t, d) \tag{1}$$

Depicts the utilization scenario where FLOPS are floating operations per second, t is execution time and d is the delay. Delay cost is estimated penalty a data center pays to user. Each task submitted by the user to the data center possess some attributes given by Eq. 2.

$$TE \rightarrow f(S, N, T_a, M_t) \tag{2}$$

Here in Eq. 2 S is the service type, N is total instruction count, T_a is arrival time of task and M_t is time needed by the PE to complete the task.

Thus our aim is to optimize the

$$\Theta = \rho_1 * t(\frac{N}{FLOPS}) + \rho_2 * d \tag{3}$$

Here all the parameters of equations are already described in Eq. 1 and 2. The ρ_1 and ρ_2 are the weights and selected based on the preferences of the users wish to submit a task to particular data center PE.

The proposed hybrid algorithm will try to obtain the global optimized solution of load balancing. At First all the submitted requests are queued. The load balancer predicts the request dimension and verifies for the availability and capability of the virtual machine and returns the lightly loaded VM id to the data center controller. After finding best suited available VM from VmStateList, genetic algorithm applied to group the list of requests in packets (or chromosomes) as per fitness value.

The steps used for scheduling is as follows:

1: Start *Vm* and Present Allocation Counts.
2: Provide *Vm* list to Datacenter controller.
3: Priority wise allocate the requests to available VMs.
4: *Vm state ← vmStatesList. get(Vm_ID);*
5: If virtual machine is available go to step 6
6: As per Priority of task, processing unit cloudlet initialized, encoded in binary strings and packed individuals according to fitness function.
7: Fitness: Each task Evaluated for fitness value

$$MaxLim = (2^{maxp} - 1)$$

$$Select\ RandomVal = [0,1] * MaxLim.$$

At every iteration, Fittest *Vm* Selected as per mean fitness value of the machine to assign tasks in *Vm*.
8: Calculate bit string using genotype(chromosome).
9: Calculate fitness according to processing list of requests.
10: *do while (no of iterations = maxiterations)*
11:    If gets optimized solution {
12:        Select: Genotype with lowest fitness.
13:        Eliminate: Genotype with highest fitness value
            get bit string using step8;
                calculate length;
            }
14:        *If (fitness > Maximum Power)* then
                        Solution met
            else   Increment process and start iteration again;
15: Perform random single point crossover
16: Mutation: New offspring mutated as per mutation probability and a new index value.
17: New offspring considered as new tasks and used for next round of iteration.
18: End condition tested.
19: Use the remaining VMs and tasks for fitness evaluation.
20: Stop

5 Simulation Results and Analysis

Cloud Analyst toolkit has been used to analyze the simulation result and performance of the proposed algorithm. The obtained results with 10 user bases each of 10 requests grouping factor in data center of proposed method are matched with well-known existing algorithms such as Round Robin(RR), Equal Spread Current Execution (ESCE), Genetic Algorithm (GA). Optimize Response Time service broker policy has been selected for analysis. Obtained statistical metrics characterize overall Data Center Processing time, total response time of the system, VM utilization, and overall Processing Cost.

Simulation results in Fig. 1 proved that the Proposed GA is more efficient in processing and provide response in lesser time than the RR, ESCE and GA load balancing algorithms. As results shows that the processing cost is same for all the algorithms.

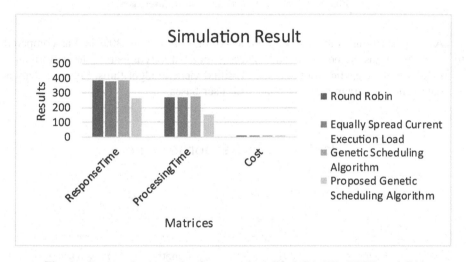

Fig. 1. Comparative analysis of proposed modified GA, RR, ESCE, and GA

The dynamic scheduling of Proposed GA allocates VMs in such a fashion that it achieves better load balancing. Appropriate packaging of task as per genetic fitness value in task scheduling help in balance task distribution among available resources based on its resource capability. Migration of tasks also minimized as resource utilized dynamically at any point of time. This process helps attain the optimal execution time in the cloud environment by allocating the job in random order to the suitable VMs according to best fit size and assign the job to the lightly loaded virtual machine. Figure 2 shows that Proposed GA handles the same jobs in less number of VMs.

Overall utilization of server resources can be improved by combining the different types of workloads. The optimum resource allocation avoids the overload in the system and contributes in load balancing with optimum server usage and migration.

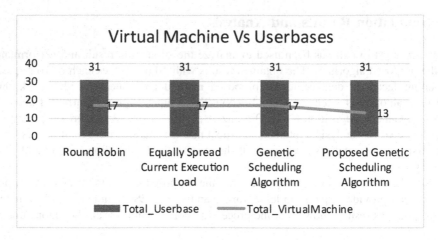

Fig. 2. Graph for virtual machine vs userbases

Average Response time taken by proposed algorithm about 30% less as compared to other algorithms. Same workload has been simulated for comparing the performance with RR, ESCE, Genetic and proposed modified Genetic algorithms. Figure 3 depicts the data centers average response time with user bases.

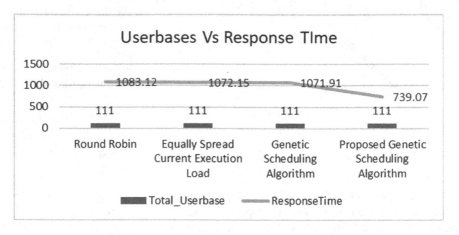

Fig. 3. Graph for userbases vs response time (ms)

As per different simulation configurations in Table 1 the result analysis shows the proposed algorithm achieves better performance on same workload.

Figure 4 shows that Proposed GA uses minimum processing time and less number of VMs in same configuration in different scenarios. Response Time and Processing Time of Proposed GA outperforms. Processing time is almost 40% less as compared to other algorithms.

Table 1. Response Time (ms), Processing Time (ms) and number of virtual machines used as per different configurations of simulation environment

Algorithm name	UBs	VMs	DCs	Response time	Processing time	Cost
RR	31	17	5	383.343	270.911	5.942
ESCE	31	17	5	382.527	270.885	5.942
GA	31	17	5	387.017	275.317	5.942
PGA	31	13	5	261.040	150.038	5.942
RR	38	17	5	356.090	250.423	6.391
ESCE	38	17	5	353.224	247.524	6.391
GA	38	17	5	345.942	240.133	6.391
PGA	38	16	5	243.608	139.000	6.391
RR	42	17	5	343.683	236.878	6.651
ESCE	42	17	5	336.402	229.745	6.651
GA	42	17	5	338.951	232.142	6.651
PGA	42	17	5	234.418	127.863	6.651

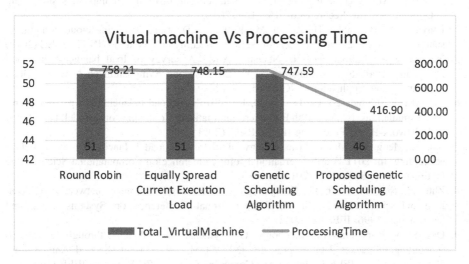

Fig. 4. Graph for virtual machine vs processing time (ms)

This proposed technique effectively transformed cloud computing environment in innovative way and provide efficient and enhanced scheduling to cloud resources, to complete the processing of user's tasks in optimum time.

6 Conclusion

This paper proposed an enhanced genetic algorithm based hybrid load balancing strategy. The proposed algorithm also used the priority to find available VM and for the scheduling. The obtained results show improvement in the response time, requirement of less processing time, efficiently utilization of the resources to balance the loads. It is experimentally found that the proposed strategy is more appropriate, to optimize the problem and produces significant results than Round Robin(RR), Equally Spread Current Execution(ESCE) and simple Genetic Algorithm (GA). Proposed hybrid GA approach is efficient load balancing strategy in virtualized cloud computing environment. As a drawback, the proposed approach is analyzed under simulated environment with limited number of jobs and resources. So, in future proposed technique could be analyzed by deploying in real environment, on heterogeneous VMs and variations of crossover and selection strategies can be considered for better optimization and more self-adaptive VM load balancing.

References

1. Buyya, R., Broberg, J., Goscinski, A.: Cloud Computing Principles and Paradigms. Wiley, New York (2011)
2. http://www.nist.gov/itl/cloud/
3. Alakeel, A.M.: A guide to dynamic load balancing in distributed computer systems. Int. J. Comput. Sci. Inf. Secur. **10**(6), 153–160 (2010)
4. Khiyaita, A., Bakkali, E.H., Zbakh, M., Kettani, E.D.: Load balancing cloud computing: state of art. In: 2012 National Days of Network Security and Systems (JNS2). IEEE (2012)
5. Nuaimi, K.A., Mohammad, N., Nuaiami, A.M.: A survey of load balancing in cloud computing: challenges and algorithms. In: 2012 Second Symposium on Network Cloud Computing and Applications (NCCA). IEEE (2012)
6. Cosenza, B., Coradasco, G., De Chiara, R.: Distributed load balancing for parallel agent-based simulations. In: 2011 19th Euromicro International Conference on Parallel, Distributed and Network-Based Processing (PDP). IEEE (2011)
7. Shi, J., Meng, C., Ma, L.: The strategy of distributed load balancing based on hybrid scheduling. In: 2011 Fourth International Joint Conference on Computational Sciences and Optimization (CSO). IEEE (2011)
8. Zhu, W., Sun, C., Shieh, C.: Comparing the performance differences between centralized load balancing methods. In: IEEE International Conference on Systems, Man, and Cybernetics, 1996. IEEE (1996)
9. Das, S., Viswanathan, H., Rittenhouse, G.: Dynamic load balancing through coordinated scheduling in packet data systems. In: INFOCOM 2003. Twenty-Second Annual Joint Conference of the IEEE Computer and Communications. IEEE Societies. IEEE (2003)
10. Armstrong, T.R., Hensgen, D.: The relative performance of various mapping algorithms in independent runtime predictions. In: Proceedings of 7th IEEE Heterogeneous computing workshop (HCW 1998), pp. 79–87 (1998)
11. Xu, Y., Wu, L., Guo, L., Chen, Z., Yang, L., Shi, Z.: An intelligent load balancing algorithm towards efficient cloud computing. In: Proceedings of AI for Data Center Management and Cloud Computing: Papers, From the 2011 AAAI Workshop (WS-11-08), pp. 27–32 (2011)
12. Liu, G., Li, J., Xu, J.: An improved min-min algorithm in cloud computing. In: Du, Z. (ed.) Proceedings of the 2012 International Conference of Modern Computer Science and Applications. Advances in Intelligent Systems and Computing, vol. 191, pp. 47–52. Springer, Heidelberg (2013). https://doi.org/10.1007/978-3-642-33030-8_8
13. Kokilavani, T., Amalarethinam, D.D.: Load balanced min-min algorithm for static meta-task scheduling in grid computing. Int. J. Comput. Appl. **20**(2), 43–49 (2011)

14. Bhoi, U., Ramanuj, P.N.: Enhanced max-min task scheduling algorithm in cloud computing. Int. J. Appl. Innov. Eng. Manage. **2**(4), 259–264 (2013)
15. Balaji, N., Umamaheshwari, A.: Load balancing in virtualized environment - a survey. Indian J. Sci. Technol. **8**(S9), 230–234 (2015)
16. Moharana, S., Ramesh, R.D., Power, D.: Analysis of load balancers in cloud computing. Int. J. Comput. Sci. Eng. **2**(2), 101–108 (2013). ISSN 2278-9960
17. Sahu, Y., Pateriya, M.K.: Cloud computing overview and load balancing algorithms. Internal J. Comput. Appl. **65**(24) (2013)
18. Ray, S., Sarkar, A.D.: Execution analysis of load balancing algorithms in cloud computing environment. Int. J. Cloud Comput. Serv. Archit. (IJCCSA) **2**(5), 1–13 (2012)
19. Mishra, R., Jaiswal, A.: Ant colony Optimization: A Solution of Load balancing in Cloud. International Journal of Web & Semantic Technology (IJWesT) **3**(2), 33–50 (2012)
20. Nishant, K., Sharma, P.: Load balancing of nodes in cloud using ant colony optimization. In: 2012 UKSim 14th International Conference on Computer Modelling and Simulation (UKSim). IEEE (2012)
21. Dasgupta, K., Mandal, B., Dutta, P., Mondal, J.K., Dam, S.: A genetic algorithm (GA) based load balancing strategy for cloud computing. In: Proceedings of Elsevier, Procedia Technology (2013)
22. Calheiros, R.N., Ranjan, R., Beloglazov, A., Rose, C., Buyya, R.: Cloudsim: a toolkit for modeling and simulation of cloud computing environments and evaluation of resource provisioning algorithms. In: Software: Practice and Experience (SPE), vol. 41, no. 1, pp. 23–50. Wiley Press, New York (2011). ISSN: 0038-0644
23. Wickremasinghe, B.R., Calheiros, N., Buyya, R.: Cloudanalyst: a cloudsim-based visual modeller for analyzing cloud computing environments and applications. In: Proceedings of Proceedings of the 24th International Conference on Advanced Information Networking and Applications (AINA2010), Perth, Australia, pp. 446–452 (2010)
24. Goldberg, D.E.: Genetic Algorithms in Search, Optimization, and Machine Learning. Addison-Wesley, Boston (1989)
25. Geetha, V., Devi, R.A., Ilavenil, T., Begum, S.M., Revathi, S.: Performance comparison of cloudlet scheduling policies. In: 2016 International Conference on Emerging Trends in Engineering, Technology and Science (ICETETS), Pudukkottai, pp. 1–7 (2016)
26. Xu, M., Tian, W., Buyya, R.: A survey on load balancing algorithms for virtual machines placement in cloud computing. Concurrency Comput. Pract. Exp. **29**(12), 4123–4138 (2017)

A Study of Deep Learning Methods for Mitotic Cell Detection Towards Breast Cancer Diagnosis

S. Kaushik$^{(\boxtimes)}$, S. Vijaya Raghavan, and B. Sivaselvan

Indian Institute of Information Technology Design & Manufacturing Kancheepuram,
Chennai, India
{ced14i032,ced14i045,sivaselvanb}@iiitdm.ac.in
http://www.iiitdm.ac.in/

Abstract. Advances in digital health records, computing and machine learning have led to the synergistic rise of machine learning techniques being applied to medical imaging tasks such as detection, diagnosis and discovery. Recent advances in computer vision and image processing have been applied to medical imaging yielding vast performance improvements over existing methods. Breast cancer is a leading cause of death among cancer patients in women. Mitotic count in biopsied breast tissue is an important biomarker for predicting breast cancer prognosis as per the Nottingham Grading System. In this work, we survey different deep learning based approaches to detect mitotic cells with the overall aim of assisting pathologists with the diagnosis of breast cancer.

Keywords: Deep learning · Mitotic cell detection · Object detection

1 Introduction

For the diagnosis of Breast Cancer, the concept of Breast cancer (BCa) grading plays an important role. A key component of the BCa grade is the mitotic count, which involves quantifying the number of cells in the process of dividing (i.e., undergoing mitosis) at a specific point in time. Currently, mitotic cell counting is done manually by a pathologist looking at multiple high power fields (HPFs) on a glass slide under a microscope, an extremely laborious and time consuming process. The development of computerized systems for automated detection of mitotic nuclei, is confounded by the highly variable shape and appearance of mitoses.

The most commonly used grading system that estimates the veracity of breast cancer is the Nottingham Grading system [3]. It is a total score based on 3 different sub-scores. The 3 sub-scores are assigned based on 3 components of how the breast cancer cells look under a microscope. Each of the 3 components is assigned a sub-score of 1, 2, or 3, with 1 being best and 3 being worst. Once the 3 sub-scores are added, a Nottingham score is obtained: the minimum score possible is 3 (1+1+1) and the maximum possible is 9 (3+3+3).

© Springer Nature Singapore Pte Ltd. 2019
M. Singh et al. (Eds.): ICACDS 2019, CCIS 1045, pp. 254–263, 2019.
https://doi.org/10.1007/978-981-13-9939-8_23

The three components of the Nottingham Score are: Tubule formation, Mitotic Cell Count and, Nuclear Pleomorphism. Of these, the mitotic cell count is quantitative and a critical problem. Mitotic cell detection is a challenging problem owing to the following reasons:

- Mitotic cell occurrences are rare when compared to the other types of cells.
- It has a very similar appearance to that of apoptotic nuclei, lymphocyte nuclei and dust particles.
- There is enormous variation in the cell appearance in terms of shape and texture as the mitotic cells undergo a variety of morphological transformations.

2 Recent Works

Early methods proposed for mitotic cell detection approached it as a classification problem. These methods [7,8] involve obtaining hand-crafted features and performing classification using random forest, Support Vector Machines (SVM) and other conventional machine-learning based classifiers. The primary disadvantage with these methods is that they were not able to capture the wide range of features required to perform classification efficiently.

To address this, deep learning methods were applied, with their ability to learn robust features, offered significant performance improvements over conventional methods.

There are different ways this problem has been modeled in the deep learning literature:

- **Classification approach**: It is modeled as a binary classification problem where the input image has to be classified into one of two classes - with mitotic cells or without mitotic cells. One method uses a standard grid size of 100 × 100, which is moved over the image pixel-wise. The extracted intermediate representation is then used to classify the image. The drawback with this method is the high computation time required as the grid has to cover the whole image exhaustively [2].
- **Segmentation approach**: Segmentation is defined as the process of partitioning an image into multiple regions or segments to extract meaningful information. This approach involves two steps. In the first step, mitotic segmentation is carried out using deep networks such as the UNet [14]. Once the segmentation mask is created, the region of interest is obtained. Classifiers are then built, which are used to differentiate the cells inside the region of interest as mitotic or non-mitotic. This resolves the high computation time issue to some extent, but the performance is not satisfactory owing to the class imbalance problem - the number of occurrences of mitotic cells is less compared to other types of cells and the mitotic cells occupy very little area [1].
- **Object Detection Approach**: Here, the mitotic cells are considered as objects that have to be detected in an image. Different object detection algorithms have been applied to detect mitotic cells. [9]. This approach has shown improvement in performance and computation time.

Our emphasis is on the object detection approach which has shown promising results. We apply different deep neural network architectures for this problem and evaluate their performance. We also attempt to qualitatively explain their performance with respect to this problem.

3   Methodology

We explore two major families of Object Detection architectures - Region based Object Detectors and Single Shot Object Detectors.

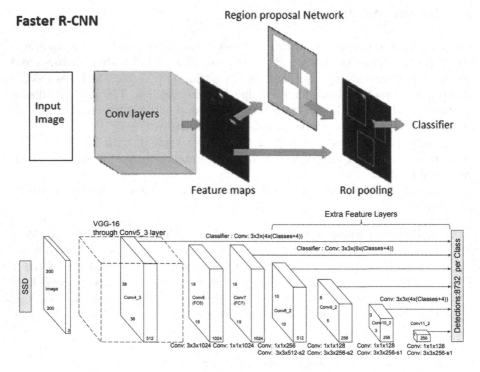

Fig. 1. Top pane: Faster RCNN architecture (image adapted from [13]). Bottom pane: Single Shot Multibox Detector architecture (image adapted from [10])

3.1   Region Based Detectors

Region based detectors are a class of object detection models that have two stages - the region proposal stage which is responsible for detecting the regions of interest and the object detection stage which performs object detection in the regions of interest.

Among the region-based detection architectures, the state-of-the-art network is FasterRCNN [13]. It has two stages - Region proposal network (RPN) and object detection network. The input image is passed to the RPN which outputs rectangular object proposals each with an objectness score. The region proposals are passed to the object detection network which then performs region of interest (ROI) pooling followed by non-maximum suppression (NMS), which is thresholded to select the relevant regions. The object detection network comprises of a classifier and regressor - the regressor's purpose is to regress the bounding box and the classifier's purpose is to classify the object in the bounding box. The loss function is multi-task - cross-entropy is used for the classification task and smooth L2 is used for the regression task.

In this study, the experiments with Faster R-CNN are carried out using the following state-of-the-art pre-trained detection models obtained from the Tensorflow Object Detection API [6]: ResNet101 [4], InceptionNet [16], NASNet [17].

3.2 Single Shot Detectors

The major difference between Region Based detectors and Single Shot Detectors is the process: Single Shot Detectors combine the bounding box prediction and classification into a single stage while Region Based predictors treat them as two different stages. Thus, the SSD approach is significantly faster than the Faster R-CNN approach. As illustrated above in Fig. 1, the SSD architecture comprises of a base convolutional network followed by several multi-box convolutional layers.

Experiments with SSD Networks are carried out using the following state-of-the-art models: MobileNet [5] and YOLO [12].

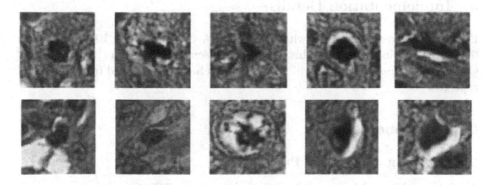

Fig. 2. Top pane: Tissue with mitotic cells. Bottom pane: Tissue without mitotic cells.

4   Dataset and Preprocessing

4.1   Dataset Description

The dataset [15] used is from the 2012 ICPR Mitosis detection contest. Images are taken from the Aperio XT scanner, with the resolution of the scanner being

$0.2456\,\mu m$ per pixel. Each HPF has an area of $512 \times 512\,\mu m^2$. The dataset consists of 50 images, with 35 training and 15 test images. Dimensions of each HPF are 2084×2084. The total number of mitotic cells in train and test images are 226 and 101 respectively. A sample of mitotic and non-mitotic cells are shown in Fig. 2.

4.2 Data Preprocessing

To maintain uniform color intensity across images, color normalization is applied using Macenko stain normalization [11], a stain color-deconvolution technique which takes into account the prior knowledge of the reference stain vector, and corrects every other image in the dataset. Also, due to the large size of each HPF image, directly using it as an input to the deep learning network would not be feasible from the hardware perspective. Resizing the image to a smaller size would not work in this scenario since mitotic cells occupy a small area of 150×150, which would result in loss of cells. A popular method to deal with this issue in deep learning literature is to divide the image into patches of uniform dimension. Patches are created from each 2084×2084 image with size 512×512 and a stride of 32. An added advantage of this method is the increase in available data, since the number of images in the dataset is very low.

Patches which do not contain the whole mitotic cell or do not contain any mitotic cell are removed. In order to further increase the dataset size, data augmentation techniques such as flipping images left/right, up/down and random rotation of images between -5 and $5°$ are applied.

5   Implementation Details

Experiments were performed with the NVIDIA GeForce GTX 1060 GPU with 6GB vRAM. Models used in this paper have been sourced from the TensorFlow Object Detection API [6], except YOLO, which has been sourced from its official repository.

6   Experiments

6.1 Training and Testing Procedure

Training. All models except YOLO use the FasterRCNN architecture, which is configured to have each model as the backbone, with anchor scales of 0.25, 0.5, 1.0 and 2.0, aspect ratios of 0.5, 1.0, 2.0 and batch size 1. Each model is trained for 20000 steps, with Stochastic Gradient Descent(SGD) optimizer and Negative Log Likelihood(NLL) Loss.

Testing. Each test image of size 2084 × 2084 is split into 512 × 512 patches with a stride of 393. This is done to prevent overlapping of regions. To infer images from many viewpoints, test-time augmentations like flip left/right and flip up/down are performed. Hence, each image is passed into the test pipeline three times, with the final detection for the image containing the union of all predictions. Each box is predicted with a certain confidence probability, and only boxes with confidence greater than the chosen confidence threshold is considered. Subsequently, NMS is performed to remove redundant predictions.

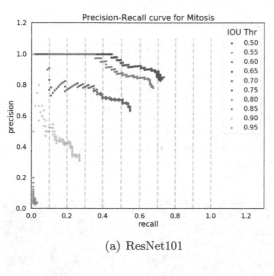

(a) ResNet101

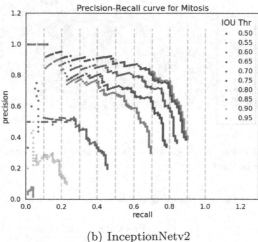

(b) InceptionNetv2

Fig. 3. Precision-Recall curves for models with varying confidence thresholds, ranging from 0.5 to 0.95 with an increment of 0.05.

6.2 Evaluation Metrics

Since the objective is to detect mitotic cells from a HPF containing various structures like tubules, nuclei and dust particles, it is essential to reduce the number of false positives (FP) and false negatives (FN) while keeping the true positive (TP) count high. Hence, we have chosen the evaluation metrics to be Precision (Pr), Recall (Rec) and F1-Score(F1), which are defined in Eq.1.

$$Pr = \frac{TP}{TP + FP}$$

$$Rec = \frac{TP}{TP + FN} \tag{1}$$

$$F1 = \frac{2 * Pr * Rec}{Pr + Rec}$$

Precision-Recall(PR) curves of ResNet101 and InceptionNet models are shown in Fig. 3. It can be observed that setting the confidence threshold to 0.5 gives the best results.

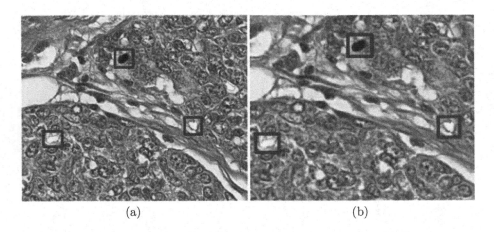

(a)   (b)

Fig. 4. Sample detection results. Blue boxes are predictions. Yellow cells are mitotic.(Color figure online)

Table 1. Results obtained. Running times are calculated for each image patch.

Architecture	Precision	Recall	F1Score	Running time(s)
FasterRCNN+ResNet101 Backbone	0.856	0.735	0.790	32.0
FasterRCNN+InceptionNet Backbone	0.764	0.801	0.782	122.5
FasterRCNN+NASNet Backbone	0.781	0.673	0.723	74.8
FasterRCNN+MobileNet Backbone	0.712	0.514	0.597	4.1
YOLO	0.650	0.772	0.705	5.8

7   Results and Discussion

Sample detections are shown in Fig. 4. A quantitative study of the results obtained from Table 1 shows that the model FasterRCNN+ResNet101 backbone and FasterRCNN+InceptionNet backbone offer the best performance in terms of the F1-Score. FasterRCNN+MobileNet is the fastest but does not perform as well owing to the fact that MobileNet is aimed at fast performance on mobile devices. Also, in order to study the speed/accuracy tradeoff between Region-based and Single shot Detectors, Fig. 5 shows the F1-Score vs Running Time plot. It can be observed from the plot that FasterRCNN+ResNet101 backbone hits the sweet spot of high accuracy and faster running time, while other region based detectors such as InceptionNet and NASNet acheive comparable accuracy with the ResNet models. On the other end of the spectrum, Single Shot detectors such as YOLO and MobileNet perform poorly accuracy-wise, but have the fastest running times. An intuitive explanation for the better performance of ResNet compared to InceptionNet and NASNet architectures could be the heavy class imbalance in each HPF. Owing to the increased depth in latter architectures, they could be biased towards predicting non-mitotic cells in the image.

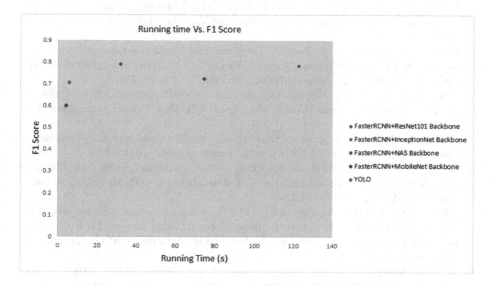

Fig. 5. Scatter Plot of F1-Score vs Running Time for all models.

8   Conclusion

Computer aided tools have been of great importance to doctors, pathologists and scientists. For the problem of breast cancer detection, mitotic cell count is an important parameter, which was estimated manually, by the pathologist involved. Advances in computer vision technology in problem areas such as image segmentation and object detection have led to their applications in medical imaging and digital pathology. In this paper, we explored the problem of mitotic cell detection using different state-of-the-art object detection algorithms. We have analyzed and discussed the results obtained qualitatively and quantitatively based on our experiments. We also explored other aspects of using these models such as the speed-accuracy tradeoff.

References

1. Chen, H., Wang, X., Heng, P.A.: Automated mitosis detection with deep regression networks. In: 2016 IEEE 13th International Symposium on Biomedical Imaging (ISBI), pp. 1204–1207, April 2016. https://doi.org/10.1109/ISBI.2016.7493482
2. Cireşan, D.C., Giusti, A., Gambardella, L.M., Schmidhuber, J.: Mitosis detection in breast cancer histology images with deep neural networks. In: Mori, K., Sakuma, I., Sato, Y., Barillot, C., Navab, N. (eds.) MICCAI 2013. LNCS, vol. 8150, pp. 411–418. Springer, Heidelberg (2013). https://doi.org/10.1007/978-3-642-40763-5_51
3. Elston, C.W., Ellis, I.O.: Pathological prognostic factors in breast cancer. I. The value of histological grade in breast cancer: experience from a large study with long-term follow-up. C. W. Elston & I. O. Ellis. Histopathology 1991; 19; 403–410. Histopathology 41(3a), 151–151 (2002). https://doi.org/10.1046/j.1365-2559. 2002.14691.x, https://onlinelibrary.wiley.com/doi/abs/10.1046/j.1365-2559.2002. 14691.x
4. He, K., Zhang, X., Ren, S., Sun, J.: Deep residual learning for image recognition. In: 2016 IEEE Conference on Computer Vision and Pattern Recognition (CVPR), pp. 770–778 June 2016. https://doi.org/10.1109/CVPR.2016.90
5. Howard, A.G., et al.: Mobilenets: efficient convolutional neural networks for mobile vision applications. CoRR abs/1704.04861 (2017). http://arxiv.org/abs/ 1704.04861
6. Huang, J., et al.: Speed/accuracy trade-offs for modern convolutional object detectors. CoRR abs/1611.10012 (2016). http://arxiv.org/abs/1611.10012
7. Irshad, H.: Automated mitosis detection in histopathology using morphological and multi-channel statistics features. J. Pathol. Inform. 4(1), 10 (2013). https:// doi.org/10.4103/2153-3539.112695
8. Khan, A.M., El-Daly, H., Rajpoot, N.M.: A gamma-gaussian mixture model for detection of mitotic cells in breast cancer histopathology images. In: Proceedings of the 21st International Conference on Pattern Recognition (ICPR2012), pp. 149– 152, November 2012
9. Li, C., Wang, X., Liu, W., Latecki, L.J.: Deepmitosis: mitosis detection via deep detection, verification and segmentation networks. Med. Image Anal. 45, 121–133 (2018). https://doi.org/10.1016/j.media.2017.12.002. http://www.sciencedirect.com/science/article/pii/S1361841517301834
10. Liu, W., et al.: SSD: single shot multibox detector. CoRR abs/1512.02325 (2015). http://arxiv.org/abs/1512.02325
11. Macenko, M., et al.: A method for normalizing histology slides for quantitative analysis. In: 2009 IEEE International Symposium on Biomedical Imaging: From Nano to Macro, pp. 1107–1110 June 2009. https://doi.org/10.1109/ISBI.2009. 5193250

12. Redmon, J., Divvala, S., Girshick, R., Farhadi, A.: You only look once: Unified, real-time object detection. In: 2016 IEEE Conference on Computer Vision and Pattern Recognition (CVPR), pp. 779–788 June 2016. https://doi.org/10.1109/CVPR.2016.91

13. Ren, S., He, K., Girshick, R., Sun, J.: Faster R-CNN: towards real-time object detection with region proposal networks. IEEE Trans. Pattern Anal. Mach. Intell. **39**(6), 1137–1149 (2017). https://doi.org/10.1109/TPAMI.2016.2577031

14. Ronneberger, O., Fischer, P., Brox, T.: U-Net: convolutional networks for biomedical image segmentation. In: Navab, N., Hornegger, J., Wells, W.M., Frangi, A.F. (eds.) MICCAI 2015. LNCS, vol. 9351, pp. 234–241. Springer, Cham (2015). https://doi.org/10.1007/978-3-319-24574-4_28

15. Roux, L., Racoceanu, D., et al.: Mitosis detection in breast cancer histological images an ICPR 2012 contest. J. Pathol. Inform. **4**, 8 (2013). https://doi.org/10.4103/2153-3539.112693

16. Szegedy, C., et al.: Going deeper with convolutions. CoRR abs/1409.4842 (2014). http://arxiv.org/abs/1409.4842

17. Zoph, B., Le, Q.V.: Neural architecture search with reinforcement learning. CoRR abs/1611.01578 (2016). http://arxiv.org/abs/1611.01578

Hybrid Approaches for Brain Tumor Detection in MR Images

Prabhjot Kaur Chahal[1], Shreelekha Pandey[1], and Shivani Goel[2(✉)]

[1] Department of Computer Science and Engineering,
Thapar Institute of Engineering and Technology, Punjab, India
{prabhjot_kaur,shreelekha.pandey}@thapr.edu
[2] Department of Computer Science Engineering, Bennett University,
Greater Noida, Delhi, India
shivani.goel@bennett.edu.in

Abstract. The growing technology in medical image processing helps in quick as well as an accurate analysis of several life threatening diseases. Interestingly, domain of brain tumor analysis has effectively utilized this trend to automate core steps, i.e. extraction, detection, and the most important proximate segmentation for tumor examination. To diagnose neurological disorders magnetic resonance (MR) imaging methods are of great help. Discussing the MR image types this paper briefs the parameters influencing the process of brain tumor detection. Also, the study proposes a hybrid segmentation approach combining k-means with fuzzy c-means (FCM) and support vector machine (SVM) with fuzzy c-means. Experimentation performed show that fusion outperforms three of the base approaches in brain tumor identification on DICOM dataset using 200 T1W and T2W MR images. The evaluation parameters show that k-means combined with fuzzy c-means produce better accuracy. Results further prove applicability of the proposal in detecting ranges and shapes of brain tumor using MR images.

Keywords: Medical images · Segmentation · Brain tumor · Magnetic resonance

1 Introduction

Brain tumor, i.e., unwanted cell formation, is one of the most prevalent life threatening diseases. Such tissues, if detected in time essentially leads to their successful elimination. In last few years researchers have contributed prodigiously in the field of medical imaging. As a result, several effective methods to extract and detect brain tumor have been discovered. For effectiveness, a range of works have also utilized capabilities of image segmentation techniques to extract meaningful content (i.e., tumor) from medical images [1–3]. But, variable shapes and presence of cerebrospinal fluid (CSF) make a difficult brain tumor detection task more complex [1]. Segmentation in medical images is governed by factors

© Springer Nature Singapore Pte Ltd. 2019
M. Singh et al. (Eds.): ICACDS 2019, CCIS 1045, pp. 264–274, 2019.
https://doi.org/10.1007/978-981-13-9939-8_24

like poor contrast, noise, and missing boundaries. For their effective control, diagnosing imaging processes like magnetic resonance (MR) imaging and compute tomography (CT) scan are employed [2]. Usage of harmless magnetic fields and radio waves make MR images preferable. These images can be segmented using manual, semi-automatic, and fully automatic techniques [3]. In absence of experts, performance of automatic techniques depends solely on knowledge bases. Researchers have proposed several methods to improve such knowledge bases and thus the capability of tumor detection systems [4,5]. Segmentation of MR images needs to be very efficient for proper tumor analysis. This paper thus focuses mainly on segmentation techniques used specifically for MR images to design and implement a hybrid system. It also discusses several parameters used to differentiate various types of MR images. The proposed approach individually combines fuzzy c-means with k-means and support vector machine. Comparison with base line approaches proves that combinations are promising.

The rest of the paper is organized in four sections. Section 2 gives an overview of MR imaging and contrast parameters. Section 3 summarizes the existing literature. Section 4 explains the proposed hybrid combinations. Comparison results with the existing techniques are discussed in Sect. 5. Finally, conclusion followed by highlights of future directions is presented in Sect. 6.

2   MR Imaging and It's Types

Irrespective of superiority of employed segmentation technique, segmentation quality depends greatly on contrast, amount of noise, and incomplete boundaries. In medical images good contrast supersedes all other basic requirements, as abnormal structure identification is completely based on certain contrast characteristics. However, image contrast is influenced by certain parameters listed in Table 1. These parameters are tuned for obtaining proper contrast to differentiate tumor from normal brain tissues (fat, gray matter, white matter, and CSF). Shape, size, and integrity of tumor tissues can be identified by keen analysis of MR images. Different compositions of tissue types result in varying MR image signals and hence various MR images like T1-weighted (T1W),

Table 1. Parameters influencing image contrast

Intrinsic (Brain tissues)	Extrinsic (Image physical characteristics)
–Proton Density (PD)	–Magnetic Field Strength (MFS)
–Longitudinal Relaxation Tme (T1)	–Radio Frequency (RF)
–Transverse Relaxation Time (T2)	–Repetition Time (TR)
–Chemical Shift	–Echo Time (TE)
–Susceptibility	–Inversion Time (TI)
	–RF pulse amplitude (Flip angle)
	–b-value

T2-weighted (T2W), fluid attenuated inversion recovery (FLAIR), and proton density weighted (PDW) [5, 6]. Diffusion based MR images like diffusion weighted image (DWI) and apparent diffusion coefficient (ADC) are also used for early diagnosis and longitudinal evaluations. This study uses the two most common MR image types T1W and T2W.

3   Related Work

A novel approach, KIFCM combines k-means with fuzzy c-means for effective detection in minimal time [7]. Results obtained on three datasets and are compared with conventional algorithms. Combination reports good accuracy ranging from 90.5% to 100% on different datasets. A study focuses on reducing the computational time by presenting bacteria foraging optimization (BFO) based modified fuzzy k-means algorithm (MFKM) algorithm [8]. Dataset with T1W, T2W images for diseases like astrocytoma, metastatic bronchogenic carcinoma, meningioma, and primitive neuro ectodermal tumor are utilized. The reported computation time is 1.98 min with acceptable similarity index (95.77%), sensitivity (97.14%), and specificity (93.94%). One of the works compares k-means with fuzzy c-means (FCM) on scales like better segmentation and computation time [9]. Experimental results proves dominance of FCM over k-means in terms of mean squared error (MSE) and peak signal to noise ratio (PSNR). Computationally as well FCM (8.639 s) performs better than k-means (22.831 s).

A novel user friendly segmentation approach using one-class SVM is presented [10]. It's able to learn non-linear distribution of image data without prior knowledge and attains sensitivity of 83% on T1W, CE-T1W images. Another novel development combines daubechies-4 wavelet transform with support vector machine (SVM) as well as self-organizing maps (SOM) for classification of human brain tumor from MR images [11]. Results show that accuracy with SOM turned to be 94% and with SVM its 98%. Another study integrates SOM with fuzzy K means (FKM) to achieve efficient segmentation [6]. The technique is verified using the clinical images obtained from four patients, along with the images taken from Harvard Brain Repository. SVM is also explored in union with genetic algorithm (GA) to classify brain tissues in magnetic resonance images (MRI) [12]. Results on Harvard medical school dataset having 83 T2W MR images obtain accuracy in between 94.44% to 98.14% and sensitivity stretch from 91.4% to 97.3%. SVM is also explored in combination with fuzzy c-mean for effective segmentation and classification [13]. Comparison results on 120 patients are considered and compared using different classifiers. Following observations are made: ANN is better for larger number of cases where as SVM works better with smaller number. The combination outperforms by reporting better accuracy and lesser error rates.

As per the survey systems based on k-means segmentation are fast and simple, but suffer from partial tumor detection, mainly for malignant cases. In contrast, systems using FCM retain more information and detect malignant tumors accurately. However, they are sensitive to noise, outliers, and have longer execution time. Also, for overlapped data sets FCM performs better as concept of membership helps in better clustering. Combination has benefits of both the algorithms, i.e. it effectively deals with issues like noise, illumination factor, and large data sets, etc. and thus boost system's performance in brain tumor detection.

In case of FCM and SVM, the SVM is robust to noise and over-fits lesser, however it is not efficient in terms of computational time. The reason is due to heavy computational steps and calculations involved. Furthermore, pair-wise classifications method may be used (i.e. for all classes, one class against all others in case of multi-class classification) which FCM withstands.

4   The Fusion Approach

The system presented here combines k-means and support vector machine with Fuzzy C-means. Starting with working principle illustrations of all the mentioned approaches, the hybrid approach description is followed.

4.1   Preliminary Concept

K-means clustering aims to partition n observations into k clusters such that each observation belongs to a cluster with the nearest means, serving as a prototype of the cluster. Let X = x1, x2, ..., xn be the set of data points and V = v1, v2, .., vc be the pool of centres, then k-means is based on minimization of the objective function representing the total intra-cluster variance (Eq. 1). Here, is the distance measure between every data point xi and cluster centre vi, c represents number of cluster centres and ci represents number of data points in ith cluster. Firstly, number of clusters and their respective prototypes are initialized. k-means works by attributing the closest cluster to each data point. Then recalculate new prototypes by averaging values of all the data points linked with the cluster using Eq. 2.

$$J(V) = \sum_{i=1}^{c} (||x_i - v_i||)^2 \tag{1}$$

$$\mu_i = \frac{1}{|c_i|} \sum_{x_i \epsilon c_i} x_j \tag{2}$$

Fuzzy c-means (FCM) is one the oldest clustering algorithms introduced by Professor Jim Bezdek in 1981 [14]. The algorithm attempts to partition finite pool of n data points, X = x1, x2, ..., xn, into c fuzzy clusters using some criteria. It maps data points to nearest cluster centres depending upon the distance values between cluster centres and data points. The algorithm is based on optimizing an objective function that defines the goodness of a solution and is given as in Eq. 3. Here, m is the fuzziness exponent which is a real number greater than 1 and number of iterations to be performed depends on it. μ_{ij} represents degree of membership of data point x_i in j^{th} cluster and is defined as in Eq. 4. Here d_{ij} represents distance of data point xi and centre of jth cluster.

$$J_m(U,V) = \sum_{i=1}^{n} \sum_{j=1}^{c} (\mu_{ij})^m (||x_i - v_i||)^2 \tag{3}$$

$$\mu_{ij} = \frac{1}{\sum_{k=1}^{c} (d_{ij} - d_{ik})^{\frac{2}{m-1}}} \tag{4}$$

Support vector machine (SVM) is a supervised learning technique used for data analysis and classification. SVM classifier has a quick learning rate even in extensive data; however it is utilized for two or more class classification difficulties. SVM depends on the conception of decision planes, which isolates between a lot of things having distinctive class memberships. In this paper, SVM is utilized as the segmentation as well as classification strategy. In the first approach used with Fuzzy c-means and k-means, the combination segments the image whereas SVM is used to classify the tumor. In the second approach SVM is completely used as segmentation technique. The utilization of SVM includes two essential strides of training and testing.

In the SVM the classes are supposed to be represented as x, and the decision boundary is estimated as $y = 0$, So by using the Eq. 5

$$y = \sum_{i=1}^{N} w_i x_i + b = x_i w + b \tag{5}$$

where the input patterns, w is the weight vector, b is the offset. Since the classes are defined as ± 1 the equation for the line isolating the classes will be:

$$wx_i + b \geq 1 \; if \; y_i = 1 \tag{6}$$

$$wx_i + b < 1 \; if \; y_i = -1 \tag{7}$$

The distance from the hyper plane $wx_i + b = 0$ to the origin is $\frac{-b}{||w||}$, where $||w||$ the norm of w. The distance from the hyper-plane to the origin is: $M = \frac{2}{||w||}$, where M is the margin. So the maximum margin is obtained by minimizing $||w||$.

Hybrid Approaches (Fuzzy C-Means with K-Means, Fuzzy C-Means with SVM). This work attempts to individually combine FCM with k-means as well as with SVM. Approach I is clustering-clustering, i.e. it combines two clustering algorithms FCM and k-means. Whereas, in Approach II is clustering-classifier, i.e. it integrates FCM with SVM. Approach II aims to verify the applicability of SVM in different phases. Figure 1 shows process flow of the system implemented with the hybrid approach FCM + k-means (FKM) and FCM with SVM (FSVM). Procedure starts by taking original MR image as an input which undergoes pre-processing mainly for noise removal. In current implementation Gaussian low pass filter is applied. Next step is skull scripting, an important phase of brain segmentation process to separate out normal tissues like white matter, grey matter, and CSF. Thus, for improved and effective detection Otsu's thresholding is utilized in this work followed by segmentation using hybrid approach, FKM and FSVM. Lastly, to accentuate tumor shape morphological filtering using two basic operations (dilation, i.e., shrinking the foreground and erosion, i.e., expanding the foreground) is done. The highlighted white region in the obtained image signifies tumor and the system finally classifies the image as tumorous accordingly.

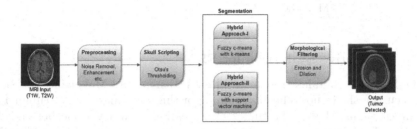

Fig. 1. The generic flow diagram of the proposed hybrid system

5   Results and Discussion

Performances of the combinations FKM and FSVM are analyzed using Digital Imaging and Communications in Medicine (DICOM) dataset. Experiments are performed using 200 MR brain images from different modality types, namely T1-weighted and T2-weighted. All images have 256×256 pixels. DICOM dataset has images of cerebrum influenced by cerebrum sore. A normal human brain is characterized by symmetry in axial, sagittal, and coronal brain images whereas an asymmetry strongly signifies abnormality. Hybrid approaches are mainly meant for segmentation, thus visual results are presented. In addition, results of FKM and FSVM are compared with k-means, SVM, and FCM on DICOM dataset using accuracy performance measures. All the algorithms are implemented in MATLAB 2014a. System runs on Window 8 and has Intel core i5 processor with 4GB RAM. Classification accuracy is defined as the probability that diagnostic test is performed correctly and is given as in Eq. 8. It is computed using confusion matrix parameters including true positive rate (TP), true negative rate (TN), false positive rate (FP), and false negative rate (FN).

$$Accuracy = \frac{TP + TN}{TN + FN + TP + FP} \times 100 \qquad (8)$$

where, $TP = \frac{Number\ of\ tumorous\ MR\ brain\ images}{Total\ number\ of\ MR\ images\ in\ dataset}$,

$TN = \frac{Number\ of\ non-tumorous\ MR\ brain\ images}{Total\ number\ of\ MR\ images\ in\ dataset}$

$FP = \frac{Number\ of\ non-tumorous\ MR\ brain\ images\ detected\ as\ tumorous}{Total\ number\ of\ MR\ images\ in\ dataset}$

$FN = \frac{Number\ of\ tumorous\ MR\ brain\ images\ detected\ as\ non-tumorous}{Total\ number\ of\ MR\ images\ in\ dataset}$

Table 2. Accuracy values (in %) obtained with various segmentation approaches using SVM classifier for four different kernels

	RBF	LINEAR	POLY	QUADRATIC
FCM	74	85	60	45
SVM	70	88	85	50
FSVM	85	93	79	57
k-means	55	70	46	50
KFM	86	96	69	60

5.1   Comparative Evaluation for FKM

DICOM dataset contains two tumor classes, Benign and Malignant. Classification accuracy shows how effectively an algorithm identifies type of tumor from MR image scans. Higher the tumor classification accuracy value better is the algorithm. Each of the three segmentation approaches are tested using four SVM classifiers with varying kernels, namely linear, polynomial, Gaussian (RBF), and quadratic. Table 2 compares base clustering approaches k-means and FCM with hybrid FKM approach on classification accuracy for all the kernels. Clearly, k-means reports the lowest accuracy values with all the kernels except quadratic. For quadratic kernels the performance of FCM is the lowest, in fact this is the minimum accuracy (45% only) reported during the experiments. However, FKM reports maximum accuracy with three out of four kernels. The highest accuracy of 96% is obtained when FKM is used with linear kernel. Thus the hybrid approach k-means + FCM is found to classify tumor in a better way in comparison to any of the two individual approaches. Moreover, one study develops KIFCM and reports an accuracy of 90.5% using only 22 DICOM images [24]. In comparison, the hybrid system achieves 96% accuracy with almost more than 10 times of DICOM images.

In addition to accuracy algorithms are compared by means of visual examination as is shown in Figs. 2 and 3. In Fig. 2, an MR image having malignant tumor type is taken for examination whereas in Fig. 3 benign tumor type is used. Benign brain tumors are non-cancerous and less dangerous. Malignant primary brain tumors are cancerous that originate in the brain itself, typically grow faster than benign tumors, and aggressively invade surrounding tissue. Intermediate results obtained with five segmentation approaches (k-means, FCM, SVM, FKM and FSVM) are compared. In every case, same original brain MR image is given as an input to the system followed by preprocessing and then using Otsu thresholding. Figures 2(a) and 3(a) are depicting the outputs for k-means; clearly formed clusters are far away from the actual tumor region which may lead to an inaccurate identification. Thus, for the considered image k-means is not able to detect the affected region properly even after the completion of all the required iterations. Looking at the depiction obtained for FCM (Figs. 2(b) and 3(b)), though better than k-means but highlights all high intensity brain regions rather than the crucial tumor region. Further in case of SVM (Figs. 2(c)

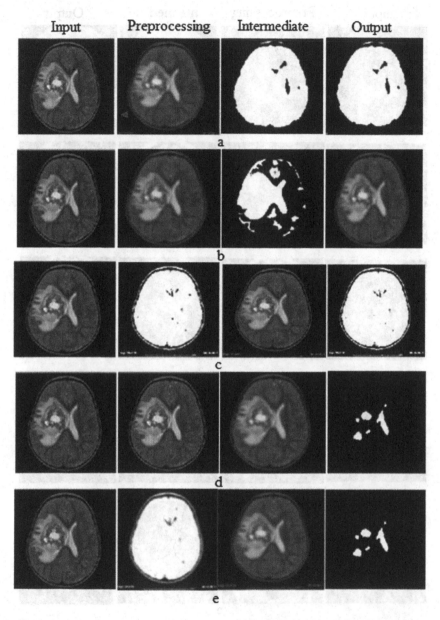

Fig. 2. Visual representation of malignant tumor using T1-W MRI at various stages (a) k-means (b) FCM (c) SVM (d) FKM (e) FSVM

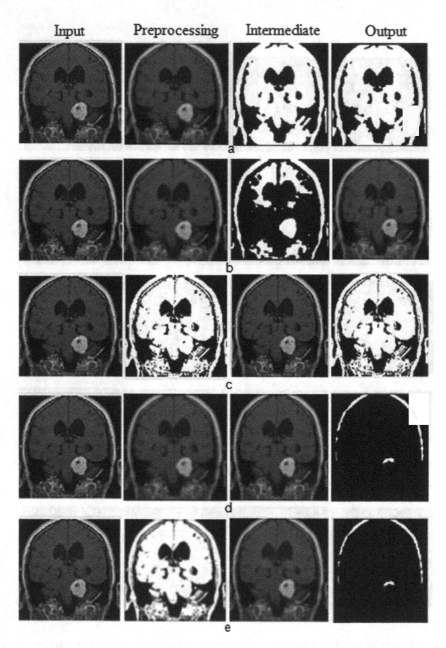

Fig. 3. Visual representation of benign tumor using T1-W MRI at various stages (a) k-means (b) FCM (c) SVM (d) FKM (e) FSVM

and 3(c)) the intensity ranges to extreme level that the tumor area is no visible at all. In contrast, intermediate result obtained using the hybrid approaches in both the cases (Figs. 2(d)–(e) and 3(d)–(e)) better converge towards the tumor region. Intensity variations are evident in the formed clusters, which thus helps in segmenting tumorregion easily as well as effectively. The end result obtained in FKM and FSVM are nearly same, however varies in the second level where preprocessing and thresholding techniques are applied.

5.2 Comparative Evaluation for FSVM

In case of Approach-II the base algorithms are FCM and SVM, and thus FSVM is compared against them (Table 2). Performance of integrated approach outperforms the base approaches. The linear accuracy of FSVM is 93% with is just 3–4% less than FKM approach. No doubt the comparison on this scale is not possible as human errors prevail during the experimentation. However, the difference of both hybrid approaches with bases ones (k-means, FCM and SVM) definitely depicts a great leap in terms of efficiency. Moreover, any combination may it be clustering-clustering or clustering-classifier, the performance surely varies from the traditional ones. The loop holes of one algorithm overshadow the other algorithm. The SVM is computationally slow as it involves complex computational steps in its processing which in return may affect FSVM, however, FCM is computational better than SVM so it boost the processing time than SVM as alone.

6 Conclusion and Future Scope

Efficient tumor identification, extraction, and classification are some of the challenging tasks for physicians and radiologists. Automation of these modules thus occupies a major proportion of research in the domain of medical imaging. Several existing segmentation techniques are shown to achieve good performance on different tumor datasets. Irrespective of the accuracy percentage reported by any automatic tumor detection system using the best segmentation approach, a second opinion is still required for better diagnosis in any of the case. MR image contrast is a significant factor as it highly influences the process of brain tumor detection. Similarly, systems combining two or more techniques are observed to report better performance. The combination FKM is also observed to report overall enhancement in terms of accuracy as well as computation time as compared to traditional approaches (k-means/FCM/SVM) and even hybrid FSVM to a minute extend. In future, a common tumor detection platform able to work effectively on numerous tumor types using appropriate MR image can be thought of by integrating capabilities of segmentation techniques successfully. Lastly, it's hard to fully automate these systems as human assistance is a critical issue. So another future direction can be the development of a feedback driven system that learns from each result.

hello [9]

References

1. Clark, M.C., Hall, L.O., Goldgof, D.B., Velthuizen, R., Murtagh, F.R., Silbiger, M.S.: Automatic tumor segmentation using knowledge-based techniques. IEEE Trans. Med. Imaging **17**(2), 187–201 (1998)
2. Kaus, M.R., Warfield, S.K., Nabavi, A., Black, P.M., Jolesz, F.A., Kikinis, R.: Automated segmentation of MR images of brain tumors. Radiology **218**(2), 586–591 (2001)
3. Gordillo, N., Montseny, E., Sobrevilla, P.: State of the art survey on MRI brain tumor segmentation. Magn. Reson. Imaging **31**(8), 1426–1438 (2013)
4. Georgiadis, P., et al.: Improving brain tumor characterization on MRI by probabilistic neural networks and non-linear transformation of textural features. Comput. Methods Programs Biomed. **89**(1), 24–32 (2008)
5. Dvorak, P., Bartusek, K., Kropatsch, W., Smékal, Z.: Automated multi-contrast brain pathological area extraction from 2D MR images. J. Appl. Res. Technol. **13**(1), 58–69 (2015)
6. Vishnuvarthanan, G., Rajasekaran, M.P., Subbaraj, P., Vishnuvarthanan, A.: An unsupervised learning method with a clustering approach for tumor identification and tissue segmentation in magnetic resonance brain images. Appl. Soft Comput. **38**, 190–212 (2016)
7. Abdel-Maksoud, E., Elmogy, M., Al-Awadi, R.: Brain tumor segmentation based on a hybrid clustering technique. Egypt. Inform. J. **16**(1), 71–81 (2015)
8. Vishnuvarthanan, A., Rajasekaran, M.P., Govindaraj, V., Zhang, Y., Thiyagarajan, A.: An automated hybrid approach using clustering and nature inspired optimization technique for improved tumor and tissue segmentation in magnetic resonance brain images. Appl. Soft Comput. **57**, 399–426 (2017)
9. Srinivas, B., Rao, G.S.: Unsupervised learning algorithms for MRI brain tumor segmentation. In: 2018 Conference on Signal Processing And Communication Engineering Systems (SPACES), pp. 181–184, January 2018
10. Zhou, J., Chan, K., Chong, V., Krishnan, S.M.: Extraction of brain tumor from MR images using one-class support vector machine. In: IEEE Engineering in Medicine and Biology 27th Annual Conference, vol. 2006, pp. 6411–6414. IEEE (2005)
11. Chaplot, S., Patnaik, L., Jagannathan, N.: Classification of magnetic resonance brain images using wavelets as input to support vector machine and neural network. Biomed. Signal Process. Control **1**(1), 86–92 (2006)
12. Kharrat, A., Gasmi, K., Messaoud, M.B., Benamrane, N., Abid, M.: A hybrid approach for automatic classification of brain MRI using genetic algorithm and support vector machine. Leonardo J. Sci. **17**(1), 71–82 (2010)
13. Singh, A., et al.: Detection of brain tumor in MRI images, using combination of fuzzy C-means and SVM. In: 2015 2nd International Conference on Signal Processing and Integrated Networks (SPIN), pp. 98–102. IEEE (2015)
14. Ehrlich, R., Bezdek, J.C., Full, W.: FCM the fuzzy C-means clustering algorithm. Comput. Geosci. **10**(2–3), 191–203 (1984)

SeLF: A Deep Neural Network Based Multimodal Sequential Late Fusion Approach for Human Emotion Recognition

Anitha Modi[(⊠)] and Priyanka Sharma

Department of Computer Science and Engineering,
Nirma University, Ahmedabad, India
{anitha.modi,priyanka.sharma}@nirmauni.ac.in

Abstract. Computer vision domain consists of algorithms and techniques to enhance computers with the ability to see and perceive. Human emotion recognition using computer vision is a challenging research area. Facial expression may not always give accurate judgment of emotion hence needs to be combined with other modalities such as voice, text and physiological signals. Several fusion approaches such as direct, early and late were introduced but the problem still persists. This paper focuses on deep neural network (NN) based sequential late fusion approach to identify emotions from various available modalities. Modalities are integrated into the system sequentially at the decision level. A deep CNN was trained to identify face emotions. Short videos were analyzed to recognize emotions. Further, frames were extracted and the emotions were analyzed. The voice channel was processed and transcripts were generated. Each channel outcome was compared for accuracy. The opinion was recorded manually for conformance of results. The opinion matched with the emotion classified by the system.

Keywords: Emotion recognition · Deep neural network · Multimodal features · Late fusion · Sequential approach

1 Introduction

Emotions are the inherent feature of human being. The ability to express emotions and the intensity of expressing emotions depends on the stimulus given. The key challenge is to recognize the distinguished pattern and develop a robust system to identify the expressed emotions. Further, there is a need towards automating the emotion recognition system which would assist in a situation such as identifying boredom and improvising visual experience required to maintain interestingness in gaming, website and online tutorials [22].

There is a specific pattern involved while expressing emotions. Ekman, Pulchik, Parrot [1–3] concentrated on clustering emotions based on their expressive state, intensity and relationship among them. These were first studied and encoded in the form of AU(Action Units) and FACS [4] for images and FAP's [5] for videos.

The face was primarily studied as a key to recognizing emotions experienced by a human being. Face images were extensively analyzed since FACS was introduced [6].

© Springer Nature Singapore Pte Ltd. 2019
M. Singh et al. (Eds.): ICACDS 2019, CCIS 1045, pp. 275–283, 2019.
https://doi.org/10.1007/978-981-13-9939-8_25

With the introduction of various face image databases in 2D such as CK, CK+ [7], 3D [8] and 4D [9], the study intensified. Apart from RGB other formats of images such as thermal [10] was also taken into account for studies. It was evident from the research that automatic face emotion recognition system with the highest accuracy failed in real scenarios. It failed due to inaccuracy in the training dataset or other factors such as regional, cultural, gender and age group dependencies. The approach broadened with the introduction of other modalities for studies such as voice [11], text [12, 14] and physiological signals [13]. The methods to recognize human emotions spanned across modalities. The multimodal approach combines different modalities to produce desired efficiency and accuracy. The combination of the modalities was done such as face and voice [13], face and physiological signal [15]. The major drawback in the available dataset is that they are acquired under an experimental environment which is quite unrealistic categorized as a posed expression.

Several works have been carried out on the dataset in wild acquired under realistic environment. Such studies are subjected to practical problems such as non-availability of the frontal face as most of these algorithms work on the frontal face. Gesture-based studies were conducted to eliminate this issue [16]. Further research is carried out towards defining a process to combine the extracted features and produce desired results in less computation time. Combining modalities is compute intensive process as the complexity increases with an increase in features.

2 Related Work

Several feature fusion approaches such as direct, early, late and sequential fusion were introduced based on correlation, synchronous or asynchronous nature of features and their availability in time.

Direct [17] fusion approach is advantageous if the dataset is a rich feature source and are correlated both in the spatial and temporal domain. Feature level fusion before training the system was experimented in early [18, 19] method but required synchronous feature source. There is a higher dimension of features leading to overfitting.

Late fusion [20] is applicable at the decision level either through polling or maximization process and can handle asynchronous data sources. But the decision needs to be taken at the initial level regarding the feature sources that are experimented for the purpose. Integration of features in sequential order is the key feature of sequential fusion [21] approach such as rule-based and is less studied. The details of fusion approaches are described in Table 1.

Further, with the introduction of different deep neural network architectures, there was a change in choice of deep neural network architecture to increase the accuracy of the system. A bimodal (video and voice) late fusion was applied on videos in which the voice channel was extracted and processed [23]. A similar study was done using 3D CNN for video and 2D CNN for voice [24]. Text and voice correlations in expressing emotions were studied using CNN architecture [25]. Feature level fusion approach was explored using LSTM architecture [26]. Hardware acceleration was used to speed up the process for reduced computation time [27].

Table 1. Fusion approaches with different modalities and the number of emotions detected.

Author	Fusion approach	Modalities	Dataset	No. of Emotions	Model description	Results	Open issues
Ranganathan et al. [17]	Direct	Audio, face video, body video, physiological signals	emoFBVP	23	DBN (Deep Belief Networks) and CDBN (Convolutional Deep Belief Networks) were used to study	SVM baseline: 75.67% DBN: 76.54% CDBN: 81.41%	Requires rich feature source with the high temporal and spatial correlation between data sources
Huang et al. [18]	Early with Plain fusion	Audio and face	Author collected dataset	6	Prosodic feature for voice, feature based study for video	Audio: 75% Video: 69.4% Audio + video: 91.7%	Requires synchronous feature source
Gunes et al. [19]	Early and late	Face and body	Face and upper body gesture dataset generated by the author	6	C4.5 and BayesNet were used for classification. Feature fusion approach for early and decision level fusion for late was used	Early fusion overall: 96% Late fusion Sum rule: 86% Product rule: 80% Weight rule: 82%	High dimensional feature sources were used
Yoshitomi et al. [20]	Late fusion	Voice and face	Author-generated voice, thermal (IR) and visible images (VR)	5	HMM for voice, Neural Network for image classification with a weighted sum for multimodal late fusion approach	VR: 85% IR: 75% VR + IR: 95% Voice: 84% Voice + VR: 92.5%	Availability of IR data source for classification as there is a change in the initial decision regarding data source for experimentation
Chen et al. [21]	Sequential rule-based approach	Video images and voice	An author-generated dataset of video clips and voice samples	4	F0 contours for voice and Fourier Transforms (FT) features fed into HMM for videos. A rule-based approach which exploits the relationship between the two modalities	Low accuracy due to insufficient data and features	Well defined rules need to be established well in advance before integration of features at the initial level

The earlier work requires a fixed and predefined set of input sources towards building a highly accurate system. Further there no scope for inclusion of any other available data sources with rich features in the existing system. The main focus of our work is to build a dynamic system which can incorporate a classification model for various available data sources with different modalities.

3 Proposed Approach

The proposed approach provides a framework to recognize emotions based on the devices and modality of data available during the data gathering process. Initially, the available modality is used to classify the emotion. Based on the output class probability we sequentially integrate the next available data channel from a different source into the model. Then the output class probability of the modalities is compared. The process is repeated till the same class labels are acquired with output probability greater than the desired threshold.

Currently, videos recorded during conversation such as project review meeting are used to build and test the model. The selected videos contain interactions that are conducted in a realistic environment without any specialized lab setup or devices. The recorded video clips are fed to the system and the emotion is recognized and further subjected to emotional analysis. The proposed system flow diagram is depicted in Fig. 1.

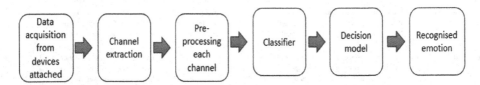

Fig. 1. Flow diagram of the proposed system.

4   System Architecture

A deep convolution neural network (CNN) was used to train FER2013 face emotion dataset. The dataset comprises of 35887 pre-cropped, 48×48 size grayscale images of faces. Each face image was labeled with one of the seven emotion classes: anger, disgust, fear, happiness, sadness, surprise and neutral. A small snapshot of images is shown in Fig. 2. Deep CNN model was trained on NVIDIA GPU system with adadelta optimizer and softmax classifier and achieved an accuracy of 61%.

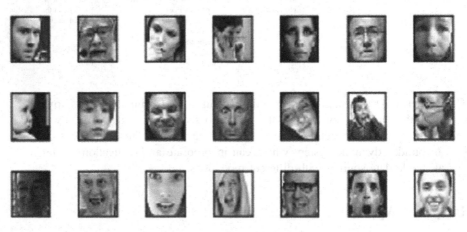

Fig. 2.   FER2013 dataset

The voice component is extracted from the video using open source audio extractor. The extracted audio was pre-processed using open source software Audacity. Noise and silence were removed. The transcript of the pre-processed voice was generated. The video clippings were fed to the system. The entire video summarized to one emotion. The system extracted frames from a video containing a face and fed to a trained deep CNN model. The output is a class probability representing six basic emotion classes. The detailed architecture is shown in Fig. 3. Frame wise detailed study was conducted to analyze the recognized emotion.

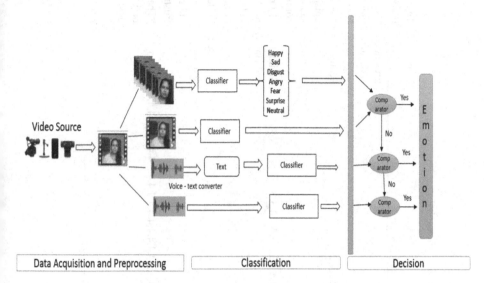

Fig. 3. System architecture

5 Results

The proposed architecture focuses on sequential approach towards a fusion of modalities. Table 2 summarizes the results. For experimental purpose short video of a few minutes were taken.

The numerical value depicted in Table 2 indicates the following results:

- 0 - 'Angry'
- 1 - 'Disgust'
- 2 - 'Fear'
- 3 - 'Happy'
- 4 - 'Sad'
- 5 - 'Surprise
- 6 - 'Neutral'

Figure 4 gives a frame-wise classification for better analysis of the results. Further short sentences extracted from the transcript were summarized and analyzed manually and observation was included. At decision level, the frame outcome and video outcome is matched based on a max count on frames.

Table 2. Summarization of results

Video	Duration	Emotion identified	Frame extracted	Emotion per frame	Opinion	Text analysis from transcript
Vid_gen_1	65 s	4	16	3,4,3,2,6,4,2,3,6,4,4,2,3,4,3,6	Frustrated and sad	"Not happening "; indicates sad and frustrated
Vid_stud_2	90 s	2	20	4,0,2,0,0,0,2,2,4,2,2,2,2,2,2,4,2	Scared	"Sorry, I couldn't finish": indicates sad and fearful for comments
Vid_stud_3	30 s	3	27	2,4,2,3,3,4,2,2,4,2,3,3,3,4,4,4,3,3,3,4,4,4,3,3	Smiling and Happy	"I finished the module" Yes.: indicated a sense of happiness
Vid_stud_4	60 s	4	13	4,4,4,3,4,3,4,4,4,4,4	Confused and sad	"I don't know what to do": indicated frustration
Vid_gen_2	52 s	4	38	4,4,4,4,4,4,3,4,3,3,3,4,4,4,4,4,4,4,4,4,3,4,4,4,4,4,4,3	Not so happy	"The results will be improved in next meet". Indicated unhappiness

It was noted that frame extraction count varies due to non-availability of face region for recognition. Experiments were repeated on Vid_gen_2 with different frame count to study the effect. Table 3 and Fig. 4 shows the results for random count value.

Table 3. Frame count analysis.

Count	Emotion for extracted frames	No. of frames extracted
10	4, 4, 4, 4, 4, 4, 4, 4, 3, 4, 3, 3, 3, 4, 4, 4, 4, 3, 3, 4, 4, 4, 4, 4, 4, 4, 4, 4, 4, 3, 4, 4, 4, 4, 4, 4, 4	37
20	4, 4, 4, 4, 3, 3, 3, 4, 4, 3, 4, 4, 4, 4, 4, 4, 4, 4, 4	19
30	4, 4, 4, 4, 3, 3, 3, 4, 4, 3, 4, 4, 3	13

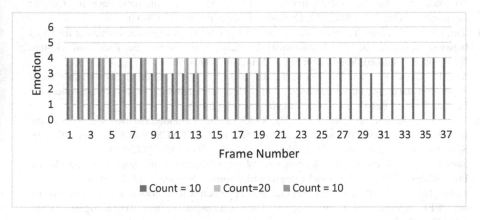

Fig. 4. Frame analysis with varied count values for a particular experimental video Vid_gen_2.

6 Conclusion

Multimodal emotion is compute intensive. The purpose of this paper is to provide a framework to integrate modalities at a later stage only if there is a difference in the outcome of any two available modalities. In our current study, the outcome video emotions matched with the frame outcome and further matched with the manual opinion. Choice of modality plays a vital role and depends on the situation and device attached for data gathering. The availability of channels with required data such as face region might not be present always in a real scenario. Under such circumstances, our approach assists in proceeding towards the next available modality. Further, the experiments can be conducted with various illumination, orientation, camera quality and an initial selection of modality.

However, our work required manual conformance of results for text and audio channel. Hence it is a semi-automated system. This partial automation can be further extended to a fully automated system with minimal manual observation for conformance of results.

References

1. Ekman, P.: An argument for basic emotions. Cogn. Emot. **6**(3-4), 169–200 (1992)
2. Plutchik, R., Kellerman, H.: Emotion, Theory, Research, and Experience, vol. 1. Academic Press, London (1980)
3. Parrott, W.G. (eds.): Emotions in Social Psychology: Essential Readings. Psychology Press, New York (2001)
4. Eckman, P., Friesen, W.V.: Manual for the Facial Action Coding System. Consulting Psychologists Press, Palo Alto (1977)
5. MPEG Video and SNHC, Text of ISO/IEC FDIS 14 496-3: Audio, Atlantic City MPEG Mtg (1998)
6. Ekman, P., Friesen, W.V.: Facial Action Coding System: A Technique for the Measurement of Facial Movement. Consulting Psychologists Press, Mountain View (1978)
7. Kanade, T., Cohn, J.F., Tian, Y.: Comprehensive database for facial expression analysis. In: Proceedings of the Fourth IEEE International Conference on Automatic Face and Gesture Recognition (Cat. No. PR00580), Grenoble, France, pp. 46–53 (2000)
8. Yin, L., Wei, X., Sun, Y., Wang, J., Rosato, M.J.: A 3D facial expression database for facial behavior research. In: 7th International Conference on Automatic Face and Gesture Recognition (FGR06), Southampton, pp. 211–216 (2006)
9. Yin, L., Chen, X., Sun, Y., Worm, T., Reale, M.: A high-resolution 3D dynamic facial expression database. In: Proceedings of 8th IEEE International Conference on Automatic Face & Gesture Recognition, Amsterdam, pp. 1–6 (2008)
10. Nguyen, H., Kotani, K., Chen, F., Le, B.: A thermal facial emotion database and its analysis. In: Klette, R., Rivera, M., Satoh, S. (eds.) PSIVT 2013. LNCS, vol. 8333, pp. 397–408. Springer, Heidelberg (2014). https://doi.org/10.1007/978-3-642-53842-1_34
11. Paeschke, A., Kienast, M., Sendlmeier, W.F.: F0-contours in emotional speech. In: Proceedings of 14th International Congress of Phonetic Sciences, vol. 2 (1999)
12. Binali, H., Wu, C., Potdar, V.: Computational approaches for emotion detection in text. In: 4th IEEE International Conference on Digital Ecosystems and Technologies, Dubai, pp. 172–177 (2010)
13. Thushara, S., Veni, S.: A multimodal emotion recognition system from video. In: International Conference on Circuit, Power and Computing Technologies (ICCPCT), Nagercoil, pp. 1–5 (2016)
14. Strapparava, C., Mihalcea, R.: Learning to identify emotions in text. In: Proceedings of the 2008 ACM Symposium on Applied Computing. ACM (2008)
15. Huang, Y., Yang, J., Liao, P., Pan, J.: Fusion of facial expressions and EEG for multimodal emotion recognition. Comput. Intell. Neurosci. **2017**, 8 (2017)
16. Kapur, A., Kapur, A., Virji-Babul, N., Tzanetakis, G., Driessen, P.F.: Gesture-based affective computing on motion capture data. In: Tao, J., Tan, T., Picard, R.W. (eds.) ACII 2005. LNCS, vol. 3784, pp. 1–7. Springer, Heidelberg (2005). https://doi.org/10.1007/11573548_1
17. Ranganathan, H., Chakraborty, S., Panchanathan, S.: Multimodal emotion recognition using deep learning architectures. In: 2016 IEEE Winter Conference on Applications of Computer Vision (WACV), Lake Placid, New York, pp. 1–9 (2016)
18. Huang, T.S., Chen, L.S., Tao, H., Miyasato, T., Nakatsu, R.: Bimodal emotion recognition by man and machine. In: ATR Workshop on Virtual Communication Environments, vol. 31 (1998)

19. Gunes, H., Piccardi, M.: Affect recognition from face and body: early fusion vs. late fusion. In: 2005 IEEE International Conference on Systems, Man and Cybernetics, Waikoloa, HI, vol. 4, pp. 3437–3443 (2005)
20. Yoshitomi, Y., Kim, S.-I., Kawano, T., Kilazoe, T.: Effect of sensor fusion for recognition of emotional states using voice, face image and thermal image of face. In: Proceedings of the 9th IEEE International Workshop on Robot and Human Interactive Communication. IEEE RO-MAN 2000, Osaka, Japan, pp. 178–183 (2000)
21. Chen, L.S., Huang, T.S., Miyasato, T., Nakatsu, R.: Multimodal human emotion/expression recognition. In: Proceedings of the Third IEEE International Conference on Automatic Face and Gesture Recognition, Nara, pp. 366–371 (1998)
22. Kołakowska, A., Landowska, A., Szwoch, M., Szwoch, W., Wróbel, M.R.: Emotion recognition and its applications. In: Hippe, Z.S., Kulikowski, J.L., Mroczek, T., Wtorek, J. (eds.) Human-Computer Systems Interaction: Backgrounds and Applications 3. AISC, vol. 300, pp. 51–62. Springer, Cham (2014). https://doi.org/10.1007/978-3-319-08491-6_5
23. Song, K., Nho, Y., Seo, J., Kwon, D.: Decision-level fusion method for emotion recognition using multimodal emotion recognition information. In: 15th International Conference on Ubiquitous Robots (UR), Honolulu, HI, pp. 472–476 (2018)
24. Hossain, M.S., Muhammad, G.: Emotion recognition using deep learning approach from audio-visual emotional big data. Inf. Fusion **49**, 69–78 (2019)
25. Choi, W.Y., Song, K.Y., Lee, C.W.: Convolutional attention networks for multimodal emotion recognition from speech and text data. In: Proceedings of Grand Challenge and Workshop on Human Multimodal Language (Challenge-HML), pp. 28–34 (2018)
26. Tan, Z.X., Goel, A., Nguyen, T.-S., Ong, D.C.: A multimodal LSTM for predicting listener empathic responses over time. arXiv preprint arXiv:1812.04891 (2018)
27. Sonawane, B., Sharma, P.: Acceleration of CNN-based facial emotion detection using NVIDIA GPU. In: Bhalla, S., Bhateja, V., Chandavale, A.A., Hiwale, A.S., Satapathy, S.C. (eds.) Intelligent Computing and Information and Communication. AISC, vol. 673, pp. 257–264. Springer, Singapore (2018). https://doi.org/10.1007/978-981-10-7245-1_26

Animal-Vehicle Collision Mitigation Using Deep Learning in Driver Assistance Systems

Mudit Goswami[1](✉), V. Prem Prakash[1], and Dhruv Goswami[2]

[1] Dayalbagh Educationl Institute, Agra 282005, UP, India
muditgos29@gmail.com, vpremprakash@dei.ac.in
[2] Cholamandalam MS Risk Services, George Town, Chennai 600001,
Tamil Nadu, India
dhruvgoswami@cholams.murugappa.com
https://www.dei.ac.in/dei/, http://www.cholarisk.com/

Abstract. The significant rise in the rate of animal-vehicle collision on Indian roads in recent years underline the imperative need for effective technological interventions that help mitigate animal-vehicle collisions in real-time. This paper proposes a deep learning approach for the implementation of the Real-Time Animal Vehicle Collision Mitigation System. The paper makes a comparative study of three deep learning based object detection frameworks: (1) Mask R-CNN; (2) You Only Look Once (YOLOv3); and (3) MobileNet-SSD. These object detectors are implemented, evaluated and compared with each other on the basis of their mean average precision (mAP) and processing times. The results show that the MobileNet-SSD architecture gives the best trade-off between the mAP and processing time and is best suited for Real-Time Animal Detection among the three approaches considered. Using the trained model of MobileNet-SSD based object detection framework, an Animal Vehicle Collision Mitigation System is implemented and shown to perform well on several real-world test scenarios.

Keywords: Animal-Vehicle Collision (AVC) · Deep learning · Driver assistance

1 Introduction

In 2017, approximately 4,64,910 accidents were reported in India [1]. These collisions resulted in 1,34,796 fatal accidents, 1,47,913 human fatalities, 4,70,975 human reported injuries and over 4.34 lakh crores of government property was damaged [1]. In 2014–2017, a total of 8642 animal vehicle collisions were reported in India [1–4]. In the year 2017, the share of accidents due to animals increased from 0.5% to 0.8%. The top 10 Indian states with the highest number of animal

© Springer Nature Singapore Pte Ltd. 2019
M. Singh et al. (Eds.): ICACDS 2019, CCIS 1045, pp. 284–295, 2019.
https://doi.org/10.1007/978-981-13-9939-8_26

vehicle collisions were Uttar Pradesh, Jharkhand, Gujarat, Tamil Nadu, Madhya Pradesh, Punjab, Andra Pradesh, Karnataka, Jammu & Kashmir, and Haryana [1–4].

Human fatalities due to the animal-vehicle collision have also increased substantially. According to the data made available by the Ministry of Road Transport and Highways (MORTH), India shows that there were 1893 human fatalities in 2014, while in 2017 this number increased to 3611 [1,4]. Figure 1 show the state wise distribution of the accidents from the year 2014 to 2017 due to animal-vehicle collision for the five Indian states.

S. No.	Name of State	Animal-Vehicle Collision Between 2014-2017		
		No. of accidents	No. of fatalities	No. of Injured people
1	Uttar Pradesh	1269	667	1043
2	Madhya Pradesh	857	145	599
3	Gujarat	714	285	652
4	Jharkhand	728	163	332
5	Punjab	543	421	289

Fig. 1. State-wise distribution of Road Accidents due to animals from 2014–2017 [1–4]

Currently, In India the network of roads are increasing at a rate of 26.9 km per day [1]. These roads pose a serious threat to the natural habitat of the animals, as the national highways and expressways are being constructed through the forests, causing sudden interruptions on the road by the animals.

According to the proposed architectures for the AVC mitigation in [5,6]. The animal-vehicle collision system architectures have been implemented mainly using two broad approaches, (1) Passive Methods and (2) Active Methods. In Passive methods, an effort is made to keep the animals away from the road using methods like ultrasonic noise, big lights mounted on vehicles, electronic mats, animal reflectors, road side refractors and so on. In Active methods, an emphasis is laid on animal detection. In [6], it is observed that the best way for animal detection is to use camera-based methods. The use of camera for animal detection seems viable as due to the advent of new technologies. The size of the cameras are decreasing and the computation power of the devices is increasing, resulting in more robust animal detection systems. The major disadvantage with camera-based system is due to their field of view, however many positions for a camera can be tested to obtain the best view of the road. In this paper, a computer vision approach based on deep learning is used to detect animals on the road and generate a warning signal in order to provide assistance to the driver.

This paper can be divided into six section. In Sect. 2, we discuss the various existing work on the animal-vehicle collision mitigation system and also the detection algorithms that are being used for animal detection. In Sect. 3, we propose our solution for the animal-vehicle collision mitigation system and how deep learning could be used for improving the animal detection algorithms. In Sect. 4, we compare the three deep learning object detection framework namely, Mask R-CNN, YOLOv3 and MobileNet-SSD and discuss the details about the various components included in the framework. In Sect. 5, we present the comparative analysis between the three deep learning based object detection framework and compare them on the basis of Mean Average Precision (mAP), Processing time of each frame and the detection results. We perform all the tests on a CPU. In Sect. 6, we conclude the paper and determine that the MobileNet-SSD provides the best object recognition in Real-Time and could be used for the animal detection in driver assistance systems.

2   Related Work

Substantial amount of work has been done on the development of animal detection algorithms using traditional Image Processing and Machine Learning approaches. In [7], it is shown that a driver can take control of the car during a collision, within a response time of 150 ms. However, the human eyes cannot look continuously on the road and need rest while driving. In [8], a face detection algorithm is used which detects the face of the animals by analyzing their pose. However, this approach has limited applicability as the animals may arrive at the scene in different poses and from different directions which may not be conducive for effective detection. In [9], background subtraction algorithm is used to determine underwater animals using a static camera, however this technique cannot be used for dynamic cameras due to the restriction of the background subtraction algorithm that require a reference frame for comparison. In [10], visual models of animals are proposed using Haar-based methods. Animals detection is performed using the following three techniques: (1) Histogram of Textons; (2) Intensity Normalized Patch Pixel Values; (3) Scale Invariant Feature Transform (SIFT) descriptor. The performance of the system is good, but is limited to the lateral view of the animals. In [13], a wireless sensor network based approach is described that can be integrated on the road sides to alert the drivers in real-time through the road sign. The authors provide a smart management system for the road signs. However, this approach is region based and cannot be implemented on a large scale. In [14], an approach using FLANN (Fast Approximate Nearest Neighbour) Based Matcher and FLANN search library is proposed. The proposed system uses FLANN along with background subtraction and foreground enhancement to improve the accuracy of detecting elephants over railway tracks and then alerting the concerning authorities. This techniques is limited to the application of a stationary camera and cannot be used with moving cameras. In [15], a comparative study between three detectors: (1) Haar-Adaboost; (2) Histogram of Oriented Gradient (HOG)-Adaboost; and (3) Local Binary Pattern (LBP)-Adaboost is made. Based on this comparative study, a two stage architecture is proposed. In the first stage, the proposed architecture detects the region of interest using LBP-AdaBoost, while the second stage is based on support vector machine classifiers trained using HOG features. This work is limited to the lateral view of the animal (moose) and the second stage of the system has shown to have limited capabilities during the night time.

In [12], a vision based approach is described to detect animals on the road. The proposed system implements the HOG and LBP feature extractors and the extracted features are then classified using the Support Vector Machine (SVM) and AdaBoost classifiers. The proposed system was validated on well known datasets. In [11], the authors present a multiclass vehicle detection system based on tensor decomposition and object proposal. The bounding boxes are selected based on feature ranking after tensor decomposition. Object proposal methods, local features and image region similarities are summed up with learned weights to compute the reliability score of each proposal. The proposed system is tested on various nigh-time multiclass vehicle dataset for evaluation. However, detection in the proposed system is limited to the four classes of vehicles only, with an accuracy of 95.82%. A deep learning framework called Region-based Convolutional Neural Networks (RCNN) is used in [16] for the detection of Kangaroos. Due to the scarcity of labelled data on kangaroos in traffic environment, a state-of-the-art data generation pipeline was used to generate 17000 synthetic depth images of traffic scenes with kangaroos instances annotated in them. The mAP for the testing dataset was 92%. An improvement of 37% was achieved over the other existing methods of animal detection. However, the application of this work to real-time animal detection is limited to the use of a GPU and would not facilitate real-time animal detection with low cost devices (such as Raspberry Pi and Arduino micro-controllers).

3   Proposed System and Design

Little work has been done so far in the development of effective and portable systems for real-time animal vehicle collision detection. Existing systems have been implemented using Road Side Units (RSUs) and warn the driver through warning signs but these systems are not portable and do not scale well with large segments of roads. This paper proposes a deep learning framework that can be implemented on a dashboard system. The proposed dashboard system would be easily portable and could provide more assistance to the driver by generating a message signal whenever there is an animal detected in the camera frame.

The proposed system is tested on several images and videos of animals commonly encountered on Indian roads, and shown to perform effectively. Taking into consideration the top-5 states (Fig. 1) prone to animal-vehicle collisions, the animal classes considered in this work are: Dog, Cow, Cat, Horse, Sheep, Nilgai, and Bullock. Other animals commonly found in India include Elephants, Camels, Lions, and Tigers. The proposed deep learning architecture, MobileNet-SSD, consists of two parts namely the object detection framework and the base network, which fits into the object detection framework. The Base Detector is responsible for classifying the input image using the MobileNets architecture, and the object detection framework - SSD takes the input image and generates the bounding boxes for the class detection. MobileNet-SSD was trained on the COCO dataset [17] and then fine-tuned on the PASCAL VOC - 2007 & 2012 (0712) dataset [18], that is VOCO-0712, to achieve a mean accuracy of 72.7%.

The model was trained for only 20 object, which included animals like Cat, Cow, Dog, Horse, Sheep and so on. Since the objective of this system is to correctly detect the presence of an animal in real-time, it is allowed to classify other unlabelled objects into the category of animals. For instance, a Camel is classified and detected as a Horse or Cow, an Elephant is classified and detected as a Dog or Cow or Sheep, since it is more crucial here to correctly identify an animal. Such an approach has proven to be surprisingly effective as the results presented in Sect. 6 show.

4   Object Detection Frameworks

In this section, the three Object Detection Frameworks, namely, (1) Mask R-CNN [22]; (2) YOLOv3 [23]; and (3) MobileNet-SSD [20,21], are described in detail on the basis of their architecture, mAP and running time. In the next section, a comparative study between the three architectures is performed on the basis of mAP and processing time. Based on the results, a deep learning Object Detection Framework is proposed for real-time detection for mitigating animal-vehicle collisions.

4.1   Mask-RCNN

The basic architecture of the Mask R-CNN is mainly built upon the Faster R-CNN [24] detector. The Faster R-CNN consists of two stages: the first stage is responsible for generating object bounding box over the proposed candidate using the Region Proposal Network (RPN), while in the second stage, features are extracted using the RoIPool from each candidate and then the classification and bounding box regression is performed. In Mask R-CNN, a third stage is introduced in which a branch is added in parallel to the existing second stage of Faster R-CNN to predict and determine the object mask. Mask R-CNN runs at 5 frames per second on a GPU, and hence is not fast enough for practical real-time applications. In Mask R-CNN, during training the multi-task loss on each sampled RoI is defined as the sum of the loss during the classification (L_{cls}), bounding box (L_{box}) and the mask (L_{mask}). The L_{mask} enables the network to generate masks for every class without competition among the other classes available. The parallel architecture helps in generating the masks on the detected objects using the information provided by the classification branch. The RoI*Align* layer helps in removing the harsh quantization of the RoIPool [24], using the bi-linear interpolation [26] to compute the exact input feature value at four regularly sampled locations in each RoI bin, which results in properly aligning the extracted features with the input. The network architecture of the Mask R-CNN extends to the Faster R-CNN box heads from ResNet [27] and FPN [28].

Mask R-CNN makes use of the Regional Proposal Networks (RPN) to locate and generate regions on the image that potentially contain the object. Each of the regions is characterized by its Objectness Score. In Mask R-CNN, a total of 300 regions are selected for detection, which are then passed onto the three parallel branches of the networks: (1) Label Prediction; (2) Bounding Box Prediction; and (3) Mask Prediction. During the prediction, the 300 regions undergo the Non-Maxima Supression, which results in top 100 regions, where each region is a 4D tensor denoted as $100 \times L \times 15 \times 15$. Here, L denoted the number of labelled classes and $15 * 15$ is the size of the original mask generated, which is the scaled to the input image.

4.2 You Only Look Once - YOLOv3

YOLO [29] defines the object detection problem as a regression problem and proposes to spatially separate the bounding boxes and the associated class probabilities. Using a single convolutional neural network, YOLO predicts the class and class probabilities directly from full images in one evaluation. YOLO base network runs at 45 fps with no batch processing on a GPU, hence rendering it more suitable for real-time applications using CNNs. YOLO outperforms the Fast R-CNN [25]; it makes less than half the number of background errors. YOLO is quite applicable to new and unexpected inputs due to its highly generalizable representation of the object. However, the tradeoff in YOLO is that of speed versus accuracy: good speed is achieved by lowering the accuracy levels.

YOLO design helps to achieve end-to-end training and real-time speeds. The input to the network is a $S \times S$ grid, if the center of any grid is same as that of the object, then that grid is responsible for the detection of the object. Each grid is responsible for producing B bounding boxes,confidence and C (per grid) class probabilities. The final prediction scores are encoded as $S x S x (B*5) + C$.

In 2016, a better version of YOLO known as YOLOv2 [30] was introduced which was capable of detecting more than 9000 object categories. YOLOv2 gets 76.8 mAP on VOC 2007 at 67 fps. YOLOv2 proposes a method to jointly train on object detection and classification. YOLO9000 was simultaneously trained on the COCO detection dataset and ImageNet classification dataset. YOLO9000 achieved 19.7 mAP for ImageNet detection and get 16.0 mAP on the 156 classes not in COCO. Further, an improved version of YOLO known as YOLOv3 [23] was released, which marked in an increase in the speed and accuracy. 320×320 YOLOv3 runs in 22 ms at 28.2 mAP.

4.3 MobileNet-SSD

In this section, the Object Detection Framework - SSD and the Base Network - MobileNets are described separately. Towards the end of the section, we combine the MobileNet Network and the SSD framework to perform Real-Time Object Detection at 33 frames per second on an Intel i5 (7th gen) 2.5 GHz processor. Due to their small size these object detectors may be used on devices like Raspberry Pi to run light-weight, deep neural networks.

1. **Single Shot Multibox Detector (SSD)** [21] is based upon the use of the feed forward convolutional neural networks for generating bounding boxes of different fixed-size and then providing scores on the basis of the presence of object class instances in the bounding boxes. The SSD network consists of VGG16 [19] as a base network which is used for high quality image classification, followed by an auxiliary structure for the purpose of detection. The key features of the auxiliary structure are as follows: (1) Multi-scale feature map for detection; (2) Convolutional predictors for detection; (3) Default box and aspect ratio. These operation are followed by a Non-Maximum Supression for finding the final bounding boxes. For a 300 × 300 input image, SSD achieves an accuracy of 74.3 mAP on VOC2007 dataset at 59 fps on Nvidia TitanX and for a 512 × 512 input image, SSD achieves an accuracy of 76.9 mAP.

2. **MobileNets** [20] - These models are used for various mobile and embedded vision applications. The model is based on depth-wise separable convolutions. The depth-wise separable convolutions perform factorization over standard convolution to divide them into depth-wise convolutions and a 1 × 1 point-wise convolution. The depth-wise convolution applies a single filter to each input channel, while the point-wise convolution consisting of a 1 × 1 convolution combines the output of the depth-wise convolution. A standard convolution is responsible for filtering and combining the input into a new set of output. The depth-wise separable convolution is divided into two layers: (1) Layer for filtering; and (2) Layer for combining. The factorization helps in reducing the computational time and the model size. The MobileNets use 3 × 3 depth-wise separable convolutions which reduce the computation by 8 to 9 times, as compared to the standard convolutions.

   MobileNets are as accurate as the base network - VGG16, but the model size of MobileNets is 32 times smaller than that of VGG16 and the model is 27 times faster than the VGG16. Hence, the MobileNets provide a better model for the base network due to their speed and accuracy tradeoff with the VGG16 base network.

MobileNet-SSD [20], in this Object Detection Framework, the SSD and MobileNet are combined to provide a better real time object detection. In this framework, the VGG16 base network is replaced with a fast and accurate MobileNet base network. The MobileNet-SSD is initially trained on the COCO dataset and then fine-tuned on the VOC0712 dataset to achieve an accuracy of 72.7 mAP. The MobileNet-SSD outperforms the existing framework having VGG16 as the base network in terms of the number of parameters: for a SSD framework with a VGG16 model the number of parameters are 33.1 million, whereas with SSD framework and the MobileNet model, the number of parameters reduces drastically to 6.1 million.

5   Comparison Between Object Detection Framework

To evaluate the performance of the Object Detection Framework, the following metrics have been used: (1) Processing Time; (2) Mean Average Precision (mAP); and (3) Detection results. The Pre-trained deep learning models are used for object detection. The main objective at this point is to detect the animal on the road rather than specify the correct class of the animal being detected. The experimental work presented here was performed on an Intel core i5-7th gen 2.50 GHz dual core processor with 8 GB RAM.

5.1 Processing Time

The processing time for each of the three Object Detection Frameworks is based on the frames processed per second. From Fig. 2(a), it may be seen that the time taken by Mask R-CNN to process a single frame is 2750 ms and by YOLOv3 is 1926 ms, whereas MobileNet-SSD processes a single frame in 300 ms, thus outperforming the other two Object Detection Frameworks. These results were obtained by running the deep learning frameworks on a CPU, and only MobileNet-SSD was able to perform the Real-Time Object Detection. However, as we observe in the next section, the mAP for the MobileNet-SSD is reduced due to the increased speed (Fig. 2).

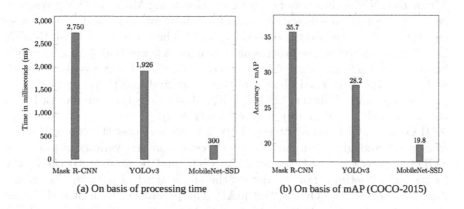

(a) On basis of processing time   (b) On basis of mAP (COCO-2015)

Fig. 2. Comparison of the Object Detection frameworks

5.2 Mean Average Precision - mAP

This section describes the detailed overview of the mean average precision for the Object Detection Frameworks. From Fig. 2(b), we can easily see that the mAP is highest for Mask R-CNN with a value of 35.7 and for YOLOv3 it is 28.2, whereas for MobileNet-SSD mAP value is the lowest being 19.8. A detailed comparison is done on the basis of the mAP values for the VOC 2007, VOC 2012 and COCO 2015 dataset. The speed of each of the deep learning frameworks in terms of the frames per second is described as recorded on a NVIDIA TeslaX GPU (Fig. 3).

Method	Backbone	Stage	Test Size	VOC2007	VOC2012	COCO - 2015	Speed (fps)
Mask R-CNN	ResNet-101-C4	Two Stage	N/A	N/A	N/A	35.7%(0.5:0.95)	5
Mask R-CNN	ResNetXt-101-FPN	Two Stage	N/A	N/A	N/A	37.1%(0.5:0.95)	17
YOLOv1	Darknet	OneStage	448 x 448	63.4	57.9	N/A	45
YOLOv2	DarkNet-19	One Stage	448 x 448	78.6	73.4	21.6%(0.5:0.95), 44%(0.5)	40
YOLOv3	Darknet-53	One Stage	320 x 320	N/A	N/A	28.2%(0.5:0.95)	91
SSD	VGG16	One Stage	300 x 300	77.2	75.8	25.1%(0.5:0.95), 43.1%(0.5)	23.2
SSD	VGG16	One Stage	512 x 512	79.8	78.5	28.8%(0.5:0.95), 48.5%(0.5)	26.8
SSD	MobileNet	One Stage	300 x 300	68	72.4	19.3(0.5:0.95)	23.3

Fig. 3. Comparative analysis of the Object Detection framework using mAP

5.3   Detection Results

In this section, we present the results of various object detection (animals) performed using the deep learning based Object Detection Frameworks. Results obtained for Mask R-CNN, YOLOv3 and MobileNet-SSD respectively are presented in sequence.

1. **Mask R-CNN** - The task of object detection using Mask R-CNN gives very good detection results on various objects of different shape and size and also generates a mask around the detected objects. The accuracy of Mask R-CNN is 35.7 mAP. However, the processing time of each frame is around 2.9 s which hampers its ability to detect objects in real-time. Mask R-CNN is able to mark and detect the unlabelled objects of the same kind and therefore facilitates animal detection. However, Mask R-CNN object detection framework is not able to provide real-time object detection (Fig. 4).

2. **YOLOv3** - YOLO-based object detection outperforms the Mask R-CNN framework and gives comparably good results on the various object. The YOLOv3 detector is able to detect medium and large size objects in the frame but sometimes fails to detect the small sized objects in the frame. The accuracy of YOLOv3 is 28.2 mAP. The processing time of each frame is around 1.926 s on a CPU and hence it does not provide real-time object detection. YOLOv3 is able to detect the unlabelled objects and can classify them using labelled objects of the same kind and facilitates animal detection. In summary, YOLOv3 shows substantial improvement in the speed of detection but is not suitable for running on low computing devices (Fig. 5).

3. **MobileNet-SSD** - The MobileNet-SSD outperforms Mask R-CNN and YOLOv3 in terms of processing speed of each frame at the cost of accuracy. MobileNet-SSD detector performs good object detection on medium and large size objects but sometime fails to detect small objects. The accuracy of MobileNet-SSD is 19.8 mAP. The processing time for each frame is around 0.2 s on a CPU and hence it easily provides real time object detection. MobileNets-SSD also detects the unlabelled objects of the same kind and is able to perform animal detection with Cat, Cow, Dog, Horse, and Sheep as labelled animals. MobileNet-SSD provides good tradeoff between the speed and accuracy to provide real-time object detection on a CPU or a low computing device (Fig. 6).

Fig. 4. Results for the mask R-CNN detection

Fig. 5. Results for the YOLOv3 detection

Fig. 6. Results for the MobileNet-SSD detection

6   Conclusions

A comparative study of three different Object Detection frameworks is made and the MobileNet-SSD Object Detection Framework is found to be best suited for Real-Time Animal-Vehicle Collision Mitigation. The single stage architecture of the SSD Network facilitates detection in the least time (0.2 s on the test system) and generally gives good results, whereas the other two frameworks are seen to fail in performing effective real time object detection on the CPU. However, the real-time detection hampers the ability of the MobileNet-SSD framework to detect small objects in the frame which decreases the detection accuracy of network. The MobileNet-SSD framework used is trained on a small dataset of 20 objects, however the number of classes can be increased by fine-tuning the network with new classes. The MobileNet-SSD object detection framework can be easily implemented on a low cost device like Raspberry Pi and could result in the advent of a low-cost portable driver assistance system. The system only detects a small class of labelled objects including animals, however it provides detection to unlabelled objects also, using the labelled objects. The proposed system has the added advantage that it can be easily implemented on a portable device and installed for use on vehicle dashboards.

References

1. Road Accidents in India - 2017 Transport Research Wing (India) (Govt. of India, Ministry of Roads and Transport), New Delhi (2017)
2. Road Accidents in India - 2016 Transport Research Wing (India) (Govt. of India, Ministry of Roads and Transport), New Delhi (2016)
3. Road Accidents in India - 2015 Transport Research Wing (India) (Government of India, Ministry of Roads and Transport), New Delhi (2015)
4. Road Accidents in India - 2014 Transport Research Wing (India) (Govt. of India, Ministry of Roads and Transport), New Delhi (2014)
5. Sharafsaleh, M.A., et al.: Evaluation of an animal warning system effectiveness phase two-final report. Department of Transport, Institute of Transportation Studies, University of California, Berkeley, CA, USA, Technical report, UCB-ITS-DPRR-2012-12 (2012)
6. Knapp, K., et al.: Deer-vehicle crash countermeasure toolbox: a decision and choice resource. Midwest Regional University Transportation Center, Deer-Vehicla Crash Information Clearinghouse, University of Wisconsin-Madison, Madison, WI, USA, Technical report, DVCIC-02 (2004)
7. Fabre-Thorpe, M., Delorme, A., Marlot, C., Thorpe, S.: A limit to the speed of processing in ultra-rapid visual categorization of novel natural scenes. J. Cognit. Neurosci. 13(2), 171–180 (2001)
8. Burghardt, T., Calic, J.: Analysing animal behaviour in wildlife videos using face detection and tracking. Proc.-Vis. Image Signal Process. 153(8), 305–312 (2006)
9. Walther, D., Edgington, D., Koch, C.: Detection and tracking of objects in underwater video. In: Proceedings of the IEEE Computer Society Conference on Computer Vision and Pattern Recognition (CVPR), Washington, DC, USA, June/July 2004, pp. 544–549 (2004)
10. Ramanan, D., Forsyth, D.A., Barnard, K.: Building models of animals from video. IEEE Trans. Pattern Anal. Mach. Intell. 28(8), 1319–1334 (2006)
11. Kuang, H., Chen, L., Chan, L.L.H., Cheung, R., Yang, H.: Feature selection based on tensor decomposition and object proposal for night-time multiclass vehicle detection. IEEE Trans. Syst. Man Cybern. Syst. 49, 71 (2019)
12. Dhulekar, P.A., Gandhe, S.T., Bagad, G.R., Dwivedi, S.S.: Vision based technique for animal detection. In: International Conference on Advances in Communication and Computing Technology (ICACCT), February 2018
13. Viani, F., Polo, A., Giarola, E., Robol, F., Benedetti, G., Zanetti, S.: Performance assessment of a smart road management system for the wireless detection of wildlife road-crossing. In: IEEE International Smart Cities Conference (ISC2), September 2016

14. Suju, D.A., Jose, H.: FLANN: fast approximate nearest neighbour search algorithm for elucidating human-wildlife conflicts in forest areas. In: Fourth International Conference on Signal Processing, Communication and Networking (ICSCN), March 2017

15. Mammeri, A., Zohu, D., Boukerche, A.: Animal-vehicle collision mitigation system for automated vehicles. IEEE Trans. Syst. Man Cybern. Syst. **46**(9), 1287 (2006)

16. Saleh, K., Hossny, M., Nahavandi, S.: Effective vehicle-based kangaroo detection for collision warning systems using region-based convolutional networks. Sensor MDPI **18**, 1913 (2018)

17. COCO: Common Object in Context. http://cocodataset.org/#home

18. PASCAL VOC (Visual Object Classes - 2007 & 2012). http://host.robots.ox.ac.uk/pascal/VOC/voc2007/

19. Simonyan, K., Zisserman, A.: Very deep convolutional networks for large-scale image recognition. arXiv preprint, arXiv:1409.1556 (2014)

20. Howard, A.G., et al.: MobileNets: efficient convolutional neural networks for mobile vision applications. arXiv preprint, arXiv:1704.04861v1 (2017)

21. Liu, W., Anguelov, D., Erhan, D., Szegedy, C., Reed, S.: SSD: Single shot multibox detector. arXiv preprint, arXiv:1512.02325 (2015)

22. Ren, S., He, K., Girshick, R., Sun, J.: Faster R-CNN: towards real-time object detection with region proposal networks. In: Advances in Neural Information Processing Systems, pp. 91–99 (2015)

23. Redmon, J., Farhadi, A.: YOLOv3: an incremental improvement. arXiv preprint arXiv:1804.02767v1 (2018)

24. Ren, S., He, K., Girshick, R., Sun, J.: Faster R-CNN: towards real-time object detection with region proposal networks. In: NIPS (2015)

25. Girshick, R.: Fast R-CNN. In: ICCV (2015)

26. Jaderberg, M., Simonyan, K., Zisserman, A., Kavukcuoglu, K.: Spatial transformer networks. In: NIPS (2015)

27. He, K., Zhang, X., Ren, S., Sun, J.: Deep residual learning for image recognition. In: CVPR (2016)

28. Lin, T.-Y., Dollar, P., Girshick, R., He, K., Hariharan, B., Belongie, S.: Feature pyramid networks for object detection. In: CVPR (2017)

29. Redmon, J., Divvala, S., Girshick, R., Farhadi, A.: You only look once: unified, real-time object detection. arXiv preprint, arXiv:1506.02640v5 (2016)

30. Redmon, J., Farhadi, A.: YOLO9000: better, faster, stronger. arXiv preprint, arXiv:1612.08242v1 (2016)

Classification of Parkinson's Disease Using Various Machine Learning Techniques

Tamanna Sood[(⊠)] and Padmavati Khandnor[(⊠)]

Punjab Engineering College (Deemed to be University),
Chandigarh 160012, India
tamanna.sood1893@gmail.com, padmavati@pec.ac.in

Abstract. Parkinson's Disease is one of the most wide spread diseases in elderly people. This disease largely limits the patient's movement and speech abilities. The patient develops a tendency to fall frequently hence, ending up hurt with various injuries. Thus, it is very important to monitor and notify either the patients or their caregivers about the severity of the disease. This work showcases a comparative study of the various datasets, algorithms and techniques available for the classification of Parkinson's Disease. This paper also presents the classification of Parkinson's Disease based on various machine learning algorithms for UCI Spiral dataset for Parkinson's Disease.

Keywords: Parkinson's disease · Machine learning · KNN · Random Forest · Decision Tree · Convolutional Neural Networks

1 Introduction

Parkinson's disease (PD) is a long-term disorder of the brain. It is a neuro-degenerative disorder, mainly caused by the low level of the dopamine-producing cells of the brain. The main causes of this disease remain unidentified, but according to researchers, this disease may be caused by either genetic or environmental factors. It is an incurable condition; however, treatment may help control the symptoms. This disease majorly affects the cognitive and speech abilities of the patient [1]. The symptoms of Parkinson's disease can be categorized into two major categories: motor symptoms and non-motor symptoms [2] as shown in Fig. 1.

1.1 Stages of Parkinson's Disease

Parkinson's disease can be broadly categorized into 5 stages [3]. The symptoms during each stage vary significantly.

- **Stage 1:** Mild symptoms which do not interfere with the daily life activities of the patient.
- **Stage 2:** Daily activities take more time to complete with worsened symptoms.
- **Stage 3:** Mid-stage Parkinson's disease. Impaired daily life activities due to worsened symptoms. Patient experiences loss of balance, moves slowly and falls easily.

© Springer Nature Singapore Pte Ltd. 2019
M. Singh et al. (Eds.): ICACDS 2019, CCIS 1045, pp. 296–311, 2019.
https://doi.org/10.1007/978-981-13-9939-8_27

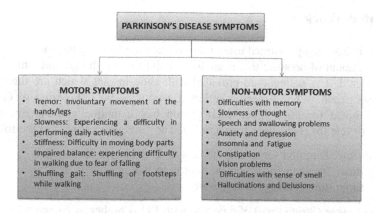

Fig. 1. Symptoms of Parkinson's disease

- **Stage 4:** Patient needs assistance while walking and performing other daily life activities as the symptoms become severe.
- **Stage 5:** The Most advanced stage of the disease, the patient is bed-ridden and will require assistance while walking or performing any activity.

1.2 Unified Parkinson's Disease Rating Scale (UPDRS)

The Medical Diagnostic Society's - Unified Parkinson's Disease Rating Scale (MDS-UPDRS) is a standard used to assess the severity of Parkinson's disease [4]. It is used to categorize the disease into one of the 5 categories based on the severity of a number of symptoms. The stages of the UPDRS scale are shown in Table 1.

Table 1. Categories of the UPDRS scale [4]

UPDRS	Category	Symptoms
0	Normal	Recovers with one or two steps
1	Slight	Three to Five steps, but patient recovers unaided
2	Mild	More than Five steps, but patient recovers unaided
3	Moderate	Stand safely, but with the absence of postural response; falls if not caught by the examiner
4	Severe	Very unstable, tends to lose balance spontaneously or with just a gentle pull on the shoulders

2 Related Work

Gait analysis has been performed using various machine learning techniques [5]. In this paper, the amount of pressure that is applied by the foot on the ground while walking was considered. The patients are provided with shoe insoles which are fitted with 8 force sensors each. When a person suffers a tremor or FoG (Freezing of Gait), the reading is noted for 60 s. Since each person has a unique gait pattern, the gait pattern/gait cycle for each subject is recorded. The gait cycle consists of the following:

Stance time: Duration for which the foot is in contact with the floor
Swing time: Duration for which the foot is in the air
Stride time: Stance time + Swing time

The gait cycle (Stride time) of a person with PD is higher as compared to the gait cycle (Stride time) of a normal person. This is because while walking, a person suffering from PD offers higher friction to the ground while walking. The collected data was then classified using SVM and an accuracy of 92.7% was achieved.

The authors designed a Fuzzy Inference System to quantify tremors [6]. Each patient was asked to wear a sensor on each of the limbs (one on the hand and other on the foot/ankle). Then the movements/tremor of the patient was recorded and analyzed. The data of 57 patients (123 measurements) were recorded and used in the analysis of the system. Several different combinations of features were extracted from this data and then classified into tremor and non-tremor. The detected tremors were then sorted into descending order and three features based on the amplitude average of tremors which are higher than 90%, between 90%–70%, and 70%–50% were extracted. After the extraction of the features, the data was fed to a Takagi-Sugeno Fuzzy Inference System. When a tremor is observed between 1 and 3, the rating is mild; however, a tremor between 3 and 10 is rated as severe.

The authors have incorporated a sensor system with an auditory feedback mechanism [7]. This auditory feedback mechanism will inform the patient of FoG once detected. Two types of devices have been studied. The first device is Sensors in the Headset (SHE). This device is worn as a headband and consists of a direct auditory feedback system. It has a higher sensitivity to trunk oscillations or the upper body movements. Once a tremor of FoG is detected, the patient is informed. The second device is the Sensors on the Shin (S3). As the name suggests a sensor is placed on the shin of the patient. Best performance is guaranteed by this device in terms of sensitivity, specificity, precision, and accuracy in case of a FoG event. The only drawback is that an additional device is required for the auditory feedback. All the data collected by both the devices is analysed and classified using Artificial Neural Networks (ANN). The accuracy is higher in S3 (95.6%) as compared to SHE.

The authors proposed a system for the detection of various types of tremors [8]. Tremors may be classified into two types, namely:

- Rest tremor- Tremors which occur when the patient is at rest and
- Postural tremor- Tremors which occur when the patient is at a certain position.

Three types of sensor placements have been compared. One, where the sensor is placed at the wrist only, second where the sensor is placed at the finger only and third, where the sensor is placed at both the wrist and the finger. The patient is asked to perform finger tapping exercises. The data collected is then pre-processed using MATLAB. After that various features were extracted and the data was classified using an SVM classifier. Depending upon the placement of the sensor, 80% accuracy has been achieved.

The authors proposed a PD monitoring architecture for smart cities [9]. This system uses speech analysis to classify the patients. The architecture is as follows: Once the voice has been uploaded, as many as 22 linear and non-linear features are extracted and then analyzed. The classification of voice signals was performed using SVM and ANN. The data set was divided into four parts. Three parts were used for training while the 4th part was used for testing. The same process was used until each part was tested. This was done to remove biases in the data if any. The accuracy of SVM is greater as compared to that of ANN.

[10] Focuses specifically on the turning during gait. The patient is made to wear an IMU consisting of an accelerometer, a gyroscope, and a magnetometer. Then the patient is made to walk a distance of 10 m then make a turn of 180 and then return to the original position. A video recording is also done for this movement. Four features such as the total number of steps, the total time taken, the number of continuous steps and the number of hesitation steps are extracted from the data collected. These features are then fed into a Fuzzy Inference System, where they are analyzed and the UPDRS score is obtained as the output. Also, the results are verified with the results obtained from the experts (who calculated the UPDRS score with the help of the video recording). The two results are compared and a high level of accuracy is obtained.

The authors have focused on minimizing the time taken to calculate the UPDRS; also the method used reduces the computation time and improves the prediction accuracy of Parkinson's disease [11]. The Incremental Support Vector Regression (ISVR) is used for the prediction of Total-UPDRS and Motor-UPDRS, the Non-Linear Iterative Partial Least Squares (NIPALS) is used for the reduction in the dimensionality of the data meanwhile retaining most of the data information, and Self Organizing Map (SOM) is used for the data clustering. 16 features of the UCI telemonitoring dataset are used. The prediction model was trained on a 4 GHz processor PC with Microsoft Windows 7 running MATLAB 7.10 (R2010a). An error of about 0.8158 for Motor-UPDRS and 0.8004 for about Total-UPDRS is observed. The main advantage of this research is that this method is efficient in memory requirement and can be implemented effectively for large datasets.

A comparative study of various nature-inspired algorithms for the extraction of optimal features required for the aiding in the classification of the patients from the control subjects has been presented in [12]. A real-life dataset of 166 people (Gait Monitoring Dataset), comprising of both patients and control subjects is used. First optimal feature selection process is applied then, the classification is done using neural networks. The Bat Algorithm (BBA) uses 6 features and depicts an accuracy rate of 93.6%. The Modified Cuckoo Search algorithm (MCS) uses 6 features depicting an accuracy rate of 97.84%. Particle Swarm Optimization (PSO) uses 5 features depicting an accuracy rate of 80.38%. Genetic Algorithms (GA) use 8 features depicting an accuracy rate of 79.93%.

The authors created a model for the home monitoring of early Parkinson's disease symptoms which works in real time and operates on a cloud platform [13]. The data had been collected using mobile phones and various other wearable sensors. Along with identifying the severity of Parkinson's disease, this model also evaluates the patient's voice disorders or dysphonia. Along with the collected data the UCI Tele-monitoring dataset is also used. The collected data is classified by applying various machine learning algorithms. Decision tree algorithm depicts the highest accuracy rate (100%), followed by KNN algorithm (99.65%), then by SVM algorithm (94.99%), then by Naïve Bayes algorithm (85.1%) and finally Random tree algorithm (79.93%). The main advantage of this model is that it enables remote supervision of Parkinson's patients.

Early diagnosis in Parkinson's disease is very critical, [14] analyses the effectiveness of vocal features in the early tele-diagnosis of Parkinson's disease. A two-step approach has been used. Only the patient data is used in the first step. The UPDRS score is used to identify the patient group with higher severity of speech impairment. In the second step, the data sample of the above patient group is excluded from the dataset. A new dataset of patients having less speech impairment severity and healthy subjects is created. A combination of three classification methods is used to address the binary classification problem. The classification methods used are: SVM (Linear and RBF), ELM (Extreme Learning Machine) and KNN. The highest accuracy achieved is 96.4% and the Mathew's Correlation Coefficient (MCC) of 0.77 is obtained. Further, the author wants to extend the model to identify the patient group with milder motor symptoms using a dataset consisting of the UPDRS subscores.

The authors make the diagnosis of Parkinson's disease easier. A novel approach of using Echo State Networks (ESN) to classify patients with Parkinson's disease has been introduced [15]. The time series of the UCI Spiral Dataset is used without applying any feature extraction or pre-processing techniques. The Deep ESN yields an accuracy of 94.27% while the Shallow ESN yields an accuracy of 91.60%.

The authors aim to identify the severity in the actions of Parkinson's patients by, the analysis of their movement and speech patterns [16]. A Deep Multi-Layer Perceptron (DMLP) was proposed for the behavior analysis for the estimation of severity. The speech and movement data was measured with the help of an accelerometer of the smartphone. Along with the collected data, the UCI telemonitoring dataset was also used. Along with DMLP, other machine learning algorithms were also used for the classification of patients. The highest accuracy was obtained by DMLP (80%), followed by Linear Regression (77.5%), M5 (75%), KNN (72.5%) and Random Forest (65%). Further, a security feature could be added to the model so as to restrict the access to the patient and/or the caregiver only.

A model to diagnose Parkinson's disease with the help of handwriting samples of individuals has been proposed [17]. The dataset collected by the authors comprised of data from 74 patients (59 male and 15 female) and 18 control subjects (6 male and 12 female). Each individual was asked to draw a set of images/patterns. The image data was then converted into a time series pattern. This data was used in the training of a Convolutional Neural Network model. The accuracy of the model was observed to be 80.75% $\pm$ 2.08%.

The UPDRS score is a measure of the extent of Parkinson's disease. This score ranges from 0 to 176; 0 being perfectly healthy and 176 representing total disability. The authors have created an ensemble model for the prediction of the UPDRS score [18]. This model predicts the UPDRS score with the help of the speech signal as an input. The UCI telemonitoring dataset is used for the training of the model. The said model has the ability to identify more relevant and informative patient-specific risk factors and generate more accurate UPDRS score and. A combination of the K-means algorithm with the CART (Classification and Regression Tree) algorithm is used. An accuracy of 92.9% is achieved when 22 features of the dataset are used.

Another model for the prediction of severity of Parkinson's disease is built in [19]. This model used Deep Neural Networks. The authors calculate the total UPDRS score (0–176) and the motor UPDRS score (0–108). 16 features of the UCI telemonitoring dataset have been used. The data was pre-processed by normalizing into a range of 0–1 using min-max normalization. The model has been built on a system with Intel Core i5-5200U CPU @2.20 GHz and 8 GB RAM. The tensorflow library of python was used to implement the Deep Neural Network. 80% of the data is used for training and 20% for testing the model. 94.44% classification accuracy and 62.74% test accuracy is obtained for the total UPDRS score, while 83.37% classification accuracy and 81.67% test accuracy is obtained for motor UPDRS score.

The authors have presented an effective and efficient model for the diagnosis of Parkinson's disease using fuzzy k-nearest neighbor approach [20]. 22 features of the UCI telemonitoring dataset are used. Feature reduction is done using PCA (Principle Component Analysis). The input parameter vector is transformed into a feature vector, thereby, reducing its dimensionality. Min-Max normalization is employed to avoid feature values in greater numerical ranges dominating those in smaller numerical ranges. This model has been compared with various SVM based approaches and has been found to be significantly better. The best classification accuracy of the said model is 96.07% using a 10-fold cross-validation method. Further, the authors wish to extend the model for the classification of diseases others than Parkinson's disease.

Dysphonia is an impairment of voice or difficulty in speaking. Dysphonia is one of the major symptoms of Parkinson's disease. Several dysphonia features, feature reduction/selection techniques and classification algorithms have been proposed by various researchers. In [21], the proposed model is based on a hybrid intelligent system that is capable of feature pre-processing using the Model-based clustering Gaussian mixture model. The feature reduction/selection is performed using principal component analysis (PCA) along with Linear discriminant analysis (LDA), sequential forward selection (SFS) and sequential backward selection (SBS). The classification is done using a combination of three supervised classifiers, namely, least-square support vector machine (LS-SVM), probabilistic neural network (PNN) and general regression neural network (GRNN). 22 features of the UCI telemonitoring dataset have been used. Maximum classification accuracy of 100% has been achieved with this model. The proposed model can be applied to other medical datasets to enhance the discriminatory power of the clinical features.

The author draws a comparison among the many techniques for the classification of Parkinson's disease using the UCI telemonitoring dataset [22]. The variable selection component reduced the number of inputs by setting the status of the unrelated variable as rejected. The data partitioning component provides two mutually exclusive datasets for testing and training purposes. After performing the above two steps, the following methods are applied (testing accuracies indicated): Regression (88.6%), DM Neural (84.3%), Decision tree (84.3%) and Neural Network (92.9%).

The authors present a hybrid model to increase the classification accuracy for the prediction of Parkinson's disease [23]. 22 features of the UCI telemonitoring dataset have been used in building the model. The presented method is a combination of the Particle Swarm Optimisation (PSO) algorithm and the Naïve Bayes algorithm. The best training data and intended parameters for the Naïve Bayesian training are chosen using the PSO algorithm. The model is trained for Naïve Bayesian classification using the selected data. This process yields a very high accuracy of 97.95%. It is thus concluded, that to increase the accuracy of a model, a new algorithm is not always required, rather the best training data needs to be selected.

An expert disease diagnostic system for Parkinson's disease is presented [24]. This model is based on Genetic Algorithm (GA-) Wavelet Kernel (WK-) Extreme Learning Machine (ELM). The UCI telemonitoring dataset has been used. This dataset comprises of 192 samples of each patient, and each sample consists of 22 features. Thus, a matrix of dimensions 192×22 is created. 128 samples have been used for training while the remaining samples have been used for testing. The calculated highest classification accuracy of the GA-WK-ELM method was found to be 96.81%. The optimum values of these wavelet kernel parameters and the numbers of hidden neurons of WK-ELM were calculated by using GA. The output of WK-ELM makes decisions about the diagnosis of Parkinson's disease.

The authors make use of acoustic features automatically extracted from the replicated voice recording to discriminate the people suffering from Parkinson's disease from the healthy subjects [25]. The Naranjo voice dataset has been used. This dataset comprises of 240 recordings from 80 people (40 patients and 40 healthy subjects). Each voice recording was processed to yield 44 features per recording i.e. a 44 dimension vector. Correlation-based variable reduction is performed where the number of redundant variables is reduced while keeping the different information provided in each group. This is followed by the Least Absolute Shrinkage and Selection Operator (LASSO) regression method which increases and enhances the prediction accuracy and interpretability of the model by performing variable selection and regularization. A net accuracy of 86.2% is obtained.

The authors used more than one unique neural network to reduce the possibility of decision (classification) with error [26]. The predictive accuracy of Parkinson's disease prediction based on vocal recordings is increased with the help of Parallel neural networks. The model is made up of two steps. In the first step, a set of feedforward neural networks are trained with the Levenberg-Mar-quardt backpropagation training algorithm. In the second step, the output of each neural network is evaluated using a rule base. A key feature of this model is that during each step the unlearned data of the neural network is used for the training of the next neural network. This model was implemented using the neural network toolbox in MATLAB. The designed parallel neural networks increase the robustness of the model, thus yielding an accuracy of 91.4%.

The kinematic and pressure features in handwriting can be used for the differential diagnosis of Parkinson's disease have been depicted [27]. Also, a new dataset PaHaW dataset (Parkinson's disease Handwriting dataset), consisting of handwriting samples from 37 patients and 38 healthy subjects is presented. The dataset consists of eight writing tasks per subject. The handwriting features (20 kinematic and pressure features) were computed from on-surface movements and pressures. Three different classifiers were used for classification of patients from the healthy controls. The highest accuracy was depicted by SVM (81.3%), followed by AdaBoost (78.9%) and K-NN (71.7%). This model could be further used to perform deeper spiral analysis and extract spiral specific features.

The authors aim at studying the differences in hand movement and muscle coordination while using a pen and tablet device to identify a Parkinson's disease patient from a healthy control subject [28]. A total of 59 subjects participated in the study out of which 24 suffered from Parkinson's disease. Each subject was asked to draw a horizontal line on the tablet keeping the velocity of the pen constant. For each line drawn, the score vector was calculated. Then, each subject's score vectors were averaged. This averaged score was then fed into various classifiers. The accuracy of the classifiers is as follows: Naïve Bayes (90.9%), AdaBoost (J48) (88.63%), Logistic Regression (86.36%) and SVM (86.36%). The authors wish to further identify non-PD related movement impairments by recording various other lines and trajectories; so as to provide an insight to whether Parkinson's disease could be identified based on its characteristic symptoms.

2.1 Comparison of Various Techniques for the Classification of PD

Table 2 presents the comparison of the existing techniques for the classification of PD with respect to the dataset used, algorithms used accuracy and the features used.

Table 2. Comparison of the various existing techniques

Paper reference number	Dataset used	Algorithms used	Accuracy	Features used
[5]	Vertical Ground Reaction Force (VGRF) by Physionet	SVM	92.7%	–
[6]	Collected from observation of 57 patients	Takagi Sugeno FIS	–	–
[7]	A group of sixteen patients was monitored	Artificial neural network (ANN)	95.6%	–
[8]	Data was acquired from 14 subjects	SVM	80%	12

(continued)

Table 2. (*continued*)

Paper reference number	Dataset used	Algorithms used	Accuracy	Features used
[9]	Voice samples from 31 male and 31 female participants	ANN SVM	90% (ANN) 97.2% (SVM)	22
[10]	46 patients (92 readings)	Fuzzy Inference System	High	–
[11]	UCI telemonitoring	Hybrid method of Self-organizing maps (SOM), Incremental Support Vector Regression (ISVR), Non-Linear Iterative Partial Least-Squares (NIPALS)	MAE: 0.4656	16
[12]	UCI telemonitoring and gait monitoring dataset (MCS)	Bat Algorithm (BBA), Modified Cuckoo Search (MCS), Particle Swarm Optimization (PSO), Genetic Algorithms (GA)	BBA: 93.6%, PSO: 80.38%, MCS: 97.84%, GA: 79.93%	BBA-6, PSO-5, MCS-6, GA-8
[13]	UCI telemonitoring	Decision tree, Random tree, SVM, Naive Bayes and KNN	Decision tree-100%, Naïve Bayes: 85.1%, KNN: 99.65%, Random Tree: 79.93%, SVM: 94.99%	–
[14]	UCI telemonitoring	SVM (Support Vector Machine) SVM-linear and SVM-RBF, ELM (Extreme Learning Machine), K-NN	ELM: 83.70%, SVM-RBF: 77.59%, k-NN: 78.64%	16
[15]	UCI spiral Dataset for Parkinson's Disease	Deep Echo state network (based on Recurrent Neural Network)	Deep ESN: 94.27%, Shallow ESN: 91.60%	–
[16]	UCI telemonitoring, dataset collected by author via smartphone sensors	KNN, Random Forest, Linear Regression, M5P Regression Tree, Deep Multilayer Perceptron	KNN: 72.5%, Random Forests: 65%, Linear Regression: 77.5%, M5): 75%, DMLP-5: 76%, DMLP-10: 80%	–
[17]	Consists of 92 individuals (18 control and 74 patients)	Convolutional Neural Networks	80.75% ± 2.08%	–
[18]	UCI telemonitoring	k-means with CART (Classification and Regression Tree) algorithm	92.9%	–
[19]	UCI Telemonitoring	Deep Neural Networks	Total UPDRS score: 94.44%; Motor UPDRS Score: 83.36%	16
[20]	UCI Telemonitoring	Fuzzy K-nearest neighbour	95.7%	22
[21]	UCI Telemonitoring	SVM, probabilistic neural networks (PNN), General regression neural network (GRNN)	91.4%	22

(*continued*)

Table 2. *(continued)*

Paper reference number	Dataset used	Algorithms used	Accuracy	Features used
[22]	UCI Telemonitoring	Neural Networks, DMneural, Regression and Decision Tree	Neural network: 92.9%; DMNeural: 84.3%; Regression: 88.6%; Decision tree: 84.3%	–
[23]	UCI Telemonitoring	Naïve Bayesian classification and PSO algorithm	97.95%	22
[24]	UCI Telemonitoring	Genetic Algorithm-Wavelet Kernel-Extreme Learning Machine (GA-WK-ELM)	96.81%	22
[25]	Naranjo; 240 voice recordings from 80 people (40 patients + 40 non patients)	Correlation-based variable reduction followed by LASSO regression	86.2%	10 out of 44
[26]	UCI Telemonitoring	Parallel neural networks	91.4%	–
[27]	Parkinson's disease handwriting (PaHaW) database	K-nearest neighbours (K-NN), ensemble AdaBoost classifier, and support vector machines (SVM)	SVM: 81.3%; KNN: 71.7%; Adaboost: 78.9%	–
[28]	Collected by the author comprising of 44 individuals (20 control, 24 patients)	Naïve Bayes, AdaBoost (J48), Logistic Regression, SVM	Naïve Bayes: 90.9%; AdaBoost (J48): 88.63%; Logistic Regression: 86.36%; SVM: 86.36%	–

3 Methodology

The UCI Spiral dataset consists of handwriting samples of 77 individuals among which 62 are People with Parkinson (PWP), while the remaining are healthy subjects. In this work, the dataset has been classified using various machine learning and deep learning techniques.

3.1 Using Machine Learning Techniques

Preprocessing
Preprocessing is an important step performed for the transformation of the dataset. Preprocessing is done to remove the noise present in our dataset. In this paper, we have calculated the average and standard deviation of fields for the preprocessing part. The various features used are as shown in Fig. 2, and also as listed below:

1. Mean of Acceleration in the X-direction
2. Mean of Acceleration in the Y-direction
3. Mean of Acceleration in the Z-direction
4. Mean of Pressure

5. Mean of Grip Angle
6. Standard Deviation of Acceleration in the X-direction
7. Standard Deviation of Acceleration in the Y-direction
8. Standard Deviation of Acceleration in the Z-direction
9. Standard Deviation of Pressure
10. Standard Deviation of Grip Angle

X-AVG	Y-AVG	Z-AVG	PRESSURE-AVG	GRIP ANGLE-AVG	X-SD	Y-SD	Z-SD	PRESSURE-SD	GRIP ANGLE-SD	CATEGORY
197.2469	210.0797	0.57931	899.0698276	721.1689655	95.52397	90.5969	2.620226	80.53794681	152.6919308	Control
200.7321	213.6854	0.653852	856.1059428	841.3118122	97.48691	92.08916	2.753935	100.4151651	161.5956683	Control
225.5475	250.1245	0.735856	878.6098414	924.2562758	110.4607	101.7489	2.885446	77.50833011	109.0694556	Control
197.671	218.2048	0.737273	917.3332788	997.4480275	98.58249	92.43531	2.966946	82.50267945	152.0234159	Control
196.4864	207.1053	0.606003	936.6419724	742.0366841	93.0196	89.92375	3.104192	88.39914365	169.2424405	Control
197.053	212.3821	0.662596	884.4532204	852.4719322	95.02154	88.50074	2.963231	85.83979541	150.3459874	Control
200.1914	213.5982	0.655516	928.4569892	862.2142573	94.46997	87.43382	2.978581	89.04222743	137.9825746	Control
199.7035	217.3014	0.246582	568.7410289	1392.987837	92.63021	91.35624	2.013463	77.68842031	151.4512078	Control
210.1753	224.5515	40.62072	674.0211707	1437.93246	96.45109	88.27911	126.1229	226.2010216	180.1288014	Control

Fig. 2. Dataset after preprocessing

This section presents the classification of the dataset using various machine learning techniques such as: K-Nearest Neighbor (KNN), Decision Tree (DT) and Random Forest (RF), which are all described below:

- **Decision Tree**: DT is a type of supervised learning method used for classification problems. It is a graphical representation of all the possible solutions to a decision. The decisions which are made are based on some conditions and can be explained easily. Each DT is a flow chart like structure, where each internal node denotes a test on an attribute, each branch represents an outcome of the test and each leaf or the terminal node holds a class label.
- **Random Forest**: It is a type of supervised learning method. RF builds multiple decision trees and merges them together to get more accurate and stable predictions. They correct the decision tree's habit of overfitting to their training dataset. They are capable of handling the missing values and maintain accuracy from missing data and are also able to handle large datasets with high dimensionalities.
- **K- Nearest Neighbor**: KNN is a method for classifying objects based on the closest training examples in the feature space, by storing all the available cases and classifying the new cases based on the similarity measure. The 'K' in the KNN algorithm is the number of neighbors we wish to take the vote from. This is a type of instance-based or lazy learning method where all the computation is delayed until classification. It is one of the simplest classification algorithms where little or no prior knowledge about the distribution data is required.

The Decision Tree, Random Forest, and KNN models have been built in Python with the help of the Scikit-learn library. 75% of the data has been used for training while 25% has been used for testing in each model.

3.2 Using Deep Learning Techniques

This section presents the classification of the dataset using various deep learning techniques: Convolutional Neural Networks with VGG16 implementation and Convolutional Neural Networks with MobileNet implementation, which are described as follows:

- **Convolutional Neural Networks**: CNNs are a category of neural networks that have been proven very effective in image recognition and classification. A CNN is made up of four basic layers: (i) Convolution layer, (ii) Non-Linearity or the ReLu (Rectified Linear Unit) layer, (iii) Pooling or Sub-Sampling layer and (iv) Classification or the Fully-Connected layer.
- **Convolutional Neural Networks with VGG16 model**: The VGG16 is a pre-trained model built using tensorflow. This model has been trained to classify the data into 1000 classes. A total of 16 layers (Convolution layer, Pooling layer, and Fully Connected layer) are present in this model. In an attempt to increase the accuracy the simple CNN model was modified and a fine-tuned CNN model using VGG16 model was built.
- **Convolutional Neural Networks with MobileNet model**: MobileNet [29] is another pre-trained network designed specifically by google for small datasets and is light weighted as compared to the VGG16 model. The main advantage of the MobileNet model is that it avoids overfitting. MobileNet consists of around 88 layers. To further analyze the accuracy of, a simple CNN model was built over a MobileNet model.

The CNN models are built in Python with the help of keras library using theano backend. 80% of the data has been used for training while 20% has been used for testing in each model.

The performance of each model is evaluated in terms of classification accuracy, confusion matrix, True positive rate (TPR)/Sensitivity and True negative rate (TNR)/Specificity for each model separately.

$$TPR/\text{Sensitivity} = \frac{Number\ of\ true\ positives}{number\ of\ true\ postives + Number\ of\ false\ negatives} \quad (1)$$

$$TNR/\text{Specificity} = \frac{Number\ of\ true\ negatives}{number\ of\ true\ negatives + Number\ of\ false\ positives} \quad (2)$$

4   Results and Discussions

4.1   Machine Learning Techniques

The UCI dataset was classified using Decision Tree, Random Forest, and KNN. These models were run for 10 iterations each. The average accuracy, specificity, and sensitivity of each model is tabulated in Table 3. The Random Forest depicts an accuracy of 92.1%, with the confusion matrix (of the best performing iteration) as shown in Fig. 3 (a). The Decision tree model depicts an accuracy of 90.6%, with the confusion matrix (of the best performing iteration) as shown in Fig. 3(b). The KNN model depicts an average accuracy of 89%, with the confusion matrix (of the best performing iteration) as shown in Fig. 3(c).

The Random Forest model performs better as compared to the Decision Tree and the KNN models.

Table 3. Accuracy, sensitivity and specificity of the various models over 10 iterations (in %)

Model	Iteration No.	1	2	3	4	5	6	7	8	9	10	Average
Random Forest	Accuracy	95	100	91	88	84	95	88	90	100	90	92.1
	Sensitivity	100	100	100	100	93	95	100	100	100	89	97.7
	Specificity	94	100	89	82	88	100	82	89	100	100	92.4
Decision Tree	Accuracy	95	90	95	85	90	90	95	100	75	95	90.6
	Sensitivity	100	100	100	100	88	94	93	100	64	100	93.9
	Specificity	94	88	94	83	100	94	93	100	100	94	94
KNN	Accuracy	85	90	85	90	80	90	90	90	90	100	89
	Sensitivity	50	93	89	93	88	94	88	94	88	100	87.7
	Specificity	33	93	94	93	88	94	100	94	100	100	88.9

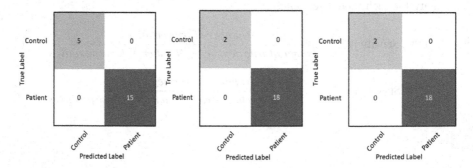

Fig. 3. Confusion matrix for (a) Decision Tree (b) Random Forest (c) KNN

4.2 Deep Learning Techniques

The images in the UCI spiral dataset were classified using CNN, CNN with VGG16 and CNN with MobileNet.

The CNN model with VGG16 implementation depicts an average classification accuracy of 63.15% over 10 epochs, with the confusion matrix as shown in Fig. 4(a). The CNN model with MobileNet implementation depicts an average classification accuracy of 84.62% over 10 epochs, with the confusion matrix as shown in Fig. 4(b).

The accuracy, sensitivity, and specificity of various models is depicted in Table 4. The table indicates 84.62% accuracy has been achieved using CNN with MobileNet model and 66.67% accuracy has been achieved using CNN with VGG16 model. The CNN with MobileNet model performs better as compared to the CNN with VGG16 model.

Table 4. Accuracy, sensitivity and specificity of the deep learning models

Parameter	CNN with VGG16	CNN with MobileNet
Accuracy	66.67%	84.62%
Sensitivity	66.67%	100%
Specificity	66.67%	66.67%

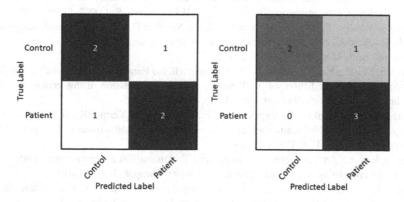

Fig. 4. Confusion matrix for (a) VGG16 model (b) MobileNet model

5 Conclusion and Future Scope

Parkinson's disease is a long-term disorder of the brain. This disease mainly affects the cognitive and motor abilities of the patient. In this paper, the classification of Parkinson's disease has been performed using machine learning models such as Random Forest, Decision Tree and K-Nearest Neighbour on the time series data of the UCI spiral dataset for Parkinson's disease. Also, deep learning models such as Convolutional Neural Network with VGG 16 implementation and Convolutional Neural Network with MobileNet implementation based on the UCI Spiral dataset for Parkinson's disease have been implemented. The further direction is the classification of Parkinson's disease based on real-time data collected in the form of images.

References

1. NIA: Parkinson's disease (2018). https://www.nia.nih.gov/health/parkinsons-disease. Accessed 02 Sept 2018
2. NHS: Parkinson's disease - nhs (2018). https://www.nhs.uk/conditions/parkinsons-disease/. Accessed 27 Aug 2018
3. Parkinson's Foundation: Parkinson's foundation: better lives. Together (2018). https://parkinson.org/Understanding-Parkinsons/What-is-Parkinsons/Stages-of-Parkinsons. Accessed 03 Sept 2018
4. MDS-UPDRS: MDS rating scales (2018). https://www.movementdisorders.org/MDS/Education/Rating-Scales.htm. Accessed 25 Aug 2018
5. Abdulhay, E., Arunkumar, N., Narasimhan, K., Vellaiappan, E., Venkatraman, V.: Gait and tremor investigation using machine learning techniques for the diagnosis of Parkinson disease. Future Gener. Comput. Syst. **83**, 366–373 (2018)
6. Sanchez-Perez, L.A., Sanchez-Fernandez, L.P., Shaout, A., Martinez-Hernandez, J.M., Alvarez-Noriega, M.J.: Rest tremor quantification based on fuzzy inference systems and wearable sensors. Int. J. Med. Informatics **114**, 6–17 (2018)
7. Lorenzi, P., Rao, R., Romano, G., Kita, A., Irrera, F.: Mobile devices for the real-time detection of specific human motion disorders. IEEE Sens. J. **16**(23), 8220–8227 (2016)
8. Alam, M.N., Johnson, B., Gendreau, J., Tavakolian, K., Combs, C., Fazel-Rezai, R.: Tremor quantification of Parkinson's disease-a pilot study. In: 2016 IEEE International Conference on Electro Information Technology (EIT), pp. 0755–0759. IEEE (2016)
9. Islam, M.M., Razzaque, M.A., Hassan, M.M., Ismail, W.N., Song, B.: Mobile cloud-based big healthcare data processing in smart cities. IEEE Access **5**, 11887–11899 (2017)
10. Ornelas-Vences, C., Sanchez-Fernandez, L.P., Sanchez-Perez, L.A., GarzaRodriguez, A., Villegas-Bastida, A.: Fuzzy inference model evaluating turn for Parkinsons disease patients. Comput. Biol. Med. **89**, 379–388 (2017)
11. Nilashi, M., Ibrahim, O., Ahmadi, H., Shahmoradi, L., Farahmand, M.: A hybrid intelligent system for the prediction of Parkinson's disease progression using machine learning techniques. Biocybern. Biomed. Eng. **38**(1), 1–15 (2018)
12. Shrivastava, P., Shukla, A., Vepakomma, P., Bhansali, N., Verma, K.: A survey of nature-inspired algorithms for feature selection to identify Parkinson's disease. Comput. Methods Programs Biomed. **139**, 171–179 (2017)
13. Almogren, A.: An automated and intelligent Parkinson disease monitoring system using wearable computing and cloud technology. Cluster Comput. 1–8 (2018)
14. Sakar, B.E., Serbes, G., Sakar, C.O.: Analyzing the effectiveness of vocal features in early telediagnosis of Parkinson's disease. PLoS ONE **12**(8), e0182,428 (2017)
15. Gallicchio, C., Micheli, A., Pedrelli, L.: Deep echo state networks for diagnosis of Parkinson's disease. arXiv preprint arXiv:180206708 (2018)
16. Wan, S., Liang, Y., Zhang, Y., Guizani, M.: Deep multi-layer perceptron classifier for behavior analysis to estimate Parkinsons disease severity using smartphones. IEEE Access **6**, 36825–36833 (2018)
17. Pereira, C.R., et al.: Handwritten dynamics assessment through convolutional neural networks: an application to Parkinson's disease identification. Artif. Intell. Med. **87**, 67–77 (2018)
18. Zhang, J., Xu, W., Zhang, Q., Jin, B., Wei, X.: Exploring risk factors and predicting UPDRS score based on Parkinson's speech signals. In: eHealth Networking, Applications and Services (Healthcom), pp. 1–6. IEEE (2017)

19. Grover, S., Bhartia, S., Yadav, A., Seeja, K., et al.: Predicting severity of Parkinsons disease using deep learning. Procedia Comput. Sci. **132**, 1788–1794 (2018)
20. Chen, H.L., et al.: An efficient diagnosis system for detection of Parkinsons disease using fuzzy k-nearest neighbor approach. Expert Syst. Appl. **40**(1), 263–271 (2013)
21. Hariharan, M., Polat, K., Sindhu, R.: A new hybrid intelligent system for accurate detection of Parkinson's disease. Comput. Methods Programs Biomed. **113**(3), 904–913 (2014)
22. Das, R.: A comparison of multiple classification methods for diagnosis of Parkinson disease. Expert Syst. Appl. **37**(2), 1568–1572 (2010)
23. Ghanad, N.K., Ahmadi, S.: Combination of PSO algorithm and Naïve Bayesian classification for Parkinson disease diagnosis. Adv. Comput. Sci. Int. J. **4**(4), 119–125 (2015)
24. Avci, D., Dogantekin, A.: An expert diagnosis system for Parkinson disease based on genetic algorithm-wavelet kernel-extreme learning machine. Parkinsons Dis. (2016)
25. Naranjo, L., Pérez, C.J., Martín, J., Campos-Roca, Y.: A two-stage variable selection and classification approach for Parkinsons disease detection by using voice recording replications. Comput. Methods Programs Biomed. **142**, 147–156 (2017)
26. Åström, F., Koker, R.: A parallel neural network approach to prediction of Parkinsons disease. Expert Syst. Appl. **38**(10), 12470–12474 (2011)
27. Drotár, P., Mekyska, J., Rektorová, I., Masarová, L., Smékal, Z., Faundez-Zanuy, M.: Evaluation of handwriting kinematics and pressure for differential diagnosis of Parkinson's disease. Artif. Intell. Med. **67**, 39–46 (2016)
28. Kotsavasiloglou, C., Kostikis, N., Hristu-Varsakelis, D., Arnaoutoglou, M.: Machine learning-based classification of simple drawing movements in Parkinson's disease. Biomed. Signal Process. Control **31**, 174–180 (2017)
29. Howard, A.G., et al.: MobileNets: efficient convolutional neural networks for mobile vision applications. arXiv preprint arXiv:170404861 (2017)

Detection of Malignant Melanoma Using Deep Learning

Savy Gulati$^{(\boxtimes)}$ ⓘ and Rosepreet Kaur Bhogal ⓘ

Lovely Professional University, Phagwara, India
savygulati99@gmail.com, rosepreetkaurl2@gmail.com

Abstract. Malignant melanoma is the most vicious and dangerous type of skin cancer, as it can easily diffuse to other regions of the body. This is the reason that mortality rates of melanoma are so immense. The deadly stats about melanoma can be overshadowed by the fact that melanoma can be cured if detected early. So, it is prominent to distinguish melanocytic and non-melanocytic lesions at initial stages. For this, use of Computer Aided Diagnosis systems are in vogue as they does not involve painful procedures and are effective in diagnosis. In this work, CAD system is developed based on deep learning concept, as in recent times this concept is becoming widely popular for yielding higher accuracies. Most popular deep neural network namely Convolutional neural networks are exploited. Two pretrained networks AlexNet and VGG16 have been used in two different ways. These ways are transfer learning and usage as feature extractor. It has been seen that transfer learning based concept yields efficient results for both CNNs, as AlexNet with transfer learning gives 95% of accuracy while AlexNet as a feature extractor provides accuracy of 90%. Same is observed with VGG16 as it shows accuracy of 97.5% for the former case and 95% for the latter case. Lastly, comparison of all techniques is carried out and it is evident that VGG16 with transfer learning outperform all by exhibiting accuracy, sensitivity and specificity of 97.5%, 100% and 96.87% respectively. Comparison of this method with other state-of-art methods has also been carried out and it is seen that our methodology outperform them. Apart from this, sensitivity achieved for both transfer learning based architectures is 100%, it means that all of the melanoma cases are diagnosed correctly.

Keywords: Melanoma · Deep learning · Convolutional neural networks · AlexNet · VGG16 · Transfer learning · Feature extractor

1 Introduction

The outer covering of a body known as Skin, is a largest organ of a body, as it constitute total area of almost 20 sq. feet and put up 16% of body mass. It serves as a shield against foreign particles and damaging ultraviolet radiations of sun [1]. Despite of its utter importance, skin as organ is not treated like other organs of the body and is subjected to more negligence, thus leading to many skin disorders [2]. Malignant Melanoma commonly called as melanoma is the most dreadful type of skin cancer because it can easily and quickly invade to other parts of a body, thus leads to death of a person [3]. It occurs in melanocytes cells which generate melanin pigment. Colour of

© Springer Nature Singapore Pte Ltd. 2019
M. Singh et al. (Eds.): ICACDS 2019, CCIS 1045, pp. 312–325, 2019.
https://doi.org/10.1007/978-981-13-9939-8_28

skin depends upon this brown coloured pigment. When UV rays penetrate into melanocytes, large amount of melanin is produced, which results in formation of dark-coloured moles, these lesions become uncontrollable and take shape of cancerous tumours which has ability to spread [4].

Statistics related to melanoma are so dreadful that death of one person takes place each hour [5] and number of people suffering from melanoma is increasing from past thirty years [6]. It is the fifth frequent cancer in males strata and sixth frequent cancer in females strata [7]. Increase of 53% is seen in melanoma patients from 2008 to 2018 [5]. Various regions like, North America, Australia and Europe are adversely affected by the evil of melanoma. Malignant melanoma is the most frequent cancer in United States of America. Currently more than one million Americans are suffering from melanoma. Moreover, it has been found that one in five American will likely to suffer from this skin cancer in their life period [8]. These alarming facts can be overshadowed by detecting melanoma in its initial stages, as from stats it is well cleared that malignant melanoma can be cured if diagnosed early [3, 8, 9]. So, it is significant to distinguish melanoma and non-melanoma lesions which is quite challenging and burdensome task. Images for both melanoma and non-melanoma lesions are provided in Fig. 1.

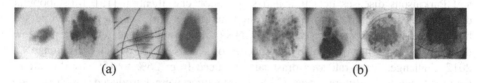

(a)   (b)

Fig. 1. Illustration of (a) Benign lesions, (b) Melanoma lesions [30].

To differentiate melanoma both invasive as well as non-invasive procedures are available which include Biopsy and Dermoscopy respectively. In Biopsy, sample of affected skin tissue is taken out and its examination is performed so that diagnosis can be made whether the resultant mass is melanocytic or not. Apart from being painful, it involves other risk factors like infection and accidental injury to other organs/areas [10]. Further, Dermoscopy is basically a skin surface based microscopy, which is also known as epiluminoscopy. In this, high resolution image of the affected area is taken and accessed by the experts with the device called Dermoscope. This device reduces surface reflections and allow dermatologists to access microstructures as well as deeper layers. To introspect dermoscopic images highly experienced dermatologists are required so that chances of misinterpretation of melanocytic lesions can be reduced. But if medical experts have not been trained adequately then detection accuracy reduces [11]. So accurate diagnosis of melanocytic lesions is challenging for non-experts.

To address these issues, computer aided diagnosis systems are prevalent as in these systems diagnosis is carried out by the system itself. These systems can assist dermatologists for effective melanoma detection, apart from this, these can also be used as stand-alone systems. CAD systems demand image of affected area only. By utilising image, examination is performed and output is generated that whether the inputted image is of melanocytic or non-melanocytic lesion. Vast literature exists for CAD systems based on machine learning that is classical computer vision process. These CAD systems are laid on image processing concepts which include: image acquisition, pre-processing, segmentation, handcrafted feature extraction, feature selection and classification. In case of conventional computer vision methods, the load is on the developer as they need engineering expertise and algorithms to extract features from images and provide them to the classifier. Contrary to this, Deep neural networks only require raw images as an input while bypassing all the complex and trivial steps mentioned above [12]. Comparison of classical machine learning and computer vision based CAD systems and deep neural network based CAD systems is provided in Fig. 2. Sometimes deep neural networks require little pre-processing procedures to refine the results.

In recent times, Deep learning is gaining huge popularity as they make process automated and generate appreciable improvements in comparison to the traditional machine learning based algorithms [13]. Deep learning have opened new doors in the field of medical image analysis and have provided prominent results in different fields such as Diabetic retinopathy, histological and Microscopical elements detection, Gastrointestinal diseases detection, Cardiac Imaging, Tumor Detection, Alzheimer's and Parkinsons diseases detection and skin lesion classification [13]. Most popular deep neural architectures are Convolutional neural networks as they had witnessed huge success since past few years [14]. CNNs are known in research since past few decades but came in vogue after the success of AlexNet [15], which won ImageNet 2012 challenge. Error rate was drastically reduced from 26% to 15% by this architecture. Since then, different new CNN architectures were introduced which include VGGNet [27], GoogleNet, ResNet and many more. These architectures are widely used and yield effective results, thus this field is emerging rapidly and efficiently.

In this work, classification of melanoma and non-melanoma has been carried out using AlexNet and VGG16 by employing transfer learning and usage as feature extractor. It has been investigated that which technique yields optimum results and comparison with other existing methods has also been carried out. Rest of the paper is structured as: Sect. 2 includes literature survey, Sect. 3 is comprised of methodology which has been followed, Sect. 4 includes Experimental results and Sect. 5 is dedicated for conclusion.

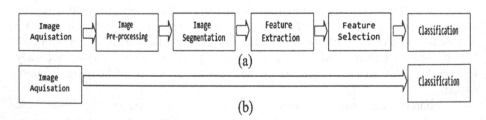

Fig. 2. Comparison (a) Conventional computer vision, (b) Deep neural networks (CNNs).

2 Literature Survey

Convolutional neural networks can be used in three different ways to carry out classification of cancerous and non-cancerous moles. So we can say that to deal with one problem three possible solutions can be employed. First, CNN as a feature extractor, in this instead of evaluating hand crafted features, readymade features are extracted by CNN architecture and these features are fed into classifier for distinction of melanoma and non-melanoma. Pomponiu, Nejati and Cheung [16] proposed CNN architecture and utilised it as a feature extractor and provide these features to K nearest neighbour classifier. Features are taken from last three fully connected layers. Individual performance accessed using features obtained from these layers. It has been seen that results obtained using last layer features, yields better results than others. Kawahara, BenTaieb and Hamarneh [17] performed image normalization and then evaluated features using AlexNet. Obtained features are fed to Logic Regression classifier for melanoma detection. Yu et al. [18] carried out resizing of images and passed them to AlexNet architecture. From network, features are taken out and then they are concatenated with fisher vector. Finally SVM classifier is used to distinguish cancerous moles. Dorj et al. [19] extract features using AlexNet and pass them to ECOC SVM to diagnose melanoma, squamous cell carcinoma, actinic keratosis and basal cell carcinoma. Second method is Transfer learning in this pre-trained model is used directly with little modifications as per the requirement. This eases out the task of user as it doesn't demand huge number of images which is a severe problem in case of medical datasets. Georgakopoulos et al. [20] carried out task of melanoma classification and four differential structures. Augmentation of images performed using LOG, hessian matrix, gabor filter bank and Gaussian filter. Then transfer learning carried out using AlexNet and one more CNN to achieve desired tasks.

Nasr-Esfani et al. [21] acquired clinical images and pre-process them to remove illumination and noise. These pre-processed images are augmented to increase the dataset. These augmented images are provided to proposed CNN and by performing transfer learning paradigm melanoma and non-melanoma lesions are classified. Kalouche [22] took images using standard camera and these images are pre-processed and segmented. After this, images are transferred to three models namely logistic regression, deep neural network and VGG16 for classification of melanoma. It is seen that VGG16 outperformed all. Menegola, Fornaciali and Pires [23] used pretrained CNNs namely VGG16, VGGM and train them on ISBI 2016 and atlas of Dermoscopy datasets to carry out transfer learning for malignant melanoma detection. Third method is to generate complete architecture from scratch that is complete responsibility is on the developer itself to adjust weights, biases, epochs, layers and all other parameters. Li and Shen [24] considered three tasks: Lesion segmentation, lesion dermoscopic features extraction and lesion classification. Two fully connected residual networks (FCRN) for producing segmentation and classification results. Lesion index calculation unit for refining coarse classification results by obtaining distance heat maps. LIN architecture is for segmentation and classification whereas LFN architecture is for dermoscopic feature extraction. LIN's performance is superior as compared to other existing pre-trained networks. Gonzalez-Diaz [25] incorporated knowledge of dermatologists and created dermatologists knowledge network, in this specific features of skin lesion are considered which are of prime interest to dermatologists. Several blocks included in CNN like dermoscopic structure segmentation block, modulation block, polar pooling block and asymmetry block. It has been seen that proposed model yields significant results.

3 Methodology

3.1 Image Pre-processing

To refine images for further processing and prevent deviation from actual results, input images are pre-processed. Hairs present on the body are major obstacle which can make the diagnosis process worse. So, to eliminate hairs DullRazor [26] has been used. Resultant images and their related masks obtained after performing pre-processing are given in Fig. 3. After removing hairs, images are resized to make them compatible with the pre-trained nets. In this work, AlexNet and VGG16 are used, so modifications in size are performed according to these nets. AlexNet accepts images of size 227 × 227, whereas VGG16 requires images of size 224 × 224. So as per need the resizing operation has been applied.

Fig. 3. Pre-processed Images including original images, hair masks and hair excluded images

3.2 AlexNet and VGG16

In this study, two ImageNet based pre-trained multi-layer Convolutional neural networks namely AlexNet and VGG16 are used. ImageNet is a large publicly available and reputable dataset which include approximate of 1.2 million images of thousand different categories. This dataset was built to use in visual based object detection software research. ImageNet project conducts annual competition named Large Scale Visual Recognition Challenge (ILSVRC). In 2012, Krizhevsky et al. [15] won this challenge by presenting novel deep convolutional neural network to perform classification of images present in ImageNet. This proposed architecture reduced error rate drastically from 26% to 15%. It was the AlexNet which brought back CNNs into existence again and confronted its ability to achieve high accuracies and efficient results. AlexNet's first layer is the input layer which requires images of 227 × 227 × 3 having zero-center normalization. Further it have five convolutional layers followed by max-pooling layers. Also there are three fully connected layers and about crores of trainable parameters. Last is the output layer which evaluate the performance of a network based on the probabilities.

VGGNet [27] become prevalent by accomplishing markable performance in ImageNet ILSVRC-2014. This net scored first rank in localization challenge by beating GoogleNet, though it was a first runner up in image classification task. It works in various configurations that is with different number of weight layers. VGG16 is a very deep pre-trained convolutional network with 16 weight layers and consists of about 138 million parameters. Input layer of this net require images of size $224 \times 224 \times 3$. Images are then fed to 5 convolutional blocks. Each block involve a 2D convolutional layer. In this, small filters of 3×3 receptive field are present. Hidden layers include Rectifier Linear Units and max pooling layers. Apart from these, 3 fully connected layers and one softmax layer is also present.

As, both the pre-trained networks include 1000 different kinds of classes but our task is to distinguish only two classes that is melanoma and non-melanoma. So, to make fully connected layer to perform binary classification, we changed the number of classes from thousand to two. Original architectures of AlexNet and VGG16 are provided in Figs. 4 and 5 respectively. Classification of melanoma and benign lesion can be carried out using three different approaches. First is by training AlexNet and VGG16 from scratch that is instead of ImageNet, networks are trained using different database. Due to less number of availability of labelled medical images this method do not provide fruitful results. That's why other methods are employed in this work. Others methods include transfer learning and using pre-trained networks as a feature extractor. These two methods have been carried out with both AlexNet as well as VGG16 Convolutional neural networks. Details on these methods are provided below.

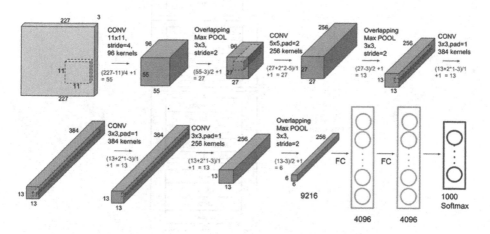

Fig. 4. Original AlexNet network taken from [28]

Transfer Learning. As dermatological datasets generally have less number of images. To overcome this issue, ImageNet based pre-trained nets AlexNet and VGG16 are modified and learning is carried out to train them and perform melanoma recognition task. Fine-tuning of a pretrained network is comparatively much faster and easier than constructing and training a network from scratch. In this, quick learning is executed to diagnose malignant melanoma using a smaller set of training images. The significance of using transfer learning is that both the pretrained networks have already learnt a rich set of features, as they were trained on large number of images. To perform transfer learning, all the layers are kept frozen except top layers that is last fully connected and classification layer. These last layers are trained on domain specific features. Here, domain specific denotes the features of both melanoma and non-melanoma lesions. All the frozen layers which are based on ImageNet make the network learn generic features which are useful for all applications.

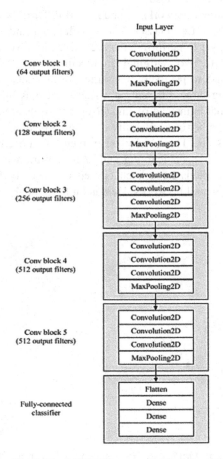

Fig. 5. Original VGG16 network taken from [29]

Use Pre-trained Network as Feature Extractor. In this both convolutional neural networks are basically used to extract features. These obtained features are then fed into classifier which will classify melanoma lesions. Low level layers are fixed so that generic features can be obtained, whereas complete feature sets are obtained from the fully connected layers. These features from fully connected layers are provided to ECOC SVM to distinguish melanocytic lesions. This technique reduces the complexity and does not require any domain or engineering expertise, as there is no need to develop algorithms to extract hand-crafted features. Moreover the complete load is on the CNN itself to obtain both generalized as well as domain specific details.

4 Experimental Results

4.1 Dataset

In this work, dataset used is PH^2 [30], which has been acquired at Dermatology Service of Hospital Pedro Hispano, Portugal. It is free and reputable public database, which has been used as a bench mark for many research works in the field of melanoma diagnosis. It has 200 images of lesions, out of which 160 images are of benign lesions and remaining 40 images are of melanoma lesions.

4.2 Evaluation Metrics

Performance has been evaluated using three different parameters namely accuracy, sensitivity and specificity. Accuracy gives the overall detection rate that is, it involves correct detection of both melanocytic and non-melanocytic lesions. Sensitivity gives detection rate of melanocytic lesions. Specificity gives detection rate of non-melanocytic lesions. These metrics can be obtained using Eqs. (1), (2) and (3) respectively, where True positive (TP) determines number of melanoma lesions identified correctly. True negative (TN) determines number of non-melanoma lesions identified correctly, False Positive (FP) determines number of non-melanoma lesions misclassified and False Negative (FN) determines number of melanoma lesions misclassified.

$$Accuracy = \frac{TP + TN}{TP + TN + FP + FN} \tag{1}$$

$$Sensitivity = \frac{TP}{TP + FN} \tag{2}$$

$$Specificity = \frac{TN}{TN + FP} \tag{3}$$

4.3   Implementation Details

PH^2 database is randomly segregated into two sets namely training and testing sets. From total, 80% of images are used for training and 20% images are utilised for testing. Training is done using stochastic gradient descent with momentum (SGDM) method. Learning rate is set to 0.01 so that algorithm, converges optimally towards true solution. Number of epochs taken for all tasks are 20. For AlexNet using transfer learning and as feature extractor minibatch size of 128 is used, whereas for VGG16 experiments minibatch size of 32 is taken because VGG16 is more deeper convolutional neural network as compare to the AlexNet, also it has huge number of trainable parameters which are excessive for the GPU used in this work to handle it at 128 batch size. Complete work has been carried out on a system enabled with NVIDIA GeForce 940MX GPU.

4.4   Results

Firstly, classification of melanoma and non-melanoma lesions has been carried out using AlexNet in two different ways. Transfer learning paradigm used in which top layers are modified and trained with dermoscopic images. Then, AlexNet is used to extract feature and provide them to SVM-ECOC for classification purpose. It can be seen from Table 1 that transfer learning method yields optimum results by providing accuracy, sensitivity and specificity of 95%, 100% and 93.75%, whereas in terms of specificity AlexNet as feature extractor provide comparable results. Secondly identification of malignant melanoma done using VGG16 architecture by both transfer learning as well as feature extractor approach, obtained results are compared in Table 2. Here also VGG16 with transfer learning outperformed other by yielding accuracy of 97.5%, sensitivity of 100% and specificity of 96.87%.

Table 1. Comparison of AlexNet results

AlexNet	Accuracy (%)	Sensitivity (%)	Specificity (%)
Transfer Learning (TL)	95	100	93.75
As feature Extractor (FE)	90	75	93.75

Table 2. Comparison of VGG16 results

VGG16	Accuracy (%)	Sensitivity (%)	Specificity (%)
Transfer Learning (TL)	97.5	100	96.87
As feature Extractor (FE)	95	87.5	96.87

In Table 3 comparison of all results obtained using both AlexNet and VGG16 by applying two different methods of transfer (TL) and feature extractor (FE) has been performed and respective confusion matrices obtained for all techniques are given in Table 4. It is evident that VGG16 generates more effective results as compare to the AlexNet in terms of both techniques. Maximum accuracy of 97.5% achieved when VGG16 employed with transfer learning. As VGG16 has deeper layers as compare to the AlexNet which help to yield more features of melanocytic as well as non-melanocytic lesions, thus making learning efficient. Training plots for transfer learning approach of both the architectures are provided in Fig. 6, Whereas ROC curves for all the experiments are given in Fig. 7. Area under the curve in receiver operating curve also serves as evaluation measure, more the value of AUC is close to unity better is the performance. Results are also compared with other methods in Table 5 and it is seen that our method outperform other state-of-art methods. To make justice, comparison is carried out with those works which are also implemented with PH^2 database.

Table 3. Comparison of all techniques

Techniques	Accuracy (%)	Sensitivity (%)	Specificity (%)
AlexNet (TL)	95	100	93.75
VGG16 (TL)	**97.5**	**100**	**96.87**
AlexNet (FE)	90	75	93.75
VGG16 (FE)	95	87.5	96.87

Table 4. Confusion Matrices

Techniques	TP	TN	FP	FN
AlexNet (TL)	8	30	2	0
VGG16 (TL)	8	31	1	0
AlexNet (FE)	6	30	2	2
VGG16 (FE)	7	31	1	1

Table 5. Comparison with other works

Work cited in	Accuracy (%)
[31]	93
[32]	92.5
[33]	86
Ours using AlexNet (TL)	**95**
Ours using VGG16 (TL)	**97.5**

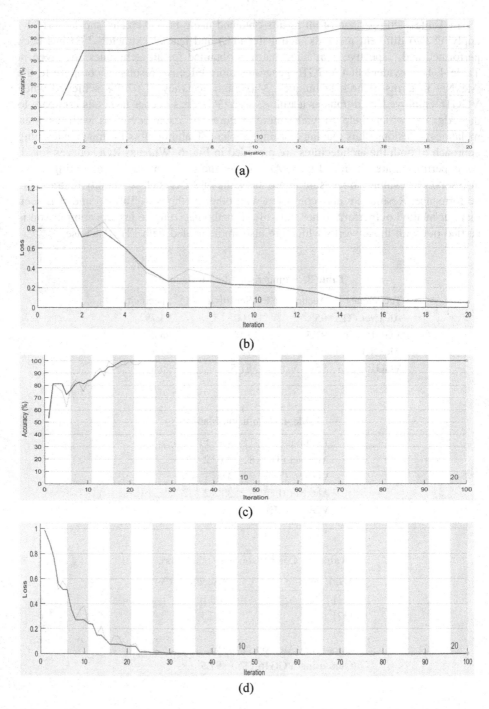

(a)

(b)

(c)

(d)

Fig. 6. Training plots. (a), (b) Accuracy and loss v/s iteration plot for AlexNet (Transfer learning), (c), (d) Accuracy and loss v/s iteration plot for VGG16 (Transfer learning) [Solid lines indicate smoothed training and dotted lines indicate actual training]

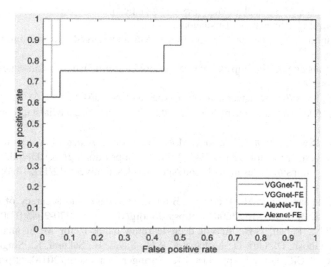

Fig. 7. ROC curves

5 Conclusion

In this work, classification of melanoma and non-melanoma lesions has been carried out by exploiting concept of deep learning. Here most popular deep neural network namely convolutional neural networks are employed. Detection of melanocytic lesions has been performed using AlexNet and VGG16 in two different ways. These ways include transfer learning and usage of pre-trained networks as feature extractor. It has been analysed that transfer learning concept yields optimum results for both CNNs, as AlexNet used for transfer learning gives 95% of accuracy whereas AlexNet as a feature extractor yields 90% of accuracy. Similar is the case with VGG16 as it provides 97.5% for the former case and 95% accuracy for the latter case. When overall comparison of all the techniques is made it has been observed that VGG16 with transfer learning paradigm exhibit appreciable results for malignant melanoma classification by providing accuracy, sensitivity and specificity of 97.5%, 100% and 96.87% respectively. Moreover it has been seen that sensitivity achieved for both transfer learning based architectures is 100%, it means that all of the melanoma cases are diagnosed perfectly. Apart from this, performance is also compared with other existing methods in which our method exhibit better performance. In future, task is to exploit bigger datasets and other pre-trained convolutional neural networks to enhance the performance of melanoma classification.

References

1. WebMD. https://www.webmd.com/skin-problems-and-treatments/picture-of-the-skin#1
2. verywellhealth. https://www.verywellhealth.com/what-is-skin-cancer-3010808
3. Lacy, K., Wisam, A.: Skin cancer. Medicine **41**(7), 402–405 (2013). https://doi.org/10.1016/j.mpmed.2013.04.00

4. Mayoclinic. https://www.pharmacytimes.com/perspectives/management-of-melanoma/burd en-and-disease-characteristics-of-melanoma
5. Skin Cancer Foundation. https://www.skincancer.org/skin-cancer-information/skin-cancerfacts
6. American Cancer Society. https://www.cancer.org/cancer/melanoma-skin-cancer/about/key-statistics.html
7. Cancer.Net. https://www.cancer.net/cancer-types/melanoma/statistics
8. American Academy of Dermatology. https://www.aad.org/media/stats/conditions/skin-cancer
9. Geller, A.C., Swetter, S.M., Weinstock, M.A.: Focus on early detection to reduce Melanoma deaths. J. Invest. Dermatol. **135**, 947–949 (2015). https://doi.org/10.1038/jid.2014.534
10. Mercola. https://articles.mercola.com/sites/articles/archive/2012/11/21/biopsy-complica tions.aspx
11. Kittler, H., Pehamberger, H., Wolff, K., Binder, M.: Diagnostic accuracy of dermoscopy. Lancet Oncol. **3**(3), 159–165 (2002). https://doi.org/10.1016/S1470-2045(02)00679-4
12. Sultana, N.N., Puhan, N.B.: Recent deep learning methods for Melanoma detection: a review. In: Ghosh, D., Giri, D., Mohapatra, R.N., Savas, E., Sakurai, K., Singh, L.P. (eds.) ICMC 2018. CCIS, vol. 834, pp. 118–132. Springer, Singapore (2018). https://doi.org/10. 1007/978-981-13-0023-3_12
13. Razzak, M.I., Naz, S., Zaib, A.: Deep learning for medical image processing: overview, challenges and the future. In: Dey, N., Ashour, A.S., Borra, S. (eds.) Classification in BioApps. LNCVB, vol. 26, pp. 323–350. Springer, Cham (2018). https://doi.org/10.1007/ 978-3-319-65981-7_12
14. Kwasigroch, A., Mikołajczyk, A., Grochowski, M.: Deep neural networks approach to skin lesions classification — a comparative analysis. In: 22nd International Conference on Methods and Models in Automation and Robotics (MMAR), Miedzyzdroje, pp. 1069–1074. IEEE Press (2017). https://doi.org/10.1109/mmar.2017.8046978
15. Krizhevsky, A., Sutskever, I., Hinton, G.: ImageNet classification with deep convolutional neural networks. In: 25th International Conference on Neural Information Processing Systems (NIPS), Lake Tahoe, pp. 1097–1105. ACM (2012). https://doi.org/10.1145/ 3065386
16. Pomponiu, V., Nejati, H., Cheung, N.-M.: Deepmole: deep neural networks for skin mole lesion classification. In: IEEE International Conference on Image Processing (ICIP), Phoenix, pp. 2623–2627. IEEE Press (2016). https://doi.org/10.1109/icip.2016.7532834
17. Kawahara, J., BenTaieb, A., Hamarneh, G.: Deep features to classify skin lesions. In: IEEE 13th International Symposium on Biomedical Imaging (ISBI), Prague, pp. 1397–1400. IEEE Press (2016). https://doi.org/10.1109/ISBI.2016.7493528
18. Yu, Z., et al.: Hybrid dermoscopy image classification framework based on deep convolutional neural network and Fisher vector. In: 14th International Symposium on Biomedical Imaging (ISBI 2017), Melbourne, pp. 301–304. IEEE Press (2017). https://doi. org/10.1109/ISBI.2017.7950524
19. Dorj, U.O., Lee, K.K., Choi, J.Y., et al.: The skin cancer classification using deep convolutional neural network. Multimed. Tools Appl. **77**, 9909 (2018). https://doi.org/10. 1007/s11042-018-5714-1
20. Georgakopoulos, S.V., Kottari, K., Delibasis, K., et al.: Improving the performance of convolutional neural network for skin image classification using the response of image analysis filters. Neural Comput. Appl. (2018). https://doi.org/10.1007/s00521-018-3711-y

21. Nasr-Esfahani, E., et al.: Melanoma detection by analysis of clinical images using convolutional neural network. In: 38th Annual International Conference of the IEEE Engineering in Medicine and Biology Society (EMBC), Orlando, pp. 1373–1376. IEEE Press (2016). https://doi.org/10.1109/EMBC.2016.7590963
22. Kalouche, S.: Vision-based classification of skin cancer using deep learning (2016)
23. Menegola, A., Fornaciali, M., Pires, R., Bittencourt, F.V., Avila, S., Valle, E.: Knowledge transfer for melanoma screening with deep learning. In: IEEE 14th International Symposium on Biomedical Imaging (ISBI 2017), Melbourne, pp. 297–300. IEEE Press (2017). https://doi.org/10.1109/ISBI.2017.7950523
24. Li, Y., Shen, L.: Skin lesion analysis towards melanoma detection using deep learning network. Sensors (Basel, Switzerland) 18(2), 556 (2018). https://doi.org/10.3390/s18020556
25. Gonzalez Diaz, I.: DermaKNet: incorporating the knowledge of dermatologists to Convolutional Neural Networks for skin lesion diagnosis. IEEE J. Biomed. Health Inform. (2017). https://doi.org/10.1109/jbhi.2018.2806962
26. Lee, T., Ng, V., Gallagher, R., Coldman, A., McLean, D.: DullRazor: a software approach to hair removal from images. Comput. Biol. Med. 27, 533–543 (1997)
27. Karen, S., Zisserman, A.: Very deep convolutional networks for large-scale image recognition. J. CoRR, abs/1409.1556 (2014)
28. https://www.learnopencv.com/understanding-alexnet/
29. Romero Lopez, A., Giro-i-Nieto, X., Burdick, J., Marques, O.: Skin lesion classification from dermoscopic images using deep learning techniques. In: 23th IASTED International Conference on Biomedical Engineering (BioMed), Innsbruck, pp. 49–54. IEEE Press (2017). https://doi.org/10.2316/P.2017.852-053
30. Mendonça, T., Ferreira, P.M., Marques, J.S., Marcal, A.R., Rozeira, J.: PH^2 - a dermoscopic image database for research and benchmarking. In: 35th International Conference of the IEEE Engineering in Medicine and Biology Society, Osaka, pp. 3–7. IEEE Press (2013). https://doi.org/10.1109/EMBC.2013.661077
31. Salido, J.A.A., Ruiz Jr., C.: Using deep learning for melanoma detection in dermoscopy images. Int. J. Mach. Learn. Comput. 8(1), 61–68 (2018). https://doi.org/10.18178/ijmlc.2018.8.1.664s
32. Maia, L.B., Lima, A., Pinheiro Pereira, R.M., Junior, G.B., de Almeida, J.D.S., de Paiva, A.C.: Evaluation of melanoma diagnosis using deep features. In: 25th International Conference on Systems, Signals and Image Processing (IWSSIP), Maribor, pp. 1–4. IEEE Press (2018). https://doi.org/10.1109/IWSSIP.2018.8439373
33. Roy, S.S., Haque, A.U., Neubert, J.: Automatic diagnosis of melanoma from dermoscopic image using real-time object detection. In: 52nd Annual Conference on Information Sciences and Systems (CISS), Princeton, pp. 1–5. IEEE Press (2018). https://doi.org/10.1109/CISS.2018.8362245

SARPS: Sentiment Analysis of Review(S) Posted on Social Network

Sumedha🅳 and Rahul Johari$^{(\boxtimes)}$🅳

SWINGER: Security, Wireless, IoT Network Group of Engineering
and Research, University School of Information, Communication,
and Technology (USICT), Guru Gobind Singh Indraprastha University,
Sector-16C, Dwarka, Delhi, India
{swinger, rahul}@ipu.ac.in

Abstract. Today's environment is witnessing a change in the shopping scenario as most of the urban user of all the age group prefers to buy and sell the
product online. The companies allow the buyer to give feedback and reviews
related to the product and with this user can easily share their views about any
product, brand, services, hotel etc. Before making the purchase the customer
nowadays always go-through the reviews which are present on the portal or
vortal because it gives them the idea about the quality and service given by the
company related to that product or brand. Not always the reviews are genuine
but fake reviews are also available to promote and de-promote the product and
one cannot easily distinguish which one is real and which one is fake. The
positive reviews build a good impact on the user for buying the product whereas
the negative reviews always restrict the user from buying a particular product.
The proposed work classifies the reviews on the basis of rating ranging from 1 to
5. The review whose rating is greater than 3.5 is considered as the positive
reviews and whose rating is less than 3.5 is considered as the negative reviews.
The simulation of proposed work has been done in jupyter notebook and the
results are encouraging.

Keywords: Social network · Reviews · Sentiment analysis · Opinion mining

1 Introduction

Social Network is the collection of the various program over the internet through which
people can share ideas, media, do business, and connect with friends and family.
Nowadays with the advancement in technology the many e-commerce sites such as
Amazon, Flipkart, Snapdeal, etc. have emerged. With the help of these sites, anyone
can buy and sell the products online. Due to the increase in e-commerce sites, online
purchasing also increases. To buy the product, online reviews play an important role
for the other customers who want to buy online. Sentiment Analysis is the process of
extracting useful information from the source information using natural language
processing to make it meaningful. On the basis of polarity, the information is distinguished as positive, negative or neutral. Opinion mining is the subfield of sentiment
analysis as it extracts the user opinion about any product or service and categorizes

© Springer Nature Singapore Pte Ltd. 2019
M. Singh et al. (Eds.): ICACDS 2019, CCIS 1045, pp. 326–337, 2019.
https://doi.org/10.1007/978-981-13-9939-8_29

them into different classes. It deals with the emotions of the user about any product. In the current research work, the main emphasis is on the review analysis. A review is a feedback from the customers to inquire about the service, quality, brand, details etc. for the particular product, book, mobile phones etc. The review analysis investigates the reviews and tags them into two classes positive and negative. The reviews which can be against any particular item or brand can be considered as the negative review. The reviews which are in the favor of the item, mobile phone, service etc. can be considered as the positive review or as the authentic review. False reviews are the unauthenticated reviews for de promoting the product or service. If the user frequently comments about an item or content length is not precise then there is a chance that it is a false review. Nowadays people are hired by the company for posting the reviews on the shopping portal. They are paid just for degrading the reputation of the item or brand. They can be hackers who want to degrade the quality, service, and details of the specific item. The advantages and disadvantages of SARPS: Sentiment Analysis of Reviews Posted on Social Network are as follows:

1.1   Advantages of Obtaining Reviews

- The online reviews help in promoting the product.
- The reviews are needed for an advertising point for online shopping.
- Online reviews are helpful as they provide the suggestion for a particular item for making it better than before.

1.2   Disadvantage of Obtaining Reviews

- Nowadays online review is the medium for de-promoting the product.
- The reviews are used as the method for degrading the company's reputation.
- Sometimes checking reviews is the waste of time especially when the review is lengthy and fake.

2   Problem Statement and Motivation

The problem of fake reviews was that it misguides many genuine users who want to buy a specific product. Many people were hired by the company to de-promote the brand or other product. These problem associated with fake reviews motivate us to undertake the research work.

3   Related Work

In the paper [1] author presents a model to construct three different types of features which involve review density, semantic and emotion for finding the fake reviews from various websites. For capturing the category, store and time character of fake reviews the feature was proposed. The classifier used in detecting the nonreal reviews was decision tree, SVM, Naïve Bayes. When the behavior feature was used with all the three classifiers the precision result is very low whereas when the review density, semantics ad emotion features were used the Naïve Bayes performance was weak when compared to SVM and decision tree.

In the paper [2] authors described the different machine learning algorithms for classification of sentiments of datasets. There were two cases for analyzing the reviews as positive and negative. Firstly the algorithm was applied to a dataset having stop words and secondly applied without the stop words. The supervised learning techniques were used for sentiment analysis to differentiate between the real and the fake movie reviews. The four techniques used were (SVM) support vector machine, k- nearest neighbor, decision tree and naïve Bayes. It shows the comparison of various sentiment classifications using weka tool to categorized them into fake and real reviews From all the four techniques the more accurate results were given by the SVM in both the cases and for finding fake reviews as well.

In the paper [3] author(s) incorporated the sentiment analysis to detect the spam, malicious and fake reviews and filter them with vulgar and curse words. Based on the demand of the product they analyze the various features from the Amazon dataset for calculation of sentiment score and ratings. The results were shown graphically. They made a dictionary based on the weight given according to its polarity to a sentiment word and then present a method with various rules for computation of sentiment score.

In the paper [4] author identified the opinion spam detection indicators based on the behavior, feature of the reviewers. To recognize the real and similar reviews they present two algorithms for analyzing the relation between the content and the topic. The proposed algorithms used automatic word segment techniques. The percentage of finding the real and fake reviews given by them was 54.7% and 46%.

In the paper [5] author(s) focused on finding the non-real reviews based on the relational and semantic discovery. It detects the relation between the products, reviewers and the reviews. The data mining techniques were used to extract the relational and semantic features and based on the features they used the SVM, logistic regression, Random forest and Naïve Bayes techniques for classification of fake and non-fake reviews.

In the paper [6] author(s) takes into account the reviews in the form of text and stars as well. The model involved five parts which were

Feedback comments analysis
Mining of feedback comments
Computation of dimensions weights and trust
Classification of fake and authentic comments
Seller trusted profile.

For detecting real and non-real reviews the various supervised learning algorithms were used. The fake reviews were found based on the writing style, level of details, understandability etc.

In the paper [7] author(s) used sentiment analysis and temporal to detect fake and authentic product reviews. It detected out that normal reviewer generally reviews during weekends and holidays whereas the fake reviewer does review during working hours. The methodology used follows the following steps: data collection, procedure, and sentiment analysis and calculated the sentiment score and kappa score. It also concluded that the fake reviewers post positive comments whereas the genuine reviewers post both positive as well as negative comments.

In the paper [8] author(s) present two types of features and apply supervised learning algorithms on Yelp data for classification. The features involved were readability and topic features. It uses the behavioral features related to reviewers and reviews for learning. The classifiers used were SVM, K- nearest neighbor, Naïve Bayes, and logistic regression. From all the classifiers the LR gave the best result with 97.2% accuracy.

In the paper [9] author detected fake reviews by created a model which classifies the editorial articles and using sentiment analysis used different classifier for finding the polarity of the review. The methodology includes three stages: pre-processing, processing and post-processing. The dataset includes English news websites. The results were shown using different classifiers like KNN, Naïve Bayes and support vector machines and classified as positive, negative and neutral.

In the paper [10] the author examined spam detection methods based on machine learning. It uses the decision-making process which is done with combining spam filtering software and human analysis and then shows the different results on different datasets. The improper dataset was concerned as the major problem in detection of spam.

In the paper [11] presented a novel utilization of internet-based life investigation by gathering tweets sent from vitality purchasers to their vitality suppliers. It focuses at delayed consequences of estimation examination on customer's tweets teaming up with the Big Six (Britain's greatest and most prepared gas and power suppliers) versus three new competitors essentialness providers and mainly discussed the tweets revolving around the use of practical power source.

In the paper [12] author proposed a model to extract sentiments from reviews dataset. The techniques used were supported vector machine, LDA model and aspect extraction. The proposed model was implemented in the R language of programming. The output from lda model was used to trained the support vector machine and calculated the precision, recall, f score and mean accuracy.

In [13] and [14], author(s) have conducted a statistical survey on data mining techniques with demonstrations done on MongoDB. Author(s) have also described the importance of big data, its techniques, and applications. To show the effectiveness of data mining techniques, simulations have been carried out of real-time dataset where queries have been run on MongoDB.

In [15], a comparative study between big data and big data analytics has been conducted. Comparative analysis between two real-time Indian traffic datasets has been demonstrated where simulations have been done on MongoDB.

In [16], author(s) have described predictive modeling in the context of social networks. Firstly, the theoretical description has been provided. Then, a thorough predictive analysis has been carried out on a real-time social network dataset of a conference.

In the paper [17] author(s) used a method to extract the opinion target and an opinion word. For finding the confidence the graph based co-ranking model was used. The partially supervised algorithm for word alignment with hill climbing model for opinion detection was used and finally shows that the opinion word is more productive when semantics and opinion both were considered.

4 Methodology Adopted

The real-time authentic schema was created for mobile phone(s) by aggregating the data from various Online Shopping Web Portal and is described as follows (Tables 1, 2 and 3).

Table 1. Schema from flipkart

S. no.	Mobile	Camera	Battery	Value
1	Honor 7A	3.0	2.4	4.7
2	Redimi 6	3.8	2.8	4.8
3	Realme 2	3.4	4.7	4.8
4	MotoX4	4.1	3.4	4.3
5	Nokia 6.1	3.5	3.3	4.6

Table 2. Schema of amazon

S. no.	Mobile	Camera	Battery	Value
1	Honor 7A	4.0	3.8	4.1
2	Redimi 6	4.0	4.3	4.1
3	Realme 2	4.2	4.2	4.4
4	MotoX4	4.0	3.6	3.9
5	Nokia 6.1	3.4	3.6	3.5

Based on the following mathematical equations were performed.

Table 3. Equations used

$Mean = \sum_{i=1}^{5} Xi.$ [19]
$covariance\,xy = (X - X.mean) * (Y - Y.mean).$ [20] $cov\,xy = xy.mean.$
$standard\,deviation_x = X.std().$ [21] $standard\,deviation_y = Y.std().$
$covariance_{xy} = \dfrac{cov_{xy}}{std_x * std_y}.$ $cov_{xy} = xy.mean.$

5 Experiment Performed

The ratings from review table were collected and the experiment was performed. There were two variable one is dependent and other is independent. The battery is considered as a dependent variable and value is considered as an independent variable. The graph plotted is between battery and value. Then a line graph, correlation matrix, and bar graph were plotted for all the variables.

5.1 Dataset

The reviews were taken from the flipkart and amazon sites. The ratings given by user were taken to analyze and various mathematical equations were performed such as mean, covariance, and correlation.

5.2 Tool

The tool used is jupyter notebook in anaconda navigator. The version of the jupyter notebook is 5.4.0. Jupyter notebook is used with ipython to create notebooks.

5.3 Algorithm

Univariate Analysis- It is the analysis on the one variable at a time and finds a pattern. It doesn't deal with the relationship.

5.4 Following Steps Were Performed for the Simulation Work

- The input file was loaded.
- Co-variance and correlation were calculated on the Dataset, using the mathematical formula as detailed below: $xy = (X - X.mean()) * (Y - Y.mean())$ and $cov\_xy = xy.mean()$
- Select dependent and independent variables were selected.
- Conversion data (data cleaning) were performed.
- Apply linear transformation, standardization, normalization and data mining
- Line graph, correlation matrix, and bar graph were displayed.

6 Results Obtained

Snapshot obtained after doing computation on jupyter notebook is as follows:

Line graph, correlation matrix and its related bar graph obtained after compilation of the dataset are as follows (Figs. 1, 2, 3 and 4).

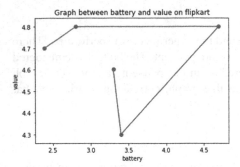

Fig. 1. Battery v/s Value Graph on flipkart

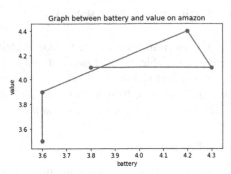

Fig. 2. Battery v/s Value Graph on amazon

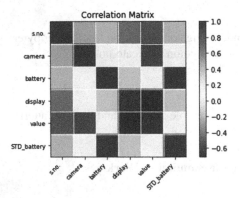

Fig. 3. Correlation matrix on flipkart

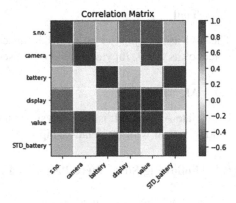

Fig. 4. Correlation matrix on amazon

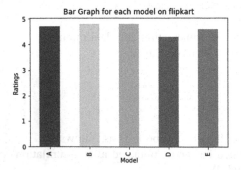

Fig. 5. Ratings bar graph on flipkart

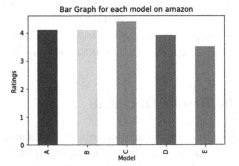

Fig. 6. Ratings bar graph on amazon

Legends used in Figs. 5 and 6 are depicted in Table 4:

Table 4. Model number with their respective phone names

Model number	Phone name
A	HONOR 7A
B	REDIMI 6
C	REAL ME2
D	MOTOX4
E	NOKIA 6.1

7 Steps for Detection of Fake Reviews

1. To send OTP to customer registered mobile number which he would use at the time of giving reviews.
2. To send email to registered Email id and given the link for feedback.
3. Shooting the URL at the registered mobile numbers and redirecting it to the web portal for giving feedback of the product.
4. The frequent buyers should give membership such as Gold, Silver and platinum membership according to their purchases.
5. Employees of the same company are debarred from posting the review of the item.

8 Fake Review Detection Tools

Fake Spot: It is the tool used for detecting the unauthorized and false reviews present on various web portals and e-commerce sites. The method used by this tool is that it first scans, examines the comment and then identifies the type of review. The tool inspects the comments and finds the untruthful pattern about the product and the item which is reviewed by the user.

Review Meta: The review data is a website used for study the reviews and gives them the type as a good review and bad review. It totally does twelve tests for finding the doubtful reviews and categorizes them into one out of three types. The three different types are as follow:

1. Pass
2. Warn
3. Fail

The working of the tool includes the three following steps. The data is collected that is the product review url. The collected data is executed using the review meta analyzer, And finally a report card is generated to show the type of review as pass, fail or warn. The report ard generated from review meta for honor 7 A phone is shown below (Figs. 7, 8 and 9).

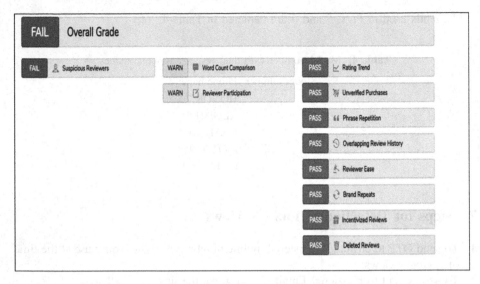

Fig. 7. Reportcard for Honor 7A [22]

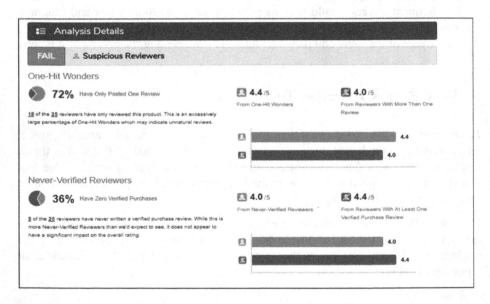

Fig. 8. Analysis of review by analyzer [22]

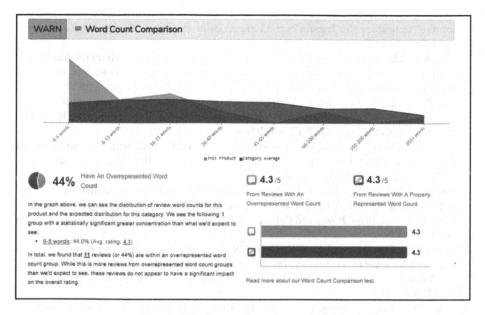

Fig. 9. Word count by review meta [22]

9 Conclusion and Future Scope

From the above experiment, we can conclude that for the same product the customer rating varies with the two different social network sites. The ratings above 3.5 are considered as the authentic review whereas the ratings below 3.5 are considered as the fake review. The company can start the reward ceremony for honest reviewers. It can also build some incentive scheme to encourage the reviewers for doing the positive comment such as 5% to 10% discount on the purchase of next product, Review along with a photograph of the customer on the website and Voucher for tourist excursion. The future work includes fetching the large data from different websites, social sites to reduce human effort and work. The research can be used to improve the existing algorithms for review analysis. For the future work, the reviews in the form of comments and text can be considered for computation and detection of reviews.

Acknowledgment. The Author(s) wishes to express their gratitude to their institution Guru Gobind Singh Indraprastha University for providing a great exposure to accomplish research oriented tasks and providing a strong platform to develop skills and capabilities.

References

1. Li, Y., Feng, X., Zhang, S.: Detecting fake reviews utilizing semantic and emotion model. In: 2016 3rd International Conference on Information Science and Control Engineering (ICISCE), pp. 317–320. IEEE, July 2016

2. Elmurngi, E., Gherbi, A.: An empirical study on detecting fake reviews using machine learning techniques. In: International Conference on Innovative Computing Technology, pp. 107–114 (2017)
3. Chauhan, S.K., Goel, A., Goel, P., Chauhan, A., Gurve, M.K.: Research on product review analysis and spam review detection. In: 2017 4th International Conference on Signal Processing and Integrated Networks (SPIN), pp. 390–393. IEEE, February 2017
4. Liu, P., Xu, Z., Ai, J., Wang, F.: Identifying indicators of fake reviews based on spammer's behavior features. In: 2017 IEEE International Conference on Software Quality, Reliability and Security Companion (QRS-C), pp. 396–403. IEEE, July 2017
5. Runa, D., Zhang, X., Zhai, Y.: Try to find fake reviews with semantic and relational discovery. In: 2017 13th International Conference on Semantics, Knowledge and Grids (SKG), pp. 234–239. IEEE, August 2017
6. Sathyanandani, S., Sreedharan, D.: An e-commerce feedback review mining for a trusted seller's profile by classifying fake and authentic feedback comments. In: 2017 International Conference on Circuit, Power and Computing Technologies (ICCPCT), pp. 1–6. IEEE, April 2017
7. Wang, C.C., Day, M.Y., Chen, C.C., Liou, J.W.: Temporal and sentimental analysis of a real case of fake reviews in Taiwan. In: Proceedings of the 2017 IEEE/ACM International Conference on Advances in Social Networks Analysis and Mining 2017, pp. 729–736. ACM, July 2017
8. Wang, X., Zhang, X., Jiang, C., Liu, H.: Identification of fake reviews using semantic and behavioral features. In: 2018 4th International Conference on Information Management (ICIM), pp. 92–97. IEEE, May 2018
9. Samonte, M.J.C.: Polarity analysis of editorial articles towards fake news detection. In: Proceedings of the 2018 International Conference on Internet and e-Business, pp. 108–112. ACM, April 2018
10. Radovanović, D., Krstajić, B.: Review spam detection using machine learning. In: 2018 23rd International Scientific-Professional Conference on Information Technology (IT), pp. 1–4. IEEE, February 2018
11. Ikoro, V., Sharmina, M., Malik, K., Batista-Navarro, R.: Analyzing sentiments expressed on twitter by UK energy company consumers. In: 2018 Fifth International Conference on Social Networks Analysis, Management and Security (SNAMS), pp. 95–98. IEEE, October 2018
12. Vamshi, K.B., Pandey, A.K., Siva, K.A.: Topic model based opinion mining and sentiment analysis. In: 2018 International Conference on Computer Communication and Informatics (ICCCI), pp. 1–4. IEEE, January 2018
13. Seth, S., Johari, R.: Evolution of data mining techniques: a case study using MongoDB. In: Proceedings of the 12th INDIA Com; INDIACom 2018; IEEE Conference ID: 42835 2018 5th International Conference on "Computing for Sustainable Global Development", 14–16 March 2018 (in-print)
14. Seth, S., Johari, R.: Statistical survey of data mining techniques: a WalkThrough approach using MongoDB. In: International Conference on Innovative Computing and Communication, 5–6 May 2018
15. Seth, S., Johari, R.: Data analytics using MongoDB: a case study on Indian traffic dataset. In: International Conference on Computational Intelligence and Data Analytics, 26–27 October 2018 (underprint)
16. Seth, S., Johari, R.: Data analytics using MongoDB: a case study on Indian traffic dataset. In: Intelligent Data Analysis: From Data Gathering to Data Comprehension
17. Seth, S., Johari, R.: SNAP: social network analysis using predictive modelling. In: Intelligent Data Analysis: From Data Gathering to Data Comprehension (underprint)

18. Mathapati, S., Shreelekha, B.S., Tanuja, R., Manjula, S.H., Venugopal, K.R.: Co-extraction of opinion targets and opinion words from online reviews based on opinion and semantic relations. In: 2018 Fifteenth International Conference on Wireless and Optical Communications Networks (WOCN), pp. 1–6. IEEE, February 2018
19. https://en.wikipedia.org/wiki/Mean
20. https://www.dummies.com/education/math/business-statistics/how-to-measure-the-covariance-and-correlation-of-data-samples/
21. http://www.datasciencemadesimple.com/standard-deviation-function-python-pandas-row-column/
22. https://reviewmeta.com/amazon-in/B07DKGTVCD

Impact of Feature Extraction Techniques on a CBIR System

Ghanshyam Raghuwanshi[1] and Vipin Tyagi[2(✉)]

[1] Manipal University Jaipur, Jaipur, Rajasthan, India
ghanshyam.raghuwanshi@jaipur.manipal.edu
[2] Jaypee University of Engineering and Technology,
Raghogarh, Guna, MP, India
dr.vipin.tyagi@gmail.com

Abstract. Feature extraction is a key step and plays a deciding role for the performance of an image retrieval system. Success of a Content Based Image Retrieval System depends on the used features of the image. This paper includes a wide-range of survey on the various feature extraction process and their impact on the working behavior of an image retrieval system. This impact is calculated on the basis of retrieval accuracy, retrieval time, space complexity and feature extraction time. Comprehensive survey on the recent trends and challenges to the retrieval system has also been discussed. Furthermore, directions and suggestions, based on the real world applications are also suggested for encouraging the researchers in the area of image processing for adopting the optimized feature extraction process. This survey also tries to fill the gap between the traditional approaches and recent trends of feature extraction. More importantly, this paper also surveyed the issues with the feature extraction techniques in spatial as well as spectral domain.

Keywords: Image retrieval · LBP · DLEP · DTRCWF · TBIR · CBIR

1 Introduction

It is always challenging to handle large multimedia data with the rapid advancement in the high computational facilities. Dependency of organizations on multimedia data has attracted many researches to develop new data processing and retrieval techniques to achieve better retrieval performance. Now-a-days, propagation of better quality and economical imaging devices has motivated the research community for enhancing the existing methods of multimedia data processing. This enhancement can further reduce the burden on the database handlers in maintaining large image databases. One of the most challenging issue with multimedia data is to retrieve it with acceptable accuracy and time. However, invention of the multimedia data retrieval started from Text based image retrieval (TBIR). Various researchers made their precious efforts towards TBIR based approaches [16, 17, 20, 21, 23, 24, 26]. TBIR system is good only for small size databases but if the database size increases then it creates hurdle not only for database manager but for the end user also. TBIR approach requires huge annotation and increases the semantic hole between the view of the user and system understanding.

© Springer Nature Singapore Pte Ltd. 2019
M. Singh et al. (Eds.): ICACDS 2019, CCIS 1045, pp. 338–348, 2019.
https://doi.org/10.1007/978-981-13-9939-8_30

In this article a comprehensive survey is done for analyzing the current trends of the image retrieval system and also the future aspects for the betterment of image retrieval.

Further the limitations of the TBIR approach by introducing the Content Based Image Retrieval (CBIR) approach are reduced [52]. CBIR approach works on the extracted visual features like color [5–8] and shape [9–13] instead of the textual information. Present work surveyed CBIR with the variation of feature set.

This paper is organized in the following subsection: Sect. 2 specifies the types of visual features, description and their impact analysis using spatial domain is presented in the Sect. 2.1. Section 2.2 does the analysis of space and time complexity in spatial domain. Feature Extraction in spectral domain is explained in Sect. 2.3. Effect of multiple features is described in Sect. 2.4. Finally, conclusion is presented in the Sect. 3.

2 Types of Visual Features

CBIR systems use visual features such as color, texture, shape and spatial location of objects in images. Performance of the CBIR system depends on the types of features, method adopted for feature extraction and also the nature of the features.

Basically, features are extracted in the spatial and spectral domain (Fig. 1). Spatial domain approaches work directly on the pixels and the relation of the pixel values with the neighboring pixels whereas in spectral domain approaches, work is done on the frequency or signals. Various methods of feature extraction have been proposed till date which deal in the spatial domain and spectral domain.

2.1 Feature Extraction in Spatial Domain

Binary patterns come under the spatial domain approach. Many researchers have contributed in developing the different methods of binary pattern generation. These patterns are further used for feature vector creation.

Spatial domain approaches like Local Binary Pattern (LBP) [32], Center Symmetric Local Binary Pattern (CSLBP) [34], Block level LBP (BLK-LBP) [33], Local Tetra Pattern (LTP) [49], Local Neighborhood Intensity Pattern (LNIP) [42], etc. are the some of the representatives of spatial domain approaches. Local Edge Pattern for Segmentation and Image Retrieval (LEPSEG and LEPINV) [43] are the other binary patterns. LBP is one of the most widely used method of feature extraction. All of these methods are used to generate the binary pattern also the histograms of the generated patterns. LBP considers all the neighbors of the central pixels and generates the eight-bit binary pattern whereas CSLBP generates the four-bit pattern by limiting the number of neighboring pixels in the horizontal and vertical direction only.

LBP and CSLBP both use single threshold for pattern generation. Next enhancement came by introducing the Local Ternary Pattern (LTP) which generates two binary patterns by using lower and upper threshold (Eq. 1).

$$LTP(c_p)\begin{cases} 1 & if\ n_p > c_p + t \\ 0 & if\ n_p > c_p - t\ and\ n_p < c_p + t \\ -1 & if\ n_p < c_p - t \end{cases} \qquad (1)$$

Since LBP, CSLBP and LTP work at the global level and are not able to evaluate geometry of the image at block or region-level. However, block-level processing is added in the pattern generation step of BLK-LBP (Eq. 2) to overcome the issues raised in the LBP.

Total number of pixels which take part in the pattern generation at block level are almost less than half as compared to the pixels used in pattern generation phase.

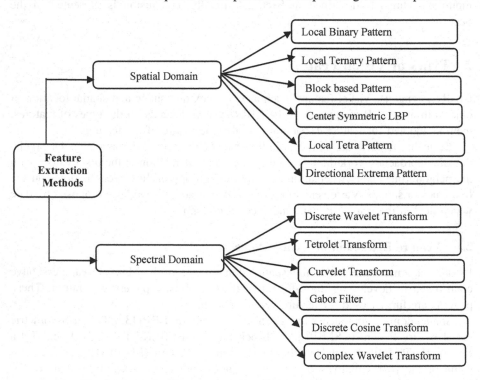

Fig. 1. Feature extraction methods of spatial and spectral domain

$$BLK\text{-}LBP_{P,R}(bl) = \sum_{bl=1}^{BL} \sum_{a=1}^{P} 2^{(a-1)} \times f_1(I(g_a) - I(g_c))$$

$$f_1(x) = \begin{cases} 1 & if\ x > 0 \\ 0 & otherwise \end{cases} \qquad (2)$$

where bl is the numbering of block that has to be considered for processing, BL represents the number of total blocks contained by the images. P is the number of pixels to be considered as neighboring pixel and R is the radius. Directional information is added in the pattern by the Directional Local Extrema Pattern (DLEP) [31].

Binary pattern is calculated in the four different directions for the single pixel. It computes the binary feature vector in four principle path such as *horizontal, vertical,* 45°, 135°. It is used for calculating the spatial relationship of the pixels in four directions which results in the local extrema pattern. Each time central pixel is evaluated against the neighboring pixels in the specific direction at a given angle as:

$$D(g_i) = I(g_c) - I(g_i) \qquad for\, i = 1\ldots\ldots\ldots 8 \tag{3}$$

The local extremas are extracted using

$$f(D(g_j) = \begin{Bmatrix} 0 & D(g_a) \times D(g_b) \geq 0 \\ 1 & else \end{Bmatrix}$$
$$l_\alpha(g_c) = f(D(g_j) \tag{4}$$

The DLEP for the central pixel in α direction is defined as:

$$DLEP(I(g_c)_\alpha = \{l_\alpha(g_c):,l_\alpha(g_1),l_\alpha(g_2)_\alpha\ldots\ldots\ldots\ldots\ldots l_\alpha(g_8)\} \tag{5}$$

Since images are retrieved from the databases of larger sizes so size of the feature vector and feature extraction time are also the issue of concern. CBIR system will be practical and able to deal with the real life problems if extracted features and time in feature extraction both are optimized along with the precision of the CBIR system. Block level Directional Local Extrema Pattern (BLK-DLEP) [40] resolves the issues of DLEP.

2.2 Time and Space Complexity

It is important to analyze the time and space performance of the extracted features. We have surveyed the space and time complexities of the various binary pattern based techniques. Figure 2 shows the relation of feature pattern size of various binary patterns for the image of size 128 * 128.

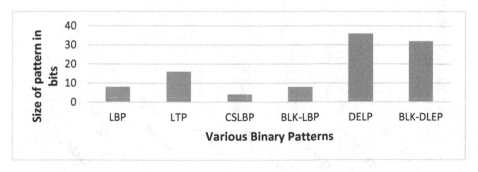

Fig. 2. Relation of pattern size with binary patterns

Relation of space complexity among the variants of LBP in terms of pattern size is as follows:

$$CS\text{-}LBP > BLK\text{-}LBP > LBP > LTP > BLK\text{-}DLEP > DLEP$$

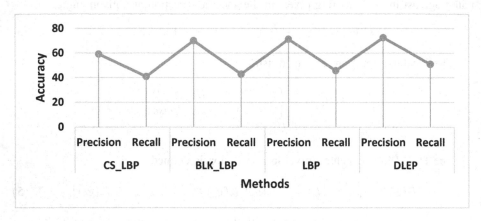

Fig. 3. Accuracy of methods based on binary pattern

Time complexity of the image retrieval system is affected by the two parameters: time required for the feature extraction and time required for searching the image in the feature database. Presence of multi-feature in the feature vector certainly increases the total retrieval time of the system. Total retrieval time of the CBIR system is calculated as follows:

$$time\_complexity = feature\ extraction\ time + searching\ time$$

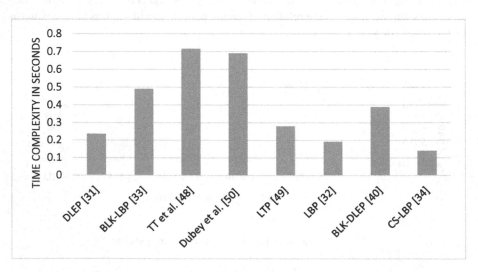

Fig. 4. Time complexity of the methods based on binary pattern on Brodatz [39] database

Accuracy of these methods on the Brodatz database [39] is shown in the Fig. 3. Accuracy of the DLEP is better among all the binary pattern based approach because it generates the pattern in four different directions. Figure 4 shows the total time complexity of the existing binary pattern based CBIR systems. It can be observed that the method which have less number of bits in the pattern, results in the less time complexity. Space and time complexities are the primary concerns if the database size is large. Space complexity can be compromised on the databases of smaller sizes.

2.3   Feature Extraction in Spectral Domain

Methods presented in the previous section suffer from the center pixel dependency problem. Sudden change in the intensity value of central pixel results in the huge change in the generated pattern. Dependency on the central pixel is reduced by using the frequency domain analysis of the image features [18, 19, 22, 27–30]. Features in the spectral domain are more robust and take lesser time in the computation in comparison to features extracted in the spatial domain. Discrete wavelet transform (DWT) was initially adopted by spectral domain approaches. Gabor wavelet transform [37] is used for more robust feature extraction. However, initially only horizontal and vertical directions were used for feature extraction purposes.

Complex Wavelet Transform (CWT), Dual Tree Complex Wavelet Transform (DTCWT) [36] adds more directional analysis in the extracted features. Combination of DT-CWT with the RCWF [38] produces better image features in total of twelve directions. Better adaptability in the feature extraction is provided by the Tetrolet transform [35]. Further, Tetrolet transform is processed at block level to provide the more discriminative power [40]. Figure 5 shows the comparison of the time complexities of spatial and spectral domain approaches.

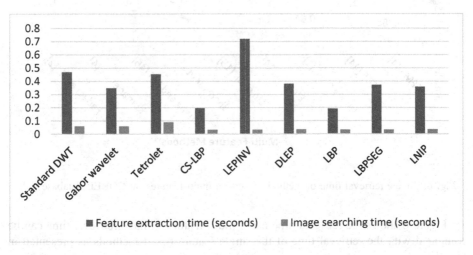

Fig. 5. Comparison of time complexities among spatial and spectral domain approaches on VisTex [53] database

2.4   CBIR Based on Multiple Features

Methods explained in the earlier section are related to the single feature. It is desirable to achieve the better accuracy with minimum retrieval. Unfortunately, single feature methods retrieve the images in less time but the accuracy is compromised sometimes. Mostly methods based on single-feature are designed to analyze, evaluate and retrieve images from the specific domain due to its narrow discriminative information. This problem can be solved by embedding more features in the feature set. Inclusion of supplementary features may degrade the performance sometimes. This problem is identified and solved by methods [14, 15, 25, 41]. Some of the methods like ElAlami [14] and Lin et al. [15] control the effect of ill features by assigning the weights to the features (Eq. 6).

$$Similarity = D_1 \times feature_{color} + D_2 \times feature_{texture} \tag{6}$$

D_1 and D_2 are the adaptive weights for the features (texture and color). Weights are the deciding the factor for each of the feature at the time of image matching. Assigned weights are adaptive in nature and varies according to the image. Sometimes, it is better to assign the weights to the block of the image [41] instead of allocating weights to the features. However, selection of the weights must be adaptive and according to the image geometry. Static weight assignment to the regions or features is not the proper solution. Feature selection approaches use the concept of weight assignment at the time of image similarity calculation.

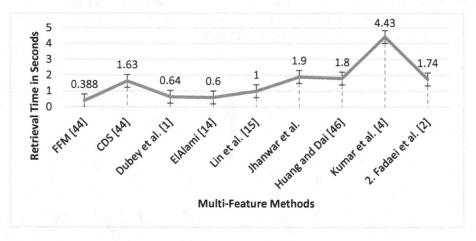

Fig. 6. Image retrieval time of methods based on multi-features on COREL database [54]

Figure 6 shows the retrieval time using multi-features. Image retrieval time can be compared with the retrieval time of the single feature based methods as presented in Fig. 4.

It can be observed from Fig. 6 that retrieval time for the multi-feature methods is more than the methods presented in Fig. 4.

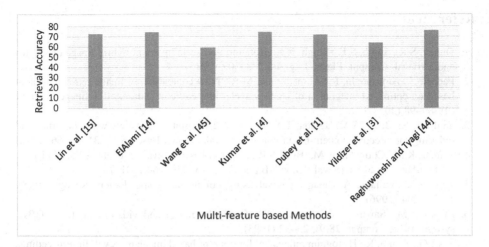

Fig. 7. Image retrieval accuracy of methods based on multi-features on COREL database [54]

However, the retrieval accuracy of the methods based on the multi-feature is better than the single-feature methods. Accuracy of the methods like FFM [25, 44] and also ElAlami [14] is better among the other methods as shown in Fig. 7, since these methods provide the treatment for the ill features. Region based analysis of the image also plays a crucial role in the image processing. Some of the representative methods [10–12, 40, 41] are used for extracting the region level features. Multiple features can also be extracted at block-level for providing the better discriminative power to the features.

Initially, image is divided into non-overlapping regions then each of the non-overlapping region is processed separately Region based features are extracted by dividing the image into non-overlapping regions and processing of each region separately, results in the region level features. Another way of region level processing is to apply the better segmentation technique.

Integrating Region Matching (IRM) [51] is done for matching the all integrating regions of the image. Similarity score is calculated by normalizing the combined effect of all the regions.

3 Conclusion

Feature extraction is the key process in the image processing and works as a backbone for various image retrieval approaches. The feature database stores the information about the visual content of the image. In this paper, recent as well as past trends of feature extraction with their effects have been discussed. Broad and open research issues related to feature extraction with the future research directions are suggested.

Image retrieval system can be effective and scalable if its feature set is pertaining acceptable space and time complexity as well.

References

1. Dubey, S.R., Singh, S.K., Singh, R.K.: Rotation and scale invariant hybrid image descriptor and retrieval. Comput. Electr. Eng. **46**, 288–302 (2015)
2. Fadaei, S., Amirfattahi, R., Ahmadzadeh, M.R.: New content-based image retrieval system based on optimised integration of DCD, wavelet and curvelet features. IET Image Proc. **11**(2), 89–98 (2017)
3. Yildizer, E., Balci, A.M., Jarada, T.N., Alhajj, R.: Integrating wavelets with clustering and indexing for effective content-based image retrieval. Knowl.-Based Syst. **31**, 55–66 (2012)
4. Kumar, K.M., Chowdhury, M., Bulo, S.R.: A graph-based relevance feedback mechanism in content-based image retrieval. Knowl.-Based Syst. **73**, 254–264 (2015)
5. Jain, A.K., Vailaya, A.: Image retrieval using colour and shape. Pattern Recogn. **29**(8), 1233–1244 (1996)
6. Flickner, M., Sawhney, H., Niblack, W.: Query by image and video content: the QBIC system. IEEE Comput. **28**(9), 23–32 (1995)
7. Pass, G., Zabith, R.: Histogram refinement for content-based image retrieval. In: Proceedings of the Workshop on Applications of Computer Vision, pp. 96–102 (1996)
8. Huang, J., Kuamr, S., Mitra, M.: Image indexing using colour correlogram. In: Proceedings of the CVPR, pp. 762–765 (1997)
9. Zhang, D., Lu, G.: Review of shape representation and description techniques. Pattern Recogn. **37**(1), 1–19 (2004)
10. Yang, C., Dong, M., Fotouhi, F.: Image content annotation using Bayesian framework and complement components analysis. In: Proceedings of the ICIP (2005)
11. Mezaris, V., Kompatsiaris, I., Strintzis, M.G.: An ontology approach to object-based image retrieval. In: Proceedings of the ICIP, pp. 511–514 (2003)
12. Zhang, D., Islam, M.M., Lu, G.: Semantic image retrieval using region based inverted file. In: Proceedings of the DICTA, pp. 242–249 (2009)
13. Yang, M., Kpalma, K., Ronsin, J.: A survey of shape feature extraction techniques. Pattern Recogn. 43–90 (2008)
14. ElAlami, M.E.: A novel image retrieval model based on the most relevant features. Knowl.-Based Syst. **24**(1), 23–32 (2011)
15. Lin, C.-H., Chen, R.-T., Chan, Y.-C.: A smart content-based image retrieval system based on color and texture feature. Image Vis. Comput. **27**(6), 658–665 (2009)
16. Chang, N.S., Fu, K.S.: A relational database system for images. Technical report TR-EE 79–28, Purdue University (1979)
17. Chang, N.S., Fu, K.S.: Query-by pictorial-example. IEEE Trans. Software Eng. **SE-6**(6), 519–524 (1980)
18. Chang, T., Kuo, C.-C.J.: Texture analysis and classification with tree-structured wavelet transform. IEEE Trans. Image Proc. **2**(4), 429–441 (1993)
19. Gross, M.H., Koch, R., Lippert, L., Dreger, A.: Multiscale image texture analysis in wavelet spaces. In: Proceedings of the IEEE International Conference on Image Processing (1994)
20. Chang, S.-F., Eleftheriadis, A., McClintock, R.: Next-generation content representation, creation and searching for new media applications in education. Proc. IEEE **86**(5), 884–904 (1998)
21. Chang, S.K.: Pictorial data-base systems. IEEE Comput. **14**, 13–21 (1981)
22. Smith, J.R., Chang, S.-F.: Automated binary texture feature sets for image retrieval. In: Proceedings of the ICASSP 1996, Atlanta, GA (1996)
23. Chang, S.-K., Hsu, A.: Image information systems: where do we go from here? IEEE Trans. Knowl. Data Eng. **4**(5), 431–442 (1992)

24. Chang, S.-K., Yan, C.W., Dimitroff, D.C., Arndt, T.: An intelligent image database system. IEEE Trans. Software Eng. **14**(5), 681–688 (1988)
25. Shrivastava, N., Tyagi, V.: An efficient technique for retrieval of color images in large databases. Comput. Electr. Eng. (2014). http://dx.doi.org/10.1016/j.compeleceng.2014.11. 009
26. Tamura, H., Yokoya, N.: Image database systems: a survey. Pattern Recogn. **17**(1), 29–43 (1984)
27. Kundu, A., Chen, J.-L.: Texture classification using QMF bank-based subband decomposition. CVGIP Graph. Models Image Process. **54**(5), 369–384 (1992)
28. Laine, A., Fan, J.: Texture classification by wavelet packet signatures. IEEE Trans. Pattern Recogn. Mach. Intell. **15**(11), 1186–1191 (1993)
29. Smith, J.R., Chang, S.F.: Transform features for texture classification and discrimination in large image databases. In: Proceedings of the IEEE International Conference on Image Processing (1994)
30. Wallace, I., Wintz, P.: An efficient three-dimensional aircraft recognition algorithm using normalized Fourier descriptors. Comput. Graph. Image Process. **13**, 99–126 (1980)
31. Murala, S., Maheshwari, R.P., Balasubramanian, R.: Directional local extrema patterns: a new descriptor for content based image retrieval. Int. J. Multimedia Inf. Retrieval **1**(3), 191–203 (2012)
32. Ojala, T., Pietikäinen, M., Harwood, D.: A comparative study of texture measures with classification based on featured distributions. Pattern Recogn. **29**, 51–59 (1996)
33. Takala, V., Ahonen, T., Pietikäinen, M.: Block-based methods for image retrieval using local binary patterns. In: Kalviainen, H., Parkkinen, J., Kaarna, A. (eds.) SCIA 2005. LNCS, vol. 3540, pp. 882–891. Springer, Heidelberg (2005). https://doi.org/10.1007/11499145_89
34. Heikkil, M., Pietikainen, M., Schmid, C.: Description of interest regions with local binary patterns. Pattern Recogn. **42**, 425–436 (2009)
35. Raghuwanshi, G., Tyagi, V.: Texture image retrieval using adaptive tetrolet transforms. Digit. Signal Proc. **48**, 50–57 (2016)
36. Kingsbury, N.G.: Image processing with complex wavelet. Philos. Trans. R. Soc. Lond. Ser. A Contain. Pap. Math. Phys. Character **357**, 2543–2560 (1999)
37. Manjunath, B.S., Ma, W.Y.: Texture features for browsing and retrieval of image data. IEEE Trans. Pattern Anal. Mach. Intell. **18**, 837–842 (1996)
38. Kokare, M., Biswas, P.K., Chatterji, B.N.: Texture image retrieval using new rotated complex wavelet filter. IEEE Trans. Syst. Man Cybern. **35**(6), 1168–1178 (2005)
39. Brodatz, P.: Textures: A Photographic Album for Artists and Designers. Dover, New York (1996)
40. Raghuwanshi, G., Tyagi, V.: Texture image retrieval based on block level directional local extrema patterns using tetrolet transform. In: Singh, M., Gupta, P.K., Tyagi, V., Flusser, J., Ören, T. (eds.) ICACDS 2018. CCIS, vol. 905, pp. 449–460. Springer, Singapore (2018). https://doi.org/10.1007/978-981-13-1810-8_45
41. Raghuwanshi, G., Tyagi, V.: A novel technique for content based image retrieval based on region-weight assignment. Multimedia Tools Appl. **77**(2), 1889–19111 (2018)
42. Prithaj, B., Ayan, K.B., Avirup, B., Partha, P.R., Subrahmanyam, M.: Local Neighborhood Intensity Pattern – a new texture feature descriptor for image retrieval. Expert Syst. Appl. (2018). https://doi.org/10.1016/j.eswa.2018.06.044
43. Yao, C.H., Chen, S.Y.: Retrieval of translated, rotated and scaled color textures. Pattern Recogn. **36**(4), 913–929 (2002)
44. Raghuwanshi, G., Tyagi, V.: Feed-forward content based image retrieval using adaptive tetrolet transforms. Multimedia Tools Appl. **77**(18), 23389–234101 (2018)

45. Wang, X.-Y., Yu, Y.-J., Yang, H.-Y.: An effective image retrieval scheme using color, texture & shape features. Comput. Stan. Interfaces **33**(1), 59–68 (2011)
46. Jhanwar, N., Chaudhuri, S., Seetharaman, G., Zavidovique, B.: Content based image retrieval using motif co-occurrence matrix. Image Vis. Comput. **22**, 1211–1220 (2004)
47. Huang, P.W., Dai, S.K.: Image retrieval by texture similarity. Pattern Recogn. **36**(3), 665–679 (2003)
48. Van, T.T., Le, T.M.: Content based image retrieval based on binary signatures cluster graph. Expert Syst. (2017). https://doi.org/10.1111/exsy.12220
49. Murala, S., Maheshwari, R.P., Balasubramanian, R.: Local tetra patterns: a new feature descriptor for content-based image retrieval. IEEE Trans. Image Process. **21**(5), 2874–2886 (2012)
50. Dubey, S.R., Singh, S.K., Singh, R.K.: Boosting local binary pattern with bag-of-filters for content based image retrieval. In: Proceedings of the IEEE UP Section Conference on Electrical, Computer and Electronics (UPCON) (2015)
51. Jia, L., James, Z.W., Gio, W.: IRM: integrated region matching for image retrieval. In: ACM International Conference on Multimedia, pp. 147–156 (2000)
52. Tyagi, V.: Content-Based Image Retrieval: Ideas, Influences, and Current Trends. Springer, Singapore (2017). https://doi.org/10.1007/978-981-10-6759-4
53. https://vismod.media.mit.edu/vismod/imagery/VisionTexture/vistex.html
54. http://wang.ist.psu.edu/docs/related/

Convolutional Feature Extraction and Neural Arithmetic Logic Units for Stock Prediction

Shangeth Rajaa$^{(\boxtimes)}$ and Jajati Keshari Sahoo

Department of Mathematics, BITS Pilani Goa Campus, Sancoale, Goa, India
shangethrajaa@gmail.com, jksahoo@goa.bits-pilani.ac.in

Abstract. Stock prediction is a topic undergoing intense study for many years. Finance experts and mathematicians have been working on a way to predict the future stock price so as to decide to buy the stock or sell it to make profit. Stock experts or economists, usually analyze on the previous stock values using technical indicators, sentiment analysis etc. to predict the future stock price. In recent years, many researches have extensively used machine learning for predicting the stock behaviour. In this paper we propose data driven deep learning approach to predict the future stock value with the previous price with the feature extraction property of convolutional neural network and to use Neural Arithmetic Logic Units with it.

Keywords: Deep learning · Convolutional Neural Network · Neural Arithmetic Logic Units · Stock prediction

1 Introduction

A large number of people buy and sell stocks everyday in an aim to make maximum profit. Many mathematical methods and models have been developed which analyses the movement of the stock price. But its not sure if the future stock prices can actually be predicted due to its dependency on various factors and its dynamic nature.

In recent years, machine learning and deep learning are being used in almost all the industries including finance. Machine learning in one way can be viewed as a function approximation (or a complex multiple dimensional curve fitting) for a given data. Machine learning can analyse and learn the complex multiple dimensional features of the data which humans cannot visualize or learn.

Although there are several mathematical models and techniques for stock prediction, this paper focuses on data driven machine learning approach with least knowledge in finance. The future stock price is to be predicted given the past prices. This paper tries to use and analyse the complex feature extraction ability of deep learning to learn the pattern of the stock price movement and predict the future price.

© Springer Nature Singapore Pte Ltd. 2019
M. Singh et al. (Eds.): ICACDS 2019, CCIS 1045, pp. 349–359, 2019.
https://doi.org/10.1007/978-981-13-9939-8_31

2   Machine Learning

In recent times machine learning research in finance has been steadily increasing. There are generally 2 types of tasks in machine learning, classification and regression. Supervised machine learning regression model will be used for this stock prediction task.

2.1   Classical Machine Learning Algorithms

Classical machine learning algorithms are much more easier to interpret and understand than deep learning as we have a thorough understanding of underlying algorithms. These algorithms works better even on smaller data set and are computationally cheaper than deep learning techniques. Many researches have been done in predicting the stock price using classical machine learning algorithms. The author of [1] has used Support Vector Machine (SVM) for financial forecasting and also did experimental analysis of parameters for SVM. Random forest techniques are also used in financial data, in [2]. Random forest, Naive bayes and support vector machine are used for classification the direction of movement of financial data.

2.2   Deep Learning

Although many machine learning algorithms exists and are successful, the evolution of deep learning marked a great milestone in the field of Artificial intelligence. The base work for deep learning started in 1940s, but it became more popular recently due to availability of more data and cheap computation devices. The performance of deep learning models increased exponentially every year and is projected to increase more. Image classification task is performed in [3] using a Artificial Neural networks. After Neural Networks, many new models were invented to increase the performance of deep learning in images, videos and time series data such as text, voice, etc. Convolutional Neural Network [4] won the imagenet competition as it was good in extracting features of images/frames. Then Recurrent Neural networks [5] were used for series data such as text and voice which needed a memory to remember the previous data features. Deep learning also performs very good in unsupervised models such as Auto Encoder [6], General Adversarial Networks (GAN) [7] and in Reinforcement Learning.

3   Deep Learning in Finance

3.1   Artificial Neural Networks (ANN)

ANNs are models comprised of densely connected computation nodes (neurons). These neural networks have the ability to learn complex features of the input data and perform the task. ANNs are series of matrix multiplication with nonlinear function to make the whole network non linear to learn more complex features.

$$h_1 = \phi(X \cdot W_1 + b_1) \tag{1}$$

$$h_i = \phi(h_{i-1} \cdot W_i + b_i) \tag{2}$$

$$\hat{y} = \phi(h_n \cdot W_n + b_n) \tag{3}$$

where n is the number of layers in the network, h is the hidden unit, $\hat{y}$ is the prediction in forward pass through the model abd ϕ is the activation function.

[8] and [9] uses Artificial Neural Networks to predict the stock price and direction of movement of the price. Dimensionality reduction techniques such as Principle Component Analysis (PCA) are used in [10] for stock prediction. Artificial neural networks are also experimented for the task of predicting close price after 5 time interval(days/hour/minute). Data got from data processing steps explained in Proposed Approach was used and Tensors of shape (n, 20) was used as input data, where n is the number of data. And tensor of shape (n, 1) was the label. The model consists of 4 layers of Fully Connected Dense Layer with dropouts and ReLU Non Linearity.

3.2 Convolutional Neural Network

Convolutional Neural Network (CNN)s are stacks of convolution operations between input which is passed through the network and filters (kernels) which extract the features of the input. The network is also activated with some activation function like ReLU for non linearity. The dimension of the layers are reduced with Pooling layers to reduce computation and it can also be viewed as increasing the feature concentration.

[11] shows the potential of convolutional neural network for finance stock prediction. 1-d convolutional network [12] is also used to predict the stock movement as a classification model with 1 day close, open, high, low, volume data.

For this experiment, since the data is 1 dimensional, Conv1d (1 dimensional convolutional layers) of Pytorch is used with 3 convolutional layers with Max-Pooling and ReLU activation. Then the convolutional layers are flattened into tensor of shape (n, 1, −1), where n is the number of data in the batch and −1 represents length of the layer multiplied by number of channels in the last convolutional layer. Followed by 3 layers of Dense or Fully Connected Layers with ReLU activation and Dropouts to avoid over fitting of the data.

3.3 Recurrent Neural Networks

Recurrent Neural network predicts an output given an input but in a sequential manner. The inputs and outputs are in sequence like text or audio.

$$h_t = \phi(X_t \cdot W_x + h_{t-1} \cdot W_h) \tag{4}$$

$$\hat{y}_t = \phi(h_t \cdot W_y) \tag{5}$$

where W_x, W_y, W_y are the weights, h_t is the hidden state or memory state of state/time t and ϕ is the activation function. The financial data can be seen as a sequential data, the future stock price is predicted in [13] using LSTM network. A hybrid model RNN was used in [14] to predict the stock price.

3.4   Neural Arithmetic Logic Units

Neural Networks, although can perform several tasks nearly to human level accuracy, but they seem to fail when it encounters quantities outside the range of training data, like extrapolation. This shows that the models actually try to fit the data rather than to generalize and learn it. [15] proposed a new module Neural Accumulator and Neural Arithmetic Logic Units which can be added to any neural network architecture which helps in generalizing quantities to neural network and helps the model to generalize for tasks like extrapolation.

Stock prediction in one way can also be seen as an extrapolation task, where we are trying to predict the stock price in the future which can be above or below the range of out training data. In this paper we propose to use the ability of the Neural Arithmetic Logic Units to generalize and extrapolate to our task of stock prediction.

4   Proposed Approach

4.1   Data

Historical stock price data of India from Feb, 2015 to Aug, 2018 was used for this research. The data contains columns like Date, Close, High, Low, Open, Volume. This data changes every 1 h, a total of around 6200 price data. The data set is checked for missing data and removed. Only Close prices are taken. All the other columns such as Date, High, Low, Open, Volume are omitted in the data. The goal is to predict stock closing price after 5 interval, with the closing price of past 20 intervals. This is a regression task to predict the exact closing price. For computational reasons and faster convergence, the data is scaled to a range of 0–1. The stock values are scaled with (Fig. 1)

$$x_{scaled} = \frac{x - x_{min}}{x_{max} - x_{min}} \tag{6}$$

Fig. 1. Closing stock prices data

Table 1. Scaled close prices data

Close price	411.15	414.05	410.20	410.25	410.00
Scaled close	0.1840	0.1874	0.1828	0.1829	0.1826

After scaling, the data is split into input and label. Input contains past 20 scaled close prices and the label contains the scaled stock prices after 5 intervals (Table 1).

Facebook's PyTorch framework was used to design the computation graph and for training the model. The arrays of data are converted into tensors and are split into batches for faster computation using the advantage of Matrix operations. So the input X will be a vector of shape (20, 1) and label will be of shape (1, 1).

The data was split into training and testing data in the ration of (8:2). And a batch size of 1232 was used to split the data into 5 equal batches. So 4 batches of 1232 data for training set and 1 batch for test set.

Each batch of data will be a tensor of shape (1232, 20) for Artificial Neural network models and tensor of shape (1232, 1, 20) for Convolutional Neural Network models.

4.2 Neural Arithmetic Logic Units (NALU) Based Model for Stock Prediction

Instead of PyTorch's nn.Linear layers, a self defined NALU module which is defined by

Neural Accumulator (NAC):

$$a = Wx \tag{7}$$

$$W = \tanh(\hat{W}) \circledast \sigma(\hat{M}) \tag{8}$$

Neural Arithmetic Logic Unit (NALU):

$$y = g \circledast a + (1 - g) \circledast m \tag{9}$$

$$m = \sigma(\, W(log(|x| + \epsilon))) \tag{10}$$

$$g = \sigma(Gx) \tag{11}$$

Sigmoid function was used in the calculation of m instead of exponential function which was used originally in the Neural Arithmetic Logical units paper. Four layers of Neural Arithmetic Logic Units are stacked like fully connected layers using defined pytorch NALU module. Dropouts are added in between each layer as a regularization technique to avoid over fitting the data. Relu activation function is added in between the NALU layers.

$$ReLU(x) = \begin{cases} 0 & x \leq 0 \\ x & x > 0 \end{cases} \tag{12}$$

Finally sigmoid activation is used to make the prediction in the desired range of 0–1 (as the data is scaled to 0–1 range) (Fig. 2).

$$Sigmoid(x) = \frac{1}{1 + e^{-x}} \tag{13}$$

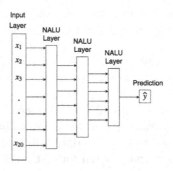

Fig. 2. Architecture of NALU Network

The output of the network is compared with the true value using Squared L2 Norm (Mean Squared Error) loss function.

$$MSELoss(y, \hat{y}) = \frac{1}{m} \sum_{i=1}^{m} (y^{(i)} - \hat{y}^{(i)})^2 \tag{14}$$

where $y^{(i)}$ is the true label value and $\hat{y}^{(i)}$ is the model prediction for i^{th} training data. To minimize the loss, back propagation algorithm is used with Adam optimizer. A cyclic learning rate [16] scheduler has been used with the optimizer as an attempt to escape the problem of local minimum of loss. When the algorithm is stuck in a local minimum or narrow minimum, increasing the learning rate help it escape the local space and reach a better or wider minimum space. Each data batch is has been used 500 times to learn and update the weight parameters of the model so as to reduce the total loss. As we use cyclic learning rate, the loss tends to go high when the learning rate increases, so we save the model state with lowest loss.

4.3 Convolutional Feature Extraction and NALU Based Model for Stock Prediction

Convolutional Neural Network has been used to predict the stock in the past. This paper proposes a new model using the feature extraction ability of convolutional neural network with the Neural Arithmetic Logic Units. As the stock data is 1 dimensional series data, 1 dimensional convolutional layers using nn.Conv1d in Pytorch are used and stacked 3 layers of 1-d convolutional layers to extract the features of stock price movements. Kernel size of 4 has been used in the network for all the convolutional layers. The number of kernels/filters in each layers are 1, 16, 32 and 64. Max pooling layers are added in between every convolutional layer to reduce the dimension, kernel size of 1 or 2 is used and stride is also 2, which will reduce the layer length to half. ReLU activation function is used to make the network non linear (Fig. 3).

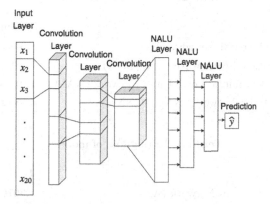

Fig. 3. Architecture of CNN-NALU Network

Convolutional layers are followed by 2 layers of Neural Arithmetic Logic Units and 2 layers of Fully connected layers as the regressor. ReLU activation function is used in between the linear and NALU layers with dropouts to avoid overfitting of the data. We use sigmoid activation function in the last layer of the network to make the prediction in the range of 0–1.

Squared L2 Norm loss function was used to get the loss after the forward pass, Adam optimizer was used for optimization and Cyclic learning rate scheduler was used to change the learning rate in cycle from 10^{-6} to 10^{-2}.

5   Results

Different models were used in this research to find which model is able to learn the trend of the stock price and predict the future price given the last 20 prices better. In each iteration after training the models using training set, the testing set is used to check how good the model has learned and how good it can predict unseen data. After training the model, the whole stock close data is predicted using the trained model and plotted to visualize how good the model performs on the data as a whole.

Table 2 gives the training loss of each of the model. It can be observed that Models with Neural Arithmetic Logic Units learned better ANN and CNN models. Table 3 gives the loss of the models on testing set. Models with Neural Arithmetic Logic Units was able to predict the stock price better than ANNs and CNNs on unseen data. After the training and validating the testing set, the model was used to test the complete data. Previous 20 data points were given and the model predicted the close price after 5 intervals. The loss of the model with the whole data set is given by Table 4. This value has to be re scaled back to the original interval to compare with the actual price (Figs. 4, 5, 6 and 7).

Table 2. Training loss of models

Model	Training loss
Artificial Neural Network (ANN)	8.04649e−06
Convolutional Neural Network (CNN)	5.58822e−06
Neural Arithmetic Logic Units Network (NALU)	1.91356e−06
NALU CNN Network (NALU-CNN)	5.58499e−07

Table 3. Testing loss of models

Model	Testing loss
Artificial Neural Network (ANN)	1.30709e−06
Convolutional Neural Network (CNN)	5.99638e−07
Neural Arithmetic Logic Units Network (NALU)	4.31875e−07
NALU CNN Network (NALU-CNN)	3.05196e−07

Table 4. Loss of models in the whole data set

Model	Total loss
Artificial Neural Network (ANN)	1.29998e−06
Convolutional Neural Network (CNN)	1.07971e−06
Neural Arithmetic Logic Units Network (NALU)	3.97540e−07
NALU CNN Network (NALU-CNN)	3.30627e−07

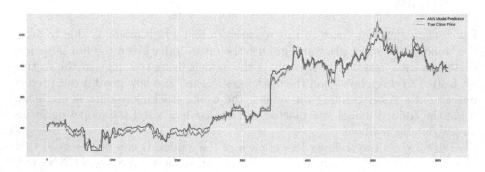

Fig. 4. Prediction plot of Artificial Neural Network Model

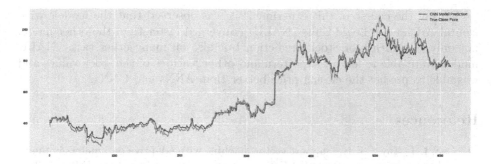

Fig. 5. Prediction plot of Convolutional Neural Network Model

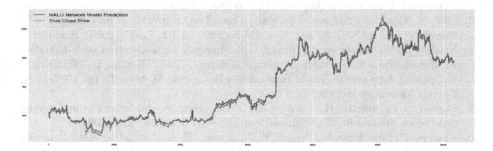

Fig. 6. Prediction plot of NALU Network Model

Fig. 7. Prediction plot of CNN-NALU Network Model

6 Conclusion

In this paper we proposed to use the feature extraction property of convolutional neural networks and the extrapolation and arithmetic ability of Neural Arithmetic Logic Units to predict the stock price 5 days later.

During the course of this experiment it was observed that the models with Neural Arithmetic Logic Units (NALU) converged faster than the other model not only in the task of Stock prediction but also on many other tasks. NALU models were able to learn the pattern and other features of the stock values and was able to predict the closing price better than ANNs and CNNs.

References

1. Cao, L.J., Tay, F.E.H.: Support vector machine with adaptive parameters in financial time series forecasting. IEEE Trans. Neural Netw. **14**(6), 1506–1518 (2003)
2. Patel, J., Shah, S., Thakkar, P., Kotecha, K.: Predicting stock and stock price index movement using trend deterministic data preparation and machine learning techniques. Expert Syst. Appl. **42**(1), 259–268 (2015)
3. Shah, S., Gandhi, V.: Image classification based on textural features using artificial neural network (ANN). J. Inst. Eng. (India): Ser. A **84**, 72–77 (2004). Springer
4. Krizhevsky, A., Sutskever, I., Hinton, G.E.: ImageNet classification with deep convolutional neural networks. In: Pereira, F., Burges, C.J.C., Bottou, L., Weinberger, K.Q. (eds.) Advances in Neural Information Processing Systems 25, pp. 1097–1105. Curran Associates Inc. (2012)
5. Connor, J.T., Martin, R.D., Atlas, L.E.: Recurrent neural networks and robust time series prediction. IEEE Trans. Neural Netw. **5**(2), 240–254 (1994)
6. Vincent, P., Larochelle, H., Bengio, Y., Manzagol, P.-A.: Extracting and composing robust features with denoising autoencoders. In: Proceedings of the 25th International Conference on Machine Learning, ICML 2008, pp. 1096–1103. ACM, New York (2008)
7. Goodfellow, I., et al.: Generative adversarial nets. In: Ghahramani, Z., Welling, M., Cortes, C., Lawrence, N.D., Weinberger, K.Q. (eds.) Advances in Neural Information Processing Systems 27, pp. 2672–2680. Curran Associates Inc. (2014)
8. Kara, Y., Boyacioglu, M.A., Baykan, Ö.K.: Predicting direction of stock price index movement using artificial neural networks and support vector machines: the sample of the Istanbul stock exchange. Expert Syst. Appl. **38**(5), 5311–5319 (2011)
9. Abhishek, K., Khairwa, A., Pratap, T., Prakash, S.: A stock market prediction model using artificial neural network. In: 2012 Third International Conference on Computing, Communication and Networking Technologies (ICCCNT 2012), pp. 1–5, July 2012
10. Tsai, C.-F., Hsiao, Y.-C.: Combining multiple feature selection methods for stock prediction: union, intersection, and multi-intersection approaches. Decis. Support Syst. **50**(1), 258–269 (2010)
11. Chen, J., Chen, W., Huang, C., Huang, S., Chen, A.: Financial time-series data analysis using deep convolutional neural networks. In: 2016 7th International Conference on Cloud Computing and Big Data (CCBD), pp. 87–92, Nov 2016
12. Chen, S., He, H.: Stock prediction using convolutional neural network. IOP Conf. Ser. Mater. Sci. Eng. **435**(1), 012026 (2018)
13. Chen, K., Zhou, Y., Dai, F.: A LSTM-based method for stock returns prediction: a case study of China stock market. In: Proceedings of the 2015 IEEE International Conference on Big Data (Big Data), BIG DATA 2015, pp. 2823–2824. IEEE Computer Society, Washington, DC (2015)
14. Rather, A.M., Agarwal, A., Sastry, V.N.: Recurrent neural network and a hybrid model for prediction of stock returns. Expert Syst. Appl. **42**(6), 3234–3241 (2015)

15. Trask, A., Hill, F., Reed, S.E., Rae, J., Dyer, C., Blunsom, P.: Neural arithmetic logic units. In: Bengio, S., Wallach, H., Larochelle, H., Grauman, K., Cesa-Bianchi, N., Garnett, R. (eds.) Advances in Neural Information Processing Systems 31, pp. 8046–8055. Curran Associates Inc. (2018)
16. Smith, L.N.: No more pesky learning rate guessing games. CoRR, abs/1506.01186 (2015)

VMProtector: Malign Process Detection for Protecting Virtual Machines in Cloud Environment

Preeti Mishra[1]([✉]), Akash Negi[1], E. S. Pilli[2], and R. C. Joshi[1]

[1] Department of Computer Science and Engineering,
Graphic Era Deemed to be University, Dehradun, India
dr.preetimishranit@gmail.com, aakaxh07@gmail.com, rcjoshi.geu@gmail.com
[2] Department of Computer Science & Engineering,
Malaviya National Institute of Technology Jaipur, Jaipur, India
espilli.cse@mnit.ac.in

Abstract. Cloud computing provides delivery of computing resources as a services pay-as-you-go basis. It represents a shift from products being purchased, to products being subscribed as a service, delivered to consumers over the internet from a large scale data center. The main issue with cloud services is security from attackers who can easily compromise the Virtual Machines (VMs) and applications running over it. In this paper, we present a VMProtector mechanism to detect malign processes which generate attacks against VMs running in cloud. VMProtector extracts the n-grams and applies Principal Component Analysis (PCA) algorithm to select relevant n-gram patterns. It further applies fusion technique using three classifiers Random Forest (RF) and K-Nearest Neighbour (KNN) and Logistic Regression (LR) to learn and detect system call pattern of malign processes. The approach is implemented using University of New Maxico (UNM) dataset and provides promising results.

Keywords: Cloud security · Intrusion detection · System call traces · Machine learning · Malign process detection

1 Introduction

Cloud computing services are highly growing day by day and so as the attack surface in cloud environment [1]. One of the Cloud security report [2] showed that 90% of data are lost due to unauthorized access to legitimate resources by using malicious code or malware. Some of the malware modify the legitimate program and try to perform malicious activity leading to disclosure of user's sensitive data. Hence, the primary concern of the service provider is the secure delivery of services to the users. Some of the key security concerns are virtual machine (VM) security, network security, hypervisor security, hardware security, software security and application security etc. A virtual machine (VM) is one of the untrusted domains in cloud that can be easily compromised by attackers.

M. Singh et al. (Eds.): ICACDS 2019, CCIS 1045, pp. 360–369, 2019.
https://doi.org/10.1007/978-981-13-9939-8_32

An malicious user can install malicious software that targets the root privileges of the guest OS.

To resolve such kind of security issues researchers are still working on different security domains [3]. The security techniques for detecting intrusions can be broadly divided into two types: signature-based [4] and behavior-based [5]. Signature-based techniques looks for specific signature in the database for detecting the attacks. The main disadvantage with signature based techniques is that they cannot detect variants of attacks. Behavior-based techniques learns the expected behavior of the system and detect the attacks based on the learned patterns. Behavior-based techniques can detect variants of attacks and generally works in two phases: learning and detection. During learning phase, the behaviour of system is learned using machine learning techniques in both anomalous and normal scenarios and decision model is generated. In detection phase model, decision model is used to classify the unknown patterns in normal or attack classes. This process minimizes the response time for alert generation and provides good accuracy specially for detecting attack variants. Behavior analysis can be performed by two ways: static analysis and dynamic analysis. In static analysis, program behavior is analyzed without running them where as dynamic analysis analyses the run time behavior of the programs.

In this paper, we have proposed a dynamic analysis approach, called VMProtector to detect malign processes running on VMs. VMProtector captures and analyses the behaviour of the VMs in the form of system call traces generated by programs running inside VMs. The system call traces are converted in many short sequences of system calls, called n-grams. A numeric feature vector is generated <b1,b2,b3,b4 ——bk> for each trace where each bi represents the occurrence of n-grams in the trace. The important features are selected through Principal Component Analysis (PCA) [6] which have potential to perform feature selection. It selects a number of individual features from all feature components [6]. Further, fusion technique is applied which uses three classifiers: Random Forest (RF) [7], K-nearest neighbour (KNN) [8] and Logistic Regression (LG)[9] to learn the behaviour pattern of monitored programs. A maximum voting scheme is used make a final prediction based on the output of three classifiers. The main contributions of our work are as follows:

- To propose a malign process detection approach, based on PCA based n-grams and ensemble learning.
- To compare the results of proposed approach with existing approaches and discuss the benefit of our technique over others.

There are a total V sections in the paper. Section 2 describes the similar work done in the field of malware detection in cloud. Section 3 describes the various security modules of VMProtector in detail. In Sect. 4, a detailed experiment and result analysis is carried out and our work is compared with existing work. Section 5 provides concluding remarks at the end with future work.

2   Related Work

Varadharajan et al. [10] put forward an intrusion detection system (IDS) which is comprised of intrusion detection engine, packet differentiator, Operating system library and repository (OSLR), shared packet buffer and analyzer in a virtual environment. This is embedded into host OS or Virtual Machine Manager.

Alarifi et al. [11] showed the use of bag of system call (BOS) for feature extraction method to secure their virtual machines in the cloud environment. They initially assumed that VM were not malicious in data collection phase and services limited. In this technique, each trace system call are pre-processed under BOS method, where every value represent the frequency of trace. In their extended work, they used some other method but used Markov model for generating appropriate normal behaviour. Their technique is more prone to false alarms.

VMWatcher [12] proposed the prototype implementation of the guest view casting technique, used for extracting the VM memory information from hypervisor. Basically the author used Signature based technique for detecting the attacks by looking specific signature of the attack in database. The main disadvantage with signature based technique is that it cannot detect the attacks from unknown criterion. They only checked the presence of hidden processes and do not performed behaviour based analysis.

Gupta et al. [13] proposed an anomaly based algorithm called immediate system call sequence(ISCS) to detect malware's, rootkits, VM escape etc in cloud environment. Their approach fails to detect malware that hides its presence from security tool. Nitro is a framework for tracing system calls for KVM hyper visor, based on interrupt forcing mechanism. It is restricted to KVM hypervisor and not publicly available. Nitro can be used as a module in KVM-based cloud security tool for tracing system call.

Deshpande et al. [14] made a host based IDS system for cloud computing environment that create generates the system call logs and used n-gram for feature extraction. They used KNN classifier only for homogeneous data that is sensitive to parameter K (number of nearest neighbour). Ensemble algorithm is not applied that could have given better results.

Varsha et al. [15] developed a malware detection using N-gram based file signature based method technique basically the author used N-gram technique to detect the signature of the malware and analysed it. Signature based technique cannot detect the different pattern of unknown criterion. So using N-gram technique as signature matching can create many false alarm.

3   VMProtector: Security Design

In this section, a detailed description of the security design of VMProtector is provided. VMProtector consists of four detection components named (i) Program Execution Tracer (PET), (ii) Program Trace Pre-processor (PTP), (iii) Program Behaviour Detection Engine (PBDE) and (iv) Alert and Log Generator (ALG). PET performs the execution tracing of monitored programs and collects the execution logs in form system call traces. PTP performs the feature extraction and feature selection of traces. PBDE learns and detects the malicious program behavior. ALG generates the alerts on detection of malicious activity. The execution flow is shown in Fig. 1.

The details of each components are given below:

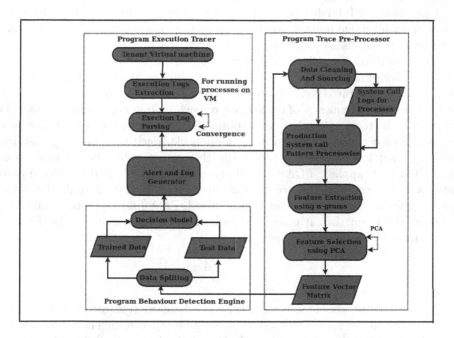

Fig. 1. Execution flow chart of malware detection technique.

3.1   Program Execution Tracer (PET)

Program Execution Tracer (PET) is responsible for collecting the execution tracing logs of the monitored programs running inside the VMs. There are different utilities available for various OSes for system call log extraction. For Linux-VM, VMProtector attaches a system call tracer (strace) to all the running processes to create the individual system call trace log for each of them. The strace utility produces the traces of monitored programs. Monitored programs can either be decided by the tenant member and communicated to cloud admin at the time of registration or automatically taken from program file of monitored machine. The strace of monitored program produces a long list of system calls, called a trace. Each trace log is stored in form of the two columns where first column represents the process id and second column represents the ordered sequence of system calls. All the trace logs of the monitored programs are merged to create a behavior log which is later processed by other components to represent the TVM profile.

3.2   Program Trace Pre-processor

The extracted system call logs are not enough for behaviour analysis. They are pre-processed to extract the meaningful information out of them using n-gram technique. In pre-processing phase, initially, each trace is converted into many n-grams using a sliding window of size k and gradually shifting the window by 1 position. PTT further pre-processes the n-grams and stores the frequency count of each unique n-gram occurring in a trace. For example, let us consider a trace $T_i = \{$s1s2s3s4s5s3s2s6s7$/$ where each si is a system call. Each trace is first converted into collection of n-grams: <m1,m2,m3,m4—-ml> where l is total number of n-grams obtained after processing the trace T_i. A numeric feature vector is generated for T_i represented by <b1,b2,b3,b4,b5..bq> where each bi represents the frequency of occurrence of each unique n-gram in the trace Ti where q is the total unique n-grams obtained. Numeric feature vectors are generated for each trace and stored in a common file. Each n-gram is representing a feature and its frequency is presenting the feature value. For feature selection, PCA [6] is applied. PCA find a linear projection of high dimensional data into lower dimensional subspace like the variance retained is maximized and the least square reconstruction error is minimized. PCA find the center data and subtract the mean then it calculate the dxd co-variance matrix. The Feature vector matrix (FVM) log is generated.

$$c = \frac{A^T A}{N} \tag{1}$$

Now PCA calculate the eigenvector of the co-variance matrix (orthogonal). Eigenvalues to be the new spaces dimension. Now the variance in each new dimension is given by the eigenvalues. So we have a final optimized dataset [6]. The algorithmic steps for feature extraction and selection are shown in Algorithm 1.

3.3   Program Behaviour Detection Engine

In this phase, Program Behaviour Detection Engine (PBDE) analyses the feature matrix log which represents the program behavior in both normal and malign scenarios. Heterogeneous ensemble learning is used to learn and detect the malign process behavior. Three different machine learnings such as RF [7], KNN [8] and LR [9] are used to learn the behavior of the monitored programs. The algorithmic steps are shown in Algorithm 2.

Let us first discuss each classifier briefly. A RF classifier is a ensemble learning classifier that consisting of a collection of randomized base regression trees or decision trees. It is a generic principle of classifier combination that use L tree-structured base classifiers. Every decision tree is made by randomly selecting the data from the available data. At the end, all the trees are combined to form a aggregated regression estimated [7].

Algorithm 1: Algorithm for Feature Extraction and Feature-Pre-processing

---

Result: for every VM, system calls log generation
Log_pre-processing() $VM_i = 1$
while $VM_i! = n$ **do**
    Execution_log=PET(monitored progs)
    while *Execution_log !=EMPTY* **do**
        Label=Extract_name(New_Trace$_i$);
        `# labelling: normal or malign`
        while *Trace_ i$\neq$ EOF* **do**
          | *FVM=PTP(Trace$_i$)*
        end
        Trace$_i$ + +;
    end
    VM$_i$ + +;
end
X_data=FVM[,2:n-1]; `# Features of the dataset`
Y_data=FVM[1] `# Target of the dataset`
pca=PCA(); `# feature selection using PCA`
pca.fit(X_data);
New_data=pca.fit_transform(X_data,Y_data);

Algorithm 2: Algorithm for PBDE for learning and detecting the behavior of malware running inside VMs

---

Result: Result about the Malicious behaviour
Learning_mod()
Xtr,Xts,Ytr,Yts(New_data,Y,test_size=0.3) `Data split for testing and`
  `training`
clf1=RandomForestClassifier();
clf2=KNeighborsClassifier();
clf3=logisticRegression();
Decision_Model1=clf1.fit(Xtr,Yts);
Decision_Model2=clf2.fit(Xtr,Yts);
Decision_Model3=clf3.fit(Xtr,Yts);
detection_Engine_model( )
pred1=model1.predict(Xtr,Ytr);
pred2=model2.predict(Xtr,Ytr);
pred3=model3.predict(Xtr,Ytr);
final_prediction=[];
while *i!=length(Xts)* **do**
    final_prediction=append(final_prediction,statistics(
    pred1[i],pred2[i],pred3[i])
    i++;
end

The KNN classifier is an instance-based conventional and simplest classifier that stores all the examples as training data and classifies them until a query is presented. Every instance in the example is examined and a set of similar instances are presented to classify the query. Therefore this conventional pattern classification has no model for approximation but many local approximations are made depending on the target function for each new query [8]. LR describes the dataset and the relationship between one dependant variable and one or more nominal, ordinal interval or ratio-level independent variable. The dependent variable should be dichotomous in nature. Their should be no outlier in the data, which can be converted into the continuous predictor to standardized the scores [9].

The results of three classifiers are combined using maximum voting based fusion technique to achieve better detection rate as shown in Eq. 2.

$$C(X) = argmax \sum_{j=1}^{B} P_{ij} \qquad (2)$$

Where B is the total number of classifiers and P_{ij} is the prediction probability of classifier j for class i. Once a process is identified as malicious, an event signal is communicated to ALG, described next.

3.4   Alert and Log Generator (ALG)

ALG generates an alarm to cloud administrator if malign behaviour is found. Cloud administrator can then take appropriate action for preventing the malicious activities further. The logs generated by PBDE are share with cloud administrator to know more details about the processes generating the malicious behavior. He/she can kill the process or can even isolate the VM for performing detailed analysis.

4   Experiments and Results

In this phase, we describe the dataset, the configuration details of testbed and detailed experimental analysis.

VMProtector have been validated using University of New Maxico Dataset (UNM) [16]. Each UNM dataset represents the system call trace of privileged process such as login, send-mail etc. The following experimental set up have been used for developing a prototype: Linux machine with 8 GB RAM and 2 TB hard-disk and Ubuntu 18.04 as Host OS, and one VM with Ubuntu 16.04 and Xen 4.9 hypervisor. We used python 3.1 and spyder tool for as a programming framework.

We executed and compared the results of various classifier such as RF, NB, KNN and ensemble of these classifiers using fusion technique.

The ensemble machine learning algorithm considers different heterogeneous classifiers: rule-based, distance-based and probability-based. The reason for considering the different types of classifiers is that the limitations associated with one type of classifier can be overcome by other type of classifier. PCA has been applied as a feature selection algorithm with all these classifiers, as shown in Table 1. Out of all these classifiers, NB is providing the poor results for all the UNM datasets. The highest accuracy (92.37%) is achieved by fusion of all the classifiers for CERT syn sendmail dataset. RF achieved slightly low accuracy 91%, KNN achieved 88.13% whereas NB is achieving very poor accuracy of 54.23% for CERT syn sendmail. For UNM ps dataset also, fusion technique is achieving highest accuracy of 83.30% which is far better than accuracy achieved by other classifiers that is between 75% 9%. For UNM live named dataset, NB is achieving providing very poor accuracy of 80.8%. KNN is providing better performance than NB and is achieving 90.30% accuracy. RF is achieving an accuracy of 92.0% for UNM live named dataset. Fusion technique is again achieving the highest accuracy of 93.30% for same dataset. For most of the UNM datasets, the results achieved by other classifiers are lesser than the fusion technique.

Table 1. Accuracy comparison among different classifier's on UNM datasets

Data sets	PCA + RF + KNN + LR	PCA + RF	PCA + KNN	PCA + NB	Mishra et al.'s [10]
CERT syn.sendmail	92.37	91	88.13	54.23	96.217
UNM mixed xlock	96.87	96.87	96.87	84.25	96.54
UNM ps	83.30	75.0	79.16	75.0	89.20
UNM live named	93.30	92.30	90.30	80.8	83.12
UNM synthetic lpr	99.52	99.3	99.4	84.61	98.11
UNM login	85.71	85.1	85.51	64.28	72.10
UNM live inetd	92.15	92.15	92.30	84.61	81.10
UNM ftp	80.0	80.0	80.0	60.3	NA

We have compared VMProtector with existing technique (MSCSD [10]) for securing virtual machines from in cloud environment as shown in Table 1. MSCSD [10] uses decision tree (DT) algorithm for learning the behavior of programs and DT is unstable because it uses a tree model for making decisions. The accuracy of DT totally depends on conditional control statement. There are higher chances of DT to overfit over the large dataset. For UNM live inetd, MSCSD is achieving the 81.10% accuracy whereas VMProtector achieves an a better accuracy of 92.15%. Even for UNM login, VMProtector is providing an accuracy of 85.71% which is higher than the accuracy (72.10%) achieved by MSCSD. For UNM live named, there is 10% difference in the accuracy of both the methods. VMProtector is achieving better accuracy in this case as well. For UNM synthetic lpr also, VMProtector is achieving slightly better accuracy than MSCSD. For a few dataset, VMProtector and MSCSD are proving more or same results. This may be because of the smaller size of such datasets. However, overall, VMProtector can be considered as an improved over MSCSD for detecting intrusions in VMs running in cloud environment.

Table 2. Detailed performance analysis of VMProtector

Data sets	TPR	TNR	FPR	FNR
CERT syn. sendmail	89.79	94.20	5.79	10.20
UNM mixed xlock	100	94.4	5.55	0
UNM ps	80	85.71	14.28	20.0
UNM live named	100	85.71	14.28	0
UNM synthetic lpr	99.33	100	0.66	0
UNM login	100	75	25	0
UNM live inetd	87.5	100	0	12.5
UNM ftp	66.6	100	0	33.3

The detailed performance results of VMProtector is shown in Table 2. For CERT synthetic sendmail, it is providing a detection rate/True Positive Rate (TPR) of 89.79% with 5.79% false positives. The overall detection rate lies from 66.6% to 100% and false positive alarm (FPR) ranges from 0% to 14.28% which is acceptable performance. The false negative rate is also not too high for most of the datasets. For some of the datasets like UNM mixed xlock, UNM login and UNM live named, very good performance is achieved. The details about other datasets can be refereed in Table 2.

5   Conclusion

We proposed a malign process detection system, called VMProtector for detecting malicious behaviour of the programs running inside the virtual machines for a cloud environment based system call analysis. VMProtector extracts the program behavior in terms of n-grams of execution traces of programs and applies PCA to select important n-grams. The use of n-gram technique eliminates the need of storing large sequence of system call traces. The use PCA results in optimized storage requirement and also decreases the execution time of algorithms on reduced dataset. VMProtector applies fusion based ensemble machine for learning and detecting the behaviour of attacks and their variants. The fusion based ensemble machine learning algorithm uses Random forest (RF), K-Nearest Neighbour (KNN) and Logestic regression (LR). It has been validated that fusion technique is providing the most accurate results.

In future, we would like to add clustering module in VMProtector for detecting completely unseen attacks.

References

1. Kumar, S., Goudar, R.: Cloud computing-research issues, challenges, architecture, platforms and applications: a survey. Int. J. Future Comput. Commun. **1**(4), 356 (2012)
2. Oracle: "oracle report" (2018). https://assets.kpmg/content/dam/kpmg/kz/pdf/Oracle-and-KPMG-Cloud-Threat-Report_2018_Limited.pdf
3. Singh, A., Shrivastava, D.M.: Overview of attacks on cloud computing. Int. J. Eng. Innovative Technol. (IJEIT) 1(4) (2012)
4. Kumar, V., Sangwan, O.P.: Signature based intrusion detection system using snort. Int. J. Comput. Appl. Inf. Technol. **1**(3), 35–41 (2012)
5. Jain, M., Bajaj, P.: Techniques in detection and analyzing malware executables: a review. Int. J. Comput. Sci. Mobile Comput. **3**(5), 930–935 (2014)
6. Song, F., Guo, Z., Mei, D.: Feature selection using principal component analysis. In: International Conference on System Science, Engineering Design and Manufacturing Informatization, vol. 1, pp. 27–30. IEEE (2010)
7. Biau, G.: Analysis of a random forests model. J. Mach. Learn. Res. **13**(Apr), 1063–1095 (2012)
8. Bijalwan, V., Kumar, V., Kumari, P., Pascual, J.: KNN based machine learning approach for text and document mining. Int. J. Database Theory Appl. **7**(1), 61–70 (2014)
9. Hosmer Jr., D.W., Lemeshow, S., Sturdivant, R.X.: Applied Logistic Regression, vol. 398. Wiley, Hoboken (2013)
10. Mishra, P., Pilli, E.S., Varadharajan, V., Tupakula, U.: Securing virtual machines from anomalies using program-behavior analysis in cloud environment. In: IEEE 18th International Conference on High Performance Computing and Communications, pp. 991–998. IEEE (2016)
11. Alarifi, S., Wolthusen, S.: Anomaly detection for ephemeral cloud IaaS virtual machines. In: Lopez, J., Huang, X., Sandhu, R. (eds.) NSS 2013. LNCS, vol. 7873, pp. 321–335. Springer, Heidelberg (2013). https://doi.org/10.1007/978-3-642-38631-2_24
12. Dinaburg, A., Royal, P., Sharif, M., Lee, W.: Ether: malware analysis via hardware virtualization extensions. In: Proceedings of the 15th ACM Conference on Computer and Communications Security, pp. 51–62. ACM (2008)
13. Gupta, S., Kumar, P.: An immediate system call sequence based approach for detecting malicious program executions in cloud environment. Wireless Pers. Commun. **81**(1), 405–425 (2015)
14. Deshpande, P., Sharma, S., Peddoju, S., Junaid, S.: Hids: a host based intrusion detection system for cloud computing environment. Int. J. Syst. Assur. Eng. Manag. **9**(3), 567–576 (2018)
15. Phalke, N.N., Adagale, S.S., Priyadarshi, A., Shinde, V.B.: Malware detection using n-gram based file signature based method. Int. J. Recent Innovation Trends Comput. Commun. **2**(11), 3793–3795 (2014)
16. UNM: UNM Dataset (1998). http://www.cs.unm.edu/~immsec/systemcalls.htm

Comparative Analysis of Ensemble Methods for Classification of Android Malicious Applications

Meghna Dhalaria, Ekta Gandotra$^{(\boxtimes)}$, and Suman Saha

Department of Computer Science and Engineering,
Jaypee University of Information Technology, Waknaghat, Solan, H.P., India
meghna8aug@gmail.com, ekta.gandotra@gmail.com,
suman.saha@juit.ac.in

Abstract. Currently, Android smartphone operating systems are the most popular entity found in the market. It is open source software which allows developers to take complete benefit of the mobile operation device, but additionally increases sizable issues related to malicious applications. With the increase in Android phone users, the risk of Android malware is increasing. This paper compares the basic machine learning algorithms and different ensemble methods for classifying Android malicious applications. Various machine learning algorithms such as Random Forest, Logistic Regression, Support Vector Machine, K-Nearest Neighbor, Decision Tree and Naive Bayes and ensemble methods like Bagging, Boosting and Stacking are applied on a dataset comprising of permissions, intents, Application programming interface (API) calls and command signatures extracted from Android applications. The results revealed that the stacking ensemble techniques performed better as compared to the Bagging, Boosting and base classifiers.

Keywords: Android malware classification · Machine learning ·
Ensemble techniques · Bagging · Boosting · Stacking

1 Introduction

Android is the widely used mobile platform across the world with more than 85% of the market share [1]. The increasing use of Android-based applications (apps) is causing the growth of malware. Nearly 17.5 million Android users downloaded malicious applications from the official Google Play Store in 2017 [2]. These malicious apps create several serious threats such as information leakage, system damage and financial loss etc. According to the McAfee report [3], the growth of Android malware is increasing rapidly with approx 750 million in 2018. Android malware may be embedded in various applications such as gaming, educational and banking apps etc. These infected applications can compromise privacy and security by permitting unauthorized access to rooting devices, private sensitive information, etc. Earlier, most of the malware detection methods were based on signature-based approach. It uses a database of known malware signatures and compares each application against this database. The drawback of this method is that it is not suitable for detection of new

© Springer Nature Singapore Pte Ltd. 2019
M. Singh et al. (Eds.): ICACDS 2019, CCIS 1045, pp. 370–380, 2019.
https://doi.org/10.1007/978-981-13-9939-8_33

malware (i.e. zero-day malware) whose signatures do not exist in the database. Recently, researchers started to use machine learning methods for malware classification. The problem in machine learning technique is that it gives high false positive and false negative rate [4]. Ensemble techniques such as Bagging, Boosting and Stacking are applied in order to improve accuracy. The goal of this paper is to compare the different ensemble methods for Android malware classification. The paper is organized as follows: Sect. 2 provides an overview of related work. Section 3 presents the approach used. Section 4 provides the experimental results and their comparative analysis. Finally, Sect. 5 presents the conclusion.

2 Literature Review

In this section, numerous contributions have been explored with the aid of the researchers in the field of Android malware detection using machine learning. Zhou and Jiang [5] characterized existing Android malware from diverse components, including the permissions requested. They recognized the permissions which are extensively asked in both benign and malicious apps. The author found that malicious apps have a tendency to request extra permissions than benign ones. In 2012, Sanz et al. [6] introduced a new technique to detect Android malware applications through machine learning strategies with the aid of analyzing the extracted permissions from the application itself. In [7], the author presented a method MAMA that extracts numerous features from the Android manifest to build classifiers and detect malware. Huang et al. [8] presented a technique for detection of Android malicious applications based on 20 features. Their experimental results show that an individual classifier is able to detect about 81% of malware applications. In [9], the author developed a tool named Marvin that creates a risk by examining an application using static and dynamic features. In 2015, Bhandari et al. [10] developed an approach DRACO that combines both static and dynamic analysis. It explains the features that contributing to the maliciousness of the examined application and generates the score. In [11], the author introduced SigPID named as Significant Permission Identification for detection of Android malware. The detection device based totally on permission usage to deal with rapid growth in Android malware. SigPID used machine learning based classification method such as SVM and Decision tree to classify the apps into malware or benign. The results show that SVM achieves 90% of recall, precision, F-measure and accuracy. In 2015, Cen et al. [12] proposed a malware detection method primarily based on permissions and API calls. They applied probabilistic discriminative model based on RLR (Regularized Logistic Regression) and compared with other classifier named as K-NN, decision tree, SVM and Naive Bayes. Yerima et al. [13] proposed a novel classifier fusion approach named as DroidFusion which is based on the multilevel architecture that enables the combination of algorithms for improving the accuracy. They applied the various ranking algorithm on their predictive accuracy in order to drive final classifier. Their experimental results show that the fusion method performs better for improving accuracy than the ensemble learning algorithm. Wang et al. [14] applied a different machine learning algorithm named as SVM, Random Forest and Logistic regression with static analysis for detection of Android malware apps. For training machine learning algorithms they used platform-specific static features and app specific static features. Experimental results demonstrate that logistic regression performs better in comparison to other classifiers with 96% of TPR (True Positive Rate) and 0.06% of FPR (False Positive Rate). In [15], the author introduced a novel dynamic evaluation framework, referred to as EnDroid, which automatically extracts multiple varieties of dynamic features to implement effective malware detection. For effective detection of malware, they applied the stacking ensemble technique. Their experimental outcomes show that stacking perform better for the detection of Android malware. This paper presents a comparative analysis of base classifiers and ensemble methods for classification of Android applications.

3   Methodology Used

This section discusses the approach followed for comparing the machine learning algorithms and ensemble methods for detecting and classifying Android applications into malicious and benign. First of all, a dataset [5] comprising of permissions, intents, API calls and command signatures extracted from Android malicious and benign applications is downloaded. Six machine learning algorithms i.e. Naive Bayes (NB), Random Forest (RF), Logistic Regression (LR), K-Nearest Neighbor (K-NN), Decision Tree (DT) and Support Vector Machine (SVM) and three ensemble technique i.e. Bagging, Boosting and Stacking are applied on the dataset using WEKA (Waikato Environment for Knowledge Analysis) [16] library and their performance is evaluated based on different parameters. For stacking ensemble technique, the topmost four classifiers (on the basis of accuracy) are combined in the group of three making four different combinations. The LR is used as level-2 meta-classifier in stacking. Afterward, comparative analysis is carried out on the results obtained. The details of the dataset used, machine learning and ensemble algorithms used are given in the following sub-sections. Figure 1 depicts the methodology of the proposed work.

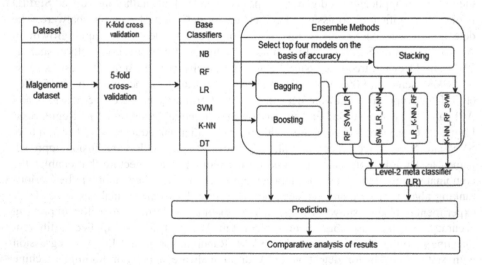

Fig. 1. Workflow of methodology used

Dataset Used

Malgenome [5] dataset is used for this work. It consists of 3800 number of instances which includes 1260 malware and 2539 benign. There are total 215 attributes which are categorized into 4 parts i.e. API Call Signature, Manifest Permission, Command Signature, and Intent. At the time of installation, the permission is granted by the users and these are declared in Android-Manifest file. API calls are needed to interact with the device. Intents are also described in the Android Manifest file. It is the conceptual information about an operation, with which we can infer the intentions of the apps.

Base Classifiers

Decision Tree

The DT [17] is used for building regression and classification model in the form of a tree structure. It focuses on an easily understandable representation form and is one of the most common learning methods. It can easily be visualized in tree structure format. A decision tree is built by iteratively splitting the dataset on the attribute that separates the data into the different existing classes until a stopping criterion is reached.

Random Forest

RF [18] is an ensemble learning method that creates numerous regression trees and aggregates their results. It trains every tree independently by the usage of a random sample of the data. This randomness allows making the model more powerful. The random forest model is excellent at managing tabular records with numerical functions or categorical functions with fewer than loads of categories.

Support Vector Machine

The SVM [19] algorithm, uses hyperplane to divide the n-dimensional space data into two regions. It calculates the maximal margin between all dimensions i.e. it is creating the largest distance between instances, which is reducing the generalization Error. The basic approach to classify the data starts by trying to create a function that splits the data points into the corresponding labels with (a) the least possible amount of errors or (b) with the largest possible margin.

Naive Bayes

NB [20] is a classification technique based on Bayes' theorem. This classifier is widely using in text estimation. For instance, many spam filters are using it in order to divide acceptable content from unacceptable. Usually, the accuracy of this method is relatively low in contrast with other approaches. However, an advantage of this technique is a very high speed of classification and also a very good level of tolerance to missing values. Additionally, NB algorithm characterized by low tolerance to redundant attributes. Continuous features are not permitted here.

K-Nearest Neighbor

K-NN [21] model is also a type of supervised learning algorithm. It is the simplest and easy than other machine learning techniques. This algorithm is representative of lazy algorithms. It is based on the assumption that records within a dataset are generally having the same properties. K-NN algorithm is relatively slow in the classification of new instances coming into the model but fast during the training process. Also, this algorithm is very sensitive to noise in the dataset.

Ensemble Techniques

Bagging: Bagging is also known as **B**ootstrap **Agg**regating. Multiple models of the same learning algorithm are generated over a subset of the training dataset using random sampling with replacement. For combining the models, the two methods are used i.e. majority voting and averaging. In majority voting, the final prediction is done on the basis of votes of each classifier. In averaging, it takes an average of the predictions of each classifier. In our work, we have used the majority vote method. Bagging helps to avoid the problem of overfitting and can reduce variance [22].

Bagging Algorithm

For training:

1. Repeat step 2 to 3 for each iteration i = 1, 2, …, n
2. Create bootstrap samples of the training dataset using random sampling with replacement.
3. Train different classifiers on these samples (NB, K-NN, DT etc.)

For testing:

1. Use a new dataset, to make predictions using base classifiers.
2. Combine the results of all models on the basis of majority voting.

Boosting: This method is used for improving the predictions of the model. Boosting technique selects instances which give the wrong prediction and modify the weights. Boosting is a little variation on bagging. In boosting, firstly equal weights are assigned to all instances. Train the classifiers to make predictions of wrongly classified instances then modify the weights of incorrectly predicted instances. In the end, take the weighted mean of all weak learners to make a strong learner i.e. final model [23]. There are different boosting algorithms such as AdaBoost, Gradient Tree Boosting and XGBoost. The AdaBoost (**Ada**ptive **Boost**ing) algorithm is used to perform boosting in our work.

Boosting Algorithm

1. Assign equal weights to all instances.
2. Train the classifier to make predictions.
3. Assign higher weights to wrongly classified instances.
4. Repeat step 2 & 3 till the classifier correctly predict the instances.

Stacking: Stacking is also known as stacked generalization. It deals with combining multiple classifiers generated by different machine learning algorithms. The process of stacking can be divided into two phases: In the first phase, all the algorithms are trained using the training data. In the second phase, the predictions from multiple models are used as input to the second level to build a new model. This model is used for the prediction on test data [24].

Stacking Algorithm

1. Select topmost four classifiers (on the basis of accuracy) combine these in the group of three making four different combinations.
2. Train these models using a complete training dataset.
3. Construct a new dataset of predictions made from multiple base-level classifiers.
4. Train a meta-model i.e. LR using the new dataset created in step 3.
5. Make predictions using this newly formed model.

4 Experimental Results

This section discusses the experimental results obtained. Six different classifiers i.e. NB, LR, RF, K-NN, DT and SVM (explained in Sect. 3) are executed on WEKA 3.8 under Intel Core i3 processor, 64 bit, 2 GB RAM. All the classification models and ensemble methods are trained using 5-fold cross-validation. The parameters used for evaluating various models are True Positive Rate (TPR), False Positive Rate, Precision, F-measure and Accuracy.

Table 1. Performance evaluation of base classifiers

Classifier	TPR	FPR	Precision (%)	F-measure (%)	Accuracy (%)
NB	0.959	0.044	95.9	95.9	95.8
RF	0.991	0.016	99.1	99.1	99.0
LR	0.974	0.026	97.4	97.4	97.3
SVM	0.990	0.011	99.0	99.0	99.0
K-NN	0.986	0.015	98.6	98.6	98.5
DT	0.970	0.037	97.0	97.0	96.9

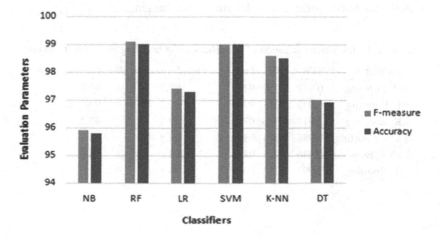

Fig. 2. Comparative analysis of base classifiers

Table 1 represents the result of six base classifiers. The results show that SVM and RF give the best accuracy i.e. 99% followed by K-NN which gives an accuracy of 98.5%. The TPR of RF and SVM is also high i.e. 0.99 and FPR is low i.e. 0.016 (RF) and 0.011 (SVM) respectively.

Figure 2 represents the comparison of six base classifiers on the basis of F-measure and Accuracy. Herein SVM and RF classifiers are proved to be the best among used base classifiers for the Malgenome dataset.

Table 2. Performance evaluation of classifiers using bagging ensemble technique

Classifier	TPR	FPR	Precision (%)	F-measure (%)	Accuracy (%)
NB_Bagging	0.961	0.042	96.1	96.1	96.0
RF_Bagging	0.992	0.016	99.2	99.2	99.1
LR_Bagging	0.979	0.021	97.9	97.9	97.9
SVM_Bagging	0.989	0.011	99.0	98.9	98.9
K-NN_Bagging	0.988	0.015	98.8	98.8	98.8
DT_Bagging	0.985	0.021	98.5	98.5	98.4

Table 2 represents the performance of six different classifiers using Bagging ensemble technique. The results show that classifiers with bagging namely NB, LR, RF, K-NN and DT give better results as compared to base classifiers. There is no improvement in results using the bagging technique in case of SVM because bagging work well with unstable classifiers. There is a minor improvement in TPR and FPR for classifiers with Bagging as compared to the base classifiers.

Table 3 depicts the performance of six classifiers using Boosting ensemble technique. The results show that all the classifiers with boosting except SVM give better results as compared to base classifiers. It is found that classifiers with AdaBoost algorithm have performed better than classifier with bagging ensemble technique with majority voting. There is an improvement in TPR and FPR for classifiers with Ada-Boost algorithm as compared to the classifiers with bagging.

Table 3. Performance evaluation of classifiers using boosting ensemble technique

Classifier	TPR	FPR	Precision (%)	F-measure (%)	Accuracy (%)
NB_Boosting	0.977	0.030	97.7	97.7	97.7
RF_Boosting	0.992	0.013	99.2	99.2	99.2
LR_Boosting	0.974	0.026	97.4	97.4	97.3
SVM_Boosting	0.988	0.014	98.8	98.8	98.8
K-NN_Boosting	0.986	0.015	98.6	98.6	98.6
DT_Boosting	0.991	0.012	99.1	99.1	99.0

Figure 3 represents the comparison of the base classifiers with bagging and boosting ensemble technique on the basis of F-measure. Both Bagging and Boosting showing better accuracy than base classifiers. Adaboost with NB and DT are performing better than their bagged versions. Bagging with LR and K-NN has better accuracy than their boosted version. Bagging and Boosting with RF is giving almost same result.

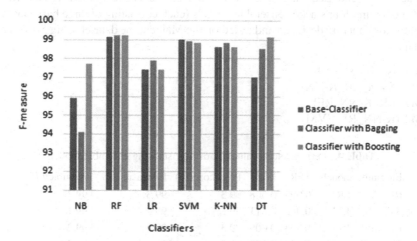

Fig. 3. Comparison of the base classifiers with bagging and boosting ensemble techniques on the basis of F-measure

Herein classifier with boosting i.e. NB, RF and DT are the best among other classifiers. The classifier with bagging is also performing better with some classifiers i.e. RF, LR and K-NN.

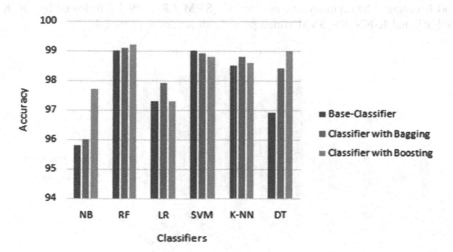

Fig. 4. Comparison of the base classifiers with bagging and boosting ensemble techniques on the basis of Accuracy

Figure 4 represents the comparison of the base classifier with bagging and boosting ensemble technique on the basis of Accuracy. Herein classifier with boosting namely NB, RF and DT are shown to be the best among other classifiers. The classifier with bagging is also performing better with some classifiers i.e. LR and K-NN.

For applying stacking ensemble method, we ranked the base classifiers on the basis of their accuracy. The ascending order of top four base classifiers is LR, K-NN, RF and SVM. Following four stacked ensemble models (each consisting of three base classifiers out of the top four) are designed and tested on the Malgenome dataset using 5-fold cross-validation.

M1 (RF_SVM_LR)
M2 (SVM_LR_K-NN)
M3 (LR_K-NN_RF)
M4 (K-NN_RF_SVM)

Table 4. Performance evaluation of four stacking ensemble models

Ensemble models	TPR	FPR	Precision (%)	F-measure (%)	Accuracy (%)
RF_SVM_LR	0.993	0.008	99.3	99.3	99.3
SVM_LR_KNN	0.992	0.011	99.2	99.2	99.1
LR_KNN_RF	0.993	0.009	99.3	99.3	99.2
KNN_RF_SVM	0.993	0.009	99.3	99.3	99.2

Stacking ensemble method uses a stack of classifiers in order to achieve better results as compared to the individual classifier. The Logistic regression is used as level-2 meta-classifier. Table 4 represents the performance of four ensemble models. The results show that almost all the four models designed using stacking ensemble techniques perform better than the base classifiers and other ensemble methods i.e. Bagging and Boosting. The accuracy obtained by RF_SVM_LR is 99.3% followed by LR_K-NN_RF and K-NN_RF_SVM which provide an accuracy of 99.2%.

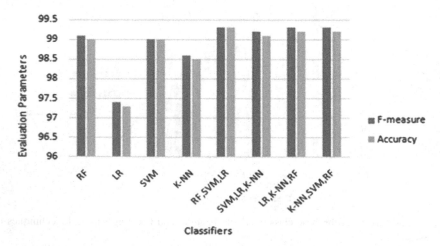

Fig. 5. Comparison of top four base models and stacking ensemble models

Figure 5 depicts the comparative analysis of the top four base models with the stacking ensemble approach in terms of F-measure and Accuracy. The stacking ensemble approach gives the highest accuracy to classify malicious apps. It is clear from the results that the models designed with stacking ensemble technique show significant improvement over base classifiers.

5 Conclusion

With the increase in Android phone users, the risk of Android malware is increasing. So there is a need to develop an effective technique for better classifying the malware. This paper presented a comparative analysis of base classifiers and three ensemble techniques i.e. Bagging, Boosting and stacking for classifying Android apps. It is concluded that ensemble techniques perform better as compared to the base classifiers. Further stacking ensemble technique outperforms in comparison to Bagging and Boosting ensemble technique. The comparison is done on the basis of F-measure and Accuracy. It is revealed from the results that the overall stacking ensemble model has improved accuracy in contrast to the base classifier accuracy. The result shows that the combination of RF_SVM_LR performs better as compared to the other ensemble models. The accuracy obtained is 99.3%.

References

1. Canalys: Over 1 billion Android-based smart phones to ship in 2017
2. Arora, A., Garg, S., Peddoju, S.K.: Malware detection using network traffic analysis in Android based mobile devices. In: 8th IEEE International Conference on Next Generation Mobile Apps, Services and Technologies, pp. 66–71 (2014)
3. McAfee Labs Threats Report: March 2018 Visit: www.mcafee.com/March2018ThreatsReport
4. Gandotra, E., Bansal, D., Sofat, S.: Malware analysis and classification: a survey. J. Inf. Secur. **5**, 56 (2014)
5. Jiang, X., Zhou, Y.: Dissecting Android malware: characterization and evolution. In: 2012 IEEE Symposium on Security and Privacy, pp. 95–109. IEEE (2012)
6. Sanz, B., Santos, I., Laorden, C., Ugarte-Pedrero, X., Bringas, P.G., Álvarez, G.: PUMA: permission usage to detect malware in Android. In: Herrero, Á., et al. (eds.) International Joint Conference CISIS'12-ICEUTE'12-SOCO'12 Special Sessions. AISC, vol. 189, pp. 289–298. Springer, Heidelberg (2013). https://doi.org/10.1007/978-3-642-33018-6_30
7. Sanz, B., et al.: MAMA: manifest analysis for malware detection in Android. Cybern. Syst. **44**, 469–488 (2013)
8. Huang, C.Y., Tsai, Y.T., Hsu, C.H.: Performance evaluation on permission-based detection for Android malware. In: Pan, J.S., Yang, C.N., Lin, C.C. (eds.) Advances in Intelligent Systems and Applications - Volume 2. SIST, vol. 21, pp. 111–120. Springer, Heidelberg (2013). https://doi.org/10.1007/978-3-642-35473-1_12
9. Lindorfer, M., Neugschwandtner, M., Platzer, C.: Marvin: efficient and comprehensive mobile app classification through static and dynamic analysis. In: 2015 IEEE 39th Annual Computer Software and Applications Conference, vol. 2, pp. 422–433. IEEE (2015)

10. Bhandari, S., Gupta, R., Laxmi, V., Gaur, M.S., Zemmari, A., Anikeev, M.: DRACO: DRoid Analyst COmbo an Android malware analysis framework. In: Proceedings of the 8th International Conference on Security of Information and Networks, pp. 283–289. ACM (2015)

11. Li, J., Sun, L., Yan, Q., Li, Z., Srisa-an, W., Ye, H.: Significant permission identification for machine-learning-based Android malware detection. IEEE Trans. Industr. Inf. **14**, 3216–3225 (2018)

12. Cen, L., Gates, C.S., Si, L., Li, N.: A probabilistic discriminative model for Android malware detection with decompiled source code. IEEE Trans. Dependable Secure Comput. **12**, 400–412 (2015)

13. Yerima, S.Y., Sezer, S.: DroidFusion: a novel multilevel classifier fusion approach for Android malware detection. IEEE Trans. Cybern. **99**, 1–14 (2018)

14. Wang, X., Wang, W., He, Y., Liu, J., Han, Z., Zhang, X.: Characterizing Android apps' behavior for effective detection of malapps at large scale. Future Gener. Comput. Syst. **75**, 30–45 (2017)

15. Feng, P., Ma, J., Sun, C., Xu, X., Ma, Y.: A novel dynamic Android malware detection system with ensemble learning. IEEE Access **6**, 30996–31011 (2018)

16. Hall, M., Frank, E., Holmes, G., Pfahringer, B., Reutemann, P., Witten, I.H.: The WEKA data mining software: an update. ACM SIGKDD Explorations Newsl **11**(1), 10–18 (2009)

17. Quinlan, J.R.: Induction of decision trees. Mach. Learn. 81–106 (1986)

18. Liaw, A., Wiener, M.: Classification and regression by randomForest. R News **2**, 18–22 (2002)

19. Keerthi, S.S., Gilbert, E.G.: Convergence of a generalized SMO algorithm for SVM classifier design. Mach. Learn. **46**, 351–360 (2002)

20. Domingos, P., Pazzani, M.: On the optimality of the simple Bayesian classifier under zero-one loss. Mach. Learn. **29**, 103–130 (1997)

21. Shakhnarovish, G., Darrell, T., Indyk, P. (eds.): Nearest-Neighbor Methods in Learning and Vision. MIT Press, Cambridge (2005)

22. Breiman, L.: Bagging predictors. Mach. Learn. **24**, 123–140 (1996)

23. Quinlan, J.R.: Bagging, boosting, and C4.5. In: AAAI/IAAI, vol. 1, pp. 725–730 (1996)

24. Ting, K.M., Witten, I.H.: Issues in stacked generalization. J. Artif. Intell. Res. **10**, 271–289 (1999)

Risk Analysis for Long-Term Stock Market Trend Prediction

Rounak Bose[✉], Amit Das, Jayanta Poray, and Supratim Bhattacharya

Techno India University,
West Bengal, EM 4/1 Salt Lake, Sector V, Kolkata 700091, India
rb1311997@gmail.com, operon.amit@gmail.com, jayanta.poray@gmail.com,
bhattacharya.supratim@gmail.com

Abstract. Stock market trend analysis is very crucial for the understanding of the way stock market attributes can fluctuate with time. Also it helps investors to analyse when to buy and/or sell financial instruments. Even though the predictions can be made with a certain degree of accuracy, the ultimate aim is to minimise the risk associated with the predictions. In this work, Linear regression, Ridge regression, Bayesian Ridge regression, Lasso regression and FBProphet forecasting models are used and compared to predict stock market prices for a particular dataset with a benchmark accuracy. Also, on the basis of the used forecasting models, we have devised a new risk function for long-term stock market predictions. This risk function is derived from the risk functions proposed by NIST and MEHARI.

Keywords: Stock market trend analysis · Time-series data analysis · Predictive modelling · Regression · Risk functions

1 Introduction

One of the most volatile and fluctuating dynamics of the world is the stock market. A stock market is essentially a huge and complex system in which stocks - shares of companies that indulge in public trading - are issued, then bought and consequently sold, and this process goes on in this cyclic fashion. As much as it is a place where the experienced people pit their expertise against others, the stock market not only takes into account people's sentiment and the public trends in general, but also the technicalities and the economic factors that play a very major role in this domain. A very noteworthy view in case of stock markets is that the stock market is a highly adversarial system of trading [14].

Importance of Stock Market Prediction: Stock market predictions are essentially what is the ruling factor of all the dynamics of every society. Stock market prices actually influence the social political and, needless to say, economic dynamics of the world we live in. Hence predicting stock market values will essentially predict the future. But then, we cannot make predictions with accuracy that is actually useful. Suppose for instance, we get predictions of

© Springer Nature Singapore Pte Ltd. 2019
M. Singh et al. (Eds.): ICACDS 2019, CCIS 1045, pp. 381–391, 2019.
https://doi.org/10.1007/978-981-13-9939-8_34

accuracy 0.8 and 0.9 respectively. Then what we actually take into account are the mis-predictions of values 0.2 and 0.1 respectively. Hence, since we cannot increase the accuracy, what we can actually do with various regression analysis techniques, is minimise the risk associated with these predictions. So the ultimate aim for stock market predictions is to minimise the risk and consequently increase the accuracy of the predictions.

It is important to note however that technical analysis does not always lead to correct or even desirable results. However, it is not correct to discredit technical analysis; since it does help the investor to take informed decisions and make knowledgable predictions with respect to certain securities/stocks [15].

Analysis, documented and properly calculated, technically, will not only help us to take appropriate decisions but also help us make near-accurate predictions about the stock market trends and values in the future. The three most significant benefits of proper technical analysis on stock market data for stock market predictions, irrespective of whether it is long-term or short-term, are:

- It will help to easily identify the support and resistance levels in that particular security.
- It will help to take informed decisions about good (or bad) entry points.
- Most significantly, it will help to easily spot trends and patterns in existing historical data and make informed and knowledgable predictions about the future with respect to the particular stock/security that is being technically analysed.

The objective of our work is to analyse the factors influencing our predictions and henceforth measure the risk for the predictions. Also, here several regression techniques are used and compared to deduce the risk that is involved in this prediction game.

2   Review of Existing Literature

Supervised learning encompasses different regression techniques. Regression analysis was first coined based on a biological phenomenon - that the descendants of ancestors who were originally very tall, had heights that were gradually decreasing towards a normal average or the mean; in other words, the values were regressing down towards the mean value [1]. This concept has, since then, been put to use in largely statistical analogies, and is now a proven way to explain the relationships between the variables that are of explanatory nature and the cumulative distribution of all the recorded responses [2].

Non-parametric forms of regression, Bayesian and Naive-Bayesian regression methodologies and multi-predictor-valued regression methodologies are some of the rather important advancements on the statistical front [3].

In their work, Pedregosa et al. developed scikit-learn, the highly beneficial machine learning library to be used complementary to the Python programming language. Some of the rather very significant objectives that have been met

by scikit-learn include fast and convenient implementations of a wide range of
regression analysis techniques and methodologies in code for machine learning
purposes [4].

2.1   Linear Regression

The linear regression model is the most basic of all the models that are a part
of the module under scikit-learn called the sklearn.linear_model. The main aim
of these modules is to implement comparatively statistically generalised models
based on linear regression analysis techniques. The *LinearRegression* module is
essentially the ordinary regression analysis taking into account the least squares,
the class definition for which is as follows:

*class sklearn.linear_model.***LinearRegression** *( )*

As far as the implementation of this statistical technique is concerned, it is
very convenient, since this method takes into account only the Ordinary Least
Squares segment. To add to the convenience, the segment has been wrapped
into an object of type predictor such that it allows for easy usage and provides
efficient and reliable solutions.

The scope of this *LinearRegression()* class is to help us make a pattern for
the prices of a stock with respect to dates, and use it to make predictions for
the unknown dates, which serves as the test data.

2.2   Ridge Regression

The implementation of Ridge Regression enters the domain of statistical analysis
with the help of the concept of Regularisation. The *Ridge* module works under the
linear_model of scikit-learn using the principles of l2 regularisation. So the main
principle behind ridge regression is to combine the least squares results obtained
in linear regression, with l2 form of regularisation; and the aim of this module is,
like that of *LinearRegression*, to minimise the cost function $J(\theta)$, where:

$$J(\theta) = \frac{1}{2m} [\sum_{i=1}^{m} (hypothesis - predicted\_values)^2 + \lambda \sum_{j=1}^{m} \theta_j^2]$$

The l2-norm of regularisation is evident from the latter half of the equation
shown above, in the segment: $\lambda \sum_{j=1}^{m} \theta_j^2$,
where the values of the weights of the parameters are squared to give the regu-
larised term, after multiplication with the regularisation factor (denoted by λ).
This form is also called Tikhonov regularisation [5]. The class definition for the
Ridge module is almost an evolution over that for *LinearRegression*, that has
been previously defined, which is as follows:

*class sklearn.linear_model.***Ridge** *( )*

2.3 Bayesian Ridge Regression

The Bayesian Ridge Regression is very much similar to the normal Ridge Regression. In fact, it is nothing more than a significant improvement over the ordinary least squares methodologies followed till now; despite the fact that as of today, there are many disagreements over the most optimised version of ridge regression [6]. The class definition for the *BayesianRidge* module, shown below, adds to that of the *Ridge* module with the implementation of fitting a particular Bayesian Ridge Regression statistical analysis model, followed by the optimisation of the significant-role-playing parameters, namely the regularisation parameter (denoted by λ) and the noise precision (denoted by α).

*class sklearn.linear_model.**BayesianRidge** ( )*

Ridge regression is by far quite capable of preventing any forms of over-fitting to given data leading to poor results on new data. The Bayesian Ridge Regression technique is essentially an almost equivalent methodology that takes merit in being a very flexible approach with respect to construction of the models for a given problem [7]. The bayesian technique is actually very intuitive when we take into the account the uncertainty about the estimations of the weights of the parameters involved, to help in the process of regularisation. The advantages of the *BayesianRidge* computational module are quite pronounced. Not only does it have provisions for the proper studying and estimation of the posterior probabilities with regards to the weight coefficients of the parameters, but also aids in easy interpretation. Adding to it, is the fact that there is an enhanced experience with respect to flexibility in the design of the models for any given problem scenario. However, the only noticeable and significantly observable drawback of this approach employing the Bayesian ridge regression is that the result predictions take significantly more time to be solved and computed.

2.4 Lasso Regression

The Least Absolute Shrinkage and Selection Operator (Lasso) is in itself a statistical method for regression analysis. The model that is analysed by the Lasso regression technique is not only more accurate with respect to the prediction scores, but is also significantly interpretable. This is because lasso not only fits the parameters, but also penalises the coefficients (or the weights) such that we can effectively assign importance levels to the coefficients, understand their significance in the analysis and the score-predictions by the model, and use this knowledge to essentially totally disregard some of the coefficients (depending on their "importance levels" of course), and make use of only the most significant ones in the prediction process [8]. The *Lasso* module strives to implement the same concept. However, the equation that implements this form of regression analysis, the lasso is as follows:

$$J(\theta) = \frac{1}{2m}[\sum_{i=1}^{m}(hypothesis - predicted\_values)^2 + \lambda \sum_{j=1}^{m}||\theta_j||][5]$$

The class definition for the *Lasso* module is given below:

*class sklearn.linear_model.**Lasso** ( )*

All the 4 modules discussed here, undertake some common set of functions, that are denoted by the pre-built methods for the same in the scikit-learn library for Python. The method-descriptions are as follows:

1. **Fitting the Model:** For fitting the linear regression model for any particular regression analysis problem, it is important to call the **fit** method, the syntax for which is: *fit (X, y, sample_weight = None)*
   The returned value is *self* - which is essentially an instance of the model itself.
2. **Getting Estimator Parameters:** To get the parameters for any given estimator, the implementation is: *get_params (deep = True)*
   This returns a mapping (*params*), from that of names of the parameters concerned to their values.
3. **Setting Estimator Parameters:** To set the parameters for any given estimator, the implementation is: *set_params (**params)*; and this works not only with single estimators, but also with pipelines and other nested objects of that nature. It is convenient in the sense that it is possible to easily update all the components of a nested object. The returned value is *self* - which is essentially an instance of the model itself.
4. **Making Predictions Using the Model:** To predict by making use of the linear regression model (the *LinearRegression()*, module to be specific), the implementation is simply: *predict (X)*, where X is an array-like shape or a sparse data-representation. The value that is returned by this function is also an array - the predicted output measurements.
5. **Checking the Performance Score:** By using *score(X, y, sample_weight = None)*, we can find the performance score of the model with respect to a particular regression analysis problem. The score of a prediction is essentially its coefficient of determination (R^2). The coefficient R^2 can be defined as $R^2 = 1 - (u/v)$, where u is essentially the residual sum after the squaring, and v is the actual cumulative sum of the squares, such that:

$$u = \sum(y\_true - y\_prediction)^2, and$$

$$v = \sum(y\_true - y\_true.mean())^2.$$

The value that is eventually returned from this method is the float-type value of the coefficient of determination (R^2), which is the prediction score for the model.

2.5 FBprophet

The FBProphet forecasting model is a relatively new development in the field of time-series forecasting. This statistical practice applies not only to linear forms of regression but also non-linear regression analysis techniques. According to Taylor et al. [9], FBProphet is providing a very practical approach to what is known as forecasting-at-scale. Prophet makes use of a decomposable model for the time-series forecasting, and has three main components, namely, trend, holidays and seasonality. It is noteworthy that the model is similar to a GAM or generalised additive model in the fact that apparently time is the only regressor, whereas many other linear (as well as non-linear) derivatives of time are the components of the model. The trend function serves to model non-linear and non-periodic changes in time-series values; the seasonality component takes care of the periodic (for instance, yearly) changes in the time-series data; and last but not the least, the holidays function makes sure that even the effect of sudden and potentially irregular changes in schedules affect the time-series data values, prominently seen over one or more days. The Prophet forecasting time series model can thus be expressed as:

$$y(t) = trend(t) + seasonality(t) + holidays(t) + \epsilon_t,$$

where, the term ϵ_t refers to idiosyncratic changes [9] in the model that are not accommodated by the same, and $y(t)$ refers to the trend of the overall model.

2.6   Risk Analysis

The primary concept worth noting with respect to the value of the bid-ask spread is to make sure that the investors would be at a disadvantage irrespective of the predicted value of the bid-ask spread [10]. A very crucial step in the domain of risk analysis and management, thereafter, is the actual calculation with respect to the risks that are actually present in the current scenario [16]. For this very reason, risk functions have been devised to streamline the process of risk calculation. Two very important and significant risk functions, among others, that have been around for quite some time now are the NIST risk function [12] devised by the NIST (the National Institute of Standards and Technologies) and the MEHARI (Method for Harmonised Analysis of Risk) risk function [11]. It is noteworthy that although other risk functions are in use, which are somewhat more efficient than the NIST or the MEHARI risk functions, these two risk functions help to properly depict the causes and the consequences when it comes to risk in long-term stock market predictions.

The NIST Risk Function: The NIST risk function is a quantitative as well as qualitative tool for the analysis and calculation of risk associated with a particular scenario [12]. This risk function takes as input, the impact of a given threat or vulnerability (or, the many factors that determine stock market prices and their fluctuations), and the likelihood of that impact factor, which is essentially the probability associated with that risk factor ever occurring. The output of the risk function is of course the "Risk" value, which is quantitatively defined on a number of scale of suitable range. Both inputs, the impact and the likelihood can have their values in qualitative as well as quantitative terms.

The MEHARI Risk Function: The MEHARI risk function is almost exactly similar to the NIST risk function, both structurally and functionally. The main difference lies in the fact that the MEHARI risk function takes into account everything in a qualitative way. Consequently, the inputs to the risk function, i.e. the impacts and the likelihoods, are both defined only qualitatively [11]. Also, the output, which is the risk associated, is defined qualitatively, and hence cannot be defined numerically.

3 Methodology

The dataset that has been used in the regression techniques have been recorded for each working day for the period of approximately 8 years. The conventional name of the financial security, of which this dataset is a part, is called the SP500. To be precise the daily SP500 values have recorded in the dataset from December 8, 2008 up until August 30, 2017. According to this dataset, there are approximately 252 entries for one full year of SP500 data.

The regression analysis resulted in:

a score of 0.936747975549684 (approximating to 0.93 over 5 rounds of testing) when *model.LinearRegresssion()* was used on the dataset,

a score of 0.9474807086816863 (approximating to 0.945 over 5 rounds of testing) when *model.Ridge()* was used on the dataset,

a score of 0.9545439315539958 (approximating to 0.954 over 5 rounds of testing) when *model.BayseianRidge()* was used on the dataset, and

a score of 0.9568207062764479 (approximating to 0.96 over 5 rounds of testing) when *model.Lasso()* was used on the dataset.

The results can be depicted on the plot as given in Fig. 1.

The prediction by the FBProphet forecasting model can be used to actually visualise the model training parallel to the actual data points. This can be visualised in Fig. 2. Likewise, the final outcome from the FBProphet forecasting model has been depicted in Fig. 3. The greyed out areas are essentially the confidence-bounds as well as the predictions for the values and the predicted confidence-bounds for the respective values, over the course of the next two years which have been used to serve the purpose of a test-dataset. The results, as can be seen, are quite consistent initially, but then diverge out (the confidence-bounds) for later periods of time. So, FBProphet might not apparently be able to perform as efficiently for the long-term predictions as compared to predictions for a shorter time.

3.1 Proposed Risk Function

To make sure that the risk associated with stock market predictions can be analysed and predicted to a certain extent, a new risk function needs to be devised that might turn out to be an improvement over the likes of the NIST and the MEHARI risk functions. The risk function that has been devised to particularly fulfill the needs for risk analysis in the domain of long-term stock

Performance Comparison of Regression models

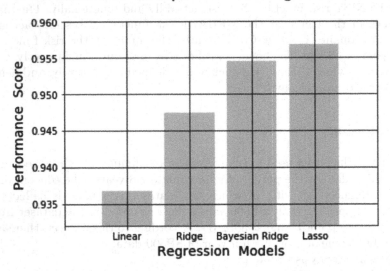

Fig. 1. Comparative study of the regression analysis techniques

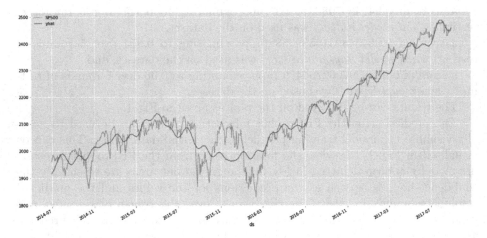

Fig. 2. The FBProphet forecast result for 8 years

market predictions is based loosely on both the NIST and the MEHARI risk functions. Like the NIST and the MEHARI risk functions, it has qualitative valuation for the inputs, "Impacts" and "Likelihoods". Complementary to that, the risk function also includes the quantitative valuation of the input parameters, allowing for scaling and suitable-range-selection for the same. However, unlike the lenience that is allowed by the NIST risk function with respect to the value-levels, the new risk function has a fixed set of 4 levels for each of the input parameters, not unlike the MEHARI risk function. The output for the newly

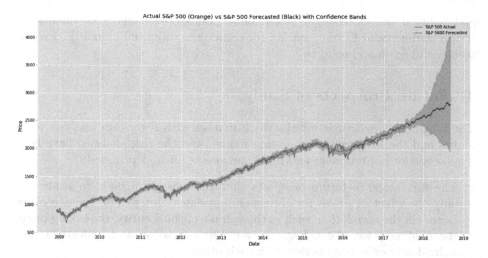

Fig. 3. The FBProphet forecast result with final predictions

devised risk function for long-term stock market predictions and risk analysis, is of course the risk associated with an investment taking into account a given impact factor for a particular likelihood. Like the NIST risk function, this output value is quantitative in nature, and akin to the MEHARI risk function, there are strictly 4 levels (or, ranges) of risk that are attributed to the quantified output value. The new risk function can be seen in Fig. 4.

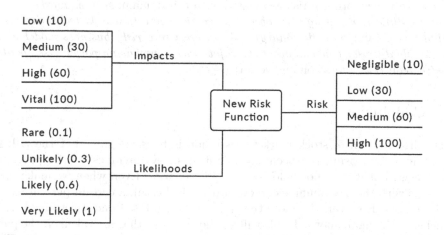

Fig. 4. The new risk function

The impact areas include, but are not limited to factors that affect the stock market namely, momentum, mean reversion, martingales, volatility, stock valuations, interest rates, economic outlooks, inflation (and/or deflation), economic and political shocks, changes in economic policies, exchange rate valuations, supply-and-demand factors, market (or sometimes, even individual [17]) sentiments, and so on and so forth.

4   Future Prospects of Study

The long-term predictions for the stock market with regression analysis techniques and the FBProphet forecasting model, and the risk analysis, have kept huge scope for improvement and future prospects for in-depth study.

1. The first scope of future prospects that this has given us is to study not only the effect of prices for corresponding dates, but to also include other factors in the correlation, such as the volume of the security, the asking price, the bidding price, the bid-ask spread [13], and so on and so forth, either individually or in conjunction with each other.
2. The second scope for improvement and future studies lies in the fact that we can now incorporate even short-term prediction studies to make sure that we can understand the economic dynamics even at a smaller time-scale, which might include other important factors such as election-effects, political fluctuations, social dynamics and day-to-day sentiments, terrorist attacks, natural calamities et cetera.

And the most significant outcome from these 2 areas of study is that we will not only be able to improve on the newly devised risk function for risk analysis in stock-market predictions, but also be able to evaluate and consequently, map and classify new forms of risk associated with this domain, such as *market-value risk, headline risk, rating risk, obsolescence risk, detection risk, legislative risk, inflationary* (and/or *deflationary) risk, interest-rate risk, business-model risk, marketability risk, convenience risk, safety risk, purchasing-power risk, political/societal risk*, and so on and so forth.

5   Conclusion

The ultimate aim of stock market prediction is to make sure that the risk is minimised. Increasing the accuracy might seem synonymous to the previous statement, but it does not hold true for all scenarios. Even when we make predictions with the maximum accuracy (in the ideal case), a certain percentage of risk persists. However, the more the risk can be analysed and ascertained with efficiency, the more knowledgable will be the decisions that are taken on the part of the investor, or any other individual entity linked to the stock market. The aim of this paper is to state that regression analysis studies and other forecasting models can predict future trends in the long-term stock market dynamics with certain accuracy, but only when it is combined with a proper risk function, to properly analyse and mitigate the risk, is it actually fruitful in terms of benefits provided to the real world. The results obtained from this study can safely suggest that, not only are we on the right track to properly work out risks associated with stock market predictions and consolidate the importances of regression analysis in stock market predictions, but also pave the way for future studies and improvements for more refined analysis strategies and efficient results.

References

1. Galton, F.: Kinship and Correlation (reprinted 1989). Statistical Science, Institute of Mathematical Statistics (1989)
2. Fisher, R.A.: The goodness of fit of regression formulae, and the distribution of regression coefficients. J. Roy. Stat. Soc. **12**, 773 (1922)
3. Aldrich, J.: Fisher and regression. Stat. Sci. **20**, 401–417 (2005)
4. Pedregosa, F., et al.: Scikit-learn: machine Learning in Python. J. Mach. Learn. Res. **12**, 2825–2830 (2011)
5. Ng, A.Y.: Feature selection, L1 vs. L2 regularization, and rotational invariance. In: Twenty-first International Conference on Machine Learning (2004)
6. Vinod, H.D.: A survey of ridge regression and related techniques for improvements over ordinary least squares. Rev. Econ. Stat. **60**, 121–131 (1978)
7. Bishop, C.M., Tipping, M.E.: Bayesian Regression and Classification. Microsoft Research (2003)
8. Friedman, J., Hastie, T., Tibshirani, R.: Regularization Paths for Generalized Linear Models via Coordinate Descent (2010)
9. Taylor, S.J., Letham, B.: Forecasting at Scale (2017)
10. Copeland, T.E., Galai, D.: Information Effects on the Bid-Ask Spread (1983)
11. CLUSIF, MEHARI* V3: Risk Analysis Guide (2004)
12. Stoneburner, A.G.G., Feringa, A.: NIST: RIsk management guide for information technology system. Special Publication 800–30. National Institute of Standards and Technology (2002)
13. Nesbitt, K., Barrass, S.: Finding trading patterns in stock market data. IEEE Comput. Graph. Appl. **24**, 45–55 (2004)
14. Boyacioglu, M.A., Avci, D.: An adaptive network-based fuzzy interference system (ANFIS) for the prediction of stock market return: the case of the Istanbul stock exchange. Expert Syst. Appl. **37**, 7908–7912 (2010)
15. Kimoto, T., Asakawa, K., Yoda, M., Takeoka, M.: Stock Market Prediction System with Modular Neural Networks (1990)
16. Yang, H., Chan, L., King, I.: Support vector machine regression for volatile stock market prediction. In: Yin, H., Allinson, N., Freeman, R., Keane, J., Hubbard, S. (eds.) IDEAL 2002. LNCS, vol. 2412, pp. 391–396. Springer, Heidelberg (2002). https://doi.org/10.1007/3-540-45675-9_58
17. Bhattacharya, S., Goswami, S., Poray, J., Bose, R., Das, A.: Study on sentiment and opinion for "Review Text" corpus. In: ICCIIoT (2018)

Evaluating Accessibility and Usability
of Airline Websites

Gaurav Agrawal[1]([✉]), Devendra Kumar[2], Mayank Singh[3],
and Diksha Dani[4]

[1] Uttarakhand Technical University, Dehradun, India
gauravagrawal1982@gmail.com
[2] College of Engineering Roorkee, Roorkee, India
devmochan@gmail.com
[3] University of KwaZulu Natal, Durban, South Africa
dr.mayank.singh@ieee.org
[4] Inderprastha Engineering College, Ghaziabad, India
dikshadani@yahoo.com

Abstract. The website has become an important factor in digitization. In recent years the airline industry has moved to online channels to increase customer base and provide timely information and services to the users. Persons with cognitive, mental, physical, sensory impairment also access these websites. To make these websites equally accessible to these disabled people, website designers should include the accessibility options in their design. An accessible website not only increases the participation of the disabled person in the digital environment but also make it more usable to everyone. Web quality parameters like usability and accessibility play an important role in customer attraction and retention. Therefore, the objective of this paper is to evaluate the quality of websites of airlines based in India. The evaluation is done on the basis of accessibility, usability, and readability of the website using online automated tools. Usability of the Indian airline websites is evaluated on various parameters of the website such as page size, page load time, number of broken links on the page. Accessibility evaluation of the website is done by checking the compliance of Indian airline website with web accessibility guideline 2.0 and evaluating the color contrast errors which makes the website inaccessible to cognitively disabled persons. Finally, the mobile-friendliness of websites is evaluated using online tools. The result of the study shows that none of the Indian airline websites satisfies the WCAG 2.0 accessibility guidelines and suffers from serious usability issues.

Keywords: Accessibility · Usability · Web accessibility guideline 2.0

1 Introduction

In the present digital world, the growing number of internet users has made web quality an important factor for accessing online services and increasing the customer base of an organization. The advances in information technology and the internet have opened new dimensions in the e-commerce industry. The traditional way of doing offline

© Springer Nature Singapore Pte Ltd. 2019
M. Singh et al. (Eds.): ICACDS 2019, CCIS 1045, pp. 392–402, 2019.
https://doi.org/10.1007/978-981-13-9939-8_35

business has been shifted to the online platform and managing an effective e-commerce website for attracting customers for business promotion is the success mantra for any industry. The international telecommunication union report of 2017 has claimed that total global internet user has reached to 3.5 billion in 2016 and expected to reach 3.9 billion by the end of 2017 which has 54% of the global population [1].

The airline industry has also been heavily impacted by the IT revolution, the adoption of the internet by the airline industry has generated a huge increase in its profit. Almost all the airlines have their own website for direct contact with customers and provide them timely information. The report of International air transport association (IATA) [2] shows that in 2016, airline website contributed to nearly 33% of the airline ticket booking and 2% of ticket booking was done using the mobile app or mobile optimal websites and by 2021, the booking through website and mobile are expected to reach 45%. IATA reports that by 2021 worldwide there will be a more number of older passengers than today. There will be 12% more people in the age range of 55 to 64 and 18.9% more people older than 65 years of age and forecast India as one of the most tourism spending country and places it on the fourth position. In the view of these facts to achieve market sustainability, Indian airline participants should have a full-fledged high-quality website that caters the need of every age group people and any elderly or physical disability should not become the barrier in web accessibility. A poorly designed website will result in users dissatisfaction in service provided and will result in a loss in sales. Websites with ease of navigation are more likely to be used by the customers and will also attract new customers. As suggested by Spencer Ivey [3] usability and accessibility of the website are the two important website design metric.

In 1998 usability is defined by International standard organization ISO9241 as "usability is the extent to which a product can be used by a specified user to achieve specified goals with effectiveness and efficiency".

The WHO report of 2011 on disability reported that 15% of the world's population is suffering from disabilities [4] and the social and economic inclusion of these people indeed is a great challenge for the developing country like India. To cater the need of these differently able people India has adopted the Right of persons with disability act on 27 December 2016 which ensures that the person with a disability to enjoy equal rights in accessing physical environment, information and communication technology to web-based services.

W3C has published Web Content accessibility guideline(WCAG) [5] to make the web accessible to all. The first version of these guidelines known as WCAG 1.0 was published in 1999, the second version WCAG 2.0 was published in 2008 which has been adopted by most of the countries as the accessibility guidelines. Recently WCAG 2.1 has been released which is based on WCAG 2.0 with some additional checkpoints.

The aim of this paper is to evaluate the usability and accessibility of the website of the Indian airline industry as many studies in the literature suggest that usability and accessibility are key factors in website development. The rest of the paper is organized as follows: Sect. 2 gives the Literature review, Sect. 3 lists the research questions, Sect. 4 gives the overview of methodology automated tools and parameters used in the study, Sect. 5 gives the overall results, and finally conclusion is discussed in Sect. 6.

2 Literature Review

Worldwide much research has been done to evaluate the quality of the airline website. The authors [6] performed the usability analysis of the airline websites operating in turkey on seven functional characteristics namely information provision, networking, participation, campaigning, online processes, mobile application, and social media application and six delivery characteristics of the website. The results revealed that websites have improved from 2012 to 2014.

In another study of turkey airline [7], the author proposed the website performance framework using hybrid multi-criteria decision-making techniques and evaluated the performance of 11 airlines on seven parameters using online diagnostics tools.

In [8] authors performed the usability evaluation of the airline website on three important airline website's functionalities namely airline ticket purchase, airline package purchase, and airline check-in service using heuristic evaluation. The results showed that the majority of websites have three major usability issues namely presence of broken links, absence of help menu and has consistency errors.

In [9], the authors proposed a method to evaluate web usability of Emirates airline website based on five user's task evaluated on three usability metrics namely time to complete the task, total mistakes done and mistake time. Results showed that out of five tasks, the task of ticket purchase fails on all three parameters and the best result is obtained for the task of flight search.

In the study of Malaysian airline website [10], the author measured the performance of airline websites using fuzzy and non-fuzzy MCDM techniques. Websites were evaluated considering load time, page size, broken link, markup validation, page rank, traffic as the web quality parameters, using online tools to collect the data. The authors also proposed a hybrid multi-criteria decision-making model approach to rank the website. The results showed that four Asian airline websites did not meet the website quality criteria and needed improvement.

A framework (ASEF) focusing on the airline industry on the Web was proposed by Apostolou et al. [11] to be used as a guide in order to improve the online services of the airline industry and also, evaluated the sites of thirty major airlines across all over the world based on the Index. The model was based on five dimensions namely interface design, site navigability, information content, the reliability of embedded software functions and appropriateness of technical implementation. This framework not only ensures the delivery of service to the customer but was also useful for developer of the airline website.

In recent studies, Oyefolahan et al. [12] evaluated the usability and accessibility of websites of Nigerian airline. The heuristic method was used to evaluate the usability and four different automated online tools for checking the compliance of the website with WCAG 2.0 accessibility guidelines. The result showed that the website under study had many functional usability and accessibility error and most of the Nigerian airline website needs improvement.

Alwahaishi et al. proposed the framework for evaluating the quality of airline website based on four parameters namely website design, Informational content, transactional content and customer support and evaluated the seven airlines of the

Arabian Gulf. Statistical correlation among various parameters was identified and finally, the author proposed an Airline Website Assessment Index (AWAI) [13].

Another similar study conducted on Indian healthcare websites evaluated the accessibility, usability and security aspects found that the hospital websites are not mature enough and they are neglecting the usability and accessibility parameters in their website design and need lots of improvement in order to meet the expectation of people and motivate them to use the digital media for health-related information [14].

3   Research Questions

In order to investigate the quality of airline websites, the following research questions were formulated

1. What is the status of accessibility of airline websites according to WCAG 2.0 accessibility guidelines?
2. What is the status of usability of Indian airline website based on the various parameters?
3. What is the readability score of the airline websites using Flesch Kincaid readability ease score?

4   Methodology

In this paper, home pages of websites of airlines based in India were investigated for usability and accessibility criteria. As shown in Table 1, a total of 9 Indian airline websites were investigated. Accessibility evaluation of website under study is based on Web Content Accessibility Guideline (WCAG). The World Wide Web consortium publishes the web content accessibility guidelines, following these guidelines makes the web accessible beyond the limitations of disabilities. Thus forming a global web quality standard. The first version WCAG 1.0 was published in the year 1999 [15].

WCAG 1.0 consists of 65 checkpoints divided under fourteen guidelines and has three conformance level A, AA, AAA. Later in the year 2008, the second version of accessibility guideline WCAG 2.0 was published [16]. WCAG 2.0 consists of twelve guidelines included under four principles namely perceivable, operable, understandable and robust. The first principle perceivable ensures that information present on the web should be easily perceived by the user irrespective of any physical disability, Operable ensures that the web interface provided is operable and provide easy navigation on the web, Understandable principle ensures that the web content and the operation should be understandable by all, Robust principle ensures that the assistive technology can be easily embedded in the web page so that web is accessible to all and any future technological advancement can be easily adapted, to implement and test these princi-ples these guidelines consist of sixty-one testable success criteria.

Indian Airline websites under study are evaluated against WCAG 2.0 guidelines.

There are many automated online tools available to check the conformance of WCAG 1.0 and 2.0. The tool employed for evaluating website accessibility in this study is Taw [17]. Taw is a set of tools for analysis of the accessibility in websites. It is an online service to check the accessibility of websites using the URL and generate a summary of an error on the analyzed page.

To evaluate the usability status of the website under study, page load time and page size are evaluated using Pingdom online tool [18], broken links of the website were evaluated through websitepulse tool [19], online version of WAVEAIM tool [20] is used to evaluate the color contrast error on the webpage, readability score of the websites are evaluated using the Webpagefx tool [21], Mobile friendliness and mobile page test is evaluated using the tool illustrated in Table 2.

Table 1. List of Airlines websites evaluated

Sr. No.	Website name
1	www.airindia.com
2	www.jetairways.com
3	www.goindigo.in
4	www.airindiaexpress.in
5	www.spiceJet.com
6	www.goair.in
7	www.airvistara.com
8	www.trujet.com
9	www.zoomair.in

Expert manual evaluation of the website under study is done to evaluate the presence of search option on the website, presence of Multilanguage option of the webpage which increases the usability, presence of sitemap and presence of screen reader on the webpage.

Table 2. Tools used

Parameter	Website
Mobile friendly	Google mobile-friendly test
Desktop web accessibility test	Taw
Broken links	Websitepulse
Color contrast errors	Wave
Load time	Pingdom
Page size	Pingdom
Readability	Webpagefx

5 Results

The result of the study for accessibility, usability, and readability are presented in the following section.

5.1   Accessibility Analysis

Accessibility errors reported by TAW tool is shown in Table 3. A total of 2643 errors, averaging 293.6 errors were found in the websites under study. The result shows that the minimum number of accessibility errors was 63 for the website of jetairways and the website of goindigo reported maximum accessibility errors (414 in number). 44% of websites had accessibility errors greater than the average number of errors of the websites under study.

Table 3. Accessibility issues reported by TAW of Perceivable (P), Operable (O), Understandable (U), Robust (R) category.

Websites	P	O	U	R	Total
www.airindia.com	14	42	13	14	83
www.jetairways.com	9	32	4	18	63
www.goindigo.in	342	141	155	176	814
www.airindiaexpress.in	59	15	19	21	114
www.spiceJet.com	189	40	88	190	507
www.goair.in	186	41	75	136	438
www.airvistara.com	121	55	53	110	339
www.trujet.com	47	17	23	30	117
www.zoomair.in	75	13	38	42	168

As shown in Fig. 1, 40% of errors reported were of the perceivable type, showing that the information presented on the webpages of the airline websites are perceived with difficulty. 28% errors were of robust type i.e., assistive technology can't interpret the information presented on the page. 18% errors were of the understandable type, resulting in content or operation on webpage beyond the understating of the end user. 14% of errors lie in the operable category, resulting in the non-operable interface.

The most frequently violated WCAG2.0 success criteria are listed in Table 4. Criteria 1.1.1 Non-text content ensures that all the non-text content of the webpage should have an equivalent text alternative. Criteria 1.3.1 ensure that information and relationship of content should be preserved while presenting the content through assistive technology tools to a disabled person. Criteria 2.4.4 and 2.4.9 ensures that the text of the hyperlink on the webpage should define the purpose of the link. Criteria 2.4.10 and 3.3.2 ensures the proper organization of web page by dividing the webpage into different sections and each section have a proper heading. It also ensures that the page should have the proper information that can guide the people with a disability while navigating and providing input through a web page. Criteria 4.1.1 and 4.1.2 ensures the compatibility of the web content with future assistive technology. Failure of these success criteria will hinder the use of the assistive technological tool on the website by the disabled people thus making it inaccessible to them.

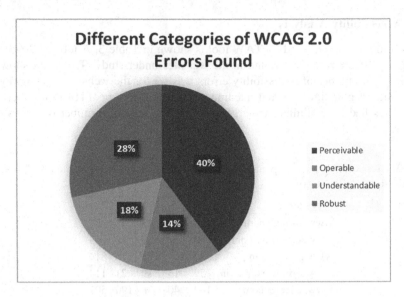

Fig. 1. Percentage of different categories of WCAG 2.0 errors

Another important factor that affects the people's ability to perceive the information presented on the web is the color contrast between the background of the web page and the text written on it. The color contrast error on the webpage will hinder the accessibility of the vision impaired person as he will not be able to recognize and distinguish between text, links and other web component present on the web page, thus decreasing the usability of website as the vision impaired person will not be able to perform simple task on airline website such as flight booking, route identification and even navigation on web page [22]. WCAG 2.0 accessibility guideline caters the need of these visually impaired people by including Success Criterion 1.4.1 and 1.4.3. The objective of former Success Criterion is to ensure that people with color vision disability should easily perceive the difference in color on the web page and later ensures the use of minimum contrast between text and background so that it can be perceivable and understandable by the people with low vision. All the websites under study had very low contrast shading with contrast errors ranging from 5(airindia express) to 164 (airvistara). Results of contrast error are shown in Table 5.

India is a diverse country in which more than 122 languages are being used so in the Indian context the webpage should present the content in other regional languages also and website should provide the option for changing the language of the web page which increases its usability so the Language of the webpage is an important criterion for increasing the accessibility of the webpage. WCAG Criteria 3.1.1. (Language of Page) ensures that user agent and assistive technology like screen reader can identify the syntax and semantics of the language used on the page so that the text of the page can be correctly rendered by them. On analyzing the website for language, it was found that almost all the websites were in English and had no other language option. Only 1 website provided the option of Hindi Language.

Another web accessibility feature important for differently abled people is the presence of a screen reader. Screen readers are audio interfaces that allow visually impaired users to use computers by reading the text on the computer screen. Only one website had a screen reader option. Results are shown in Table 5.

Table 4. Frequently occurring WCAG 2.0 violation found in airline websites

Guideline	Total errors	No. of websites
1.1.1 Non-text content(A)	503	9
1.3.1. Info and Relationship(A)	539	9
2.4.4. Link Purpose (In Context) (A)	122	9
2.4.9. Link Purpose(AAA)	178	9
2.4.10. Section Headings(AAA)	80	9
3.3.2. Labels or Instructions(A)	436	9
4.1.1. Parsing(A)	297	9
4.1.2. Name, Role, Value (A)	440	9

5.2   Usability Analysis

The usability of a website tells us how easily effectively, efficiently, and satisfactorily users use the websites and get the information they require. Apart from the content, user experience in using the website contributes greatly to increase the usability of the website and increases its user base. If the website is difficult to use, users are more likely to leave it.

The factors that affect the usability of the website include response time, loading time, broken links, search option, sitemap, and how a website is rendered on mobile devices.

Sitemaps are a visual representation of the entire website for users to understand the website's areas in a single glance. Sitemaps help users navigate the website quickly and easily. Sitemaps help a visually impaired user to jump to a specific section on the website. Only 5 websites under study had a sitemap. Average load time of websites under study was 4.6 s and the average response time was 2.1 s. The average page size was found to be 3273 kb. Larger pages take more time to load and consequently divert user's attention away from the page. Another factor impacting the usability of the website is the broken links. Broken links decrease the usability quality of the website. Broken links stop the tracking of search engine crawlers. This damages ranking by preventing search engines from indexing the pages. It has negative impact on user experience as it redirect visitors to error pages. There are not many broken links in the websites under study. All the websites were found to be mobile friendly except website of Zoomair airline for which the tool displayed the error message as the tool was restricted by the robot.txt for anaysing.

Table 5. Usability and Accessibility parameters data for airline websites

Website	Search	Multi-language	Sitemap	Load time	Page size (kb)	Broken links	Response time	Screen reader	Contrast errors
1	Y	E/H	Y	4.2	5734.4	4	2	Y	11
2	Y	E	Y	5.95	1536	3	1.199	N	31
3	Y	E	N	2.81	998.1	1	1.762	N	82
4	N	E	N	3.02	4608	2	1.48	N	164
5	N	E	N	6.04	1228.8	0	1.299	N	9
6	Y	E	Y	3.85	1228.8	2	1.526	N	23
7	N	E	Y	4.56	6246.4	1	7.641	N	5
8	N	E	N	6.25	3276.8	4	0.491	N	10
9	N	E	Y	5.06	4608	Access denied	1.58	N	30

5.3   Readability Analysis

Readability is the measure of how easy it is to read and understand the written text. It measures the complexity of the text in the content. The Internet is dynamic and fast changing. There is a very little window of opportunity to convey the message across to the users. If the content of the website is not easy to understand, the users will move on. The more readable content will also result in search engines favoring the site and help it rank higher. Therefore, it is very important that the information conveyed on the websites is easy to understand for larger masses. In order to determine the ease of readability, there are many algorithms. Flesch Kincaid Reading Ease(FKRE) is one such algorithm that is used to test the readability-ease of the website content. The scores usually range between 0 and 100. A high FKRE score indicates that the written text is easier to understand and the low value of Score symbolizes a complicated and difficult to understand text. FKRE uses the following formula to calculate the reading score:

$$\text{FKRE} = 206.835 - 1.015 * \left(\frac{words}{sentences} \right) - 84.6 * \left(\frac{syllables}{words} \right) \qquad (1)$$

For investigating the readability score of the websites under study, an online tool is used which test readability in three ways: test by URL, test by direct input and test by reference. In this study test by URL, was used to collect the readability score of websites. Result obtained is shown in Table 6.

The average readability score was found to be 53.3 which is interpreted as fairly difficult to read. While calculating the average, the readability score of jet airways whose score was reported by the tool as −62.3 was made zero as the lowest readability score could be zero.

Table 6. Flesch Kincaid Reading Ease (FKRE) score of airline website.

Website	FKRE
www.airindia.com	3.6
jetairways.com	−62.2
www.goindigo.in	65.3
www.airindiaexpress.in	74
spiceJet.com	64.5
www.goair.in	76.1
airvistara.com	70.2
www.trujet.com	60.8
www.zoomair.in	64.6

The result shows that most of the websites under study (nearly 78%) contains fairly easily understandable English text being understood by students in the age of 12 to 15 years. While 22% of the website (2 in number) has a readability score that is interpreted as very difficult to read and best understood by university graduates.

6 Conclusion

This paper evaluates the accessibility, usability, and readability of Indian airline websites. The results show that none of the websites under study satisfies the WCAG 2.0 accessibility guidelines thus making them less accessible to differently able people. These airline websites suffer from various usability issues such as broken links, lack of sitemap, larger page size resulting in poor usability and accessibility of airline website. The readability score shows that the majority of the website under study has easily understandable text. The result of the study shows that awareness regarding usability and accessibility standards are required among website designers and developers so that they can cater the needs of disabled people in terms of physical disability and language disability making a universally accessible online environment.

In June 2018 the third version of web content accessibility guideline known as WCAG 2.1 was released. WCAG 2.1 is built on WCAG 2.0 and has added seventeen new success criteria to improve the web accessibility for the user with a cognitive disability, low vision disability and disabilities of people on mobile devices, so in near future, we intend to take the evaluation of accessibility by WCAG2.1 guideline.

References

1. Sanou, B.: ICT Facts and Figures 2017 (2017)
2. Harteveldt, H.: The Future Of Airline Distribution A Look Ahead To 2017. IATA Atmospeheric Res. Gr. pp. 1–35 (2016)
3. Ivey, S.: The importance of usability and accessibility in design. https://careerfoundry.com/en/blog/ux-design/the-importance-of-usability-and-accessibility-in-design/

4. WHO: World Report on Disability - Summary. World Rep. Disabil. 2011, pp. 1–23 (2011)
5. Reid, L.G., Snow-Weaver, A.: Wcag 2.0. In: Proceedings of 2008 International Cross-disciplinary Work. Web Access - W4A 2008, p. 109 (2008)
6. Aktaş, E.B., Mutlu, Ö.: Website usability in marketing communications: the case of airline companies in Turkey. Am. J. Educ. Res. 3, 7–16 (2015)
7. Vatansever, K., Akgül, Y.: Performance evaluation of websites using entropy and grey relational analysis methods: the case of airline companies. Decis. Sci. Lett. 7, 119–130 (2017)
8. Murillo, B., Vargas, S., Moquillaza, A., Fern, L., Paz, F.: Usability Testing as a Complement of Heuristic Evaluation: A Case Study, pp. 434–444 (2017)
9. Elberkawi, E.K., El-firjani, N.F.M., Maatuk, A.M., Aljawarneh, S.A.: Usability Evaluation of Web-based Systems: A New Method and Results (2016)
10. Dominic, P.D.D., Jati, H., Sellappan, P., Nee, G.K.: A comparison of Asian e-government websites quality: using a non-parametric test. Int. J. Bus. Inf. Syst. 7, 220 (2011)
11. Apostolou, G., Economides, A.A.: Airlines Websites Evaluation Around the World, pp. 611–617 (2008)
12. Oyefolahan, I.O., Onuja, A.M., Zubairu, H.A.: An analytical approach to accessibility and usability evaluation of Nigerian airlines. Am. J. Comput. Sci. Inf. Technol. 6(2), 21 (2018)
13. Alwahaishi, S., Snášel, V., Nehari-talet, A.: Website evaluation an empirical study of Arabian Gulf airlines. Int. J. Inf. Stud. 1, 212–222 (2009)
14. Kaur, A., Dani, D., Agrawal, G.: Evaluating the accessibility, usability and security of Hospitals websites: an exploratory study. In: 2017 7th International Conference on Cloud Computing, Data Science & Engineering – Confluence, pp. 674–680. IEEE, Noida (2017)
15. Chisholm, W., Vanderheiden, G.: Web Content Accessibility Guidelines 1.0. https://www.w3.org/TR/WAI-WEBCONTENT/
16. Web content accessibility guidelines (WCAG) 2.0. https://www.w3.org/TR/2008/REC-WCAG20-20081211/
17. TAW. http://www.tawdis.net/
18. Pingdom website speed test. https://tools.pingdom.com/
19. Websitepulse. https://www.websitepulse.com/tools/
20. Web accessibility in mind. https://webaim.org/
21. Readability test tool. https://www.webfx.com/tools/read-able/
22. Ennis, A.: Testing airline web sites for accessibility compliance: use of colour. https://www.accessibilityoz.com/2015/11/testing-airline-web-sites-for-accessibility-compliance/

Amazon Reviews as Corpus for Sentiment Analysis Using Machine Learning

Akhila Ravi[1($\boxtimes$)], Akash Raj Khettry[1($\boxtimes$)],
and Sneha Yelandur Sethumadhavachar[2($\boxtimes$)]

[1] Computer Science Engineering, JSSATEB, Bangalore, India
akhilar028@gmail.com, akashrajkhettry5@gmail.com
[2] Department of CSE, JSSATEB, Bangalore, India
sneha.girisha@gmail.com

Abstract. Most of the users today, provide their reviews on the various products on the Amazon website. The reviews provided by users are usually compact and demonstrative. For this reason, it becomes an affluent source for sentiment analysis. The objective of the paper is obtaining comparisons of the working of four standard Machine Learning algorithms for classifying the sentiments of the considered Amazon product reviews dataset. In our work, we determine the performance of these algorithms, that is, how accurately can they classify the sentiment of an unknown review. The paper provides a brief insight on sentiment analysis and the comparison of the performance of the considered algorithms of the classification of the sentiments based on several performance metrics.

Keywords: Sentiment analysis · Amazon product reviews · Positive tag · Negative tag · Neutral tag · Probability of expressions

1 Introduction

Sentiment analysis is the process of recognizing positive and negative emotions and perspectives. Majority of research on sentiment analysis can be seen implemented at the complete document level, for instance differentiating a negative review from the set of positive reviews. The problem of classifying documents i.e., ascertaining if a review is of a positive or a negative sentiment, is examined by considering the overall sentiment and not by the topic of the document. However, tasks such as sentiment-oriented data interpretation, and extracting product reviews needs either sentence-level or phrase-level examination of the opinion. [8] Identifying sentiments is an arduous task. The crucial problems in sentiment analysis are identifying the representation of sentiments in textual documents and determining if the expressions suggest favourable or unfavorable view toward the subject of the document.

The sentence – "Caroline's father agreed with view of her teacher" is tagged 'positive' due to the presence of the positive sentiment word 'agreed'. If the word 'agreed' is replaced with a negative sentiment word 'disagreed', the sentence tag would change to 'negative'[5].

Sentiment analysis includes building models for two classification tasks: constructing models for classification of sentiments into positive and negative tags and a three-class classification problem of assigning positive, neutral or negative tags [10].

M. Singh et al. (Eds.): ICACDS 2019, CCIS 1045, pp. 403–411, 2019.
https://doi.org/10.1007/978-981-13-9939-8_36

Sentiment analysis involves recognition of

- Expression of sentiments,
- Probability and strength of the expressions, and
- Relationships of sentiments with the subject.

The components stated above are interrelated. For example, consider a sentence, "A conquers B", the word "conquers" indicates a favourable opinion for A and an unfavourable opinion for B [4].

A standard perspective to implementation of sentiment analysis proposes beginning with a set of positive and negative terms. In the considered sets, samples are labelled using their a priori prior probability. For example, the word 'good' indicates a positive prior probability, and the word 'worse' indicates a negative prior probability. The probability in terms of context, of the whole phrase in which a particular word occurs may be quite distinct from the prior probability of the considered word.

"Ben Thomas, chancellor of the International Energy Conservation Trust, summarizes ably the propelling of the reaction of environmental campaigns and programmes: "There is no logic behind believing that the contaminators are all of a sudden, changing to become reasonable."

In the sentence, "Trust," "ably," "logic," and "reasonable" are words which have positive prior probability, but all are not included to indicate positive sentiments. The word "logic" has negative prior probability, which makes the contextual probability of the sentence as negative. The phrase "no logic behind believing" causes changes to the probability of the proposition of the sentence which follows; since "reasonable" falls is included in the considered proposition, its contextual probability is negative. The text unit "Trust" is fragment of the considered expression and it does not convey any sentiment; hence, its contextual probability is found to be neutral. Likewise the term "contaminators": it just indicates to factories which pollute. Here, only the word "ably" has equal prior and contextual probability.

2   Background

In this section, we briefly discuss on the prior research on non topic-based text categorization. This field of work focuses on classification of the data in accordance with the style of the source or the source itself which serves as an important cue. For example, documents which involve native-language background, author, publisher (e.g., The Daily News vs. New York Times.), and "brow" (e.g., or low-brow or high-brow vs. "popular") all are under this category.

Another related field of research includes ascertaining the kind of content. One of the possible categories is the 'subjective genre'. While techniques for categorization of genre and detection of subjectivity can aid us in recognition of documents which denote a sentiment, while not proclaiming the particular classification method of ascertaining the sentiment [1].

Modern analysis on the classification based on sentiments have been partly based on knowledge. Few of the implemented work lays focus on classification of the semantic orientation of phrases or terms, using linguistic heuristics or a pre-selected group of seed words. The Prior work on categorization of the complete data based on sentiments, has frequently involved the utilisation of the manual or semi-manual construction of discriminant-word sets or models of cognitive linguistics.

Turney's effort of classifying the reviews is closest to the present work. He used a particular unsupervised learning method whose basis lies on the mutual data between the words "excellent" and "poor" and the document phrases. In distinction, we use many complete supervised machine learning techniques that are free of any prior-knowledge, with the aim of analysing the innate problem of the task.

Another work on Sentiment analysis uses natural language processing and information to extract writer's comments or reviews. In this work, Data text mining and hybrid approach of KNN Algorithm and Naïve Bayes Algorithm is used to find the sentiments of Indian people on Twitter [13].

It is shown that automatic classification of sentiment on corpus of noisy customer feedback data is also possible. Making use of vectors of large features along with technique of feature reduction, linear support vector machines can be trained which attains high classification accuracy. It is also observed that with addition of deep linguistics analysis contributes to classification accuracy [10].

3 Proposed Method

3.1 Data Corpus

The classification models are tested on an actual corpus of Amazon product reviews. In a time-frame of over two decades, several customers have contributed reviews to express their view and experiences regarding the purchased products. Each review can be analyzed to have one among the three sentiments-positive, negative or neutral.

The dataset is the standard dataset available in the 'Kaggle' website. The dataset obtained was raw and contained many redundant samples. After pre-processing of data, it was reduced to 119 distinct samples. The distribution of the Amazon product reviews dataset are presented in Table 1.

Table 1. Distribution of instances in the dataset.

Sentiment	Number of samples
Positive	65
Negative	33
Neutral	21
Total	119

3.2 Feature Extraction

The dataset gathered is utilized for extracting features which are used for training the classifier. Experiments have been implemented by considering features with n-grams and for general data extraction tasks, the number of occurrence of a keyword is an appropriate feature.

The procedure of extracting n-grams from an Amazon review is:

1. Filtering – In this step we eliminate the URL links (e.g. http://amazon.com), Amazon usernames, special words and characters.
2. Tokenization – Text is divided and tokenized by using spaces as a delimiter and removing punctuation symbols to construct a bag of words. Stemming and Lemmatization are used for further text processing.
3. Removing stop words – From the processed text, we exclude stop words-"the", "a" and "an" from the constructed set of words.
4. Constructing n-grams – We construct a corpus of n-grams from a set of continuous terms. A negation word like "not" and "no" is usually connected to a term which is prior to the term or follows it. Consider an instance, "I will not play ball" results in formation of two bigrams: "I will+not", "will+not play", "not+playball".

3.3 Naive Bayes Approach

One approach for classifying textual documents is to tag a considered record d of a class c '=argmax$_c$ P(c | d). Using Bayes' rule, derivation of the equation for the Naive Bayes classifier model. The Bayes' rule is observed as,

$$P(c|d) = \frac{P(c)P(d|c)}{P(d)} \tag{1}$$

where P(d) has no contribution in selecting c'. For estimating P(d | c), given class of d, the classifier fragments it by presuming the term fi's are conditionally independent. The proposed training function comprises of frequency estimation of P(c) and P(fi | c), by utilising smoothing [1].

3.4 Support Vector Machine Approach

Support vector machines (SVMs) are generally more effectual at standard text categorization, usually surpassing Naive Bayes. Rather than being probabilistic classifiers, these classifiers are large-margin classifiers, in distinction to Naive Bayes. For the bi-class case, the general intent backing the training method is identifying a hyperplane, denoted as vector $\hat{w}$, which not just distinguishes the records vectors in a class from another, but also ensures large margin of separation. The study correlates to a constrained optimization task. Let $c_j \in \{1, -1\}$ (denoting positive and negative respectively) be assumed as the right class for document d_j, then the equation is represented as

$$\hat{w} := \sum_j a_j c_j \hat{d}_j, a_j \geq 0 \tag{2}$$

where the α_j's can be retrieved by finding the solution for a problem which is dual optimization [1].

3.5   Random Forest Classifier Approach

The notion of ensembling decision trees is called as Random Forest, which can be obtained through integration of several decision trees. On considering single tree classifiers such as decision tree classifier, we may encounter issues such as outlier data or noisy data, which can influence the performance of the classifier function, whereas Random Forest as a classifier provides randomness and hence it is highly robust to noise and outliers. This classifier produces two kinds of randomness, one relating to data randomness and the other relating to features randomness. Since this classifier deals with integrating several Decision Trees, it includes many hyperparameters such as:

- How many trees are to be constructed for the Decision Forest.
- How many features are to be selected randomly.
- The depth of every tree.

Random Forest is regarded as an accurate and robust classifier since it involves the concept of bootstrapping and bagging [12].

3.6   K Nearest Neighbor Approach

KNN classifier is a type of instance based learning. In this approach, the classifier function is approximately local and all the computations are carried over until classification. Of all the machine learning algorithms, this is one of the simplest approach. In KNN classification, the output is class label to which a particular instance belongs to. An instance is classified by maximum scores of its neighbours with the instance being assigned to the class which has more similarity among its k nearest neighbour (here k denotes a small, positive integer). The nearest neighbour is determined using similarity index measures; generally distance functions are used. The distance functions used commonly by KNN are [13].

The Euclidean distance function is computed as

$$dist(A, B) = \sqrt{\frac{\sum_{i=1}^{m} (x_i - y_i)^2}{m}} \tag{3}$$

Manhattan distance function is computed as

$$D_{MANHATTAN}(x_i, x_j) = \sum_{k=1}^{d} |x_{ik} - x_{jk}| \tag{4}$$

3.7   Classifier

We built a sentiment analyzer classifier using four algorithms: Multinomial Naive Bayes classifier, Support vector machine, Random Forest Classifier and KNN classifier. However, among these three classifiers the Random Forest Classifier and Naive Bayes classifier yielded the best results. Performance metrics are used to obtain comparison of different classifier models implemented. We compute accuracy of the sentiment analysis classifier on the complete evaluation dataset, as

$$accuracy = \frac{N(correct\ classifications)}{N(all\ classifications)} \tag{5}$$

4   Experimental Results

The four algorithms, Naive Bayes algorithm, Support Vector Machine algorithm, Random Forest Algorithm and K-Nearest Neighbor algorithm, are implemented on the considered corpus and the following observations are obtained. The processed dataset was further split into training and testing sets of varied sizes. The different sized training and testing sets were implemented for the complete set of four algorithms and the accuracy obtained is as (Fig. 1 and Table 2).

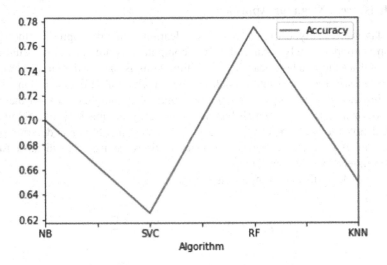

Fig. 1. Performance of the algorithms based on the accuracy

Table 2. Comparison of four algorithms for different sizes of training and testing sets.

Train size	Test size	Naive Bayes	Support Vector Machine	Random Forest	K-Nearest Neighbor
67	33	65	55.95	60.71	61.9
40	60	63.88	58.33	61.11	68.05
50	50	66.66	50	70	60
60	40	60.41	52.08	68.75	56.25

The above graph depicts accuracy produced by the four Machine Learning algorithms considered. We observe that the Random Forest classifier provides highest accuracy for the given dataset, while support vector machine provides the least accuracy (Fig. 2).

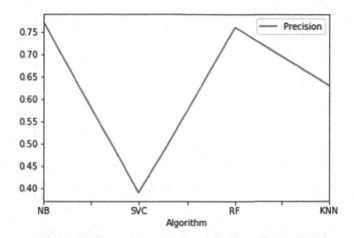

Fig. 2. Performance of the algorithms based on the precision

The above graph depicts precision of the four Machine Learning algorithms considered. We observe that the Naive Bayes classifier provides highest precision for the given dataset, while support vector machine provides the least precision (Fig. 3).

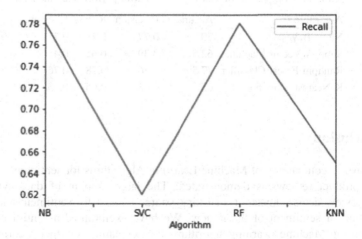

Fig. 3. Performance of the algorithms based on the recall

The above graph depicts recall of the four Machine Learning algorithms considered. We observe that the Naive Bayes classifier and Random Forest classifier provides highest recall for the given dataset, while support vector machine provides the least recall (Fig. 4).

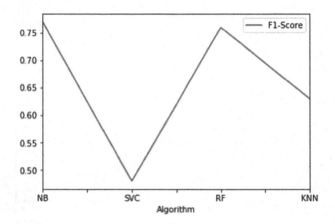

Fig. 4. Performance of the algorithms based on the F1-Score

The above graph depicts F1-Score of the four Machine Learning algorithms considered. We observe that the Naive Bayes classifier provides highest F1-Score for the given dataset, while support vector machine provides the least F1-Score (Table 3).

Table 3. Comparison of four algorithms with performance metrics.

Algorithm	Accuracy	Precision	Recall	F1-Score
Naive Bayes	70	0.77	0.78	0.77
Support Vector Machine	62.5	0.39	0.62	0.48
Random Forest Classifier	77.5	0.76	0.78	0.76
K-Nearest Neighbor	65	0.63	0.65	0.63

5 Conclusion

In this paper, a comparison of Machine Learning Algorithms for sentiment analysis of Amazon product reviews is demonstrated. The large amount of data available as Amazon review dataset makes it a striking source of data for sentiment analysis and classification of sentiment of the review. We have exemplified a sentiment analysis approach using Machine Learning algorithms for extricating sentiments corresponding to the positive or negative polarities for reviews in a text-document. However we could represent sentiments using varied interpretations which includes indirect interpretations which requires a certain amount of analytical reasoning, for a sentiment to be identified. Hence it has been challenging to show the expediency of our elementary scheme of sentiment analysis. The experimental observations obtained, however, demonstrate that insightful data on sentiments from almost all the documents, can be extracted using the proposed models. Out of the four implemented models, the Random Forest Classifier model produced the best accuracy metrics. In future work, we intend to explore even richer and sophisticated methods of linguistic analysis like, parsing, semantic analysis and topic modeling. The classifier models are capable of determining positive, negative and neutral sentiments of documents.

References

1. Pang, B., Lee, L., Vaithyanathan, S.: Thumbs up? Sentiment classification using machine learning techniques (2002)
2. Dave, K., Lawrence, S., Pennock, D.M.: Mining the peanut gallery: opinion extraction and semantic classification of product reviews (2003)
3. Yi, J., Nasukawa, T., Bunescu, R., Niblack, W.: Sentiment analyzer: extracting sentiments about a given topic using natural language processing techniques (2003)
4. Nasukawa, T., Yi, J.: Sentiment analysis – capturing favorability using natural language processing (2003)
5. Kim, S.-M., Hovy, E.: Determining the sentiment of opinions (2004)
6. Beineke, P., Hastie, T., Vaithyanathan, S.: The sentimental factor: improving review classification via human-provided information (2004)
7. Gamon, M.: Sentiment classification on customer feedback data: noisy data, large feature vectors, and the role of linguistic analysis (2004)
8. Wilson, T., Wiebe, J., Hoffmann, P.: Recognizing contextual polarity in phrase-level sentiment analysis (2005)
9. Pak, A., Paroubek, P.: Twitter as a corpus for sentiment analysis and opinion mining (2010)
10. Agarwal, A., Xie, B., Vovsha, I., Rambow, O., Passonneau, R.: Sentiment analysis of Twitter data (2011)
11. Parmar, H., Bhanderi, S., Shah, G.: Sentiment mining of movie reviews using random forest with tuned hyperparameters (2014)
12. Abirami, A.M., Gayathri, V.: A survey on sentiment analysis methods and approach (2016)
13. Goyal, S.: Review paper on sentiment analysis of Twitter data using text mining and hybrid classification approach (2017)

Blockchain for the Internet of Vehicles

R. Ramaguru$^{(\boxtimes)}$ⓘ, M. Sindhuⓘ, and M. Sethumadhavanⓘ

TIFAC-CORE in Cyber Security, Amrita School of Engineering, Coimbatore,
Amrita Vishwa Vidyapeetham, Coimbatore, India
ramaguru.90@gmail.com, sindhumsc@gmail.com, m_sethu@cb.amrita.edu

Abstract. Recent advancements in the Internet of Things and mobile internet helped the development of traditional Vehicular Adhoc-NETwork (VANET) based systems into the Internet of Vehicles (IoV). Vehicles in IoV make decisions based on the information from other vehicles and roadside infrastructure. This information helps them make critical decisions and alert the user about unpredictable situations. Security and privacy concerns in vehicles are increasing, hence it is important to address these issues, thus preventing malicious nodes transmitting falsified information or tampering critical communication data. In this paper, we propose RealTime Blockchain for the Internet of Vehicles for ensuring authentication and maintaining secure communication between the vehicles. The blockchain keeps track of communication information between vehicles to provide accountability. This paper also introduces smart contracts based vehicle services like automatic toll payment, vehicle servicing slot booking and payment, fuel payment, vehicle insurance renewal, etc. The proposed blockchain supports native cryptocurrency for the payments within the network.

Keywords: Internet of Vehicles · Automotive blockchain ·
Vehicular blockchain · Vehicular security · Blockchain for IoV

1 Introduction

Vehicles which were once just a medium of transport has transformed into huge computing and communication medium. Vehicles are getting smarter and autonomous with the rapid growth of the Internet of Things (IoT). The conventional Vehicle Adhoc Networks (VANETs) are changing into the Internet of Vehicle (IoV), which is seen as a subclass of the Internet of Things (IoT). VANET makes every participating vehicle into a wireless or mobile node, thus making vehicles to connect to each other, in turn creating a wide range network. The traditional vehicular network cannot provide global and sustainable services to customers because the objects involved are temporary, random and unstable, and the range of usage is local and discrete [1].

M. Singh et al. (Eds.): ICACDS 2019, CCIS 1045, pp. 412–423, 2019.
https://doi.org/10.1007/978-981-13-9939-8_37

1.1   Internet of Vehicles

Internet of Vehicles (IoV) can be defined as a large-scale distributed system for wireless communication and information exchange between Vehicle to X (V2X) (where X: vehicle, roadside smart device, human and the internet) according to agreed communication protocols and data interaction standards like the IEEE 802.11p standard, cellular technologies. IoV uses the IoT in the Intelligent Transport System. IoV is an integration of three networks namely an inter-vehicle network, an intra-vehicle network and vehicular mobile network [2]. IoV is an open and integrated network with high manageability, controllability, operationalization and credibility and is composed of multiple users, multiple vehicles, multiple things and multiple networks. IoV has two main technologies: vehicles' intelligence and vehicles' networking.

Vehicles' intelligence is the integration of driver and vehicle as a single entity and to make the environment intelligent by using network technologies.

Vehicles' networking consists of VANET, vehicle telematics and mobile internet. An ideal goal for IoV is to realize the in-depth integration of human-vehicle-thing-environment, reduce the cost, improves the efficiency of transportation & the service level of cities and ensure that humans are satisfied with and enjoy their vehicles [1].

As the opportunities and application provided by the IoV are more, the challenges posed by the IoV ecosystem is also multi-fold. Firstly, due to the high connectivity among the vehicles and between vehicles & roadside infrastructure, sensitive information is getting shared with unknown vehicles. Secondly, any malicious node could compromise a vehicle by sending false information which a vehicle might use for the decision-making process, resulting in a threat to the safety of the vehicle as well as the user. Thirdly, due to the access to the internet, a vehicle is accessible remotely, this poses a threat to take control of the complete vehicle.

1.2   Blockchain

A Blockchain is a decentralized computation and information sharing platform that enables multiple authoritative domains, who do not trust each other to cooperate, coordinate and collaborate in a rational decision making process [3]. Blockchain was first introduced in the well-known cryptocurrency known as Bitcoin by "Satoshi Nakamoto" through his whitepaper *Bitcoin: A Peer-to-Peer Electronic Cash System* [4]. Blockchain has gained velocity in its application in non-financial sectors like supply chain management, healthcare, global trade, provenance data, etc.

Immutability, consensus, smart contracts, shared information ledger, decentralization are some of the features seen as promising aspects of blockchain that makes it best technology for the future of IoV ecosystem to address these aforementioned challenges.

The rest of the paper is structured as follows: Sect. 2 describes the security and privacy issues in the IoV. Section 3 discusses the existing solutions and their shortcomings. Section 4 details the proposed architecture, workflow and comparative analysis with other blockchains. This paper is concluded in Sect. 5.

2   Security and Privacy Issues

Vehicles communicating to the external world and connected to internet face all the security vulnerabilities and possibly be hacked. The security risks of IoV can be mainly on four aspects namely Connected Vehicle Security, Intelligent Device Security, V2X Communication Security and Data Security.

2.1   Connected Vehicle Security

CAN Network. Controller Area Network (CAN) [5] bus is the robust vehicle bus allowing communications between microcontroller without a need of host computer. The CAN bus contains no direct support for secure communication. CAN bus offers mechanisms for data integrity, data consistency and error detection. Message spoofing is considered as one of the main threats to in-vehicle networks since it is possible to display a falsified value to a vehicle's speedometer or tachometer or even taking control of critical safety systems [6]. Some of the major issues in the CAN bus are lack of network isolation, lack of encryption, lack of authentication and access control, vulnerable to Denial of Service (DoS) attack.

OBD Interface. On-Board Diagnostics (OBD) is a computer-based system originally designed for emission control [7]. OBD systems allow the vehicle technician or the vehicle owner to access the status of various subsystems in the vehicle. OBD interface is the entry point for accessing the in-vehicle network [8]. Some of the major issues in the OBD interface are lack of authentication and inability to detect malicious code.

In-Vehicle Infotainment System. In-vehicle Infotainment is the combination of hardware and software inside a vehicle which provides information and entertainment services to users (driver and passengers). In-vehicle infotainment systems include radio, bluetooth, CD, TV, USB and the recent addition of smartphone connectivity. **Smartphone connectivity** allows the user to use the features in their smartphone through infotainment's interface. Android Auto [9], Apple CarPlay [10], Bosch mySPIN, Baidu's CarLife are applications that provide the above functionality. During this communication session, usually, the vehicle's sensitive data are sent to users smartphone.

Over the Air (OTA) Update. OTA Software upgrades are pushed from the OEM's server to the remote vehicles. This model lacks verification of the source and signature of the software going to be updated.

2.2   Intelligent Device Security

The operating system in the in-vehicle network and the mobile devices getting connected gives the vehicle computational intelligence. Vulnerabilities in the operating system and mobile applications installed in the end user device might threaten the safety of the vehicular environment.

2.3   V2X Communication Security

Various communication technologies are currently available for participating nodes to communicate between them in IoV. Some of them include Dedicated Short-Range Communications (DSRC), Long Term Evolution (LTE), World-wide Interoperability for Microwave Access (WiMAX), Infrared communications, Bluetooth, ZigBee (IEEE 803.15.4) [11]. This variety of communication technologies could be the main risk for short-range communications. Nodes acting maliciously in Vehicle to Vehicle communication and protocol cracking & man-in-the-middle in Vehicle to Network communication are threats in communication security.

2.4   Data Security

Data Security is the major security concern in the IoV. IoV involves variety and a large volume of data coming in at a faster rate. Processing and storing such a large volume of data is one of the main challenges ahead in IoV. Any mishandling of data might not only expose personally identifiable information (PII) resulting in a loss of user privacy but also harm vehicle safety, passenger safety and road management.

3   Related Work

The blockchain-based solution for connected vehicles is emerging recently along with the growth of blockchain. Three level "client-connection-cloud" model was proposed to secure data communication between nodes. This solution address security and privacy issues faced in IoV. Register Authority (RA) maintains a record of every vehicle in the network, which prevents any malicious vehicle from becoming a part of the network. The solution also addresses the flow of secure communication. Public-key cryptography is used to ensure secure communication between the vehicles [12].

CUBE Auto Blockchain is a multi-layer protection methodology to ensure a secure automotive ecosystem using Blockchain, Endpoint protection, Cloud-based intelligence along with Deep Learning and Quantum hash encryption for securing the connected car environment [13]. Their Blockchain security addresses the conventional blockchain issues through utilizing peer-to-peer hypermedia protocol and asymmetric encryption. Connected cars engage in multilateral communication from various external sources. Their Endpoint Security generates endpoints at all external connection points for protection. It uses the hash to scan, distinguish and identify over 300 million 'known attacks' with only 10 MB of storage space. For unknown attacks, its Cloud-based checkbox security is used. CUBE Cloud checkbox technology uses a transnational database which shares newly encountered malware with more than 50K corporations uploading information on a timely basis. The 'unknown attacks' are sent to the sandbox, where the files run in a virtual vehicle environment. The results are then uploaded to the database, which is shared among the vehicles. Native tokens are used as a payment medium, users gain tokens when they share their vehicle data and spend tokens when they use this data for decision making. These tokens like other cryptotokens can also be used to pay for the services at vehicle service providing centres who accept these tokens.

3.1 Shortcomings of Existing Solutions

Below are the shortcomings of the existing solutions

1. **No privacy:** The blockchain being transparent, information stored on the blockchain is available to everyone. No privacy is ensured.
2. **Usage of Heavy weight Encryption:** In IoV, vehicles most of time being in motion, using heavy weight encryption scheme would add latency to the communication and authentication mechanism. The existing solution does not explain how vehicle is interacting with roadside infrastructure and securing the communication between them.
3. **No scope for accountability:** Accountability is very important in case of autonomous vehicles. Existing solutions does not address this issue completely.

4   Proposed Work

This paper proposes to build a **Real-time Blockchain (RTBC)** platform - "**VAAHAN-Namchain**" with Artificial Intelligence capabilities to offer an end-to-end solution for IoV ecosystem's security, safety and privacy. Blockchain solution for the vehicular environment should be real-time as it is safety-critical and life-critical.

4.1 Blockchain Architecture

The proposed blockchain architecture is shown in Fig. 1

- Application is the topmost layer which interfaces the blockchain system and the users. These applications could be browser-based applications or mobile applications.
- Applications interact with smart contracts, tokens and consensus for providing intended services.

- Pluggable Byzantine Fault Tolerant consensus algorithms like Redundant Byzantine Fault Tolerance (RBFT) [14] or Quantum Byzantine Agreement (QBA) [15] is supported. The consensus algorithm employs Publicly Verifiable Secret Sharing (PVSS) [16] scheme, which ensures not only the participants can verify their own shares, but anybody can publicly verify.
- BigchainDB is the Blockchain database which is a blockchain with traditional database properties [17]. BigchainDB uses MongoDB for storage and Tendermint protocols [18] for inter-node communications. BigchainDB stores the assets (vehicle) details and communication transactions between the vehicles.
- InterPlanetary File System (IPFS) [19] is a decentralized file system for the storage which uses content-addressing and peer to peer method for storing files. IPFS is used to store vehicle logs which are typically large files. The content-address hash from the ipfs is then referenced in the blockchain transaction that is stored in BigchainDB.
- Libp2p [20] is a modular network stack that provides the peer to peer communication between various vehicles in the blockchain. This network layer is suitable for IoT communication. libp2p is transport agnostic, so it can run over any transport protocol. libp2p uses multiaddress [21], a self-describing addressing format.

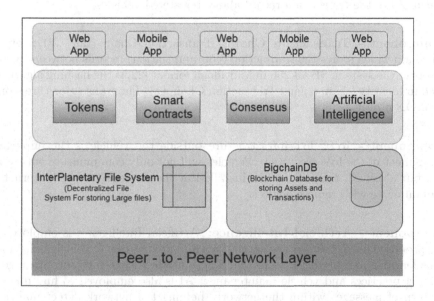

Fig. 1. Proposed blockchain architecture

4.2 Actors and Components of the Blockchain

Actors are the external participants interacting with the blockchain system through corresponding components.

Actor - Registration Authority: Registration Authority (RA) is the central government transport authority who verifies the new vehicles that are being registered and issues the Vehicle Registration Number. The importance and the need for RA is only during the initial phase of the registration.

Actor - Vehicle Owner: Vehicle Owner refers to any individual with valid identity proof of the country of residence and owns a vehicle. Vehicles are registered against the vehicle owner.

Actors - Vehicle Service Provider: Vehicle Service providers are the organization which provides vehicle-related services like fuel refill station, vehicle service station, vehicle insurance, etc.

Component - Identity Chain: Identity Chain (iota - ι) refers to the chain which stores the transaction record about registered vehicles.

Component - Transaction Chain: Transaction Chain (tau - τ) refers to the chain which stores the transaction (communication) records between various actors of the system. SHA3-256 in Multihash format [22] is the hashing algorithm used in Identity Chain (ι) and Transaction Chain (τ). The transactions are stored as JSON objects.

Component - IoT: IoT infrastructure outside the vehicle is the important component of the IoV ecosystem. Vehicles will not only communicate with vehicles but also with the IoT devices installed at the roadside and the internet to communicate with remote devices.

Component - Artificial Intelligence: Artificial Intelligence is employed in the proposed blockchain ecosystem to learn and predict user & vehicle behaviour. This learning and predict system would help the IoV system to encourage good driving practices and vehicle maintenance. AI is also employed to find unusual pattern of messages within the network, helping the network detect malicious activities and trigger corresponding actions using smart contracts.

Component - Smart Contracts: The proposed blockchain allows an organization like government agencies, vehicle service providers to deploy Smart contracts for end-user applications like insurance renewal, fuel refill payment, service payments, reward incentive, etc.

4.3   Workflow

The below section explains the workflow designed for Registration and Transaction in the proposed blockchain solution.

Registration Workflow. There is a Registration Authority (RA) who is usually the Transport Authority (Regional Transport Officer (RTO), in case of India) will be processing the new vehicle registration on receipt of application from the user through the vehicle showroom. The registration flow in the proposed blockchain is as below (as shown in Fig. 2)

1. The user submits the unique identification details (Aadhar Number) to the RTO via showroom coordinator and also present in person.
2. The vehicle showroom coordinator submits the vehicle along with the vehicle details like Engine number, Chassis number, Model number, Insurance details, etc. and the user information like Name, Address, Contact details, Nominee. This constitutes **a transaction** in the network.
3. The Registration Authority verifies the information provided and approves the transaction. This creates a block in the ι which needs to be validated.
4. The transaction is validated by the user, vehicle showroom coordinator, Nominee of the user, Transport Authority belonging to the different region, coordinator from vehicle manufacturer.
5. Once the transaction is validated, it is then added to the ι and a Distributed Identifier (DID) is given to the vehicle showroom coordinator.
6. Upon the receipt of this DID, the vehicle showroom coordinator, configures the vehicle with this DID.
7. This DID would be then used by the vehicle for communicating to the vehicles, roadside infrastructure, internet and any other IoT components part of the ecosystem.

   Distributed Identifier (DID) is an identifier that can be accessed and verified by all the participants in the network, to prove that the vehicle is a legitimate authorized node in the network. No other details stored on the ι can be accessed by others.

Transaction Workflow. All transactions other than the Registration transaction will be logged in the τ. Below usecase would describe how the τ is used to resolve security, privacy and practical issues.

   Every vehicle has a OBD unit monitoring the vehicle's health, whenever OBD identifies a malfunctioning a Diagnostic Trouble Code (DTC) is logged which would help the technician to resolve this issue. There is a diagnostics service smart contract running on the blockchain. Let us assume a vehicle's OBD has detected a critical fault and this vehicle is registered in our ι.

1. Vehicle sets the DTC inside the vehicle and sends the DTC code with the vehicle's DID, state information as a transaction to the τ.

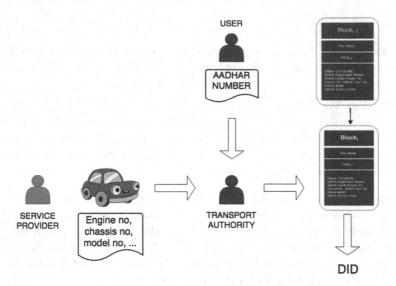

Fig. 2. Registration workflow

2. The diagnostic service smart contract running would be invoked based on this transaction. Based on the critical nature, two possible actions could be taken:
   - smart contract would ignore this transaction, if the DTC is non-critical.
   - or smart contract would add this transaction as a valid block in τ and alert the vehicle service center.
3. On receiving this, now the vehicle's service center technician can also perform two actions
   - perform a remote diagnostics to rectify the identified problem.
   - or alert the vehicle owner for immediate service, which is also logged as a transaction in τ
4. If the vehicle owner ignores this notification and if the vehicle or vehicle owner is affected because of the identified issue. Then Insurance claim for vehicle parts (incase of vehicle part failure) or free replacement of parts or insurance claim for loss of life shall not be provided, since he/she did not turn up to service center as alerted by service center technician.

Figure 3 displays the Transaction workflow as described. The above mentioned use case addresses the issue identified in the vehicle immediately and also provides accountability to avoid false and invalid insurance claims. This is only one of the many use cases that our smart contract based blockchain addresses.

4.4 Cryptocurrency

The proposed blockchain supports native cryptocurrency called "**Naanayam**". The cryptocurrency is unique tokens similar to ERC-721 tokens [23]. These can

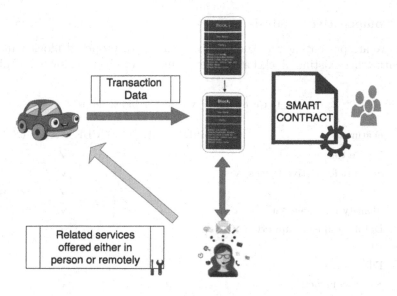

Fig. 3. Transaction workflow

be used for payment within the network like incentivization, transaction fees, as payment fee for service availed from a service provider. Below are some of the applications that uses smart contracts and cryptocurrency.

Reward for Good Driving Practices. Our proposed blockchain utilizes AI for learning and predicting user behaviour, this algorithm would also calculate a score called **driver score** based on the driving pattern, vehicle maintenance and renewal of insurance, payment of vehicle-related taxes to the government. A Reward Smart contract would distribute the reward on a timely basis to the qualified users in form of our cryptotokens. This is how the tokens are circulated within the proposed blockchain ecosystem.

Vehicle Service Booking and Payment. Smart vehicles continuously monitor their health and they could be made self-aware and decide themselves when should they visit for the servicing of the vehicle. Vehicles can automatically invoke a smart contract to book a slot for service with user consent. Once the vehicle service is completed, a smart contract would automatically deduct the corresponding charge from the user wallet.

Automatic Toll Payment. Automatic toll payment services are already available, this could be one of the applications where the usage of proposed cryptocurrency is helpful.

4.5   Comparative Analysis

Below we are presenting the comparative analysis of proposed blockchain solution with other existing blockchain system which could be used for IoV (Table 1).

Table 1. Comparison with other blockchains

Features	BigchainDB	Indy [24]	CUBE	VAAHAN
Native tokens			✓	✓
Support for native tokens	✓		✓	✓
ZKP		✓		✓
Identity management	✓	✓		✓
Database query support	✓			✓
BFT	✓	✓		✓
File storage				✓
Smart contracts		✓		✓

5   Conclusion

This paper discussed the security and privacy issues in IoV like but not limited to issues in CAN bus, OBD interface, in-vehicle infotainment, vulnerabilities in over the air software update and communication & data security. The proposed blockchain platform uses Registration authority (authorized government representative) to ensure the authentication of the vehicle as well as the user. The identity chain also provides pseudo-anonymity through a Distributed identifier. Smart contracts are used to trigger events based on communication between vehicle & service provider and vehicle & smart devices. In addition, the proposed native token can be used for incentivization for encouraging good user behaviour and payments across the network.

References

1. Yang, F., Wang, S., Li, J., Liu, Z., Sun, Q.: An overview of Internet of Vehicles. Wirel. Commun. Over ZigBee Autom. Inclin. Meas. **11**, 1–5 (2014)
2. Asia-Pacific Economic Cooperation: White Paper of Internet of Vehicles (IoV) (2014)
3. Chakraborty, S., Jayachandran, P.: Blockchain - Architecture. Design and Use cases, NPTEL Course Lecture (2018)
4. Nakamoto, S.: Bitcoin: a peer-to-peer electronic cash system (2008). www.bitcoin. org
5. Bosch CAN Specification 2.0. Robert Bosch GmbH (1991)
6. Buttigieg, R., Farrugia, M., Meli, C.: Security issues in controller area networks in automobiles. In: 18th International Conference on Sciences and Techniques of Automatic Control & Computer Engineering - STA 2017 (2017)

7. Wikipedia - On-Board Diagnostic. https://en.wikipedia.org/wiki/On-board_diagnostics. Accessed 30 Sept 2018
8. Yadav, A., Bose, G., Bhange, R., Kapoor, K., Iyengar, N.C., Caytiles, R.D.: Security, vulnerability and protection of vehicular on-board diagnostics. Int. J. Secur. Appl. **10**, 405–422 (2016)
9. Android Auto. https://www.android.com/auto/. Accessed 13 Mar 2019
10. Apple's CarPlay. https://www.apple.com/in/ios/carplay/. Accessed 13 Mar 2019
11. Ivanov, I., Maple, C., Watson, T., Lee, S.: Cyber security standards and issues in V2X communications for Internet of Vehicles. Living in the Internet of Things: Cybersecurity of the IoT, London 2018, pp. 1–6 (2018)
12. Arora, A., Yadav, S.K.: Block chain based security mechanism for Internet of Vehicles (IoV). In: 3rd International Conference on Internet of Things and Connected Technologies, (ICIoTCT), Elsevier (2018)
13. CUBE Intelligence: CUBE Whitepaper (2015). https://cubeint.io
14. Aublin, P., Mokhtar, S.B., Quéma, V.: RBFT: redundant byzantine fault tolerance. In: 2013 IEEE 33rd International Conference on Distributed Computing Systems, Philadelphia, PA, pp. 297–306 (2013)
15. Quantum Byzantine Agreement - Wikipedia. https://en.wikipedia.org/wiki/Quantum_Byzantine_agreement. Accessed 16 Nov 2018
16. Publicly Verifiable Secret Sharing - Wikipedia. https://en.wikipedia.org/wiki/Publicly_Verifiable_Secret_Sharing. Accessed 18 Nov 2018
17. BigchainDB GmbH: BigchainDB 2.0: The Blockchain Database (2018). www.bigchaindb.com
18. Ambili, K.N., Sindhu, M., Sethumadhavan, M.: On federated and proof of validation based consensus algorithms in blockchain. In: IOP Conference Series: Materials Science and Engineering, vol. 225, no. 1. IOP Publishing (2017)
19. IPFS - Content Addressed, Versioned, P2P File System. https://github.com/ipfs/papers/raw/master/ipfs-cap2pfs/ipfs-p2p-file-system.pdf. Accessed 08 Dec 2018
20. Libp2p - A Modular Network Stack. https://libp2p.io. Accessed 22 Oct 2018
21. Multiaddress Format. https://multiformats.io/multiaddr/. Accessed 22 Oct 2018
22. Multihash Format. https://multiformats.io/multihash/. Accessed 22 Oct 2018
23. Ethereum Request for Comments (ERC)-721. http://erc721.org. Accessed 02 Oct 2018
24. Hyperledger Indy. https://www.hyperledger.org/projects/hyperledger-indy. Accessed 02 Oct 2018

Implementation of Smart Indoor Agriculture System and Predictive Analysis

Md. Salah Uddin[1], Md. Asaduzzaman[2(✉)], Rafia Farzana[3(✉)],
Md. Samaun Hasan[1(✉)], Mizanur Rahman[1(✉)],
and Shaikh Muhammad Allayear[1(✉)]

[1] Department of Multimedia and Creative Technology,
Daffodil International University, Dhaka, Bangladesh
{salah.mct, hasan.mct, mizan.mct}@diu.edu.bd,
headmct@daffodilvarsity.edu.bd
[2] Instalogic Inc., Dhaka, Bangladesh
muhid.ewu@gmail.com
[3] Leotech, Dhaka, Bangladesh
rafiaborna8@gmail.com

Abstract. Day by day Indoor Agricultural system is becoming more popular and enhancing agricultural productivity. Smart agriculture systems call on different type of Internet of Things (IoT) capabilities to improve farming production and deliver new monitoring facilities. In Smart agriculture system, sensors are placed within the ground may record real-time data on soil moisture, temperature and pH. The main challenges of a smart agriculture system are the integration of these sensors and tying the sensor data to the analytics driving automation and response activities. When integrated, the use of data analytics can reduce the overall cost of agriculture and contribute to higher production from the same amount of area through precise control of water, fertilizer and light. The aim of this paper is to develop an automatic decision making system to watering, lighting and airing the plants based on sensor data. Finally, the paper gives an idea of a prediction formula to find the value of the sensors which will reduce the cost of the sensor.

Keywords: Agriculture · Sensors · Temperature and humidity · Light ·
Moisture · Arduino Uno · Prediction formula

1 Introduction

At present time, the most popular and fastest growing industry is Indoor Agriculture. The amounts of available arable land and water to support conventional agriculture are dwindling due to huge population. To provide food supply for huge population farmers are opening up indoor agriculture system. Farmers are using different types of technology and artificial intelligent to monitor the plants inside indoor agriculture system. Increased control allows for a higher degree of precision and also allows growers a wider range of crop selection. Maintaining optimal climate control is the most important factor for indoor farmers. The future of the agriculture industry is data and technology

© Springer Nature Singapore Pte Ltd. 2019
M. Singh et al. (Eds.): ICACDS 2019, CCIS 1045, pp. 424–435, 2019.
https://doi.org/10.1007/978-981-13-9939-8_38

based. Using modern technology, it is possible to control the climate. If we control the climate it is possible to increase the productivity in indoor agriculture system.

At present time, Farmers use different type of sensors to measure the environmental parameters according to the plant requirement in a smart agriculture system. The farmer also can create a cloud server for remotely accessing using IoT. The manual monitoring is totally eliminated here. The Arduino Uno enables the data processing and it is an open-source platform used for building electronics projects. Arduino consists of both a physical programmable circuit board and IDE (Integrated Development Environment) that runs on computer. The smart indoor agriculture system uses some sensors to provide information of the light levels, pressure, humidity, and temperature. These sensors can control the actuators automatically turn on lights, control a heater, turn on a mister or turn on a fan, all controlled through the Arduino Uno.

The paper is organized as follows: Sect. 2 contains an overview of existing approaches; Sect. 3 introduces proposed method and the algorithms to solve the issue; Sect. 4 explains the performance of the system; finally, Sect. 5 concludes the paper with limitations of the proposed approach.

2   Overview of Existing Approaches

Ref. no.	Proposed system	Technology used	Advantages	Disadvantages
[1]	Used remote controlled system for control the agriculture management	IoT, Wi-fi, Li-fi	Remote controlled farm	Controlling system is not automated
[2]	Their system can monitor temperature and humidity of the field	They have used Camera to interface with CC3200 for capture images	Making use of IoT on agriculture	Used expensive instruments
[3]	Agricultural cultivation technology with indoor aquaponics.	IoT, Smartphone	Monitoring the plants	Need to remember the ON/OFF switch

An agriculture-based survey says that indoor can give more productivity than normal cultivation in USA. Indoor agriculture can provide 4000 times more productivity than outdoor cultivation [5].

3   Proposed Method

The "Smart Indoor Agriculture System" is an automatic system where sensors are used for collecting data of temperature, humidity, light, moisture of soil. A smart automation watering system has been developed for watering the plants, LEDs for lighting, and a 12 V fan for air flow (it effects on heavy cold or dry season).

Based on sensors sense data, our developed automatic system can watering, lighting and airing the plants which is controlled by the code written in Arduino Uno.

The system is for indoor which is controlled by only the sensors. Here, LEDs are used for increasing the time of the day. So, it is not necessary to monitor the plants time as a result cost of the land will be decreased. The proposed technique is providing some features such as:

- The collected data provides the information about different environmental factors (humidity, light, air, temperature) which helps to monitor the system.
- Secondly, it includes smart control and intelligent decision making based indoor agriculture system on accurate real time field data.

3.1   Proposed Sensor Based Agricultural Monitoring System

In this project, several types of sensors are used to monitor the plants. Although, the system is in indoor so the climate change is not noticeable. The automation watering system, lighting system, airing system is the best part of the project which makes easier the agriculture system.

The actual code loads on Arduino Uno and relay module control the voltage of the device. This was the basic part of this project. Here, the materials that used for implementation of Smart Indoor Agriculture system.

DHT11 (Digital Humidity and Temperature Sensor)
The DHT11 is an ultra-low-cost digital temperature and humidity sensor which senses the steam of the environment and a thermistor to measure the surrounding air. It has digital input pins (Fig. 1).

Fig. 1.   DHT11 module

LDR (Light Dependent Resistor)
LDR is a light-controlled variable resistor and detect the darkness (Fig. 2).

Fig. 2. LDR (Light Dependent Resistor)

Soil Moisture

Soil moisture sensors are used to measure the volume of water content in soil (Fig. 3).

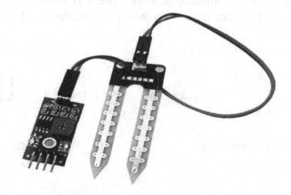

Fig. 3. Soil moisture sensor module

pH Meter

A pH meter is a tool that has capability to measures the hydrogen-ion activity in water-based solutions and indicates its acidity (Fig. 4).

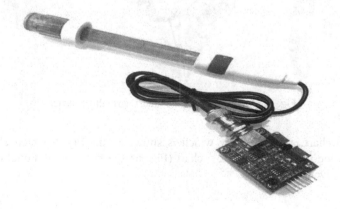

Fig. 4. pH meter

The pseudocode of the indoor agriculture system is:

1. **Input** Temperature, Humidity, pH, Soil Moisture, Light
2. **IF** Temperature>30 Or Humidity <30 **THEN**
3. Start Fan
4. **IF** Soil Moisture<45 **THEN**
5. Start Water Motor
6. **IF** Light <500 **THEN**
7. Start LED
8. **END IF**
9. **WRITE** Temperature, Humidity, pH, Soil Moisture, Light

Algorithm 1: Indoor Agriculture System

The architecture for the smart agriculture system is shown in the Fig. 5 which contains various services from the sensors when it is needed for the plants.

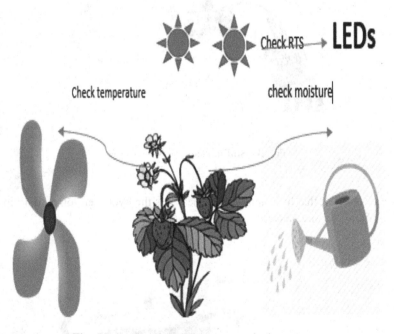

Fig. 5. Architecture of the smart agriculture system

The flowchart is given below which is shown in the Fig. 6 which clearly make sense about the project. In the Flow chart (Fig. 6) and Fig. 7 conditional on/off of an Actuator is given.

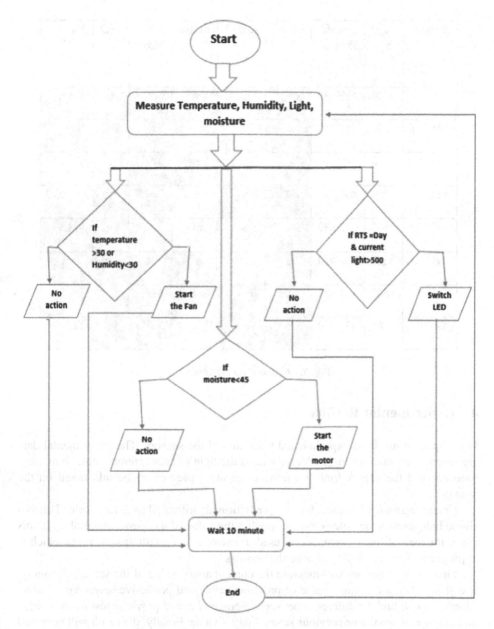

Fig. 6. Flow chart of smart agriculture system

After calculating proper situation to start or stop Actuator this simple graph can make full visual.

Moisture	Light in Day	Temp& Hum	Relay1	Relay2	Relay3	Water Motor	LED	FAN
>45	>500	>30‖<30	No	Yes	Yes	No	Yes	Yes
>45	>500	<30‖>30	No	Yes	No	No	Yes	No
>45	<500	>30‖<30	No	No	Yes	No	No	Yes
>45	<500	<30‖>30	No	No	Yes	No	No	Yes
<45	>500	>30‖<30	Yes	Yes	Yes	Yes	Yes	Yes
<45	>500	<30‖>30	Yes	Yes	No	Yes	Yes	No
<45	<500	>30‖<30	Yes	No	Yes	Yes	No	Yes
<45	<500	<30‖>30	Yes	No	Yes	Yes	No	Yes

Fig. 7. Actuator on/off condition.

4 Experimental Results

In this project has been experimented with data of the sensors. The experimental data are recorded in an excel sheet which contains the light intensity, temperature, humidity, moisture and the pH. A trial was done to create a prediction formula based on the results.

Linear regression is a most famous prediction algorithm all over the world. This is a single independent variable is used to predict the value of a dependent variable. In this paper the idea of linear regression is used to create a new prediction formula which is appropriate for predict the value of the sensors.

Firstly, the algorithm will measure the current actual value of the sensor. Secondly, it will calculate the average value of previous actual and predictive seven day's value. Thirdly, it will find the difference between average of actual previous seven day's value and average of predictive previous seven 7 day's value. Finally, the result will be added with the current actual value of the sensor. The pseudo code is shown below.

1. Input: Xn= Regularization value of 7th day,
   a[100] ←Actual value of previous seven days,
   b[100]←predictive value of previous seven days
2. Output: Xn+1= Desirable predictive value of tomorrow
3. Initialize sum=0, sum1=0
4. n←Input value
5. For i=0 to n-7 do
6. sum←sum+a[i]
7. End for
8. sum=sum/7
9. X1=sum←average of actual value of seven days
10. For j=0 to n-7 do
11. sum1←sum1+b[j]
12. End for
13. Sum1=sum1/7
14. X2=sum1←average of predictive value of seven days
15. Xn+1=Xn+(X1-X2)
16. End

Algorithm 2: The prediction formula

After using the above formula, the values of sensors at Night are recorded in an excel sheet and plotted in a graph. The graph is shown in Figs. 8, 9, 10, 11, 12, 13, 14, 15, 16 and 17). This is the visualization of the difference on the graph and X axis stands for the Day and Y axis stands for the value (Actual and predict) of the DHT11 sensor.

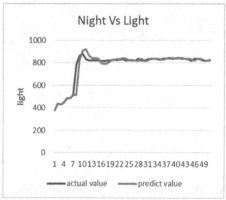

Fig. 8. Actual value Vs predict Light value at Night

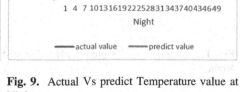

Fig. 9. Actual Vs predict Temperature value at Night

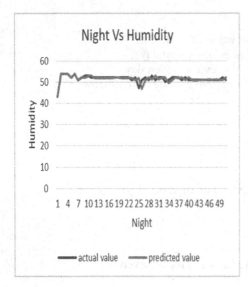

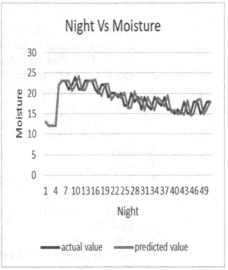

Fig. 10. Actual value Vs predict Humidity value at Night

Fig. 11. Actual value Vs predict Moisture value at Night

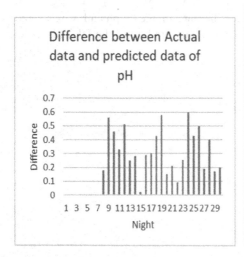

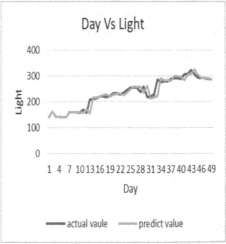

Fig. 12. Actual value Vs predict pH value at Night

Fig. 13. Actual value Vs predict Light value at Day

On the above graph (Figs. 8, 9, 10, 11 and 13) the blue series is the actual value of the sensor and the orange series is the predict value. It shows the difference between actual and predict value graphically.

In case of Day the value of the sensors are very different. The data of sensors at Day has been recorded in an excel sheet and plotted graphs using same formula.

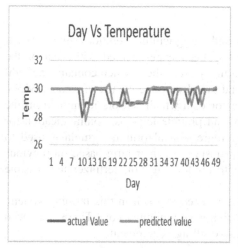

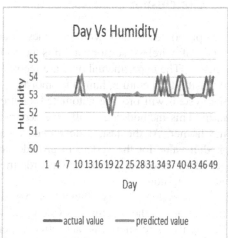

Fig. 14. Actual Vs predict Temperature value at Day

Fig. 15. Actual value Vs predict Humidity value at Day

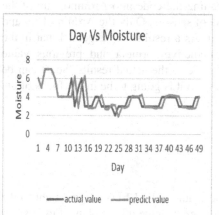

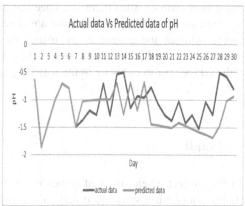

Fig. 16. Actual value Vs predict Moisture value at Day

Fig. 17. Actual value Vs predict pH value at Day

On the above graph (Figs. 14, 15, 16 and 17) the blue series is the actual value of the sensor and the orange series is the predict value. It shows the difference between actual and predict value graphically.

This is the visualization of the difference on the graph and X axis stands for the Day and Y axis stands for the value (Actual and predict) of the DHT11 sensor.

5 Conclusion

The proposed research work provides smart indoor agriculture solution using different types of wireless sensor and this project has been experimented with data of the sensors. The experimental data are recorded in an excel sheet which contains the light intensity, temperature, humidity, moisture and the pH. Due to the use of smart devices, the system will provide automated solution for data which sensors monitor from the farm. This methodology will give accuracy and provide low-cost communication for the farmer. At the last, a developed linear regression algorithm formula is used to predict value for the system to provide farmer status of their farm based on previous actual value to take decision about crop monitoring for irrigation, fertilizer and possible future decision.

This system is very efficient as they do not need any soil in this farming system. Instead of soil the system uses Coco-peat which is very popular now. There is no need for highly toxic chemicals and other expensive till age equipment.

Future Work
Future work should focus on implementing framework based model on the predictive value where there is no use of sensor. Our aim is to reduce cost of the sensor, and based on the predictive methodology and it is expected that the framework shows accurate results. This research paper future aim is uploading the code into Arduino Uno of the prediction formula, then there is no need to use of sensors. Only the Arduino Uno and the actuators like LEDs, Fan, motor are needed. As a results it is expected that in the future without using sensor, by using the predictive formula and previous value Arduino Uno will give a result that will very close to the actual results. So, it can be reduced the cost to cultivate in the way of smart. So it is going to be in the focus of the authors' future research.

Appendix

In this project when low light comes in the room automatic LED can give light to the plant. Water Airflow can also make the growing environment of a plant (Fig. 18).

Fig. 18. The main prototype for smart indoor agriculture system

References

1. Shareef Mekala, M., Viswanathan, P.: A novel technology for smart agriculture based on IoT with cloud computing. IEEE, pp. 75–85 (2017). (17224855)
2. Prathibha, S., Hongal, A., Jyothi, M.: IOT based monitoring system in smart agriculture. In: IEEE Conferences, pp. 81–84 (2017)
3. Priyadharsnee, K., Rathi, S.: AN IoT based smart irrigation system. Int. J. Sci. Eng. Res. **8**(5) (2017). ISSN 2229-5518
4. Vernandhes, W., Salahuddin, N., Kowanda, A., Sari, S.: Smart aquaponic with monitoring and control system based on IO. In: 2017 Second International Conference on Informatics and Computing (ICIC), Jayapura, Indonesia, pp. 1–6. IEEE (2018)
5. Taylor, L.: Agrilyst reports indoor agriculture over 4k times more productive than outdoor commodity crop production, pp. 1–2 (2018). agfundernews.com
6. Badhiye, S.S., Sambhe, N.U., Chatur, P.N.: KNN technique for analysis and prediction of temperature and humidity data. Int. J. Comput. Appl. **61**(14), 7–13 (2013)
7. Ray, P.: Indoor Aeromycroflora at Institute of Agriculture Library (Visva-Bharati): a study. SRELS J. Inf. Manag. **54**(1), 37 (2017)
8. Apel, A., Weuster-Botz, D.: Engineering solutions for open microalgae mass cultivation and realistic indoor simulation of outdoor environments. Bioprocess Biosyst. Eng. **38**(6), 995–1008 (2015)
9. Kleinstiver, P., Speechley, M.: PHP25: does the past predict the future? Value Health **6**(3), 207 (2003)
10. Kim, Y., Yarlagadda, P.: Sensors, measurement and intelligent materials (n.d.)
11. CityCrop: CityCrop—Automated Indoor Farming (2018). https://www.citycrop.io/. Accessed 5 Apr 2018

Data Dimensionality Reduction (DDR) Scheme for Intrusion Detection System Using Ensemble and Standalone Classifiers

Ashu Bansal$^{(\boxtimes)}$ and Sanmeet Kaur$^{(\boxtimes)}$

Department of Computer Science and Engineering,
Thapar Institute of Engineering and Technology, Patiala, India
ashubansal8@gmail.com, sanmeetkbhatia@gmail.com

Abstract. The growth in IT sector is touching new pinnacles day by day, and hence the number of devices that are connected through Internet have increased tremendously, resulting into Big Data issue, more computation time and an increased rate of malicious activities. Thus, to provide more security, Intrusion Detection System (IDS) were introduced which played a major role in the past few years, when it comes to security. With an intent to develop a more efficient IDS, one needs to explore several Data Mining Strategies in the domain of Data Analytics. While consulting the domain of Data Analytics one fundamental problem that is encountered is high dimensional data. Hence, for reducing the dimensions of data a Data Dimensionality Reduction Scheme has been proposed which minimizes the number of features, dimensions and tuples in the Training set in order to increase detection rates for IDS. The scheme proposed has been evaluated with two approaches - Ensemble approach and the Standalone Classifier approach. The dataset used for the experiment is benchmark dataset NSL-KDD and latest intrusion dataset CICIDS 2017.

Keywords: Intrusion Detection System (IDS) ·
Data Dimensionality Reduction (DDR) · Ensemble · Standalone

1 Introduction

Last decade witnessed exceptional growth of devices communicating over Internet. The growth has already touched acme, hence, opening a pool of opportunities for Hackers. Evidently, the side effect could be analyzed by realizing, that, the number of malicious activities like MITM, DDoS, Spoofing have also become more common in today's generation of computing. On the other hand, we have shields like Intrusion Detection System (IDS) for Cyber Security, which have defended such attacks and would possibly protect our devices in future too. Intrusion Detection System is the automated controller of network traffic or the events occurring in the network and it examines them by searching for mischievous activities [1]. Additionally, it scrutinizes the attacks done by the hacker to ruin the Confidentiality, Integrity, and Availability (CIA). IDS and the humongous amount of data it uses are inter-related when it comes to speed and time. Data being collected from data packets contains a lot of irrelevant information which adds to the increased size and dimension of data sets used by IDS, hence leading

© Springer Nature Singapore Pte Ltd. 2019
M. Singh et al. (Eds.): ICACDS 2019, CCIS 1045, pp. 436–451, 2019.
https://doi.org/10.1007/978-981-13-9939-8_39

to the high dimensionality problem. No doubt, IDS encounters lot many problems such as low detection rate, high false positive rates due to the intense quantity of data.

In order to overcome the challenges like high dimensional data [2], we hereby propose a strategy for reducing dimension of data or Data Dimensionality Reduction (DDR) Scheme. Often, Data Reduction Schemes subjects to loss of information in the Training phase [15], but they also hold credit for high running time during the same Training phase. The DDR scheme so proposed promises less computation time for building classifier and would also lead to increase in detection rates. This high accuracy is yielded through the usage of Standalone and Ensemble classifier approach. Further, each of the classifier approach is divided into two categories, such as Extreme Gradient Boosting algorithm (XGBoost) and Conditional Inference tree (CTree) fall under Ensemble approach and Support Vector Machine (SVM) and Neural Network (NNet) could be grouped as the Standalone classifier.

This paper has been arranged in the following way - Sect. 2 discusses the related work about data reduction challenges. The proposed scheme has been introduced in Sect. 3. Further, Sect. 4 provides the brief introduction about the chosen datasets. For Experimentation and description of used classifiers, Sect. 5 could be referred and ultimately, the conclusion and future work are outlined in Sect. 6.

2   Related Work

One major issue in the domain of Big Data is Dimensionality Reduction. In IDS Training and Testing of models consume a lot time as the datasets are high in dimensions. This causes more consumption of resources and hence less detection stability. In order to make the detection more accurate and stable, the data must be relevant with lesser dimensions. This could be done by eliminating the data that doesn't contribute to detection before the training of classifiers. Therefore, a need to develop an effective feature reduction policy [35], [36] is a must thing, as it can reduce time and provide more accurate results with IDS. Data Dimensionality reduction can be done either in tuple (instance) or in terms of column (features) [13]. Apparently, three methods have been proposed so far: feature selection [16–18], tuple selection [19–21] and hybrid technique, where feature and tuple selection are grouped as discussed in [13, 14].

Various researchers use different kind of approaches to find better results. As like, Chou et al. [22] describe the feature selection on the basis of correlation. They used Symmetric Uncertainty algorithm for finding the correlation between features. Ahmad et al. [23] uses Principal Component Analysis method for finding the related feature and select feature through Genetic Algorithm by choosing highest Eigen values. Sharma et al. [24] chooses an entropy-based filter for feature selection followed by Naïve Bayes classifier to find an intrusion.

Al-Jarrah et al. [25] selects the feature based upon Random Forest approach, that is actually not a suitable idea for selecting the feature, because, on the basis of this classifier we cannot judge the selection. Their result leads to huge information loss. In [26], SVM and simulated annealing is used to define the feature set. This approach selected 23 features out of 41 in KDDCUP 99 dataset. Like [20, 21] describes the instance or tuple reduction strategy for a large dataset, but in this there is the issue with the runtime.

Furthermore, in [27] feature selection is done through the mutual information among the feature and the class. However, this mutual information gave unbalanced sample distribution set which has a great impact on the IDS performance. Wang et al. [28] describes the wrapper approach for feature selection. This approach utilizes the classifier for the selection process, that takes too much time to build the model for IDS. Saurabh et al. [30] describe the vitality based feature reduction approach which can identify important feature and anomalies in IDS through Naïve Bayes classifier.

Shantharajah et al. [31] use the NSL-KDD dataset and SVM and Naïve Bayes, also Decision tree (C4.5, J48) has been implemented on it. From their findings, it was noticed that the best accuracy for all kinds of attack was given by C4.5, considering that the normal data possess 6 feature subsets. Shadi et al. [32] describe the voting algorithm to finding the reduced feature set. They find only 8 features to train the classifier. This technique has a great loss of useful information for finding an attack in an accurate manner. Even they utilized the NSL-KDD dataset for intrusion detection.

Considering all the existing approaches, we can say that they have many pros and cons in terms of accuracy and loss of useful information when it comes to finding an attack. Even the redundant data has increased the complexity of the IDS. Hence, depending on literature survey, we hereby propose an intelligent IDS through this study which also showcases a feature selection algorithm that selects only those features that have a great impact.

3   Proposed Methodology

In this section, we introduce Data Dimensionality Reduction (DDR) scheme more profoundly. As shown in Fig. 1, DDR contains various steps including preprocessing, Feature Selection, Dimensionality Reduction and Tuple Reduction. First, Data numericalization has been performed on training dataset (D). In this step the normal traffic is represented as 0 and rest of the traffic i.e. abnormal traffic is represented by 1. After that, Data Dimensionality Reduction has been performed on training dataset.

The selected methods calculate the correlation amongst an attribute and class with the use of different measures and after analyzing, we found that the most frequently used metrics are entropy based (Information Gain, Gain Ratio, and Symmetric-Uncertainty), Statistical based (ChiSquared) and Instance-based (ReliefF, oneR) [13]. Our approach is based on three algorithms one from each category i.e. Symmetric-Uncertainty (SU), Chi-squared (CHI) and ReliefF (RF). Moreover, in [14], Information Gain algorithm has been chosen for the entropy-based filter, which has a problem with their criterion as mentioned in [5] because it is biased towards feature with fewer values. In the proposed approach, Symmetric-Uncertainty has been used as entropy-based filter.

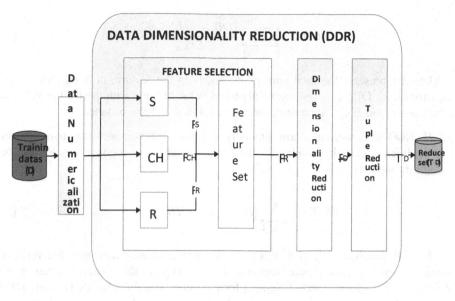

Fig. 1. Scheme for Data Dimensionality Reduction (DDR)

Symmetric-Uncertainty (SU) [13] measures the amount of information regarding feature related to the class or label. The SU is measured by using the below formula.

$$SU(P, Q) = \frac{H(P) - H(Q) - H(P, Q)}{H(Q) + H(P)} \tag{1}$$

Where H(P) illustrates the entropy for variable P (i.e. Features). Let $p(a)$ be the prior probabilities of all the features represents as of P and Q is another random variable (i.e. class). H(P) (or H(Q)) computed through the following formula.

$$H(P) = - \sum_{a \in P} p(a) log_2 p(a) \tag{2}$$

H(P, Q) measure the conditional entropy that defines the uncertainty of P for the given variable Q. $H(P, Q)$ is computed through the below formula.

$$H(P, Q) = \sum_{b \in Q} p(b) \sum_{a \in P} p(a|b) log_2 p(a|b) \tag{3}$$

Where $p(a|b)$ describe the posterior probability of a given the value of b of Q.

Chi-Squared (CHI) [33] is a statistical metric which computes the correlation amongst the features and class. Pearson chi-square static has been used to measure the correlation and it is computed through the below formula.

$$CHI = \sum_{m=1}^{t} \sum_{n=1}^{n_l} \frac{\left(OB_{m,n} - EX_{m,n}\right)^2}{EX_{m,n}} \tag{4}$$

Where t represents the total number of values in the feature, n_l is the number of labels (or class). $OB_{m,n}$ represents the observed value of tuple with the feature value m in the class n and $EX_{m,n}$ represents the expected mean of the instance.

ReliefF (RF) [34] measures how uniquely a feature differentiates the instances for same or different class by looking for the nearest neighbor of the instance. RF can be measure through the following formula.

$$RF(P) = \frac{1}{h} \sum_{e=1}^{h} [DF(g_i, g_a) - DF(g_i, g_b)] \tag{5}$$

Where, P represents a feature, h is the total number of instances, g_i is the value of feature. Then the differentiate function $DF()$ compare the feature values from $DF(g_i, g_a)$ for the former and $DF(g_i, g_b)$ for the latter. The differentiate function $DF()$ is defined below, where g_{min}, g_{max} are the minimum and maximum values of P respectively.

$$DF(P_1, P_2) = \frac{|g_1 - g_2|}{g_{max} - g_{min}} \tag{6}$$

In Feature and Tuple Selection of DDR scheme Symmetric-Uncertainty algorithm (F_{SU}) obtains a score (S_{SU}), which assigns a score $S_f \in S_{SU}$ to every feature f given their relevance. For this, when F_{SU} equals S_{SU}, its score mean μ_{SU} can be computed. In case feature f meets the value $S_{SU} > \mu_{SU}$, then f is assigned to feature set F_{SU}. For other algorithms, the same strategy has been applied to get features. Reduced feature F_R is obtained by $F_{SU} \cup F_{CHI} \cup F_{RF}$. After selecting the reduced feature set (F_R), Dimensionality Reduction step has been performed in which the columns representing all features f does not belong to F_R. Consequently, we obtained a reduced data set (R_D). Later on, in tuple reduction, the removal of duplicate instances from the R_D, who has same feature values and same class and get the final reduced dataset (TR_D). This approach is illustrated in Algorithm 1.

Algorithm 1: Feature and Tuple Selection Algorithm

Step 1: Input original dataset D after data numericalization that include features P
and target class (= Label) Q.

Step 2: Repeat step 3 to step 5 in parallel order.

Step 3: For each feature P_i

Step 3.1: Calculate score S_{su} for each feature f using Symmetric-
Uncertainty ($S_f \in S_{su}$).

Step 3.2: Sort S_{su} in descending order.

Step 3.3: Compute mean μ_{su} for score (S_{su}).

Step 3.4: if feature f satisfy $S_{su} > \mu_{su}$.

Step 3.5: Feature f is assigned to feature subset F_{su}.

Step 4: For every feature P_i

Step 4.1: Evaluate score S_{CHI} for each feature f using chi-squared ($S_f \in S_{CHI}$).

Step 4.2: Arrange S_{CHI} in decreasing order.

Step 4.3: Compute mean μ_{CHI} for score (S_{CHI}).

Step 4.4: if feature f satisfy $S_{CHI} > \mu_{CHI}$.

Step 4.5: Feature f is assigned to feature subset F_{CHI}.

Step 5: for every feature P_i

Step 5.1: Evaluate score S_{RF} for each feature f using reliefF ($S_f \in S_{RF}$).

Step 5.2: Sort S_{RF} in descending order.

Step 5.3: Compute mean μ_{RF} for score (S_{RF}).

Step 5.4: if feature f satisfy $S_{RF} > \mu_{RF}$.

Step 5.5: Feature f is assigned to feature subset F_{RF}.

Step 6: Reduced feature set $(F_R) = F_{su} \cup F_{CHI} \cup F_{RF}$.

Step 7: Remove the feature f from D which are not available in F_R and

get reduced dataset R_D.

Step 8: Remove the duplicate tuple from R_D and get final reduced dataset TR_D.

4 Dataset Description

For the experimental purpose and DDR scheme's evaluation, two datasets have been considered, which are benchmark NSL-KDD dataset and CICIDS 2017 dataset.

NSL-KDD Dataset: This dataset is the revised form of KDD Cup 99 dataset. It almost covers the inherent drawbacks of KDD Cup 99 dataset. NSL-KDD is the finest version of KDD Cup 99 dataset. In NSL-KDD, a number of records in train and test sets are acceptable. This improvement makes the dataset consistent and comparable. The dataset consists of 40 features and one label by which abnormal behavior is detected. Furthermore, NSL-KDD dataset has training and testing sets which include 125973 and 22544 instances respectively. Table 1 depicts the name of that 40 features and one Label (normal and attack).

Table 1. Features of NSL-KDD

S no.	Feature name	S no.	Feature name
1	Duration	22	Is_guest_login
2	Protocol_type	23	Count
3	Service	24	Serror_rate
4	Src_bytes	25	Rerror_rate
5	Dst_bytes	26	Same_srv_rate
6	Flag	27	diff_srv_rate
7	Land	28	Srv_count
8	Wrong_fragment	29	srv_serror_rate
9	Urgent	30	srv_rerror_rate
10	Hot	31	srv_diff_host_rate
11	Num_failed_logins	32	Dst_host_count
12	Logged_in	33	Dst_host_srv_count
13	Num_compromised	34	Dst_host_same_srv_count
14	Root_shell	35	Dst_host_diff_srv_count
15	Su_attempted	36	Dst_host_same_src_port_rate
16	Num_root	37	Dst_host_srv_diff_host_rate
17	Num_file_creation	38	Dst_host_serror_rate
18	Num_shells	39	Dst_host_srv_serror_rate
19	Num_access_files	40	Dst_host_rerror_rate
20	Numoutbound_cmds	41	Dst_host_srv_rerror_rate
21	Is_hot_login	42	Label

CICIDS 2017 Dataset: The CICIDS 2017 dataset [3, 4] has been created by the Canadian Institute of Cybersecurity (CIC) in 2017 which is used in this research and it comprises of mandatory and revised attacks such as DoS, DDoS, Brute Force, XSS, SQL injection, Infiltration, Port scan, and Botnet. The earlier publically available datasets lack traffic diversity, volumes, anonymized packet information payload, restraints on the variety of attacks, lack of the feature set and metadata. Thus, CICIDS 2017 overpower the issues like various protocols such as HTTP, HTTPS, FTP, SSH and email protocol are present. The dataset listed on Wednesday has been chosen which consists of a diverse type of DoS Attack. Subsequently by capturing the network traffic, the .pcap file is converted to CSV file using CICFlowMeter [5]. Denial-of-Service attacks present in this dataset have been categorised into five classes, namely DOS Slow Loris, DOS Slowhttptest, DOS Huk, DoS Goldeneye and recently talked about attack called Heartbleed. The dataset consists of 79 features suggested by CIC [5] presented in Table 2.

Table 2. Features of CICIDS 2017

No	Feature	No	Feature	No	Feature
1	Source Port	28	Bwd IAT Total	55	Average Packet Size
2	Destination Port	29	Bwd IAT Mean	56	Avg Fwd Segment Size
3	Protocol	30	Bwd IAT Std	57	Avg Bwd Segment Size
4	Flow Duration	31	Bwd IAT Max	58	Fwd Avg Bytes/Bulk
5	Total Fwd Packets	32	Bwd IAT Min	59	Fwd Avg Packets/Bulk
6	Total Backward Packets	33	Fwd PSH Flags	60	Fwd Avg Bulk Rate
7	Total Length of Fwd Pck	34	Bwd PSH Flags	61	Bwd Avg Bytes/Bulk
8	Total Length of Bwd Pck	35	Fwd URG Flags	62	Bwd Avg Packets/Bulk
9	Fwd Packet Length Max	36	Bwd URG Flags	63	Bwd Avg Bulk Rate
10	Fwd Packet Length Min	37	Fwd Header Length	64	Subflow Fwd Packets
11	Fwd Pck Length Mean	38	Bwd Header Length	65	Subflow Fwd Bytes
12	Fwd Packet Length Std	39	Fwd Packets/s	66	Subflow Bwd Packets
13	Bwd Packet Length Max	40	Bwd Packets/s	67	Subflow Bwd Bytes
14	Bwd Packet Length Min	41	Min Packet Length	68	Init_Win_bytes_fwd
15	Bwd Packet Length (avg)	42	Max Packet Length	69	act_data_pkt_fwd
16	Bwd Packet Length Std	43	Packet Length Mean	70	min_seg_size_fwd
17	Flow Bytes/s	44	Packet Length Std	71	Active Mean
18	Flow Packets/s	45	Packet Len. Variance	72	Active Std
19	Flow IAT Mean	46	FIN Flag Count	73	Active Max
20	Flow IAT Std	47	SYN Flag Count	74	Active Min
21	Flow IAT Max	48	RST Flag Count	75	Idle Mean
22	Flow IAT Min	49	PSH Flag Count	76	Idle packet
23	Fwd IAT Total	50	ACK Flag Count	77	Idle Std
24	Fwd IAT Mean	51	URG Flag Count	78	Idle Max
25	Fwd IAT Std	52	CWE Flag Count	79	Idle Min
26	Fwd IAT Max	53	ECE Flag Count	80	Label
27	Fwd IAT Min	54	Down/Up Ratio		

5 Experimentation

This section, showcases the performance of recommended DDR scheme on the benchmark NSL-KDD and CICIDS 2017 dataset in presence of both, ensemble and standalone classifiers. The experiments are executed on Intel Quad Core 3.2 GHz processor having 8 GB RAM. R Studio has been used for conducting experiments. The details of chosen classifiers are presented as followed:

5.1 Ensemble Approach

Extreme Gradient Boosting classifier (XGBoost) [9] is extended version of Gradient Boosting Machine. It integrates the weak learner into an individual strong learner in a repetitive method. The whole algorithm is based on assigning weights to the learner. To find, a strong learner uniform distribution is used by assigning the weights. Uniform distribution has been finding through the following formula.

$$D_t(i) = \frac{D_t \exp(-\alpha_t \, y_i \, h_t(x_i))}{Z_t} \tag{7}$$

Where D_t is the distribution, α is the learning rate, h is the weak learner, x is the training fragment (attribute), y is the label class and Z_t is the previous distribution. The same formula has been used to find Z_t.

Conditional Inference Tree (CTree) [10] is the statistical approach for recursive portioning. It covers the two fundamental problems of exhaustive search procedures are handled by CTree. It reduces over-fitting and also reduces the biasing of covariates missing values and multiple splits.

5.2 Standalone Classifier

SVM [11] has been used for analyzing classification generally using two class labels. SVM allows choosing several kernels like linear, polynomial and radial bias function. In this study, we chose radial bias function for binary classification as normal or intrusion.

Neural Network (Nnet) [12] is a computational model influenced by the design of biological neural network. It includes an interconnected group of artificial neurons which process information. It is also known as a feed-forward neural network.

5.3 Experimental Results

This section highlights the results evaluated by our proposed strategy using the above-mentioned classifiers. For evaluating we use the two datasets: KDDCUP 1999 (benchmark dataset) and CICIDS 2017. For **NSL-KDD**, the training set D_{NSL} contains 125,973 instances which contain both normal traffic and abnormal traffic (attack). Each instance containing 41 features which contain both discrete (9 features) and continuous

(32 features) features. Afterward, we apply DDR strategy on $D_{(NSL)}$ for data reduction we get reduced dataset $TR_{D(NSL)}$. $TR_{D(NSL)}$ contains 119,220 instances and 22 features which is less than as discussed in [26] and [27]. A reduction of around 6% of the number of instances has been observed from D_{NSL}. For **CICIDS 2017**, the total dataset has 692,703 instances. We split the dataset for training and testing the classifiers. After splitting the training dataset D_{CIC} contain 500,000 instances and 79 features. Moreover, every instance is identified as normal or an attack. By implementing DDR on D_{CIC}, a compressed dataset $TR_{D(CIC)}$ was achieved with 117,200 instances and 36 features. Approximately 18% of the number of instances in D_{CIC} has been observed. The chosen feature from the NSL-KDD dataset has been described in Tables 3 and 4 depicts the chosen feature for the NSL-KDD dataset and CICIDS 2017 dataset respectively.

Table 3. Selected feature of NSL-KDD.

Features	Selected feature
22	6, 27, 4, 24, 29, 26, 38, 39, 3, 12, 5, 34, 35, 23, 33, 8, 7, 2, 13, 11, 10, 20

Table 4. Selected feature for CICIDS 2017

Features	Selected feature
36	1, 2, 21, 78, 4, 26, 7, 65, 39, 23, 75, 18, 20, 31, 42, 24, 19, 44, 45, 11, 56, 9, 73, 43, 79, 29, 28, 68, 25, 71, 40, 55, 37, 17, 35, 3

Before applying the classifiers, we apply the normalization on the reduced dataset. As we know training set consists of huge number of instances and every instance has multiple features, a challenge about training dataset is that values in the features. Some attributes have the values that have maximum scope among the minimum and maximum value, for this large scope, we normalize the features using logarithmic scaling method for obtaining the ranges and to get the values in the range [0, 1] through the following formula (8).

$$A_j[i] = \frac{A_j[i] - A_{min}[i]}{A_{max}[i] - A_{min}[i]} \tag{8}$$

Where $A_j[i]$ represents the value of ith feature of jth data instance. $A_{min}[i]$ depicts the lowest value of ith feature in the dataset A (A = R_D), while $A_{max}[i]$ depicts the largest value among the values in that feature.

For NSL-KDD dataset, three attributes such as "duration", "src_bytes", "dst_bytes" are there on which we apply normalization steps. There are also some attributes are there in CICIDS 2017 like "Flow Duration", "Fwd Packet Length Std", "Flow Bytes/s", " Flow Packets/s", "Flow IAT Mean", "Flow IAT max", etc. on which we apply the normalization process to get the values in range between [0,1].

Now we apply the classifiers on reduced dataset R_D. Table 5 describes the accuracy of detecting an intrusion between the classifiers, time comparison has been represented in Figs. 2 and 3 for NSL-KDD and CICIDS 2017 datasets respectively. Figures 4 and 5 describes the True Positive Rate comparison between the classifiers for the NSL-KDD and CICIDS 2017 datasets respectively.

Table 5. Accuracy comparison

Accuracy (%)	NSL-KDD		CICIDS 2017	
	Without DDR	With DDR	Without DDR	With DDR
XGBoost	94.3	98.85	95.3	98.42
CTree	85.45	92.51	85.56	95.90
SVM	73.34	79.25	79.56	85.32
Nnet	71	73.2	78.5	80.25

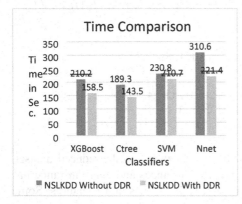

Fig. 2. Time comparison for NSL-KDD   **Fig. 3.** Time comparison for CICIDS 2017

Figure 6 represents the error comparison for the NSL-KDD dataset and Fig. 7 depicts the error comparison for CICIDS 2017 dataset. In this experiment, we only compare the measurements for NSL-KDD with other proposed methodology, because they choose only KDD dataset for their experiment as shown in Fig. 8. Confusion matrix for various classifiers has been represented in Table 6 (Attack and Normal). Moreover, in this proposed model other evaluation metrics for NSLKDD has been performed after applying DDR scheme. The evaluation metrics has been described in Table 7.

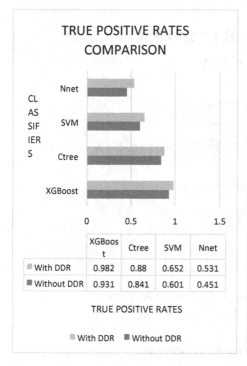

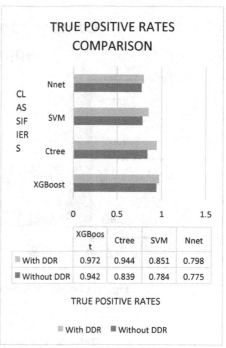

Fig. 4. TPR comparison for NSL-KDD dataset

Fig. 5. TPR comparison for CICIDS 2017 dataset

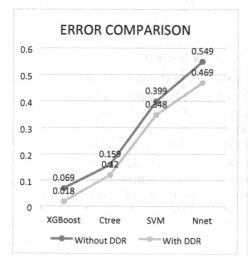

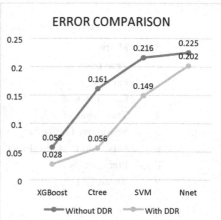

Fig. 6. Error comparison for NSL-KDD

Fig. 7. Error comparison for CICIDS2017

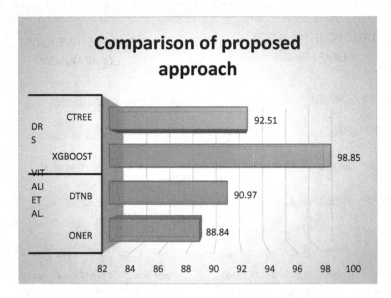

Fig. 8. Comparison between DRS and Vitali et al. [13]

Table 6. Confusion matrix for NSL-KDD

		XGBoost		CTree		SVM		Nnet	
				Predicted					
		Attack	Normal	Attack	Normal	Attack	Normal	Attack	Normal
Actual	Attack	12584	40	11455	133	8490	4513	6820	6020
	Normal	229	9690	1565	9390	180	9360	214	9487

Table 7. Evaluation metrics for NSL-KDD

S.No	Metrics	XGBoost	CTree	SVM	Nnet
1	True positive	12584	11455	8490	6820
2	False negative	229	1565	4513	6020
3	False positive	40	133	180	214
4	True negative	9690	9390	9360	9487
5	Sensitivity (TPR)	0.982	0.879	0.652	0.531
6	False Alarm Ratio (FPR)	0.0041	0.0139	0.0188	0.0220
8	Precision (%)	99.68	98.45	97.13	96.95
9	Recall (%)	97.3	84.1	72.4	70.1

6   Conclusion

Dimensionality reduction without affecting the classifier's accuracy is one of the biggest challenge faced by data sets with plenty of dimensions. In order to suggest a solution to cope up with the challenge of high dimension, DDR scheme has been proposed which reduces dimensions without compromising with the accuracy of classifiers. The scheme so proposed uses SymmetricUncertainty, Chi-Squared and ReliefF in a combined way, to chalk out important and useful features. Moreover, the scheme covers various processes like data numericalization, feature selection, dimensionality reduction and tuple selection as well.

For the experiment we used two datasets NSL-KDD and CICIDS 2017. CICIDS 2017 is the recent intrusion dataset, which is very descriptive in nature. It covers almost all the protocol types and hots down attack diversity too. CICIDS 2017 hasn't been used by the researchers to find the intrusion till date, for this reason we chose this dataset for our experiment. CICIDS 2017 has in all 79 features which are like hurdle in the way to find the malicious activity in an efficient way. Our proposed DDR scheme is very suitable for this kind of volumetric data. Also the elapsed time for building the classification model, is considerably reduced by the usage of DDR scheme making it as one of the most advantageous feature of our proposed scheme. Apart from this, both ensemble approach and standalone classifier approach give better result when applied with the DDR scheme, with regard to accuracy and computation time. The study will also boost up the researchers in the field of big data and data science in their concern work, and would yield more Data analysis opportunities in the domain of cyber security.

The work so proposed, can be enhanced to achieve the optimal set of features with the help of fuzzy logic, and other correlation feature selection method. The efficiency of system can be further improvised by using deep learning techniques. Deep learning techniques like Convolutional Neural Network and Long Short Term Memory (LSTM) network can be used to find the accurate results without reducing the features from the datasets.

Acknowledgement. This Publication is an outcome of the R&D work undertaken in the project under the Visvesvaraya PhD Scheme of Ministry of Electronics & Information Technology, Government of India, being implemented by Digital India Corporation (formerly Media Lab Asia).

References

1. Scarfone, K., Peter, M.: Guide to intrusion detection and prevention systems (IDPs). NIST special publication 800.2007, 94 (2007)
2. Zuech, R., Khoshgoftaar, T.M., Wald, R.: Intrusion detection and big heterogeneous data: a survey. J. Big Data **2**(1), 1–41 (2015)
3. Sharafaldin, I., Gharib, A., Habibi Lashkari, A., Ghorbani, A.A.: Towards a reliable intrusion detection benchmark dataset. Softw. Netw. **2017**, 177–200 (2018)

4. Shiravi, A., et al.: Toward developing a systematic approach to generate benchmark datasets for intrusion detection. Comput. Secur. **31**(3), 357–374 (2012)

5. Karimi, Z., Kashani, M.M.R., Harounabadi, A.: Feature ranking in intrusion detection dataset using combination of filtering methods. Int. J. Comput. Appl. **78**(4) (2013)

6. Azad, C., Jha, V.K.: Data mining based hybrid intrusion detection system. Indian J. Sci. Technol. **7**(6), 781–789 (2014)

7. MeeraGandhi, G., Appavoo, K., Srivasta, S.: Effective network intrusion detection using classifiers decision trees and decision rules. Int. J. Adv. Netw. Appl. **2** (2010)

8. Tama, B.A., Rhee. K.-H.: An in-depth experimental study of anomaly detection using gradient boosted machine. Neural Comput. Appl. **31**, 1–11 (2019)

9. Dieci, L., Friedman, M.J.: Continuation of invariant subspaces. Numer. Linear Algebr. Appl. **8**(5), 317–327 (2001)

10. Hothorn, T., Hornik, K., Zeileis, A.: Unbiased recursive partitioning: a conditional inference framework. J. Comput. Graph. Stat. **15**(3), 651–674 (2006)

11. Bennett, K.P., Campbell, C.: Support vector machines: hype or Hallelujah? SIGKDD Explor. **2**(2), 1–3 (2000)

12. Ripley, B., Venables, W.: Maintainer Brian Ripley: Package 'net'. R package version, 7-3 (2016)

13. Herrera-Semenets, V., et al.: A data reduction strategy and its application on the scan and backscatter detection using rule-based classifiers. Expert Syst. Appl. **95**, 272–279 (2018)

14. Chen, T., Zhang, X., Jin, S., Kim, O.: Efficient classification using parallel and scalable compressed model and its application on intrusion detection. Expert Syst. Appl. **41**(13), 5972–5983 (2014)

15. Aggarwal, C.C.: Data Mining: The Textbook. Springer, Heidelberg (2015). https://doi.org/10.1007/978-3-319-14142-8

16. Cheng, X., Cai, H., Zhang, Y., Xu, B., Su, W.: The optimal combination of feature selection and classification via local hyperplane based learning strategy. BMC Bioinform. **16**(1), 2–19 (2015)

17. Ganapathi, N.P., Duraivelu, V.: A knowledgeable feature selection based on a set theory for web intrusion detection system. In: Suresh, L., Dash, S., Panigrahi, B. (eds.) Artificial Intelligence and Evolutionary Algorithms in Engineering Systems, vol. 325, pp. 51–59. Springer, New Delhi (2015). https://doi.org/10.1007/978-81-322-2135-7_7

18. Xia, J., Fang, A.C., Zhang, X.: A novel feature selection strategy for enhanced biomedical event extraction using the Turku system. Biomed. Res. Int. **2014**, 1–12 (2014)

19. García, S., Luengo, J., Herrera, F.: Data Preprocessing in Data Mining. Springer, Switzerland (2015). https://doi.org/10.1007/978-3-319-10247-4

20. de Oliveira Moura, S., de Freitas, M.B., Cardoso, H.A., Cavalcanti, G.D.: Choosing instance selection method using meta-learning. In: 2014 IEEE International Conference on Systems, Man, and Cybernetics (SMC), pp. 2003–2007. IEEE (2014)

21. Silva, D.A., Souza, L.C., Motta, G.H.: An instance selection method for large datasets based on Markov geometric diffusion. Data Knowl. Eng. **101**, 24–41 (2016)

22. Chou, T.-S., et al.: Correlation-based feature selection for intrusion detection design. In: 2007 Military Communications Conference, MILCOM 2007. IEEE (2007)

23. Ahmad, I., Abdulah, A.B., Alghamdi, A.S., Alnfajan, K., Hussain, M.: Feature subset selection for network intrusion detection mechanism using genetic eigen vectors. In: Proceedings of CSIT, vol. 5 (2011)

24. Mukherjee, S., Sharma, N.: Intrusion detection using naive Bayes classifier with feature reduction. Procedia Technol. **4**, 119–128 (2012)

25. Al-Jarrah, O.Y., et al.: Machine-learning-based feature selection techniques for large-scale network intrusion detection. In: 2014 IEEE 34th International Conference on Distributed Computing Systems Workshops (ICDCSW). IEEE (2014)
26. Lin, S.-W., et al.: An intelligent algorithm with feature selection and decision rules applied to anomaly intrusion detection. Appl. Soft Comput. **12**(10), 3285–3290 (2012)
27. Manzoor, I., Kumar, N.: A feature reduced intrusion detection system using ANN classifier. Expert Syst. Appl. **88**, 249–257 (2017)
28. Zhang, F., Wang, D.: An effective feature selection approach for network intrusion detection. In: 2013 IEEE Eighth International Conference on Networking, Architecture and Storage (NAS). IEEE (2013)
29. Greenwood, P.E., Nikulin, M.S.: A Guide to Chi-Squared Testing, vol. 280. Wiley, Hoboken (1996)
30. Mukherjee, S., Sharma, N.: Intrusion detection using naive Bayes classifier with feature reduction. In: Proceedings in 2nd International Conference on Computer, Communication, Control and Information Technology, C3IT-2012 (2012). Procedia Technol. **4**, 119–128
31. Dhanabal, L., Shantharajah, S.P.: A study on an NSL-KDD dataset for intrusion detection system based on classification algorithms. Int. J. Adv. Res. Comput. Commun. Eng. **4**, 446–452 (2015)
32. Aljawarneh, S., Aldwairi, M., Yassein, M.B.: Anomaly-based intrusion detection system through feature selection analysis and building the hybrid efficient model. J. Comput. Sci. **25**, 152–160 (2017)
33. Lessmann, S., Baesens, B., Mues, C., Pietsch, S.: Benchmarking classification models for software defect prediction: a proposed framework and novel findings. IEEE Trans. Softw. Eng. **34**(4), 485–496 (2008)
34. Liu, Y., Khoshgoftaar, T.M., Seliya, N.: Evolutionary optimization of software quality modeling with multiple repositories. IEEE Trans. Softw. Eng. **36**(6), 852–864 (2010)
35. Abdulhammed, R., Musafer, H., Alessa, A., Faezipour, M., Abuzneid, A.: Features dimensionality reduction approaches for machine learning based network intrusion detection. Electronics **8**(3), 322 (2019)

Short Term Forecasting of Agriculture Commodity Price by Using ARIMA: Based on Indian Market

Anil KumarMahto[✉], Ranjit Biswas, and M. Afshar Alam

Department of CSE, Jamia Hamdard, Hamdard Nagar, New Delhi, India
anil.fiem16@gmail.com

Abstract. The Forecasting of agriculture commodity price plays an important role in the developing country like India, whose major population directly or indirectly depends upon farming. There are several forecasting techniques like Time series analysis, regression techniques, learning techniques. We used Auto Regressive Integrated Moving Average (ARIMA) model under Time series analysis for forecasting, which consider only the historical data. We selected price of sunflower seed for the period 1st January 2011 to 31st December 2016, gathered from "data.gov.in" for the market Kadiri, Anantpur district, Andhra Pradesh, India. We used the data from 1st Jan, 2011 to 31st Dec 2015 for training purpose and the data from 1st Jan, 2016 to 31st Dec 2016 for testing purpose. Based on the training data, ARIMA(1, 1, 2) selected as best model. Mean Average Percentage Error (MAPE) for the selected model is calculated as 2.30%. The Root Mean Square Percentage Error (RMSPE) observed by the model as 3.44%.

Keywords: Forecasting · ARIMA · Time series analysis ·
Agriculture commodity price

1 Introduction

As India is developing country and the larger population depends upon the farming. The agriculture commodity price affects all the human beings directly or indirectly specially the farmers, whose sole income depends upon the selling price of agriculture commodities. There are several factors like demand, supply, geographical location etc., which can affect the agriculture commodity price.

1.1 Short Term Forecasting Techniques

Based on the duration, Forecasting categories into three major parts: "long term, medium term and short term". Long term forecasting refers to the predicting the price for years, while medium term forecast ranged between 2–5 years. The short term forecasting techniques used to predict in the range of day to one year. Forecasting can be done by daily basis, weekly basis, monthly basis, quarterly basis or yearly basis. The forecasting techniques mainly divided into two parts: Based on economical factors and based on historical data. Here we mainly focused on techniques based on historical data.

© Springer Nature Singapore Pte Ltd. 2019
M. Singh et al. (Eds.): ICACDS 2019, CCIS 1045, pp. 452–461, 2019.
https://doi.org/10.1007/978-981-13-9939-8_40

1.2   ARIMA Model

ARIMA model stands for "Autoregressive Integrated Moving Average Model" sometime also referred as Box-Jenkins model. This model contains three parameters namely p, d and q and represented as ARIMA(p, d, q). The parameter p is associated with Autoregressive model i.e.; AR(p), parameter d is associated with Integrated model i.e.; I(d) and the parameter q is associated with Moving Average model i.e.; MA(q). This model totally depends upon the past data and do the prediction.

1.3   Model Building Strategy

Box-Jenkins [7–10] proposed "model building strategy" which consist three parts, as shown in Fig. 1. The first part is model identification, in which we analyze the time series data on the basis of various facts like: different plots of the data, our subjective knowledge in that particular area, statistic etc. By analyzing we mainly choose the model.

Fig. 1. Model building strategy

The second part of this strategy is to finding the optimal parameters by fitting the chosen model in first part. The third and last step of the model is to analyze the accuracy of the fitted mode. If we get the desired accuracy for the model, then we can accept the model, otherwise we iterate this three step strategy, until we get the desired model.

In [1], Razali et al., used ARIMA and GARCH model for forecasting of crude palm oil and black pepper for Malaysian market. They concluded that best models for crude palm oil and for black pepper are ARIMA(1, 1, 1) and ARIMA(2, 1, 1) respectively.

In [2], Ussenbayev, et al., used Dynamic Model Averaging (DMA) for forecasting of commodity price and compare the accuracy with the ARIMA model.

In [4], Idrees *et al.,* used ARIMA model for forecasting of stock price, based on Indian stock market. In [5] Kibona et al., used ARIMA model to forecast the price of Maize. Based on the chosen data, ARIMA(3, 1, 1) was the best model (Fig. 2).

1.4   Data Preprocessing

The price of sunflower seed is taken from the website "data.gov.in" for the period 1st January 2011 to 31st December 2016. The sample format of data is shown in the given table. As we can see that the price is not available for the date 20/01/2016. So we assume that,

Price on date (X) = Price on date (X − 1)

The data is divided in two sets: Training set and Testing Set, the data from 1st Jan, 2011 to 31st Dec 2015 for training purpose and the data from 1st Jan, 2016 to 31st Dec 2016 for testing purpose (Table 1).

Table 1. Daily sunflower seed price in Indian market

State	District	Market	Commodity	Arrival date	Price
Andhra Pradesh	Anantapur	Kadir	Sunflower seed	14/01/2016	4800
Andhra Pradesh	Anantapur	Kadir	Sunflower seed	15/01/2016	4800
Andhra Pradesh	Anantapur	Kadir	Sunflower seed	16/01/2016	4800
Andhra Pradesh	Anantapur	Kadir	Sunflower seed	17/01/2016	3900
Andhra Pradesh	Anantapur	Kadir	Sunflower seed	18/01/2016	3900
Andhra Pradesh	Anantapur	Kadir	Sunflower seed	19/01/2016	4000
Andhra Pradesh	Anantapur	Kadir	Sunflower seed	20/01/2016	NA
Andhra Pradesh	Anantapur	Kadir	Sunflower seed	21/01/2016	4000
Andhra Pradesh	Anantapur	Kadir	Sunflower seed	22/01/2016	3800

1.5   Challenges in Forecasting of Agriculture Commodity Price

Forecasting of agriculture commodity price is complex in nature. As per the nature of agriculture commodity, its price depends upon several factors like- time, season, status of monsoon, geographical location supply, demand etc. ARIMA model totally rely on the historical data. In the time series data there are several practical issues like: missing data, the size of the series, conversion from daily price to weekly price/monthly price/quarterly price or conversion from weekly price to monthly price/quarterly price.

2   Methodology

2.1   ARIMA

This model contains three parameters namely p, d and q and represented as ARIMA(p, d, q). The parameter p is associated with Autoregressive model i.e.; AR(p), parameter d is associated with Integrated model i.e.; I(d) and the parameter q is associated with Moving Average model i.e.; MA(q).

2.2   Autoregressive (P)

AR(P) is also known as autoregressive model of order 'p'. Autoregressive means regression on themselves. Here 'p' denotes the number of past terms of the series involved to find the next term. Suppose Y_t

$$" Y_t = \varphi_1 Y_{t-1} + \varphi_2 Y_{t-2} + \ldots \varphi_p Y_{t-p} + e_t \, "$$

In AR(p), p is the order of autoregressive process, denotes the number of previous terms involve in the regression analysis for the series Y. For example, ARIMA(2, 0, 0) is equivalent to AR(2). The AR(2) can be is represented as

$$" Y_t = \varphi_1 Y_{t-1} + \varphi_2 Y_{t-2} + e_t \, "$$

Here, φ_1 and φ_2 are model parameters, e_t is the error term.

2.3   Moving Average (Q)

A moving average (MA(q)) component is mainly used for specifying the error of the model. The error can be obtained by the combining the previous error terms. Here the parameter 'q' represent the total number of previous error terms required to specify the present error.

$$" Y_t = e_t - \theta_1 e_{t-1} - \theta_2 e_{t-2} \ldots - \theta_q e_{t-q} \, "$$

Here $\theta_1, \theta_2, \ldots - \theta_q$ are the weights which applied on the error terms e_{t-1}, e_{t-2}, ...e_{t-q}, respectively.

2.4   Integrated (D)

In Integrated (d) component, d represent the degree of differencing. It is used to stabilizing the series when the time series is non-stationary. We can get the stationary series from non-stationary series by subtracting the current value of the series from the previous value of the series 'd' times.

2.5   Framework for ARIMA

The first step in ARIMA framework is to visualize the time series data. On the basis of visualization we analyze that whether the series is stationary or non-stationary. As ARIMA model works with stationary series only. The second step of ARIMA is to stationarize the series. A series is stationary or not that depends upon expectation, variance and co-variance. For example if the expectation of a series is time dependent then the series will be non-stationary. There are several methods like differencing, detrending to stationarise the series. The third step of ARIMA is to apply model building strategy to find the optimal parameters p and q. These parameters can be obtained by using ACF plot (autocorrelation) and partial autocorrelation function (PACF plot) [11]. After getting the parameters p, d and q we apply ARIMA model to forecast.

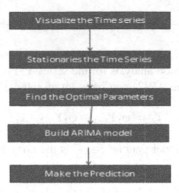

Fig. 2. Framework for ARIMA

3 Result and Analysis

Step-1: Analyzing the Time Series Data
For analysis, We have taken the dataset of daily wholesale price of sunflower seed in various Indian market (during January 2011 to December 2016) from the website www.data.gov.in. Implementation work is done in R programming language. Figure 3, shows the plot of daily price of sunflower seed during 2011 to 2016 by using the following code:

"tsData = ts(MyData$Price, frequency = 365, start = c(2011))
     plot(tsData, main = "Wholesale Price of Sunflower in 2011–16")"

Wholesale Price of Sunflower in 2011-16

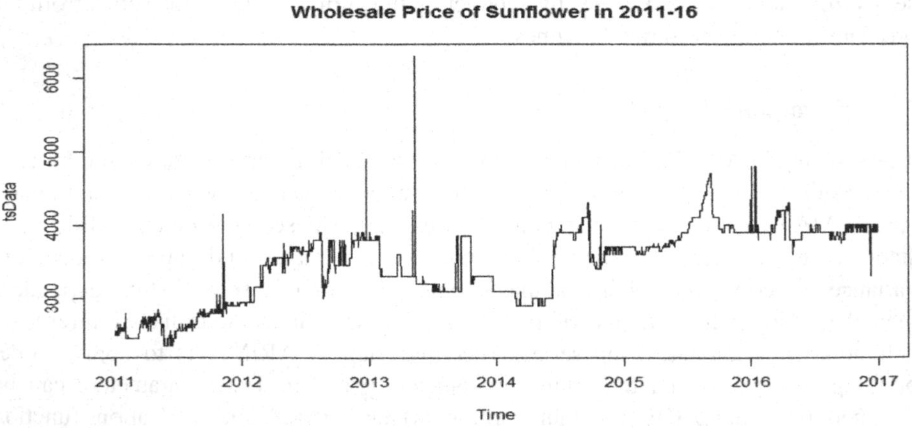

Fig. 3. Daily price of sunflower seed for Jan, 2011 to Dec, 2016

From Fig. 3, we can say that the given series is time dependent. The price is at peak generally in September to December of every year and while the price is lower in the season of February to May.

Step-2: Components of Time Series Data

Whenever we analyze any time series data, generally we get following components: Seasonality, Cycle and Trend. As from the Fig. 1, it is clear that the dataset containing seasonal component (Price at peak and low at particular point of every calendar year) as well as trend (refers that over the period of time whether the time series follows some pattern or not. For example with time whether price is increasing or decreasing). Decomposition of the sunflower time series data is shown in Fig. 5 (Fig. 4).

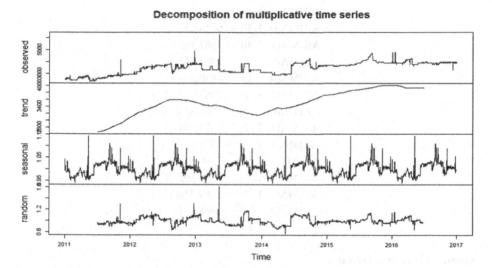

Fig. 4. Components of time series data

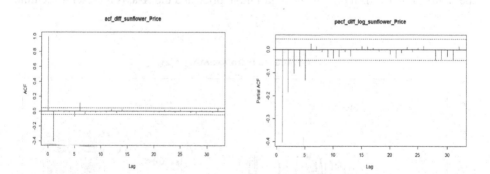

Fig. 5. ACF and PACF plot

Step-3: Stationarize the series

As from the Fig. 3, it is clear that the series is not stationary. ARIMA model cannot be applied on non-stationary series. Hence we applied Augmented Dickey-Fuller Test for getting the stationary series.

Step-4: Find the optimal parameter p, d, q for ARIMA

We used the function "auto.arima()" for finding the optimal parameter p, d and q. In Table 2, the various ARIMA model with respective drift values shown, obtained by the auto.arima() function. The best model after refitting, chosen by this function is ARIMA (1, 1, 2) with drift value −7379.147.

Table 2. Various ARIMA model with parameters

Model	Drift value
ARIMA(2, 1, 2)	−7367.08
ARIMA(0, 1, 0)	−6948.638
ARIMA(1, 1, 0)	−7267.765
ARIMA(0, 1, 1)	−7368.718
ARIMA(0, 1, 0)	−6950.554
ARIMA(1, 1, 1)	−7367.672
ARIMA(0, 1, 2)	−7368.356
ARIMA(1, 1, 2)	−7371.344
ARIMA(1, 1, 2)	−7371.827
AHJMA(0, 1, 2)	−7369.831
ARIMA(2, 1, 2)	−7368.505
ARIMA(1, 1, 3)	−7369.316
ARIMA(2, 1, 3)	−7368.691

Step-5: Make prediction

We apply the model ARIMA(1, 1, 2) for forecasting of sunflower seed price for the period of 1st January 2016 to 31st December 2016. The forecasted result is shown in the figure. The Y-axis represent the logarithmic price and the X-axis represents the time (Fig. 6).

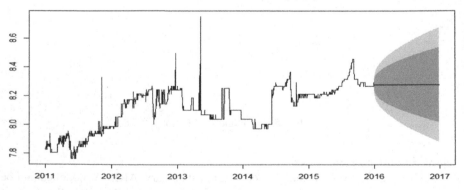

Fig. 6. Forecasting by ARIMA model

4 Error Analysis

We compared the forecasted price with the actual price as shown in Fig. 7, and calculated the two important parameters: Mean Absolute Percentage Error (MAPE) and Root Mean Square Percentage Error (RMSPE) (Fig. 8).

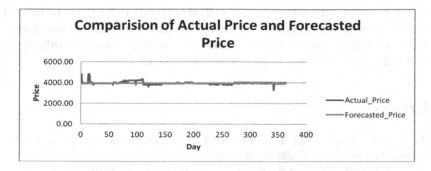

Fig. 7. Comparison of actual price and forecasted price

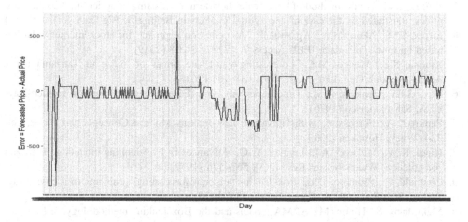

Fig. 8. Daily error

Absolute Percentage Error = (|Actual Price − Forecasted Price|) * 100/Actual Price

$$MAPE = \left(\sum \text{Absolute Percentage Error} \right)/n$$

Here, n is the number of days, for which the forecasting is done.

The MAPE and RMSEP of ARIMA(1, 1, 2) for sunflower seed is 2.30 and 3.44 respectively. In Fig. 9, we plotted the error (Actual Price − forecasted price).

5   Conclusion and Future Work

As we know that, ARIMA model is one of the model used for forecasting based on time series analysis. We consider wholesale price of sunflower seed, taken from "www.data.gov.in" for the period of 1st January, 2011 to 31st December, 2016 from one of the Indian market. ARIMA(1, 1, 2) selected as the best model. For accuracy measurement, we considered two parameters: MAPE and Root Mean Square Percentage error. The MAPE for the selected model ARIMA(1, 1, 2) is 2.30. As we know that, time series data for the agriculture commodity price is non-linear in nature and the ARIMA model deals with the stationary time series model. Hence the artificial neural network can give more accurate result in terms of accuracy.

References

1. Drachal, K.: Some novel Bayesian model combination schemes: an application to commodities prices. Sustainability **10**(8), 2801 (2018)
2. Razali, J.B., Mohamad, A.M.B.: Modeling and forecasting price volatility of crude palm oil and sarawak black pepper using ARMA and GARCH model. Adv. Sci. Lett. **24**(12), 9327–9330 (2018)
3. Wu, H., et al.: A new method of large-scale short-term forecasting of agricultural commodity prices: illustrated by the case of agricultural markets in Beijing. J. Big Data **4**(1), 1 (2017)
4. Idrees, S.M., Alam, M.A., Agarwal, P.: A prediction approach for stock market volatility based on time series data. IEEE Access **7**, 17287–17298 (2019)
5. Kibona, S.E., Mbago, M.C.: Forecasting wholesale prices of maize in Tanzania using ARIMA model. Gen. Lett. Math. **4**(3), 131–141 (2018)
6. Box, G.E.P., Jenkins, G.M.: Time Series Analysis: Forecasting and Control. Holden-Day, USA, San Francisco (1976)
7. Pankratz, A.: Forecasting with Univariate Box-Jenkins Models: Concepts and Cases, vol. 224. Wiley, Hoboken (2009)
8. Hipel, K.W., McLeod, A.I., Lennox, W.C.: Advances in Box-Jenkins modeling: 1. Model construction. Water Resour. Res. **13**(3), 567–575 (1977)
9. Chatfield, C., Prothero, D.L.: Box-Jenkins seasonal forecasting: problems in a case-study. J. Roy. Stat. Soc. Ser. A (General) 295–336 (1973)
10. Makridakis, S., Hibon, M.: ARMA models and the Box-Jenkins methodology. J. Forecast. **16**(3), 147–163 (1997)
11. Dickey, D.A., Fuller, W.A.: Distribution of the estimators for autoregressive time series with a unit root. J. Am. Stat. Assoc. **74**(366), 427–431 (1979)
12. Contreras, J., et al.: ARIMA models to predict next-day electricity prices. IEEE Trans. Power Syst. **18**(3), 1014–1020 (2003)
13. Zhang, G.P.: Time series forecasting using a hybrid ARIMA and neural network model. Neurocomputing **50**, 159–175 (2003)
14. Cryer, J.D., Chan, K.-S.: Time Series Analysis: With Application in R. STS. Springer, New York (2008). https://doi.org/10.1007/978-0-387-75959-3
15. Brockwell, P.J., Davis, R.A., Calder, M.V.: Introduction to Time Series and Forecasting, vol. 2. Springer, New York (2002)
16. Atsalakis, G.S., Valavanis, K.P.: Surveying stock market forecasting techniques–Part II: soft computing methods. Expert Syst. Appl. **36**(3), 5932–5941 (2009)

17. https://www.datascience.com/blog/introduction-to-forecasting-with-arima-in-r-learn-data-science-tutorials
18. Bourke, I.J.: A comparison of price forecasting models for the United States manufacturing beef market. Research Report, Market Research Centre, Massey University, 20, p. 76 (1978)
19. Liu, K., et al.: Comparison of very short-term load forecasting techniques. IEEE Trans. Power Syst. **11**(2), 877–882 (1996)
20. Montgomery, D.C., Johnson, L.A., Gardiner, J.S.: Forecasting and Time Series Analysis. McGraw-Hill, New York (1990)
21. https://data.gov.in/catalog/variety-wise-daily-market-prices-data-sunflower-seed.   Accessed 15 Feb 2019
22. https://otexts.com/fpp2/practical.html

Recent Research on Data Analytics Techniques for Internet of Things

Chetna Dabas[(✉)]

Department of Computer Science and Engineering,
Jaypee Institute of Information Technology, Noida, India
chetna.dabas@jiit.ac.in

Abstract. The factor driving the lucrative IoT (Internet of Things) domain is the amalgamation of diverse technologies and their associated solution strategies. This research paper reports the recent review work on IoT for data analytics methods and applications. It also work IoT data classification holding diverse dimensions. In addition, a recent and intense survey of different kinds of data analytics techniques pertaining to different applications with datasets picked up from diverse domains are unfolded and packed into domain categories for usage in IoT in this work. In the present heterogeneous IoT scenario, this recent survey is dedicated to the ones who wish to loom towards this complex domain and dream to bestow upon its research and development. A wide spectrum of visions related to data techniques for IoT is presented along with the intense review of the allied enabling technologies. Open research issues and future directions of research are also presented.

Keywords: IoT · Data analytics · Cloud computing · Fog computing

1 Introduction

The Internet of Things (IoT) technology is comprised up of the integration of smart heterogeneous constrained devices or smart real world objects or things which may include thousands of mini computers, sensors, supercomputers, televisions, chair, animals to name a few with almost no human intervention. These real world entities are responsible for collecting all sorts of unstructured, semi-structured, structured data which is available on any kind of social media platform for humans or any integrated smart machine (Yan et al. 2014). The lead objective associated with IoT is to offer to the users, a flexible, scalable and usable infrastructure using middleware software and communication protocols (interoperable in nature) to establish connections amongst heterogeneous devices present in the complex environment. Further, there comes a box full of challenges and research issues when it comes to the low cost and scalable integration of Internet of Things with other technologies like cloud computing. (Díaz et al. 2016). The IoT environment as depicted above consists up of a huge number of smart things with different architectures and communication mechanisms. The demands for these kinds of systems are consistently rising and bringing a lot of associated challenges as well like information retrieval, storage and management to name a few (Alaba et al. 2017). Specifically, the IoT network is responsible for

© Springer Nature Singapore Pte Ltd. 2019
M. Singh et al. (Eds.): ICACDS 2019, CCIS 1045, pp. 462–476, 2019.
https://doi.org/10.1007/978-981-13-9939-8_41

touching human lives in numerous ways by generating magnanimous amount of data which needs to be semantically and intelligently processed, restored and managed. The IoT data also requires monitoring, controlling, evaluation and testing to deliver efficient performance in complex integrated environments (Zhou et al. 2018). Figure 1 is a pyramid of Internet of Things with Cloud and Fog technologies. Cloud computing is a technology that is responsible for offering the countless virtualized resources over the network as services (Dabas et al. 2010). Fog computing primarily expands the idea of central networks used in cloud computing to edge networks (Ning et al. 2019).

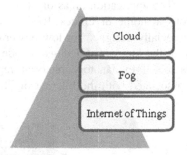

Fig. 1. Pyramid of Internet of Things with Cloud and Fog technologies

This study presents recent literature works related to the data analytics mechanisms related to the Internet of Things paradigm. The prime target of this research paper is to figure out crucial categories for some of these very significant and widely used techniques. This will further enhance the research on data analytics for Internet of Things systems in the time to come. In specific, the contributions of this research work can be summarized as below:

1. This research paper exposes the reviews on prime architectural components of Internet of Things.
2. This research work presents the data classification for Internet of Things paradigm from interesting dimensions
3. The author figures out six prime data analytics categories for Internet of Things.
4. This paper exposes a number of open issues and presents research directions to instil future research in the Internet of Things environment integrated with other technologies.
5. Finally, a conclusion is drawn at the end of this research work.

The remainder of this research paper is organized in the following manner. Section 2 presents the prime architectural components for the Internet of Things paradigm. Section 3 depicts the Internet of Things data classification. Section 4 instigates six prime data analytics categories for the Internet of Things in extensively. Section 5 focuses on the open research issues. Section 6 throws light on the directions for future research. Conclusion of this recent research work study is written in Sect. 7.

2   Internet of Things: Prime Architectural Components

Figure 2 presents the prime components (https://www.postscapes.com/internet-of-things-protocols/) associated with the Internet of Things technology. These components include hardware devices, internet mechanism, communication protocols, and application domains and data analytic techniques. The Infrastructure protocols which may be applied in the Internet of Things arena to the smallest of constrained devices and the examples include 6LoWPAN, IPv4/IPv6 and RPL. 6LoWPAN is a name assigned to Internet protocol version 6 (IPv6) over low power wireless PANs (personal area networks) at lower data rates. The application areas of 6LowPAN include entertainment and automation applications at home or offices. RPL refers to routing protocol for wireless sensor networks specially designed for low power consumption. The internet communication protocols for the Internet of Things include MQTT, AMQP, CoAP to name a few. Figure 2 is a self explanatory pictorial representation of the prime architectural components associated with the Internet of Things paradigm.

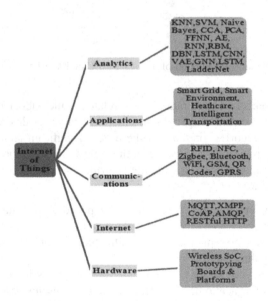

Fig. 2. Prime architectural components of Internet of Things (https://www.postscapes.com/internet-of-things-protocols/)

3   Internet of Things (IOT) Data Classification

The Internet of Things Data comes from various sources, carries a number of attributes, holds a numbers of associated phases and has data analytics techniques associated with it.

   This classification of the Internet of Things data is presented in Fig. 3 above. Sources of the Internet of Things data include the data originations from different kinds of sensors, smart entities to name two. Then there are attributes related to the big kind of Internet of Things data like its value, visualization, volatility, validity, vulnerability, validity, veracity, variability, variety, velocity and volume. Internet of data is acquired from various sources which also include sensors and other low power memory constrained devices. Other phases of Internet of Things data include processing, retention, transportation, processing and data leveraging to multiple uses and applications in diverse domains. In the future generation Internet of Things systems, there will be dire need to express semantically intelligent and optimized decisions which will require to keep all the above data ingredients into consideration along with the most appropriate data analytic technique to be applied catering to the needs of context specific micro services and micro applications. In the light of the above discussion, Sect. 4 is coming up with six identified categories of data analytic methods for the Internet of Things systems.

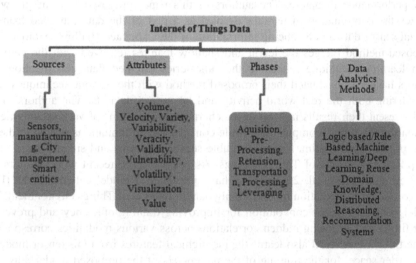

Fig. 3. Internet of Things data classification

4 Internet of Things: Data Analytics Techniques

4.1 Logic/Rule Based Learning

As per a research work, the authors of a paper (Darshan et al. 2015) presented an application related to the healthcare system which presents a review on the implications of the Internet of Things. The authors of this work have highlighted that it is important to predict the Chronic Disorders as early as possible. The authors of this work proposed a methodology inferring both knowledge and information in context with the healthcare data. Their methodology consisted primarily of three phases namely data pruning, data prediction and data presentation. Further a number of reviews and challenges have been addressed in this work and holds an example of rule based learning in the IOT arena considering the domain of healthcare system.

4.2   Machine Learning/Deep Learning

Reported by a recent research work (Martis et al. 2018), Internet of Things and Machine Learning along with big data form prime ingredients for the design of future computing systems which are artificial intelligence oriented. This study has presented trans-disciplinary kind of trans-informative review work in the above specified research areas. Two examples include the discussion of the enhanced version of Computer Aided Diagnostic method to evaluate cancer with the analysis of masses which are mammographic. For the relieving of the probable attacks, this work also presents a discussion on the median data issue while using vernacular resources in order to enable the Internet of Things techniques. The research work projected by (Ravi et al. 2017) highlights the intensity of the role of deep learning in the environment of constrained low powered IOT devices for efficiently utilizing the computing platform which are high performance in nature. The authors of this paper proposed a technique which utilizes the combination of features derived as a part of the data retrieved from the inertial sensor data and balancing information of the associated shallow features. Their proposed method merges the learnt and shallow features retrieved with the help of a deep learning technique related to the time-series oriented data classification. The authors have also evaluated their proposed method with the existing techniques while considering both the real world activity and laboratory datasets. The authors of this work present their results in form of pie charts and histograms of various activities by comparing the times (computation) while considering the limitations related to the on-node processing (real-time) using wearable sensor platforms and smart phones which composes the Internet of Things settings. As per one more recent work, authors of a research paper (Li et al. 2018a, b, c) have presented a model called DCCM (Deep Convolutional computation model) for nig data in Internet of Things environment. This model considers tensor convolution for improving training efficiency and preventing over fitting and exposing hidden correlations across various modalities corresponding to the things. Further, it also learns the hierarchical features from this tensor model. In high-order space, for the training of the parameters of the proposed model, this work also proposed a technique called HBP (high-order back propagation) where the minimization of the reconstruction of the loss function is performed. Their proposed model is evaluated while making use of the datasets namely *SNAE2*, *CUAVE*, and *STL-10*.

Further, a recent study (Li et al. 2018a, b, c) suggests the extraction of accurate information from the complex Internet of Things infrastructure with raw data (sensor) while making use of deep learning. Further, it connects the multiple layers of this environment to the edge computing environment with constrained computing capabilities. In the edge computing scenario, the authors have specifically taken up the issue of scheduling the network layers corresponding to the Internet of Things deep learning environment and carried out performance evaluation in the Python (Version 2.7) programming language. The results of this research work are plotted in terms of operations versus reduced data size ratio related to the number of layers in the Internet of Things deep learning environment. The authors of this work further claims that their proposed solution can accommodate the rise in the tasks (deployed in edge servers) to a higher number while maintaining better Quality of Service (QoS) necessities in the complex and resource constrained scenarios like IoT. In a more recent research work (Fekade et al. 2018) for telemetry applications in the Internet of Things, a probabilistic method is proposed for recovering the incomplete data from the sensors located embedded inside IoT environment. Here, the proposed method works in a sequential execution of three phases namely the K-means technique for the clustering of sensors in the IoT environment, PMF (Probability Matrix Factorization) for recovering the missing data (in each cluster), EPMF (Extended Probability Matrix Factorization) for the improvement of the data recovery precision. For the experimental evaluation of the proposed work, the authors have utilized diverse sensors planted in the *Intel Berkeley Research Laboratory*. The results of this work are tabulated while presenting the RMSE (Root Mean Square Error) enhancement with the proposed PMF technique as compared with the other existing Support Vector Machine and Deep Neural Network techniques. In one more recent hot vaporizing research work (Diro and Chilamkurti 2018), in cyber-security, an attack detection technique (distributed) for social Internet of Things scenario is presented using deep learning methodology. For Fog-to-things networks, the authors have also presented distributed attack detection architecture. The *NSL-KDD* dataset has been used as an intrusion dataset in this work. For normal and attack, the 2-class categories have been utilized and for normal, probe, DoS a 4-class category has been used in this work. An algorithm for local training and parameter exchange has been discussed. This work has been compared with the other existing shallow methods in terms of Precision, Recall and F1 Measure and the results are tabulated. The authors of (Mohammadi et al. 2018) have proposed a Deep Reinforcement Learning (DRL) methodology consisting up of a network (deep variational auto-encoder type) which bears semi-supervised form. This work has been carried out for the services related to the Internet of Things environment and considering smart city applications. Here, the dataset arrived from a deployment (real-world) in form of a campus library area consisting up of a grid of iBeacons and in relation with the learning agent, the use of both unlabeled as well as labelled data has been made for the improvisation of the accuracy and performance has been made in this work. The results are projected in form of accuracies related to various feature sets inside a DNN (Deep Neural Network) in the Internet of Things environment. The authors of this paper specifically reveal that the learning agents can be significantly benefitted by the context-awareness being applied to the unlabeled data for improving the accuracy and performance in an Internet of Things scenario. According to the authors of a research work (Zhang et al. 2018), a huge count of attributes is associated with the big data samples especially in the portable devices (constrained and low power) like those found in the common settings of Internet of Things. This fact further puts hinderances on the performance of the HOPCM (High-Order Possibilistic c-means) techniques. For the clustering of big data in the IoT environment, the authors of this work have investigated and proposed methods which are inclined on TT-HOPCM (tensor-train network) and CP-HOPCM (canonical polyadic decomposition) and forms variants of HOPCM. The datasets exploited in this work are *SNAE2* and *NUS-WIDE-14*. The results of this work signifies that for saving the memory in heterogeneous samples in the Internet of Things systems, a soaring compression rate can be achieved by the proposed TT-HOPCM and CP-HOPCM techniques while merely effecting the accuracy (clustering) on the lower side.

4.3 Re-use Domain Knowledge

In a book (Höller et al. 2014) the visions for machine to machine and its evolution in the direction of Internet of Things have been presented explaining how the existing domain knowledge can be reused.

4.4 Linked Stream Processing

The authors of research work (Soldatos et al. 2015) pertaining to the applications in the arena where semantic portability carries due importance, proposed open source solution which are meant for the Internet of Things paradigm. They gave it a name called OpenIoT. This is further based on the SSN (W3C Semantic Sensor Networks) containing both virtual and physical sensors in the Internet of Things sensors and services scenario. In this work, different capabilities of the OpenIoT platform has been investigated conceptually like registration, data-acquisition, and deployment related to the sensors (X-GSN), inter-connected objects and data-streams, authenticated and authorized access to the resources and others in an Internet of Things environment. The authors of (Hromic et al. 2015) presents the analysis of the sensor data associated with the IoT environment while performing real time event processing and clustering. This work has utilized OpenIoT platform which offers an extensive back up for the stream processing in IoT systems. In this work, in order to carry out a correlation analysis for the IoT sensors, crowd-sensed data had been utilized. Specifically, SenseZG Air dataset with its time range, number of data points and unique co-ordinates has been considered. A modified version of the existing K-means algorithm has been utilized to perform the geographical partitioning (of the dataset).

One more research work (Dastjerdi et al. 2016) presents a conceptual introduction on the association of Fog computing with Internet of Things considering different applications. The authors in specific mention that the IoT paradigm is capable of enabling innovations which can improve the quality of life as in activity tracking and healthcare for example. The authors of the research work (Qin et al. 2016) reveals that since the IoT paradigms comes with volatile and changing environments with voluminous data which is noisy and continuously generated, one of the basic issue pertaining to these kinds of systems still remains IoT data management. This research work presents an exhaustive study of the data-centric IoT systems. For example, Data stream processing, complex event processing in the Internet of Things environment has been extensive discussed using the data centric perspective in this research paper. Open research issues in relation with the data management for IoT are highlighted by the authors of this research work. In order to exploit the analytics associated with real time computing scenarios catering to the complex IoT, Fog Computing and Edge scenarios, the research paper (Gupta et al. 2017) presents a toolkit for simulation and modelling and simulation of resource managing methods. The authors of this research work describe policies related to resource management in an Internet of Things environment. The authors of (Malek et al. 2017) have thrown light on the continuous real-time data stream processing and monitoring for the usage of Internet of Things along with the big data technologies. In this work real case scenario related to Kaa and Storm applications has been presented and their experimental study is carried out using different types of sensors like temperature, pulse and CO_2 sensors in the Internet of Things environment.

4.5 Distributed Reasoning

For Internet of Things oriented smart homes, in a very recent research work, the authors (Tao et al. 2018) proposed a framework offering multi-layer cloud structure (to address heterogeneity) along with an ontology oriented service (for security) during interoperations. Future directions and challenges in the similar context have been also discussed towards the conclusions of this paper. In association with sensor data fusion and treatment in the context of the Internet of Things pervasive systems, the authors of (Rodríguez-Valenzuela et al. 2014) have proposed a service-based approach which is distributed in nature. Here, the authors discuss that Unified Modelling Language is useful in representing the Internet of Things system and a component diagram for modelling an IoT system has been presented by the authors of this paper. Further a full composition map and deployment diagram of the IoT system has been presented. Here, the results of network traffic analysis for the IoT environment has also been shown as graphical snapshots and for composite services the fluctuations in the execution times are also presented as a part of this work. The very recent research paper (Su et al. 2018) on the edge of IoT, presents the distribution associated with the semantic reasoning. The edge and cloud oriented Internet of Things architectural structure is described in this research work. In order to show the demonstration of the facilitation of edge computing for the Internet of Things paradigms, three experiments have been performed by the authors. Further, the impact on the performance of the system has been evaluated by the analyzing the association of tasks corresponding to distributed reasoning which happens amongst edge and cloud devices in an IoT environment. Another very recent paper (Ploennigs et al. 2018) discusses the materialistic aspects corresponding to the cognitive Internet of Things. The authors of this work proposed a cognitive IoT architecture which is adapted to different buildings and kept its name as CIoT (Cognitive Internet of Things). The authors have also discussed the brick ontology. In relation with physical relationships, the authors have also presented a semantic knowledge graph. For learning the behaviour of the building, the authors of this paper claim that their proposed model has incorporated numerous numbers of sensors and it guides its users in detection of unwanted events. Further this work claims that their proposed CIoT architecture is adaptable and scalable in the IoT environment. For cognitive IoT arena, the authors of one recent work (Li et al. 2018a, b, c) have investigated the distributed behaviour oriented model orchestration where the chances related to the application of cognitive computing are explored in relation with the instrumented and interconnected worlds. Further in this work, the chances related to the application of DDDAS (Dynamic Data-Driven Application System) oriented techniques with real-time decision support and analyzing capacities in the Internet of Things environment are discussed.

4.6   Recommendation Systems

For IoT related to healthcare, recently, a research work (Ali et al. 2018) proposed Type-2 fuzzy (ontology-aided) recommendation systems in order to effectively suggest diets pertaining to specific drugs and foods for monitoring the patient's body. As an implication of this recommendation system proposed by the authors who make use of sensors, patient risk factors are extracted and prescriptions are suggested for medicine box (smart) as well as food for refrigerator (smart). The accuracy related to prediction of the patient's condition as well as precision rate corresponding to the drug with food suggestions is found to be appreciably enhanced with the usage of fuzzy ontology and T2FL (type-2 fuzzy logic). This work has made use of OWL-2 (Web Ontology Language), SWRL (Semantic Web Rule Language), DL (Description Language), Simple protocol and SPARQL queries for different purposes. Results of the recommender system proposed by the authors depict efficiency to extract the patient risk factors along with prescriptions related to diabetes in the Internet of Things environment. For Internet of Things to be capable to process and store sensor data (scalable) related to healthcare domain, another recent work (Manogaran et al. 2018) presents an architectural model for smart and secure healthcare alerting and monitoring system using prediction method which is Mapreduce oriented. The proposed work primarily is composed up of architectural components namely MF-R (Meta Fog-Redirection) along with GC (Grouping and Choosing) for storage and collection of sensor data from a wide variety of sensors in the IoT environment. It is for securing integration of fog computing with cloud computing. Here, the proposed framework makes use of the MapReduce oriented prediction model for predicting the heart diseases and also provides security services. Metrics for performance like accuracy throughput, f-measure and sensitivity are tabulated in this work to measure efficiency of the prediction model and the designed framework. A survey of crowd sensing methods (Liu et al. 2018) was carried out recently for the IoT applications. This study is an exhaustive literature review of the existing state of art research work based on crowd sensing techniques while paying special attention to the Quality of Service and low resource cost. This work addresses wide range of methods, systems, techniques and models for mobile crowd sensing in the Internet of Things domain. Future directions are also discussed as a part of this work. A PLD (power level decision) method (Chen et al. 2018) was discussed recently related to Internet of Things in the e-Healthcare sector. For each node, for transmission of data every bit, this work enabled the selection of power level (optimum) leading to less energy expenditure. Further, a PPD (packet size decision) method gets discussed for deciding the packet size which is optimal. Also, another method called GLD (global link decision) is presented by the authors for reducing the delay and improving the reliability in. All these methods are proposed by the authors for providing recommendations in the IoT environment in the e-healthcare domain. Knowledge management scheme was discussed in a recent research work (Santoro et al. 2018) for the IoT domain. Investigations related to samples containing hundreds of Italian companies hailing from diverse domains were considered in order to carry out research employs modelling (structural equation). Investigation by the authors of this paper signifies the creation of collaborative and open environments for the knowledge management systems in an Internet of Things paradigm and depicts the recommendations of managerial decisions. The pros and cons of the above discussed techniques are given in Table 1. The summary of the above Internet of Things data analytics techniques is tabulated in Table 2.

Table 1. Pros and cons of data analytic techniques for IoT

Technique orientation	Pros	Cons
Logic	Logical intelligence	High latency
Machine/Deep learning	Improved business insights	Moderate latency
Re-use domain knowledge	Improved customer experiences	Moderate latency
Linked stream processing	Continuous pattern detection, low cost	Filtering noisy data
Distributed stream processing	Scalability, low latency	Filtering noisy data
Recommender systems	Product improvement	High costs

Table 2. Data analytics techniques for Internet of Things

Category name	Ref	Methods	IoT environment/Datasets	Application/Case study/Product
Logic/Rule based	Darshan and Anandakumar (2015)	Presents conceptual modeling of data pruning, data prediction and data presentation phases	Google web standard for IoT	IoT facilitated remote health monitoring system
Machine/Deep learning	Martis et al. (2018)	Study of transdisciplinary work in Big Data analytics, IoT and Machine Learning	Review work	Healthcare diaganostics and behavioral sciences
	Ravi et al. (2017)	Proposes deep learning technique with time-series classification of inertial sensor data	ActiveMiles, WISDM v1.1, WISDM v2.0, DaphnetFog datasets	Human activity, smartphones
	Li et al. (2018a)	Proposed a tensor convolution operation and a backpropagation method (high-order) for deep convolutional neural networks	CUAVE, SNAE2, STL-10 datasets	Tensor Model
	Li et al. (2018b)	Designed offloading mechanism for optimizing performance of Internet of Things based deep learning applications in edge computing scenarios	Python 2.7 Language, Intel Core i7 7770 CPU, NVIDIA Geforce GTX 1080, Caffe.	Edge Computing
	Fekade et al. (2018)	Probabilistic approach is presented for recovering incomplete Data using k-mean algorithm	Intel Berkeley Research Laboratory deployed 54 Mica2Dot sensors, Pycharm	Intel Berkeley Research Laboratory sensor data
	Diro and Chilamkurti (2018)	For social IoT and Fog to Things networks, presented a deep learning technique in cybersecurity for enabling the detection of attacks	NSL-KDD dataset. Distributed Fog nodes, 1-n encoding technique	Cybersecurity

(*continued*)

Table 2. (*continued*)

Category name	Ref	Methods	IoT environment/Datasets	Application/Case study/Product
	Mohammadi et al. (2018)	Proposes algorithm for semi-supervised DRL model for learning agent's enhanced performance	Grid of iBeacons and RSSI	Indoor localization in the smart city context
	Zhang et al. (2018)	Presented a Double-Projection Deep Computation Model (DPDCM) for feature learning of the associated big data in cloud and IoT scenarios	NUS-WIDE-14 and Animal-20 datasets	Laboratory of Computer Architecture and Cloud Computing
Re-use domain knowledge	Holler et al. (2014)	Presented the derivation of information and its integration into enterprise tasks	IETF 6LoWPAN, IETF RPL, IETF CoAP	Real world services
Linked stream processing	Soldatos et al. (2015)	Discusses semantic interoperability between Internet of Things and the Cloud	Open IoT, X-GSN Sensor	Phenonet Experiment, Urban Crowdsensing Application, Smart Campus Application
	Hromic et al. (2015)	OpenIoT oriented method for data stream analytics and cloud environments with acquisition, processing and analysis of real time sensor data	OpenIoT, X-GSN Sensor	Air quality monitoring related to Urban crowd sensing
	Dastjerdi and Buyya (2016)	Conceptual presentation of the integration of IoT and Fog Computing	Conceptual discussion	Activity tracking in Healthcare
	Qin et al. (2016)	Performed study associated with data-centric Internet of Things systems	Review work	Universities
	Gupta et al. (2017)	Propose iFogSim simulator related to modelling for the Fog and Internet of Things and scenarios	iFogSim	iFogSim
	Malek et al. (2017)	Investigation and analysis associated with vital signs prediction on buildings' occupants to the exposure of bioeffluent and pure carbon dioxide	Non-invasive biomedical sensors	Kaa and Storm
Distributed reasoning	Tao et al. (2018)	Proposed architecture for multilayer cloud in Internet of Things environment	Cloud server, IoT nodes	Smart Homes
	Rodríguez-Valenzuela et al. (2014)	Proposed a method for handling data fusion and acquisition (on a distributed service) for the Internet of Things pervasive systems	Five raspberry pies, ANROID tablet, MPL115A2	Weather forecasting system
	Su et al. (2018)	Performed data analytics for Edge computing for IoT systems for assessing semantic reasoning	IoT nodes Edge nodes, Cloud Amazon M4 Deca Cloud, MQTT server	Taxi cabs smart systems

(*continued*)

Table 2. (*continued*)

Category name	Ref	Methods	IoT environment/Datasets	Application/Case study/Product
	Ploennigs et al. (2018)	Conceived CIoT architecture for diagnosing anomalies related to temperature using machine learning. Proposed solutions with automated analytics and semantic meta-data modelling in the IoT environment	Smart devices, meta-deta API, Six buildings containing 3300 sensors	Buildings
	Li et al. (2018c)	Applied cognitive computing for Internet of Things in a conceptual manner	Progressive data maps	Energy applications, Health monitoring
Recommendation systems	Ali et al. (2018)	IoT-based theoretical health prescription assistant is discussed.	Theoretical work	Healthcare
	Manogaran et al. (2018)	Proposed architectural structure for IoT for storing along with processing sensor data (scalable) for health care applications	Fog Nodes, IoT Nodes	Smart Healthcare monitoring and alerting system
	Liu et al. (2018)	Discussed resource limitations, QoS issues and solutions for mobile crowdsensing in IoT environment	Survey work	Natural Environment Monitoring
	Chen et al. (2018)	Proposed mechanisms for Packet size decision and global link decision for Internet of Things paradigm	IoT Nodes	e-Healthcare
	Santoro et al. (2018)	Investigation is performed for the relationship amongst open innovation, knowledge management in IoT scenario	Sample of 298 Italian firms	Italian firms knowledge management systems

5 Open Research Issues

Some of the data management techniques in the IoT domain are still not adapted to parallelism. A lot of issues like security, privacy, scalability, data management, interoperability, device–network–human interfaces needs dire attention. Further, threats related to linkable components comes in packages like data sanitization, data, publication, data access to name a few and all in the Internet of things environment. Plenty of other issues like voluminous data, heterogeneity of devices, vertical and horizontal scalability, needs attention when the Internet of Things is working in collaboration with other technologies for big data analytics still remain as open research issues.

6 Future Directions of Research

Data vernacularism, security and analytical aspects with respect to the integration of Internet of Things along with other technologies like Fog Computing, Edge Computing, Cloud Computing, Blockchain, Radio Frequency Identification (RFID) shows the future directions of research. Workability of Internet of Things data analytical techniques using polyglot approaches still remain crucial ingredient for future direction of research.

7 Conclusion

In this sensory IoT world integrated with numerous of data oriented complex environments, wise decisions will take the time investment in the data analytical techniques discussed as a part of the presented research work for future system optimization in multiple ways. This paper reports the Internet of Things data classification from interesting dimensions and presents the data analytics techniques in a recent research oriented fashion. Here, an exhaustive survey was performed related to the existing state of art data analytics techniques for Internet of Things was performed. Precisely, this survey included the application domains, datasets specifications, approaches followed, performance notes, evaluation mechanism and usability with respect to other technologies (to name a few) with respect to diverse data analytics techniques for Internet of Things. In specific, this research work is directed to equip the audience of this paper for handling data analytics for the future Internet of Things environment. Finally, this work ponders open research issues and projects future research directions targeting at the complex heterogeneous IoT environment handling large scale data.

References

Yan, Z., Zhang, P., Vasilakos, A.V.: A survey on trust management for Internet of Things. J. Netw. Comput. Appl. **42**, 120–134 (2014)

Díaz, M., Martín, C., Rubio, B.: State-of-the-art, challenges, and open issues in the integration of Internet of things and cloud computing. J. Netw. Comput. Appl. **67**, 99–117 (2016)

Alaba, F.A., Othman, M., Hashem, I.A.T., Alotaibi, F.: Internet of Things security: a survey. J. Netw. Comput. Appl. **88**, 10–28 (2017)

https://www.postscapes.com/internet-of-things-protocols/

Darshan, K.R., Anandakumar, K.R.: A comprehensive review on usage of Internet of Things (IoT) in healthcare system. In: 2015 International Conference on Emerging Research in Electronics, Computer Science and Technology (ICERECT), pp. 132–136. IEEE, December 2015

Martis, R.J., Gurupur, V.P., Lin, H., Islam, A., Fernandes, S.L.: Recent advances in big data analytics, Internet of Things and machine learning. Future Gener. Comput. Syst. **88**, 696 (2018)

Ravi, D., Wong, C., Lo, B., Yang, G.Z.: A deep learning approach to on-node sensor data analytics for mobile or wearable devices. IEEE J. Biomed. Health Inform. **21**(1), 56–64 (2017)

Li, P., Chen, Z., Yang, L.T., Zhang, Q., Deen, M.J.: Deep convolutional computation model for feature learning on big data in Internet of Things. IEEE Trans. Industr. Inf. **14**(2), 790–798 (2018a)

Li, H., Ota, K., Dong, M.: Learning IoT in edge: deep learning for the Internet of Things with edge computing. IEEE Netw. **32**(1), 96–101 (2018b)

Fekade, B., Maksymyuk, T., Kyryk, M., Jo, M.: Probabilistic recovery of incomplete sensed data in IoT. IEEE Internet Things J. **5**(4), 2282–2292 (2018)

Diro, A.A., Chilamkurti, N.: Distributed attack detection scheme using deep learning approach for Internet of Things. Future Gener. Comput. Syst. **82**, 761–768 (2018)

Mohammadi, M., Al-Fuqaha, A., Guizani, M., Oh, J.S.: Semisupervised deep reinforcement learning in support of IoT and smart city services. IEEE Internet Things J. **5**(2), 624–635 (2018)

Zhang, Q., Yang, L.T., Chen, Z., Li, P.: High-order possibilistic c-means algorithms based on tensor decompositions for big data in IoT. Inf. Fusion **39**, 72–80 (2018)

Höller, J., Boyle, D., Karnouskos, S., Avesand, S., Mulligan, C., Tsiatsis, V.: From Machine-to-Machine to the Internet of Things, pp. 1–331. Academic Press, Cambridge (2014)

Soldatos, J., et al.: OpenIoT: Open source Internet-of-Things in the cloud. In: Podnar Žarko, I., Pripužić, K., Serrano, M. (eds.) Interoperability and Open-Source Solutions for the Internet of Things. LNCS, vol. 9001, pp. 13–25. Springer, Cham (2015). https://doi.org/10.1007/978-3-319-16546-2_3

Hromic, H., et al.: Real time analysis of sensor data for the Internet of Things by means of clustering and event processing. In: 2015 IEEE International Conference on Communications (ICC), pp. 685–691. IEEE, June 2015

Dastjerdi, A.V., Buyya, R.: Fog computing: helping the Internet of Things realize its potential. Computer **49**(8), 112–116 (2016)

Qin, Y., Sheng, Q.Z., Falkner, N.J., Dustdar, S., Wang, H., Vasilakos, A.V.: When things matter: a survey on data-centric Internet of Things. J. Netw. Comput. Appl. **64**, 137–153 (2016)

Gupta, H., Vahid Dastjerdi, A., Ghosh, S.K., Buyya, R.: iFogSim: a toolkit for modeling and simulation of resource management techniques in the Internet of Things, edge and fog computing environments. Softw. Pract. Exp. **47**(9), 1275–1296 (2017)

Malek, Y.N., et al.: On the use of IoT and big data technologies for real-time monitoring and data processing. Procedia Comput. Sci. **113**, 429–434 (2017)

Tao, M., Zuo, J., Liu, Z., Castiglione, A., Palmieri, F.: Multi-layer cloud architectural model and ontology-based security service framework for IoT-based smart homes. Future Gener. Comput. Syst. **78**, 1040–1051 (2018)

Rodríguez-Valenzuela, S., Holgado-Terriza, J.A., Gutiérrez-Guerrero, J.M., Muros-Cobos, J.L.: Distributed service-based approach for sensor data fusion in IoT environments. Sensors **14**(10), 19200–19228 (2014)

Su, X., et al.: Distribution of semantic reasoning on the edge of Internet of Things. In: 2018 IEEE International Conference on Pervasive Computing and Communications (PerCom), pp. 1–9. IEEE, March 2018

Ploennigs, J., Ba, A., Barry, M.: Materializing the promises of cognitive IoT: how cognitive buildings are shaping the way. IEEE Internet Things J. **5**(4), 2367–2374 (2018)

Li, C.S., Darema, F., Chang, V.: Distributed behavior model orchestration in cognitive Internet of Things solution. Enterp. Inf. Syst. **12**(4), 414–434 (2018c)

Ali, F., et al.: Type-2 fuzzy ontology–aided recommendation systems for IoT–based healthcare. Comput. Commun. **119**, 138–155 (2018)

Manogaran, G., Varatharajan, R., Lopez, D., Kumar, P.M., Sundarasekar, R., Thota, C.: A new architecture of Internet of Things and big data ecosystem for secured smart healthcare monitoring and alerting system. Future Gener. Comput. Syst. **82**, 375–387 (2018)

Liu, J., Shen, H., Narman, H.S., Chung, W., Lin, Z.: A survey of mobile crowdsensing techniques: a critical component for the internet of things. ACM Trans. Cyber-Physical Syst. **2**(3), 18 (2018)

Chen, X., Ma, M., Liu, A.: Dynamic power management and adaptive packet size selection for IoT in e-Healthcare. Comput. Electr. Eng. **65**, 357–375 (2018)

Santoro, G., Vrontis, D., Thrassou, A., Dezi, L.: The Internet of Things: building a knowledge management system for open innovation and knowledge management capacity. Technol. Forecast. Soc. Chang. **136**, 347–354 (2018)

Dabas, C., Gupta, J.P.: A cloud computing architecture framework for scalable RFID. In: Proceedings of the International MultiConference of Engineers and Computer Scientists, vol. 1, March 2010

Ning, Z., Huang, J., Wang, X.: Vehicular fog computing: enabling real-time traffic management for smart cities. IEEE Wirel. Commun. **26**(1), 87–93 (2019)

Zhou, Y., Tuzel, O.: Voxelnet: End-to-end learning for point cloud based 3d object detection. In: Proceedings of the IEEE Conference on Computer Vision and Pattern Recognition, pp. 4490–4499 (2018)

Information Delivery System for Early Forest Fire Detection Using Internet of Things

Ravi Tomar[1][(✉)], Rahul Tiwari[1], and Sarishma[2]

[1] University of Petroleum and Energy Studies, Dehradun, India
Ravitomar7@gmail.com, rahultiwari596@gmail.com
[2] Uttarakhand Technical University, Dehradun, India
sarishmasingh@gmail.com

Abstract. The frequency of occurrence of forest fires have increased exponentially in India in the past few decades. This can be attributed to the increasing human settlements and involvement in the forest area. Forest fires can be controlled if proper information about them is being made available to appropriate authorities at the right time so that they can take timely action to prevent it from turning into a major disaster. We propose an information delivery system along with its associated algorithm which uses different parameters, wireless technologies, sensors and Internet of Things along with cloud computing so as to deliver real time information about the forest fire occurrences. The probability of fire occurrence is transmitted to the user in the form of interactive charts and images along with latitude, longitude of the location. The system will have a Service Oriented Architecture and will transmit information to the local as well as central authorities.

Keywords: Sensors · Wireless Sensor Networks · Cloud computing · Internet of Things · Service oriented architecture

1 Introduction

Forest fire refers to the act of witnessing uncontrolled fire which causes a devastating loss to resources, both human as well as natural. In recent times, the total incidents of forest fires have increased due to multidimensional reasons. Forest fire is one scenario where early detection and prevention can be very helpful if the appropriate authorities are informed about it. In this paper we will primarily focus upon the in-time acknowledgment of the occurrence of forest fire and the design of the information delivery system for faster delivery of information so that quick and prompt action can be taken in minimum possible time in order to minimize the loss of resources.

There are two terms generally used for forest fires. One is surface fire [1] which only burns at the surface level igniting the senescent leaves falling on the floor. This type of fire occurs primarily in autumn season when dry leaves availability is quite high than normal. Surface fires are also helpful in natural regeneration of forests and increase the overall microbial activity of the soil. The other one is known as crown fire [1] where the surface fire increases in density and burns the entire suburbs of trees and shrubs. It is a very dangerous type of fire and spreads fast uphill than downhill.

© Springer Nature Singapore Pte Ltd. 2019
M. Singh et al. (Eds.): ICACDS 2019, CCIS 1045, pp. 477–486, 2019.
https://doi.org/10.1007/978-981-13-9939-8_42

The causes leading to forest fires can be either man-made or natural. Factors such as lightning, favorable environmental conditions that may lead to ignition of fire etc. all come under the category of natural causes of forest fire whereas anthropogenic factors include electricity sparks, cigarette, man-made flames etc. Indian forests have been affected by fires but in recent times with increased human settlement in and around the forests, have led to increased cases of forest fires being caused by manmade factors. After ignition, factors such as air pressure, wind, moisture level etc. all lead to an increase in the intensity of forest fires in the affected area.

Forests account for nearly 22% [1] of the total land area of India and one of the major reasons of degradation and reduction of forest cover in India is forest fires. The forests in the northern India are more prone to fire incidents as compared to our south and north eastern forests. The months of April, May and June experience the most fierce of forest fires due to present of dry leaves and increased temperature of forests in the daytime. Mostly, such incidents are initiated by human error which soon turns into the worst nightmares for the most of us. The historic fires of Uttarakhand [2] are still fresh in the hearts of most of us. On an average, nearly 20 thousand fire incidents are reported yearly in India.

There are varied impacts of forest fire on the environment as it leads to forest degradation and other damages which can be in the social, ecological and economic dimensions. Fires lead to loss of timber, biodiversity, vegetation and extinction of flora and fauna in the affected area. It leads to soil erosion, decrease in forest cover and carbon sink and correspondingly also leads to an increase in global warming and the percentage of harmful gases in the environment such as carbon monoxide, carbon dioxide etc. In some cases, it also affects the livelihood of the people residing in the area, mostly tribal and rural population.

Currently helicopters [3] are used to spray water and fire restricting materials to bring fire under control. However such methods are highly expensive and uneconomical for the country in the long run. Another method is to contain the fire within a restricted area by making barriers [3] around it which are beforehand cleaned so that they become devoid of vegetation. One more method used is to set a counter fire in response to the fire, when both the fires meet at a point, the fire is extinguished.

There are major health effects of forest fire on people who go close to it in order to contain it. Lack of breathable oxygen in the near vicinity of fire leads to asphyxia [3]. Especially in the people who are involved in the process of extinguishing it. Asphyxiation combined with dehydration may lead to fatal effects on the person.

The Forest Survey of India [4] states that we have nearly 63 million hectares of forest out of which 38 million hectare are dense forests. Considering the Indian demography, we are currently using our 1% of world's resources to satisfy the day to day needs of 16% of world's population along with the needs of 19% of world's cattle population which we account for. This clearly represents the level of pressure under which we currently are as a country to save our forests.

In this paper, we will deploy the latest technologies to develop such a model which can be implemented in Indian scenario with an effective integration of forest personnel in the process [17]. The use of wireless technology will enable the effective dissemination of information to the appropriate authorities in real time. The authorities will then be able to take care of the situation before it gets out of hand and turns into a disaster [18].

The rest of the paper is divided as: Sect. 2 gives a brief introduction of the latest technologies being leveraged in the paper which form a background of the paper. Section 3 will give the detailed description of our proposed system along with the architecture of the system. Section 4 showcases the proposed algorithm and describe the implementation of the model in the Indian administrative scenario. Section 5 will elaborate upon the security considerations of the system, after which the paper is concluded.

2 Background

With the onset of a technology oriented world, now these days almost every field is leveraging the reach of latest technologies in order to benefit themselves and achieve their means in the best possible manner [11]. As for the same case, the following technologies are used in the implementation of our project and a brief introduction of each of these technologies is provided as:

(a) *Cloud computing:* Cloud computing [7] provides a paid on the go service of computing to the user on a dynamic and subscription basis. It has revolutionized the aspect of computing as a service and has made computing ability a resource which is easily available through an online service portal and is most affordable compared to other means. We use cloud computing resources so as to generate graphs, charts and other visual data based on the information received.

(b) *Wireless Sensor Networks:* A wireless sensor network [6] is a network consisting of automated nodes in form of sensors which are primarily targeted at observing and exchanging data about the physical environment surrounding the sensors at any given point of time [9].

(c) *Communication technologies:* There are various communication protocols which are now available to be used while using wireless communication [5, 10]. Many such technologies are there such as General Packet Radio Service used to communicate via packets over a 2G, 3G or 4G connection of Global System for Mobile communication, protocols and standards such as ZigBee and IEEE 802.11 are the most affordable, efficient and reliable technologies available for wireless communication [13].

(d) *Internet of Things:* Internet of Things [8] refers to a network of sensors where sensors acts as nodes in the network and these nodes are capable of small computation and communication. They work on reception of some particular input and generate signals based on the results obtained by the computation carried on the input [21]. Recently, sensors have been used in all the trending fields so as to obtain real time on the go information about the environment in which they are deployed.

3 Proposed System

Many systems have been proposed for forest fire detection in near past [4, 5] but most of them suffer from the anomaly of raising false alarms. This problem has led to wastage of resources due to false alert as well as due to negligence in cases when a forest fire has indeed occurred. In order to detect the occurrence of fire in a forest with least number of false alarms [9], we propose a system which leverages the technologies such as Internet of Things, Cloud Computing and other wireless technologies and aims at providing an efficient, smart, tracking facility for forest fires [14, 15].

The resultant model is intelligent and uses different types of sensors to detect fire. These sensors when scattered in the forest at appropriate distances, sense the data and keep on transmitting it to their master nodes. After receiving the data, it will be forwarded to the user in charge [12]. The user will be at the receiving end and will keep on getting updates about the possibility of occurrence of fire with respect to time and the rest of measured parameters [19].

Once the user is notified through the user application programs, steps can be taken in time to extinguish the fire so as to minimize the overall losses [21]. The purpose of proposing this model is to minimize the false alarms as well to as to reduce the human effort which is needed to patrol the forests, especially in the months of March, April and May [3] when the probability of forest fire occurrence is greatly increased in tropical regions [2].

The proposed system will be self-dependent and autonomous in functioning with minimum need of outside interference and support. The entire stretch of forest area to be covered will be categorized and divided into three layers. The first layer will cover the outermost area and will contain multiple sensors, which are termed as sub nodes over here. The second layer will lie in the middle of the forest and will contain multiple sensors called as nodes. Nodes will be receiving data from sub nodes and process it accordingly. The last layer will be containing master nodes which are responsible for processing of data and forwarding it to the cloud service.

Types of Sensor Nodes: The sensors being scattered over the entire area of forest are categorized on the basis of level of authority and data reporting.

(a) *Sub Nodes:* These are the most primitive nodes which will collect all the basic environmental data depending upon the type of sensors being deployed. The data about the environmental conditions such as temperature and relative humidity (DHT22), smoke, light, carbon dioxide intensity, carbon monoxide intensity is sensed by these nodes. The list of parameters being sensed can be decreased or increased depending upon the cost of infrastructure or the criticality of the forest on which they are being implemented.

(b) *Nodes:* The data being sensed and collected by the sub nodes will be forwarded to these nodes which will act as a master node for the sub nodes.

(c) *Master nodes:* Master nodes are embedded with a GSM or GPRS module along with a Wi-Fi backup in adverse situations. Master nodes will sense the information regarding the net wind speed and direction and will integrate it with the information obtained by the other nodes so as to generate useful set of data. This data is forwarded to the could computing based services through GPRS/GSM module. The services then process the data and visualizes it in the form of graphs and charts which are then sent to the user application, so as to make it very descriptive and informative to the user.

In a normal scenario, considering the environmental conditions, there are numerous natural factors which support the sustaining forest fires. Temperature, humidity level, wind, presence of dry mass etc. all account for such factors. In [10], the rule of 30 is proposed which states that if three critical factors surpass their threshold values then there is a high probability of catching fire. The rule states that if the temperature of a forest is more than 30 °C, the humidity value or moisture content in the air is more than 30% and finally if the wind speed in that area is more than 30 km/h then there might be chances of occurrence of fire in the area.

In our proposed model, we will be using a fuzzy logic function which will take few parameters as input and will be generating the output in the form of graph. The parameters listed below will be observed and transmitted by the sensors which will be dispersed along the geographical area of the forest. Different sensors will be evaluating different parameters. Since sensors have a very limited battery life, it is proposed hereby that they should be equipped with solar panels so that they can function autonomously for as long as possible before we need to manually change their batteries which may be needed in 10 months or so [11]. To further save the battery life, we propose that sensors should remain in any of the three states:

Table 1. Power consumption of sensors

S.no.	Mode of operation	Power consumed
1.	Sleep	62 μA
2.	On	9 mA
3.	Hibernate	0.7 μA

The mean separation for deployment of sensors is proposed to be around 75 m from each other where they can communicate using ZigBee protocol [12] and in case of emergency can also use GPRS for transmission of alerts. The placement of sensors is done in such a manner so as to form a grid of sensors [16] which cover each and every section of the forest. ZigBee offers a frequency of 2.4 GHz with a −96 dBm sensitivity index and a range of 75 m. The alert probability will be calculated using the algorithm proposed in the next section. The model will be using a service oriented architecture which is briefly given as [17, 18]:

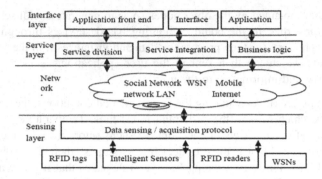

Fig. 1. Service oriented architecture

4 Proposed Algorithm

This section deals with the details of the algorithm which is being implemented for the proper functioning of the system. The algorithm takes in input in the form of data being transmitted by the sensors and then executes its function so as to provide most accurate results to the user (Table 2).

Table 2. Notations of parameters used

Parameter	Symbol
Temperature	T
Wind	W
Relative humidity	H
Air pressure	P
Smoke	S
Light	L
Sub-node	Sn
Node	N
Master node	Mn
Sn (counter, max. no.)	Sn(i,x)
N (counter, max. no.)	N(j,y)
Mn (counter, max. no.)	Mn(k,z)
Status (on, off)	(1,0)
Time (minutes)	&
Graphs and charts	Gr

The following table details out the modules being used in the model whereby every module is responsible for some or other functioning of the system.

Table 3. The list and function constituent modules

Module	Functionality
Start()	Awakes the entire system and the corresponding modules
Mobile_app()	A user interface through which information will be transferred
Sub_node_data(t,s,l,h)	This function is used to report the sensed data to the nodes in tier 2
Node_data(t,s,l,h,p,w)	This function is used to report the sensed data to the nodes in tier 3
Master_node_data(res)	It takes input and produces the output based upon a function
Sense(&, sub_node)/Sense(&, node)/Sense (&, master_node)	This function will make the parameter to sense and report data as and when the function is called
Exec_func(t,s,l,h,p,w)	A fuzzy logic based function which will predict the forest fire occurence
Status(on,off)	When invoked, all the working nodes will broadcast 1 to mark that they are alive
Send_result(res)	Sends the processed result to cloud service
Visualize(res)	The obtained result is put into graphs and charts
Notify_user(res, gr)	The user is notified via the mobile application
Cloud_service()	Data will be sent by master node to remote cloud services
Tag()	Keeps track of information such as serial number, status, product ID etc.
Sleep()	Allows the nodes to go into hibernate mode

Considering the above mentioned parameters, the algorithm which uses the parameters as well as modules is given as:

1) Start (&) where &={5,10} for February to May; &={10,15} for June-October and &={20,25} for November-January
2) Start Mobile_app();
3) From (i=0 to x)
    Start_Sn(i)
    Sense (&, Sn(i));
4) From (j=0 to y)
    Start_N(j)
    Sense (&, N(j));
5) From (k=0 to z)
    Start_Mn(k)
    Sense (&, Mn(k));
6) Sub_node_data(t,s,l,h)→Node(ij);
7) Node_data(t,s,l,h,p,w)→Master_Node(jk);
8) Master_Node(t,s,l,h,p,w)→Exec_func();
9) Exec_func()=tslhpw(q)=min[μt(q),μs(q),μl(q),μ(q),μp(q),μw(q)];
10) Exec_func()→res→Master_node();
11) Master_node(res) →Cloud_service();
12) Cloud_service(res) →Visualize();
13) Visualize(gr) →Cloud_service();
14) Cloud_service(gr) →Mobile_app();
15) Repeat till &=∞;
16) End.

The above mentioned algorithm when implemented using a test case over the iFog simulator generates correct results for nearly 9 out of 10 cases. The data for the test cases is as provided in the table:

Table 4. Prediction of fire results

Temp	Light	Humidity	Smoke	Wind	Fire
20	300	80	30	10	27.8
80	300	80	30	10	41
20	300	80	80	15	33.8
20	900	80	30	12	39.7
20	300	100	30	20	19.3
20	300	80	30	10	30.3
80	300	80	80	8	50
80	800	80	80	50	53.6
80	800	40	80	10	63.1
100	800	40	80	20	70.1

The obtained results are in accord with our model and algorithm. The user interface and the mobile application can further be divided into two types where one user interface can be for the professionals guarding the forest and the other is for the people who are the administrators. A link to it can also be made to the emergency response services such as fire brigades, helicopters etc. which will serve as quick hand measures in action of extinguishing the fire or controlling it.

5   Security Considerations

With the rapid advancement in technology and numerous information dissemination techniques, the rate of information breach and hacking frequency has also been increased at an exponential rate [19]. The proposed system is aimed at information delivery to the appropriate authorities so as to minimize the overall loss of resources. The system does not focus ample enough to strengthen the security of its constituting components. Since the available resources that we have at our disposal are quite low therefore the computation ability is preserved to keep the system up and running for longest period of time which leads to sidelining of security. However as per the resources available, we always have an opportunity to deploy another layer which will handle the security related aspects of the system. Various encryption techniques can be used which can be expended up to 128 bits of keys [21] which can be used to encrypt and decrypt the data. This domain of security is open for future research by the aspiring researchers.

6 Conclusion

In order to effectively manage the occurrence of forest fires, it is paramount that the instant information about it is being provided to appropriate authorities on time. We propose a model along with its working algorithm whereby we predict the probability of occurrence of forest fire on the basis of some parameters. These parameters are being sensed using various sensors which will form a wireless sensor network and it will use a service oriented architecture along with leveraging the concept of Internet of Things and cloud computing. The paper concludes with the outline of the due considerations of security perspective on the system.

References

1. Lele, N., Joshi, P.K.: Analyzing deforestation rates, spatial forest cover changes and identifying critical areas of forest cover changes in North-East India during 1972–1999. Environ. Monit. Assess. **156**(1–4), 159 (2009)
2. Barrett, S.W., Arno, S.F.: Indian fires as an ecological influence in the northern rockies. J. Forest. **80**(10), 647–651 (1982)
3. Bahuguna, V.K., Upadhay, A.: Forest fires in India: policy initiatives for community participation. Int. Forest. Rev. **4**(2), 122–127 (2002)
4. Champion, S.H., Seth, S.K.: A revised survey of the forest types of India (1968)
5. Karafyllidis, I., Thanailakis, A.: A model for predicting forest fire spreading using cellular automata. Ecol. Model. **99**(1), 87–97 (1997)
6. Yuan, C., Liu, Z., Zhang, Y.: Aerial images-based forest fire detection for firefighting using optical remote sensing techniques and unmanned aerial vehicles. J. Intell. Rob. Syst. **88**(2–4), 635–654 (2017)
7. Khanna, A.: RAS: a novel approach for dynamic resource allocation. In: 2015 1st International Conference on Next Generation Computing Technologies (NGCT), pp. 25–29. IEEE, September 2015
8. Atzori, L., Iera, A., Morabito, G.: The Internet of Things: a survey. Comput. Netw. **54**(15), 2787–2805 (2010)
9. Zhang, J., Li, W., Yin, Z., Liu, S., Guo, X.: Forest fire detection system based on wireless sensor network. In: 4th IEEE Conference on Industrial Electronics and Applications, ICIEA 2009, pp. 520–523. IEEE, May 2009. Zhang, J., Li, W., Han, N., Kan, J.: Forest fire detection system based on a ZigBee wireless sensor network. Front. Forestry China 3(3), 369-374 (2008)
10. Yu, L., Wang, N., Meng, X.: Real-time forest fire detection with wireless sensor networks. In: 2005 International Conference on Wireless Communications, Networking and Mobile Computing, Proceedings, vol. 2, pp. 1214–1217. IEEE, September 2005
11. Hefeeda, M., Bagheri, M.: Wireless sensor networks for early detection of forest fires. In: IEEE International Conference on Mobile Adhoc and Sensor Systems, MASS 2007, pp. 1–6. IEEE, October 2007
12. Collins, B.M., Stevens, J.T., Miller, J.D., Stephens, S.L., Brown, P.M., North, M.P.: Alternative characterization of forest fire regimes: incorporating spatial patterns. Landscape Ecol. **32**(8), 1543–1552 (2017)
13. Arrue, B.C., Ollero, A., De Dios, J.M.: An intelligent system for false alarm reduction in infrared forest-fire detection. IEEE Intell. Syst. Appl. **15**(3), 64–73 (2000)

14. Garcia-Jimenez, S., Jurio, A., Pagola, M., De Miguel, L., Barrenechea, E., Bustince, H.: Forest fire detection: a fuzzy system approach based on overlap indices. Appl. Soft Comput. **52**, 834–842 (2017)
15. Sahana, M., Ganaie, T.A.: GIS-based landscape vulnerability assessment to forest fire susceptibility of Rudraprayag district, Uttarakhand, India. Environ. Earth Sci. **76**(20), 676 (2017)
16. Singhal, A., Tomar, R.: Intelligent accident management system using IoT and cloud computing. In: 2016 2nd International Conference on Next Generation Computing Technologies (NGCT), pp. 89–92. IEEE, October 2016
17. Hua, L., Shao, G.: The progress of operational forest fire monitoring with infrared remote sensing. J. Forestry Res. **28**(2), 215–229 (2017)
18. Alkhatib, A.A.: Smart and low cost technique for forest fire detection using wireless sensor network. Int. J. Comput. Appl. **81**(11), 12 (2013)
19. Mengod, P.C., Bravo, J.A.T., Sardá, L.L.: The influence of external factors on false alarms in an infrared fire detection system. Int. J. Wild Fire **24**(2), 261–266 (2015)
20. Khanna, A., Sarishma: Mobile Cloud Computing Principles and Paradigms. IK International, New Delhi (2015)
21. Kim, H., Park, H., Jang, S.S.: An energy-efficient location-aware routing scheme for mobile wireless sensor networks. J. Next Gener. Inf. Technol. (JNIT) **4**(6) (2013)

An Experimental Analysis of Similarity Measures Effect for Identification of Software Component Composition of Services Based on Use-Cases

Amit Kumar Srivastava[✉] and Shishir Kumar

Jaypee University of Engineering and Technology, Guna 473226, India
amitsri1983@gmail.com, dr.shishir@yahoo.com

Abstract. The current business environment made helpless to rethink that how software component is developed so that in future if similar feature required then it could be reused. For the reuse process the component-based software engineering was useful. In component-based development scenario the challenging task is to identify the software logical components. In the literature there are various clustering techniques with expert judgment are available to identify logical software components. In this context, all the previous methods use the similarity measure technique for finding the software cohesion. It has been observed that if any change has been made to similarity measure then it reflects changes in value of software cohesion. So, the goal of this paper is to show the effect of similarity measure for identify the logical software component of software system. For the validation and justification various feature-based similarity measures and standard parameter (Precision, Recall and Accuracy etc.) are used for software cohesion for the design of Online Broker System (case study).

Keywords: Logical component · Data mining · Software Cohesion · Software coupling · Software complexity · Similarity measure

1 Introduction

In component-based software development process, collection of similar types of component is a challenging task. There are various clustering techniques along with expert judgment methods are used to collect the component, and it gives remarkable assurance for the similar type of the logical software component for software system. Such combinatorial problem is known as NP-hard problem. In previous techniques various corelational/non-corelational or distance-based similarity measures are used to predict the similar type of logical components for a software system. All generic techniques were performed the sensitivity analysis in respect of weight value over feature parameters. But none of them describe the generalize hypothesis of similarity measure for such type of NP-hard problem. In this paper, author concentrate on experimental evaluation of effect of similarity measure in identification of logical components and in the results, it shows that there may be the possibility to improve the

© Springer Nature Singapore Pte Ltd. 2019
M. Singh et al. (Eds.): ICACDS 2019, CCIS 1045, pp. 487–499, 2019.
https://doi.org/10.1007/978-981-13-9939-8_43

result. As observed in previous techniques, similarity measure plays a vital role in identification of logical components and It is responsible as prerequisite point for have similar type of component for the base point of designing of software architecture [1]. It is a challenging task to decompose the system by identifying the similar feature-based logical component without using any tool support [2]. Researcher are used several correlation, Non-correlation or distance-based Binary similarity measure in form of automatic or semi-automatic methods to avoid the conflict situation or biasing condition about functionality during the identification of logical components. Out of all available standard methods some of the clustering methods [3–5] and some of the based-on optimization [6, 7] are also used the binary similarity measure for identification of logical components. In all cases fitness function indirectly depend on the similarity measure. In each method the fitness function variable e.g., Software Cohesion has computed by binary similarity measure [8–15]. The selection of a feature similarity measure is also a NP-hard problem.

Choi et al. [19] done a few comprehensive surveys on binary measures and he collected in three categories of feature vector i.e. correlation, non-correlation and distance-based binary similarity measures used over last century. In this paper for performing the experimental evaluation we used Choi, S.S. et al. listed binary similarity measure for calculation of fitness variable which is mentioned in Tables 5 and 7. It has been observed that each similarity measure gives different value for software cohesion and these values give the resultant change in fitness function value. This is shown by the Fig. 1. The experimental evaluation of effect shown by using real world example online broker system (OBS) [7]. The OBS is real world example of software which is used for automate the traditional stock trading using internet and gives faster access to stock reports, current market trends and real-time stock prices. The OBS case consist of 30 use cases (UC_1, …, UC_{30}), 04 actors (A_1, A_2, A_3, A_4), 22 analysis classes and 6 entity classes (AC_1, AC_2, …, AC_6). The component diagram of OBS is mapped with the actors with use cases is given in Eqs. (1)–(4).

$$Actor(A_1) \rightarrow \{UC_1...UC_{18}, UC_{19}, UC_{20}, UC_{26}, ..., UC_{30}\} \tag{1}$$

$$Actor(A_2) \rightarrow \{UC_2, UC_3, UC_4, UC_{21}, ..., UC_{25}\} \tag{2}$$

$$Actor(A_3) \rightarrow \{UC_{12}\} \tag{3}$$

$$Actor(A_4) \rightarrow \{UC_2 UC_3 UC_4 UC_{12} UC_{15}...UC_{20}\} \tag{4}$$

The use case matrix Table 1 is arrange in the 30×10 metrics size which gives the feature relation between the Actor, Entity classes and use cases. If any use case mapped with the any actor or entity-class then it represented by binary value 1 otherwise 0. For evaluation the SCI-GA [7] fitness equation (5) is use for showing the effect of similarity.

$$FF = SoftCoh - (SoftCoup + SoftComp) \tag{5}$$

Where, SoftCoh = Software Cohesion, SoftCoup = Software Coupling and SoftComp = Software Complexity

$$SoftCoh = \sum_{c=1}^{n} \frac{CC(cmp_c)}{n},$$ (6)

$$SoftCoup = \sqrt{\frac{\sum_{c=1}^{n}(CCR(cmp_c))^2}{No.\ of\ usecases}}$$ (7)

$$SoftComp = \sqrt{\frac{\sum_{c=1}^{n}(CompComp(cmp_c))^2}{No.\ of\ usecases}}$$ (8)

$cmp_c = c^{th}$ component, $CC\ (cmp_c)$ = Cohesion of cth component, n = number of the component and $CCR\ (cmp_c)$ = Coupling of the cth component.

Table 1. Use case matrix of online broker system case study

Use case	Actor(A_i) i = 1, 2, 3, 4				Entity Class (AC_j) j = 1, 2, 3, 4, 5, 6						Use Case	Actor(A_i) i = 1, 2, 3, 4				Entity Class (AC_j) j = 1, 2, 3, 4, 5, 6					
	1	2	3	4	1	2	3	4	5	6		1	2	3	4	1	2	3	4	5	6
UC_1	1	0	0	0	0	1	0	0	0	0	UC_{16}	1	0	0	1	0	0	0	0	0	1
UC_2	1	1	0	1	0	1	0	0	0	0	UC_{17}	1	0	0	1	0	0	0	0	0	1
UC_3	1	1	0	1	0	1	0	0	0	0	UC_{18}	1	0	0	1	0	0	0	0	0	1
UC_4	1	1	0	1	0	1	0	0	0	0	UC_{19}	1	0	0	1	0	0	0	0	0	1
UC_5	1	0	0	0	1	1	0	0	0	0	UC_{20}	1	0	0	1	0	0	0	0	0	1
UC_6	1	0	0	0	1	1	0	0	0	0	UC_{21}	0	1	0	0	0	0	0	0	0	0
UC_7	1	0	0	0	1	1	0	1	0	0	UC_{22}	0	1	0	0	0	1	0	0	0	0
UC_8	1	0	0	0	1	1	0	0	0	0	UC_{23}	0	1	0	0	0	1	0	0	0	0
UC_9	1	0	0	0	1	1	0	1	0	0	UC_{24}	0	1	0	0	0	1	0	0	0	0
UC_{10}	1	0	0	0	0	0	1	0	0	1	UC_{25}	0	1	0	0	0	1	0	0	0	0
UC_{11}	1	0	0	0	0	0	1	0	0	0	UC_{26}	1	0	0	0	1	0	0	1	1	1
UC_{12}	1	0	1	1	0	0	0	0	0	1	UC_{27}	1	0	0	0	1	0	0	1	1	1
UC_{13}	1	0	0	0	0	0	0	0	0	1	UC_{28}	1	0	0	0	0	0	0	1	0	1
UC_{14}	1	0	0	0	0	0	1	0	0	1	UC_{29}	1	0	0	0	1	0	0	1	1	1
UC_{15}	1	0	0	1	0	0	0	0	0	1	UC_{30}	1	0	0	0	1	0	0	1	1	1

2 Literature Review

In previous suggested methods several clustering methods like (a) RBR (b) RB (c) Agglomerative (d) Direct (e) Graph-Based (f) FCM (g) Hierarchical clustering and (h) Competitive Neural Network are used for identification of software component. In methods (a) to (e) based on the similarity matrix using CLUTO tool [16]. In methods (e) and (h) clustering is performed on feature matrix of use cases using MATLAB software [17]. Shahmohammadi et al. suggested a clustering-based approach for identification of logical component and he was used coefficient of Jaccard construct a similarity matrix for binary features [5]. He was performed sensitivity analysis of weight for binary and continuous similarity matrix and concludes that weight value 0.5 is suitable for binary and continuous similarity metrics. Because already it concluded by R. Xu et al. that in both the cases problem is related to information loss [18]. As on effect of weight value in method SCI-GA [7] use the simple coefficient approach for similarity measure. But in this work the result shows that improve is possible by other similarity measure coefficient. Numerous correlation and non-correlation binary similarity measure are used in various fields. Each of them considers the different synaptic properties. Some of similarity coefficients include the similarity measure and some of do not consider it. These binary similarity coefficients were applied in various field i.e. biological data set [20, 21], ethnology [22], taxonomy [23], image retrieval [24], geology [25], and chemistry [26] etc. Recently, they have been frequently used to solve the NP-hard problem like identification problems in biometrics such as fingerprint [27], iris images [28], and recognition [29, 30]. Various research articles [20, 31–34] elaborate their properties and features.

3 Experimental Evaluation

Similarities have direct geometric interoperability; they express the relative positions of points in the multidimensional space. If the points represent a random sample from a statistical population, then the strength of correlation can be tested for significance by methods well-known from univariate statistics. It can be said that the pair wise similarity of objects is meaningful only if it calculated based on characters present in at least one of the objects, and those characterizing only some others in the simple are irrelevant.

Similarity measure is processing to compute the completely similar types of object. Usually the completely similar or up to the maximum similarity is described by the value 1 ($Sij = 1$) and if Si and Sj is not similar or minimum similarity then it is denoted by the 0 ($Sij = 0$). If binary variables are in fact two-state nominal characters (i.e., the presence/absence from is just a "disguise"), then coding by 0 and 1 is arbitrary: 1 does not mean more than 0. Here in this paper authors are use the use-case matrix for the feature of software component. For the validation of use-case property recall and precision are calculating as follows;

3.1 Precision (p)

In binary classification context precision is referred to as positive predictive value. For the Table 1 (use-case matrix of Online Broker System) the calculated precision p is given in Table 2. In Table 2 the rows are shows the exactness between two use case pair like in first row the precision value of UC_1 to $UCj\varepsilon_{1, 2, 3....,30}$ are shown. The value of UC_1 to UC_1 is 1 that means 100% like each other. The UC_1 to UC_2 value is 0.5 shows that only 50% similarity is present in both the use case pair.

Table 2. Precision for OBS Use case

UC$_i$, where i = {1, 2, 3, 4, 5, 6, 7, 8, 9, 10, 30}	UC$_j$, where j = {1, 2, 3, 4, 5, 6, 7, 8, 9, 10, ..., 30}																							
	1.0	0.5	0.5	0.5	0.7	0.7	0.5	0.7	0.5	0.3	0.5	0.3	–	0.3	0.0	0.5	0.5	0.5	0.5	0.2	0.2	0.3	0.2	0.2
	1.0	1.0	1.0	1.0	0.7	0.7	0.5	0.7	0.5	0.3	0.5	0.5	–	0.7	1.0	1.0	1.0	1.0	1.0	0.2	0.2	0.3	0.2	0.2
	1.0	1.0	1.0	1.0	0.7	0.7	0.5	0.7	0.5	0.3	0.5	0.5	–	0.7	1.0	1.0	1.0	1.0	1.0	0.2	0.2	0.3	0.2	0.2
	1.0	1.0	1.0	1.0	0.7	0.7	0.5	0.7	0.5	0.3	0.5	0.5	–	0.7	1.0	1.0	1.0	1.0	1.0	0.2	0.2	0.3	0.2	0.2
	–	–	–	–	–	–	–	–	–	–	–	–	–	–	–	–	–	–	–	–	–	–	–	–
	0.5	0.3	0.3	0.3	0.7	0.7	0.8	0.7	0.8	0.7	0.5	0.5	–	0.7	0.0	0.0	0.0	0.0	0.0	1.0	1.0	1.0	1.0	1.0
	0.5	0.3	0.3	0.3	0.3	0.3	0.5	0.3	0.5	0.7	0.5	0.5	–	0.7	0.0	0.0	0.0	0.0	0.0	0.6	0.6	1.0	0.6	0.6
	0.5	0.3	0.3	0.3	0.7	0.7	0.8	0.7	0.8	0.7	0.5	0.5	–	0.7	0.0	0.0	0.0	0.0	0.0	1.0	1.0	1.0	1.0	1.0
	0.5	0.3	0.3	0.3	0.7	0.7	0.8	0.7	0.8	0.7	0.5	0.5	–	0.7	0.0	0.0	0.0	0.0	0.0	1.0	1.0	1.0	1.0	1.0

3.2 Recall (r)

In binary classification the recall is out of all items i.e. completely true, how many are items classified by the similarity measures or classifiers. For the Table 1 (use-case matrix of Online Broker System use case only) the calculated recall is given in Table 3 below.

The above Table 3 shows the recall value for all use-cases of OBS component.

Table 3. Recall (Sensitivity) for OBS use case

UC$_i$, where i = {1, 2, 3, 4, 5, 6, 7, 8, ..., 30}	UC$_j$, where $_j$ = {1, 2, 3, 4, 5, 6, 7, 8, 9, 10, ..., 30}																							
	1.0	1.0	1.0	1.0	0.2	0.2	0.3	1.0	1.0	0.5	0.5	0.5	–	0.5	0.0	0.5	0.5	0.5	0.5	0.5	0.5	0.5	0.5	0.5
	0.5	1.0	1.0	1.0	0.3	0.3	0.3	0.5	0.5	0.3	0.3	0.5	–	0.3	0.3	0.5	0.5	0.5	0.5	0.3	0.3	0.3	0.3	0.3
	0.5	1.0	1.0	1.0	0.3	0.3	0.3	0.5	0.5	0.3	0.3	0.5	–	0.3	0.3	0.5	0.5	0.5	0.5	0.3	0.3	0.3	0.3	0.3
	0.5	1.0	1.0	1.0	0.3	0.3	0.3	0.5	0.5	0.3	0.3	0.5	–	0.3	0.3	0.5	0.5	0.5	0.5	0.3	0.3	0.3	0.3	0.3
	–	–	–	–	–	–	–	–	–	–	–	–	–	–	–	–	–	–	–	–	–	–	–	–
	0.2	0.2	0.2	0.2	0.3	0.3	0.4	0.4	0.6	0.4	0.2	0.4	–	0.3	0.0	0.0	0.0	0.0	0.0	1.0	1.0	0.6	1.0	1.0
	0.3	0.3	0.3	0.3	0.2	0.2	0.3	0.3	0.7	0.7	0.3	0.7	–	0.3	0.0	0.0	0.0	0.0	0.0	1.0	1.0	1.0	1.0	1.0
	0.2	0.2	0.2	0.2	0.3	0.3	0.4	0.4	0.6	0.4	0.2	0.4	–	0.3	0.0	0.0	0.0	0.0	0.0	1.0	1.0	0.6	1.0	1.0
	0.2	0.2	0.2	0.2	0.3	0.3	0.4	0.4	0.6	0.4	0.2	0.4	–	0.3	0.0	0.0	0.0	0.0	0.0	1.0	1.0	0.6	1.0	1.0

3.3 F-Measure

The F-measure is a measure of a similar type of use cases test's accuracy. It considers both the positive predictive value (Precision: p) and the sensitivity of data (Recall: r) of the test to compute the measure: Precision (p) is the number of correct positive results divided by the number of all positive results, and Recall (r) is the number of correct positive results divided by the number of positive results that should have been classified.

For the Table 1 (use-case matrix of Online Broker System use case only) the calculated F-Measure for pair of use-cases is given in Table 4 below.

Table 4. F-Measure for OBS use cases

UCi, where i = {1, 2, 3, 4, 5, 6, 7, 8, 9, ..., 30}	UCj, where J = {1, 2, 3, 4, 5, 6, 7, 8, 9, 10, ..., 30}																						
	1.0	0.7	0.7	0.7	0.3	0.3	0.3	0.8	0.7	0.4	0.5	–	0.4	0.0	0.5	0.5	0.5	0.5	0.3	0.3	0.4	0.3	0.3
	0.7	1.0	1.0	1.0	0.4	0.4	0.4	0.6	0.5	0.3	0.3	–	0.4	0.4	0.7	0.7	0.7	0.7	0.2	0.2	0.3	0.2	0.2
	0.7	1.0	1.0	1.0	0.4	0.4	0.4	0.6	0.5	0.3	0.3	–	0.4	0.4	0.7	0.7	0.7	0.7	0.2	0.2	0.3	0.2	0.2
	0.7	1.0	1.0	1.0	0.4	0.4	0.4	0.6	0.5	0.3	0.3	–	0.4	0.4	0.7	0.7	0.7	0.7	0.2	0.2	0.3	0.2	0.2
	–	–	–	–	–	–	–	–	–	–	–	–	–	–	–	–	–	–	–	–	–	–	–
	0.3	0.2	0.2	0.2	0.4	0.4	0.5	0.5	0.7	0.5	0.3	–	0.4	0.0	0.0	0.0	0.0	0.0	1.0	1.0	0.8	1.0	1.0
	0.4	0.3	0.3	0.3	0.2	0.2	0.4	0.3	0.6	0.7	0.4	–	0.4	0.0	0.0	0.0	0.0	0.0	0.8	0.8	1.0	0.8	0.8
	0.3	0.2	0.2	0.2	0.4	0.4	0.5	0.5	0.7	0.5	0.3	–	0.4	0.0	0.0	0.0	0.0	0.0	1.0	1.0	0.8	1.0	1.0
	0.3	0.2	0.2	0.2	0.4	0.4	0.5	0.5	0.7	0.5	0.3	–	0.4	0.0	0.0	0.0	0.0	0.0	1.0	1.0	0.8	1.0	1.0

3.4 Accuracy

Accuracy is defined as to the closeness of a measured value to a given threshold or standard. For the Table 1 (use-case matrix of Online Broker System use case only) the calculated Accuracy is given in Table 5 below.

Table 5. Accuracy for OBS use cases

Uci, where i = {1,2,3,4,5,6, 7,8,9,10,.......,30}	UCj, where J = {1,2,3,4,5,6,7,8,9, 10, ...,30}																						
	1.0	0.8	0.8	0.8	0.9	0.9	0.8	0.2	0.2	0.2	0.2	–	0.2	0.2	0.2	0.2	0.2	0.2	0.2	0.2	0.2	0.2	0.2
	0.8	1.0	1.0	1.0	0.7	0.7	0.6	0.4	0.4	0.4	0.4	–	0.5	0.4	0.4	0.4	0.4	0.4	0.4	0.4	0.4	0.4	0.4
	0.8	1.0	1.0	1.0	0.7	0.7	0.6	0.4	0.4	0.4	0.4	–	0.5	0.4	0.4	0.4	0.4	0.4	0.4	0.4	0.4	0.4	0.4
	0.8	1.0	1.0	1.0	0.7	0.7	0.6	0.4	0.4	0.4	0.4	–	0.5	0.4	0.4	0.4	0.4	0.4	0.4	0.4	0.4	0.4	0.4
	0.8	0.8	0.8	0.8	0.7	0.7	0.6	0.2	0.2	0.2	0.2	–	0.4	0.2	0.2	0.2	0.2	0.2	0.2	0.2	0.2	0.2	0.2
	0.8	0.8	0.8	0.8	0.7	0.7	0.6	0.2	0.2	0.2	0.2	–	0.4	0.2	0.2	0.2	0.2	0.2	0.2	0.2	0.2	0.2	0.2
	0.5	0.3	0.3	0.3	0.6	0.6	0.7	0.5	0.5	0.5	0.5	–	0.5	0.5	0.5	0.5	0.5	0.5	0.5	0.5	0.5	0.5	0.5
	0.5	0.3	0.3	0.3	0.6	0.6	0.7	0.5	0.5	0.5	0.5	–	0.5	0.5	0.5	0.5	0.5	0.5	0.5	0.5	0.5	0.5	0.5
	0.7	0.5	0.5	0.5	0.6	0.6	0.7	0.3	0.3	0.3	0.3	–	0.5	0.3	0.3	0.3	0.3	0.3	0.3	0.3	0.3	0.3	0.3
	0.5	0.3	0.3	0.3	0.6	0.6	0.7	0.5	0.5	0.5	0.5	–	0.5	0.5	0.5	0.5	0.5	0.5	0.5	0.5	0.5	0.5	0.5
	0.5	0.3	0.3	0.3	0.6	0.6	0.7	0.5	0.5	0.5	0.5	–	0.5	0.5	0.5	0.5	0.5	0.5	0.5	0.5	0.5	0.5	0.5

3.5 On the Basis of Correlation Similarity Measures

For evaluation we are using Sokal & Sneath-II measure for computing the similarity measures.

$$S_{Sokel\&Sneath-II} = \frac{2(a+d)}{2a+b+c+2d} \tag{9}$$

Where, a = Number of variables present in both the object Si & Sj value having 1, b = Number of variables present in object (S$_i$) and absent from object (S$_j$), c = Number of variables present in object (S$_j$) and absent from object (S$_i$), d = Number of variables absent from both the objects.

For OBS real world example the value of a, b, c & d for UC_1 to UC_1 and UC_1 to UC_2 is calculated in the Table 6. Sokel & Sneath-II applied on OBS case study and finding the fitness parameter using Eq. (9).

Table 6. The parameter value for UC_1 to UC_1 and UC_1 to UC_2

Use case pair	a (TT)	b (TF)	c (FT)	d (FF)
UC_1-UC_1	2	0	0	8
UC_1-UC_2	2	2	0	6

Similarly, we can calculate the other object value of use cases. Now the Sokal & Sneath-II similarity measure for UC_1 to UC_2 is: Sim $(UC_1, UC_2) = 2(2 + 6)/(2 * 2 + 2 + 0 + 2 * 6) = 16/18 = .88$

Similarly, we can compute the similarity measure for all combination of use cases, calculated value is given in Table 7.

Table 7. Similarity Metrix/Proximity Metrix for OBS use cases

	UC_1	UC_2	UC_3	UC_4	UC_5	UC_6	UC_7	–	UC_{24}	UC_{25}	UC_{26}	UC_{27}	UC_{28}	UC_{29}	UC_{30}
UC_1	1.00	0.89	0.89	0.89	0.95	0.95	0.89	–	0.89	0.89	0.67	0.67	0.82	0.67	0.67
UC_2		1	1	1	0.82	0.82	0.75	–	0.89	0.89	0.46	0.46	0.67	0.46	0.46
UC_3			1	1	0.82	0.82	0.75	–	0.89	0.89	0.46	0.46	0.67	0.46	0.46
UC_4				1	0.82	0.82	0.75	–	0.89	0.89	0.46	0.46	0.67	0.46	0.46
UC_5					1	1	0.95	–	0.82	0.82	0.75	0.75	0.75	0.75	0.75
UC_6						1	0.95	–	0.82	0.82	0.75	0.75	0.75	0.75	0.75
–	–	–	–	–	–	–	–	–	–	–	–	–	–	–	–
UC_{25}							–		1	0.46	0.46	0.67	0.46	0.46
UC_{26}							–			1	1	0.89	1	1
UC_{27}							–				1	0.89	1	1
UC_{28}							–					1	0.89	0.89
UC_{29}							–						1	1
UC_{30}							–							1

According to the sensitivity analysis [5] both the properties i.e. Actor and Entity classes have high impact in logical design of software component. Software cohesion is core point of design of software system. Here for calculation of software cohesion we use Eq. 6. The CC (cmp_c) is cohesion of cth component and n is the number of component. The cohesion of component is calculated by Eq. 10. If number of use case in component is only one, then the cohesion value of that component is 1 otherwise it is calculated by the similarity measure between two feature objects (use case) and that will have divided by the combination of m_c to 2.

Hence, For OBS component diagram the cohesion of the component 1 is:

$$CC(cmp_c)_{[0,1]} = \left(\frac{sim(UC_1, UC_2) + sim(UC_1, UC_3) + sim(UC_2, UC_3)}{3!/\{2!(3-2)!\}} \right) \tag{10}$$

Similarly, we can compute cohesion value for all six components. According to the Eq. (6) the OBS software cohesion value using $S_{\text{Sokel \& Sneath-II}}$ is 0.944. The effect of similarity measures of other method's results is shown in Table 8.

Table 8. Calculated software cohesion result for OBS case study by corelational similarity coefficient

Use-Case	Measure	Formula/Method	Soft. Cohn.	Soft. Coupl.	Soft. Compl.	Fit. Fun. Value
OBS	S_{Jaccard}	**COMO(CRUD-Based)** (Lee, S.D., Yang, Y.J., Cho, F.S., Kim, S.D., & Rhew, S.Y. (1999))	0.825	0.171	0.079	0.575
		Clustering Based (Shahmohammadi, G., Jalili, S., & Hasheminejad, S.M.H. (2010))	0.927	0.163	0.083	0.681
		FCA Based (Cai, Z.G., Yang, X.H., Wang, X.Y., & Kavs, A.J. (2011))	0.919	0.183	0.087	0.649
	$S_{\text{SimpleCoffecient}}$	$\frac{a+d}{a+b+c+d}$/**SCI-GA** (Hasheminejad, S.M.H., & Jalili, S. (2013))	0.969	0.159	0.0771	0.733
	$S_{\text{Pearson \&Heron-I}}$	$\frac{ad-bc}{\sqrt{(a+b)(a+c)(b+d)(c+d)}}$	0.796	0.159	0.0771	0.560
	$S_{\text{Pearson \&Heron-II}}$	$\cos\left(\frac{\pi\sqrt{bc}}{\sqrt{ad}+\sqrt{bc}} \right)$	0.99	0.159	0.0771	0.754
	S_{Michael}	$\frac{4(ad-bc)}{(a+d)^2+(b+c)^2}$	0.769	0.159	0.0771	0.533
	$S_{\text{Kulczynski-II}}$	$\frac{\frac{a}{2}(2a+b+c)}{(a+b)(a+c)}$	0.885	0.159	0.0771	0.649
	$S_{\text{Driver\&Kroeber}}$	$\frac{a}{2}\left(\frac{1}{a+b} + \frac{1}{a+c} \right)$	0.884	0.159	0.0771	0.648
	$S_{\text{Braun-Blanquet}}$	$\frac{a}{max(a+b,a+c)}$	0.783	0.159	0.0771	0.547
	$S_{\text{Sokel\&Sneath-I}}$	$\frac{a}{a+2b+2c}$	0.698	0.159	0.0771	0.462
	$S_{\text{Sokel\&Sneath-II}}$	$\frac{2(a+d)}{2a+b+c+2d}$	0.944	0.159	0.0771	0.708
	$S_{\text{Sokel\&Sneath-IV}}$	$\frac{\frac{a}{(a+b)} + \frac{a}{(a+c)} + \frac{d}{(b+d)} + \frac{d}{(c+d)}}{4}$	0.778	0.159	0.0771	0.542

3.6 On the Basis of Non-correlation Similarity Measures

For evaluation based on non-correlation Similarity measure Gower & Legendre similarity measure Eq. (11) is used to explain the procedure for calculation of software cohesion.

$$S_{Gower\&Legendre} = \frac{a+d}{a+0.5(b+c)+d} \tag{11}$$

Using Table 6, similarity measure of OBS case study by Gower & Legendre is as follows:

$$Sim(UC_1, UC_2) = \frac{(2+6)}{2+0.5(2+0)+6} = 0.888$$

Now similarly can be calculating similarity measure for other component. The Software Cohesion has been calculated based on Gower & Legendre similarity measure is 0.959. The other non-corelational similarity coefficient results are shown in Table 9.

Table 9. Calculated software cohesion result for OBS case study by non-corelational similarity coefficient

Use-Case	Similarity	Formula/Method	Soft. Cohn.	Soft. Coupl	Soft. Compl.	Fitness function value
OBS	$S_{3W\text{-}Jaccard}$	$\frac{3a}{3a+b+c}$	0.922	0.159	0.0771	0.686
	$S_{Russell\&Rao}$	$\frac{a}{a+b+c}$	0.806	0.159	0.0771	0.570
	S_{Dice}	$\frac{2a}{2a+b+c}$	0.895	0.159	0.0771	0.659
	$S_{Roger\&Tanimoto}$	$\frac{a+d}{a+2(b+c)+d}$	0.876	0.159	0.0771	0.640
	$S_{Sokel\&Michener}$	$\frac{a+d}{a+b+c+d}$	0.925	0.159	0.0779	0.729
	S_{Faith}	$\frac{a+0.5d}{a+b+c+d}$	0.589	0.159	0.0771	0.749

4 Result Analysis

It has been observed in literature survey that various software component identification approach uses the use-case property for composition of services in software component. By using the feature of usecase the software component design recomposed based on the fitness function value. The fitness function value computed by the software cohesion, software coupling and software complexity. Higher fitness function value shows that the composition of use cases is adequate for software component of system design. As explained in section experimental evaluation: the software cohesion is calculated by the similarity coefficient. But due to the various approach of similarity coefficient, the software cohesion value is not fixed for a same use case composition. So, it is not possible to conclude that obtained fitness function value is accurate with highest accuracy. As authors have shown in Tables 8 and 9 on different similarity coefficient gives the different cohesion value for same feature value of OBS case study. Authors observed that the selection of similarity coefficient is a NP-hard problem.

By using Precision, Recall, Accuracy & F-Measure obtained values authors computed various similarity measures like $S_{Jaccard}$, S_{YuleQ} etc. For example, row no. 1 of Table 10 shows the value corresponding to Precision (0.5, 0.5, 1), Recall (0.5, 0.5, 1), Accuracy (0.8, 0.8, 1) and F-measure (0.7, 0.7, 1) for component 1. Based on these standard parameter values, coefficient parameters (a, b, c & d) and similarity measure $S_{Jaccard}$ (as defined in Table 8) authors obtained similarity measure $S_{Jaccard} = [0.8, 0.8, 1]$.

The results in the Tables 10 and 11 shows that the use-case feature of software component is valid. By experimental evaluation authors observed that a pattern which concludes that software cohesion accuracy is depending upon the selection of similarity measure coefficient. For example, tuple no 3 & 6 in Table 10 on computed value of precision, recall, accuracy and f-measure the different similarity coefficient gives same result i.e. S_{YuleQ} [1] and $S_{Pearson\&Heron-II}$ [1] but when authors compute the software cohesion value by both similarity coefficient using both the value he get different value cohesion result. By the similarity coefficient S_{YuleQ} is not applicable for computation and $S_{Pearson-Heron-II}$ gives .99. In Table 10: Validation and similarity in between the usecases by corelational similarity coefficients shows that the usecase feature property is suitable for the composition of similar functionality of services.

Table 10. Validation and similarity in between the use cases by corelational similarity coefficients

Sr. No.	Precision			Recall			F-Measure			Accuracy			Similarity			
	UC_1–UC_2	UC_1–UC_3	UC_2–UC_3	UC_1–UC_2	UC_1–UC_3	UC_2–UC_3	UC_1–UC_2	UC_1–UC_3	UC_2–UC_3	UC_1–UC_2	UC_1–UC_3	UC_2–UC_3	Method	UC_1–UC_2	UC_1–UC_3	UC_2–UC_3
1	0.5	0.5	1	0.5	0.5	1	0.7	0.7	1	0.8	0.8	1	$S_{Jaccard}$	0.8	0.8	1
2	0.5	0.5	1	0.5	0.5	1	0.7	0.7	1	0.8	0.8	1	$S_{SimpleCoff}$	0.8	0.8	1
3	0.5	0.5	1	0.5	0.5	1	0.7	0.7	1	0.8	0.8	1	S_{YuleQ}	1	1	1
4	0.5	0.5	1	0.5	0.5	1	0.7	0.7	1	0.8	0.8	1	S_{YuleW}	1	1	1
5	0.5	0.5	1	0.5	0.5	1	0.7	0.7	1	0.8	0.8	1	$S_{Pearson\&Heron-I}$	0.61	0.61	0.04
6	0.5	0.5	1	0.5	0.5	1	0.7	0.7	1	0.8	0.8	1	$S_{Pearson\&Heron-II}$	1	1	1
7	0.5	0.5	1	0.5	0.5	1	0.7	0.7	1	0.8	0.8	1	$S_{Sokel\&Sneath-IV}$	0.81	0.81	NA

Table 11. Performance validation based on all measures and result of various non-corelational similarity coefficients

Sr. No.	Precision			Recall			F-Measure			Accuracy			Similarity			
	UC_1 UC_2	UC_1 UC_3	UC_2 UC_3	UC_1 UC_2	UC_1 UC_3	UC_2 UC_3	UC_1 UC_2	UC_1 UC_3	UC_2 UC_3	UC_1 UC_2	UC_1 UC_3	UC_2 UC_3	Method	UC_1 UC_2	UC_1 UC_3	UC_2 UC_3
1	0.5	0.5	1	0.5	0.5	1	0.7	0.7	1	0.8	0.8	1	$S_{3W-Jaccard}$	0.75	0.75	1
2	0.5	0.5	1	0.5	0.5	1	0.7	0.7	1	0.8	0.8	1	$S_{Russell\&Rao}$	0.5	0.5	1
3	0.5	0.5	1	0.5	0.5	1	0.7	0.7	1	0.8	0.8	1	S_{Dice}	0.66	0.66	1
4	0.5	0.5	1	0.5	0.5	1	0.7	0.7	1	0.8	0.8	1	$S_{Roger\&Tanimoto}$	0.8	0.8	1
5	0.5	0.5	1	0.5	0.5	1	0.7	0.7	1	0.8	0.8	1	$S_{Sokel\&Michener}$	0.8	0.8	1
6	0.5	0.5	1	0.5	0.5	1	0.7	0.7	1	0.8	0.8	1	$S_{Tanimoto}$	0.5	0.5	1
7	0.5	0.5	1	0.5	0.5	1	0.7	0.7	1	0.8	0.8	1	S_{Faith}	0.5	0.5	1

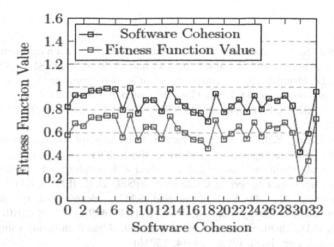

Fig. 1. The effect of software cohesion of fitness function value.

According to the experimental evaluation it is proof that fitness function value for identification of software component development is directly proportional to the software cohesion. It has been observed that the highest software cohesion value 0.99 gives the highest fitness value for a use case matrix of Table 1. According to the experimental analysis the best similarity coefficient for OBS case type data set is Pearson & Hearon-II.

5 Conclusions and Feature Works

This experimental evaluation performed for validation of use-case features and effect of similarity coefficient for identification of software logical component. According to the use-case feature a use-case metrics is prepared in combination of four actor and six entity class. In second step a similarity/proximity metrics obtained by similarity coefficients listed in Tables 8 and 9. By using similarity metrics and Eq. (6) the software cohesion is calculated. In result of experimental evaluation, it is observed that for such type of use case feature data the Pearson & Hearon-II similarity coefficient gives better result in comparison to other similarity measure coefficient. It is observed that the software cohesion by similarity coefficient is not admissible heuristic. There may be a possibility of some other optimum value (in terms of maximum) that can be predicted with same data structure.

Since, there is bunch of measures used in the literature for the computation of similarity measures; one can work for finding the generalized criteria instead of using various similarity measures that is further used in the computation of design parameters.

References

1. Kim, J., Park, S., Sugumaran, V.: DRAMA: a framework for domain requirements analysis and modeling architectures in software product lines. J. Syst. Softw. **81**(1), 37–55 (2008)
2. Birkmeier, D., Overhage, S.: On component identification approaches – classification, state of the art, and comparison. In: Lewis, G.A., Poernomo, I., Hofmeister, C. (eds.) CBSE 2009. LNCS, vol. 5582, pp. 1–18. Springer, Heidelberg (2009). https://doi.org/10.1007/978-3-642-02414-6_1
3. Kim, S.D., Chang, S.H.: A systematic method to identify software components. In: 11th Asia-Pacific Software Engineering Conference. IEEE (2004)
4. Lee, J.K., et al.: Component identification method with coupling and cohesion. In: Eighth Asia-Pacific Software Engineering Conference, APSEC 2001. IEEE (2001)
5. Shahmohammadi, G., Jalili, S., Hasheminejad, S.M.H.: Identification of system software components using clustering approach. J. Object Technol. **9**(6), 77–98 (2010)
6. Menéndez, H.D., Otero, F.E.B., Camacho, D.: Medoid-based clustering using ant colony optimization. Swarm Intell. **10**(2), 123–145 (2016)
7. Hasheminejad, S.M.H., Jalili, S.: SCI-GA: software component identification using genetic algorithm. J. Object Technol. **12**(2), 3:1 (2013)
8. Albani, A., Overhage, S., Birkmeier, D.: Towards a systematic method for identifying business components. In: Chaudron, M.R.V., Szyperski, C., Reussner, R. (eds.) CBSE 2008. LNCS, vol. 5282, pp. 262–277. Springer, Heidelberg (2008). https://doi.org/10.1007/978-3-540-87891-9_17
9. Cai, Z.-g., et al.: A fuzzy formal concept analysis-based approach for business component identification. J. Zhejiang Univ. Sci. C **12**(9), 707 (2011)
10. Jain, H., et al.: Business component identification-a formal approach. In: Proceedings of the Fifth IEEE International Enterprise Distributed Object Computing Conference, EDOC 2001. IEEE (2001)
11. Peng, L., Tong, Z., Zhang, Y.: Design of business component identification method with graph segmentation. In: 3rd International Conference on Intelligent System and Knowledge Engineering, ISKE 2008, vol. 1. IEEE (2008)
12. Wang, Z., Xiaofei, X., Zhan, D.: A survey of business component identification methods and related techniques. Int. J. Inf. Technol. **2**(4), 229–238 (2005)
13. Ganesan, R., Sengupta, S.: O2BC: a technique for the design of component-based applications. In: 39th International Conference and Exhibition on Technology of Object-Oriented Languages and Systems, TOOLS 39. IEEE (2001)
14. Lee, S.D., et al.: COMO: a UML-based component development methodology. In: Proceedings of the Sixth Asia Pacific Software Engineering Conference, APSEC 1999. IEEE (1999)
15. Cui, J.F., Chae, H.S.: Applying agglomerative hierarchical clustering algorithms to component identification for legacy systems. Inf. Softw. Technol. **53**(6), 601–614 (2011)
16. Karypis, G.: CLUTO: A Clustering Toolkit. Department of Computer Science, University of Minnesota, USA (2002)
17. Demuth, H., Beale, M.: Neural Network Toolbox, For use with MATLAB, Version8 (2008)
18. Xu, R., Wunsch, D.: Survey of clustering algorithms. IEEE Trans. Neural Networks **16**(3), 645–678 (2005)
19. Choi, S.-S., Cha, S.-H., Tappert, C.C.: A survey of binary similarity and distance measures. Systemics Cybern. Informetics **8**, 43–48 (2010)
20. Hubalek, Z.: Coefficients of association and similarity, based on binary (presence-absence) data: an evaluation. Biol. Rev. **57**–4, 669–689 (1982)

21. Michael, E.L.: Marine ecology and the coefficient of association: a plea in behalf of quantitative biology. Ecology **8**, 54–59 (1920)
22. Driver, H.E., Kroeber, A.L.: Quantitative Expression of Cultural Relationships. University of California Press, Berkeley (1932)
23. Sokal, R.R., Sneath, P.H.: Principles of Numeric Taxonomy. W.H Freeman, San Francisco (1963)
24. Smith, J.R., Chang, S.-F.: Automated binary texture feature sets for image retrieval. In: International Conference on Acoustic, Speech, and Signal Processing, Atlantic (1996)
25. Michael, H.: Binary coefficients: a theoretical and empirical study. Math. Geol. **8**(2), 137–150 (1976)
26. Willett, P., Barnard, J.M., Downs, G.M.: Chemical similarity searching. Chem. Inf. Comput. Sci. **38**, 983–996 (1998)
27. Willett, P.: Similarity-based approaches to virtual screening. Biochem. Soc. Trans. **31**, 603–606 (2003)
28. Cha, S.-H., Yoon, S., Tappert, C.C.: Enhancing binary feature vector similarity measures. J. Pattern Recogn. Res. **1**(1) (2006)
29. Cha, S.-H., Srihari, S.N.: A fast nearest neighbor search algorithm by filtration. Pattern Recogn. **35**, 515–525 (2000)
30. Cha, S.-H., Tappert, C.C.: Optimizing binary feature vector similarity measure using genetic algorithm. In: ICDAR, Edinburgh (2003)
31. Cormack, R.M.: A review of classification. J. R. Stat. Soc. Ser. A **134**, 321–353 (1971)
32. Goodman, L.A., Kruskal, W.H.: Measures of association for cross classifications. J. Am. Stat. Assoc. **49**, 732–764 (1954)
33. Goodman, L.A., Kruskal, W.H.: Measures of association for cross classifications II. Further discussion and references. J. Am. Stat. Assoc. **54**, 123–163 (pp. 35–75) (1959)
34. Goodman, L.A., Kruskal, W.H.: Measures of association for cross classifications III. Approximate sampling theory. J. Am. Stat. Assoc. **58**, 310–364 (1963)

Quantitative Analysis of Drinking Water Quality for Long Term Water Borne Diseases

Kamidi Prasanth[✉], Sabbi Vamshi Krishna, Sanniti Rama Krishna, and Kondapalli Jayaram Kumar

Department of Electronics and Communication Engineering, Godavari Institute of Engineering and Technology, Rajahmahendravaram, India
prasanth.kamidi26@gmail.com,
prof.svkrishna@gmail.com, krishna2014mtech@gmail.com,
jramworld@gmail.com

Abstract. The quality of drinking water is being deteriorated due to rapid increment of industrialization and population in India. This issue results in the interest of research by several researchers to check the prominence of drinking water quality from different parts of India in view of the physicochemical properties of drinking water just as the nearness of different pathogenic microorganisms. Microbial impurities in water are a noteworthy general well-being anxiety. Pathogens have been recognized as an essential danger to stream water quality in the India, conceivably affecting drinking and water system water sources and recreational waters. The aim of this paper is to ensure the providing of safe drinking water quality that must be monitored within a existent time of applications and are utilized for the physical as well as chemical requirements of the water can be studied. These requirements such as physical and chemical substances that can be determines to their size depending on the properties of water based on their nature. Utilizing Geological Information framework and statistical software (SPSS and SAS) connections of affirmed Giardiasis have been contrasted and accessible atmosphere and hydrologic information. The research in this paper suggest that there is no visible difference in illness event related with measure of precipitation or extraordinary disease occurrence. In India, there is a seasonal disease occurrence due to the temperature. For this purpose, the samples were collected from different southern India's region watersheds.

1 Introduction

The waterborne diseases like diarrhea, systematic illnesses and gastrointestinal are increasing day by day and approximately per year 2.3 million deaths occurs due to these diseases which becomes a global burden [1, 2]. The most effect of these diseases is children that are about 1.5 million. About 12 billion US dollars economic loss are estimated worldwide [3]. Waterborne diseases are brought about by ingestion, airborne or contact with polluted water by an assortment of irresistible specialists which incorporates microscopic organisms, infections, protozoa and helminths. Worldwide about 2.6 billion people do not have access to improved sanitation and about 790 million people are not using the purified water sources. About 3.3% yearly death is due

M. Singh et al. (Eds.): ICACDS 2019, CCIS 1045, pp. 500–508, 2019.
https://doi.org/10.1007/978-981-13-9939-8_44

to lacking of purified water and sanitation worldwide [4]. World Health Organization suggested that only with improving the quality of water, about 5% deaths can be reduced worldwide [5].

Water is the universally significant and greatest esteemed inherent assets. It is an embodiment of something in the existence of all subsisting bodies by the simplest plant with respect to the most composite subsisting system recognized as human body [6]. A person can live without food for five weeks or more, but without water he can survive for only a few days. Water is an association of hydrogen and oxygen atoms with a chemical compound as H2O and the greatest part of generous synthesis (70%) with regard to the earth's exterior [7]. It is a finite resource and is necessary for land management, conscientiousness and for creatures alive on earth including human beings. Lots of people don't be aware of the true importance of drinking sufficient water every day. A huge quantity of water can be misspending in so many ways of human occupation [8]. Water is an outstanding asset caused by its unique chemical and physical characteristics. It is a pivotal element for evolution and the superiority of living creatures in crowded countries. In distinctive dreary region it has similarly come to be a reality constituent [9]. Therefore, "water situated for human swallowing not necessary contain pathogen-microbes or injurious of chemicals", by virtue of water attenuates with micro-organisms in the causation of ubiquitous [10]. Namely, good drinking water is not a splendor but one of the majorities crucial necessity of life intrinsically. Water constructs the majority weight of human body weight of roundly two-third of its weight, human brain is composed of 94% of water, lungs can be composed by 90% of water and blood can be 83%. Although in progressive countries possess the continues from an inadequacy of retrieved to have secured drinking water from improved references and to acceptable disinfection amenities [11]. The WHO [12] brings to light specifically seventy-five percent in every respective injury in progressive countries develops caused by mistreated drinking water.

Accordingly, water standards deal with the frequently of the majority crucial constituent of considering the quality acquires to rectified water authorities. A sufficient water standard depicts the protection of drinking water with regarded to physical, chemical as well as biological parameters. Worldwide and also regional areas are accepted those requirements and describes the physio-chemical standard requirements of drinking water [13]. The complication related with chemical compounds of drinking water proceeds essentially from their proficiency provoke the unpropitious or harmful health injuries sustained the succeeding time of intervals in relevant of certain concerns are toxins that have collecting poisonous attributes such as substantial metals and contents that are destructive injuries [14]. The general complications in household employment of water provides may be solidity, iron, sulfates, sodium-chlorides, alkalinity, acidity and dissolved solids and some chemical contamination [15]. The slightly description of water requirements of drinking water quality about their properties such as physical, chemical and also biological properties are examined below Fig. 1.

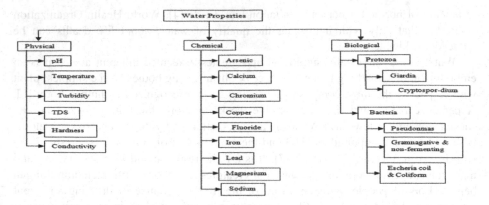

Fig. 1. Graphical representation of water nature requirements

2 Why Can't Waterborne Pathogens Be Eliminated?

We can find the Microorganisms anywhere in our environment. With bare eyes, we can-not find them. Water, air, soil and sustenance having tremendous quantities of these organisms. In spite of the fact that people are basically free of microorganisms before birth, consistent conditions of introduction (e.g., breathing, eating, and drinking) speedily permit the basis of innocuous microbial lushness in our bodies [16].

Microbial pathogens (microorganisms fit for causing illness), nonetheless, can and frequently do harm the individuals who become infected. Also, illnesses that healthy people "climate" well may demonstrate lethal to people with traded off resistant frameworks. Now and again, a contamination can persevere to make a "bearer state" where a disease-causing operator is harbored by the body (and spread) with no clear manifestations. Waterborne sicknesses are normally viewed as those illnesses coming about because of ingestion of sullied water. Extra pathways of contamination being contemplated by EPA incorporate inward breath of water vapors just as body contact amid washing (deft pathogens) in the emergency clinic condition [17].

Since intentional water ingestion (drinking water) and washing are all inclusive practices and unintentional ingestion amid recreational exercises (e.g., swimming, water skiing, swimming) is normal, lacking security of water respectability could prompt across the board episodes (the Centers for Disease Control characterizes a flare-up to be at least two instances of ailment that can be followed to a typical source). Since side effects can be mellow and fleeting, it is assessed that just a small quantity of waterborne flashes is apparent, announced and explored. Also, specialists trust that some food related illness episodes may begin with a fundamental illness (e.g., of an eatery laborer) brought about by polluted drinking water. Microscopic organisms, to wipe out these pathogens from our water, particularly from our drinking water, appears to be hypothetically direct. Basically, blend in a disinfectant, permit satisfactory contact time to guarantee inactivation (rendering the organisms unfit to create infection), and siphon the water into the circulation lines [18].

3 Abundant Physical Parameters of Drinking Water Quality

The physical features of water quality principles can be evaluated and to analyses the quality features of water samples. That is pH, Turbidity, Conductivity, Hardness, Total Dissolved salts, Dissolved Oxygen can be listed below:

3.1 pH

The word pH stands for potential of hydrogen. It deals with measure of hydrogen ion concentration in water. And it decides the nature of water that is dyspepsia or alkalinity nature of water. If the pH value of nearly 1, it acts as acidic nature of water. The value of pH at its specific range of 14, its essential nature of the particular specimens is in strongly basic or alkaline nature. The standard value of pH is 7 (that is Neutral) [19]. Generally, the pH value of drinking water is ranges between 6.5–8.5. It is considered to be a standard level concentration of standard organizations. The range exceeds degree level of concentration causes the harmful effects to consumers. The study concluded that the supreme of admissible limit of water of their pH is 6.5–8.5 (Table 1) as prescribed by WHO and BSI.

Table 1. Analysis of pH parameter.

Property	Range (mg/l)	Effects
pH	<4.0	Critical danger effects for health due to dissolved poisonous metal ions
	4.0–6.0	Poisonal impacts integrated with dissolved metals, which involves lead
	6.0–9.0	No health effects, Aluminum solubility and amphoteric oxides begins to increase at pH 6 and 8.5 respectively
	9.0–11.0	Possibility of noxious impacts integrated with deprotonated nature expands sharply. Water savouracetous at a pH of greater than 9
	>11.0	Critical jeopardy for health

3.2 Dissolved Oxygen

Dissolved oxygen (DO) can be described insides the units of milligrams of oxygen gas (O2) dissipate in respective liter of water (i.e. mg/L) or as a grade of the supreme constitute of DO is specifically realizable within the water body at a designate condition and also the degree of salt nature (% saturation) of water [18]. DO collections are based on environmental coercion, along with this is taken into consequence for the time of factor register. The substantial distinction between DO engrossment at the facade of water and the intricacy in water bodies can marks from arrangement of the water formation, because of febrile or saturation effects. Such realizes are mostly definite in the summer times the instant waters exterior are great deals with warmer than obscured waters. Excessiveness of DO can lead to 'electrocute globule injuries' in fishes, where oxygen globule can build in the vacuole system, pale stratum and eyes, amongst contrasting organs, which can lead to demise. It can evaluate the both (mg/L and % saturation) should be recorded. The study concluded that the extreme admissible limit of Dissolved oxygen in water of 5 and 3 prescribed by WHO and BSI respectively.

3.3   Hardness

In drinking water, hardness is principally responsible for highly dissolved minerals of calcium and magnesium. It is a function of physical structure area of horizontal surface of water is syndicated. Water is elementary by means of limestone are susceptible towards hard water since rainfall, which is inherently acidic for the reason it accommodates the CO_2 gas, it repeatedly dissolves and carries the cations to the water. The permitted desirable boundary of complete hardness is 300 mg/L, whereas the apex boundary is 600 mg/L. It can be classified as smooth, fairly, hardened and very hardened. In accordance with this categorization most of the specimens occur under the fairly to hardened categories. Due to this origin of categorizing it has been surveyed that no water specimens are smooth but all the sustained values were surrounded by the permissible merits of BIS (300 mg/L) and WHO (500 mg/L) as prescribed in the Table 2.

Table 2.   Analysis of total hardness.

Property	Range (mg/l)	Effects
Total hardness	50–100	Fairly smooth
	100–150	A little bit hardened
	150–200	Fairly hardened
	200–300	Hardened
	>300	Especially hardened

4   Hypothesis of the Research

A general objective of the investigation is to decide the degree of waterborne exposures to pathogenic microorganisms. This can be practiced through the investigation of the spatial and transient changeability of affirmed announced human instances of a microorganism, for example, Giardia. Giardia is a decent reference pathogen for a few reasons: (1) it is a standout amongst the most normally distinguished etiologic specialists in waterborne ailment flare-ups; (2) it has a huge number of ecological sources that might be affected by watershed hydrology; (3) it is more impervious to ordinary treatment than the bacterial pathogens. Hence affirmed human cases are required to be bound to happen from a waterborne course (when contrasted with different pathogens that are all the more effectively expelled by treatment forms). Consequently, the connections between precipitation, streamflow, expansive watershed qualities and affirmed human instances of Giardia for southern India will be analyzed.

(A) Infection rates for waterborne pathogens are because of contact with untreated water and will be identified with recreational practices, occasional access and utilization of recreational water. Specific Aim (1) To decide whether regular patterns in affirmed human instances of Giardia diseases agree with occasional recreational water use.

(B) Characteristics and states of watersheds impact the worldly and spatial bounty of waterborne pathogens and related gastrointestinal sickness. Explicit Aim (2) To look at general wellbeing information from Southern India from an assortment of watersheds to decide whether a connection exists between waterborne ailments and watershed conditions and attributes (land use appropriation of the watersheds, presence of a particular highlights in. Explicit Aim (3) To decide the effect of land use (urban versus provincial) on the recurrence of affirmed Giardia cases.

(C) Combined Sewer Overflows (CSO's) enable untreated water to pollute drinking water sources bringing about expanded presentation to waterborne pathogens. Explicit Aim (4) Evaluate the distinctions in recurrence of affirmed Giardia cases in watersheds with and without Combined Sewer Overflows (CSOs) upstream of drinking water sources.

(D) High spillover instigated by overwhelming precipitation makes a more prominent inundation of pathogens drinking water sources prompting higher contamination rates from waterborne pathogens after these precipitation occasions. Explicit Aim (5): To look at the worldly relationship between high precipitation occasions and flare-ups of Giardia cases.

5 Result and Discussion

5.1 Comparison of Watersheds (Urban Vs Rural)

Of enthusiasm for this investigation was a correlation of dispersion of instances of affirmed giardiasis among different watersheds in southern India. These destinations were of enthusiasm for their portrayal of urban, rustic and CSO in drinking water framework separately. These gatherings were contrasted two at any given moment with grant appraisals of provincial versus urban, rustic versus CSO and urban versus CSO. For these investigations, two example t-test were performed. The needy variable for these examinations was the quantity of affirmed cases per 10,000.

5.2 Student t-Test

Utilizing SPSS, understudy's t-tests were performed to assess the impacts of land use and CSOs on human instances of giardiasis. It was discovered that there was no noteworthy distinction (P = 0.546) between the urban watershed and the country watershed with respect to pathologically affirmed instances of giardiasis.

The Table 3 demonstrates the predominance rates of giardiasis saw in different investigations in India however there is a plausibility that a higher number of cases might be identified with a higher populace thickness inside the watersheds.

Table 3. Prevalence rates of Giardiasis observed in southern India.

Site of study	Population	% Prevalence
Bangalore	Children in urban slum	8–10
Pune	Children in urban slum	7.9
Chennai	Rural population	16
Chennai	Semi-urban and urban population	22.6
Karnataka	Rural population	37.1
Karnataka	Semi-urban and urban population	2.5
Vellore	Rural population	53.8
Vellore	Semi-urban and urban population	28.2

So as to beat that predisposition we determined yearly Giardiasis cases in per 10,000 populaces for every one of the watersheds. Figure 2 speaks to the absolute yearly number of cases per 10,000 individuals for the three watersheds. As found in the figure, there is an expansion in the quantity of giardiasis cases in the Deerfield watershed in contrast with the Blackstone watershed when determined per 10,000 populaces which could be because of some announcing predisposition.

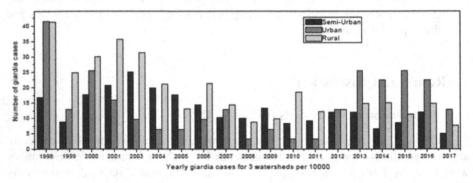

Fig. 2. Total annual confirmed Giardia cases per 10000 populations in the semi-urban, urban, and rural watersheds.

In this way, the crude number of giardiasis cases (before normalizing with 10,000 populaces) may have been affected by the bigger watershed territory and populace thickness (Fig. 3). Likewise there is a plausibility of detailing inclination. In any case, the Vellore rustic Watershed keeps on appearing number of giardiasis cases even after standardized per 10,000 populaces.

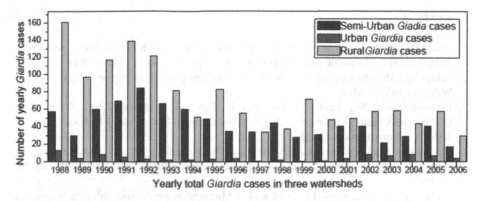

Fig. 3. Before normalization total annual confirmed Giardia cases in the semi-Urban, urban, and rural watersheds.

6 Conclusion and Future Scope

A large portion of the recorded waterborne sickness flare-ups in provincial territories were from recreational waters that included new lake/lake water. A restriction of our informational collection is that most of the detailed illness information is with no data concerning the causative media or wellspring of the contamination. Next to no data is accessible with respect to the beginning of these revealed diseases, for example, regardless of whether these cases are nourishment borne or waterborne. In any case, these sorts of constraints in wellbeing office information are normal. Human instances of gastrointestinal ailments are commonly underreported. Thusly, the data predisposition may have an effect on the outcomes. People may likewise obtain ailments outside of their watershed limits.

Another serious issue of getting exact information of gastrointestinal sickness is under detailing. In the vast majority of the cases the accessible malady information from Department of Public Health is gathered from self-detailing techniques. Along these lines, the possibility of announcing predispositions cannot be maintained a strategic distance from. Such kind of predisposition isn't exceptionally phenomenal with gastrointestinal malady related research. Mohanty revealed in 1997 in Hyderabad, the first number of gastrointestinal cases were multiple times higher in contrast with under announcing of Disease. No noteworthy distinction (P = 0.546) between the urban watershed and the Semi-Urban watershed has been found with respect to affirmed instances of giardiasis.

The provincial watershed had fundamentally higher quantities of affirmed instances of Giardia disease (P = 0.003) when contrasted with the urban and semi-urban watershed which may have originated from its tainted drinking water source this is affected by CSOs. The affirmation is just conceivable in the event that it very well may be contrasted and another watershed in country territory with CSOs and all similar criteria. One piece of our goal is affirmed that a connection exists between waterborne maladies and watershed conditions and qualities and effect of land use has some connection with of announced Giardia cases in country territories.

References

1. World Health Organization (WHO): Water Sanitation and Health (2015). https://www.who.int/water_sanitation_health/monitoring/midtermeval.pdf. Accessed 17 Mar 2019
2. Bitton, G.: Microbiology of Drinking Water Production and Distribution, 1st edn, p. 312. Wiley, Hoboken (2014)
3. Ingerson-Mahar, M., Reid, A.: Microbes in Pipes: The Microbiology of the Water Distribution System a Report on an American Academy of Microbiology Colloquium, p. 26. ASM Academy, Boulder (2012)
4. Alhamlan, F.S., Al-Qahtani, A.A., Al-Ahdal, M.N.: Recommended advanced techniques for waterborne pathogen detection in developing countries. J. Infect. Dev. Ctries. **9**, 128–135 (2015)
5. Leclerc, H., Schwartzbrod, L., Dei-Cas, E.: Microbial agents associated with waterborne diseases. Crit. Rev. Microbiol. **28**, 371–409 (2002)
6. Centers for Disease Control and Prevention (CDC): Global Water, Sanitation, and Hygiene (WASH). http://www.cdc.gov/healthywater/global/. Accessed 17 Feb 2015
7. APHA: Standard Methods for Examination of Water and Waste Water, 15th edn. American Public Health Association, Washington D.C. (1995)
8. BIS Bureau of Indian Standards IS: 10500, Manak Bhavan, New Delhi, India (1998)
9. Vijayakumar, N., Ramya, R.: The real time monitoring of water quality in IoT environment. Int. J. Sci. Res. (2013)
10. Dhoble, S.B., Choudhari, N.K., Chaudhari, A.R.: Sensor based electronics system for evaluation of water quality. Res. J. Eng. Sci. **3**(11), 6–10 (2014)
11. Faruq, M.O., Emu, I.H., Haque, M.N., Dey, M., Das, N.K., Dey, M.: Design and implementation of cost effective water quality evaluation system. In: IEEE Region 10 Humanitarian Technology Conference (R10-HTC) (2017)
12. WHO: Guidelines for Drinking-water Quality. World Health Organization, Geneva (2004)
13. Patil, P.T.: Evaluation of groundwater quality and its suitability for drinking purpose in Budhgaon, Kavalapur and Karnal Villages of Sangli District, Maharashtra, India. Int. J. Res. Eng. Technol. (2016)
14. Dwivedi, A.K.: Researches in water pollution: a review. Int. Res. J. Nat. Appl. Sci. **4**(1) (2017). Pollution and Environmental Assay Research Laboratory (PEARL), Department of Botany, DDU Gorakhpur University, Gorakhpur-273009, U.P., India
15. Water and Health. Springer Nature America, Inc. (2014)
16. Kot, M., Castleden, H., Gagnon, G.A.: Unintended consequences of regulating drinking water in rural Canadian communities: examples from Atlantic Canada. Health Place **17**(5), 1030–1037 (2011)
17. Frazier, L.M., Miller, V.A., Horbelt, D.V., Delmore, J.E., Miller, B.E., Paschal, A.M.: Comparison of focus groups on cancer and employment conducted face to face or by telephone. J. Qual. Health Res. **20**(5), 617–627 (2010)
18. Dunn, G., Harris, L., Cook, C., Prystajecky, N.: A comparative analysis of current microbial water quality risk assessment and management practices in British Columbia and Ontario, Canada. Sci. Total Environ. **468**, 544–552 (2014)
19. Ontario Ministry of Health and Long-Term Care: Drinking water protocol (2014). www.health.gov.on.ca/en/pro/programs/.../oph.../drinking_water.pdf

Author Index

Printed in the United States
By Bookmasters